Windows Server Cookbook™

Other Microsoft Windows resources from O'Reilly

Related titles
Learning Windows Server 2003

Securing Windows Server 2003

DNS on Windows Server 2003

Windows Server 2003 in a Nutshell

Windows Server Hacks™

Windows Books Resource Center
windows.oreilly.com is a complete catalog of O'Reilly's Windows and Office books, including sample chapters and code examples.

oreillynet.com is the essential portal for developers interested in open and emerging technologies, including new platforms, programming languages, and operating systems.

Conferences
O'Reilly brings diverse innovators together to nurture the ideas that spark revolutionary industries. We specialize in documenting the latest tools and systems, translating the innovator's knowledge into useful skills for those in the trenches. Visit *conferences.oreilly.com* for our upcoming events.

Safari Bookshelf (*safari.oreilly.com*) is the premier online reference library for programmers and IT professionals. Conduct searches across more than 1,000 books. Subscribers can zero in on answers to time-critical questions in a matter of seconds. Read the books on your Bookshelf from cover to cover or simply flip to the page you need. Try it today with a free trial.

Windows Server Cookbook™

Robbie Allen

O'REILLY®

Beijing · Cambridge · Farnham · Köln · Paris · Sebastopol · Taipei · Tokyo

Windows Server Cookbook™
by Robbie Allen

Published by O'Reilly Media, Inc., 1005 Gravenstein Highway North, Sebastopol, CA 95472.

O'Reilly books may be purchased for educational, business, or sales promotional use. Online editions are also available for most titles (*safari.oreilly.com*). For more information, contact our corporate/institutional sales department: (800) 998-9938 or *corporate@oreilly.com*.

Editor:	Andy Oram
Production Editor:	Matt Hutchinson
Production Services:	Octal Publishing, Inc.
Cover Designer:	Ellie Volckhausen
Interior Designer:	David Futato

Printing History:

March 2005:	First Edition.

 This book uses RepKover™, a durable and flexible lay-flat binding.

ISBN: 0-596-00633-0
[M]

To Betty Parsons (Granna):
Without you, I would not be who I am today.
Thank you for your love and friendship.

Table of Contents

16. Domain User, Group, and Computer Accounts 505

Foreword

It's a privilege to write a few words about this book, which I'm sure will become worn with use as it becomes an essential resource for you. Managing a Windows network is a challenging job. Between learning how to manage and administer server applications, configuring Active Directory security, defining group policies, and performing general maintenance, your hands are always full and there's always a fire to put out. As with most activities, efficient management of a Windows network requires a thorough understanding of the tools that are available to you. There are many cases where performing a task or solving a problem can become more difficult or even be impossible without the right tool.

For example, knowing how to leverage command-line tools and support mechanisms can save you both time and effort. For example, if you have to create 100 user accounts you can either create the accounts one by one using the Users and Computers MMC snapin, or you can do the same thing in a fraction of the time with a simple batch file or WMI script. Configuring a network adapter on a system through a user interface requires you to access the system physically or through a remote-access application, but you can use a script to do the same thing with one command from anywhere in your network.

Whether you are a new or veteran Windows administrator, you've almost certainly found that the difficult part of the management recipe is not using the tools, but identifying the best ones to use for various tasks. Some tools ship with Windows, some are provided by Microsoft on the support CD, from the Resource Kit, or from its web site, and yet others are available on the web. In many cases there are several tools or ways to accomplish the same task, but some ways are more efficient than others in certain circumstances.

That's why you need a book like this. Robbie has done a fantastic job identifying common Windows management tasks, investigating the tools available for those tasks, figuring out how to get the most out of them, testing them in real-world environments, and serving it to you in a no-nonsense reference. This book will save you precious time that will reimburse your investment in it many times over.

—Mark Russinovich
Austin, TX

Preface

From my admittedly biased viewpoint, system administrators don't get enough credit. The system administration profession doesn't get the same kind of respect as the law or medical communities, even though system administrators are constantly asked to diagnosis highly technical problems and perform intricate surgery on both hardware and software issues. And sometimes there may even be lives at stake! OK, perhaps I'm over-dramatizing the situation, but my point is that system administrators are the unsung heroes of the IT revolution and don't get the recognition they deserve.

There are thousands of programs, tools, commands, screens, scripts, buttons, tabs, applets, menus, and settings that system administrators need to know about and understand to do their job. And it has only been in the past couple of years that Microsoft's documentation has actually been more of a help than a hindrance. But it still isn't enough. What Windows system administrators really need is quick and easy ways to find what they need to get the job done.

There are plenty of books that go into all sorts of detail about the theory behind a particular technology or application, but what if you don't need that? What if you know the theory but just can't (or don't want to) remember the exact command-line or graphical sequence to configure an application? Or perhaps you need some bare-bones code to help automate a task. There are very few books that cut through the fluff and provide only the essentials for getting the job done. This book is intended to do just that. This book also provides added value by describing exactly when a task can come in handy and listing additional pointers for more information.

Based on my own experience, hours of research, and years of hanging out on news-groups and mailing lists, I've compiled over 300 recipes that should answer many of the "How do I..." questions one could pose about Windows Server. And just as in the Perl community where the *Perl Cookbook* was a latecomer that sells well even today, I believe the *Windows Server Cookbook* will also be a great addition to any Windows system administrator's library.

Who Should Read This Book

As with many of the books in the Cookbook series, *Windows Server Cookbook* can be useful to anyone who has to deploy, administer, or automate Windows Server 2003 or Windows 2000. This book can serve as a great reference for those who have to work with Windows Server on a day-to-day basis. And because of all the scripting samples, this book can be really beneficial to programmers who want to accomplish various tasks in an application. For those without much programming background, the VBScript solutions are straightforward and should be easy to follow and expand on.

If you like the format of this book, but crave more recipes on Active Directory, I highly recommend checking out *Active Directory Cookbook*. It is similar to this book in structure, except has over 320 recipes devoted only to Active Directory. I gave up trying to remember all the nerd knobs and tweaks you could do to Active Directory; I wrote *Active Directory Cookbook* so I would have them all in one place. O'Reilly is in the process of publishing additional Cookbooks on topics such as Windows XP, Exchange Server, and Windows Server Security to name a few.

What's in This Book

This book consists of 17 chapters. Here is a brief overview of each chapter.

- Chapter 1, *Introduction*, sets the stage for the book by covering where you can find the tools used in the book, VBScript and Perl issues to consider, and where to find additional information. It also contains code for many generic scripts, such as reading data from an Excel spreadsheet, or sending the output of a script via email, which you can plug into code samples in later chapters.

- Chapter 2, *System Configuration*, covers some basic configuration tasks that most administrators will need to do after installing a server. Some of these include setting the time, configuring page files, joining the server to a domain, and configuring failure options.

- Chapter 3, *Disks, Drives, and Volumes*, covers disk quotas, converting between disk types, creating drives, mapping drives, and managing volumes.

- Chapter 4, *Files, Folders, and Shares*, covers file and folder manipulation, creating shortcuts and links, modifying file properties, and managing share points.

- Chapter 5, *Running and Scheduling Tasks*, covers the primary ways you can run and schedule tasks on Windows Server.

- Chapter 6, *Processes*, covers both basic and advanced process management. It includes how to create, suspend, and kill processes along with how to view the DLLs and APIs used by a process.

- Chapter 7, *Services*, covers starting and stopping services, running scripts as services, searching for services, and viewing various service properties.

- Chapter 8, *Event Logs*, covers how to create and view events, create and manage event logs, and search event logs.

- Chapter 9, *Registry*, covers basic registry administration. It includes recipes on how to create and delete registry keys and values, exporting and importing registry files, restricting access to the registry, and monitoring registry activity.

- Chapter 10, *Network Configuration*, covers tasks related to configuring network adapters, viewing network configuration, viewing network traffic, and installing IPv6 support.

- Chapter 11, *Security Best Practices*, covers several tasks related to securing Windows Server 2003, including auditing, screen saver locking, creating strong passwords, and disabling unused accounts.

- Chapter 12, *Internet Information Services 6.0*, covers basic IIS 6.0 administration, including installing IIS, creating web and FTP sites, enabling SSL, and running executable content.

- Chapter 13, *Domain Name System (DNS)*, covers installation and maintenance of the DNS Server, including creating and viewing zones, creating resource records, converting a zone to be AD-integrated, scavenging old resource records, and enabling debug logging.

- Chapter 14, *DHCP Server*, covers installing the DHCP Server, authorizing a DHCP Server, configuring server options, creating scopes, viewing and managing leases, and maintaining a DHCP.

- Chapter 15, *Active Directory*, covers basic Active Directory administration, including creating a forest, raising the functional level, backing up and restoring of Active Directory, searching a domain, creating and modifying objects, importing and exporting objects, finding and managing FSMO role holders, and managing trusts.

- Chapter 16, *Domain User, Group, and Computer Accounts*, covers how to create, modify, and configure user, group, and computer objects in Active Directory.

- Chapter 17, *Exchange Server 2003*, covers some basic tasks related to installing and configuring Exchange. It also includes mailbox and distribution list administration tasks.

There are also six appendixes included with this book:

- Appendix A, *Introduction to WSH*, provides an overview of using Windows Script Host.

- Appendix B, *Introduction to WMI*, is a short introduction to scripting with Windows Management Instrumentation.

- Appendix C, *Introduction to ADSI*, covers the basics of Active Directory Services Interface programming.

- Appendix D, *List of Default Environment Variables*, contains a list of environment variables that are available by default.
- Appendix E, *List of Default Processes*, contains a list of processes that run by default.
- Appendix F, *List of Default Services*, contains a list of services that are installed by default.

This book covers hundreds of tasks you'll need to do at one point or another with Windows Server. If you feel something important has been left out that should be included, let me know. I'll work to get it in a future edition. For contact information, see the "We'd Like to Hear from You" section.

Conventions Used in This Book

The following typographical conventions are used in this book:

Constant width
> Indicates command-line elements, computer output, and code examples.

Constant width italic
> Indicates placeholders (for which you substitute an actual name) in examples and in registry keys.

Constant width bold
> Indicates user input.

Italic
> Introduces new terms and URLs, commands, file extensions, filenames, directory or folder names, and UNC pathnames.

Bold
> Indicates labels on buttons and menu items.

 Indicates a tip, suggestion, or general note. For example, I'll tell you if you need to use a particular version or if an operation requires certain privileges.

 Indicates a warning or caution. For example, I'll tell you if Active Directory does not behave as you'd expect or if a particular operation has a negative impact on performance.

Using Code Examples

This book is here to help you get your job done. In general, you may use the code in this book in your programs and documentation. You do not need to contact us for permission unless you're reproducing a significant portion of the code. For example, writing a program that uses several chunks of code from this book does not require permission. Selling or distributing a CD-ROM of examples from O'Reilly books *does* require permission. Answering a question by citing this book and quoting example code does not require permission. Incorporating a significant amount of example code from this book into your product's documentation *does* require permission.

We appreciate, but do not require, attribution. An attribution usually includes the title, author, publisher, and ISBN. For example: "*Windows Server Cookbook* by Robbie Allen. Copyright 2005 O'Reilly Media, Inc., 0-596-00633-0."

If you feel your use of code examples falls outside fair use or the permission given above, feel free to contact us at *permissions@oreilly.com*.

Safari Enabled

 When you see a Safari® Enabled icon on the cover of your favorite technology book, it means the book is available online through the O'Reilly Network Safari Bookshelf.

Safari offers a solution that's better than e-books. It's a virtual library that lets you easily search thousands of top tech books, cut and paste code samples, download chapters, and find quick answers when you need the most accurate, current information. Try it for free at *http://safari.oreilly.com*.

We'd Like to Hear from You

The information in this book has been tested and verified to the best of my ability, but mistakes and oversights do occur. Please let the publisher know about errors you may find, as well as your suggestions for future editions, by writing to:

> O'Reilly Media, Inc.
> 1005 Gravenstein Highway North
> Sebastopol, CA 95472
> (800) 998-9938 (in the United States or Canada)
> (707) 829-0515 (international or local)
> (707) 829-0104 (fax)

O'Reilly maintains a web page for the book, which lists errata, examples, and any additional information. You can access this page at:

> *http://www.oreilly.com/catalog/winsckbk*

Examples can also be found at my web site:

> *http://www.rallenhome.com/books/winsckbk/*

To comment or ask technical questions about this book, send email to:

bookquestions@oreilly.com

For more information about O'Reilly books, conferences, software, Resource Centers, and the O'Reilly Network, see O'Reilly's web site at:

http://www.oreilly.com

Acknowledgments

Instead of saving the best for last, I think it is high time I mention my wife first when it comes to acknowledgments. Without her, I'd probably be stuck in some small apartment with nothing but TV dinners in the refrigerator. She is a constant reminder (especially when the grass gets tall) that there is more to life than my occupation. Thank you for being my best friend.

As far as O'Reilly goes, there isn't a better publisher in the business. I'd like to give special thanks to John Osborn for listening to all of my crazy ideas. And I am especially grateful to Andy Oram for ensuring I stay on a path to lucidity. Andy has been a great role model for a certain up-and-coming editor.

I was very fortunate to have a very talented group of technical reviewers for this book. Without them, this book would have been much weaker. In alphabetical order, they are Rick Kingslan, Carlos Magalhaes, Tony Murray, Joe Richards, Michael B. Smith, and Mitch Tulloch.

Joe Richards, of Joeware (*http://www.joeware.net/*) fame, wrote Chapter 17 and did an excellent job. Now if I could only convince him to write a book of his own…

Mitch Tulloch, well-known author (*http://www.mtit.com/*), wrote all of the content for Chapter 12, except for the scripting solutions. He did a great job, and I'm really pleased with how it turned out. Mitch is a class act.

Alistair Lowe-Norris wrote most of the content contained in Appendixes A and C.

I also want to thank Mark Russinovich for taking time out of his busy schedule to write the foreword for this book. And thanks for all of the great Sysinternals tools as well.

CHAPTER 1

Introduction

The Windows Server operating system (OS) has come a long way in the past ten years. In the early days of Windows NT, system crashes were common annoyances that administrators had to learn to deal with. There were few tools to manage the OS, and the ones that were available, which mainly consisted of the graphical variety, were limited in functionality and didn't scale well. Also at that time, Microsoft was not yet serious about providing intuitive scripting interfaces, which would enable administrators to automate repetitive tasks. The result was that administrators were forced to do a lot with a little.

The tides changed dramatically with the release of Windows 2000, which turned out to be much more scalable and manageable. Microsoft began to improve in the management areas it had previously lacked by adding more tools and introducing several new scripting interfaces that were robust and easy to use.

But in many ways, Windows 2000 felt like a first version release of a major piece of software, which it was. Windows 2000 did a lot of things right, but there were still major gaps in terms of manageability. Windows Server 2003, Microsoft's latest server OS, is a much more mature platform. It isn't as big of an upgrade as Windows NT to Windows 2000, but Microsoft smoothed out a lot of the rough edges that were present in Windows 2000.

So what are we left with? If I had to sum it up into a single sentence: Windows Server 2003, and Windows 2000 to a lesser degree, is a sophisticated OS that has been built from the ground up to be both scalable and manageable, and supports all of the major information technology services you need to run a business or organization. The result is that administrators now have to do a lot with a lot.

You can't get all of this capability wrapped up into a single OS without some trade-offs. To be able to take full advantage of Windows 2000 Server or Windows Server 2003, you have to know lots of gory technical details. You have to know how to navigate through the hundreds of dialogs and menus. You have to know which command-line utilities are available to accomplish various specific tasks, where to find them, and which options you should use for each utility. You have to know what scripting interfaces are available to automate tasks so you can keep your support costs low. We take it for granted, but that is a lot for any one person to know. I've been doing Windows system administration for eight years and I still have a difficult time recalling the correct tool or command or scripting interface for certain tasks.

And that is the purpose of this book: to be a comprehensive reference so I don't have to waste time (and brain cells) trying to remember that Windows Management Instrumentation (WMI) doesn't have any scripting interfaces for creating or modifying page files; or how to use Group Policy to run a task on a group of workstations; or how to find all of the files that are currently open on a system. This book covers general system administration duties, but it also covers a great deal more. There are dedicated chapters on many of the major services you'll end up running at one point including IIS, DNS, DHCP, Active Directory, and Exchange.

Approach to the Book

If you are familiar with the O'Reilly Cookbook format that you can find in other popular books such as *Active Directory Cookbook*, *Perl Cookbook*, or *DNS and BIND Cookbook*, then the layout of this book will not be new to you. It is composed of 17 chapters, each containing 10–30 recipes that describe how to perform a particular task. Most recipes contain four sections: *Problem*, *Solution*, *Discussion*, and *See Also*. The Problem section briefly describes the task the recipe addresses and when you might need to use it. The Solution section contains step-by-step instructions on how to accomplish the task. Depending on the task, there could be up to three different sets of solutions covered. The Discussion section goes into detail about the solution(s). The See Also section contains references to additional sources of information that can be useful if you still need more information after reading the discussion. The See Also section may reference other recipes, Microsoft Knowledge Base (MS KB) (*http://support.microsoft.com/*) articles, or documentation from the Microsoft Developers Network (MSDN) (*http://msdn.microsoft.com*).

At Least Three Ways to Do It

People like to work in different ways. Some prefer graphical interfaces (GUIs) while others like to work from the command-line interface (CLI). And experienced system administrators like to automate tasks using scripts. Since people prefer different methods, and no one method is necessarily better than another, I decided to write solutions to recipes using one of each. That means instead of a single solution per recipe, I include up to three solutions using GUI, CLI, and scripting examples. That said, some recipes cannot be accomplished with one of the three methods or it may be very difficult to do with a particular method. In that case, I cover only the applicable methods.

In the GUI and CLI solutions, I use standard tools that are readily accessible. There are other freeware, shareware, or commercial tools that I could have used that would have made some of the tasks easier to accomplish, but I wanted to make this book as useful as possible without requiring you to hunt down the tools or purchase an expensive software package.

I took a similar approach with the scripting solutions. While I prefer Perl, I use VBScript due to its widespread use among Windows administrators. It is also the most straightforward from a coding perspective when using WMI and Windows Script Host (WSH). For those familiar with other languages, such as Visual Basic, Perl, and JScript, it is very easy to convert code from VBScript. See the sidebar "Differences Between VBScript and Perl" for more information on how to convert between those two languages.

For those of you who wish that all of the solutions were written with Perl instead of VBScript, you are in luck. I've posted companion Perl scripts for each VBScript example on the book's web site. Go to *http://www.rallenhome.com/books/* to download the code.

Windows 2000 Versus Windows Server 2003

Another challenge with writing this book was determining which operating system version to cover. Many organizations still run Windows 2000, but Windows Server 2003 has been a big seller (at least according to Microsoft). Since Windows Server 2003 is the latest and greatest version and includes a lot of new tools that aren't present in Windows 2000, my approach is to make everything work under Windows Server 2003 first, and Windows 2000 second. In fact, the majority of the solutions will work unchanged with Windows 2000. For the recipes or solutions that are specific to a particular version, I include a note mentioning the version it targets. Most GUI and scripting solutions work unchanged with either version, but Microsoft introduced several new command-line tools with Windows Server 2003, many of which cannot be run on Windows 2000 as certain system application programming interfaces (APIs) have changed from Windows 2000 to Windows Server 2003. Typically, you can still use these newer tools on a Windows XP or Windows Server 2003 computer to manage Windows 2000.

Where to Find the Tools

For the GUI and CLI solutions to mean much to you, you need access to the tools that are used in the examples. For this reason, in the majority of cases and unless otherwise noted, I used only tools that are part of the default operating system or available in the Resource Kit or Support Tools. There are two exceptions to this rule that I'll explain shortly.

Differences Between VBScript and Perl

Here are some of the main differences between VBScript and Perl:

- With Perl, you have to use the `Win32::OLE` module and `Win32::OLE->GetObject` method to access the WMI, WSH, or ADSI scripting interface. With VBScript, you simply need to call the built-in `GetObject` function.
- Perl uses the arrow operator (->) to invoke a method on an object, whereas VBScript uses a dot (.).
- In Perl, the backslash (\) character is the escape character, so you need to use two backslashes when using it within double quotes.
- Perl uses special characters to distinguish variables, whereas VBScript doesn't use a character. With Perl, the basic convention is the dollar sign for scalar variables (e.g., $string), the at sign for arrays (e.g., @elements), and the percent sign for hashes (e.g., %dictionary).
- Perl is generally case sensitive, whereas VBScript is not.
- VBScript requires an underscore to continue a statement to the next line, whereas Perl does not.
- Perl uses the dot (.) for string concatenation, whereas VBScript uses the ampersand (&).
- Perl requires that each statement end with a semicolon (;), whereas VBScript assumes the end of the line is the end of the statement (unless the underscore continuation character is used).
- Perl uses the `my` keyword to predefine variables, whereas VBScript uses the `Dim` keyword.
- Perl uses pound (#) for comments, whereas VBScript uses a single quote (').

If you can keep these differences in mind, along with being able to convert basic language constructs (`for` loops, `if then else` conditionals, etc.), you should have no problems converting VBScript to Perl.

The Resource Kits for Windows 2000 Server and Windows Server 2003 are invaluable sources of information, and provide numerous tools that aid administrators in their daily tasks. More information on the Resource Kits can be found at the following web site: *http://www.microsoft.com/windows/reskits/*. Some tools are freely available online, but others must be purchased as part of a Resource Kit. The Windows 2000 Support Tools, which are called the Windows Support Tools in Windows Server 2003, contain many "must have" tools for people that work with Windows Server. The installation MSI for the Windows Support Tools can be found on a Windows 2000 Server or Windows Server 2003 CD in the *\support\tools* directory.

Even though many of the same tools are available in both the Windows 2000 Support Tools and Windows Server 2003 Support Tools, several have been enhanced in the latter version including LDP, Dsacl, and LDIFDE.

The biggest source of tools that I use that don't come from Microsoft can be found on the Sysinternals web site: *http://www.sysinternals.com/*. Mark Russinovich and Bryce Cogswell have developed a suite of extremely useful tools that every Windows Server system administrator should be familiar with. These tools are free and they often come with complete source code for the tool.

Another good source of tools, especially for Active Directory, is Joe Richards' Joeware site: *http://www.joeware.net/*. Joe wrote many of his tools, some in executable form and others in Perl, to help in daily system administration tasks, so they are all very practical and useful. And like Sysinternals, most are free.

Running Tools with Alternate Credentials

A best practice for managing Windows Server systems is to create separate administrator accounts with elevated privileges, instead of letting administrators use the same user account with which they access network resources. This is beneficial because an administrator who wants to use elevated privileges must explicitly log on with his admin account instead of having the rights all the time, which could lead to accidental changes. Assuming you employ this method, you have to provide alternate credentials when using tools to administer systems unless you log on (locally or with Terminal Services) to the target machine with the admin credentials.

There are several ways to specify alternate credentials when running tools. Many GUI and CLI tools have an option to specify a user and password for authentication. If the tool you want to use does not have that option, you can use the *runas.exe* command instead. The following command runs the *enumprop.exe* command under the credentials of the administrator account in the *rallencorp.com* domain:

```
> runas /user:administrator@rallencorp.com /netonly "enumprop LDAP://dc1/
dc=rallencorp,dc=com"
```

Sometimes it is convenient to create a MMC console that runs under administrator privileges. In this case, simply use *mmc.exe* as the command to run from *runas*:

```
> runas /user:administrator@rallencorp.com /netonly "mmc.exe"
```

This will create an empty MMC console from which you can add consoles for any snap-in that has been installed on the local computer. This is beneficial because all of the consoles that you add will be run under that administrative account. If you don't want to type that command over and over, simply create a shortcut on your desktop and put the command as the target path. By doing this, you eliminate one of the common complaints about using alternate credentials; that is, it makes the job more tedious.

 The /netonly option is necessary if the user you are authenticating with does not have local logon rights on the computer from which you are running the command, or if you want to authenticate with an account from a nontrusted domain.

There is another option for running MMC snap-ins or any GUI program with alternate credentials. Click on the Start menu and browse to the tool you want to open, hold down the Shift key, and then right-click on the tool. If you select **Run As**, you will be prompted to enter alternate credentials with which to run the tool.

A Brief Word on Windows Scripting

Much has been said over the years about how unfriendly Windows Server is to experienced system administrators who want to automate tasks with scripts. I'm pleased to say that Microsoft has made some great strides in this area over the past three or four years so that now there are very few tasks that you cannot automate with a script.

Microsoft has developed three primary scripting interfaces over the years: WSH, WMI, and ADSI. Note that I said that these are interfaces, not languages. In generic terms, a scripting interface is just a framework for how a script calls functions or methods to perform tasks. WSH is the scripting engine that acts as the interpreter for the scripting languages that are native to Windows (i.e., VBScript and Jscript). It has an interface for doing basic scripting such as printing out to a console or displaying a dialog box, processing command-line arguments, and other basic system administration tasks such as reading and writing files and manipulating the Registry. WMI is the high-octane system management interface. With it you can query and often configure many of the components within Windows. WMI is to computers what ADSI is to Active Directory. ADSI is the primary scripting interface for querying and manipulating objects in Active Directory. You can also use it to manage local users and groups on a computer as well as the IIS Metabase.

For a more thorough introduction to each of these interfaces, check out Appendixes A, B, and C.

Getting the Most Out of Your Scripts

With the VBScript solutions, my intention is to provide the answer in as few lines of code as is reasonable. Since this book is not a pure programming book, I did not want to overshadow the graphical and command-line solutions by providing pages of code or detailed explanations on how to use WSH, WMI, or ADSI. If you are looking for such material, I recommend my book *Active Directory Cookbook* (O'Reilly) or *Windows 2000 Scripting Guide* by Microsoft Corporation (MSPress). The code in this book is meant to show you the basics for how a task can be automated and let you run with it. Most examples will take only minor tweaking to make them do something useful in your environment.

To make the code as simple as possible, I had to remove error checking and other features that are standard scripting best practices. Next, I'll describe how to incorporate these things into your own scripts so that you can quickly turn any code in this book into a robust script with all the trimmings.

Running Scripts Using Alternate Credentials

Just as you might need to run the graphical and command-line tools with alternate credentials, you may also need to run your scripts and programs with alternate credentials. One way is to use the *runas* utility when you invoke a script from the command line. Another option is to use the Scheduled Tasks service to run the script under credentials you specify when creating the scheduled task. And yet another option is to hardcode the credentials in the script. Obviously this is not very appealing in many scenarios because you do not want the username and password contained in the script to be easily viewable by others. Nevertheless, at times it is a necessary evil, especially when working against multiple servers, and I'll describe how it can be done with WMI, ADSI, and ADO.

WMI

Here is example WMI code that prints the list of disk drives on a system:

```
strComputer = "."   ' localhost
set objWMI = GetObject("winmgmts:\\" & strComputer & "\root\cimv2")
set objDisks = objWMI.InstancesOf("Win32_LogicalDisk")
for each objDisk in objDisks
    Wscript.Echo "DeviceID: " &  objDisk.DeviceID
    Wscript.Echo "FileSystem: " &  objDisk.FileSystem
    Wscript.Echo "FreeSpace: " & objDisk.FreeSpace
    Wscript.Echo "Size: " & objDisk.Size
    WScript.Echo ""
next
```

This code does the same thing, except it targets a remote computer (srv01) and authenticates as the administrator account on that system:

```
set objLocator = CreateObject("WbemScripting.SWbemLocator")
set objWMI = objLocator.ConnectServer("srv01", "root\cimv2", _
                                      "srv01\administrator", "Adm1nPa33wd")
set objDisks = objWMI.InstancesOf("Win32_LogicalDisk")
for each objDisk in objDisks
    Wscript.Echo "DeviceID: " &  objDisk.DeviceID
    Wscript.Echo "FileSystem: " &  objDisk.FileSystem
```

```
        Wscript.Echo "FreeSpace: " & objDisk.FreeSpace
        Wscript.Echo "Size: " & objDisk.Size
        WScript.Echo ""
    next
```

To authenticate as an alternate user in WMI, you simply need to replace the GetObject call with two statements. The first is a call to CreateObject, which instantiates a SWbemLocator object. With this object, you can then call the ConnectServer method and specify the credentials for authentication. The first parameter is the server name, the second is the WMI provider path, the third is the user, and the fourth is the user's password.

ADSI

With ADSI, you can use the IADsOpenDSObject::OpenDSObject method to specify alternate credentials. For example, a solution to print out the description of a domain might look like the following:

```
    set objDomain = GetObject("LDAP://dc=rallencorp,dc=com")
    WScript.Echo "Description: " & objDomain.Get("description")
```

Using OpenDSObject, it takes only one additional statement to make the same code authenticate as the administrator account in the domain.

```
    set objLDAP = GetObject("LDAP:")
    set objDomain = objLDAP.OpenDSObject( _
        "LDAP://dc=rallencorp,dc=com", _
        "administrator@rallencorp.com", _
        "MyPassword", _
        0)
    WScript.Echo "Description: " & objDomain.Get("description")
```

ADO

It is just as easy to authenticate in ADO code. Take the following example, which queries all computer objects in the *rallencorp.com* domain:

```
    strBase   = "<LDAP://dc=rallencorp,dc=com>;"
    strFilter = "(&(objectclass=computer)(objectcategory=computer));"
    strAttrs  = "cn;"
    strScope  = "subtree"

    set objConn = CreateObject("ADODB.Connection")
    objConn.Provider = "ADsDSOObject"
    objConn.Open "Active Directory Provider"
    set objRS = objConn.Execute(strBase & strFilter & strAttrs & strScope)
    objRS.MoveFirst
    while Not objRS.EOF
        Wscript.Echo objRS.Fields(0).Value
        objRS.MoveNext
    wend
```

Now, by adding two lines (shown in bold), we can authenticate with the administrator account:

```
strBaseDN  =  "<LDAP://dc=rallencorp,dc=com>;"
strFilter  = "(&(objectclass=computer)(objectcategory=computer));"
strAttrs   = "cn;"
strScope   = "subtree"

set objConn = CreateObject("ADODB.Connection")
objConn.Provider = "ADsDSOObject"
objConn.Properties("User ID")  = "administrator@rallencorp.com"
objConn.Properties("Password") = "MyPassword"
objConn.Open "Active Directory Provider"
set objRS = objConn.Execute(strBaseDN & strFilter & strAttrs & strScope)
objRS.MoveFirst
while Not objRS.EOF
    Wscript.Echo objRS.Fields(0).Value
    objRS.MoveNext
wend
```

To authenticate with ADO, you need to set the User ID and Password properties of the ADO connection object. I used the user principal name (UPN) of the administrator for the user ID in this example. Active Directory allows connections with a UPN (*administrator@rallencorp.com*), NT 4.0–style account name (e.g., *RALLENCORP\ Administrator*), or distinguished name (e.g., *cn=administrator,cn=users,dc=rallencorp,dc=com*) for the user ID.

Defining Variables and Error Checking

An important part of any script is error checking. Error checking allows your programs to gracefully identify any issues that arise during execution and take appropriate action. Another good practice when writing scripts is to define variables before you use them and clean them up after you are done with them. In this book, most of the programmatic solutions do not include any error checking, predefined variables, or variable clean up. While admittedly this does not set a good example, if I included extensive error checking and variable management, it would have made this book considerably longer with little value to you, the reader.

Error checking with VBScript is pretty straightforward. At the beginning of the script, include the following declaration:

```
On Error Resume Next
```

This tells the script interpreter to continue even if errors occur. Without that declaration, whenever an error is encountered, the script will abort. When you use On Error Resume Next, you need to use the Err object to check for errors after any step where a fatal error could occur. The following example shows how to use the Err object.

```
On Error Resume Next
set objDomain = GetObject("LDAP://dc=rallencorp,dc=com")
if Err.Number <> 0 then
```

```
    Wscript.Echo "An error occured getting the domain object: " & Err.Description
    Wscript.Quit
end if
```

Two important properties of the Err object are Number, which if nonzero signifies an error, and Description which contains the error message (when present).

As far as variable management goes, it is always a good practice to include the following at the beginning of every script:

```
Option Explicit
```

When this is used, every variable in the script must be declared or an exception will be generated when you attempt to run the script. This prevents a mistyped name from causing hard-to-trace errors. Variables are declared in VBScript using the Dim keyword. After you are done with a variable, it is a good practice to set it to Nothing so you release any resources bound to the variable, and don't accidentally reuse the variable with its previous value. The following code shows a complete example for printing the display name for a domain with error checking and variable management included:

```
Option Explicit
On Error Resume Next

Dim objDomain
set objDomain = GetObject("LDAP://cn=users,dc=rallencorp,dc=com")
if Err.Number <> 0 then
    Wscript.Echo "An error occured getting the domain object: " & Err.Description
    Wscript.Quit
end if

Dim strDescr
strDescr = objDomain.Get("description")
if Err.Number <> 0 then
    Wscript.Echo "An error occured getting the description: " & Err.Description
    Wscript.Quit
end if

WScript.Echo "Description: " & strDescr

set objDomain = Nothing
set strDescr  = Nothing
```

Using Command-Line Options in a Script

Most code samples you'll see in this book use hardcoded variables. That means when you want to change the value of a variable, you have to modify the script. A much more flexible solution is to obtain the desired value of those variables via command-line options. All good command-line programs work this way.

With WSH, you can retrieve the command-line options that are passed to a script by enumerating the WScript.Arguments object. Here is an example:

```
set objArgs = WScript.Arguments
WScript.Echo "Total number of arguments: " & WScript.Arguments.Count
for each strArg in objArgs
    WScript.Echo strArg
next
```

This works OK, but there is no structure to it. You can't retrieve the value of the /foo option by name. You can only access elements of a WScript.Arguments collection by index number. But never fear, WSH 5.6 introduced named and unnamed arguments. Let's say we invoked the following command:

```
> d:\scripts\dostuff.vbs /c:test /verbose:4
```

This bit of code shows how you can access the /c and /verbose options:

```
WScript.Echo WScript.Arguments.Named.Item("c")
WScript.Echo WScript.Arguments.Named.Item("verbose")
```

Writing the Output of a Script to a File

In most of the code in this book, I simply print the output to STDOUT using the WScript.Echo method. This is OK if you need an interactive script, but what if you want to schedule one to run periodically? Printing the output to STDOUT won't do much good. An alternative is to write the output to a file instead. This is pretty easy using WSH. The following code appends some text to a file:

```
' ------ SCRIPT CONFIGURATION ------
strFile = "<FilePath>"    ' e.g. c:\output.txt
' ------ END CONFIGURATION ---------
const ForAppending = 8
set objFSO = CreateObject("Scripting.FileSystemObject")
set objFile = objFSO.OpenTextFile(strFile, constForAppending, True)
objFile.WriteLine("Script completed: " & Now)
objFile.Close
```

There is nothing magical here. The Scripting.FileSystemObject interface is used for working with files. The OpenTextFile method supports different access options. The following script is a variation of the earlier script except it opens a file for writing out all of the running processes (overwriting any existing data in the file):

```
' ------ SCRIPT CONFIGURATION ------
strFile = "<FilePath>"    ' e.g. c:\output.txt
' ------ END CONFIGURATION ---------
constForWriting = 2
set objFSO = CreateObject("Scripting.FileSystemObject")
set objFile = objFSO.OpenTextFile(strFile, constForWriting, True)

objFile.WriteLine("Script started: " & Now)
objFile.WriteLine("List of processes:")
```

```
set objWMI = GetObject("winmgmts:root\cimv2")
for each objProcess in objWMI.InstancesOf("Win32_Process")
    objFile.WriteLine(vbTab & objProcess.Name)
next

objFile.WriteLine("Script completed: " & Now)
objFile.Close
```

Instead of WScript.Echo, you have to use the WriteLine method of the Scripting.FileSystemObject object. If you also wanted to print the results to STD-OUT, there is nothing to prevent you from putting a WScript.Echo statement right before or after a WriteLine statement.

Sending the Output of a Script in Email

When you automate a task, you are being proactive. Part of being proactive is trying to identify issues before they turn into major problems. If your scripts simply append their status to a log file, it is unlikely you'll learn about any problems in a timely manner unless you are vigilantly watching over your log files. Fortunately, you can send emails very easily from VBScript so that instead of writing to a file, you can choose to send an email when there is a serious issue.

Here is an example script that just sends simple email:

```
' This code sends an email via SMTP
' ------ SCRIPT CONFIGURATION ------
strFrom = "script@rallencorp.com"
strTo   = "rallen@rallencorp.com"
strSub  = "Script Output"
strBody = "The script ran successfully"
strSMTP = "smtp.rallencorp.com"
' ------ END CONFIGURATION ---------

set objEmail = CreateObject("CDO.Message")
objEmail.From = strFrom
objEmail.To = strTo
objEmail.Subject = strSub
objEmail.Textbody = strBody
objEmail.Configuration.Fields.Item( _
        "http://schemas.microsoft.com/cdo/configuration/sendusing") = 2
objEmail.Configuration.Fields.Item( _
        "http://schemas.microsoft.com/cdo/configuration/smtpserver") = _
        strSMTP
objEmail.Configuration.Fields.Update
objEmail.Send
WScript.Echo "Email sent"
```

This code requires the use of a SMTP-enabled mail server. The email is directed toward the mail server, which relays it to the correct destination. This script also requires Microsoft Collaboration Data Objects (CDO) to be installed on the client computer. This can be done by installing Outlook or by installing CDO separately from the Microsoft site (search for "CDO" on *http://msdn.microsoft.com/*).

Reading and Writing from Excel

A common question I see on newsgroups has to do with reading and writing Excel spreadsheets from scripts. Why would you want to do this, you might ask? Well, let's suppose that I manage over 20 servers. I put together a small spreadsheet to keep track of them. Now, if I want to perform a task on all of my servers with a script, all I need to do is read information about each of the servers from the Excel spreadsheet and I don't have to worry about hardcoding the servers within the script.

This next script shows how to iterate over the rows in a worksheet until the script comes across a row that does not have the first cell populated:

```
' ------ SCRIPT CONFIGURATION ------
strExcelPath = "c:\data.xls"
intStartRow = 2
' ------ END CONFIGURATION ---------
On Error Resume Next
set objExcel = CreateObject("Excel.Application")
if Err.Number <> 0 then
  Wscript.Echo "Excel application not installed."
  Wscript.Quit
end if
On Error GoTo 0

objExcel.WorkBooks.Open strExcelPath
set objSheet = objExcel.ActiveWorkbook.Worksheets(1)

intRow = intStartRow
do while objSheet.Cells(intRow, 1).Value <> ""
  WScript.Echo "Row " & intRow
  WScript.Echo "Cell 1: " & objSheet.Cells(intRow, 1).Value
  WScript.Echo "Cell 2: " & objSheet.Cells(intRow, 2).Value
  WScript.Echo "Cell 3: " & objSheet.Cells(intRow, 3).Value
  WScript.Echo "Cell 4: " & objSheet.Cells(intRow, 4).Value
  intRow = intRow + 1
  WScript.Echo
loop

objExcel.ActiveWorkbook.Close
objExcel.Application.Quit
Wscript.Echo "Done"
```

In this case, I just printed the values from the first four cells. You could obviously do more complex stuff with that information.

Now suppose I wanted to analyze the process information of a system. I could use the *taskmgr.exe* program, but it doesn't really give me the flexibility I need. Instead I can write a script to output that information to a spreadsheet. Here is the code to do that:

```
' ------ SCRIPT CONFIGURATION ------
strComputer = "."
strExcelPath = "d:\procs.xls"
' ------ END CONFIGURATION ---------
```

```
On Error Resume Next
set objExcel = CreateObject("Excel.Application")
if Err.Number <> 0 then
  Wscript.Echo "Excel application not installed."
  Wscript.Quit
end if
On Error GoTo 0

' Create a new workbook.
objExcel.Workbooks.Add

' Bind to worksheet.
Set objSheet = objExcel.ActiveWorkbook.Worksheets(1)
objSheet.Name = "Processes"

' Populate spreadsheet cells with user attributes.
objSheet.Cells(1, 1).Value = "Process Name"
objSheet.Cells(1, 2).Value = "Command Line"
objSheet.Cells(1, 3).Value = "PID"
objSheet.Cells(1, 4).Value = "Owner"
objSheet.Range("A1:D1").Font.Bold = True

' Query process information
set objWMI = GetObject("winmgmts:\\" & strComputer & "\root\cimv2")
intProcessCount = 1
for each objProcess in objWMI.InstancesOf("Win32_Process")
   ' For each process, write the name, command-line options and process ID
   ' to the spreadsheet
   intProcessCount = intProcessCount + 1
   objSheet.Cells(intProcessCount,1).Value = objProcess.Name
   objSheet.Cells(intProcessCount,2).Value = ObjProcess.CommandLine
   objSheet.Cells(intProcessCount,3).Value = ObjProcess.ProcessID
   objProcess.GetOwner strUser,strDomain
   objSheet.Cells(intProcessCount,4).Value = strDomain & "\" & strUser
next

' This formats the columns
objExcel.Columns(1).ColumnWidth = 20
objExcel.Columns(2).ColumnWidth = 50
objExcel.Columns(3).ColumnWidth = 5
objExcel.Columns(4).ColumnWidth = 30

' Save the spreadsheet, close the workbook and exit.
objExcel.ActiveWorkbook.SaveAs strExcelPath
objExcel.ActiveWorkbook.Close
objExcel.Application.Quit

WScript.Echo "Done"
```

I included comments in the code to help you follow along with what is happening. Pretty straightforward, isn't it? Keep in mind that Excel must be installed on the computer in order to run this script.

Where to Find More Information

While it is my hope that this book provides you with enough information to perform the majority of Windows system administration tasks you are likely to do, it is not realistic to think every possible task can be covered. In fact, there are easily another five or six chapters I could have included in this book, but due to space and time considerations it was not possible for this edition. There is a wealth of additional resources and information you can find on the Internet or in a bookstore. In this section I cover some of the ones I use most frequently.

Help and Support Center

Windows Server 2003 comes with a new feature called the Help and Support Center, which is available directly off the Start menu. It is a great resource of information and it serves as the central location to obtain help information about the operating system, applications, and installed utilities.

Command-Line Tools

If you have any questions about the complete syntax or usage of a command-line tool used in the book, you should first look at the help information available with the tool. The vast majority of CLI tools provide syntax information by simply passing /? as a parameter. For example:

```
> netsh /?
```

Microsoft Knowledge Base

The Microsoft Help and Support web site is a great source of information and is home to the Microsoft Knowledge Base (MS KB) articles. Throughout the book I include references to pertinent MS KB articles where you can find more information on a topic. You can find the complete text for a KB article by searching on the KB number at the following web site: *http://support.microsoft.com/default.aspx*. You can also append the KB article number to the end of this URL to go directly to the article: *http://support.microsoft.com/?kbid=*.

Microsoft Developers Network

MSDN contains a ton of information on Windows Server and programmatic interfaces such as WMI. Throughout the book, I'll sometimes reference MSDN pages in recipes where applicable. Unfortunately, there is no easy way to reference the exact page I'm referring to unless I provided the URL or navigation to the page, which would more than likely change by the time the book was printed. Instead, I provide the title of the page, which you can search for via the following site: *http://msdn.microsoft.com/library/*.

Web Sites

These web sites are great starting points for information that helps you perform the tasks covered in this book:

Microsoft Windows Server home pages (http://www.microsoft.com/windowsserver2003/default.mspx; http://www.microsoft.com/windows2000/)
> These sites are the starting point for Windows Server information provided by Microsoft. They contain links to whitepapers, case studies, and tools.

Microsoft webcasts (http://support.microsoft.com/default.aspx?scid=fh;EN-US;pwebcst)
> Webcasts are on-demand audio/video technical presentations that cover a wide range of Microsoft products. There are numerous webcasts related to Windows Server technologies that cover such topics as disaster recovery, Windows Server 2003 upgrade, and Terminal Services deployment.

Google (http://www.google.com/)
> Google is my primary starting point for locating information. Google is often quicker and easier to use to search the Microsoft web sites (e.g., MSDN) than the search engines provided on those sites.

MyITForum (http://www.myitforum.com)
> The MyITForum site has very active online forums for various Microsoft technologies. It also has a large repository of scripts.

LabMice (http://www.labmice.net/)
> The LabMice web site contains a large collection of links to information on Windows Server including MS KB articles, whitepapers, and other useful web sites.

Robbie Allen's home page (http://www.rallenhome.com/)
> This is my personal web site, which has information about the books I've written and links to download the code contained in each (including this book).

Microsoft Technet script center (http://www.microsoft.com/technet/community/scriptcenter/default.mspx)
> This site contains a large collection of WSH, WMI, and ADSI scripts.

Newsgroups

Most of the Windows Server–related Microsoft newsgroups are very active and have one or more of Microsoft's Most Valuable Professionals (MVPs) actively responding to questions. If you have a question and can't find an answer, try posting to the pertinent newsgroup.

These are general-purpose Windows Server newsgroups:

- microsoft.public.windows.server.general
- microsoft.public.win2000.general

Each of these newsgroups covers a specific Windows Server technology:

- microsoft.public.windows.server.security
- microsoft.public.win2000.security
- microsoft.public.inetserver.iis
- microsoft.public.windows.server.active_directory
- microsoft.public.win2000.active_directory
- microsoft.public.windows.server.dns
- microsoft.public.win2000.dns
- microsoft.public.exchange2000.general

These are the scripting-related newsgroups:

- microsoft.public.scripting.vbscript
- microsoft.public.scripting.wsh
- microsoft.public.windows.server.scripting
- microsoft.public.win32.programmer.wmi
- microsoft.public.adsi.general
- microsoft.public.active.directory.interfaces

If you have a question about a particular topic, a good starting point is to search the newsgroups using Google Groups (*http://groups.google.com/*). Just like Google's web search engine, Google's group search engine is an invaluable resource. Another good resource is the following Yahoo! Group: *http://groups.yahoo.com/group/adsianddirectoryservices*.

Books

In addition to the Resource Kit books, the following books are invaluable resources for Windows Server system administration:

The Ultimate Windows Server 2003 System Administrator's Guide by Robert Williams and Mark Walla (Addison-Wesley)
 This book is a good all-purpose tutorial on Windows Server 2003.

Windows Server 2003 in a Nutshell by Mitch Tulloch (O'Reilly)
 This is a great reference guide for Windows Server 2003.

Microsoft Windows 2000 Scripting Guide by Microsoft Windows Server Resource Kit Team (MS Press)
 This book is one of the best available on scripting with Windows 2000.

Active Directory Cookbook by Robbie Allen (O'Reilly)
 If you like the book you are reading now and want to learn more about Active Directory, you'll want to check out this book.

Magazines

A good way to stay current with the latest industry trends and system administration techniques is by reading magazines. Here are a few good ones you should consider subscribing to:

Windows IT Pro Magazine (http://www.windowsitpro.com/)
> This is a general-purpose monthly magazine for system administrators that support Microsoft products. The articles contributed by industry experts are informative and provide unique insight into common issues system administrators face.

Windows Scripting Solutions (http://www.winnetmag.com/WindowsScripting/)
> This is a useful monthly newsletter that covers all aspects of scripting in the Windows environment. You'll see a little bit of everything in this newsletter.

Security Administrator (http://www.winnetmag.com/WindowsSecurityIndex.cfm)
> Security is an important part of any system administrator's job these days. With this newsletter you'll be able to stay abreast of the latest Windows security issues.

CHAPTER 2

System Configuration

2.0   Introduction

There are many useful customizations you can make after installing the operating system. Some of the configuration options I cover in this chapter include setting the time and date, joining a server to a domain, configuring page files, and configuring startup and failure options. I then cover some settings that disable annoying Windows features. These aren't terribly important from a performance point of view, but are down-right necessary to reduce your frustration level when dealing with a server. Good examples of this include disabling the Manage/Configure Your Server Wizard and the Windows Server 2003 Shutdown Tracker.

Using a Command-Line Interface

Commands to help configure Windows Server are not in short supply. In Table 2-1, I list all the command-line utilities I use in this chapter along with where each can be found.

Table 2-1. Command-line tools used in this chapter

Tool	Windows Server 2003	Windows 2000 Server	Recipes
bootcfg	*%SystemRoot%\system32*	N/A	2.14
compname	*http://www.willowhayes.co.uk/*	*http://www.willowhayes.co.uk/*	2.8
date	CMD shell	CMD shell	2.7
dsmod	*%SystemRoot%\system32*	N/A	2.10
hostname	*%SystemRoot%\system32*	*%SystemRoot%\system32*	2.8
msoobe	*%SystemRoot%\system32\oobe*	N/A	2.1
net	*%SystemRoot%\system32*	*%SystemRoot%\system32*	2.2, 2.7
netdom	Windows 2003 Support Tools	Windows 2000 Support Tools	2.8–2.10
nltest	Windows 2003 Support Tools	Windows 2000 Support Tools	2.10
psinfo	*http://sysinternals.com/*	*http://sysinternals.com/*	2.6, 2.16

Table 2-1. Command-line tools used in this chapter (continued)

Tool	Windows Server 2003	Windows 2000 Server	Recipes
reg	%SystemRoot%\system32	Windows 2000 Support Tools	2.2, 2.3, 2.7, 2.12, 2.15, 2.17, 2.18
setx	Windows 2003 Support Tools	Windows 2000 Resource Kit	2.11
shutdown	%SystemRoot%\system32	Windows 2000 Resource Kit	2.8, 2.19
srvinfo	Windows 2003 Resource Kit	Windows 2000 Resource Kit	2.6, 2.16
systeminfo	%SystemRoot%\system32	N/A	2.6, 2.12, 2.16
time	CMD shell	CMD shell	2.7
wmic	%SystemRoot%\system32\wbem	N/A	2.6, 2.11, 2.15

Using VBScript

When it comes to querying and configuring basic system properties of a server, WMI fits the bill in most cases. I use a variety of WMI classes throughout the chapter, which I've listed in Table 2-2.

Table 2-2. WMI classes used in this chapter

WMI Class	Recipes
StdRegProv	2.3, 2.8, 2.17, 2.18
Win32_BIOS	2.6
Win32_ComputerSystem	2.6, 2.8, 2.9, 2.14
Win32_Environment	2.11
Win32_Localtime	2.7
Win32_OSRecoveryConfiguration	2.15
Win32_OperatingSystem	2.6, 2.8, 2.16, 2.19
Win32_PageFileUsage	2.12
Win32_Processor	2.6
Win32_TimeZone	2.7
Win32_WindowsProductActivation	2.1

2.1   Activating Windows Server 2003

Problem

You want to activate or view the activation status of a Windows Server 2003 system. Microsoft requires that you activate Windows Server 2003 within 30 days of installation to validate you have a legal copy of the software.

Solution

Using a graphical user interface

1. From the Start menu, select All Programs → Activate Windows.
2. Select whether you want to activate by phone or over the Internet.

Using a command-line interface

The following command opens the Activation wizard described in the previous section:

```
> %systemroot%\system32\oobe\msoobe /a
```

There are no options that can activate the computer silently from the command line.

Using VBScript

```
' This code activates a Windows Server 2003 system.
' ------ SCRIPT CONFIGURATION ------
strComputer = "."

boolActivateOnline = True  ' If this is true, boolActivateOffline should
                           ' be false

boolActivateOffline = False ' If this is true, boolActivateOnline should
                            ' be false
strOfflineConfirmationCode = "1234-5678" ' if Activating offline, you need
                                         ' specify a confirmation code
' ------ END CONFIGURATION ---------
set objWMI = GetObject("winmgmts:\\" & strComputer & "\root\cimv2")
set colWPA = objWMI.InstancesOf("Win32_WindowsProductActivation")
for each objWPA in colWPA
   WScript.Echo "Activation Settings:"
   Wscript.Echo "  Activation Required: " & objWPA.ActivationRequired
   Wscript.Echo "  Caption: " & objWPA.Caption
   Wscript.Echo "  Description: " & objWPA.Description
   Wscript.Echo "  Notification On: " & objWPA.IsNotificationOn
   Wscript.Echo "  Product ID: " & objWPA.ProductID
   Wscript.Echo "  Remaining Eval Period: " & objWPA.RemainingEvaluationPeriod
   Wscript.Echo "  Remaining Grace Period: " & objWPA.RemainingGracePeriod
   Wscript.Echo "  Server Name: " & objWPA.ServerName
   Wscript.Echo "  Setting ID: " & objWPA.SettingID
   WScript.Echo

   if objWPA.ActivationRequired = True then
      if boolActivateOnline = True then
         intRC = objWPA.ActivateOnline
         if intRC <> 0 then
            WScript.Echo "Error activating online: " & intRC
         else
            WScript.Echo "Successfully activated online"
         end if
      end if
```

```
       if boolActivateOffline = True then
          intRC = objWPA.ActivateOffline(strOfflineConfirmationCode)
          if intRC <> 0 then
             WScript.Echo "Error activating offline: " & intRC
          else
             WScript.Echo "Successfully activated offline"
          end if
       end if
    end if
 next
```

Discussion

Microsoft estimates that it has lost billions of dollars due to pirated, or illegally copied, software. Microsoft Product Activation (MPA) is a new technology used to reduce software piracy. Microsoft has integrated MPA into their most recent operating systems (i.e., Windows XP and Windows Server 2003) and some consumer applications (e.g., Microsoft Office). MPA is designed to prevent casual copying. For example, let's say you buy a single copy of Windows XP from Best Buy, install it on your computer, and then lend the CD to a friend who installs it on his computer. The second copy is considered pirated and not legitimate under MPA.

MPA is an umbrella term for the various Microsoft activation technologies such as Windows Product Activation (WPA) and Office Activation Wizard (OAW). You can run an unactivated copy of Windows for up to 30 days before you must activate it to use the system further. Over those 30 days, you are periodically reminded to activate Windows via a pop-up window from the system tray. The longer you wait the more frequent these notifications become. And they can be down right aggravating if you don't plan to activate the system for a number of days. Fortunately, you can disable these notifications. Here is a small script that does it:

```
strComputer = "."
set objWMI = GetObject("winmgmts:\\" & strComputer & "\root\cimv2")
set colWPA = objWMI.InstancesOf("Win32_WindowsProductActivation")
for each objWPA in colWPA
   objWPA.SetNotification(0)
next
```

Just don't forget that you still need to activate the system!

The activation process is an anonymous and relatively quick operation. No personally identifiable information is needed to activate the product. There are three different ways you can activate Windows. First, you can use a broadband connection over the Internet. This requires that ports 80 and 443 (HTTP and HTTPS) are open through your firewall, which if you use the Internet they undoubtedly are. Second, WPA can automatically connect to the Internet using a modem. And third, you can call a toll-free number to activate it over the phone.

If you have questions about WPA, see MS KB 302878, which is the MPA FAQ.

See Also

MS KB 291983 (Ports That Are Used by Windows Product Activation), MS KB 291997 (How to Activate Windows XP Using an Unattend.txt File), MS KB 302806 (Description of Microsoft Product Activation), MS KB 302878 (Frequently Asked Questions about Microsoft Product Activation), MS KB 325510 (Support WebCast: Microsoft Windows XP and Office XP: Understanding the New Mandatory Product Activation), and MS KB 326851 (Activation and Registration of a Microsoft Product)

2.2   Configuring Automatic Updates

Problem

You want to configure how updates are applied using the Automatic Updates feature.

Solution

Using a graphical user interface

To configure Automatic Updates locally on a system, do the following:

1. Open the System applet in the Control Panel.
2. Select the **Automatic Updates** tab.
3. Check the box beside **Keep my computer up to date** to enable Automatic Updates.
4. Once you have done that, the radio buttons under **Settings** will become active. Select how you want to be notified about new updates and whether you want to automatically install them.
5. Click **OK** when you are done.

To configure Automatic Updates using Group Policy, do the following:

1. Open the Group Policy Management Console.
2. In the left pane, navigate to the group policy object (GPO) you want to modify.
3. Right-click the target GPO and select **Edit**.
4. In the left pane of the Group Policy Object Editor, expand **Computer Configuration** → **Administrative Templates** → **Windows Update**.
5. In the right pane, double-click the setting you want to configure.

Using a command-line interface

The following commands enable Automatic Updates to automatically download new updates and notify when installation is ready to proceed:

```
> reg add HKLM\Software\Policies\Microsoft\Windows\WindowsUpdate\AU /t REG_DWORD /v
NoAutoUpdate /d 0
```

```
> reg add HKLM\Software\Policies\Microsoft\Windows\WindowsUpdate\AU /t REG_DWORD /v
AUOptions /d 3
> net stop wuauserv
> net start wuauserv
```

You must restart the Automatic Updates service before the changes take effect. See the Discussion for the complete list of Automatic Updates–related registry values.

The following commands, placed in a batch file, will enable Automatic Updates to automatically download new updates from a Software Update Services (SUS) v1.1 Server and notify when installation is ready to proceed:

```
set SUSSERVER=<SUSServerName>
net stop wuauserv
if exist temp.reg del temp.reg

echo Windows Registry Editor Version 5.00>>temp.reg
echo.>>temp.reg
echo [HKEY_LOCAL_MACHINE\SOFTWARE\Policies\Microsoft\Windows\WindowsUpdate]>>temp.reg
echo "WUServer"="http://%SUSSERVER%">>temp.reg
echo "WUStatusServer"="http://%SUSSERVER%">>temp.reg
echo.>>temp.reg
echo [HKEY_LOCAL_MACHINE\SOFTWARE\Policies\Microsoft\Windows\WindowsUpdate\AU]>>
temp.reg
echo "NoAutoUpdate"=dword:00000000>>temp.reg
echo "AUOptions"=dword:00000003>>temp.reg
echo "UseWUServer"=dword:00000001>>temp.reg
echo "ScheduledInstallDay"=dword:00000001>>temp.reg
echo "ScheduledInstallTime"=dword:00000003>>temp.reg
echo.>>temp.reg
echo [HKEY_LOCAL_MACHINE\SOFTWARE\Microsoft\Windows\CurrentVersion\WindowsUpdate\Auto
Update]>>temp.reg
echo "AUState"=dword:00000002>>temp.reg
echo "LastWaitTimeOut"="2000.01.01 00:00:01">>temp.reg
echo "SusServerVersion"=dword:00000001>>temp.reg
echo "ConfigVer"=dword:00000001>>temp.reg

regedit /s temp.reg
del temp.reg
net start wuauserv
```

Thanks to Michael B. Smith for providing this code.

Discussion

Patching systems is a critical issue system administrators face today. Many of the viruses and worms that spread like wildfire throughout the Internet could have been prevented if administrators had been more diligent in applying security updates.

With Windows 2000 SP2, Microsoft introduced Automatic Updates, which lets your computers automatically download and install these updates from Microsoft.

In the late 1990s, you couldn't blindly trust new patches from Microsoft, so you had to test them thoroughly before deploying them. Now, patches are much more reliable. You also don't have as much time to test them to ensure they won't introduce new problems. These factors make Automatic Updates a good solution to solve the problem. You can have updates download automatically and decide whether they should be installed automatically, periodically, or manually.

If you have many computers, you should consider using Software Update Services, SUS, (*http://www.microsoft.com/windowsserversystem/sus/default.mspx*) or Windows Update Services, WUS. These tools let you download updates to a central server from which internal computers can install the updates. There are two distinct advantages to this approach. First, you can optimize network utilization for the updates by downloading them only once. Second, you can selectively choose which updates clients will install. This gives you more control over how and where updates are installed in your environment.

The command-line batch file presented in the command-line solution is suitable, with modifications for your environment, to use for deploying SUS via registry control. While not as elegant as a group policy-based solution, it has the advantage of allowing you to easily customize SUS options for differing groups of computers (for example, you may wish for workstation computers to automatically reboot after patch application, but you almost certainly do not wish that to occur for server computers). This is a feature that will be built into WUS.

The command-line batch file also illustrates a mechanism for forcing the Automatic Updates service to restart a full update cycle. The last four echo commands cause the service to basically behave as if it had never been executed before. This corrects what I see as a bug in SUS—if additional patches are approved after a computer has already downloaded patches, but before it has installed them (and rebooted if necessary), then the Automatic Updates service will not process them until all of the prior patches have been installed.

There are desired scenarios that cannot feasibly be automated with SUS. Most of these limitations are expected to be overcome in WUS when it is released some time in 2005.

Using this batch file, in combination with *psexec* and the *shutdown* tool can allow you to fully manage your patch application needs for small- to medium-sized environments. For an example of a well-developed and full-featured script utilizing this concept, see *http://googleit.aptonline.net/pages/cmdscripts.html#SUSUR*. Large environments will likely be utilizing Microsoft's SMS or another centralized deployment application.

The SUS whitepaper (Patch Management Using Software Update Services 1.0 SP1 available at *http://www.microsoft.com/downloads/details.aspx?FamilyId=38D7E99B-E780-43E5-AA84-CDF6450D8F99&displaylang=en*) contains detailed information about all of the Automatic Updates service registry keys and their impact on SUS. MS KB 328010 contains a much more concise set of material suitable for most needs.

See Also

MS KB 294871 (Description of the Automatic Updates feature in Windows), MS KB 327850 (How to configure and use Automatic Updates in Windows 2000), MS KB 327838 (HOW TO: Schedule Automatic Updates in Windows XP, Windows 2000, or Windows Server 2003), and MS KB 328010 (How to configure automatic updates by using Group Policy or registry settings)

2.3   Disabling Windows Update

Problem

You want to prevent a user from running Windows Update or Automatic Updates.

Solution

Using a graphical user interface

1. Open the Group Policy Management Console.
2. In the left pane, navigate to the GPO you want to modify.
3. Right-click the target GPO and select **Edit**.
4. In the left pane of the Group Policy Object Editor, expand **User Configuration** → **Administrative Templates** → **Start menu and Taskbar**.
5. In the right pane, double-click **Remove links and access to Windows Update** (for Windows Server 2003) or **Disable and Remove Links to Windows Update** (for Windows 2000).
6. Select **Enable** and click **OK**.

Using a command-line interface

To disable Windows Update for all users who haven't logged in previously, run the following command:

```
> reg add HKU\.DEFAULT\Software\Microsoft\Windows\CurrentVersion\Policies\Explorer /t
REG_DWORD /v NoWindowsUpdate /d 1
```

To disable Windows Update for the user who is currently logged on, run the following command:

```
> reg add HKCU\Software\Microsoft\Windows\CurrentVersion\Policies\Explorer /t REG_
DWORD /v NoWindowsUpdate /d 1
```

Using VBScript

```
' This code disables Windows Update in the .Default profile.
' ------ SCRIPT CONFIGURATION ------
strComputer = "."
' ------ END CONFIGURATION ---------
const HKEY_USERS = &H80000003
strKey = ".DEFAULT\Software\Microsoft\Windows\CurrentVersion\Policies\Explorer"
set objReg=GetObject("winmgmts:\\" & strComputer & "\root\default:StdRegProv")
objReg.SetDwordValue HKEY_USERS, strKey, "NoWindowsUpdate", 1
WScript.Echo "Windows Update disabled in .Default profile"
```

Discussion

If you are using SUS or some other patch management system to distribute updates to your client-base, you may not want your clients accessing the Microsoft Windows Update site *(http://windowsupdate.microsoft.com/)*. One of the reasons to use something like SUS is so your users don't have to download the same updates over the Internet from Microsoft. If you leave Windows Update turned on, there is nothing to prevent them from doing it.

Fortunately, there is an easy way to disable it. You can use Group Policy to force the change to apply across a group of users (the Windows Update disablement settings are available only in the User Configuration section of a GPO). Or you can use the command-line or VBScript solutions to disable it via a login script or manually if need be.

Once this setting is in effect, a user will not see the Windows Update link in the Start Menu or Internet Explorer, and if the user attempts to access the Windows Update site, he will get a message indicating that Windows Update has been disabled for his computer.

See Also

MS KB 326686 ("Windows Update Was Disabled by Your System Administrator" Error Message)

2.4 Installing or Uninstalling a Windows Component

Problem

You want to install or uninstall a Windows Component.

Solution

Using a graphical user interface

1. From the Control Panel, open the Add or Remove Programs applet.
2. Click on **Add/Remove Windows Components**.
3. Click on the component you are interested in.
4. If there are subcomponents, the **Details** button will become active. Click on it. Check the box beside the components you want to install. When you are done, click **OK**.
5. Click **Next**. At this point the component(s) will be installed.
6. Click **Finish** to close the screen.

Using a command-line interface

Create an answer file using a text editor, such as *notepad.exe*. Here is an example answer file that would install the DNS Server service:

```
[netoptionalcomponents]
dns=1
```

See the Discussion section for more on answer files.

Next, run the *sysocmgr* utility with following parameters (assuming you named the answer file *c:\comp_install.txt*):

```
> sysocmgr /i:%windir%\inf\sysoc.inf /u:c:\comp_install.txt
```

 The *sysocmgr* utility has additional options for suppressing dialog boxes (/x and /q). For the complete list of *sysocmgr* options, run sysocmgr /? from a command line.

Using VBScript

Unfortunately, there are no scripting interfaces for installing Windows Components. However, you can run the *sysocmgr* command from the previous section directly within a batch script (*.bat* extension) or using the WScript.Shell Run method within VBScript.

```
' This code simulates the same steps from the command-line solution.
' First, an answer file is created containing the parameters to install
' the DNS Server. Then the sysocmgr command is invoked to perform the
' installation.
strFile = "c:\comp_install.txt"

constForWriting = 2
set objFSO = CreateObject("Scripting.FileSystemObject")
set objFile = objFSO.OpenTextFile(strFile, constForWriting, True)
objFile.WriteLine("[netoptionalcomponents]")
```

```
objFile.WriteLine("dns=1")
objFile.Close

set objWshShell = WScript.CreateObject("WScript.Shell")
intRC = objWshShell.Run("sysocmgr /i:%windir%\inf\sysoc.inf /u:" & _
                        strFile, 0, TRUE)
if intRC <> 0 then
   WScript.Echo "Error returned from sysocmgr command: " & intRC
else
   WScript.Echo "Windows Component installed"
end if
```

Discussion

A Windows Component is an optional feature of the operating system. A Windows Component can be anything from server service, such as DNS, to a small application, like Calculator. You've undoubtedly used the steps I described in the graphical solution to install a Windows Component before. Fewer people are as familiar with the command-line (and VBScript) solutions.

You can script the installation (and uninstallation for that matter) of Windows Components using the *sysocmgr.exe* utility. All you need is an answer file that contains the components to install or uninstall. This can in fact be the same answer file you use to do unattended installations. *Sysocmgr.exe* reads only the [Components] and [Netoptionalcomponents] sections of an answer file. To see all the available components you can include in these sections, you need to look at the unattended reference documentation that is available on the Windows Server CDs for Windows 2000 and Windows Server 2003.

On a Windows 2000 CD, navigate to *\SUPPORT\TOOLS* and open the *deploy.cab* file. Within *deploy.cab* is a file named *unattend.doc*, which you'll need to extract and open. This file contains all answer file settings. On a Windows Server 2003 CD, you also need to open *\SUPPORT\TOOLS\deploy.cab*, but instead you want to extract *ref.chm* from it. Within *ref.chm* is a section entitled *Unattend.txt*, which contains all of the settings.

Again, you'll want to look at the [Components] and [Netoptionalcomponents] sections of the reference documentation. For [Components] there are over 80 different entries you can use and for [Netoptionalcomponents] there are 13 possible entries. One difference to note about the two sections is that you enable or disable components in the [Components] section using on (to install) or off (to uninstall) and for the [Netoptionalcomponents] section you use 1 (to install) or 0 (to uninstall).

Here is a sample answer file that installs IIS and the DNS Server service:

```
[Components]
 iis_common = on
 iis_www = on
 iis_www_vdir_scripts = on
 iis_inetmgr = on
```

```
fp_extensions = on
iis_ftp = on
netoc = on

[NetOptionalComponents]
dns=1
```

 Answer files are case insensitive, so DNS=1 is the same as dns=1.

See Also

MS KB 222444 (How to Add or Remove Windows Components with Sysocmgr.exe)

2.5 Installing an Application or Service Pack via Group Policy

Problem

You want to push an application or service pack to a group of users or computers using group policy.

Solution

Using a graphical user interface

1. Open the Group Policy Management snap-in.

2. In the left pane, navigate to the GPO you want to modify. Left-click on it and select **Edit**.

3. If you want to publish an application to computers the GPO applies to, expand **Software Settings** under **Computer Configuration**. If you want it to apply to users, expand **Software Settings** under **User Configuration**.

4. Right-click **Software installation** and select **New** → **Package**.

5. Enter the UNC path of the location of the MSI installation file (even if it resides on a local drive on the domain controller.

6. Select the MSI file and click **Open**.

7. Select **Assigned** if you want this application to be installed automatically on each client the GPO applies to. Select **Published** if you want this application to be downloaded and made available to be installed via an **Add/Remove Programs** applet if the client chooses to install it (this option is only available for the User Configuration section of a GPO).

8. Click **OK**.

Discussion

You can use group policy to install applications, hotfixes, and service packs on servers. The preferred method for installation is to use Microsoft Installer files, but you can also use something called a ZAW down-level application package (ZAP) file to do non-MSI–based installations (for example, using *Setup.exe* instead). ZAP installations can be configured only in the **User Configuration** section of a GPO. For more on ZAP installations, see MS KB 231747.

When you *assign* an application to the **User Configuration** section of a GPO, the application is automatically installed the next time targeted users log into a computer. When an application is assigned to the **Computer Configuration** section of a GPO, it is installed the next time the GPO is refreshed on targeted computers (or when the computers reboot). In both cases, the application installation is finalized the first time a user actually runs the program.

Publishing an application is a little different. You can publish an application only in the **User Configuration** section of a GPO, not the **Computer Configuration** section. After you publish an application, it will show up in the **Add/Remove Programs** applet and be available for the user to install on demand.

 You can force a GPO to be refreshed on a client using the secedit or gpupdate utilities. For more information, see MS KB 203607 for Windows 2000 or MS KB 298444 for Windows XP and Windows Server 2003.

You can do much more than just basic assigning and publishing of applications with GPOs. You can also upgrade and remove applications. For a quick overview of those processes, see MS KB 314934. You can also use the GPO software installation feature to install service packs on your clients. See MS KB 278503 for more information on how to install a service pack using a GPO.

See Also

MS KB 203607 (HOW TO: How to Modify the Default Group Policy Refresh Interval), MS KB 257718 (HOW TO: Create Third-Party Microsoft Installer Package (MSI)), MS KB 278503 (Best Practices for Using Update.msi to deploy Service Packs), MS KB 302430 (How to assign software to a specific group by using a Group Policy), MS KB 314934 (HOW TO: Use Group Policy to Remotely Install Software in Windows 2000), MS KB 324750 (HOW TO: Assign Software to a Specific Group By Using a Group Policy in the Windows Server 2003 Family), and MS KB 816102 (HOW TO: Use Group Policy to Remotely Install Software in Windows Server 2003)

2.6   Viewing System Properties

Problem

You want to view the system properties of a server. These properties include operating system version, system manufacturer and model, processors, memory, and logon domain to name a few.

Solution

Using a graphical user interface

From the Start menu, select **All Programs** (or **Programs** on Windows 2000) → **Accessories** → **System Tools** → **System Information**.

You can also get some system information by going to **Start** → **Run**. Type **WinVer** and click **OK**.

If you want to view the installed hardware on a machine, go to **Start** → **Run**. Type **devmgmt.msc** and click **OK**.

Using a command-line interface

There are numerous ways to get system information from the command line. You can run the new Windows Server 2003 utility, *systeminfo.exe* against Windows 2000, Windows XP, or other Windows Server 2003 systems. Use the /s option to run the command against a remote server as in this example:

```
> systeminfo /s <ServerName>
```

The *srvinfo.exe* utility, which is available in the Windows Server 2003 and Windows 2000 Resource Kits, can also retrieve system information remotely. It displays a list of installed services, service packs, and hotfixes.

```
> srvinfo \\<ServerName>
```

Lastly, the Sysinternals *psinfo.exe* tool retrieves similar information for a local or remote system. The tool has options for viewing hotfixes (-h option), software (-s option), and disk volume (-d option) information.

```
> psinfo -h -s -d \\<ServerName>
```

Using VBScript

```
' This code prints system information similar to the systeminfo command.
' ------ SCRIPT CONFIGURATION ------
strComputer = "."   ' e.g. rallen-srv01
' ------ END CONFIGURATION ---------

set dicProductType = CreateObject("Scripting.Dictionary")
dicProductType.Add 1, "Workstation"
dicProductType.Add 2, "Domain Controller"
dicProductType.Add 3, "Standalone Server"
```

```
set objWMIDateTime = CreateObject("WbemScripting.SWbemDateTime")

set objWMI = GetObject("winmgmts:\\" & strComputer & "\root\cimv2")
set colOS = objWMI.InstancesOf("Win32_OperatingSystem")
for each objOS in colOS
    Wscript.Echo "Host Name: " & objOS.CSName
    Wscript.Echo "OS Name: " & objOS.Caption
    Wscript.Echo "OS Version: " & objOS.Version & " Build " & objOS.BuildNumber
    Wscript.Echo "OS Manufacturer: " & objOS.Manufacturer
    Wscript.Echo "OS Configuration: " & dicProductType.Item(objOS.ProductType)
    Wscript.Echo "OS Build Type: " & objOS.BuildType
    Wscript.Echo "Registered Owner: " & objOS.RegisteredUser
    Wscript.Echo "Registered Organization: " & objOS.Organization
    Wscript.Echo "Product ID: " & objOS.SerialNumber
    objWMIDateTime.Value = objOS.InstallDate
    Wscript.Echo "Original Install Date: " & objWMIDateTime.GetVarDate
    objWMIDateTime.Value = objOS.LastBootUpTime
    Wscript.Echo "System Up Time: " & objWMIDateTime.GetVarDate
    Wscript.Echo "Windows Directory: " & objOS.WindowsDirectory
    Wscript.Echo "System Directory: " & objOS.SystemDirectory
    Wscript.Echo "BootDevice: " & objOS.BootDevice
    Wscript.Echo "System Locale: " & objOS.Locale
    Wscript.Echo "Time Zone: " & "GMT" & objOS.CurrentTimezone
    Wscript.Echo "Total Physical Memory: " & _
                round(objOS.TotalVisibleMemorySize / 1024) & " MB"
    Wscript.Echo "Available Physical Memory: " & _
                 round(objOS.FreePhysicalMemory / 1024) & " MB"
    Wscript.Echo "Page File: Max Size: " & _
                 round(objOS.TotalVirtualMemorySize / 1024) & " MB"
    Wscript.Echo "Page File: Available: " & _
                 round(objOS.FreeVirtualMemory / 1024) & " MB"
next

set colCS = objWMI.InstancesOf("Win32_ComputerSystem")
for each objCS in colCS
    Wscript.Echo "System Manufacturer: " & objCS.Manufacturer
    Wscript.Echo "System Model: " & objCS.Model
    Wscript.Echo "System Type: " & objCS.SystemType
    WScript.Echo "Domain: " & objCS.Domain
    Wscript.Echo "Processor(s): " & objCS.NumberofProcessors & _
                " Processor(s) Installed."
next

intCount = 0
set colProcs = objWMI.InstancesOf("Win32_Processor")
for each objProc in colProcs
    intCount = intCount + 1
    Wscript.Echo vbTab & "[" & intcount & "]: " & _
                objProc.Caption & " ~" & objProc.MaxClockSpeed & "Mhz"
next

set colBIOS = objWMI.InstancesOf("Win32_BIOS")
for each objBIOS in colBIOS
    Wscript.Echo "BIOS Version: " & objBIOS.Version
next
```

Discussion

One command-line tool I didn't mention in the solutions is *wmic.exe*. While it isn't available for Windows 2000, it is very handy on Windows Server 2003. I can simulate pretty much everything that the scripting solution does in four commands. Here they are:

```
> wmic os list full
> wmic computersystem list full
> wmic cpu list full
> wmic bios list full
```

These commands actually print out more information than the scripting solution because they display all of the properties from the associated classes, not just the ones I chose to display. To run *wmic* against a remote computer, use the /node option and be sure to enclose the target server name in quotes:

```
> wmic /node:"srv01" os list full
```

2.7   Setting the System Time, Date, and Time Zone

Problem

You want to set the system time, date, and time zone.

Solution

Using a graphical user interface

1. From the Control Panel, open the Date and Time applet. This can also be accomplished by double-clicking the clock on the system tray or running *timedate.cpl* from the command line.

2. You can configure the year, month, day, and time on the **Date & Time** tab and the time zone on the **Time Zone** tab.

3. On Windows Server 2003, you can configure clock synchronization (Network Time Protocol (NTP) settings) from the **Internet Time** tab if the system is not part of a domain. If it is member of a domain, then the clock is synchronized automatically from an Active Directory domain controller.

Using a command-line interface

The following commands set the time to 11:02 p.m. and the date to November 1, 2005:

```
> time 23:02:00
> date 11/01/2005
```

The date format may vary depending on your locale.

Run this command to display the current date, time, and time zone:

```
> date /t & time /t & w32tm -tz
```

You can use this command to display time zone information from the registry:

```
> reg query \\<ServerName>\HKLM\SYSTEM\CurrentControlSet\Control\TimeZoneInformation
```

This command sets the SNTP server list:

```
> net time /setsntp:<ServerList>
```

For example:

```
> net time /setsntp:mytime.rallencorp.com,time.windows.com
```

This command queries the SNTP server:

```
> net time /querysntp
```

This command forces the local system to sync its time from the time source:

```
> net time /set
```

Using VBScript

```
' This code displays the local date, time, and time zone on a target computer
' ------ SCRIPT CONFIGURATION ------
strComputer = "."    ' e.g. rallen-srv01
' ------ END CONFIGURATION ---------
WScript.Echo "Current time using Now function: "
WScript.Echo vbTab & Now

set dicDaysOfWeek = CreateObject("Scripting.Dictionary")
dicDaysOfWeek.Add 0, "Sun"
dicDaysOfWeek.Add 1, "Mon"
dicDaysOfWeek.Add 2, "Tue"
dicDaysOfWeek.Add 3, "Wed"
dicDaysOfWeek.Add 4, "Thu"
dicDaysOfWeek.Add 5, "Fri"
dicDaysOfWeek.Add 6, "Sat"

set objWMI = GetObject("winmgmts:\\" & strComputer & "\root\cimv2")
set objDateTime = objWMI.Get("Win32_Localtime=@")
WScript.Echo "Current time using WMI: "
WScript.Echo vbTab & dicDaysOfWeek.Item(objDateTime.DayOfWeek) & " " & _
        objDateTime.Month & "/" & objDateTime.Day & "/" & _
        objDateTime.Year & " " & objDateTime.Hour & ":" & objDateTime.Minute
WScript.Echo "Time zone:"
set colTZ = objWMI.ExecQuery("select * from Win32_TimeZone")
for each objTZ in colTZ
    Wscript.Echo vbTab & objTZ.Caption
next
```

The easiest way to set the time and date via a script is by shelling out to the *time* and *date* commands, but this means the script must be run locally. Here is an example:

```
WScript.Echo "Current time: " & Now

strCommand = "cmd.exe /c time 23:02:00"
set objWshShell = WScript.CreateObject("WScript.Shell")
intRC = objWshShell.Run(strCommand, 0, TRUE)
if intRC <> 0 then
   WScript.Echo "Error returned from time command: " & intRC
else
   WScript.Echo "time command completed successfully"
end if

strCommand = "cmd.exe /c date 11/01/2004"
intRC = objWshShell.Run(strCommand, 0, TRUE)
if intRC <> 0 then
   WScript.Echo "Error returned from date command: " & intRC
else
   WScript.Echo "date command completed successfully"
end if

WScript.Echo "New time: " & Now
```

 If you want to set the time remotely, use the *psexec* command.

Discussion

If your server is part of a workgroup or NT 4 domain, you must manually configure the time and date settings on it. You can either set the time and date based on some external time source (such as your watch) or you can configure the server to synch from a time server. The latter is the preferred method because as long as the time server you are pointing your servers to has the correct time, your servers will have the correct time. If your server is part of an Active Directory domain, it will automatically sync its time from a domain controller.

Time and date synchronization is handled by the Windows Time service (W32Time), which was originally developed for Windows 2000 and is a compliant implementation of RFC 1769—Simple Network Time Protocol (SNTP). For Windows Server 2003, W32Time was updated to support NTP, a more accurate protocol than SNTP.

W32Time is highly configurable via the registry. See MS KB 223184 for the list of registry settings you can configure for Windows 2000. A similar KB article has not been produced yet showing the differences for Windows Server 2003.

For a good whitepaper on the Windows 2000 Time service, visit the following URL: *http://www.microsoft.com/windows2000/docs/wintimeserv.doc.*

For more on the Windows Server 2003 Time service, visit the following URL: *http://www.microsoft.com/Resources/Documentation/windowsserv/2003/all/techref/en-us/W2K3TR_times_intro.asp.*

See Also

RFC 1305, RFC 1769, MS KB 216734 (How to Configure an Authoritative Time Server in Windows 2000), MS KB 223184 (Registry Entries for the W32Time Service), MS KB 247873 (Description of Date and Time Format Standards), MS KB 258059 (How to Synchronize the Time on a Windows 2000-Based Computer in a Windows NT 4.0 Domain), MS KB 262680 (A List of the Simple Network Time Protocol Time Servers That Are Available on the Internet), and MS KB 816043 (HOW TO: Turn On Debug Logging in the Windows Time Service)

2.8   Setting the Name of a Server

Problem

You want to configure the host name for a server.

Solution

Using a graphical user interface

1. From the Control Panel, open the System applet.
2. Select the **Computer Name** tab (or **Network Identification** on Windows 2000).
3. Click the **Change** button (or **Properties** on Windows 2000).
4. Enter the new name in the **Computer name** field.
5. If the computer is a member of the domain, you will be prompted for credentials to use for renaming the account in the domain unless you are logged in with a domain administrator account.
6. Click **OK**.
7. Click **OK** to confirm that you'll need to restart (this won't actually restart the computer).
8. Click **OK** again.
9. Click **Yes** if you want to restart now or **No** to restart later.

Using a command-line interface

Use this command to display the current computer name:

```
> hostname
```

The *compname.exe* utility, which is available from *http://www.willowhayes.co.uk/*, can also display the current computer name:

```
> compname /s
```

But this command can also do a whole lot more. This changes a computer's name:

```
> compname /c <NewServerName>
```

The truly powerful feature of *compname* is its ability to name a system based on certain variables (or what it calls templates). You can name a computer based on its serial number, UUID, MAC address, and date, among other things. The following example changes a computer name to contain its serial number at the end:

```
> compname /c pc-?s
```

Run compname /? for more information on the available templates.

This is a registry-based method for setting a computer's name:

```
> reg add \\<CurrentServerName>\HKLM\SYSTEM\CurrentControlSet\Services\Tcpip\
Parameters /v "NV Hostname" /d <NewServerName>
> reg add \\<CurrentServerName>\HKLM\SYSTEM\CurrentControlSet\Control\ComputerName\
ComputerName /v ComputerName /d <NewServerName>
> shutdown \\<CurrentServerName> /r
```

If the computer is already part of a domain and you use either the *compname* or registry methods, the computer's domain account will become out of sync and it will no longer be able to function in the domain. To rename a computer that is part of a domain, use the *netdom.exe* command:

```
> netdom renamecomputer <CurrentServerName> /newname:<NewServerName> /userd:
<DomainUserName>
```

Using VBScript

```
' This code changes the name of a computer.  It does NOT modify
' the computer's account in the domain if one exists.
' ------ SCRIPT CONFIGURATION ------
strComputer = "<CurrentServerName>"
strNewName = "<NewServerName>"
' ------ END CONFIGURATION ---------
const HKLM    = &H80000002
strKeyPath    = "System\CurrentControlSet\Control\ComputerName\ComputerName"
set objReg = GetObject("winmgmts:\\" & strComputer & _
                       "\root\default:StdRegProv")
intRC = objReg.SetStringValue(HKLM, strKeyPath, "ComputerName", strNewName)
if intRC <> 0 then
   WScript.Echo "Error setting ComputerName value: " & intRC
else
   WScript.Echo "Successfully set ComputerName value to " & strNewName
end if

strKeyPath    = "System\CurrentControlSet\Services\Tcpip\Parameters"
intRC = objReg.SetStringValue(HKLM, strKeyPath, "NV Hostname", strNewName)
```

```
if intRC <> 0 then
    WScript.Echo "Error setting NV Hostname value: " & intRC
else
    WScript.Echo "Successfully set NV Hostname value to " & strNewName
end if

WScript.Echo "Rebooting system..."
set objWMI = GetObject("winmgmts:\\" & strComputer & "\root\cimv2")
for each objOS in objWMI.InstancesOf("Win32_OperatingSystem")
    objOS.Reboot( )
next


' This code renames a computer in its domain and on the computer itself.
' This script works only against Windows XP and Windows Server 2003 computers.
' ------ SCRIPT CONFIGURATION ------
strComputer      = "<ComputerName>"         ' e.g., joe-xp
strNewComputer   = "<NewComputerName>"      ' e.g., joe-pc
strDomainUser    = "<DomainUserUPN>"        ' e.g., administrator@rallencorp.com
strDomainPasswd  = "<DomainUserPasswd>"
strLocalUser     = "<ComputerAdminUser>"    ' e.g., joe-xp\administrator
strLocalPasswd   = "<ComputerAdminPasswd>"
' ------ END CONFIGURATION ---------
' Connect to Computer
set objWMILocator = CreateObject("WbemScripting.SWbemLocator")
objWMILocator.Security_.AuthenticationLevel = 6
set objWMIComp = objWMILocator.ConnectServer(strComputer, _
                                  "root\cimv2", _
                                      strLocalUser, _
                                      strLocalPasswd)
set objWMICompSys = objWMIComp.Get("Win32_ComputerSystem.Name='" & _
                                  strComputer & "'")
' Rename Computer
intRC = objWMICompSys.Rename(strNewComputer, _
                           strDomainPasswd, _
                           strDomainUser)
if intRC <> 0 then
    WScript.Echo "Rename failed with error: " & intRC
else
    WScript.Echo "Successfully renamed " & strComputer & " to " & strNewComputer
end if

WScript.Echo "Rebooting system..."
Set colOS = objWMIComp.InstancesOf("Win32_OperatingSystem")
for each objOS in colOS
    objOS.Reboot( )
next
```

Discussion

Setting the name of a computer is a straightforward operation, but it does require a reboot. If the computer is member of an Active Directory domain, the corresponding computer account must also be renamed. Some of the solutions I described do this automatically and some do not.

 In some cases, renaming a computer can adversely affect services running on the computer. For example, you cannot rename a machine that is a Windows 2000 domain controller, Exchange 2000 or 2003 server, or a Windows Certificate Authority without first removing those services.

Using a command-line interface

The renamecomputer option in *netdom* is new to Windows Server 2003. You can run it against a remote computer and it includes a /Reboot option that allows you to automatically reboot the computer after the rename is done.

Using VBScript

The Win32_ComputerSystem::Rename method must be run on the local machine unless the computer is a member of a domain. Unlike the graphical and command-line solutions, you cannot specify alternate credentials for the connection to the computer other than domain credentials. For this reason, the user and password you use with the Rename method must have administrative privileges on the target machine (i.e., part of the Administrators group) and on the computer object in Active Directory.

 This method is new in Windows XP and Windows Server 2003, and is not available on Windows 2000 and earlier machines.

See Also

MS KB 228544 (Changing Computer Name in Windows 2000 Requires Restart), MS KB 238793 (Enhanced Security Joining or Resetting Machine Account in Windows 2000 Domain), MS KB 260575 (HOW TO: Use Netdom.exe to Reset Machine Account Passwords of a Windows 2000 Domain Controller), MS KB 325354 (HOW TO: Use the Netdom.exe Utility to Rename a Computer in Windows Server 2003), and MSDN: Win32_ComputerSystem::Rename

2.9   Joining a Server to a Domain

Problem

You want to join a server to an Active Directory domain so that users in the domain can access resources on the server.

Solution

Using a graphical user interface

1. Log onto the computer you want to join and open Control Panel → System applet.
2. Click the **Computer Name** tab.
3. Click the **Change** button.
4. Under **Member of**, select **Domain**.
5. Enter the domain you want to join and click **OK**.
6. You may be prompted to enter credentials that have permission to join the computer.
7. Reboot the computer.
8. Note that the tabs in the **System** applet vary between Windows 2000, Windows XP, and Windows Server 2003.

Using a command-line interface

The following command joins a computer to a domain:

```
> netdom join <ComputerName> /Domain <DomainName> /UserD <DomainUserUPN> /PasswordD *
/UserO <ComputerAdminUser> /PasswordO * /Reboot
```

 The last character in the /UserO and /PasswordO options is the letter O, not the number 0.

Using VBScript

```
' This code joins a server to a domain.
' ------ SCRIPT CONFIGURATION ------
strComputer     = "<ComputerName>"       ' e.g. joe-xp
strDomain       = "<DomainName>"         ' e.g. rallencorp.com
strDomainUser   = "<DomainUserUPN>"      ' e.g. administrator@rallencorp.com
strDomainPasswd = "<DomainUserPasswd>"
strLocalUser    = "<ComputerAdminUser>"  ' e.g. administrator
strLocalPasswd  = "<ComputerUserPasswd>"
' ------ END CONFIGURATION ---------
' Constants
Const JOIN_DOMAIN             = 1
Const ACCT_CREATE            = 2
Const ACCT_DELETE            = 4
Const WIN9X_UPGRADE          = 16
Const DOMAIN_JOIN_IF_JOINED  = 32
Const JOIN_UNSECURE          = 64
Const MACHINE_PASSWORD_PASSED = 128
Const DEFERRED_SPN_SET       = 256
Const INSTALL_INVOCATION     = 262144
```

```
' Connect to Computer
set objWMILocator = CreateObject("WbemScripting.SWbemLocator")
objWMILocator.Security_.AuthenticationLevel = 6
set objWMIComp = objWMILocator.ConnectServer(strComputer, _
                                    "root\cimv2", _
                                    strLocalUser, _
                                    strLocalPasswd)
set objWMICompSys = objWMIComp.Get( _
                        "Win32_ComputerSystem.Name='" & _
                        strComputer & "'")
' Join Computer
intRC = objWMICompSys.JoinDomainOrWorkGroup(strDomain, _
                                    strDomainPasswd, _
                                    strDomainUser, _
                                    vbNullString, _
                                    JOIN_DOMAIN)
if intRC <> 0 then
    WScript.Echo "Join failed with error: " & rc
else
    WScript.Echo "Successfully joined " & strComputer & " to " & strDomain
end if
```

Discussion

To join a computer to Active Directory, a computer account must be created in the domain. You can create this account before joining the computer or, in some cases, the account can be created during the join operation.

Using a graphical user interface

If you have the correct permissions in Active Directory, you can actually create a computer object at the same time as you join it to a domain via the instructions described in the graphical solution. Since the System applet doesn't allow you to specify an OU for the computer object, if it needs to create a computer object it will do so in the default cn=Computers container. However, the computer object may be pre-created in an alternate OU if you so desire.

 With Windows Server 2003 Active Directory you can change the default container for computer objects. See Recipe 8.12 in *Active Directory Cookbook* (O'Reilly).

Using a command-line interface

The *netdom.exe* command attempts to create a computer object for the computer during a join if one does not already exist. An optional /OU option can be added to specify the OU in which to create the computer object. To do so, you'll need to have the necessary permissions to create and manage computer objects in the specified OU.

There are some restrictions on running the netdom join command against a remote machine. If a Windows XP machine has the ForceGuest security policy setting enabled, you cannot join it to a domain remotely. Running the `netdom` command directly on the machine works regardless of the ForceGuest setting.

Using VBScript

In order for the `Win32_ComputerSystem::JoinDomainOrWorkGroup` method to work remotely, you have to use an `AuthenticationLevel` equal to 6 so that the traffic between the two machines (namely the passwords) is encrypted. You can also create computer objects using `JoinDomainOrWorkGroup` by using the `ACCT_CREATE` flag in combination with `JOIN_DOMAIN`.

 This function works only with Windows XP and Windows Server 2003 and is not available for Windows 2000 and earlier machines.

Just as with the *netdom* utility, you cannot run this script against a remote computer if that computer has the ForceGuest setting enabled.

See Also

Recipe 8.12 in *Active Directory Cookbook* (O'Reilly) for more on changing the default computers container, the following URL for more information on the ForceGuest setting: *http://www.microsoft.com/technet/prodtechnol/winxppro/reskit/prde_ffs_ypuh.asp*, MS KB 238793 (Enhanced Security Joining or Resetting Machine Account in Windows 2000 Domain), MS KB 251335 (Domain Users Cannot Join Workstation or Server to a Domain), MS KB 290403 (How to Set Security in Windows XP Professional That Is Installed in a Workgroup), and MSDN: Win32_ComputerSystem::JoinDomainOrWorkgroup, and MSDN: NetJoinDomain

2.10 Testing and Resetting the Secure Channel

Problem

You want to test the secure channel of a server in a domain.

Solution

The following command tests the secure channel for a computer:

```
> nltest /server:<ComputerName> /sc_query:<DomainName>
```

The following command resets the secure channel for a computer:

```
> nltest /server:<ComputerName> /sc_reset:<DomainName>
```

The following solutions describe how to reset a computer account.

Using a graphical user interface

1. Open the **Active Directory Users and Computers** snap-in.

2. If you need to change domains, right-click on **Active Directory Users and Computers** in the left pane, select **Connect to Domain**, enter the domain name, and click **OK**.

3. In the left pane, right-click on the domain and select **Find**.

4. Beside **Find**, select **Computers**.

5. Type the name of the computer and click **Find Now**.

6. In the **Search Results**, right-click on the computer and select **Reset Account**.

7. Click **Yes** to verify.

8. Click **OK**.

9. Rejoin the computer to the domain as I described in Recipe 2.5.

Using a command-line interface

You can use the *dsmod.exe* utility to reset a computer's password. You will need to rejoin the computer to the domain after doing this.

```
> dsmod computer "<ComputerDN>" -reset
```

Another option is to use the *netdom.exe* command, which can reset the computer so that you do not need to rejoin it to the domain.

```
> netdom reset <ComputerName> /Domain <DomainName> /User0 <UserUPN> /Password0 *
```

Using VBScript

```
' This code resets an existing computer object's password to the
' initial default. You'll need to rejoin the computer after doing this.
set objComputer = GetObject("LDAP://<ComputerDN>")
objComputer.SetPassword "<ComputerName>"
```

Discussion

Every member computer in an Active Directory domain establishes a secure channel with a domain controller. The computer's password is stored locally on the machine in the form of a Local Security Authority (LSA) secret and also in Active Directory with the computer's account. The NetLogon service on the computer uses this password to establish the secure channel with a domain controller. If for some reason the LSA secret and computer password become out of sync, the computer will no longer be able to authenticate in the domain. The nltest /sc_query:<DomainName> and nltest /sc_verify:<DomainName> commands can query a computer to verify its secure channel is working. Here is sample output from the nltest /sc_query command when things are working:

```
Flags: 30 HAS_IP  HAS_TIMESERV
Trusted DC Name \\dc1.rallencorp.com
```

```
Trusted DC Connection Status Status = 0 0x0 NERR_Success
The command completed successfully
```

If its secure channel is failing, you'll need to reset the secure channel. If that doesn't work, you'll need to reset the computer account. Here is sample output when things are not working or if you are logged in with cached credentials:

```
Flags: 0
Trusted DC Name
Trusted DC Connection Status Status = 1311 0x51f ERROR_NO_LOGON_SERVERS
The command completed successfully
```

To reset the computer, set the computer account password to the name of the computer. This is the default initial password for new computers. Every 30 days Windows 2000 and newer systems automatically change their passwords in the domain. After you've set the password, you'll need to rejoin the computer to the domain since it will no longer be able to communicate with a domain controller due to unsynchronized passwords. However, the netdom reset command will try to reset the password on both the computer and in Active Directory. If successful, you won't have to manually rejoin the computer to the domain. Unfortunately, the actions executed by netdom reset cannot be done either from the GUI or from VBScript.

See Also

Recipe 2.9 for joining a computer to a domain, MS KB 156684 (How to Use NLT-EST to Force a New Secure Channel), MS KB 216393 (Resetting Computer Accounts in Windows 2000 and Windows XP), and MS KB 325850 (HOW TO: Use Netdom.exe to Reset Machine Account Passwords of a Windows Server 2003 Domain Controller)

2.11 Viewing and Setting Environment Variables

Problem

You want to view the current environment variables or create new ones.

Solution

Using a graphical user interface

1. From the Control Panel, open the System applet.
2. Select the **Advanced** tab.
3. Click the **Environment Variables** button.

4. Click the **New** button under the **User variables** or **System variables** box depending on whether you want to create an environment variable that is visible only to the currently logged-on user or system-wide.

5. Enter the variable name and value and click **OK** until all windows are closed.

 The new variable(s) will not be available in any CMD windows that are currently open. You'll need to close and reopen any CMD sessions in which you want to use the new variable(s).

Using a command-line interface

To view environment variables, run the *set* command. You can also view a subset of environment variables by running *set* and specifying the first letters of the variable(s). This command displays all environment variables that begin with USER:

```
> set user
```

You can use the *wmic* utility to print environment variables on a remote system:

```
> wmic /node:"<ServerName>" environment list full
```

You can print the value of an environment variable using echo:

```
> echo %systemroot%
```

To set an environment variable for use in the current CMD session, use the *set* command. The following command sets the FOOBAR environment variable:

```
> set FOOBAR=test
```

FOOBAR will be valid only for the life of the CMD session you set it in. If you need to create a permanent environment variable, use *setx.exe*:

```
> setx FOOBAR test
```

Just as with *set*, you will *not* be able to use the new variable in any CMD sessions you had open before creating it (other than the one in which it was created).

With the Windows Server 2003 version of *setx* (which comes with the OS), you can even set new environment variables on a remote server:

```
> setx FOOBAR test /s <ServerName> /u <UserName> /p <Password>
```

Using VBScript

```
' This code prints the environment variables.
' ------ SCRIPT CONFIGURATION ------
strComputer = "."
' ------ END CONFIGURATION ---------
set objWMI = GetObject("winmgmts:\\" & strComputer & "\root\cimv2")
set colVars = objWMI.InstancesOf("Win32_Environment")
for each objVar in colVars
   WScript.Echo objVar.Name & ": " & objVar.variableValue & _
              " (" & objVar.Username & ")"
next
```

```
' This code shows how to expand an environment variable.
set objShell = CreateObject("WScript.Shell")
WScript.Echo objShell.ExpandEnvironmentStrings("%systemroot%\notepad.exe")


' This code creates a new system environment variable called FOOBAR.
' ------ SCRIPT CONFIGURATION ------
strVarName = "FOOBAR"
strVarValue = "Foobar Value"
strComputer = "."
' ------ END CONFIGURATION ---------
set objVarClass = GetObject("winmgmts:\\" & strComputer & _
                            "\root\cimv2:Win32_Environment")
set objVar = objVarClass.SpawnInstance_
objVar.Name = strVarName
objVar.VariableValue = strVarValue
objVar.UserName = "<SYSTEM>"
objVar.Put_
WScript.Echo "Created environment variable " & strVarName
```

Discussion

Environment variables are very similar in concept to the variables you'd find in a programming language: there is a variable identifier and an associated value. This is extremely handy because it means that you don't always have to know the exact path or name of certain settings on the system.

For example, let's say you wanted to view the NetLogon log file on a remote system. After you log on to the system, you have to locate the file. On your computer it is located in *C:\WINNT\Debug*, but that directory might not exist on the remote computer. You then perform a search for the file and find it is located in *D:\Windows\ Debug*. If you used environment variables, finding the file would have been a lot easier. On your machine, the *Debug* directory lives in the *C:\WINNT* directory, which is the default system root path. On the remote server it was *D:\Windows*. The default system root directory on Windows Server 2003 is *\Windows*, but since it is on the D: drive in this case, that means whoever installed the OS chose a nondefault drive (which is fine). Regardless of where the system root is, the SystemRoot environment variable defines this path for us. By simply enclosing SystemRoot in percent signs (%), we could have found our file much quicker (*%systemroot%\debug\netlogon.log*).

There are many different environment variables, which you can view by running the *set* command without any parameters from the command line. You can see the default environment variables provided by the OS in Appendix D.

See Also

Appendix D—List of Default Environment Variables, MS KB 41246 (How to Use Environment Variable Substitution in Batch Files), MS KB 104011 (HOW TO: Propagate

Environment Variables to the System), MS KB 185652 (Environment Variable Processing Order in Windows 2000), and MSDN: Win32_Environment

2.12 Configuring Page Files

Problem

You want to configure the page files on a system. It is a common practice to move the default page file stored on the system root drive (typically C:) to a different disk to improve performance. The page files and system drive are frequently accessed by the operating system and separating them on different disks can improve performance. You may also want to increase the size of the page file or spread your page file across multiple volumes based on the needs of your system.

Solution

Using a graphical user interface

1. From the Control Panel, open the System applet.

2. Select the **Advanced** tab.

   On Windows Server 2003:

   a. Under **Performance**, click the **Settings** button.

   b. Click the **Advanced** tab.

   c. Under **Virtual memory**, click the **Change** button.

   d. You'll see a list of all volumes and any page files that have been configured on them. To modify the size of an existing page file, highlight the drive the page file is on, modify the **Initial size** and/or **Maximum size**, and click **Set**. You can also select **System managed** size to let the system control the size of the page file. To add a new page file, select a drive that currently does not have a page file and select either **Custom size** or **System managed size**. If you select the former, enter the **Initial size** and **Maximum size**. Click **Set** when you are done. A performance tip is to set the initial size the same as the maximum size to reduce unnecessary I/O operations.

   On Windows 2000:

   a. Click the **Performance Options** button.

   b. Click the **Change** button.

   c. You'll see a list of all attached disks and any page files that have been configured on them. To modify the size of an existing page file, highlight the drive the page file is one, modify the **Initial size** and/or **Maximum size**, and click **Set**. To add a new page file, select a drive that currently does not have a page file, enter the **Initial size** and **Maximum size**, and click **Set**.

Using a command-line interface

Page file information is stored in the registry, so you can use the *reg.exe* command to display current settings:

```
> reg query "\\<ServerName>\HKLM\System\CurrentControlSet\Control\Session Manager\
Memory Management" /v PagingFiles
```

For Windows Server 2003, you can also use the *systeminfo.exe* command to display page file usage:

```
> systeminfo | findstr Page
```

The list of page files is stored in a REG_MULTI_SZ value called PagingFiles in the registry. By using the *reg add* command you can overwrite the current settings in PagingFiles and specify the page files you want. This command configures only one page file on the system located at *d:\pagefile.sys*:

```
> reg add "\\<ServerName>\HKLM\System\CurrentControlSet\Control\Session Manager\
Memory Management" /v PagingFiles /t REG_MULTI_SZ /d "d:\pagefile.sys 580 1024"
```

The first number after *d:\pagefile.sys* is the initial size in megabytes for the page file and the second number is the maximum size.

This command causes there to be two page files, one on the C: drive and the other on the D: drive:

```
> reg add "\\<ServerName>\HKLM\System\CurrentControlSet\Control\Session Manager\
Memory Management" /v PagingFiles /t REG_MULTI_SZ /d "C:\pagefile.sys 512 1024\0D:\
pagefile.sys 512 1024\0"
```

You'll need to reboot for the changes to take effect.

Using VBScript

```
' This code displays the current page files on the system.
' ------ SCRIPT CONFIGURATION ------
strComputer = "."
' ------ END CONFIGURATION ---------
set objWMI = GetObject("winmgmts:\\" & strComputer & "\root\cimv2")
set colPF = objWMI.InstancesOf("Win32_PageFileUsage")
for each objPF in colPF
   Wscript.Echo objPF.Name
   Wscript.Echo "  Initial Size: " & objPF.AllocatedBaseSize
   Wscript.Echo "  Max Size: " & objPF.CurrentUsage
   WScript.Echo "  Peak Usage: " & objPF.PeakUsage
   WScript.Echo
next
```

You cannot change the size of a Page file with the Win32_PageFileUsage class (or any other WMI class), you can only retrieve a page file's properties.

Discussion

There are two types of memory on computers: random access memory (RAM) (or physical memory) and virtual memory. RAM is stored on specialized chips and is very fast, whereas virtual memory is stored on hard drives and is comparatively slow. On Windows systems, paging files are used to allocate space for virtual memory.

The operating system uses RAM when possible, but when the limits of RAM are exceeded it turns to virtual memory. When the system needs to make room in RAM (e.g., when you open a new application), it pages out the most infrequently used sections of RAM to virtual memory. That means the system has to perform disk reads and writes during this process. Your goal with virtual memory should be to configure the paging files so that they are big enough to handle virtual memory demands and can be accessed quickly.

In fact, your page file configuration can have a significant impact on system performance. When the Windows operating system is first installed, a page file is created (called *pagefile.sys*) on the drive the operating system is installed on. As I mentioned in the Problem section, you should consider moving this page file to a separate drive so that there isn't a lot of contention for disk I/O when the system needs to access virtual memory. An even better practice is to create two page files. It is a good idea to have a page file on a non-system partition, but you may still want a page file on the system partition to handle memory dumps. If there is no page file on the system drive and a system crash (blue screen) occurs, the system will not be able to write out a memory dump that can be used to troubleshoot the crash. Windows uses the page file on the least busy partition, so it should primarily use the non-system partition page file for virtual memory. It is also worth noting that you shouldn't bother with creating two page files unless you have at least two disks. Creating multiple paging files on the same disk doesn't buy you much in terms of performance.

Regarding the size of the page files, the general rule of thumb is to have at least 1.5 times the amount of RAM, which is the default configuration. So if you had 1 GB of RAM, you should have at least a 1.5-GB paging file. The largest any one page file can be on a single disk is 4 GB.

Another issue to consider if security is a concern for you is clearing the paging files during system shutdown. Some applications write sensitive information, such as passwords, to RAM. If that data gets paged out to virtual memory, it can end up in a page file. That information can remain in the page file for a considerable amount of time (even after reboot) until that space is needed for something else. While the page files are protected by the operating system, it is possible (although not very easy, mind you) for an attacker that has gained control over the system to read that file and any data within it. The solution for this is to clear the page files whenever the system shuts down. To enable this you need to modify a registry setting and reboot the computer. See MS KB 182086 for more information.

Using a graphical user interface

The System Managed option I described in the graphical solution is only available in Windows Server 2003. It is a new feature that lets the system determine how big the page file needs to be. It is a good practice to use this setting unless you have a very good reason not to do so.

Using a command-line interface

Be careful when configuring the page files from the command line. Thoroughly test your command before trying it on a production system. The last thing you want to do is mess up the page files on your systems!

Using VBScript

None of the WMI classes allow you to configure the page files directly—you can only view them. If you need to do it programmatically, your best bet would be to use the Registry WMI provider to set the corresponding registry values for page files as I described in the command-line solution.

See Also

MS KB 182086 (How to Clear the Windows Paging File at Shutdown), MS KB 197379 (Configuring Page Files for Optimization and Recovery), and MS KB 237740 (How to Overcome 4,095-MB Paging File Size Limit in Windows)

2.13 Putting System Information on the Desktop

Problem

You want to put information on the desktop wallpaper so that when you log into a server you can automatically see its configuration.

Solution

Using a graphical user interface

1. Open the Sysinternals BGInfo program on the target server.
2. The default configuration information is displayed. You can modify it directly or select a new setting in the **Fields** box and click the **Add** button. You can also create your own custom settings by clicking the **Custom** button.
3. Click the **Background** button to customize the background color or bitmap.
4. Click the **Position** button to customize where the BGInfo is displayed on the desktop.

5. Click the **Desktops** button to configure the desktops where you want this information displayed. You can put it only on your desktop, on all console users' desktops, or on Terminal Services user's desktop.

6. Click the **Preview** button to see what the new background would look like.

7. Click the **Apply** button to commit the changes.

Discussion

If you maintain more than three or four servers, it can be difficult to distinguish them when you are logged onto the console or logged on with Terminal Services. And if you support multiple vendor models that have different hardware, it can be even more difficult to remember what is installed on each computer. Fortunately, there is a simple, yet elegant solution. Why not just put system information on the desktop background so that as soon as you log in, you can see how much memory is installed, view the disk configuration, find out how many CPUs are installed, etc.? The guys at Sysinternals have come through for us yet again by providing the BGInfo utility that can do exactly this. It is a highly customizable tool that lets you put just about anything you could think of on the desktop background.

You can configure where the information should be positioned in the background, you can use any background color or wallpaper you want, and you can even choose to configure whether only Terminal Services users should see it or whether it should be available to anyone that logs on. Figure 2-1 shows the default configuration screen for BGInfo.

If you'd like to use this across a set of servers, consider running BGInfo as part of a Group Policy logon script. It is fully scriptable from the command line. Run bginfo /? for more details.

2.14   Configuring System Startup Options

Problem

You want to configure the system startup options for a server.

Solution

Using a graphical user interface

1. From the Control Panel, open the System applet.

2. Select the **Advanced** tab.

3. Under **Startup and Recovery**, click the **Settings** button.

4. Under the **System Startup** heading, you can modify the default operating system and the amount of time the system waits before loading the default OS.

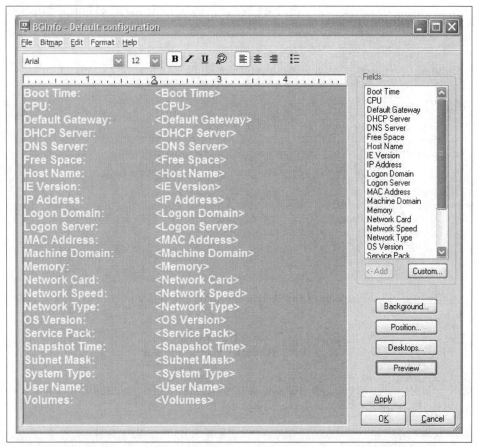

Figure 2-1. BGInfo default configuration

5. To change additional startup options on Windows Server 2003, you can click the **Edit** button to modify the *boot.ini* file. See the Discussion section for how to do this on Windows 2000.

6. Click **OK** until all of the windows are closed.

Using a command-line interface

Windows Server 2003 includes a new tool called *bootcfg.exe* (also available with Windows XP) that lets you examine and modify the system startup options (including *boot.ini*) from the command line. To get a list of the current startup options, run *bootcfg* without any parameters:

```
> bootcfg
```

The following command changes the timeout setting for the default OS option to 15 seconds:

```
> bootcfg /timeout 15
```

The following command adds the /DEBUG and /SOS options to the OS option defined by ID 2 (which you can see by running *bootcfg* without any options):

```
> bootcfg /Raw "/DEBUG /SOS" /A /ID 2
```

For the complete list of *bootcfg* options, run bootcfg /? from the command line.

Using VBScript

```
' This code displays the system startup settings.
' ------ SCRIPT CONFIGURATION ------
strComputer = "."   ' e.g., rallen-srv01
' ------ END CONFIGURATION ---------
set objWMI = GetObject("winmgmts:\\" & strComputer & "\root\cimv2")
set colCompSys = objWMI.InstancesOf("Win32_ComputerSystem")
for Each objCompSys in colCompSys
    WScript.Echo "Startup Delay: " & objCompSys.SystemStartupDelay
    for each strOption in objCompSys.SystemStartupOptions
        WScript.Echo "Operating System: " & strOption
    next
next

' This code sets the startup delay to 10 seconds.
' ------ SCRIPT CONFIGURATION ------
strComputer = "."   ' e.g., rallen-srv01
' ------ END CONFIGURATION ---------
set objWMI = GetObject("winmgmts:\\" & strComputer & "\root\cimv2")
set colCompSys = objWMI.InstancesOf("Win32_ComputerSystem")
for Each objCompSys in colCompSys
    WScript.Echo "Startup Delay Before: " & objCompSys.SystemStartupDelay
    objCompSys.SystemStartupDelay = 10
    objCompSys.Put_
    WScript.Echo "Startup Delay After: " & objCompSys.SystemStartupDelay
next
```

Discussion

For a list of options that are supported in *boot.ini*, see MS KB 833721.

Using a graphical user interface

The **Edit** button is available only on Windows Server 2003. If you want to modify the *boot.ini* file on Windows 2000, you'll have to use the procedures described next in the command-line solution.

Using a command-line interface

Since Windows 2000 doesn't come with the *bootcfg* utility, you have to modify the *boot.ini* file directly. First, make the file editable:

```
> attrib %SystemDrive%\boot.ini -h -r -s
```

Then edit the file:

```
> edit %SystemDrive%\boot.ini
```

And finally, make the file read-only and hidden again:

```
> attrib %SystemDrive%\boot.ini +h +r +s
```

Using VBScript

None of the scripting interfaces support modifying the *boot.ini* file (aside from direct file manipulation).

See Also

MS KB 99743 (Purpose of the BOOT.INI File in Windows 2000 or Windows NT), MS KB 102873 (BOOT.INI and ARC Path Naming Conventions and Usage), MS KB 242443 (Boot Menu Is Not Displayed and Timeout Value Is Not Used), MS KB 291980 (A Discussion About the Bootcfg Command and Its Uses), and MS KB 316739 (How to Use the /USERVA Switch in the Boot.ini File to Tune /3GB Configurations)

2.15 Configuring System Failure Options

Problem

You want to configure what happens when a server encounters a critical failure and crashes.

Solution

Using a graphical user interface

1. From the Control Panel, open the System applet.
2. Select the **Advanced** tab.
3. Under **Startup and Recovery**, click the **Settings** button.
4. All of the system failure options are located under the **System Failure** heading. Modify the settings as necessary.
5. Click **OK** until all of the windows are closed.

Using a command-line interface

The system failure and recovery options are stored in the registry. You can view the current settings by enumerating the HKLM\SYSTEM\CurrentControlSet\Control\ CrashControl subkey:

```
> reg query \\<ServerName>\HKLM\SYSTEM\CurrentControlSet\Control\CrashControl
```

On Windows Server 2003, you can also use the *wmic* utility to view these settings:

```
> wmic /node:<ServerName> recoveros list /format:list
```

To modify these settings, use either the *reg add* command (on Windows 2000) or the *wmic* command (on Windows Server 2003). Next, I'll show some examples using *wmic*.

To disable admin alerts after failure, do the following:

```
> wmic recoveros set SendAdminAlert = False
```

To disable automatic reboot after failure, do the following:

```
> wmic recoveros set AutoReboot = False
```

To not write any information to a memory dump file after failure, do the following:

```
> wmic recoveros set DebugInfoType = 0
```

To set the mini-dump directory to *d:\minidumps* (only available with Windows Server 2003), do the following:

```
> wmic recoveros set MiniDumpDirectory = d:\minidumps
```

To set the location of the dump file to *D:\Dump\Mem.dmp*, do the following:

```
> wmic recoveros set DebugFilePath = D:\Dump\Mem.dmp
```

To not overwrite an existing dump file, do the following:

```
> wmic recoveros set OverwriteExistingDebugFile = 0
```

Using VBScript

```
' This code displays the current failure and recovery settings.
' ------ SCRIPT CONFIGURATION ------
strComputer = "."   ' e.g., rallen-srv01
' ------ END CONFIGURATION ---------
set objWMI = GetObject("winmgmts:\\" & strComputer & "\root\cimv2")
set colRecoveryConfig = objWMI.InstancesOf("Win32_OSRecoveryConfiguration")
for each objConfig in colRecoveryConfig
    Wscript.Echo objConfig.Name
    Wscript.Echo "  Auto reboot: " & objConfig.AutoReboot
    Wscript.Echo "  Debug File Path: " & objConfig.DebugFilePath
    Wscript.Echo "  Debug Type: " & objConfig.DebugInfoType
    Wscript.Echo "  Expanded Debug File Path: " & objConfig.ExpandedDebugFilePath
    Wscript.Echo "  Kernel Dump Only: " & objConfig.KernelDumpOnly
    Wscript.Echo "  Overwrite Existing: " & objConfig.OverwriteExistingDebugFile
    Wscript.Echo "  Send Admin Alert: " & objConfig.SendAdminAlert
    Wscript.Echo "  Write Debug Info: " & objConfig.WriteDebugInfo
    Wscript.Echo "  Write to System Log: " & objConfig.WriteToSystemLog
next

' This code modifies the system failure and recovery settings.
' ------ SCRIPT CONFIGURATION ------
strComputer = "."   ' e.g., rallen-srv01
' ------ END CONFIGURATION ---------
set objWMI = GetObject("winmgmts:\\" & strComputer & "\root\cimv2")
set colRecoveryConfig = objWMI.InstancesOf("Win32_OSRecoveryConfiguration")
```

```
for each objConfig in colRecoveryConfig
    Wscript.Echo objConfig.Name

    ' Uncomment the settings you want to modify:
    ' objConfig.AutoReboot = True
    ' objConfig.DebugFilePath = "d:\dumps\memory.dmp"
    ' objConfig.DebugInfoType = 1   ' Only available on W2K3
    ' objConfig.KernelDumpOnly = False
    ' objConfig.MiniDumpDirectory = "d:\minidumps" ' Only available on W2K3
    ' objConfig.OverwriteExistingDebugFile = True
    ' objConfig.SendAdminAlert = True
    ' objConfig.WriteDebugInfo = True
    ' objConfig.WriteToSystemLog = True

    objConfig.Put_
next
WScript.Echo "Successfully modified settings."
```

Discussion

Microsoft operating systems have had a reputation for frequent crashes, which can cause the system to freeze and become unusable until it is rebooted. A crash is sometimes referred to as a system failure, bug check, stop error, or blue screen of death (for the blue screen that is displayed after the crash). System failures were especially common in the days of Windows 3.51 and Windows 9x. Fortunately, Microsoft has steadily improved in this area and now Windows 2000 and Windows Server 2003 are two of the most stable operating systems available. Nevertheless, Microsoft hasn't been able to completely rid itself of occasional crashes due to bugs in the OS or bad third-party drivers.

There are several settings you can configure to control what happens after a system crash. By default, when a system crashes, it writes the contents of memory to a debug file in the system root called *memory.dmp*. This file will be one of the first things Microsoft asks for if you open a support case about the crash (see MS KB 314103 for more information). After the debug file is written, an event is written to the System Event log and, if configured, an administrative alert is sent to the administrator of the system. See MS KB 310490 for more on configuring administrative alerts. Lastly, the system automatically reboots. You may want to give some thought about this last option because I've seen more than one case where a system continuously reboots itself because it experienced the failure during system startup. Also, if you automatically reboot and are not closely monitoring your systems, there could be sporadic undetected crashes.

Table 2-3 lists all of the system failure options and their corresponding graphical, registry, WMIC, and WMI settings.

Table 2-3. System failure settings

Graphical interface	Registry value	WMIC and WMI property	Description
Automatically restart	AutoReboot	AutoReboot	Determines if system automatically reboots after a system crash. The default is true.
Dump file	DumpFile	DebugFilePath	Path to the debug (or dump) file. The default is *%SystemRoot%\MEMORY.DMP*.
Write debugging information	CrashDumpEnabled	DebugInfoType	Determines if debug information is written to the debug file after a system crash. Values include: 0 (none), 1 (complete), 2 (kernel memory), and 3 (small memory). The default is 1. This setting is new in Windows Server 2003.
Write debugging information	KernelDumpOnly	KernelDumpOnly	This setting is deprecated in favor of DebugInfoType.
Small dump directory	MinidumpDir	MiniDumpDirectory	Path to the directory where the small memory dump file will be stored. The default is *%SystemRoot%\MiniDump*.
Overwrite any existing file	Overwrite	OverwriteExistingDebugFile	Determines if an existing debug file will be overwritten. If true (the default), then overwrite the debug file if it already exists. If false, then do not write a debug file if one already exists.
Send an administrative alert	SendAlert	SendAdminAlert	Determines if an administrative alert will be sent to the administrator after a system crash. If true (the default), an alert will be sent. If false, an alert will not be sent.
N/A	N/A	WriteDebugInfo	This setting is deprecated in favor of DebugInfoType.
Write an event to the system log	LogEvent	WriteToSystemLog	Determines if an event will be written to the System event log. If true (the default), an event is written. If false, an event is not written. This feature cannot be turned off on Windows 2000 Server or Windows Server 2003.

See Also

MS KB 307973 (HOW TO: Configure System Failure and Recovery Options in Windows), MS KB 310490 (HOW TO: Set Up Administrative Alerts in Windows XP), and MS KB 314103 (Preparation Before You Contact Microsoft After Receiving a STOP Message on a Blue Screen)

2.16 Viewing System Uptime

Problem

You want to find out how long a server has been running since the last restart.

Solution

Using a command-line interface

All three of the following commands display the system uptime:

```
> psinfo \\<ServerName> | findstr Uptime
> srvinfo \\<ServerName> | findstr /c:"Up Time"
> systeminfo /s <ServerName> | findstr /c:"Up Time"
```

Using VBScript

```
' This code prints system uptime for a host.
' ------ SCRIPT CONFIGURATION ------
strComputer = "."    ' e.g., rallen-srv01
' ------ END CONFIGURATION ---------
set objWMIDateTime = CreateObject("WbemScripting.SWbemDateTime")
set objWMI = GetObject("winmgmts:\\" & strComputer & "\root\cimv2")
set colOS = objWMI.InstancesOf("Win32_OperatingSystem")
for each objOS in colOS
   objWMIDateTime.Value = objOS.LastBootUpTime
   Wscript.Echo "System Up Time: " & objWMIDateTime.GetVarDate
next
```

Discussion

In the early days of Windows NT 3.51 and 4.0, it wasn't uncommon for servers to reboot or need to be rebooted on a regular basis. Applications were not as well behaved as they are today and the operating system wasn't as stable. This changed with Windows 2000, when unexpected failures became much less common. But there were still a lot of hotfixes and patches to install on a regular basis, most of which required reboots. Hopefully Windows Server 2003 will continue the upward trend in availability and further reduce the number of reboots that are required.

It is a good idea to pay attention to the uptime on your servers to make sure their availability jives with what you think it should be. Perhaps a server rebooted due to a blue screen or even worse, because another administrator (or attacker!) did something they shouldn't have. Looking at system uptime is the poor man's availability monitor. You may even want to create a script that runs at system startup on your servers, which can serve as a notification mechanism anytime your servers reboot.

2.17 Disabling the Manage/Configure Your Server Screen

Problem

You want to disable the **Manager Your Server** and **Configure Your Server** screens from being displayed when you log into a server.

Solution

Using a graphical user interface

The following directions disable the screen for the currently logged on user only. See the command-line solution for how to disable it for all users by default.

For Windows Server 2003:

1. From the Start menu, select **All Programs** → **Administrative Tools** → **Manage Your Server**.
2. At the bottom lefthand corner of the screen, check the box beside **Don't display this page at logon**.

For Windows 2000:

1. From the Start menu, select **Programs** → **Administrative Tools** → **Configure Your Server**.
2. At the bottom of the screen, uncheck the box beside **Show this screen at startup**.

Using a command-line interface

Run the following command against a Windows Server 2003 or Windows 2000 machine to prevent the Manage/Configure Your Server screen from displaying for all users:

```
> reg add "\\<ServerName>\HKU\.DEFAULT\Software\Microsoft\Windows NT\CurrentVersion\
Setup\Welcome" /v srvwiz /t REG_DWORD /d 0
```

If a user logged in before you set the previous registry value, then you'll need to run this command to disable it for the logged-in user (note: this command must be run locally):

```
> reg add "HKCU\Software\Microsoft\Windows NT\CurrentVersion\Setup\Welcome\srvWiz"
/ve /t REG_DWORD /d 0
```

Using VBScript

```
' This code disables the Manage/Configure Your Server screen for all users
' (this only applies to users that have not logged in yet)
' ------ SCRIPT CONFIGURATION ------
intEnable = 0                   ' 0 = disable screen; 1 = enable screen
```

```
strComputer = "<ServerName>"  ' name of target server
' ------ END CONFIGURATION ---------
const HKU   = &H80000003
strKeyPath  = ".DEFAULT\Software\Microsoft\Windows NT\CurrentVersion\" & _
              "Setup\Welcome"
strValue = "srvwiz"
set objReg = GetObject("winmgmts:\\" & strComputer & _
                       "\root\default:StdRegProv")
intRC = objReg.SetDwordValue(HKU, strKeyPath, strValue, intEnable)
if intRC <> 0 then
   WScript.Echo "Error setting registry value: " & intRC
else
   WScript.Echo "Successfully disabled screen"
end if


' This code disables the Manage/Configure Your Server screen for
' the currently logged on user.
' ------ SCRIPT CONFIGURATION ------
intEnable = 0    ' 0 = disable screen; 1 = enable screen
strComputer = "."
' ------ END CONFIGURATION ---------
const HKCU   = &H80000001
strKeyPath   = "Software\Microsoft\Windows NT\CurrentVersion\" & _
               "Setup\Welcome\srvWiz"
set objReg = GetObject("winmgmts:\\" & strComputer & _
                       "\root\default:StdRegProv")
intRC = objReg.SetDwordValue(HKCU, strKeyPath, "", intEnable)
if intRC <> 0 then
   WScript.Echo "Error setting registry value: " & intRC
else
   WScript.Echo "Successfully disabled screen"
end if
```

Discussion

When you log into a Windows 2000 Server or Windows Server 2003 system for the first time, the Configure Your Server or Manage Your Server screens, respectively, are displayed. These screens are intended to make managing a server easier by providing links to install services and obtain help information. These screens are displayed for every user that logs on until the user checks the box on the screen to stop the screen from running at logon.

A setting in the registry controls whether this screen is displayed by default. When a user logs on for the first time, the subkeys and values in the HKEY_USERS\.DEFAULT key are copied to HKEY_USERS\<UserName>, which is the same as HKEY_CURRENT_USER for the currently logged on user. Under the .DEFAULT key, the Software\Microsoft\Windows NT\CurrentVersion\srvWiz value dictates if the Configure/Manage Your Server screen displays at logon. A value of 0 disables the screen from displaying and 1 enables it. If you set it to 0 before any user logs on to the system, that screen will never display.

See Also

MS KB 289080 (HOW TO: Disable the Configure Your Server Wizard in Windows 2000) and MS KB 312580 (How to Suppress the Configure Your Server Wizard)

2.18   Disabling Shutdown Tracker

Problem

You want to disable the Shutdown Tracker from running at system startup on lab or test systems because it is annoying. Shutdown Tracker is a new feature of Windows Server 2003 that prompts you to provide a description of the reason why a server is being shut down or restarted. If the server unexpectedly restarted, you are prompted during logon for this information.

Solution

You need to reboot the system for the changes to take effect after performing one of the following.

Using a graphical user interface

1. Open the Registry Editor (*regedit.exe*) and connect to the target machine.
2. In the left pane, expand **HKEY_LOCAL_MACHINE → SOFTWARE → Policies → Microsoft → Windows NT**.
3. If there is no subkey called **Reliability**, create it by right-clicking **Windows NT**, selecting **New → Key**, and typing **Reliability**.
4. Right-click **Reliability** and select **New → DWORD Value**.
5. In the right pane, type **ShutdownReasonOn** and hit enter. Leave the default value set to 0.

You can also disable Shutdown Tracker using group policy. The settings for it are located in **Computer Configuration → Administrative Templates → System → Display Shutdown System Tracker**.

Using a command-line interface

The following command disables the Shutdown Tracker:

```
> reg add "\\<ServerName>\HKLM\SOFTWARE\Policies\Microsoft\Windows NT\Reliability" /v
ShutdownReasonOn /t REG_DWORD /d 0
```

Using VBScript

```
' This code disables the Shutdown Tracker from running.
' ------ SCRIPT CONFIGURATION ------
intEnable = 0        ' 0 = disable; 1 = enable screen
```

```
strComputer = "."   ' e.g., rallen-srv01
' ------ END CONFIGURATION ---------
const HKLM = &H80000002
strKeyPath = "SOFTWARE\Policies\Microsoft\Windows NT\Reliability"
set objReg = GetObject("winmgmts:\\" & strComputer & _
                       "\root\default:StdRegProv")
intRC1 = objReg.CreateKey(HKLM,strKeyPath)
intRC2 = objReg.SetDwordValue(HKLM, strKeyPath, "ShutdownReasonOn", intEnable)
if intRC1 <> 0 or intRC2 <> 0 then
    WScript.Echo "Error setting registry value: " & intRC
else
    WScript.Echo "Successfully disabled shutdown tracker"
end if
```

Discussion

Don't get me wrong, I think the Shutdown Tracker is a very useful feature. In fact, I'm glad Microsoft added it, but it can be annoying on test systems that you want to restart or shut down frequently. After Shutdown Tracker runs, it creates event 1074 in the System event log. Here is an example:

```
Event Type:     Information
Event Source:   USER32
Event Category:    None
Event ID:      1074
Date:          10/11/2003
Time:          6:50:42 PM
User:          rallen-w2k3\administrator
Computer:      RALLEN-W2K3
Description:
The process Explorer.EXE has initiated the restart of computer RALLEN-W2K3 on behalf
of user RALLEN-W2K3\Administrator for the following reason: Other (Planned)
 Reason Code: 0x85000000
 Shutdown Type: restart
 Comment: Just installed a hotfix.

For more information, see Help and Support Center at http://go.microsoft.com/fwlink/
events.asp.
Data:
0000: 00 00 00 85        ...
```

You can even customize Shutdown Tracker if you want. You can create your own shutdown reasons. There are eight by default. All it takes is some more registry changes. See MS KB 293814 for more information.

See Also

Recipe 2.19 for restarting or shutting down a server, and MS KB 293814 (Description of the Shutdown Event Tracker)

2.19   Restarting or Shutting Down a Server

Problem

You want to restart or shut down a server.

Solution

Using a graphical user interface

With Windows Server 2003 and Windows 2000 you can obviously shut a machine down by going to Start → Shut Down, but I'll describe the new graphical interface with the *shutdown.exe* command, which is available in Windows Server 2003.

1. From the Start menu select **Run**.
2. Type *cmd.exe* and click **OK**.
3. In the CMD window, type *shutdown /i* and hit enter.
4. Click the **Add** button, type the names of the server(s) you want to shut down or restart, and click **OK**.
5. Select whether you want to restart or shut down the server(s).
6. Enter the number of seconds to warn logged on users (or uncheck to not warn).
7. Configure the **Shutdown Event Tracker** options.
8. Click **OK**. In the CMD window, you'll see a status message stating if the operation was successful.

Here is another option that is available from either Windows 2000 or Windows Server 2003:

1. Open the Computer Management snap-in.
2. If you want to target a remote system, right-click on the **Computer Management** icon in the left pane and select **Connect to another computer**. Enter the computer name beside **Another computer** and click **OK**.
3. Right-click on the **Computer Management** icon in the left pane and select **Properties**.
4. Click the **Advanced** tab.
5. Under **Startup and recovery**, click the Settings button.
6. Click the **Shut Down** button.
7. Select from the list of actions and options under **Forced Closed Apps**.
8. Click **OK**.

Using a command-line interface

The following two commands work with the Windows Server 2003 version of *shutdown.exe*. This shuts a server down after the 30 seconds (default wait timer):

```
> shutdown /m \\<ServerName> /s /c "Server requires reboot due to app install"
```

This command restarts a server after 20 seconds:

```
> shutdown /m \\<ServerName> /r /t 20 /c "Server is going down for repairs"
```

You can use the /f option to force applications to close.

On Windows 2000, the *shutdown* options are a little different. This command shuts down a server (in 30 seconds by default):

```
> shutdown \\<ServerName> "Server is going down for repairs"
```

And this restarts (/r option) a server in 15 seconds:

```
> shutdown \\<ServerName> /r /t:15 "Server requires reboot due to app install"
```

You can force all applications to close by using the /c option.

Using VBScript

```
' This code shuts a server down.
' ------ SCRIPT CONFIGURATION ------
strComputer = "<ServerName>"    ' e.g., rallen-srv01
' ------ END CONFIGURATION ---------
set objWMI = GetObject("winmgmts:\\" & strComputer & "\root\cimv2")
set colOS = objWMI.InstancesOf("Win32_OperatingSystem")
for each objOS in colOS
   intRC = ObjOS.Shutdown( )
   if intRC <> 0 then
      WScript.Echo "Error attempting to shutdown server: " & intRC
   else
      WScript.Echo "Shutting down server..."
   end if
next


' This code forcefully shuts a server down.
' ------ SCRIPT CONFIGURATION ------
strComputer = "<ServerName>"    ' e.g., rallen-srv01
intFlag = 1 + 4     ' Flag for forceful shut down
' ------ END CONFIGURATION ---------
set objWMI = GetObject("winmgmts:\\" & strComputer & "\root\cimv2")
set colOS = objWMI.InstancesOf("Win32_OperatingSystem")
for each objOS in colOS
   intRC = ObjOS.Win32Shutdown(intFlag)
   if intRC <> 0 then
      WScript.Echo "Error attempting to shutdown server: " & intRC
   else
      WScript.Echo "Shutting down server..."
   end if
next
```

```
' This code reboots a server.
' ------ SCRIPT CONFIGURATION ------
strComputer = "<ServerName>"   ' e.g. rallen-srv01
' ------ END CONFIGURATION ---------
set objWMI = GetObject("winmgmts:\\" & strComputer & "\root\cimv2")
set colOS = objWMI.InstancesOf("Win32_OperatingSystem")
for each objOS in colOS
    intRC = ObjOS.Reboot()
    if intRC <> 0 then
        WScript.Echo "Error attempting to reboot server: " & intRC
    else
        WScript.Echo "Rebooting server..."
    end if
next
```

Discussion

When you shut down or restart a Windows server, a signal is sent to all devices, services, and programs running on the system. This signal announces that the system is preparing to shut down so everything needs to close gracefully, if possible. A normal shutdown will wait for a response from all devices and processes to make sure they have saved any files and can close before proceeding with the shutdown. If you've ever had Notepad or Word open with an unsaved file, you've seen the message asking if you want to save the file before the application closes.

If you need to automate the shutdown or restart of a system, then politely asking each application to close can be problematic. If someone had an open unsaved file on the target system, the shutdown wouldn't proceed as expected. That's why Windows also supports forcefully shutting down a system. With the *shutdown.exe* command, you can specify an additional option (/f on Windows Server 2003 and /c on Windows 2000) to force all applications to close. If an application like Notepad is running, it automatically closes any unsaved files and your unsaved changes will be lost.

On the programmatic side, the Win32_OperatingSystem class supports two shutdown methods. The first one (Shutdown), performs a normal shutdown. It will not forcefully close files. The second, however, Win32Shutdown, will. Table 2-4 contains all of the flags that can be set with Win32Shutdown.

Table 2-4. Bitmapped Win32Shutdown flags

Value	Meaning
0	Log off
0 + 4 = 4	Forcefully log off
1	Shutdown
1 + 4 = 5	Forcefully shutdown
2	Restart
2 + 4 = 6	Forcefully restart

Table 2-4. Bitmapped Win32Shutdown flags (continued)

Value	Meaning
8	Power off
8 + 4 = 12	Forcefully power off

So you can perform a forceful shutdown with a command line and from a script. How about from the GUI? You sure can. Just hit Ctrl+Alt+Del on your keyboard. Using the Tab key move to the Shut Down button. Hold the Ctrl key down and click Enter. Click OK to confirm the shutdown.

One other thing that you may need to do at some point is schedule a server to reboot or shutdown at a specific time. This is sometimes needed if an entire network or data center needs to move or go down for maintenance. You could automate this job pretty quickly using a combination of the scripting solutions and the Task Scheduler, but there is another way using the command line. The *at.exe* command lets you schedule a task to run either locally or remotely at a specified time.

This command causes a server to shut down at 20:00 (8 P.M.) tonight:

```
> at \\<ServerName> 20:00 shutdown.exe /s /c "Datacenter move"
```

This command causes the server to restart at 21:00 (9 P.M.) every Friday night:

```
> at \\<ServerName> 21:00 /every:F shutdown.exe /r /c "Weekly restart"
```

See Also

MS KB 232399 (How to Enable Logon Screen Shutdown Button in Windows 2000 Server), MS KB 324268 (HOW TO: Troubleshoot Shutdown Problems in Windows Server 2003), MS KB 325343 (HOW TO: Perform an Emergency Shutdown in Windows Server 2003), MS KB 325376 (HOW TO: Enable Verbose Startup, Shutdown, Logon, and Logoff Status Messages in the Windows Server 2003 Family), MS KB 816569 (HOW TO: Make the Shutdown Button Unavailable in the Logon Dialog Box in Windows Server 2003), and MS KB 821287 (The Computer Does Not Automatically Shut Down When the Shutdown.exe Command Is Invoked)

CHAPTER 3

Disks, Drives, and Volumes

3.0 Introduction

Before you can start using a filesystem on a server, you have to configure the disks, drives, and volumes. You have to split up the disks into volumes and assign drive letters to the volumes. You have to format a volume with a filesystem such as NTFS or FAT32. Filesystems are what give you features such as security, compression, and encryption of files and folders. Once you have usable volumes in place, there are many ongoing maintenance tasks you should do to keep your disks healthy. You'll want to periodically defragment your volumes so that new files aren't spread across many separate chunks, which decreases file access performance. You'll want to check your volumes for errors to ensure there aren't any bad sectors. And if you start running low on space, you may want to clean up a volume or see which users are using the most space. If disk space usage is a concern for you, you can implement the Windows quota feature that lets you limit the amount of space users' use. In this chapter, I cover all of these tasks and more.

Using a Graphical User Interface

The two primary graphical interfaces for managing disks, drives, and volumes are Windows Explorer and the Disk Management snap-in. With Windows Explorer, you can right-click a drive, select Properties, and perform functions such as enabling quotas, running disk cleanup, performing defragmentation, and running an error check.

The Disk Management snap-in lets you perform lower-level disk administration and volume management. With it you can create new volumes, assign drive letters, format volumes with a particular filesystem, and convert basic disks to dynamic disks.

Using a Command-Line Interface

Several important new command-line utilities have been added to Windows Server 2003 to help with managing disks and volumes. Tools such as *diskpart* and *fsutil* allow you close to complete control over disks, drives, and volumes from the command line.

Most of these new command-line tools also provide interfaces for running in batch mode, which make them easy to script. It is worth your time to get familiar with the capabilities of these tools.

Table 3-1 lists the command-line tools used in this chapter.

Table 3-1. Command-line tools used in this chapter

Tool	Windows Server 2003	Windows 2000 Server	Recipes
chkdsk	%SystemRoot%\system32	%SystemRoot%\system32	3.10
cleanmgr	%SystemRoot%\system32	%SystemRoot%\system32	3.7
compact	%SystemRoot%\system32	%SystemRoot%\system32	3.9
defrag	%SystemRoot%\system32	N/A	3.8
diruse	Windows 2003 Support Tools	Window 2000 Resource Kit	3.14
diskpart	%SystemRoot%\system32	N/A	3.1, 3.2, 3.5
diskperf	%SystemRoot%\system32	%SystemRoot%\system32	3.3
diskuse	Windows 2003 Resource Kit	Windows 2000 Resource Kit	3.14
format	%SystemRoot%\system32	%SystemRoot%\system32	3.4
fsutil	%SystemRoot%\system32	N/A	3.15–17
label	%SystemRoot%\system32	%SystemRoot%\system32	3.6
net use	%SystemRoot%\system32	%SystemRoot%\system32	3.12
subst	%SystemRoot%\system32	%SystemRoot%\system32	3.13
vrfydsk	Windows 2003 Resource Kit	N/A	3.10
writeprot	http://joeware.net	N/A	3.11

Using VBScript

Just as several new command-line tools were added to Windows Server 2003, so were some important new WMI classes. Specifically, the Win32_Volume class allows you to perform a variety of volume management tasks including running a chkdsk, defragmentation, and format of a volume.

Table 3-2 lists the WMI classes used in this chapter. The only important exception to note is that I use the MapNetworkDrive WSH method in Recipe 3.12.

Table 3-2. WMI classes used in this chapter

WMI class	Description	Recipes
CIM_Datafile	Enumerate and manage files.	3.14
Win32_Directory	Enumerate directories.	3.9
Win32_DiskDrive	Enumerate and manage physical disks.	3.1
Win32_DiskQuota	Enumerate the quota usage for a particular user.	3.16-17
Win32_LogicalDisk	Enumerate and manage logical disks.	3.1, 3.10, 3.16, 3.17

Table 3-2. WMI classes used in this chapter (continued)

WMI class	Description	Recipes
Win32_MappedLogicalDisk	Enumerate and manage mapped network drives.	3.1
Win32_QuotaSetting	Enumerate and manage disk quota settings on volumes. This class is available only with Windows XP and Windows Server 2003.	3.15
Win32_Volume	Enumerate and manage volumes. This class is available only with Windows Server 2003.	3.4–3.6, 3.8

3.1 Viewing the Disk, Drive, and Volume Layout

Problem

You want to see how the disks, drives, and volumes are laid out on a server.

Solution

Using a graphical user interface

1. Open the Computer Management snap-in.
2. In the left pane, expand **Storage** and click on **Disk Management**. The right pane will display the disk, volumes, and drives.

Using a command-line interface

On Windows Server 2003, you can use the *diskpart* utility to view the disk, drive, and volume configuration. First, get into interactive mode:

```
> diskpart
```

Next, to view the list of disks, run the following:

```
> list disk
```

Now, to see the list of volume and assigned drive letters, run the following:

```
> list vol
```

 Unfortunately, there isn't an equivalent utility on Windows 2000.

Using VBScript

```
' This code enumerates the physical and logical disks on a system.
' ------ SCRIPT CONFIGURATION ------
strComputer = "."
' ------ END CONFIGURATION ---------
WScript.Echo "Physical Disks:"
set objWMI = GetObject("winmgmts:\\" & strComputer & "\root\cimv2")
```

```
    set colDisks = objWMI.ExecQuery("select * from Win32_DiskDrive")
    for each objDisk in colDisks
        WScript.Echo " Caption: " & vbTab &  objDisk.Caption
        WScript.Echo " Device ID: " & vbTab &  objDisk.DeviceID
        WScript.Echo " Manufacturer: " & vbTab & objDisk.Manufacturer
        WScript.Echo " Media Type: " & vbTab &  objDisk.MediaType
        WScript.Echo " Model: " & vbTab &  objDisk.Model
        WScript.Echo " Name: " & vbTab &  objDisk.Name
        WScript.Echo " Partitions: " & vbTab & objDisk.Partitions
        WScript.Echo " Size: " & vbTab &  objDisk.Size
        WScript.Echo " Status: " & vbTab &  objDisk.Status
        WScript.Echo
    next

    WScript.Echo
    WScript.Echo "Logical Disks:"
    set colDisks = objWMI.ExecQuery("select * from Win32_LogicalDisk")
    for each objDisk in colDisks
        WScript.Echo " DeviceID: " & objDisk.DeviceID
        WScript.Echo " Description: " & objDisk.Description
        WScript.Echo " VolumeName: " & objDisk.VolumeName
        WScript.Echo " DriveType: " & objDisk.DriveType
        WScript.Echo " FileSystem: " & objDisk.FileSystem
        WScript.Echo " FreeSpace: " & objDisk.FreeSpace
        WScript.Echo " MediaType: " & objDisk.MediaType
        WScript.Echo " Name: " & objDisk.Name
        WScript.Echo " Size: " & objDisk.Size
        WScript.Echo
    next
```

Discussion

The solutions show how to enumerate all the disks and volumes on a server, but if
you have any mapped drives, it won't show those. The easiest way to see mapped
drives is to open Windows Explorer and look at My Computer or run net use from a
command line. From VBScript, you can use the Win32_MappedLogicalDisk WMI class,
which is new to Windows Server 2003 and Windows XP. Here is some sample code:

```
    strComputer = "."
    set objWMI = GetObject("winmgmts:\\" & strComputer & "\root\cimv2")
    set colDrives = objWMI.ExecQuery("select * from Win32_MappedLogicalDisk")
    WScript.Echo "Mapped Drives:"
    for each objDrive in colDrives
        WScript.Echo " Device ID: " & objDrive.DeviceID
        WScript.Echo " Volume Name: " & objDrive.VolumeName
        WScript.Echo " Session ID: " & objDrive.SessionID
        WScript.Echo " Size: " & objDrive.Size
        WScript.Echo
    next
```

See Also

Recipe 3.12 for mapping a network drive.

3.2 Converting a Basic Disk to Dynamic

Problem

You want to convert a basic disk to a dynamic disk.

Solution

Using a graphical user interface

1. Open the Computer Management snap-in.
2. In the left pane, expand Storage and click on **Disk Management**.
3. In the lower-right pane, right-click the disk you want to convert and select **Convert to Dynamic Disk** (on Windows XP and Windows Server 2003) or **Upgrade to Dynamic Disk** (on Windows 2000).
4. Check the box beside the disk(s) you want to convert and click **OK**.
5. Click **Convert** (on Windows XP and Windows Server 2003) or **Upgrade** (on Windows 2000) and click **Yes** to confirm the conversion.

Using a command-line interface

On Windows Server 2003, you can use the *diskpart* utility to convert a disk to dynamic. First, run diskpart to enter interactive mode:

```
> diskpart
```

You need to get a list of disks so you can select the one you want to convert:

```
> list disk
```

In the following example, I'll select disk 0:

```
> select disk 0
```

Now, run the following command to convert the disk:

```
> convert dynamic
```

You may be asked to reboot for the change to take effect.

Using VBScript

None of the WMI classes support converting a disk to a dynamic disk.

Discussion

By default, disks are initialized as basic on both Windows 2000 and Windows Server 2003. You can convert a disk to dynamic to take advantage of features such as the ability to dynamically extend partitions. Some additional benefits of dynamic disks include:

- You can perform disk and volume management without needing to restart the operating system.
- You can organize dynamic disks into disk groups. Configuration information for all disks in a group is shared and kept up-to-date even if a dynamic disk fails or is moved to another system.
- You have more options for configuring volumes. Dynamic disks support the following dynamic volumes: simple volumes, spanned volumes, striped volumes, mirrored volumes, and RAID-5 volumes.
- You are not limited on the number of volumes you create on a dynamic disk. With a basic disk you can create up to four primary partitions or three primary partitions and one extended partition.

 Once you convert a disk to dynamic, you cannot convert it back to basic unless you delete all of the dynamic volumes on the disk.

See Also

MS KB 175761 (Dynamic vs. Basic Storage in Windows 2000), MS KB 309044 (How To Convert to Basic and Dynamic Disks in Windows XP Professional), MS KB 254105 (Dynamic Disk Hardware Limitations), and MS KB 314343 (Basic Storage Versus Dynamic Storage in Windows XP)

3.3   Enabling Disk Performance Statistics

Problem

You want to monitor disk performance and you need to enable performance statistics.

Solution

On Windows 2000 Server, run the following command and then reboot:

```
> diskperf -y
```

On Windows Server 2003, all disk performance statistics are enabled by default.

Discussion

With Windows NT, both logical and physical disk performance counters were disabled by default. With Windows 2000, physical disk counters were enabled and logical disk counters were disabled. With Windows Server 2003, both logical and physical disk counters are enabled. Logical and physical disk counters were disabled by default in previous versions of the OS because of the concern that the impact to performance would be too great to have them on all the time. As disk access times have steadily improved over the years, the performance hit has become negligible. Now, you can safely have both physical and logical disk counters enabled on either Windows 2000 or Windows Server 2003.

 Within Performance Monitor, the LogicalDisk and PhysicalDisk objects contain the counters that are available when disk performance statistics are enabled.

See Also

MS KB 253251 (Using Diskperf in Windows 2000)

3.4   Formatting a Volume

Problem

You want to reformat an existing volume or initialize a new one.

Solution

Using a graphical user interface

1. Open Windows Explorer.
2. Right-click on the drive letter for the volume you want to format and select **Format**.
3. Leave **NTFS** selected for **File system** unless you have a very good reason to use **FAT32**. The same goes for the **Allocation unit size**; use the default selected unless you have a good reason.
4. Type a description under **Volume label**.
5. Check the box beside **Quick Format** if you've previously formatted the volume with the same filesystem and just want to delete the file table (i.e., links to all the files and folders).
6. Check the box beside **Enable Compression** if you want to compress the contents of the volume.
7. Click **Start**.

Using a command-line interface

The following command formats the D: drive using NTFS and sets the volume label to Data:

```
> format D: /fs:ntfs /v:Data
```

You will be prompted to enter the current label of the D: drive. Type it in and press Enter. Then you'll be asked for confirmation to continue by typing **Y** and pressing Enter.

Add the /q option to the previous command line to perform a quick format and add the /c option to enable compression on the volume. You can use the /x option to force a dismount in case someone has a handle open on the volume.

Using VBScript

```
' This code formats a volume.
' The Win32_Volume class is new in Windows Server 2003.
' ------ SCRIPT CONFIGURATION ------
strComputer = "<Server>"
strDrive = "<Drive>"  ' e.g., D:

strFS = "NTFS"
boolQuick = False
intClusterSize = 4096
strLabel = "Data"
boolCompress = False
' ------ END CONFIGURATION ---------
set objWMI = GetObject("winmgmts:\\" & strComputer & "\root\cimv2")
set colVol = objWMI.ExecQuery("select * from Win32_Volume where Name = '" & _
                             strDrive & "\\'")
if colVol.Count <> 1 then
   WScript.Echo "Error: Volume not found."
else
   for each objVol in colVol
      intRC = objVol.Format(strFS,boolQuick,intClusterSize, _
                           strLabel,boolCompress)
      if intRC <> 0 then
         WScript.Echo "Error formatting volume: " & intRC
      else
         WScript.Echo "Successfully set formatted volume."
      end if
   next
end if
```

Discussion

Before you can use a volume, you first need to format it with a filesystem. On Windows 2000 and Windows Server 2003, you can format a volume with FAT, FAT32, or NTFS. Unless you have a good reason, you should use NTFS due to its increased security features.

Another option when formatting a volume is whether to perform a quick format or normal format. Both options erase the table that tracks file locations on the filesystem. The difference is that a normal format will scan the entire volume for bad sectors. This scan is responsible for most of the time required to do a format. A quick format bypasses this, so you should only use it when the volume has been previously formatted with a filesystem and you are confident the disk isn't damaged.

You can also enable compression on a newly formatted volume. See Recipe 3.9 for more on the effects of compression.

See Also

MS KB 140365 (Default Cluster Size for FAT and NTFS) and MS KB 313348 (How to partition and format a hard disk in Windows XP)

3.5   Setting the Drive Letter of a Volume

Problem

You want to set the drive letter of a volume.

Solution

Using a graphical user interface

1. Open the Computer Management snap-in.
2. In the left pane under **Storage**, click on **Disk Administrator**.
3. In the bottom right pane, right-click the target volume or disk and select **Change Drive Letter and Paths**.
4. Click the **Change** button.
5. Beside **Assign the following drive letter**, select the new drive letter from the drop-down list and click **OK**.
6. Click **Yes** to confirm.

Using a command-line interface

The *diskpart* command lets you assign driver letters from the command line on Windows Server 2003 and Windows XP. First, start by running the command in interactive mode:

```
> diskpart
```

List the current volumes on the system:

```
> list vol
```

From the output, select the volume in which you want to set the driver letter. In the following command, I'm selecting volume 0:

```
> select vol 0
```

Now, assign the drive letter you want. In the following example, I'm assigning letter F:

```
> assign letter=F
```

Using VBScript

```
' This code sets the drive letter of a volume.
' The Win32_Volume class is new in Windows Server 2003
' ------ SCRIPT CONFIGURATION ------
strComputer = "."
strOldDrive = "I:"
strNewDrive = "J:"
' ------ END CONFIGURATION ---------
set objWMI = GetObject("winmgmts:\\" & strComputer & "\root\cimv2")
set colVol = objWMI.ExecQuery("select * from Win32_Volume where Name = '" & _
                              strOldDrive & "\\'")
if colVol.Count <> 1 then
   WScript.Echo "Error: Volume not found."
else
   for each objVol in colVol
       objVol.DriveLetter = strNewDrive
       objVol.Put_
       WScript.Echo "Successfully set drive letter for volume."
   next
end if
```

Discussion

When volumes are made active and removable media are added to a system, they are automatically assigned the next available drive letter (in alphabetical order starting from C:). It is a straightforward operation to change the letter of a drive, but you need to be sure nothing references the prior drive letter. If you attempt to assign a different drive letter to an existing drive that is currently in use, the system will let you do it and allows both the old drive letter and new drive letter to be used until the system is rebooted. After the system restarts, the old drive letter will go back into the pool of available drive letters.

If you want to change the drive letter of the system drive, you have to follow special procedures. See MS KB 223188 for more information.

See Also

MS KB 234048 (How Windows 2000 Assigns, Reserves, and Stores Drive Letters) and MS KB 223188 (How To Restore the System/Boot Drive Letter in Windows)

3.6 Setting the Label of a Volume

Problem

You want to set the label of a volume.

Solution

Using a graphical user interface

1. Open Windows Explorer.
2. Right-click the drive you want to clean up and select **Properties**.
3. Click the **General** tab if it isn't opened by default.
4. The lone input box on this tab is the label for the volume. Modify it as necessary and click **OK**.

Using a command-line interface

Use the *label* command to set the label of a volume. The following example sets the label for the C: drive to be System Volume:

```
> label c: System Volume
```

 Do not put quotes around multiword labels. The *label* command captures everything after the drive parameter so no quotes are necessary.

Using VBScript

```
' This code sets the label of a volume.
' The Win32_Volume class is new in Windows Server 2003
' ------ SCRIPT CONFIGURATION ------
strComputer = "."
strDrive = "<Drive>"  ' e.g., C:
strLabel = "<Label>"  ' e.g., System Volume
' ------ END CONFIGURATION ---------
set objWMI = GetObject("winmgmts:\\" & strComputer & "\root\cimv2")
set colVol = objWMI.ExecQuery("select * from Win32_Volume where Name = '" & _
                             strDrive & "\\'")
if colVol.Count <> 1 then
   WScript.Echo "Error: Volume not found."
else
   for each objVol in colVol
       objVol.Label = strLabel
       objVol.Put_
       WScript.Echo "Successfully set label for volume."
   next
end if
```

Discussion

The label of a volume is nothing more than a short description that is displayed in tools such as Windows Explorer when you view the list of drives. A label can contain up to 32 characters. You can use a mix of alphanumeric and special characters. Also, labels do not have to be unique across volumes, but it defeats the purpose of having labels in the first place if you configure multiple volumes with the same one. And unlike setting drive letters, you can modify the label of a volume regardless of whether the volume is the system volume or has files that are locked.

3.7   Cleaning Up a Volume

Problem

You want to clean up unused or unneeded files on a volume to reclaim space.

Solution

Using a graphical user interface

1. Open Windows Explorer.
2. Right-click the drive you want to clean up and select **Properties**.
3. Click the **General** tab if it isn't opened by default.
4. Click the **Disk Cleanup** button. Depending on the size of the volume you are scanning, this can take a while to complete.
5. Under **Files to delete**, check the boxes beside the type of files you want to remove.
6. When you are done with your selections, click **OK**.
7. Click **Yes** to confirm that you want to delete the files.

Using a command-line interface

You can launch the Disk Cleanup tool from the command line by running the following command:

```
> cleanmgr
```

To target a specific drive, use the /d option:

```
> cleanmgr /d E:
```

You can automate the Disk Cleanup tool to run against all the drives on a system in a couple of steps. First, you need to configure the types of files you want to clean up. Run the *cleanmgr* utility with the /sageset: option following by an integer. The integer represents a Disk Cleanup profile. In the following example, I'll use 1:

```
> cleanmgr /sageset:1
```

This opens the Disk Cleanup Settings property page. Under **Files to delete**, check the boxes beside the types of files you want to clean up. Click **OK** when you are done. Now, use the /sagerun: option followed by the same number we just used (1 in this case):

```
> cleanmgr /sagerun:1
```

This command enumerates all drives on the system and performs a disk clean up according to the profile we just created.

Discussion

Disk Cleanup is a tool to help you remove unneeded files on your system, which are doing nothing more than taking up space. It can find temporary files used by Internet Explorer and old setup files for applications such as Microsoft Office and let you delete them.

After you've analyzed a particular volume, you can click on a file type—e.g., Temporary Internet Files—to see a description of that file type at the bottom of the dialog box. As you check or uncheck boxes, you'll see the number beside **Total amount of disk space you gain** increase or decrease, respectively. Depending on the file type, a **View Files** button will be displayed, which when clicked, opens a Windows Explorer window to the location of the files. The list of file types will vary depending on the volume you are looking at. Only file types that apply to a particular volume are displayed.

The **Compress old files** option is a good way to minimize disk bloat over time. When enabled, it will compress files that haven't been accessed in a certain number of days. It won't delete any files, just compress them. That means files you rarely accessed are compressed and the impact to the disk is minimized.

The **More Options** tab provides buttons for opening the Windows Components and Add/Remove Programs screens and a button for removing all but the most recent system restore point. Depending on how much space you need to reclaim, all three of these can be good sources for reclaiming unused or rarely used disk space.

See Also

MS KB 253597 (Automating Disk Cleanup Tool in Windows) and MS KB 310312 (Description of the Disk Cleanup Tool in Windows XP)

3.8   Defragmenting a Volume

Problem

You want to defragment a volume to improve disk access performance.

Solution

Using a graphical user interface

1. Open Windows Explorer.
2. Right-click the drive you want to defragment and select **Properties**.
3. Click the **Tools** tab.
4. Click the **Defragment Now** button. This launches the Disk Defragmenter application.
5. Click the **Analyze** button to find out how badly the volume is fragmented. After the analysis is complete, Windows will inform you whether it believes you should defragment the volume.
6. Click the **View Report** button to view statistics about fragmentation and to see the most fragmented files.
7. Click the **Defragment** button to proceed with defragmenting the volume.

Using a command-line interface

The *defrag* utility is the command-line version of the Disk Defragmenter application (available on Windows XP and Windows Server 2003). Run the following command to perform an analysis of the D: drive:

```
> defrag d: /a
```

Add the /v option to see similar information to the View Report button in Disk Defragmenter:

```
> defrag d: /a /v
```

Finally, include the drive and /v (for verbose output) to perform a defragmentation of the volume:

```
> defrag d: /v
```

You can force a defragmentation even if disk space is low by including the /f option.

Using VBScript

```
' This code simulates the 'defrag /a /v' command except it analyzes
' all fixed disks, not just a specific one.
' The Win32_Volume class is new in Windows Server 2003
' ------ SCRIPT CONFIGURATION ------
strComputer = "."
' ------ END CONFIGURATION ---------
set objWMI = GetObject("winmgmts:\\" & strComputer & "\root\cimv2")
set colVols = objWMI.ExecQuery("Select * from Win32_Volume where DriveType = 3")

for each objVol in colVols
    WScript.Echo "Analyzing volume " & objVol.DriveLetter
```

```
        intRC = objVol.DefragAnalysis(boolDefrag, objRpt)
        if intRC = 0 then

            WScript.Echo " Volume size: " & objRpt.VolumeSize
            WScript.Echo " Cluster size: " & objRpt.ClusterSize
            WScript.Echo " Used space: " & objRpt.UsedSpace
            WScript.Echo " Free space: " & objRpt.FreeSpace
            WScript.Echo " Percent free space: " & objRpt.FreeSpacePercent
            WScript.Echo " Total fragmentation: " & _
                        objRpt.TotalPercentFragmentation
            WScript.Echo " File fragmentation: " & _
                        objRpt.FilePercentFragmentation
            WScript.Echo " Free space fragmentation: " & _
                        objRpt.FreeSpacePercentFragmentation

            WScript.Echo " Total files: " & objRpt.TotalFiles
            WScript.Echo " Average file size: " & objRpt.AverageFileSize
            WScript.Echo " Total fragmented files: " & objRpt.TotalFragmentedFiles
            WScript.Echo " Total excess fragments: " & objRpt.TotalExcessFragments
            WScript.Echo " Avg fragments per file: " & _
                        objRpt.AverageFragmentsPerFile

            WScript.Echo " Page file size: " & objRpt.PageFileSize
            WScript.Echo " Total page file fragments: " & _
                        objRpt.TotalPageFileFragments

            WScript.Echo " Total folders: " & objRpt.TotalFolders
            WScript.Echo " Fragmented folders: " & objRpt.FragmentedFolders
            WScript.Echo " Excess folder fragments: " & _
                        objRpt.ExcessFolderFragments

            WScript.Echo " Total MFT size: " & objRpt.TotalMFTSize
            WScript.Echo " MFT record count: " & objRpt.MFTRecordCount
            WScript.Echo " MFT percent in use: " & objRpt.MFTPercentInUse
            WScript.Echo " Total MFT fragments: " & objRpt.TotalMFTFragments

            if boolDefrag = True Then
                WScript.Echo "You should defragment this volume."
            else
                WScript.Echo "You do not need to defragment this volume."
            end if
            WScript.Echo
        else
            WScript.Echo "Error during defragmentation analysis: " & intRC
        end if
next


' This code simulates the 'defrag c:' command.
' The Win32_Volume class is new in Windows Server 2003
' ------ SCRIPT CONFIGURATION ------
strComputer = "."
strDrive = "<Drive>"  ' e.g. C:
boolForce = False
```

```
' ------ END CONFIGURATION ---------
set objWMI = GetObject("winmgmts:\\" & strComputer & "\root\cimv2")
set colVol = objWMI.ExecQuery("select * from Win32_Volume Where Name = '" & _
                       strDrive & "\\'")
for each objVol in colVol
   intRC = objVol.Defrag(boolForce,objRpt)
   if intRC = 0 then
      WScript.Echo "Defragmentation successful."
   else
      WScript.Echo "Error defragmenting volume: " & intRC
   end if
next
```

Discussion

When you save a file on a volume, Windows tries to save the file in one contiguous section on the disk. However, as the disk becomes full over time, the largest available contiguous sections of the disk become smaller and smaller. New files eventually become spread over multiple sections of the disk which is called fragmentation. This leads to decreased disk access performance because Windows has to access multiple sections of the disk to piece together a single file.

The Windows defragmentation feature helps alleviate this problem by scanning a disk and attempting to combine the sections of files in larger contiguous portions. To perform a full defragmentation on a volume, the target volume needs to have at least 15% free space. This is necessary because Windows needs some space to store file fragments it is trying to piece together. If you have less than 15% available, you'll need to free up some space first. See Recipe 3.7 for more details.

You can determine how badly a volume is fragmented by first analyzing the volume. All three solutions provide options for generating a report that provides details on the fragmentation level of a volume. The report will also recommend whether you should perform a defragmentation or not. This is useful only as a general guide because it may always recommend that you perform a defragmentation even after you've just run one.

You should consider performing periodic defragmentation on heavily used volumes that have become more than 50% utilized. As disk space decreases on a volume, the level of fragmentation generally increases as the number of contiguous sections of disk decrease. If you have really large disks that are rarely more than 25% used, performing a defragmentation will not likely be of much benefit.

Defragmenting a disk can take several minutes and even hours depending on the size of the disk and the level of fragmentation. Also, the disk will be continually busy during the defragmentation period, so do it during off-hours because disk access performance will definitely decrease.

Using VBScript

Both the Defrag and DefragAnalysis methods return a report object (objRpt in the VBScript solutions). This object contains details about the current state of fragmentation on the volume in question. In the second VBScript code sample, I did not enumerate the properties of the objRpt object, but you could use all of the WScript.Echo statements after if intRC = 0 then from the first code sample if you want to display the analysis after defragmentation has been performed.

In the first code sample, I perform a defragmentation analysis on all local disk volumes. With the ExecQuery method, I included DriveType = 3 in the query. The DriveType property is part of the Win32_Volume class and the number 3 represents local disks. Look up Win32_Volume in MSDN for a complete listing of other values for DriveType (although none are important in this scenario).

See Also

Recipe 3.7, MS KB 283080 (Description of the New Command Line Defrag.exe Included with Windows XP), MS KB 305781 (How To Analyze and Defragment a Disk in Windows XP), MS KB 312067 (Shadow copies may be lost when you defragment a volume), and MSDN: Win32_Volume

3.9   Compressing a Volume

Problem

You want to compress a volume.

Solution

Using a graphical user interface

1. Open Windows Explorer.
2. Right-click the drive you want to compress and select **Properties**.
3. Click the **General** tab if it isn't opened by default.
4. Check the box beside **Compress drive to save disk space** and click **OK**.
5. Select the radio button beside the option for compressing only the files contained directly under C: or compressing all subfolders and files on the drive.
6. Click **OK**.

Using a command-line interface

The following command causes files only at the root of drive D: to be compressed:

```
> compact /c d:\
```

Add the /s option to compress all files and folders on drive D:

```
> compact /c /s d:\
```

Using VBScript

```
' This code compresses a volume.
' ------ SCRIPT CONFIGURATION ------
strComputer = "."
strDrive = "<Drive>"   ' e.g., D:
boolRecursive = True
' ------ END CONFIGURATION ---------
set objWMI = GetObject("winmgmts:\\" & strComputer & "\root\cimv2")
set colFolder = objWMI.ExecQuery("select * from Win32_Directory " & _
                                  " where name = '" & strDrive & "\\'")
if colFolder.Count <> 1 then
   WScript.Echo "Error: Volume not found."
else
   for each objFolder in colFolder
      intRC = objFolder.CompressEx(strErrorFile,,boolRecursive)
      if intRC <> 0 then
         WScript.Echo "Error compressing volume: " & intRC
         WScript.Echo "Stopped on file: " & strErrorFile
      else
         WScript.Echo "Successfully compressed volume."
      end if
   next
end if
```

Discussion

Compressing an entire volume is a good idea if disk space utilization is a concern and you have really fast disks and adequate processing resources. And since support for compression is built into the NTFS filesystem, compression and decompression of files happens automatically when applications attempt to open them. That makes the use of compression largely transparent. It will, however, have an impact on system load since compressing and uncompressing files, especially large ones, can require significant processing cycles. These days, disk space is much cheaper than CPUs, so you are generally better off taking the hit in disk space than adding processing load.

If you plan on compressing a volume that has disk quotas enabled, be sure to read MS KB 320686 first. You might think that when you compress a volume, your users' quota usage would go down, but it doesn't work this way. Quotas are determined by allocated disk usage, which is the actual size of the files before compression. Due to how compressed files are stored, it is possible for users' quota usage to actually increase when you enable compression. Again, if this issue pertains to you, KB 320686 goes into a good amount of detail about why this happens.

Using VBScript

The `Win32_Directory` class has a `Compress` method in addition to the `CompressEx` method I used in this solution, but it does not provide a way to perform compression recursively. It allows you simply to compress an individual directory. With `CompressEx`, the third parameter is a Boolean that when true performs a recursive compression.

The first two parameters to `CompressEx` are the stop file and start file. The stop file will be populated if `CompressEx` encounters an error and will contain the file name the error occurred on. The start file parameter is the file name within the directory that compression should start from. This parameter is necessary only if you are attempting to catch failures from previous `CompressEx` calls. You'd pass the results from the stop file parameter you captured after the failure as the start file to the next iteration `CompressEx`. This is a little funky in my book, but it does allow you to create a robust compression script.

See Also

Recipe 4.14 for more on compressing and uncompressing individual files, MS KB 153720 (Cannot Compress a Drive with Little Free Space), MS KB 251186 (Best practices for NTFS compression in Windows), MS KB 307987 (How To Use File Compression in Windows XP), and MS KB 320686 (Disk Quota Charges Increase If You Turn On the NTFS Compression Functionality)

3.10 Checking a Volume for Errors

Problem

You want to check a volume for errors.

Solution

Using a graphical user interface

1. Open Windows Explorer.
2. Right-click the drive you want to defragment and select **Properties**.
3. Click the **Tools** tab.
4. Under **Error-checking**, click the **Check Now** button.
5. If you want to fix any file system errors that are found, check the box beside **Automatically fix file system errors**. If you want to perform a thorough scan of the disk and check for bad sectors, check the box beside **Scan for an attempt recovery of bad sectors**.
6. Check the disk options you want and click **Start**.
7. Click **OK** when the check completes.

Using a command-line interface

The *chkdsk* utility can detect problems with a volume and attempt to fix them. Specify the name of the volume you want to check to run *chkdsk* in read-only mode:

```
> chkdsk D:
```

Use the /f option to have *chkdsk* attempt to fix any errors it finds:

```
> chkdsk D: /f
```

With the /f option, *chkdsk* will try to lock the drive, so if it is in use by another process, you will only be able to schedule it to run during the next reboot. You can include the /x option with /f to force the volume to be dismounted (for a nonsystem volume).

Using VBScript

```
' This code tries to perform a chkdsk on the specified volume.
' ------ SCRIPT CONFIGURATION ------
strComputer = "."
strDrive = "<Drive>" ' e.g., D:
boolFixErrors = True  ' True = chkdsk /f, False = chkdsk
' ------ END CONFIGURATION ---------
set objWMI = GetObject("winmgmts:\\" & strComputer & "\root\cimv2")
set objDisk = objWMI.Get("Win32_LogicalDisk.DeviceID='" & strDrive & "'")
intRC = objDisk.ChkDsk(boolFixErrors)
if intRC = 0 then
   WScript.Echo "Chkdsk completed successfully."
elseif intRC = 1 then
   WScript.Echo "Chkdsk scheduled on next reboot."
else
   WScript.Echo "Error running chkdsk: " & intRC
end if
```

Discussion

On Windows Server 2003, you can use the new *vrfydsk* command to perform the same function as *chkdsk* in read-only mode. *Vrfydsk* creates a shadow copy of the target volume, assigns a drive letter to it, runs *chkdsk* (read-only mode) against that drive, unassigns the drive, and removes the shadow copy. This is useful because often when running *chkdsk* on an active volume it may report transient errors that are due to the volume being in use. With *vrfydsk*, you don't have to worry about disk activity skewing the results. If *vrfydsk* reports that errors were found, you'll want to schedule a chkdsk /f as soon as possible on the volume.

See Also

MSDN: Chkdsk Method of the Win32_Volume Class, MS KB 160963 (CHKNTFS.EXE: What You Can Use It For), MS KB 187941 (An explanation of CHKDSK and the new /C and /I switches), MS KB 191603 (Modifying the

Autochk.exe Time-out Value), MS KB 218461 (Description of Enhanced Chkdsk, Autochk, and Chkntfs Tools in Windows 2000), and MS KB 837326 (How to use the Vrfydsk.exe tool to check a volume for errors without taking the volume offline in Windows Server 2003).

3.11   Making a Disk or Volume Read-Only

 This functionality is new to Windows XP and Windows Server 2003 and is not available on Windows 2000.

Problem

You want to make a disk or volume read-only so that users or programs can't write to it.

Solution

Using a command-line interface

The Joeware (*www.joeware.net*) tool, *writeprot*, allows you to make a disk or volume read-only as long as no files are locked on that volume. The following command lists the read/write state of all disks and volumes on a system:

```
> writeprot /mview
```

The following command attempts to make the D: drive read-only:

```
> writeprot /vol d: /ro
```

The following command makes the D: drive read-write:

```
> writeprot /vol d: /rw
```

The following command attempts to make all volumes on the basic disk represented by the D: drive read-only:

```
> writeprot /vol d: /ro
```

Using VBScript

```
' This code makes a volume or disk read-only (if possible)
' ------ SCRIPT CONFIGURATION ------
strDrive = "<Drive>"  ' e.g., e:

' This assumes writeprot is in your PATH, if not, fully qualify
' the path to the command (e.g., c:\bin\writeprot.exe)
strCommand = "writeprot /vol " & strDrive & " /ro"
' ------ END CONFIGURATION ---------
set objWshShell = WScript.CreateObject("WScript.Shell")
intRC = objWshShell.Run(strCommand, 0, TRUE)
```

```
    if intRC <> 0 then
        WScript.Echo "Error returned from running the command: " & intRC
        WScript.Echo "Command attempted: " & strCommand
    else
        WScript.Echo "Command executed successfully."
    end if
```

Discussion

Volumes on basic disks and dynamic disks are treated different when it comes to enabling write protection. You can make individual volumes on a dynamic disk read-only, but for basic disks, you have to write protect the entire disk including all volumes. If you attempt to write protect a single volume on a basic disk with multiple volumes using *writeprot*, an error will be returned. You'd need to run the same command with the -unsafe option to write protect all volumes on the basic disk.

You cannot write protect any volume that has files locked for read or write access. Since files are always opened for reading on the system volume, you will not be able to write protect that volume. See Recipe 4.19 for more information on finding open files.

 It was reported by some of the technical reviewers of this book that the third-party drivers for some storage area networks devices (HP MSA-500 and MSA-1000 specifically) do NOT properly support write protection.

See Also

Recipes 4.12 and 4.18

3.12 Mapping a Network Drive

Problem

You want to map a drive to a folder on a remote computer.

Solution

Using a graphical user interface

1. Open Windows Explorer.
2. From the menu, select **Tools → Map Network Drive**.
3. Beside **Drive**, select the drive letter you want to assign.
4. Beside **Folder**, enter the UNC path to the network share you want to map.
5. If you want the drive to be persistent, make sure the box beside **Reconnect at logon** is checked.

6. By default, your current credentials will be used to access the network share, if you want to use alternate credentials, click the different username link. Enter a user name and password and click **OK**.

7. Click **Finish**.

Using a command-line interface

The following command maps a drive to a network share point:

```
> net use <Drive> <Share>
```

The following example maps \\rtp01\myshare to the N: drive using your current credentials:

```
> net use N: \\rtp01\myshare
```

The following example maps a persistent drive using alternate credentials:

```
> net use N: \\rtp01\c$ /user:amer\rallen /savecred /persistent:yes
```

The following command lists all network connections including mapped drives:

```
> net use
```

The following command deletes the N: network drive:

```
> net use N: /delete
```

Using VBScript

```
' This code creates a mapped drive to a network path.
' ------ SCRIPT CONFIGURATION ------
strDrive = "<Drive>" ' e.g., N:
strPath = "<Path>"    ' e.g., \\rtp01\c$\temp
strUser = "<User>"    ' e.g., AMER\rallen
strPassword = "<Password>"
boolPersistent = True  ' True = Persistent ; False = Not Persistent
' ------ END CONFIGURATION ---------
set objNetwork = WScript.CreateObject("WScript.Network")
objNetwork.MapNetworkDrive strDrive, strPath, boolPersistent, _
                           strUser, strPassword
WScript.Echo "Successfully mapped drive"
```

Discussion

Mapping a drive to a folder on a remote server is primarily done for convenience. There is nothing you can do with a mapped drive that you can't also do with a UNC path (e.g., \\rtp01\myshare). However, some applications may not support accessing files via a UNC path, so you might need to use a mapped drive instead. A mapped drive is more convenient if you access a remote server frequently from a tool such as Windows Explorer. Instead of typing a long UNC path, you can simple type the drive letter and access the folder much quicker. And if you need to access the remote folder using alternate credentials, creating a mapped drive can save you even more time because you can store the credentials with the mapped drive so that when your computer starts up, the drive is automatically mapped using the alternate credentials. But be warned, this approach is also a great way to create account lockouts following password changes.

 You can't use the *cd* command within a CMD session to change directories into a UNC path. You can, however, use the *pushd* command, which creates a temporary drive for the UNC path (much as if you were mapping a drive) and *cd*'s into that drive. After you end the CMD session, the drive is dismounted and the previously assigned drive letter becomes available again.

See Also

MS KB 149861 (How Authentication Works for Net Use Command) and MS KB 308582 (How to connect and disconnect a network drive in Windows XP)

3.13   Creating a Virtual Drive to Another Drive or Folder

Problem

You want to make a folder the root of a drive or you want to use multiple drive letters for the same drive.

Solution

Using a command-line interface

Use the following command to create a new drive pointing to an existing path on the system:

```
> subst <Drive> <Path>
```

The following example creates an E: drive pointing to C:\scripts:

```
> subst E: C:\scripts
```

The following example creates an F: drive pointing to C:

```
> subst F: C:\
```

Using VBScript

There aren't any WMI or WSH interfaces for creating virtual drives, but you can shell out to the *subst* command if you really want to do it via a script.

```
' This code creates a virtual drive.
' ------ SCRIPT CONFIGURATION ------
```

```
strDrive = "<Drive>"  ' e.g., e:
strPath  = "<Path>"   ' e.g., c:\scripts

' This assumes subst is in your PATH, if not, fully qualify
' the path to the command here:
strCommand = "subst " & strDrive & " " & strPath
' ------ END CONFIGURATION ---------
set objWshShell = WScript.CreateObject("WScript.Shell")
intRC = objWshShell.Run(strCommand, 0, TRUE)
if intRC <> 0 then
    WScript.Echo "Error returned from running the command: " & intRC
    WScript.Echo "Command attempted: " & strCommand
else
    WScript.Echo "Command executed successfully."
end if
```

Discussion

The *subst* command is a useful utility for making folders on a volume appear as a drive. Let's say, for example, that you like to store files in your user profile (e.g., *C:\ Documents and Settings\rallen\My Documents\scripts*) and need to frequently access those files from a command line. You are starting to shown signs of getting carpal tunnel syndrome because even with tab-completion enabled, it takes a bit of typing to type out that path. You can use *subst* to create a drive that is mapped to that folder path and save yourself a lot of typing.

There are a few caveats to be aware of when using *subst*:

The drives are removed after reboot. Perhaps the biggest drawback to virtual drives is that they are removed when a machine restarts. That means to have a persistent virtual drive you need to use a logon script to create it.

Shadow copies are not created. On Windows Server 2003, shadow copies are created for all local volumes, but this doesn't apply to virtual drives created with *subst*. Since the virtual drive corresponds to a logical volume, a shadow copy is already created for its contents.

The drives cannot be used to set quotas. Again, due to the fact the contents of a virtual drive are already part of a volume, which may already have quotas enabled, you cannot configure quotas.

Deleting the virtual drive deletes only the mapping, not the data. If you delete a virtual drive using the /d option, only the drive mapping is deleted, not the underlying contents of the drive.

See Also

Recipe 3.12, MS KB 218740 (Cannot Use Subst.exe with UNC Path), and MS KB 269163 (Drives Created with the Subst Command Are Not Connected)

3.14 Finding Large Files and Folders on a Volume

Problem

You want to find files or folders that exceed a certain size on a volume.

Solution

Using a graphical user interface

1. From the Start menu, select **Search**.
2. If you are presented with the options for what to search on, click **All files and folders**.
3. Click on **What size is it?**
4. Select the radio button beside **Specify size** and enter the size you want to search.
5. Select additional criteria if necessary and click **Search**.

Using a command-line interface

The following command finds folders that are greater than 100 MB in size on the D: drive:

```
> diruse /s /m /q:100 /d d:
```

The /s option causes subdirectories to be searched, the /m option displays disk usage in megabytes, the /q:100 option causes folders that are greater than 100 MB to be marked, and the /d option displays only folders that exceed the threshold specified by /q.

Use the *diskuse* command to find files over a certain size. The following command displays files over 100 MB in size on the D: drive:

```
> diskuse D: /x:104857600 /v /s
```

The /x:104857600 option causes files over 104,857,600 bytes to be displayed and is valid only if you include the /v option (verbose). The /s option means subdirectories from the specified path (in this case, the D: drive) are searched.

Using VBScript

```
' This code finds all files over a certain size.
' ------ SCRIPT CONFIGURATION ------
strComputer = "<ServerName>"
intSizeBytes = 1024 * 1024 * 500   ' = 500 MB
' ------ END CONFIGURATION ---------
set objWMI = GetObject("winmgmts:\\" & strComputer & "\root\cimv2")
set colFiles = objWMI.ExecQuery _
    ("Select * from CIM_DataFile where FileSize > '" & intSizeBytes & "'")
```

```
for each objFile in colFiles
    Wscript.Echo objFile.Name & "   " & objFile.Filesize / 1024 / 1024 & "MB"
next
```

Discussion

If you find that you are running out of space on a volume and want to see what is consuming the most space, you are better off using the *diruse* command-line solution. With the other solutions, you could search for all files over 100 MB, for example, but a user could have created a bunch of 10 MB MPEG files. Unfortunately, you can't use the Search dialog box or VBScript to search on folder sizes, which leaves *diruse* as the most appropriate tool in this scenario.

See Also

Recipe 3.7 and MSDN: CIM_DataFile

3.15   Enabling Disk Quotas

Problem

You want to use disk quotas on an NTFS-formatted filesystem.

Solution

Using a graphical user interface

1. Open Windows Explorer.
2. Browse to the drive on which you want to enable quotas, right-click it, and select **Properties**.
3. Click the **Quota** tab.
4. Check the box beside **Enable quota management**. This turns on disk quota tracking.
5. Check the box beside **Deny disk space to users exceeding quota limit** to turn on disk quota enforcement.
6. Configure the default quota limit if you want to have one.
7. Under the quota logging options, check the appropriate boxes if you want to have messages logged to the event log every time a user exceeds his quota warning or limit levels.
8. Click **OK**.
9. A dialog box will pop open that informs you the disk needs to be scanned to collect disk statistics. Click **OK**.

Using a command-line interface

The following command enables disk quota enforcement on drive D:

```
> fsutil quota enforce d:
```

The following command enables disk quota tracking on drive D:

```
> fsutil quota track d:
```

The following command disables disk quotas on drive D:

```
> fsutil quota disable d:
```

 You cannot modify the default limit and warning settings with *fsutil*.

Using VBScript

```
' This code enables disk quotas on a drive.
' This code works on 2003 and XP, but not 2000 systems.
' ------ SCRIPT CONFIGURATION ------
strComputer = "."
strDrive = "<Drive>"  ' e.g., D:
intEnable = 2  ' 0 = Disabled, 1 = Tracked, 2 = Enforced
intDefaultLimit  = 1024 * 1024 * 500  ' 500 MB
intDefaultWarning = 1024 * 1024 * 400 ' 400 MB
' ------ END CONFIGURATION ---------
set objWMI = GetObject("winmgmts:\\" & strComputer & "\root\cimv2")
set objDisk = objWMI.Get("Win32_QuotaSetting.VolumePath='" & strDrive & "\\'")
objDisk.State = intEnable
objDisk.ExceededNotification = True
objDisk.WarningExceededNotification = True
objDisk.DefaultLimit = intDefaultLimit
objDisk.DefaultWarningLimit = intDefaultWarning
objDisk.Put_
WScript.Echo "Quotas enabled on " & objDisk.Caption
```

Discussion

NTFS disk quotas are based on the files a user owns on a volume, not where those files are located on a volume. Quotas are set on a per-volume basis so it doesn't matter where within a volume a user owns files; they all count against any configured quota for that volume. If you have multiple volumes you want quotas on, you have to configure each separately.

When you initially enable quotas, you have an option to track quota usage or enforce quota usage. Tracking quota usage means that a message will be written to the System event log when a user exceeds his warning or limit quota thresholds. The user isn't notified of this and can continue to exceed his quota limits. Enforcing quota usage means that when the user exceeds his quota limit and attempts to add more files to the volume, he receives an "insufficient disk space" error message. Events are still logged to the System event log just as with quota tracking.

There are two default settings that you can configure when quotas are enabled. The first is the default warning threshold. After a user exceeds this size, a message is logged to the event log. The default limit threshold is the maximum amount of storage that individual users can use. If you want to apply nondefault quota parameters to specific users or groups, see Recipe 3.16.

 Quotas do not apply to the Administrator account.

You can also enable quotas using group policy if your computers are in an Active Directory domain. You can find the quota settings under *Computer Configuration\ Administrative Templates\System\Disk Quotas*. If your users have administrative rights over the machine you've enabled quotas on, those users can disable or modify the quota configuration. If you use group policy to configure quotas, users cannot change them even if they are administrators.

See Also

Recipe 3.16, MS KB 183322 (How to Enable Disk Quotas in Windows 2000), MS KB 307984 (HOW TO: Create Disk Quota Reports in Windows XP), MS KB 308664 (How To Export and Import Disk Quota Settings to Other Volumes in Windows XP), and MS KB 320686 (Disk Quota Charges Increase If You Turn On the NTFS Compression Functionality)

3.16   Configuring a Disk Quota for a User

Problem

You want to configure disk quota limits for a particular user.

Solution

Using a graphical user interface

1. Open Windows Explorer.
2. Browse to the drive on which you want to enable quotas, right-click it, and select **Properties**.
3. Click the **Quota** tab.
4. If quotas are enabled, click the **Quota Entries** button. If quotas are not enabled, enable them as described in Recipe 3.15.

5. To configure a new quota entry for a user, select **Quota → New Quota Entry** from the menu.

6. Use the object picker to locate the target user and click **OK**. The Add New Quota Entry dialog will open.

7. If you've configured a default quota, that limit will be selected by default. You can disable disk quota enforcement for this user or set new limit and warning levels. After you are done, click **OK**.

Using a command-line interface

The following command configures a quota for a particular user:

```
> fsutil quota modify <Drive> <WarningBytes> <LimitBytes> <Domain\User>
```

The following example sets a quota for user AMER\rallen with a ~381 MB warning and ~476 MB limit:

```
> fsutil quota modify d: 400000000 500000000 AMER\rallen
```

Using VBScript

```
' This code configures a quota for a particular user.
' ------ SCRIPT CONFIGURATION ------
strComputer = "."
strUser = "<User>"              ' e.g., rallen
strUserDomain = "<Domain>"      ' e.g., AMER
strDrive = "<Drive>"            ' e.g., D:
intLimit = 1024 * 1024 * 600    ' = 600 MB
intWarning = 1024 * 1024 * 350  ' = 350 MB
' ------ END CONFIGURATION ---------
set objWMI = GetObject("winmgmts:\\" & strComputer & "\root\cimv2")
set objDisk = objWMI.Get("Win32_LogicalDisk.DeviceID='" & strDrive & "'")
WScript.Echo "Found disk " & objDisk.Caption
set objUser = objWMI.Get("Win32_Account.Domain='" & strUserDomain & _
                  "',Name='" & strUser & "'")
WScript.Echo "Found user " & objUser.Name
set objQuota = objWMI.Get("Win32_DiskQuota.QuotaVolume=" & _
      "'Win32_LogicalDisk.DeviceID=""" & strDrive & """'," & _
      "User='Win32_Account.Domain=""" & strUserDomain & _
      """,Name=""" & strUser & """'")
objQuota.Limit = intLimit
objQuota.WarningLimit = intWarning
objQuota.Put_
WScript.Echo "Set quota for user " & objUser.Name
```

Discussion

If you decide that you want to delete a quota entry for a particular user, perhaps because you don't want to limit that user anymore, you have to first reassign ownership of all files owned by the user on the volume. Since quota usage is entirely determined by file ownership, you can't have files on a quota-enabled volume that belong to a user that doesn't have a quota entry. You must take ownership of the files yourself, move the files to another volume, or permanently delete the files before deleting the quota entry.

 If you don't want to go to all the trouble of transferring ownership of files, another option would be to simply set the quota for the user really high (like to the overall size of the volume).

See Also

Recipe 3.15, MS KB 183322 (How to Enable Disk Quotas in Windows 2000), MS KB 307984 (HOW TO: Create Disk Quota Reports in Windows XP), and MS KB 308664 (How To Export and Import Disk Quota Settings to Other Volumes in Windows XP)

3.17   Viewing Disk Quota Usage

Problem

You want to view the quota usage for one or more users.

Solution

Using a graphical user interface

1. Open Windows Explorer.
2. Browse to the drive on which you want to enable quotas, right-click it, and select **Properties**.
3. Click the **Quota** tab.
4. If quotas are enabled, click the **Quota Entries** button. If quotas are not enabled, enable them as described in Recipe 3.15.
5. The **Quota Entries** application contains a listing of all users that have quotas configured along with their quota limit, warning limit, and amount used. You can sort this screen by selecting **View → Arrange Items** from the menu and choosing one of the options to sort by.

Using a command-line interface

Use the following command to view the quota usage for all users on drive D:

```
> fsutil quota query d:
```

Use the following command to search the event log for all users that are violating their quota:

```
> fsutil quota violations
```

Before using the violations options of *fsutil*, be sure that you've enabled event logging of warning and limit errors (see Recipe 3.15).

Using VBScript

```
' This code displays the quota usage for users on a particular drive.
' ------ SCRIPT CONFIGURATION ------
strComputer = "."
strDrive = "<Drive>"  ' e.g., D:
' ------ END CONFIGURATION ---------
set objWMI = GetObject("winmgmts:\\" & strComputer & "\root\cimv2")
set colQuotas = objWMI.ExecQuery("select * from Win32_DiskQuota " & _
    "where QuotaVolume = 'Win32_LogicalDisk.DeviceID=""" & strDrive & """'")
for each objQuota in colQuotas
    WScript.Echo "User: "& objQuota.User
    WScript.Echo "  Volume: "& objQuota.QuotaVolume
    WScript.Echo "  Quota Limit: " & _
                    objQuota.Limit / 1024 / 1024 & "MB"
    WScript.Echo "  Warning Limit: " & _
                    objQuota.WarningLimit / 1024 / 1024 & "MB"
    WScript.Echo "  Disk Space Used: " & _
                    objQuota.DiskSpaceUsed / 1024 / 1024 & "MB"
    WScript.Echo ""
next
```

Discussion

One of the nice features of the Quota Entries application is that you can drag and drop entries in it to a spreadsheet application like Excel. Simply highlight the entries you're interested in and drag them to Excel. You can also copy and paste them using Ctrl-C and Ctrl-V.

If you've enabled compression on a volume where quotas are also enabled, you may actually see quota usage increase compared to the same volume without compression. See MS KB 320686 for more information on this issue.

See Also

Recipe 3.16, MS KB 307984 (HOW TO: Create Disk Quota Reports in Windows XP), MS KB 308664 (How To Export and Import Disk Quota Settings to Other Volumes in Windows XP), and MS KB 320686 (Disk Quota Charges Increase If You Turn On the NTFS Compression Functionality)

CHAPTER 4

Files, Folders, and Shares

4.0 Introduction

This chapter covers some of the common tasks facing administrators when it comes to managing the Windows file system. I'll not only touch on the really basic tasks such as creating, deleting, renaming, and moving files and folders, but more advanced topics such as viewing a list of all open files and identifying the process that has a file locked.

Using a Graphical User Interface

You are undoubtedly familiar with the all-purpose file, folder, and shared folder management tool, Windows Explorer. With it you can create, move, rename, and delete files and folders as well as hide, encrypt, and make them read-only. As you'll see, this is the most used graphical tool in this chapter.

You are also probably familiar with the Shared Folder MMC snap-in, which is commonly seen as a part of the Computer Management tool. This snap-in allows you to do just about anything with shares (i.e., create, delete, see who is using them, etc.).

Sysinternals produces several graphical tools that are also very helpful. These include File Monitor (Recipe 4.19), Fundelete (Recipe 4.3), and Shareenum (Recipe 4.24).

Using a Command-Line Interface

Table 4-1 lists command-line tools used in this chapter and the recipes they are used in.

Table 4-1. Command-line tools used in this chapter

Tool	Windows Server 2003	Windows 2000 Server	Recipes
attrib	*%SystemRoot%\system32*	*%SystemRoot%\system32*	4.12, 4.13
auditpol	Windows 2000 Resource Kit	Windows 2000 Resource Kit	4.18
cipher	*%SystemRoot%\system32*	*%SystemRoot%\system32*	4.15
compress	Windows 2003 Resource Kit	Windows 2000 Resource Kit	4.14

Table 4-1. Command-line tools used in this chapter (continued)

Tool	Windows Server 2003	Windows 2000 Server	Recipes
copy	CMD shell	CMD shell	4.10
creatfil	Windows 2003 Resource Kit	Windows 2000 Resource Kit	4.1
del	CMD shell	CMD shell	4.1
dir	CMD shell	CMD shell	4.5
fc	%SystemRoot%\system32	%SystemRoot%\system32	4.11
findstr	%SystemRoot%\system32	%SystemRoot%\system32	4.9
forfiles	%SystemRoot%\system32	Windows 2000 Resource Kit	4.22
handle	http://sysinternals.com/	http://sysinternals.com/	4.20
inuse	%SystemRoot%\system32	Windows 2000 Resource Kit	4.16
junction	http://sysinternals.com/	http://sysinternals.com/	4.7
linkd	Windows 2003 Resource Kit	Windows 2000 Resource Kit	4.7
mkdir	CMD shell	CMD shell	4.2
move	CMD shell	CMD shell	4.10
net file	%SystemRoot%\system32	%SystemRoot%\system32	4.19
net share	%SystemRoot%\system32	%SystemRoot%\system32	4.23, 4.24
openfiles	%SystemRoot%\system32	N/A	4.19
ren	CMD shell	CMD shell	4.10
rmdir	CMD shell	CMD shell	4.2
sdelete	http://sysinternals.com/	http://sysinternals.com/	4.4
setacl	http://setacl.sourceforge.net/	http://setacl.sourceforge.net/	4.18
shortcut	MKS Toolkit	MKS Toolkit	4.6
strings	http://sysinternals.com/	http://sysinternals.com/	4.9
subinacl	Windows 2003 Resource Kit	Windows 2000 Resource Kit	4.17, 4.25
takeown	%SystemRoot%\system32	Windows 2000 Resource Kit	4.17
where	%SystemRoot%\system32	Windows 2000 Resource Kit	4.9

Using VBScript

Between WMI and WSH, you have the ability to automate reading, writing, and searching files and folders. Unfortunately, the WMI file and folder classes don't provide the capability to do basic manipulation, which is where WSH comes in. Table 4-2 lists all of the WSH and WMI classes used in this chapter.

Table 4-2. WMI and WSH classes used in this chapter

WMI class	Description	Recipes
Cim_DataFile	WMI class that represents files	4.1, 4.5, 4.10, 4.14, 4.17, 4.22
Scripting.FileSystemObject	WSH interface for reading, writing, and manipulating files and folders	4.1, 4.2, 4.11, 4.12, 4.13

Table 4-2. WMI and WSH classes used in this chapter (continued)

WMI class	Description	Recipes
Win32_Directory	WMI class that represents folders	4.5, 4.14
Win32_ShortcutFile	WMI class that represents shortcut files (*.lnk*)	4.6
Win32_Share	WMI class that represents shared folders	4.23, 4.24

4.1 Creating and Deleting a File

Problem

You want to create or delete a file.

Solution

Using a graphical user interface

1. Open Windows Explorer.

2. In the left pane, browse to the folder where you want to create the file or that contains the file you want to delete. Click on the folder.

3. To create a new file, right-click in the right pane and select **New** and the type of file you want to create. To edit the file, double-click on it.

4. To delete a file, right-click the file in the right pane and select **Delete**. Click **Yes** to confirm. This moves the file to the **Recycle Bin**. You can also press Shift+Del to bypass the Recycle Bin and permanently delete the file.

Using a command-line interface

There aren't many options for creating files from the command line. You can create a simple text file by redirecting output from a command. Here is an example:

```
> echo hello > myfile.txt
```

One command you may not be familiar with is *creatfil.exe* from the Resource Kit. With it you can create files of arbitrary length. This is useful only if you need to create some files to test with or to test low disk space scenarios. The following command creates a 10 MB file named *foobar.txt*:

```
> creatfil foobar.txt 10240
```

To delete a file use the *del* command:

```
> del c:\scripts\foobar.vbs
```

If you want to delete a file on a remote server, you can use a *psexec.exe* command like this:

```
> psexec \\<ServerName> cmd.exe /c del c:\scripts\foobar.vbs
```

To provide alternate credentials with *psexec* use the /u and /p options to specify a username and password, respectively.

Using VBScript

See Chapter 1 for examples of creating and appending to files using VBScript.

```
' This code deletes a file
' ------ SCRIPT CONFIGURATION ------
strFilePath = "<FilePath>" ' e.g., "d:\scripts\test.txt"
' ------ END CONFIGURATION ---------
set objFSO = CreateObject("Scripting.FileSystemObject")
objFSO.DeleteFile(strFilePath)
WScript.Echo "Successfully deleted file"


' This code deletes a file using WMI
' ------ SCRIPT CONFIGURATION ------
strComputer = "."
strFilePath = "<FilePath>" ' e.g., "d:\scripts\test.txt"
' ------ END CONFIGURATION ---------
set objFile = GetObject("winmgmts:\\"& strComputer & _
                    "\root\cimv2:CIM_Datafile.Name='" & strFilePath & "'")
objFile.Delete
WScript.Echo "Successfully deleted file"
```

4.2   Creating and Deleting a Folder

Problem

You want to create or delete a folder.

Solution

Using a graphical user interface

1. Open Windows Explorer.
2. In the left pane, browse to the folder where you want to create a new folder or that contains the folder you want to delete. Click on the folder.
3. To create a new folder, right-click in the right pane and select **New** and the type of folder you want to create.
4. To delete a folder, right-click the folder in the right pane and select **Delete**. Click **Yes** to confirm. This moves the folder and its contents to the **Recycle Bin**.

> If you want a **New Folder** option when you right-click in the *left* pane of Windows Explorer, see *http://www.createwindow.com/freeware/ newfold.htm*.

Using a command-line interface

To create a folder, use the *mkdir* command (or *md* for short):

```
> mkdir c:\scripts
```

To remove a folder, use the *rmdir* command (or *rd* for short):

```
> rmdir c:\scripts
```

Use the /s option to remove a folder and all files and subfolders contained within it. Use the /q option to bypass the confirmation prompt when using /s.

To delete a folder on a remote server, use the *psexec.exe* command:

```
> psexec \\<ServerName> cmd.exe /c rmdir /s c:\temp
```

To provide alternate credentials with *psexec*, use the /u and /p options to specify a username and password, respectively.

Using VBScript

```
' This code deletes a folder
' ------ SCRIPT CONFIGURATION ------
strFolderPath = "<FolderPath>" ' e.g., "d:\temp"
' ------ END CONFIGURATION ---------
set objFSO = CreateObject("Scripting.FileSystemObject")
objFSO.DeleteFolder(strFolderPath)
WScript.Echo "Successfully deleted folder"
```

4.3   Undeleting a File

Problem

You want to attempt to undelete a file that you previously deleted.

Solution

Files that you delete with Windows Explorer can be restored using the Recycle Bin:

1. Double-click the **Recycle Bin** icon on the desktop.
2. Right-click the file you want to undelete and select **Restore**.

This assumes that you didn't use the Shift+Del key combination to delete the file or haven't emptied the Recycle Bin since the file was deleted. One problem with this method is that the Recycle Bin captures only files deleted from Explorer. None of the files that are deleted over the network, via a command prompt, or with a script are sent to the Recycle Bin.

The Sysinternals Fundelete tool can be used as a replacement for the Recycle Bin. It works just like the Recycle Bin except it does more. The Recycle Bin icon on the desktop is replaced with a Fundelete Bin icon. The Fundelete Bin captures any type

---

file deletion that occurs on the computer. And just like the Recycle Bin, you can restore files contained in the Fundelete Bin.

Fundelete hasn't been updated since 2000, so if you are looking for something that is more recently updated, Executive Software makes a product that is similar to Fundelete with even more features called Undelete. Unlike Fundelete, you have to pay for Undelete. For more information, visit: *http://www.undelete.com/*.

See Also

MS KB 136517 (How the Recycle Bin Stores Files)

4.4   Securely Deleting a File

Problem

You want to delete a file so that it cannot be retrieved by undeleting it.

Solution

Using a command-line interface

Use the Sysinternals *sdelete.exe* command to securely delete files:

```
> sdelete <FileName>
```

Use the -p option to specify the number of passes to overwrite the disk segments. The more passes, the less likely the file can be recovered.

The -s option can be used to recursively delete everything within a folder:

```
> sdelete -p 4 -s c:\logs
```

Using VBScript

```
' This code runs the sdelete command
' ------ SCRIPT CONFIGURATION ------
strCommand = "sdelete -p 5 c:\logs\tue.log"
' ------ END CONFIGURATION ---------
set objWshShell = WScript.CreateObject("WScript.Shell")
intRC = objWshShell.Run(strCommand, 0, TRUE)
if intRC <> 0 then
    WScript.Echo "Error returned from running the command: " & intRC
else
    WScript.Echo "Command executed successfully"
end if
```

Discussion

When you delete a file through Windows Explorer, it is sent to the Recycle Bin. You can use the Recycle Bin to restore the file to its original location or you can permanently delete the file by emptying the Recycle Bin. But wait a second—the file doesn't really get deleted when you empty the Recycle Bin. All that happens is that the link to the collection of bits on the hard disk that make up the file is deleted. The bits that make up the file are still present on the disk. And it stays like this until the file system overwrites those bits with a new file. That means that if a bad guy stole your computer, he could run a program to examine the hard drive and restore files that have been previously deleted and not overwritten. That is, unless you *securely* delete the file using the Sysinternals Sdelete program. Sdelete works by writing random characters to the bits that made up the file before. This prevents programs from piecing the file back together. This doesn't prevent someone from restoring a previous copy of the file from backup, but someone won't be able to take the hard drive and restore a deleted file on which you used Sdelete.

 You can also use the cipher tool to overwrite deleted data. See MS KB 814599 for more information.

See Also

MS KB 136517 (How the Recycle Bin Stores Files), and MS KB 814599 (HOW TO: Use Cipher.exe to Overwrite Deleted Data in Windows Server 2003)

4.5   Viewing the Properties of a File or Folder

Problem

You want to view the creation or last modification timestamp of a file or folder or determine whether it is encrypted, archived, compressed, etc.

Solution

Using a graphical user interface

1. Open Windows Explorer.
2. In the left pane, browse to the parent folder of the file or folder you want to view properties for. Click on the parent folder. This displays the list of subfolders and files in the right pane.
3. In the right pane, right-click on the file or folder you want to view and select **Properties**.
4. Several properties are displayed in the **General** tab. Click the **Advanced** button to see additional attributes.

Using a command-line interface

The *dir* command can be run as part of a CMD session to display the last-modified time, size, and owner of a file or directory. Here is an example:

```
> dir /q <Path>
```

You can also display other attributes of a file or folder with the /A option. Run `dir /?` for a complete list of options and parameters.

One way to view the files on a remote server is to use a UNC path. This command displays the contents of the *c:\scripts* folder on the host *fs01*:

```
> dir /q \\fs01\c$\scripts
```

You can use the *runas.exe* command to specify alternate credentials if needed or use the *psexec.exe* command.

Using VBScript

```
' This code displays the properties and attributes of a file
' ------ SCRIPT CONFIGURATION ------
strFilePath = "d:\\myfile.txt"
strComputer = "."
' ------ END CONFIGURATION ---------
set objWMI = GetObject("winmgmts:\\" & strComputer & "\root\cimv2")
set objFile = objWMI.Get("CIM_Datafile=""" & strFilePath & """")
WScript.Echo objFile.Name

WScript.Echo " 8.3 Name: " & objFile.EightDotThreeFileName
WScript.Echo " Drive: " & objFile.Drive
WScript.Echo " FileName: " & objFile.FileName
WScript.Echo " Extension: " & objFile.Extension
WScript.Echo " FileType: " & objFile.FileType
WScript.Echo " Path: " & objFile.Path
WScript.Echo " InUse Counter: " & objFile.InUseCount

WScript.Echo " Creation Date: " & objFile.CreationDate
WScript.Echo " Last Accessed: " & objFile.LastAccessed
WScript.Echo " Last Modified: " & objFile.LastModified

WScript.Echo " Archive: " & objFile.Archive
WScript.Echo " Compressed: " & objFile.Compressed
WScript.Echo " Encrypted: " & objFile.Encrypted
WScript.Echo " System: " & objFile.System
WScript.Echo " Writeable: " & objFile.Writeable
WScript.Echo " Hidden: " & objFile.Hidden


' This code displays the properties and attributes of a folder
' ------ SCRIPT CONFIGURATION ------
strDirPath = "c:\\scripts"
strComputer = "."
' ------ END CONFIGURATION ---------
```

```
set objWMI = GetObject("winmgmts:\\" & strComputer & "\root\cimv2")
set objFile = objWMI.Get("Win32_Directory=""" & strDirPath & """")
WScript.Echo objFile.Name

WScript.Echo " 8.3 Name: " & objFile.EightDotThreeFileName
WScript.Echo " Drive: " & objFile.Drive
WScript.Echo " Folder Name: " & objFile.FileName
WScript.Echo " File Type: " & objFile.FileType
WScript.Echo " Path: " & objFile.Path
WScript.Echo " InUse Counter: " & objFile.InUseCount

WScript.Echo " Creation Date: " & objFile.CreationDate
WScript.Echo " Last Accessed: " & objFile.LastAccessed
WScript.Echo " Last Modified: " & objFile.LastModified

WScript.Echo " Archive: " & objFile.Archive
WScript.Echo " Compressed: " & objFile.Compressed
WScript.Echo " Encrypted: " & objFile.Encrypted
WScript.Echo " System: " & objFile.System
WScript.Echo " Writeable: " & objFile.Writeable
WScript.Echo " Hidden: " & objFile.Hidden
```

Discussion

Another useful tool for displaying file information is Visual File Information (*vfi.exe*) from the Resource Kit. It can display file information for several files on a single screen. You start by selecting a folder and from there it enumerates every file contained within that folder and all subfolders. You can then sort by creation or modification date, size, extension, and a number of other attributes. The tool is good at enumerating over hundreds or even thousands of files very quickly, so if you wanted to find the largest file on a disk or find the most recently modified file, this would be a great tool for the job.

Figure 4-1 shows sample output from VFI.

See Also

MS KB 320050 (HOW TO: Use the File Attribute Management Script (Fileattributes.pl) in Windows 2000)

4.6   Creating a Shortcut

Problem

You want to create a shortcut to a file or folder. A shortcut is simply a file with a *.lnk* extension that redirects you to another file or folder when clicked on in Windows Explorer. You can also distinguish shortcut files from regular files by a small arrow in the bottom left side of their icons.

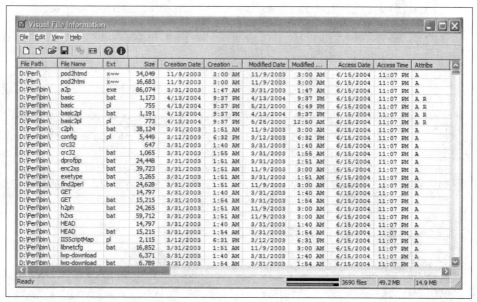

Figure 4-1. Visual File Information sample output

Solution

Using a graphical user interface

1. Open Windows Explorer.
2. Browse to the file or folder you want to create a shortcut for.
3. Right-click the file or folder and select **Create Shortcut**.
4. Move the shortcut file to desired location.

Using a command-line interface

The Windows NT Resource Kit had a tool called *shortcut.exe* that could be used to create shortcuts, but it isn't present in the Windows 2000 or Windows Server 2003 Resource Kits. The MKS Toolkit (*http://www.mkssoftware.com/products/tk/*), an excellent product that provides numerous Unix-based utilities for the Windows platform, contains a *shortcut.exe* tool, which can create shortcuts. Here is the syntax for that tool:

```
> shortcut [-f dest-file] [-a arglist] [-w workdir] [-s show-keyword]
[-i iconpath[,iconindex]] [-d description] [-D] shortcut-file

-a arglist
defines any arguments to the executable file specified with the -f dest-file option.

-d description
```

specifies descriptive text to be embedded in the link file. description is only displayed when you use the -p option to print the contents of the link file. If description includes space, the text should be enclosed in double quotes (").

-D shortcut-file
specifies the shortcut-file is on the desktop.

-f dest-file
specifies the full path and file name of the executable file to be run when the link file is double-clicked.

-i iconpath[,iconindex]
specifies the icon to be displayed for the link file. If the specified icon contains multiple images, determine which image is to be displayed by entering the appropriate number for iconindex.

-p
displays the contents of the specified shortcut file.

-s show-keyword
specifies how the executable is displayed when invoked. show-keyword can be one of the following:

SW_SHOW	starts the program in standard mode
SW_SHOWMAXIMIZED	starts the program in full screen mode
SW_SHOWMINIMIZED	starts the program minimized
SW_SHOWMINNOACTIVE	displays the program as an icon but does not start it

When this option is not specified, shortcut defaults to SW_SHOW.

-w workdir
specifies the working directory in which the program is started.

Here is an example:

```
> shortcut -f c:/perl/bin/perl.exe -a -L perl-link.lnk
```

 The MKS Toolkit isn't free and can be quite expensive, but there is another shortcut utility from this site that is free: *http://www.optimumx.com*.

Using VBScript

```
' This code creates a shortcut.

set objWSHShell = CreateObject("WScript.Shell")

' Pass the path to the shortcut
set objSC = objWSHShell.CreateShortcut("d:\mylog.lnk")
```

```
' Description - Description of the shortcut
objSC.Description = "Shortcut to MyLog file"

' HotKey - hot key sequence to launch the shortcut
objSC.HotKey = "CTRL+ALT+SHIFT+X"

' IconLocation - Path of icon to use for the shortcut file
objSC.IconLocation = "notepad.exe, 0"   ' 0 is the index

' TargetPath = Path to source file or folder
objSC.TargetPath = "c:\windows\notepad.exe"

' Arguments - Any additional parameters to pass to TargetPath
objSC.Arguments = "c:\mylog.txt"

' WindowStyle - Type of window to create
objSC.WindowStyle = 1    ' 1 = normal; 3 = maximize window; 7 = minimize

' WorkingDirectory - Location of the working directory for the source app
objSC.WorkingDirectory = "c:\"
objSC.Save
WScript.Echo "Shortcut to mylog created"

' This code finds all shortcuts on a system.
' ------ SCRIPT CONFIGURATION ------
strComputer = "."
' ------ END CONFIGURATION ---------
set objWMI = GetObject("winmgmts:\\" & strComputer & "\root\cimv2")
set colSCs = objWMI.InstancesOf("Win32_ShortcutFile")
for each objSC in colSCs
    WScript.Echo "Name:    " & objSC.Name
    WScript.Echo "Target: " & objSC.Target
    WScript.Echo
    intCount = intCount + 1
next
WScript.Echo "Total shortcuts: " & intCount
```

Discussion

Shortcuts can be useful to quickly access files and folders that are distributed across the filesystem or on remote servers. The problem with shortcuts is that they can quickly become out of date if not maintained. There is a tool in the Resource Kit to help identify dead shortcuts called *chklnks.exe*. It searches for all shortcuts whose target does not exist and displays them in a list. You can right-click on a shortcut to see the missing target location or delete selected dead shortcuts.

See Also

MS KB 140443 (How to Create a Shortcut on the Desktop)

4.7   Creating a Link or Junction Point

Problem

You want to create a link to a folder. This is sometimes referred to as a junction point. Links can be created only on NTFS file systems. Junction points are useful if you want to create a simplified path to a folder that is nested deeply in the file system.

Solution

Using a command-line interface

The *linkd.exe* command from the Resource Kit can create a link:

```
> linkd <LinkName> <Target>
```

This creates a link from folder *c:\program files\perl* to *c:\perl*:

```
> linkd c:\perl "c:\program files\perl"
```

This removes the link to *perl.exe*:

```
linkd c:\perl /d
```

You can also use the Sysinternals *junction.exe* tool to create and delete links:

```
> junction c:\perl "c:\program files\perl"
> junction /d c:\perl
```

A cool thing about *junction.exe* is that you can also use it to search for links:

```
> junction /s c:\
```

If you are browsing the file system with Windows Explorer, you won't be able to differentiate links from normal files and folders, but in a CMD session you can. A link shows up as <JUNCTION>, as shown here:

```
> dir
 Volume in drive C is System
 Volume Serial Number is F0CE-2C6F

 Directory of C:\

01/02/2002  09:08 AM                    0 build.ini
10/06/2003  01:57 PM    <DIR>            Documents and Settings
11/02/2003  12:01 AM    <DIR>            Inetpub
11/18/2003  11:43 PM    <JUNCTION>       Perl
10/06/2003  02:14 PM    <DIR>            Program Files
11/16/2003  11:25 PM    <DIR>            scripts
12/04/2003  12:45 AM    <DIR>            WINDOWS
               6 File(s)      439,283,427 bytes
               7 Dir(s)     1,575,822,336 bytes free
```

Using VBScript

```
' This code creates a link by shelling out to the linkd command.
' ------ SCRIPT CONFIGURATION ------
strLink   = "c:\perl"
strTarget = "c:\program files\perl"
' ------ END CONFIGURATION ---------
strCommand = "linkd " & strLink & " " & strTarget
set objWshShell = WScript.CreateObject("WScript.Shell")
intRC = objWshShell.Run(strCommand, 0, TRUE)
if intRC <> 0 then
   WScript.Echo "Error returned from running the command: " & intRC
else
   WScript.Echo "Command executed successfully"
end if
```

Discussion

Links, or junction points, are different from shortcuts in that they are transparent to any process or application that accesses them. A shortcut is simply a file that redirects applications to a different location. A junction point is similar to a symbolic link in Unix. When you open a junction point, applications, such as Windows Explorer, behave as if you opened the source folder. The only difference is if you delete the junction point in Windows Explorer, the source directory isn't deleted—only the junction point is deleted.

See Also

MS KB 205524 (How to create and manipulate NTFS junction points)

4.8   Creating a Program Alias

Problem

You want to create a program alias for an application or commonly accessed file. A program alias is a little different from a shortcut or link. It is similar in function to the *alias* command common on most Unix platforms. The alias name can be used as an alternative to typing the full program name. For example, let's say you use the Computer Management snap-in a lot and instead of going to Start menu → Administrative Tools → Computer Management, you prefer to type **compmgmt.msc** from the Run dialog or from the command line. You could create a program alias called *cmp* that points to *compmgmt.msc*, which reduces the number of characters you have to type by nine.

Solution

The following is how you'd create the *cmp* alias I just described.

Create a new subkey under the following key:

```
HKLM\SOFTWARE\Microsoft\Windows\CurrentVersion\App Paths
```

The name of the subkey should be the alias name. So you don't have to type an extension when using the alias, put *.exe* at the end of the name. In this case, the subkey name would be *cmp.exe*. You can, in fact, call the alias anything you want, but if the alias extension is not an executable extension such as *.exe*, you'll have to type the complete alias name when calling it. So it is perfectly fine to name the subkey *cmp.abc*, but I'd have to type **cmp.abc** instead of just **cmp** when typing it in the Run dialog.

Next, modify the default value under the new subkey; it shows up with the name (Default) in Registry Editor. Enter the full path to the program you are creating an alias for, which in this example would be *C:\Windows\system32\compmgmt.msc*. Actually, if the program is in your path, you only need to put the program name and the system will find it for you, but you are probably better off putting the complete path so there is no mistake which program you want to run.

Now you'll be able to run *cmp* from the Run dialog. From a command prompt, you can't just type **cmp** and have it launch the program. Instead you need to type **start cmp**, which will do the trick.

Discussion

There are a couple of things to keep in mind when entering the path to the program in the value under the subkey:

* Don't use environment variables such *%SystemRoot%*. It won't work.
* Passing parameters to the program (which would have made aliases even more useful) also doesn't seem to work.

You can force the program to start in a particular directory by creating a Path value under the alias subkey. Create a REG_SZ value entry named Path, and for its value put the full path to the directory where the program should start in.

4.9   Searching for Files or Folders

Problem

You want to find the files or folders that match certain criteria.

Solution

Using a graphical user interface

On Windows Server 2003, select Search from the Start menu and click **All files and folders**.

On Windows 2000, select **Search** → **For Files or Folders** from the Start menu.

1. Now you'll be able to search for a particular file or folder name (use * as the wildcard) or enter one or more words to search within text-based files.
2. Select the drive, drives, or folder you want to search.
3. Click the **Search** button (or **Search Now** on Windows 2000).
4. Below the Search button, you can select additional advanced search options, which allows you to search based on file timestamp, file size, and various file attributes.

Using a command-line interface

The *where.exe* utility searches the files in your path that match a pattern. This command finds all files that begin with *net* and have a *.exe* extension:

```
> where net*.exe
```

You can also use *where* to find files in a specific folder or tree of folders. This command finds all *.vbs* scripts whose names contain the letters foo:

```
> where /r c:\scripts *foo*.vbs
```

Windows comes with two other tools you can use to search for files that contain a certain string: *find.exe* and *findstr.exe*. The latter is more robust. If you only need to find the files in the current directory that contain the letters log, you can use this command:

```
> findstr log *
```

This next command performs a case-insensitive search (*/i*) for all nonbinary files (*/p*) on the *d:* drive (*/s*) that contain the text "confidential" (*/c*):

```
> findstr /s /p /i /c:"confidential" d:\*
```

findstr includes some regular expression support. For a list of all the features, look at the command help information (*findstr /?*).

If you want to search for strings within binary files, take a look at the Sysinternals *strings.exe* command. The following command displays any text strings contained in binary files within the *Program Files* directory:

```
> strings -s "c:\program files"
```

See Also

MS KB 185476 (HOWTO: Search Directories to Find or List Files)

4.10   Copying, Moving, or Renaming a File or Folder

Problem

You want to copy or move a set of files or folders to another location on the file system or to another server.

Solution

Using a graphical user interface

1. Open Windows Explorer.

2. In the left pane, browse to the parent folder of the file or folder you want to copy, move, or rename.

3. In the right pane, right-click the file or folder.

    a. To rename, select **Rename**, enter the new name and hit Enter.

    b. To move or copy, select **Cut** or **Copy**, respectively. Browse to the new location, right-click in the folder, and select **Paste**.

Using a command-line interface

Moving, copying, and renaming files is pretty straightforward from the command line:

```
> move <Source> <Destination>
> copy <Source> <Destination>
> ren <Source> <Destination>
```

Using VBScript

```
' This code shows how to rename (same as move in WMI) and copy a file
' or folder.
' ------ SCRIPT CONFIGURATION ------
strComputer = "."
strCurrentFile = "<CurrentFilePath>"   ' Path to existing file or folder
strNewFile     = "<NewFilePath>"       ' New path of file or folder
' ------ END CONFIGURATION ---------
set objWMI = GetObject("winmgmts:\\" & strComputer & "\root\cimv2")
set objFile = objWMI.Get("Cim_Datafile='" & strCurrentFile & "'")
WScript.Echo "Renaming " & strCurrentFile & " to " & strNewFile
intRC = objFile.Rename(strNewFile)
if intRC <> 0 then
    WScript.Echo "There was an error renaming the file: " & intRC
else
    WScript.Echo "File rename successful"
end if
```

```
' ------ SCRIPT CONFIGURATION ------
strComputer = "."
strCurrentFile = "<CurrentFilePath>" ' Path to existing file or folder
strNewFile    = "<NewFilePath>"      ' Path to copy file or folder
' ------ END CONFIGURATION ---------
set objWMI = GetObject("winmgmts:\\" & strComputer & "\root\cimv2")
set objFile = objWMI.Get("Cim_Datafile='" & strCurrentFile & "'")
WScript.Echo "Copying " & strCurrentFile & " to " & strNewFile
intRC = objFile.Copy(strNewFile)
if intRC <> 0 then
    WScript.Echo "There was an error copying the file: " & intRC
else
    WScript.Echo "File copy successful"
end if
```

4.11 Comparing Files or Folders

Problem

You want to compare the contents of two files or two folders to determine the differences.

Solution

Using a graphical user interface

1. Open the WinDiff application (*windiff.exe*) from the Resource Kit.
2. To compare two files, select **File → Compare Files** from the menu. To compare two directories, select **File → Compare Directories**.

Using a command-line interface

The *fc.exe* command compares two or more files:

```
> fc <File1Path> <File2Path>
```

Here is an example:

```
> fc c:\netdiag.log c:\old\netdiag.log
```

To compare two binary files, include the /b option in the previous command.

Using VBScript

```
' This code compares the contents of two text-based files.
' ------ SCRIPT CONFIGURATION ------
strFile1 = "<FilePath1>"  ' e.g., c:\scripts\test1.vbs
strFile2 = "<FilePath2>"  ' e.g., c:\scripts\test2.vbs
' ------ END CONFIGURATION ---------
set objFSO = CreateObject("Scripting.FilesystemObject")
set objFile1 = objFSO.opentextfile(strFile1,1)
set objFile2 = objFSO.opentextfile(strFile2,1)
```

```
arrFile1 = split(objFile1.ReadAll,vbNewLine)
arrFile2 = split(objFile2.ReadAll,vbNewLine)
objFile1.close
objFile2.close

if ubound(arrFile1) < ubound(arrFile2) then
    intLineCount = ubound(arrFile1)
    strError = strFile2 & " is bigger than " & strFile1
elseif ubound(arrFile1) > ubound(arrFile2) then
    intLineCount = ubound(arrFile2)
    strError = strFile2 & " is bigger than " & strFile1
else
    intLineCount = ubound(arrFile2)
end if

for i = 0 to intLineCount
    if not arrFile1(i) = arrFile2(i) then
        exit for
    end if
next

if i < (intLineCount + 1) then
    WScript.Echo "Line " & (i+1) & " not equal"
    WScript.Echo strError
elseif strError <> "" then
    WScript.Echo strError
else
    WScript.Echo "Files are identical."
end if
```

Discussion

Of all of the methods I described, Windiff is by far the smartest in terms of identifying when lines have been added to a file or a section of text has been moved around. By comparison, the VBScript isn't nearly as robust. It simply checks line by line to determine if two text files are identical.

See Also

MS KB 159214 (How to Use the Windiff.exe Utility)

4.12   Hiding a File or Folder

Problem

You want to hide a file or folder from view within Windows Explorer.

Solution

Using a graphical user interface

1. Open Windows Explorer.
2. Browse to the file or folder you want to hide.
3. Right-click the file or folder and select **Properties**.
4. Check the box beside **Hidden** (to hide) or uncheck the box (to unhide).
5. Click **OK**.

Using a command-line interface

To hide a file, use the *attrib.exe* command:

```
> attrib +H <Path>
```

Here is an example:

```
> attrib +H d:\mysecretscript.vbs
```

To unhide a file, use the -H option:

```
> attrib -H <Path>
```

Here is an example:

```
> attrib -H d:\mysecretscript.vbs
```

Using VBScript

```
' This code hides or unhides a file.
' ------ SCRIPT CONFIGURATION ------
strFile = "<FilePath>"   ' e.g., d:\mysecretscript.vbs
boolHide = True          ' True to hide, False to unhide
' ------ END CONFIGURATION ---------
set objFSO = CreateObject("Scripting.FileSystemObject")

' Change this to GetFolder to hide/unhide a folder
set objFile = objFSO.GetFile(strFile)

if boolHide = True then
   if objFile.Attributes AND 2 then
      WScript.Echo "File already hidden"
   else
      objFile.Attributes = objFile.Attributes + 2
      WScript.Echo "File is now hidden"
   end if
else
   if objFile.Attributes AND 2 then
      objFile.Attributes = objFile.Attributes - 2
```

```
        WScript.Echo "File is not hidden"
    else
        WScript.Echo "File is already not hidden"
    end if
end if
```

Discussion

There are many operating system files that are hidden by default. Microsoft did this so you don't get yourself into trouble by accidentally editing or deleting important system files. You also may want to do this if you don't want users to see certain files or folders. The files and folders will still be accessible if the users know the full path; they just won't be visible by default in Windows Explorer. That, however, can be easily circumvented. Windows Explorer provides an option to make all hidden files and folders viewable. From the menu, select **Tools** → **Folder Options**. Click the **View** tab. You just need to select **Show hidden files and folders** and you'll be able to see them. If you truly don't want users to be able to access certain files or folders, your best bet is to restrict access to them via NTFS permissions.

See Also

MS KB 141276 (How to View System and Hidden Files in Windows)

4.13   Making a File or Folder Read-Only

Problem

You want to prevent a file or folder from being updated by making it read-only.

Solution

Using a graphical user interface

1. Open Windows Explorer.
2. Browse to the file or folder you want to hide.
3. Right-click the file or folder and select **Properties**.
4. Check the box beside **Read-only**.
5. Click **OK**.

Using a command-line interface

To make a file read-only, use the *attrib.exe* command:

```
> attrib +R <Path>
```

Here is an example:

```
> attrib +R d:\mysecretscript.vbs
```

To make a file available for reading and writing, use the -R option:

```
> attrib -R <Path>
```

Here is an example:

```
> attrib -R d:\mysecretscript.vbs
```

Using VBScript

```
' This code enables or disables the read-only attribute of a file.
' ------ SCRIPT CONFIGURATION ------
strFile = "<FilePath>"    ' e.g., d:\mysecretscript.vbs
boolReadOnly = True       ' True = read-only, False = not read-only
' ------ END CONFIGURATION ---------
set objFSO = CreateObject("Scripting.FileSystemObject")

' Change this to GetFolder to hide/unhide a folder
set objFile = objFSO.GetFile(strFile)

if boolReadOnly = True then
    if objFile.Attributes AND 1 then
        WScript.Echo "File already read-only"
    else
        objFile.Attributes = objFile.Attributes + 1
        WScript.Echo "File is now read-only"
    end if
else
    if objFile.Attributes AND 1 then
        objFile.Attributes = objFile.Attributes - 1
        WScript.Echo "File is not read-only"
    else
        WScript.Echo "File is already not read-only"
    end if
end if
```

4.14   Compressing a File or Folder

Problem

You want to regain some space on the hard disk by compressing files or folders.

Solution

Using a graphical user interface

1. Open Windows Explorer.
2. In the left pane, browse to the parent folder of the file or folder you want to compress. Click on the parent folder. This displays the list of subfolders and files in the right pane.
3. In the right pane, right-click on the target file or folder and select **Properties**.

4. Click the **Advanced** button.

5. Check the box beside **Compress contents to save disk space**.

6. Click **OK** and **Apply**.

Using a command-line interface

The *compact* command can compress and decompress files similar to Windows Explorer. The following command compresses all files in the current directory (/c option) and all subdirectories (/s option):

```
> compact /c /s
```

This command also causes all future files added anywhere under the current directory to be compressed.

To decompress all the files in the current directory and cause all future files to not be compressed, use the /u option with /s:

```
> compact /u /s
```

The following command compresses all of the files with the *.doc* extension (i.e., Word documents) in the *c:\docs* directory:

```
> compact /c /s:c:\docs *.doc
```

The *compress.exe* utility works a little bit differently from *compact*. It doesn't compress files transparently within the filesystem using NTFS compression. Instead it creates a compressed copy of a file. Here is an example:

```
> compress largetextfile.txt compressedfile.txt
```

The source file (*largetextfile.txt*) remains unchanged and the target file (*compressedfile.txt*) is a compressed version of that file. To compress all of the files in a directory, use this command:

```
> compress -R *.*
```

This creates compressed versions of each file and names them by replacing the last character of the source file with an underscore. For example, the compressed version of *test.txt* would be named *test.tx_*.

 To decompress files that you compressed with the *compress* command, you must use the *extract* command.

Using VBScript

```
' This code compresses a folder and its contents using NTFS compression
' ------ SCRIPT CONFIGURATION ------
strComputer = "."
strFile     = "<FilePath>" ' e.g., d:\scripts\test.vbs
' ------ END CONFIGURATION ---------
```

```
set objWMI = GetObject("winmgmts:\\" & strComputer & "\root\cimv2")
set objFile = objWMI.Get("Cim_Datafile='" & strFile & "'")
WScript.Echo objFile.Name
intRC = objFile.Compress ' To uncompress change this to objFile.Uncompress
if intRC <> 0 then
   WScript.Echo "There was an error compressing the file: " & intRC
else
   WScript.Echo "File compression successful"
end if

' This code compresses a folder and its contents using NTFS compression
' ------ SCRIPT CONFIGURATION ------
strComputer = "."
strFolder   = "<FolderPath>" ' e.g. d:\scripts
' ------ END CONFIGURATION ---------
set objWMI = GetObject("winmgmts:\\" & strComputer & "\root\cimv2")
set objFolder = objWMI.Get("Win32_Directory='" & strFolder & "'")
intRC = objFolder.Compress  ' To uncompress change this to objFolder.Uncompress
if intRC <> 0 then
   WScript.Echo "There was an error compressing the folder: " & intRC
else
   WScript.Echo "Folder compression successful"
end if
```

Discussion

NTFS compression is a great feature because once you compress a file, NTFS handles decompressing it automatically for you when you attempt to view it or copy/move it to another folder. However, you shouldn't start using compression everywhere. Decompressing and compressing files is CPU intensive. Be very careful when enabling compression on frequently accessed or modified files because it can have an adverse impact on performance.

 NTFS compression works only on partitions that were formatted using a 4-KB cluster size (the default) or smaller. See MS KB 171892 for more information.

See Also

MS KB 171892 (Err Msg: The File System Does Not Support Compression), MS KB 198038 (INFO: Useful Tools for Package and Deployment Issues), MS KB 251186 (Best Practices for NTFS Compression in Windows), MS KB 307987 (HOW TO: Use File Compression in Windows XP), MS KB 314958 (How To Use the COMPRESS, COMPACT, and EXPAND Commands to Compress and Expand Files and Folders in Windows 2000), and MS KB 323425 (HOW TO: Use the COMPACT Command to Compress and Uncompress Files and Folders in Windows Server 2003)

4.15   Encrypting a File or Folder

Problem

You want to encrypt a file or folder so that other users cannot read its contents.

Solution

Using a graphical user interface

1. Open Windows Explorer.
2. In the left pane, browse to the parent folder of the file or folder you want to compress. Click on the parent folder. This displays the list of subfolders and files in the right pane.
3. In the right pane, right-click on the target file or folder and select **Properties**.
4. Click the **Advanced** button.
5. Check the box beside **Encrypt contents to secure data**.
6. Click **OK** and **Apply**.

Using a command-line interface

With the *cipher.exe* command, you can encyrpt and decrypt files and folders. Running it without any options lists the files in the current directory with a flag indicating which ones are encrypted (U = unencrypted, E = encrypted):

```
> cipher
```

The following command encrypts a single file:

```
> cipher /e /a <FileName>
```

Here is an example:

```
> cipher /e /a mysecretfile.doc
```

The following command causes any new file added to the scripts directory to get encrypted. Existing files are not encrypted:

```
> cipher /e d:\scripts
```

The following command encrypts all files in a directory and any subdirectories:

```
> cipher /e /f /a /s:d:\scripts
```

This is the same command, with /e replaced by /d, which causes everything within the *d:\scripts* directory to become unencrypted:

```
> cipher /d /f /a /s:d:\scripts
```

Discussion

NTFS supports the Encrypting File System (EFS) for encrypting the contents of files. Similar to compression, EFS is built into the file system so encryption and decryption of EFS-enabled files and folders is seamless to the enduser. And just like compression, enabling EFS should only be done after much thought about its impact. EFS can have a significant hit on the performance of a server and the access times for files.

For more on how to use EFS, including the recovery mechanisms built-in to EFS, see MS KB 324897.

See Also

MS KB 230520 (HOW TO: Encrypt Data Using EFS in Windows 2000), MS KB 298009 (Cipher.exe Security Tool for the Encrypting File System), and MS KB 324897 (HOW TO: Manage the Encrypting File System in Windows Server 2003 Enterprise Server)

4.16   Replacing a File That Is in Use

Problem

You want to replace a file that is currently locked by a process.

Solution

Using a command-line interface

You can use the *inuse.exe* command to replace a file that is locked by a process. You need to reboot after running the command for the change to take effect.

```
> inuse c:\foo.dll c:\windows\system32\foo.dll
```

In this example, the file *c:\windows\system32\foo.dll* will be replaced by *c:\foo.dll* after the system reboots.

Using VBScript

```
' This code executes the inuse command to replace a file.
' ------ SCRIPT CONFIGURATION ------
' Modify the command string as necessary
strCmdString = "inuse.exe c:\foo.dll c:\windows\system32\foo.dll"
' ------ END CONFIGURATION ---------
set objWshShell = CreateObject("WScript.Shell")
set objExec = objWshShell.Exec(strCmdString)
do while not objExec.StdErr.AtEndOfStream
    WScript.Echo objExec.StdErr.ReadLine( )
```

```
loop
do while not objExec.StdOut.AtEndOfStream
    WScript.Echo objExec.StdOut.ReadLine( )
loop
```

Discussion

Ever needed to replace a DLL or other file, but couldn't because the system said it was in use? With the *inuse* utility, you can replace files that are currently locked. Simply pass *inuse* the location of the new version of the file and the location of the currently locked file, and on reboot, the file will be overwritten. *inuse* works by setting a registry value that Windows looks at when booting up to determine if there are any pending file renames. For more information on the specific key and value, see MS KB 181345.

On Windows 2000, *inuse* is a Resource Kit tool and therefore not officially supported by Microsoft, so use it at your own risk. On Windows Server 2003, the command is part of the default installation and is supported. Also keep in mind that there is no "undo" function. So once you've overwritten a file, unless you made a copy of the original previously, you won't be able to revert back to it.

See Also

Recipe 4.20 for more on finding the process that has a file open, MS KB 181345 (How to replace in-use files at Windows restart), and MS KB 228930 (How to replace currently locked files with Inuse.exe)

4.17   Taking Ownership of a File or Folder

Problem

You want to take ownership of a file or folder. This may be necessary if you find that NTFS permissions have you locked out of a file or folder. As long as you are an administrator of the system, you should be able to take control of it and reset permissions as necessary.

Solution

Using a graphical user interface

1. Open Windows Explorer.
2. In the left pane, browse to the parent folder of the file or folder you want to take ownership of. Click on the parent folder. This displays the list of subfolders and files in the right pane.
3. In the right pane, right-click on the target file or folder and select **Properties**.
4. Select the **Security** tab.

5. Click the **Advanced** button.

6. Select the **Owner** tab.

7. Under the **Change owner to** heading select the new owner and click **Apply**.

Using a command-line interface

Use the following command to attempt to take ownership of a file:

```
> takeown <FileName>
```

For example:

```
> takeown d:\iwanna.exe
```

If you want to grant ownership to someone else, use the *subinacl.exe* command:

```
> subinacl /file <FilePath> /setowner=<User>
```

For example:

```
> subinacl /file \\rallen-svr1\docs\guide.doc /setowner=AMER\rallen
```

Or you can even grant ownership to a user over all the files in a directory:

```
> subinacl /subdirectories \\rallen-svr1\docs\* /setowner=AMER\rallen
```

Using VBScript

```
' This code transfers ownership of the specified file to the
' user running the script.  If strFile is set to a folder path
' then ownership of all files within the folder will be changed.
' ------ SCRIPT CONFIGURATION ------
strFile = "<FilePath>"         ' e.g., d:\scripts
strComputer = "<ServerName>" ' e.g., rallen-svr1 or . for local server
' ------ END CONFIGURATION ---------
set objWMI = GetObject("winmgmts:\\" & strComputer & "\root\cimv2")
set objFile = objWMI.Get("CIM_DataFile.Name='" & strFile & "'")
intRC = objFile.TakeOwnership
if intRC = 0 then
   WScript.Echo "File ownership successfully changed"
else
   WScript.Echo "Error transferring file ownership: " & intRC
end if
```

Discussion

If you are taking ownership of a file or folder because you were locked out of it, even after you take ownership you still have to go in and grant yourself the necessary NTFS permissions to access and manipulate the file or folder.

With Windows Explorer on Windows 2000, you can only assign one of the members of the local administrators group as an owner of a file or folder. With Windows Server 2003, there is a new button called Other Users or Groups that lets you use the object picker to select any user as an owner.

See Also

MS KB 268019 (HOW TO: Take Ownership of Files), and MS KB 320046 (HOW TO: Use the File Ownership Script Tool (Fileowners.pl) in Windows 2000)

4.18   Finding Who Last Opened or Modified a File

Problem

You want to find who last opened or modified a file.

Solution

To find who last opened or modified a file, you have to enable auditing on that file. To enable auditing, you have to enable auditing at the server level and then enable auditing on the particular object (in this case, a file) in which you are interested.

Using a graphical user interface

Do the following to enable auditing at the server level:

1. From the Administrative Tools, open the Local Security Policy snap-in.
2. In the left pane, expand **Local Policy** and click on **Audit Policy**.
3. In the right pane, double-click **Audit object access**.
4. Check the boxes beside **Success** or **Failure** (as needed).
5. Click **OK**.

Now you need to enable auditing on the target file(s) or folder(s):

1. Open Windows Explorer.
2. In the left pane, browse to the parent folder of the file or folder on which you want to enable auditing. Click on the parent folder. This displays the list of sub-folders and files in the right pane.
3. In the right pane, right-click on the target file or folder and select **Properties**.
4. Select the **Security** tab.
5. Click the **Advanced** button.
6. Select the **Auditing** tab.
7. Click the **Add** button.
8. Enter the user or group you want to audit access for (use the Everyone principal to audit all access) and click **OK**.
9. In the Auditing Entry dialog box, select the types of access you want to audit. You have to select Success events separately from Failure events. Click **OK** when you are done.
10. Click **Apply**.

Using a command-line interface

Use the *auditpol.exe* command to enable auditing at the server level:

```
> auditpol \\<ServerName> /enable /object:all
```

Microsoft doesn't provide a tool to configure the audit settings of files. However, you can do this with the *setacl.exe* tool. It is available for download from SourceForge at *http://setacl.sourceforge.net/*. Here is an example of setting an audit entry on the file *d:\myimportantfile.txt* for all failed access attempts by the Everyone principal:

```
> setacl -on "d:\myimportantfile.txt" -ot file -actn ace -ace "n:everyone;p:full;m:
aud_fail;w:sacl"
```

Discussion

Be careful when enabling auditing on a frequently accessed set of files or folders. The number of audit messages in the Security event log can grow quickly with just a few accesses of the file. Monitor the Security event log closely after initially enabling auditing just to make sure you don't flood it.

See Also

Recipe 11.1

4.19 Finding Open Files

Problem

You want to find the open files on a server.

Solution

There are two different categories of open files on a system. Since the days of Windows NT, the operating system has supported the capability to view the files that are open from shared folders. This is useful when you want to see who is accessing files on a file server, especially if you need to take the system down for maintenance and you want to notify the impacted users.

First seen in Windows XP and supported in Windows Server 2003 is the ability to view all open files on a system (not just shared folders). To use this feature, you first have to enable support for it. The reason this isn't enabled by default is because there is a slight system-wide performance impact when tracking all open files.

Using a graphical user interface

None of the standard graphical tools provide a list of the open files on a system. The closest thing to it would be the Sysinternals File Monitor tool. For more information, see Recipe 4.21.

To view the open files from shared folders, do the following:

1. From the Administrative Tools, open the Computer Management snap-in.
2. In the left pane, expand **System Tools** → **Shared Folders** → **Open Files**.
3. To close an open file, right-click on it in the right pane and select **Close Open File**.

Using a command-line interface

To view the open files from shared folders, run this command:

```
> net file
```

The output from that command displays open files and their associated ID. Using this ID, you can close a specific file:

```
> net file <ID> /close
```

To view all open files, first enable support for it:

```
> openfiles /local on
```

You'll need to reboot the system before this setting takes effect. At that point, you can see open files using this command:

```
> openfiles
```

Use the /s <ServerName> option to target a remote server. Similar to the net file command, you can close any open file by running this command:

```
> openfiles /disconnect /id <ID>
```

You can also disconnect all the files open by a particular user:

```
> openfiles /disconnect /a <UserName>
```

See Also

Recipe 4.21

4.20   Finding the Process That Has a File Open

Problem

You want to find the process or processes that have a file open. This is often necessary if you want to delete or modify a file, but are getting errors because it is in use by another process.

Solution

Using a graphical user interface

1. Open the Sysinternals Process Explorer (*procexp.exe*) tool.
2. Click the Find icon (binoculars) or select **Search** → **Find** from the menu.
3. Beside **Handle substring**, enter the name of the file and click **Search**.

Using a command-line interface

Use the Sysinternals *handle.exe* command to view the processes that have a lock on a file:

```
> handle <FileName>
```

This example commands shows all the processes that have a handle to the *personal.pst* file:

```
> handle personal.pst
```

Using VBScript

```
' This code prints the output from the handle.exe command
' ------ SCRIPT CONFIGURATION ------
strFilePattern = "<FileName>" ' e.g., personal.pst
strHandleExec = "handle.exe"  ' If handle.exe isn't in your PATH, you will
                              ' need to specify the full path.
' ------ END CONFIGURATION ---------
set objWshShell = CreateObject("WScript.Shell")
set objExec = objWshShell.Exec(strHandleExec & " " & strFilePattern)
do while not objExec.StdOut.AtEndOfStream
    WScript.Echo objExec.StdOut.ReadLine( )
loop
```

Discussion

Processes running on your system are constantly opening and closing files (see Recipe 4.21 for more on how to see this activity). When a process accesses a file, the process is said to have a *handle* to the file. Processes can also have handles to other system resources, such as Registry keys and values. For certain types of file accesses, a process may obtain an exclusive lock on the file (such as when it needs to write to the file), which means no other processes can modify the file; you may still be able to read the file, but you won't be able to overwrite, move, or delete it.

This may be a bit annoying if there is a file you need to do something with. You have a couple of options. First, if you determine the process that has a handle to the file is not important, you could try to kill it (see Recipe 6.3). This will often remove the lock on the file, but this isn't the most graceful approach. If you just want to replace the file, another option entails following the instructions in Recipe 4.16, which will replace a file after the next reboot.

See Also

Recipes 4.16, 4.21, 6.2, and MS KB 242131 (How to: Display a List of Processes That Have Files Open)

4.21   Viewing File Activity

Problem

You want to view the file activity on a server.

Solution

Using a graphical user interface

Open the Sysinternals File Monitor (*filemon.exe*). It automatically starts logging all file activity when it is opened.

To stop capturing file activity, click the Capture icon (magnifying glass), select **File → Capture Events** from the menu, or type **Ctrl-E**.

To search the captured data, click the Find icon (binoculars), select **Edit → Find** from the menu, or type **Ctrl-F**. The text you enter will be matched against any part of the captured data (index, time, process name, request, and file path).

To filter the captured data so that only the entries that match your filter are displayed, click the **Filter** icon, select **Options → Filter/Hightlight** from the menu, or type **Ctrl-L**.

If you double-click a particular entry in File Monitor, it will open a Windows Explorer window to the directory containing the target file.

Discussion

Ever hear your hard disks spinning or disk indicator light flashing, but you don't know why? You may not appear to have any applications open or running, but something is still accessing the hard disks. The Sysinternals File Monitor utility lets you see what processes are reading or writing files. It has some robust filter and search capability as well, which is helpful considering the fact that File Monitor can capture thousands of operations in a matter of minutes. Figure 4-2 shows sample output from File Monitor.

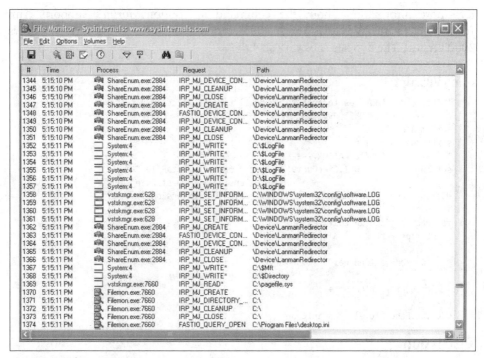

Figure 4-2. File Monitor screen

4.22 Performing an Action on Several Files at Once

Problem

You want to perform an action on several files at once.

Solution

Using a command-line interface

The *forfiles.exe* utility is a handy tool that lets you search and iterate over a group of files and perform an action against them. For example, this command searches the *d:* drive for all files with a *.zip* extension and prints out the name of each file and its size:

```
> forfiles /p d:\ /s /m *.zip /c "cmd /c echo @file : @fsize"
```

Here is another example that opens everything that ends in *.txt* with notepad. It performs a check to make sure only files are opened, not directories (@isdir==FALSE):

```
> forfiles /m *.txt /c "cmd /c if @isdir==FALSE notepad.exe @file"
```

For more information about the command-line options *forfiles* supports, run `forfiles /?` for the Windows Server 2003 version and `forfiles -h` for the Windows 2000 version. The two versions vary slightly.

Using VBScript

```
' This code shows how to iterate over all the zip files on a system
' ------ SCRIPT CONFIGURATION ------
strComputer  = "."
strExtension = "zip"
' ------ END CONFIGURATION ---------
set colFiles = objWMI.ExecQuery("select * from Cim_DataFile " & _
                                " where extension = '" & strExtension & "'")
WScript.Echo "Files with a ." & strExtension & " extension:"
intCount = 0
for each objFile in colFiles
    WScript.Echo "   " & objFile.Name

    ' Do some action here

    intCount = intCount + 1
next
WScript.Echo "Total: " & intCount
```

Discussion

If you aren't familiar with the *forfiles* command, I highly recommend that you check it out. I don't know how many times I've had to write a script or piece together a long command line to iterate over a series of files and perform some action. *Forfiles* makes the process much easier.

4.23   Creating and Deleting Shares

Problem

You want to create or delete a shared folder.

Solution

Using a graphical user interface

1. Open Windows Explorer.
2. In the left pane, browse to the folder you want to start or stop sharing.
3. Right-click on the folder and select **Sharing and Security** (or **Sharing** on Windows 2000).
4. To stop sharing the folder, select **Do not share this folder**.

5. To share the folder, select **Share this folder**. Enter the **Share name**, enter a description for the share in the **Comment** field, and specify the **User limit**.

6. Click **OK** to close the dialog box.

Using a command-line interface

The following command creates a share called `Perl Libs`:

```
> net share "Perl Libs"=d:\perl\lib /unlimited /remark:"Core Perl modules"
```

The /unlimited option means that an unlimited number of users can access the share simultaneously. You can limit the number of simultaneous users by using the /users: <Number> option instead.

This command deletes a share:

```
> net share "Perl Libs" /delete
```

Using VBScript

```
' This code creates a share.
' ------ SCRIPT CONFIGURATION ------
strComputer    = "."
strPath        = "d:\perl\lib"
strName        = "Perl Libs"
intType        = 0 ' share a disk drive resource
intMaxAllowed = 10
strDescr       = "Core Perl modules"
' ------ END CONFIGURATION ---------
set objWMI = GetObject("winmgmts:\\" & strComputer & "\root\cimv2")
set objShare = objWMI.Get("Win32_Share")
intRC = objShare.Create(strPath, strName, intType, intMaxAllowed, strDescr)
if intRC <> 0 then
   WScript.Echo "Error creating share: " & intRC
else
   WScript.Echo "Successfully created share"
end if

' This code deletes a share.
' ------ SCRIPT CONFIGURATION ------
strComputer    = "."
strName        = "Perl Libs"
' ------ END CONFIGURATION ---------
set objWMI = GetObject("winmgmts:\\" & strComputer & "\root\cimv2")
set objShare = objWMI.Get("Win32_Share.Name='" & strName & "'")
intRC = objShare.Delete
if intRC <> 0 then
   WScript.Echo "Error deleted share: " & intRC
else
   WScript.Echo "Successfully deleted share"
end if
```

Discussion

After you create a share, you need to modify the access control list (ACL) to include the users and groups that can access the contents of the share (see Recipe 4.25 for more on this).

If you want to create a hidden share, simply append "$" to the end of the share name. The only difference in a hidden share is that it won't be directly viewable when listing the shared folders on a server. Hiding shares is kind of like hiding files (Recipe 4.12); it is up to the application to display them or not. So hidden shares are not truly hidden, but they will not be visible to the casual user.

See Also

MS KB 324267 (HOW TO: Share Files and Folders over the Network in a Windows Server 2003 Domain Environment)

4.24   Viewing Shares

Problem

You want to view the list of shares on a server.

Solution

Using a graphical user interface

1. Open the Computer Management snap-in.
2. In the left pane, expand **System Tools** → **Shared Folders** → **Shared Folders**.
3. To view the properties of a share, double-click on it in the right pane. To disable a share, right-click on it and select **Stop Sharing**.

Using a command-line interface

The following command displays administrative and nonadministrative shares:

```
> net share
```

To view the list of shares on a remote server, use the Sysinternals *psexec.exe* utility to run the *net share* command against the server:

```
> psexec \\<ServerName> -u <User> net share
```

For example:

```
> psexec \\srv01 -u administrator net share
```

You can also view all of the nonadministrative shares on a remote server using this command:

```
> net view \\<ServerName>
```

Using VBScript

```
' This code displays all of the shares on a system.
' ------ SCRIPT CONFIGURATION ------
strComputer = "."
' ------ END CONFIGURATION ---------
set objWMI = GetObject("winmgmts:\\" & strComputer & "\root\cimv2")
set colShares = objWMI.InstancesOf("Win32_Share")
for each objShare in colShares
   WScript.Echo objShare.Name
   WScript.Echo "   Path:        " & objShare.Path
   WScript.Echo "   Allow Max:   " & objShare.AllowMaximum
   WScript.Echo "   Caption:     " & objShare.Caption
   WScript.Echo "   Max Allowed: " & objShare.MaximumAllowed
   WScript.Echo "   Type:        " & objShare.Type
   WScript.Echo
next
```

Discussion

The Sysinternals Shareenum program is another tool that you can use for viewing shares. It lists the shared folders on all hosts in a particular domain. Depending on the number of hosts in the domain, it can take a while to complete. It is interesting to see the output and discover what types of shared folders users have created. You may even want to periodically check the security on these shared folders to ensure that users are following your documented policies for shared folder security.

4.25   Restricting Access to a Share

Problem

You want to restrict access to a share.

Solution

There are two ways to restrict access to a share; you can set share permissions or NTFS permissions. I'm going to describe how to set share permissions, but see the Discussion section for more on NTFS permissions, the preferred method.

Using a graphical user interface

1. Open Windows Explorer.
2. In the left pane, browse to the shared folder.
3. Right-click the folder and select **Sharing and Security** (or **Sharing** on Windows 2000).
4. Select the **Sharing** tab.

5. Click the **Permissions** button.

6. From here, you can grant users or groups **Full Control**, **Read**, or **Change** access to the share.

Using a command-line interface

This command grants the AMER\rallen user with Full Control over the Perl Libs share:

```
> subinacl /share "Perl Libs" /grant=amer\rallen=F
```

This command revokes the permission:

```
> subinacl /share "Perl Libs" /revoke=amer\rallen
```

Discussion

The generally accepted way to manage share permissions is to not actually manage permissions on the shares themselves, but on the underlying files and folders using NTFS permissions. With Windows 2000, this is pretty straightforward. By default, share and NTFS permissions are both set to allow Everyone Full Control. So you create a share and just modify the NTFS permissions to include the user or groups that should have access and remove the Everyone entry.

With Windows Server 2003, it isn't as straightforward. In an effort to make things more secure, Microsoft changed the default share permissions when creating a new share to allow Everyone only Read access. That means that, regardless of whether the underlying NTFS permissions grant Write access to a group, members of that group won't be able to write to the share until you also grant Change (or more appropriately, remove the Read restriction) on the share permissions. I said that this is the generally accepted way to manage permissions because you may find some people prefer to rely on share permissions. In my mind, using share permissions makes things a little more complicated, but to each his own.

See Also

MS KB 301195 (HOW TO: Configure Security for Files and Folders on a Network (Domain) in Windows 2000), and MS KB 324267 (HOW TO: Share Files and Folders over the Network in a Windows Server 2003 Domain Environment)

4.26 Enabling Web Sharing

Problem

You want to enable web sharing for a folder. This allows users from non-Windows-based PCs to view the contents of a share using the web.

Solution

Using a graphical user interface

1. Open Windows Explorer.
2. In the left pane, browse to the folder you want to share.
3. Right-click on the folder and select **Sharing and Security** (or **Sharing** on Windows 2000).
4. Select the **Web Sharing** tab.
5. Select **Share this folder**.
6. A dialog box appears with the settings you can configure for the web share. Click **OK** when you are done.
7. Click **OK** to close the dialog box.

Discussion

To use Web Sharing, you must have IIS installed and running. When you create a web share, you are doing nothing more than creating a virtual directory in IIS. See Recipe 12.5 for more on virtual directories.

The security for a web share is a little different from a regular share: you have to select the access permissions and application permissions you want to use. Here is a list of access permissions:

Read
Allows web users to read files in the folder

Write
Allows web users to write files in the folder

Script source access
Allows web users to view the source code of scripts in the folder

Directory browsing
Allows web users to browse the folder contents

And here are the application permissions:

None
Does not allow the execution of scripts or programs

Scripts
Allows the execution of scripts, but not programs

Execute
Allows the execution of both scripts and programs

Keep in mind that NTFS and Web server permissions also apply to web shares. If the user is accessing the share without authenticating, the permissions will be based on the IUSR account IIS is running under (normally IUSER_*<computername>*). If the user authenticates, permissions will based on his or her credentials.

See Also

Recipe 12.4

4.27 Publishing a Share in Active Directory

Problem

You want to publish a share in Active Directory so that other users can find it.

Solution

Using a graphical user interface

1. Open the Active Directory Users and Computers (ADUC) snap-in.
2. In the left pane, browse to the OU in which you want to publish the share.
3. Right-click the OU and select **New → Shared Folder** (if you don't see the New heading then you don't have permission to create objects in the OU).
4. For **Name**, enter the name of the share as you want it displayed to users.
5. For **UNC Path**, enter the network path of the share (e.g., *fs01\myshare*).
6. Click **OK**.

Using VBScript

```
' This code publishes a share in AD.
' ------ SCRIPT CONFIGURATION ------
strComputer = "ad-01"  ' name of a domain controller
strShareName = "Perl Libraries"
strSharePath = "\\fs01\perl-libs"
strShareDescr = "Core Perl libraries"

set objRootDSE = GetObject("LDAP://" & strComputer & "/RootDSE")
strParentDN = "/OU=SharedFolders," & objRootDSE.Get("defaultNamingContext")
' ------ END CONFIGURATION ---------
set objOU = GetObject("LDAP://" & strComputer & strParentDN)
set objVol = objOU.Create("volume", "cn=" & strShareName)
objVol.Put "uncName", strSharePath
objVol.Put "Description", strShareDescr
objVol.SetInfo
WScript.Echo "Successfully created object: " & objVol.Name
```

Discussion

After you've created a shared folder, your users may not be able to find it or even know about it. One way to make available sby publishing them to Active Directory.

Shared folders are represented by the volume object class in Active Directory. The main pieces of information you need in order to create a volume object are the share name, the share UNC path, and a share description.

Users can search shared folders in Active Directory using the Find Users, Contacts, and Groups dialog box. You can get to this box going to My Network Places and clicking Search Active Directory in the left pane, or by running the Active Directory Users and Computers snap-in, right-clicking the target domain in the left pane and selecting Find. After the box is displayed, select Shared Folders beside Find, enter your search criteria, and click Find Now.

The one major downside to publishing shares in Active Directory is the maintenance overhead. Unlike printer publishing in Active Directory, there is no automatic pruning or maintenance process that will cleanup volume objects for shares that no longer exist. Unless you create a process to update Active Directory whenever a share is created, moved, or deleted, Active Directory will eventually become out of date and ultimately be an unreliable source of shared folder information.

 Another way to solve this problem is to use DFS whereby you have a single directory tree of shared folders, but that is beyond the scope of this chapter.

See Also

MS KB 234582 (Publishing a Shared Folder in Windows 2000 Active Directory)

CHAPTER 5

Running and Scheduling Tasks

5.0   Introduction

As a system administrator, it is important to understand how to run tasks. A task is simply a program, application, command, or script that does something useful. In the Windows environment, you need to know how to run tasks with alternate credentials, so you aren't always logged on to your workstation with administrator credentials. You need to know how to run tasks against remote servers or workstations, which enables you to do daily administration tasks without ever leaving the comfort (and security) of your workstation. Often it can be beneficial to have tasks run as soon as someone logs into a system and there are several ways you can set this up. Finally, if you are trying to automate certain tasks (as all good system administrators should), you'll need to schedule tasks to run at certain times of the day or night. I cover all of this and more in this chapter.

5.1   Running a Task with Alternate Credentials

Problem

You want to run a task using a username and password other than the one you are currently logged in with.

Solution

Using a graphical user interface

1. Open the Start Menu.
2. Browse to the application you want to open.
3. For Windows 2000, press the Shift key and right-click on the application.
4. For Windows Server 2003, right-click on the application.

5. Select **Run As**.

6. You will be prompted to enter the username, password, and domain of the user whose credentials you want use for running the task.

Using a command-line interface

The *runas.exe* command allows you to run a command with alternate credentials:

```
> runas /user:<User> "<ExectuablePath>"
```

Here is an example:

```
> runas /user:AMER\rallen.adm "mmc.exe"
```

If you want to authenticate using credentials of a user that does not have logon privileges to the local machine, you'll need to specify the /netonly option to the *runas* command.

Using VBScript

```
' This code shows how to use alternate credentials using WMI
' ------ SCRIPT CONFIGURATION ------
strServer = "<ServerName>"  ' e.g., fs01
strUser = "<User>"          ' e.g., AMER\rallen.adm
strPasswd = "<Password>"
' ------ END CONFIGURATION ---------
on error resume next
set objLocator = CreateObject("WbemScripting.SWbemLocator")
set objWMI = objLocator.ConnectServer(strServer, "root\cimv2", _
                                      strUser, strPasswd)
if Err.Number <> 0 then
   WScript.Echo "Authentication failed: " & Err.Description
end if


' Now you can use the objWMI object to get an instance of a class
' or perform a WQL query.  Here is an example:
colDisks = objWMI.InstancesOf("Win32_LogicalDisk")
' This code shows how to spawn a new process using alternate creds
' ------ SCRIPT CONFIGURATION ------
strServer = "<ServerName>"  ' e.g., fs01
strUser = "<User>"          ' e.g., AMER\rallen.adm
strPasswd = "<Password>"
strProcessPath = "<ExecutablePath>" 'e.g., Notepad.exe
' ------ END CONFIGURATION ---------
set objLocator = CreateObject("WbemScripting.SWbemLocator")
set objWMI = objLocator.ConnectServer(strServer, "root\cimv2", _
                                      strUser, strPasswd)
set objStartup = objWMI.Get("Win32_ProcessStartup")
set objConfig = objStartup.SpawnInstance_
set objProcess = GetObject("winmgmts:root\cimv2:Win32_Process")
intRC = objProcess.Create(strProcessPath, null, objConfig, intProcessID)
if intRC <> 0 then
   WScript.Echo "Error spawning process: " & intRC
```

```
else
    WScript.Echo "Successfully spawned process."
end if
```

Discussion

A best practice system administrators should follow is to log on to desktop systems using a normal user account that has no administrator level privileges other than on that system. This has three distinct advantages:

- It reduces the impact a virus can have on your network if your machine becomes infected.

- It reduces the chance of accidentally deleting important files and folders or making administrative changes unknowingly.

- It ensures the network remains secure even if someone gains physical access to your workstation while you are logged in.

If you need to access a network resource with administrator privileges, you should do so using alternate credentials as I showed in the solutions. This is also necessary if you want to access a resource on a machine in a different, untrusted domain from the one in which your account resides. For example, if you have some test systems in a lab that are not part of your domain, you'll have to use alternate credentials to access them.

Using a graphical user interface

If you need to run several different programs at the same time using alternate credentials, it can be annoying if you have to follow the graphical or command-line solution for each one. In that case, you'd probably be better off just using a remote desktop client to log on to the machine as the target user.

Another option is to open a cmd.exe session with alternate credentials. Then any programs you open with that session will also be using the alternate credentials. The following is an example:

```
> runas /user:AMER\rallen.adm cmd.exe
```

Using a command-line interface

One problem with *runas* is you cannot specify the password for the user on the command line or even by piping it in. That means *runas* will always prompt you to enter a password. Some may argue that this is intentional because it is insecure to specify passwords on the command line; however, passing a password on the command line can be useful in situations where you need *runas* capability in a batch file. Fortunately, an alternative exists in the form of the Joeware *cpau.exe* utility. It works very similar to the runas /netonly command, but you can specify the -p option to pass in a password.

```
> cpau -u <User> -p <Password> -ex "<ExectuablePath>"
```

It also has a more secure option. You can create an encrypted "job" file that contains the command to run and the password to use. If you open a job file, all you'll see is a string of letters and numbers. This prevents people from casually reading a password from a batch file.

To use this feature, you must first create the job file:

```
> cpau -u <User> -p <Password> -ex "<ExecutablePath>" -enc -file <JobFile>
```

Then to execute a job file, use the following command:

```
> cpau -dec -file <JobFile>
```

 If you don't want to type a *runas* or *cpau* command every time you open a certain tool, consider creating a shortcut that automatically does this for you. For more on creating shortcuts, see Recipe 4.6.

Using VBScript

Obviously, hard coding passwords within a script is not the most secure practice. There are a few alternatives. You can invoke a script as you would any other command-line tool using *runas* or *cpau*. Also, if you want to schedule the script to run periodically, you can specify credentials when you create the scheduled task.

See Also

MS KB 225035 (Secondary Logon (Run As): Starting Programs and Tools in Local Administrative Context)

5.2   Running a Task on a Remote Server

Problem

You want to run a task on a remote server. By this, I don't mean running a task against a remote server, but the command or script actually runs on the remote server. This is useful if the tool you want to use can only be run locally on a system, or if it generates a lot of network traffic and could work more efficiently if run locally.

Solution

Using a graphical user interface

To run a command or utility on a remote computer via a graphical interface, you'll need to use a remote desktop application like Remote Desktop or VNC.

Using a command-line interface

The following command executes the *diruse* utility on the host *fs01* to find directories that contain more than 100 MB of data:

```
> psexec \\fs01 c:\tools\diruse.exe /s /m /d /q:100 c:\
```

This assumes that *c:\tools\diruse.exe* exists on *fs01*. You can also have *psexec* copy the command you want to run from the local system to the target system by specifying the -c option. The following command executes the same one as before, except the *diruse* utility is copied to the target system:

```
> psexec \\fs01 -c diruse.exe /s /m /d /q:100 c:\
```

As with other Sysinternals tools, you can specify alternate credentials with *psexec* using the -u option. Here is an example:

```
> psexec \\fs01 -u CORP\rallen -c c:\diruse.exe /s /m /d /q:100 c:\
```

Using VBScript

```
' This code shows how to run a task on a remote server.
' ------ SCRIPT CONFIGURATION ------
strComputer = "<ServerName>"
strCommand  = "cscript.exe c:\scripts\dircheck.vbs"
' ------ END CONFIGURATION ---------
set objController = WScript.CreateObject("WSHController")
set objRemoteScript = objController.CreateScript(strCommand, strComputer)
WScript.ConnectObject objRemoteScript, "remote_"
objRemoteScript.Execute
do While objRemoteScript.Status <> 2
    WScript.Sleep 100
loop
WScript.DisconnectObject objRemoteScript
```

Discussion

If you want to use *psexec* to run a CMD command (e.g., *dir*, *date*, *set*, etc.), you can use either the /c or /k option available with *cmd.exe*. The following command simply lists the contents of the C: drive on fs01:

```
> psexec \\fs01 cmd /c dir c:\
```

Occasionally I have seen where executing a command such as *dir* will not display any results when run with *psexec*. If you encounter this, you can create an interactive CMD session on the remote server using the /k option. Here is an example:

```
> psexec \\fs01 cmd /k dir c:\
```

This will print the results of *dir*, but also leave you at a command prompt on the remote server thereby allowing you to run additional command-line utilities without calling *psexec* again.

5.3   Running a Task When a User Logs On

Problem

You want to run a task when a user logs on to a system.

Solution

There are four ways you can make tasks run automatically after a user logs on: the Registry, startup folders, login scripts, and Group Policy. I explain how to use login scripts in Recipe 5.4 and Group Policy in Recipe 5.5. Here, I'll describe the Registry and startup folder options.

Registry

There are four Registry keys that you can use to run tasks automatically. To use any of the keys, simply create a value entry of type REG_SZ under the key. Give the value any name you want and specify the full path to the program or script and any parameters as the value data. See Figure 5-1 for some example entries.

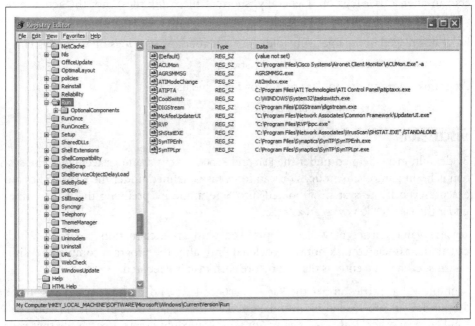

Figure 5-1. Sample Registry Run key values

Values defined under this key cause tasks to run for every user that logs on to the system:

```
HKEY_LOCAL_MACHINE\Software\Microsoft\Windows\CurrentVersion\Run
```

Values defined under this key cause tasks to run whenever the user that is currently logged on logs on to the system:

```
HKEY_CURRENT_USER\Software\Microsoft\Windows\CurrentVersion\Run
```

Values defined under this key cause a task to run the next time any user logs on to the system (and not after that):

```
HKEY_LOCAL_MACHINE\Software\Microsoft\Windows\CurrentVersion\RunOnce
```

Values defined under this key cause a task to run the next time the current user logs on to the system:

```
HKEY_CURRENT_USER\Software\Microsoft\Windows\CurrentVersion\RunOnce
```

 The values under the RunOnce keys are deleted once the tasks start.

Startup Folders

Similar to the Run and RunOnce Registry keys, programs contained in the startup folders run after a user logs on. Generally, shortcut files (*.lnk* files), not the actual programs, are placed in the startup folders, but you can do it either way.

Programs placed in the following folder are run after any user logs on to the system:

```
%ALLUSERSPROFILE%\Start Menu\Programs\Startup
```

Programs placed in this folder are run for a specific user:

```
%USERPROFILE%\Start Menu\Programs\Startup
```

Discussion

By default, tasks defined under the Run and RunOnce keys are not executed if the system is booted into Safe mode. You can force tasks defined under the RunOnce keys to execute even if the system is booted into Safe mode by prefixing the value names under the RunOnce key with an asterisk (*).

RunOnce value entries may also be prefixed with an exclamation point (!), which causes the associated task not to be deleted until after the program completes. Without this, each value entry is deleted before each task is executed.

Multiple value entries under the Run or RunOnce keys and multiple programs in the *Startup* folders are loaded in an indeterminate order, so you can't assume one will run before another. If this is an issue for you, you could create a batch file that calls the programs in a particular order and put only the batch file in the Run or RunOnce key.

There are several other Registry keys that can cause tasks to run automatically. For a complete list of all of these Registry keys and folders, see Recipe 5.6.

See Also

Recipe 5.6, MS KB 137367 (Definition of the RunOnce Keys in the Registry), MS KB 179365 (INFO: Run, RunOnce, RunServices, RunServicesOnce and Startup), and MB KB 314866 (A Definition of the Run Keys in the Windows XP Registry)

5.4   Running a Task via a Login Script

Problem

You want to set the login script for a local or domain user account.

Solution

The following solutions describe how to set the login script for a local user account on a system.

Using a graphical user interface

1. Open the Computer Management snap-in (*compmgmt.msc*).
2. In the left pane under **System Tools**, expand **Local Users and Groups**.
3. Click the **Users** folder.
4. In the right pane, double-click the user for which you want to set the login script.
5. Select the **Profile** tab.
6. Beside **Logon script**, enter the relative path (from the NETLOGON share) of the login script (e.g., *myscript.vbs*).
7. Click **OK**.

Using a command-line interface

The following command sets the login script for a local user:

```
> net user <UserName> /scriptpath:<ScriptName>
```

<ScriptName> should be the relative path of the script from the NETLOGON share.

Using VBScript

```
' This code sets the login script for a local user
' ------ SCRIPT CONFIGURATION ------
strComputer = "<ServerName>"
strUser = "<UserName>"          ' e.g., administrator
strLoginScript = "<ScriptName>" ' e.g., login.vbs
' ------ END CONFIGURATION ---------
set objUser = GetObject("WinNT://" & strComputer & "/" & strUser & ",user")
objUser.LoginScript = strLoginScript
```

```
objUser.SetInfo
WScript.Echo "Set login script for " & objuser.Name
```

The following solutions describe how to set the login script for a domain user account.

Using a graphical user interface

1. Open the Active Directory Users and Computers snap-in (*dsa.msc*).
2. In the left pane, connect to the domain that contains the user you want to set the login script for.
3. Browse to the container the user account is located in.
4. In the right pane, right-click the user and select **Properties**.
5. Select the **Profile** tab.
6. Beside **Logon script**, enter the relative path (from the NETLOGON share on the DCs) of the login script.
7. Click **OK**.

Using a command-line interface

The following command sets the login script for a domain user:

```
> net user <UserName> /domain /scriptpath:<ScriptName>
```

The following command also sets the login script for a domain user (not available on Windows 2000):

```
> dsmod user "<UserDN>" -loscr <ScriptName>
```

<ScriptName> should be the relative path of the script from the NETLOGON share on the DCs.

Using VBScript

```
' This code sets the login script for a local user
' ------ SCRIPT CONFIGURATION ------
strUserDN = "<UserDN>" ' e.g., cn=administrator,cn=users,dc=rallencorp,dc=com
strScriptPath = "<ScriptName>" ' e.g., login.vbs
' ------ END CONFIGURATION ---------
set objUser = GetObject("LDAP://" & strUserDN)
objUser.Put "scriptPath", strScriptPath
objUser.SetInfo
WScript.Echo "Login script set for " & objUser.Name
```

Discussion

A login script can be a Windows batch file (*.bat* extension) or anything supported by Windows Scripting Host on the system that runs the script. By default, this includes VBScript and JScript.

The login script setting you configure in a user's profile must contain the name of the script and the relative path from the NETLOGON share. When a user (with a local user account) logs into a system, a check is done to see if there is a login script defined for that user—let's say that *login.vbs* has been configured. The system then attempts to run *localhost**NETLOGON**login.vbs* using the credentials of the user. The default location for the NETLOGON share is *%Systemroot%\System32\Repl\Imports\Scripts*, but this path doesn't exist on member or workgroup servers. You can either create that directory structure and a NETLOGON share pointing to it, or you can use another directory. In fact, if you have your scripts in a directory called *c:\Scripts*, you can create the NETLOGON share pointing to that and forgo creating the *Repl\Imports\Scripts* directory. You can also create subdirectories under your main NETLOGON folder. If the NETLOGON share is pointing to *c:\Scripts* and I created a subdirectory under that called *Local*, then I'd need to configure my local user's login script setting to be *Local\login.vbs*.

The same logic applies to domain controllers; except that by default, the NETLOGON share already exists and points to *%SystemRoot%\sysvol\<DomainName>\Scripts*. When you add scripts to that directory, they replicate out to all domain controllers in the domain *<DomainName>* using the File Replication Service (FRS).

See Also

MS KB 258286 (HOW TO: Assign a Logon Script to a Profile for a Local User in Windows 2000) and MS KB 315245 (How to Assign a Logon Script to a Profile for a Local User)

5.5   Running a Task via Group Policy

Problem

You want to configure Group Policy so that a task runs at system startup or shutdown or when a user logs on or off.

Solution

Using a graphical user interface

1. Open the Group Policy Management Console (*gpmc.msc*).
2. In the left pane, browse to the Group Policy Object you want to edit.
3. Right-click on it and select **Edit**. This will launch the Group Policy Object Editor.
4. If you want a task to run during user logon or logoff:
   a. Expand User **Configuration** → **Windows Settings** and click on the **Scripts** icon.
   b. In the right pane, double-click on **Logon** to configure a script to run at user logon or double-click **Logoff** to configure a script to run at user logoff.

If you want a task to run during system startup or shutdown:

  a. Expand **Computer Configuration → Windows Settings** and click on the **Scripts** icon.

  b. In the right pane, double-click on **Startup** to configure a script to run at system start or double-click **Shutdown** to configure a script to run at system shutdown.

5. Click the **Add** button.

6. Fill in **Script Name** and **Script Parameters** and click **OK**.

7. Click **OK**.

Discussion

You have two options for where you can store the scripts or commands you run via group policy. One option is to specify a UNC path to the script (this could reference a remote file server), in the **Script Name** field. The key here is that all users that the Group Policy applies to must have at least read-only access to the script with their domain account. The second method is to copy the script to the folder within the Group Policy template on the file system of a domain controller (you can see this by clicking **Browse** on the **Add** screen.) If you do this, the script will be copied automatically via the File Replication Service (FRS) to all domain controllers in the domain. This is the more efficient option in terms of client performance. If you use a UNC path, the client has to access the file on a remote server, which may not be geographically close to it.

And as I described in Recipe 5.4, scripts specified in Group Policy can be a Windows batch file (*.bat* extension) or anything supported by Windows Scripting Host on the system that runs the script. By default, this includes VBScript and JScript.

 With a startup script, the credentials of the computer account are used when running the script. With a login script, the credentials of the user are used.

See Also

MS KB 198642 (Overview of Logon, Logoff, Startup, and Shutdown Scripts in Windows 2000) and MS KB 322241 (HOW TO: Assign Scripts in Windows 2000)

5.6   Listing Automatic Tasks

Problem

You want to find the tasks that run during system startup or user logon. This is interesting to check, especially after you've installed new software, to see what tasks and applications are started automatically. This often helps me identify applications that configured to run automatically without my knowledge (e.g., spyware).

Solution

Using a graphical user interface

The Sysinternals *Autoruns* utility displays all registry- and file-based entries that cause tasks to be run at system startup or user logon. Run the following from a command line or **Start → Run**:

```
> autoruns
```

You can open Registry Editor or Windows Explorer to the specific location that defines a task by right-clicking the task and selecting **Jump To**. You can delete a task by right-clicking it and selecting **Delete**.

Discussion

In Recipe 5.3, I described some of the Registry keys you can configure to make tasks run at user log on, but as you can see with Autoruns, there are many more available that can do the same thing. Figure 5-2 shows the Autoruns screen, which has a listing of all of the Registry keys, files, and folders that cause a task to run automatically.

5.7   Scheduling a Task

Problem

You want to schedule a task to run at a certain time or periodically.

Solution

Using a graphical user interface

1. From the Control Panel, open the Scheduled Tasks applet.
2. Double-click **Add Scheduled Task**.
3. Click **Next**.
4. Select the program you want to schedule to run.
5. Type a name for the task, select the frequency in which to run it, and click **Next**.
6. Enter the username and password of the user the task should run as and click **Next**.
7. If you want to go back and modify any of the settings for the task, check the box beside **Open advanced properties** and click **Finish**.

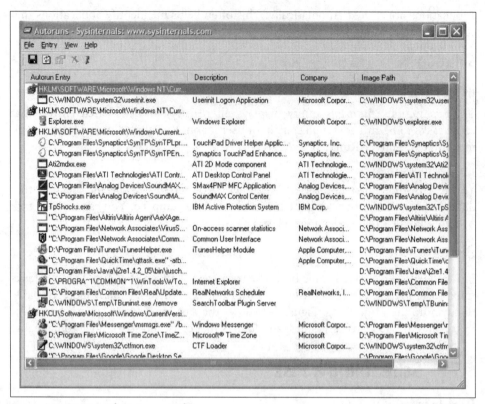

Figure 5-2. Sysinternals Autoruns utility

Using a command-line interface

On Windows Server 2003 or Windows XP, you can use the *schtasks.exe* command to schedule a task. The following command creates a task to run weekly at 1:00 AM:

```
> schtasks /create /SC WEEKLY /TN "Disk Space Checker" /TR "c:\perl\bin\perl.exe
c:\scripts\diskchecker.pl" /ST 01:00
```

On Windows 2000, you can use the *at.exe* command to schedule tasks. This command is functionally equivalent to the previous *schtasks.exe* example:

```
> at 01:00 /next:Sunday "c:\perl\bin\perl.exe c:\scripts\diskchecker.pl"
```

The *at* command is available on Windows Server 2003 as well, but you are better off using *schtasks*.

Using VBScript

```
' This code schedules a task to run every Sunday at 1:30AM.

const MON = 1
const TUE = 2
```

```
const WED = 4
const THU = 8
const FRI = 16
const SAT = 32
const SUN = 64

' ------ SCRIPT CONFIGURATION ------
strComputer  = "."
strCommand   = "c:\perl\bin\perl.exe c:\scripts\diskchecker.pl"
strStartTime = "********013000.000000-240"  ' 01:30 EDT
                'YYYYMMDDHHMMSS.MMMMMM-/+TZO
boolRepeat   = TRUE  ' Repeat the task periodically
intWeekDay   = SUN   ' Repeat task every Sunday
intMonthDay  = ""    ' Set this if you want the task to repeat monthly
boolInteract = FALSE ' Do not interact with the desktop
' ------ END CONFIGURATION ---------
set objWMI = GetObject("winmgmts:\\" & strComputer & "")
set objNewTask = objWMI.Get("Win32_ScheduledJob")
intRC = objNewTask.Create(strCommand,   _
                          strstartTime, _
                          boolRepeat,   _
                          intWeekDay,   _
                          intMonthDay,  _
                          boolInteract, _
                          intJobID)
if intRC <> 0 then
   Wscript.Echo "Error creating task: " & intRC
else
   WScript.Echo "Successfully scheduled task."
   WScript.Echo "JobID: " & intJobID
end if
```

Discussion

Recipes 5.3–5.5 describe how to set up tasks to run when a user logs on or off, or the system starts up or shuts down, but if you want to schedule a job to run at a specific time, you'll need use the Task Scheduler service. The Task Scheduler service is similar to cron on Unix; it allows you to schedule jobs using a variety of time-based criteria. You can run a job only once, once a week, every Monday and Tuesday night, etc.

The Task Scheduler service runs under the LocalSystem account by default. That means that scheduled tasks will have full access to the local system, but if the job needs to access any network resources, it won't have sufficient permissions. In this case, you can do one of two things. You can either run the Task Scheduler service under a different set of credentials (see Recipe 7.4) or you can set a user account and password the task should run as. The Scheduled Tasks applet lets you set the user account and password by entering the account name beside the **Run** as field and clicking the **Set Password** button. You can do the same thing using the *schtasks.exe* utility by specifying the /RP and /RU options. You can get more information on this by running schtasks /create /? from a command line.

Often I find that after I create a new scheduled task, I want to run it once to make sure it does what I expect. You can force a scheduled task to run immediately in the Scheduled Tasks applet by right-clicking it and selecting **Run**. Likewise, with the *schtasks* utility you can do the same using the /Run option. Here is an example:

```
> schtasks /Run /TN "Disk Space Checker"
```

With the *at.exe* command, you can create scheduled tasks, but they are a little different and less flexible than the ones you create using *schtasks* or the Scheduled Tasks applet. You cannot create a task using *at* that relies on alternate credentials like you can *schtasks*. Also, scheduled tasks created using *schtasks* cannot be displayed or modified using *at*. Another difference is that *at* tasks are represented by a number (id) that is automatically generated when you create the task; whereas with *schtasks*, you can assign a name to a given task.

Win32_ScheduledJob represents *at* jobs, so it is not possible to set alternate credentials when creating a new task with it. And if you query for all Win32_ScheduledJob objects, you are going to get only the jobs created with the at command or Win32_ScheduledJob class, not necessarily all the scheduled tasks.

See Also

Recipes 5.8, 5.9, and 7.4

5.8   Deleting a Scheduled Task

Problem

You want to delete a scheduled task.

Solution

Using a graphical user interface

1. From the Control Panel, open the Scheduled Task applet.
2. Right-click on the target task and select **Delete**.
3. Click **Yes** to confirm.

Using a command-line interface

On Windows Server 2003, you can use the *schtasks.exe* command to delete a task. The following command deletes the task named At1:

```
> schtasks /delete /tn At1
```

On Windows 2000, you need to use the *at.exe* command. The following command deletes the job associated with ID 3:

```
> at 3 /delete
```

Using VBScript

```
' This code deletes a scheduled task.
' ------ SCRIPT CONFIGURATION ------
intJobID = <JID>                    ' e.g., 1452
strComputer = "<ServerName>"    ' e.g., dns01
' ------ END CONFIGURATION ---------
set objWMI = GetObject("winmgmts:\\" & strComputer & "\root\cimv2")
Set objInstance = objWMI.Get("Win32_ScheduledJob.JobID=" & intJobID)
intRC = objInstance.Delete
if intRC <> 0 then
   Wscript.Echo "Failure deleting task id: " & intJobID
else
   Wscript.Echo "Sucessfully deleted task id: " & intJobID
end if
```

Discussion

Using a graphical user interface

The only downside is that you can't use this applet to delete a task on a remote system. However, you can still delete scheduled tasks on a remote machine. By default, a Scheduled Tasks share is created on all Windows 2000 and Windows Server 2003 servers, which contains the job files for each scheduled task. Simply browse to \\<SeverName>\Scheduled Tasks and you should see the list of scheduled tasks on that server (if you have administrator privileges). From here you can right-click a task and select Delete.

Using a command-line interface

In the command-line solutions, you need to know the task name (for *schtasks*) or the job ID (for *at*) in order to delete a task. Unless you know it off the top of your head, more than likely you'll need to query the current scheduled tasks to find the name or ID of the one you want to delete. See Recipe 5.9 for more on how to do that.

Using VBScript

You can write a script to delete all scheduled tasks by combining the code in Recipe 5.9 with this code.

See Also

Recipes 5.7, 5.9, and MS KB 310424 (HOW TO: Work with Scheduled Tasks on Remote Computers in Windows XP)

5.9   Listing the Scheduled Tasks

Problem

You want to view the list of scheduled tasks on a server.

Solution

Using a graphical user interface

From the Control Panel, open the Scheduled Task applet.

Using a command-line interface

On Windows Server 2003, the following command lists the scheduled tasks on server *dc01*:

```
> schtasks /query /s dc01
```

To get detailed information about each tasks, run the following command:

```
> schtasks /query /s dc01 /v /fo list
```

On Windows 2000, the following command lists the scheduled *at* tasks on server *dc01*:

```
> at \\dc01
```

Using VBScript

```
' This code lists the scheduled AT tasks on a computer.
' ------ SCRIPT CONFIGURATION ------
strComputer = "<ServerName>"
' ------ END CONFIGURATION ---------
set objWMI = GetObject("winmgmts:\\" & strComputer & "\root\cimv2")
set colScheduledJobs = objWMI.ExecQuery("Select * from Win32_ScheduledJob")
for each objJob in colScheduledJobs
    WScript.Echo "Job ID: " & objJob.JobID
    for each objProp in objJob.Properties_
        WScript.Echo "  " & objProp.Name & ": " & objProp.Value
    next
next
```

Discussion

Another quick way to view the scheduled tasks on a server is to simply browse the Scheduled Tasks share point on the server (*\\<SeverName>\Scheduled Tasks*). When you create a scheduled task, a job file is created that contains the settings for the task, which is placed in *%SystemRoot%\Tasks*. This directory is shared out as *Scheduled Tasks*. Unfortunately, the job files are stored in a binary format, so you cannot simply create or modify them with a text editor. You can, however, copy and paste jobs between servers. If you want to copy a job from ServerA to ServerB, open the Scheduled Tasks share point on both servers, right-click on the target job on ServerA and select Copy, then paste it into the *Scheduled Tasks* share of ServerB. Make sure any localized settings in the task are modified on ServerB after the copy is complete.

See Also

Recipes 5.7, 5.8, and MS KB 310424 (HOW TO: Work with Scheduled Tasks on Remote Computers in Windows XP)

CHAPTER 6

Processes

6.0 Introduction

Processes are a fundamental component of the Windows operating system. Anything you do on a system, whether it is deleting a file, starting a service, or writing text in Notepad, has a process behind it. Since processes are so important, it is critical that administrators understand how to manage, monitor, and troubleshoot them.

Processes use system resources, such as CPU and memory, in order to run. But not all processes are created equal. Some use more resources than others and often you'll run into situations where you need to identify processes that are using more resources than they should, which may make it difficult for other processes to do work. Processes also frequently open files, DLLs, and Registry keys and values. These resources are known as *handles* and often when a process has one open, no other process can modify or delete the resource. This can make it problematic if you need, for example, to rename a file that a process has locked.

In Appendix E, I include a list of the default processes used in Windows. There are several processes that start by default whenever a Windows server boots. Any applications you've installed that run at system startup will also have one or more processes running, all without you doing a thing. It is for this reason that you need to be able to create, query, suspend, and terminate processes on demand or else it is very easy for you to lose control over how your system performs.

In this chapter, I'll review how to identify process-related issues and cover many of the process-related tasks you should be familiar with. Now you may not need to use some of these tasks, but it is important to understand what is possible so if you run into a certain situation where, for example, you need to suspend a process, you know how to do it.

Using a Graphical User Interface

When it comes to the GUI, there are only two tools you need to be familiar with to manage processes. Task Manager (*taskmgr.exe*) is a native Windows tool that lets you view and kill any running applications or processes, and lets you view the performance of processes including CPU and memory utilization. Task Manager was updated in Windows Server 2003 to include a new Networking tab and Users tab. The Networking tab lets you view the current network activity of the system (although it doesn't show network information by process). The Users tab lets you see which users are currently logged on and lets you disconnect or log them off.

 You can type the **Ctrl-Shift-Esc** sequence to launch Task Manager quickly.

The other tool is Process Explorer (*procexp.exe*) from Sysinternals, and it is very similar to Task Manager except it provides much more process management functionality. It lets you view all the associated handles and DLLs of a process and even lets you search for specific processes, handles, and DLLs. Neither tool lets you manage processes on a remote server. To do that, you'll need to use one of the available command-line tools, of which there are many.

Using a Command-Line Interface

There are several process-related command-line tools, many of them from Sysinternals. Windows 2000 didn't provide any good process management utilities natively, but there were a few in the Resource Kit. In Windows XP and Windows Server 2003, Microsoft added the *tasklist* and *taskkill* utilities, which are installed with Windows and are very powerful. For advanced process manipulation and query tools, look no farther than Sysinternals. See Table 6-1 for a complete list of command-line tools used in this chapter along with where they can be found and what Recipes they are used in.

Table 6-1. Command-line tools used in this chapter

Tool	Windows Server 2003	Windows 2000	Recipes
handle	Sysinternals	Sysinternals	6.11
listdlls	Sysinternals	Sysinternals	6.9
netstat	%SystemRoot%\system32	%SystemRoot%\system32	6.12
netstatp	Sysinternals	Sysinternals	6.12
portqry	MS KB 310099	MS KB 310099	6.12
pslist	Sysinternals	Sysinternals	6.4, 6.5, 6.8
pskill	Sysinternals	Sysinternals	6.3, 6.14
pssuspend	Sysinternals	Sysinternals	6.2

Table 6-1. Command-line tools used in this chapter (continued)

Tool	Windows Server 2003	Windows 2000	Recipes
taskkill	*%SystemRoot%\system32*	N/A	6.3, 6.14
tasklist	*%SystemRoot%\system32*	N/A	6.4, 6.5, 6.6, 6.7, 6.13
tlist	N/A	Resource Kit Supplement 1	6.5, 6.6
top	N/A	Resource Kit Supplement 1	6.4
wmic	*%SystemRoot%\system32*	N/A	6.1, 6.4, 6.7

Using VBScript

The `Win32_Process` WMI class represents individual processes and is the only class I use extensively in this chapter. With it, you can create, terminate, and set the priority of a process. Additionally, you can get very detailed information about each process using the properties of `Win32_Process` objects. For your convenience, I've included the complete list of methods and properties available with `Win32_Process` in Tables 6-2 and 6-3.

Table 6-2. Win32_Process methods

Name	Description
AttachDebugger	Launches the registered debugger for the process.
Create	Creates a new process.
GetOwner	Returns the user name that is running the process.
GetOwnerSid	Returns the user security identifier (SID) that is running the process.
SetPriority	Changes the priority of the process.
Terminate	Kills the process.

Table 6-3. Win32_Process properties

Name	Description
Caption	Name of the process executable (e.g., notepad.exe).
CommandLine	Command line used to start the process.
CreationDate	Date the process was initially executed.
CSName	Name of the computer running the process.
Description	Name of the process executable (e.g., notepad.exe).
ExecutablePath	Path to the process executable.
Handle	Process ID (PID) of the process.
HandleCount	Total number of handles currently open by the process.
KernelModeTime	The amount of time (in 100 nanosecond units) the process has spent in kernel mode.
MaximumWorkingSetSize	Maximum working set size of the process.
MinimumWorkingSetSize	Minimum working set size of the process.
Name	Name of the process executable (e.g., notepad.exe).

Table 6-3. Win32_Process properties (continued)

Name	Description
OtherOperationCount	Number of I/O operations performed by the process that were neither read nor write operations.
OtherTransferCount	Amount of data transferred (in bytes) by the process that were neither read nor write operations.
PageFaults	Number of total page faults the process has generated.
PageFileUsage	Amount of page file space (in kilobytes) that the process is using.
ParentProcessId	Process ID (PID) of the parent process.
PeakPageFileUsage	Peak amount of page file space (in kilobytes) that the process has used.
PeakVirtualSize	Peak virtual address space (in bytes) that the process has used.
PeakWorkingSetSize	The peak working set of a process (in kilobytes).
Priority	Current priority of the process ranging from 0 to 31 (0 is the lowest and 31 is the highest).
PrivatePageCount	Number of pages allocated to the process.
ProcessId	Process ID (PID) of the process.
QuotaNonPagedPoolUsage	Quota usage of nonpaged pool for the process.
QuotaPagedPoolUsage	Quota usage of paged pool for the process.
QuotaPeakNonPagedPoolUsage	Quota usage of peak nonpaged pool for the process.
QuotaPeakPagedPoolUsage	Quota usage of peak paged pool for the process.
ReadOperationCount	Number of read operations performed by the process.
ReadTransferCount	Amount of data read (in bytes) by the process.
SessionId	Session ID that initiated the process.
TerminationDate	Date the process was terminated. A handle to the process must be held open in order to get this.
ThreadCount	Number of threads the process has opened.
UserModeTime	The amount of time (in 100 nanosecond units) the process has spent in user mode.
VirtualSize	Current size of the virtual address space (in bytes) that a process is using.
WorkingSetSize	Amount of memory (in bytes) used for the working set of the process.
WriteOperationCount	Number of write operations performed by the process.
WriteTransferCount	Amount of data written (in bytes) by the process.

Another process-related WMI class that may be of interest to you is Win32_ProcessStartup. While I don't cover it in this book, you may find it useful if you need control over how processes are created. You can pass an instance of the Win32_ProcessStartup class as a parameter when you invoke the Win32_Process.Create method. It allows you to specify various window settings and the priority of the new process. Search for Win32_ProcessStartup at *http://msdn.microsoft.com/* for more information.

6.1   Setting the Priority of a Process

Problem

You want to raise or lower the priority of a process. This is beneficial if you want to boost a CPU-starved process or limit a process that is hogging the CPU.

Solution

Using a graphical user interface

1. Open Windows Task Manager (*taskmgr.exe*).
2. Click on the **Processes** tab.
3. If you do not see the process you want to set, be sure the box beside **Show processes from all users** is checked.
4. Right-click on the target process, select **Set Priority**, and select the desired priority.

You can also accomplish the same task using the Sysinternals Process Explorer (*procexp.exe*) tool: right-click on the process and select **Set Priority**.

Using a command-line interface

With the *start* command, you can set the priority of a process when you initially run it. The following example shows how to create a process with a *high* priority:

```
> start /HIGH <ProgramPath>
```

The other valid priority options include /LOW, /NORMAL, /REALTIME, /ABOVENORMAL, and /BELOWNORMAL.

Using VBScript

```
' This code sets the priority of a process

Const NORMAL        = 32
Const IDLE          = 64
Const HIGH_PRIORITY = 128
Const REALTIME      = 256
Const BELOW_NORMAL  = 16384
Const ABOVE_NORMAL  = 32768

' ------ SCRIPT CONFIGURATION ------
strComputer = "."
intPID      = 3280          ' set this to the PID of the target process
intPriority = ABOVE_NORMAL  ' Set this to one of the constants above
' ------ END CONFIGURATION ---------
WScript.Echo "Process PID: " & intPID
set objWMIProcess = GetObject("winmgmts:\\" & strComputer & _
                    "\root\cimv2:Win32_Process.Handle='" & intPID & "'")
WScript.Echo "Process name: " & objWMIProcess.Name
```

```
intRC = objWMIProcess.SetPriority(intPriority)
if intRC = 0 Then
    Wscript.Echo "Successfully set priority."
else
    Wscript.Echo "Could not set priority. Error code: " & intRC
end if
```

Discussion

Windows 2000 and Windows Server 2003 use a priority-driven, preemptive scheduling system. This means that processes are given priorities and those with higher priorities get more CPU time and subsequently, run quicker. This is useful for administrators to know because in certain situations, it can be advantageous to play with the priorities of processes to get the desired result from your system. For example, if you find a process that is pegging the CPU on a system, if you are able to run Task Manager, you can lower the priority of that process, which should help you launch other processes or applications to diagnose and troubleshoot the badly behaving process. Another way to tackle this problem is to suspend the process, which I describe in Recipe 6.2.

Windows supports six priority classes. The following is a list of the classes and their corresponding numeric value:

Realtime (24)
> This is the highest priority class. Be extremely careful when setting this priority because it preempts all other non-realtime processes, including operating system processes. A realtime process can interrupt normal functioning of the computer, including mouse and keyboard I/O and disk read/writes. Note that realtime priority does not make a program run in realtime, it simply gives as much CPU time as the program can use and is available.

> Windows operating systems are not considered real-time operating systems because they do not (and cannot) give performance guarantees.

High (13)
> This priority class indicates that the process needs to perform time-sensitive functions that must be executed immediately upon being called. An example application that uses this priority is Task Manager, which needs a higher priority than normal processes so you can kill any that are CPU bound. Be careful when setting this priority class because a high priority process that is CPU bound can tie up the system indefinitely.

Above Normal (10)
> This is an intermediate priority class that is above Normal but below High.

Normal (8)
> This is the default priority class assigned to applications that do not require any special scheduling needs.

Below Normal (6)
> This is an intermediate priority class that is above Idle but below Normal.

Idle or Low (4)
> This priority indicates that the process only runs when the system is idle. Screen saver is an example application that utilizes this priority.

To view the current priority of all processes, run the following command:

```
> wmic process get name,processid,priority
```

You can also see the priority of processes in *pslist* output (the `Pri` column).

See Also

Recipe 6.2, MS KB 110853 (PRB: Can't Increase Process Priority), and MS KB 193846 (HOWTO: Modify the Process Priority of a Shelled Application)

6.2   Suspending a Process

Problem

You want to suspend a process from running. This is helpful if you want to temporarily stop an application from running, perhaps due to high CPU consumption, but you don't want to kill it. This can give you an opportunity to launch further diagnostic utilities to troubleshoot the process.

Solution

Using a graphical user interface

Open the Sysinternals Process Explorer tool (*procexp.exe*). To suspend a process, right-click on the target process and select **Suspend**. To resume a process, right-click on the target process and select **Resume**.

Using a command-line interface

The following command suspends a process:

```
> pssuspend <PID>
```

Replace `<PID>` with the process ID of the target process.

The following command resumes a suspended process:

```
> pssuspend -r <PID>
```

Using VBScript

Currently, no scripting API supports suspending processes. However, you can use the SuspendThread and ResumeThread functions that are defined in *kernel.lib* if you are using a high-level language such as Visual Basic or C++.

Discussion

Applications are much better behaved these days than they were a few years ago, but that still doesn't mean you won't see one from time to time peg the CPU on a system and render it virtually useless. If this happens on a remote system, it can be difficult to even use Terminal Services to access the machine. So what can you do? Well, if you can find out which process is causing the problem—perhaps by using one of the methods in Recipe 6.4—you can use *pssuspend* to remotely suspend it. You can also specify alternate credentials using the -u (user) and -p (password) options. If you specify -u without -p, it will prompt you to enter the password (this is the more secure way to do it). Here is an example command line that does this:

```
> pssuspend \\jamison -u rallen notepad.exe
```

See Also

Recipe 6.4

6.3   Killing a Process

Problem

You want to terminate a process. Even though Windows has come a long way in the past 10 years, the operating system can't prevent buggy or poorly written applications from becoming unresponsive.

Solution

Using a graphical user interface

1. Open the Windows Task Manager (*taskmgr.exe*).
2. Click on the **Processes** tab.
3. If you do not see the process you want to set, be sure the box beside **Show processes from all users** is checked.
4. Right-click on the target process, select **End Process**, and select the desired priority.

You can also accomplish the same task using the Sysinternals Process Explorer (*procexp.exe*) tool by right-clicking the process and selecting **Kill Process**.

Using a command-line interface

The following command kills a process by PID:

```
> taskkill -pid <PID>
```

And this command kills a process by name on a remote server:

```
> taskkill /s <ServerName> -im <ProcessName>
```

Use the /f option to forcefully kill the process.

The *pskill.exe* utility works in a very similar manner. Here are two examples:

```
> pskill <PID>
> pskill \\<ServerName> <ProcessName>
```

Using VBScript

```
' This code terminates the specified process.
' ------ SCRIPT CONFIGURATION ------
intPID = 2560    ' PID of the process to terminate
strComputer = "."
' ------ END CONFIGURATION ---------
WScript.Echo "Process PID: " & intPID
set objWMIProcess = GetObject("winmgmts:\\" & strComputer & _
                    "\root\cimv2:Win32_Process.Handle='" & intPID & "'")
WScript.Echo "Process name: " & objWMIProcess.Name
intRC = objWMIProcess.Terminate( )
if intRC = 0 Then
   Wscript.Echo "Successfully killed process."
else
   Wscript.Echo "Could not kill process. Error code: " & intRC
end if
```

Discussion

Manually killing processes is not something you should be in the habit of doing, but it is a necessary evil of system administration. Be selective about forcibly killing a process, because it will also terminate any child processes in an ungraceful manner and can leave lingering remnants of the process in memory, which may cause problems if you attempt to restart the process later.

There are some processes that you won't be able to manually terminate. Generally this applies to system-level process, such as *lsass*.

6.4   Viewing the Running Processes

Problem

You want to see all processes that are currently running on a system.

Solution

Using a graphical user interface

1. Open the Windows Task Manager (*taskmgr.exe*).
2. Click on the **Processes** tab.

You can also accomplish the same task using the Sysinternals Process Explorer (*procexp.exe*) tool.

Using a command-line interface

There are several options for viewing the running processes via the command line. You can use *tasklist.exe* on Windows XP and Windows Server 2003 (use the /S option to target a remote system):

```
> tasklist
```

Another Windows XP and Windows Server 2003 tool that you can use to get a process list is *wmic* as shown here (use the /node: option to target a remote system):

```
> wmic process list brief
```

The Sysinternals *pslist.exe* utility is available for Windows Server 2003 or Windows 2000 and can be run against a remote host:

```
> pslist \\<ServerName>
```

There is also the *top.exe* command, which is available in the Windows 2000 Resource Kit. It provides a continually updated view of the top running process (by CPU):

```
> top
```

 You can do something similar to *top* with *pslist* by specifying the -s option.

Using VBScript

```
' This code displays the running processes on the target computer.
' ------ SCRIPT CONFIGURATION ------
strComputer = "."  ' Can be a hostname or "." to target local host
' ------ END CONFIGURATION ---------
set objWMI = GetObject("winmgmts:\\" & strComputer & "\root\cimv2")
set colProcesses = objWMI.InstancesOf("Win32_Process")
```

```
for each objProcess In colProcesses
    WScript.Echo objProcess.Name & " (" & objProcess.ProcessID & ")"
next
```

Discussion

Sometimes it is difficult to associate an application (e.g., Internet Explorer) with its underlying process (e.g., *iexplore.exe*). In each of the command-line solutions, only the process name will be shown, which may be completely different from the name of the application. With Internet Explorer, it is pretty easy to figure out that *iexplore.exe* is probably the underlying process, but how can you tell for sure? One way is to look at Sysinternals Process Explorer. It displays a Description field that generally contains the application name of the process. Alternatively, you can specify the /v option with the *tasklist* command, which displays the Window Title field for each process. This typically includes the name of the application. Here is an example command you can run:

```
> tasklist /v /fo list
```

Unfortunately, there you can't retrieve the Window Title using the Win32_Process class.

6.5   Searching Processes

Problem

You want to find processes that match certain criteria. This is useful if you want to find processes that have a certain process name or that are utilizing a certain amount of memory.

Solution

Using a graphical user interface

1. Open the Sysinternals Process Explorer tool (*procexp.exe*).
2. From the menu, select **Find → Find Handle**.
3. Type the name of a process or handle to match (substring searches are allowed) and click the **Search** button.

Using a command-line interface

The Windows Server 2003 *tasklist.exe* command is very flexible. It provides several options for searching processes. This command searches for all *iexplore* (Internet Explorer) processes being run by the Administrator user:

```
> tasklist /FI "IMAGENAME eq iexplore*"  /FI "USERNAME eq Administrator"
```

You can also use *tasklist.exe* to perform searches based on PID, memory usage, CPU time, and other attributes. The following command finds all processes running on host *dhcp01* that are consuming more than 10 MB of memory:

```
> tasklist /S dhcp01 /FI "MEMUSAGE gt 10240"
```

On Windows 2000, you can use the *tlist.exe* (or *pslist.exe*) command in combination with *findstr.exe* to find processes. This returns all CMD processes:

```
> tlist | findstr cmd.exe
```

Using VBScript

```
' This code finds the processes that have a memory usage greater
' than the specified amount.  To search on different criteria,
' modify the WQL used in the ExecQuery call.
' ------ SCRIPT CONFIGURATION ------
strComputer = "."
intMaxMemKB = 1024 * 10000
' ------ END CONFIGURATION ---------
set objWMI = GetObject("winmgmts:\\" & strComputer & "\root\cimv2")
set colProcesses = objWMI.ExecQuery("Select * from Win32_Process " & _
                              " Where workingsetsize > " & intMaxMemKB )
WScript.Echo "Process, Size (in KB)"
for each objProcess in colProcesses
    WScript.Echo objProcess.Name & ", " & objProcess.WorkingSetSize / 1024
next
```

Discussion

Sometimes it is necessary to take a snapshot of the current status of processes in a system and have a means of documenting that status. Using the command-line and scripting solutions provides a mechanism for generating a snapshot containing custom information.

6.6   Finding the Services Run from a Process

Problem

You want to find the services being run from a process. In some cases, multiple services may be run from a single process.

Solution

Using a graphical user interface

1. Open the Sysinternals Process Explorer tool (*procexp.exe*).

2. Double-click on the process you want to view.

3. If there are services being run from the process, a **Services** tab will be available from the process properties window.

Using a command-line interface

The following command displays the services that are run from the *lsass.exe* process:

```
> tasklist /svc /FI "IMAGENAME eq lsass.exe"
```

You can also use the *tlist.exe* command from the Windows 2000 Support Tools to show similar information:

```
> tlist -s | findstr Svcs: | findstr lsass.exe
```

Using VBScript

```
' This code displays the services run from the specified process.
' ------ SCRIPT CONFIGURATION ------
strComputer = "."
strProcess = "lsass.exe"   ' name of process
' ------ END CONFIGURATION ---------
set objWMI = GetObject("winmgmts: \\" & strComputer & "\root\cimv2")
set colProcess = objWMI.ExecQuery("Select ProcessID from Win32_Process " & _
                                  " Where Name = '" & strProcess & "'" )
for each objProcess in colProcess
   intPID = objProcess.ProcessID
next

WScript.Echo "Services run from process: " & strProcess
set colProcesses = objWMI.ExecQuery("Select Name from Win32_service " & _
                                    " Where ProcessID = " & intPID)
for each objProcess in colProcesses
   WScript.Echo "  " & objProcess.Name
next
```

Discussion

It is not uncommon for a single process to host multiple services. A good example of this is the *svchost.exe* process. Typically, you'll see several *svchost* processes running at any time on a system. That is because *svchost* is a generic process that is used by services that are run from dynamic link libraries (DLLs). If all of the code for a service is housed in a DLL, it still needs a process to accept and respond to SCM requests and handle other process management functions. *svchost* provides this functionality.

 This recipe shows you how to find all of the services that a particular process is responsible for; to find the reverse of this (i.e., the process a particular service is associated with), refer to Recipe 7.9.

See Also

MS KB 250320 (Description of Svchost.exe in Windows 2000) and MS KB 314056 (A description of Svchost.exe in Windows XP)

6.7 Viewing the Properties of a Process

Problem

You want to view the properties of a process. This includes the process executable path, command line, current working directory, parent process (if any), owner, and startup timestamp.

Solution

Using a graphical user interface

1. Open the Sysinternals Process Explorer tool (*procexp.exe*).
2. Double-click the process you want to view.
3. The **Image** tab contains process properties.

Some of this information can also be viewed using Windows Task Manager (*taskmgr.exe*). After starting *taskmgr.exe*, click on the **Processes** tab. Select **View →
Select Columns** from the menu, and check the boxes beside the properties you want to see.

Using a command-line interface

The *tasklist.exe* command can display a subset of the properties described in the Problem section. Here is an example that displays properties for a specific process:

```
> tasklist /v /FI "IMAGENAME eq <ProcessName>" /FO list
```

Using VBScript

```
' This code displays the properties of a process.
' ------ SCRIPT CONFIGURATION ------
intPID = 3280    ' PID of the target process
strComputer = "."
' ------ END CONFIGURATION ---------
WScript.Echo "Process PID: " & intPID
set objWMIProcess = GetObject("winmgmts:\\" & strComputer & _
                    "\root\cimv2:Win32_Process.Handle='" & intPID & "'")
WScript.Echo "Name: " & objWMIProcess.Name
WScript.Echo "Command line: " & ObjWMIProcess.CommandLine
WScript.Echo "Startup date: " & ObjWMIProcess.CreationDate
WScript.Echo "Description: " & ObjWMIProcess.Description
WScript.Echo "Exe Path: " & ObjWMIProcess.ExecutablePath
WScript.Echo "Parent Process ID: " & ObjWMIProcess.ParentProcessId
objWMIProcess.GetOwner strUser,strDomain
WScript.Echo "Owner: " & strDomain & "\" & strUser
```

Discussion

Another option from the command line is to use *wmic* to harness the power of WMI. You can retrieve all of the properties defined by the Win32_Process class (see Table 6-3) by running this simple command:

```
> wmic process list full
```

You can also limit the output to a single process. The following example retrieves the properties for the *snmp.exe* process:

```
> wmic process where name="snmp.exe" get /format:list
```

See Also

Recipe 6.1 for a list of Win32_Process properties

6.8   Viewing the Performance Statistics of a Process

Problem

You want to view the memory, I/O, and CPU statistics of a process. This is useful if you want to examine the resources a process is using. If you find that you are running low on memory on a particular system, it can often be attributed to a single process that has consumed a large amount. If you can terminate that process, the system should go back to a stable state.

Solution

Using a graphical user interface

1. Open the Sysinternals Process Explorer tool (*procexp.exe*).
2. Double-click the process you want to view.
3. The **Performance** tab contains the process properties.

This information can also be viewed using Windows Task Manager (*taskmgr.exe*). After starting *taskmgr.exe*, click on the **Processes** tab. Select **View → Select Columns** from the menu and check the boxes beside the properties you want to see. And for yet another way to trend out process performance metrics (using more granular metrics), open Performance Monitor and look at the Process object.

Using a command-line interface

The following command displays all of the performance metrics for a process:

```
> pslist -x <ProcessName>
```

Replace *<ProcessName>* with the name of the process without its extension. For example:

```
> pslist -x iexplore
```

Using VBScript

```
' This code displays the performance stats of a process.
' ------ SCRIPT CONFIGURATION ------
intPID = 3280  ' PID of target process
strComputer = "."
' ------ END CONFIGURATION ---------
WScript.Echo "Process PID: " & intPID
set objWMIProcess = GetObject("winmgmts:\\" & strComputer & _
                    "\root\cimv2:Win32_Process.Handle='" & intPID & "'")
arrProps = Array("Name", "KernelModeTime", "UserModeTime", _
                "MaximumWorkingSetSize", "MinimumWorkingSetSize", _
                "PageFaults", "PageFileUsage", "VirtualSize", _
                "WorkingSetSize", "PeakPageFileUsage", "PeakVirtualSize", _
                "PeakWorkingSetSize", "PrivatePageCount", _
                "QuotaNonPagedPoolUsage", "QuotaPagedPoolUsage", _
                "QuotaPeakNonPagedPoolUsage", "QuotaPeakPagedPoolUsage", _
                "ThreadCount")
for each strProp in arrProps
   WScript.Echo strProp & ": " & objWMIProcess.Properties_(strProp)
next
```

Discussion

If you need to get serious about analyzing performance statistics for one or more processes, you should consider using Performance Monitor (*perfmon.exe*). With the Process performance object (click the little + icon in the **System Monitor** and select Process under **Performance object**), you can graph a variety of metrics for individual processes or all of them together using the _Total instance.

Even if you don't want to use Performance Monitor to monitor processes, the tool provides some good information about process metrics, such as Working Set. Click the **Explain** button when you view the **Process** performance object, which will cause another dialog to appear that contains additional information about what each counter means. These counters are mostly the same ones as you'll find in Task Manager, *pslist*, and Win32_Process.

6.9 Viewing the DLLs Being Used by a Process

Problem

You want to view the DLLs being used by a process or find the processes using a specific DLL. This can come in handy if you need to update a DLL and want to find out which programs are actively using it, or if you are trying to delete a DLL, but cannot due to a lock on the file by a process that is using it.

Solution

Using a graphical user interface

To view the DLLs being used by a process, do the following:

1. Open the Sysinternals Process Explorer tool (*procexp.exe*).
2. From the menu, select **View** → **Lower Pane View** → **DLLs**.
3. Click on the process you want to view. In the bottom window, the list of DLLs being used by that process is displayed.

To view the processes using a specific DLL, do the following:

1. Open the Sysinternals Process Explorer tool (*procexp.exe*).
2. From the menu, select **Find** → **Find DLLs**.
3. Type the name of the DLL (partial string accepted) and click the **Search** button.

Using a command-line interface

To view the DLLs being used by a process, use the following command:

```
> listdlls <ProcessName>
```

To view the processes using a specific DLL, use the following command:

```
> listdlls -d <DLLName>
```

Using VBScript

There are no scripting interfaces available to get this information. To get it programmatically, you must use the Win32 API or .NET Framework, or shell out to the *listdlls* utility.

Discussion

Ever visited *DLL hell*? Things aren't as bad as they once were in the early days of Windows NT, but keeping track of DLL versions for certain applications can still be a pain. DLL hell was the term given to the problem where applications would overwrite DLLs with older or incompatible versions. This would cause applications to fail in unexpected ways. Starting with Windows 2000, this problem was reduced with the introduction of the Windows File Protection (WFP). Now, applications can't replace system DLLs—only system updates can, such as when you install a service pack or hotfix.

If you really want to dig down into a process and see what it is doing, check out Recipe 6.10 where I talk about viewing the APIs that a process calls. I'll also show you another way to view the DLLs loaded by a process.

See Also

MS KB 222193 (Description of the Windows File Protection Feature) and MS KB 247957 (SAMPLE: Using DUPS.exe to Resolve DLL Compatibility Problems)

6.10 Viewing the APIs Called by a Process

Problem

You want to view the application programming interfaces (APIs) that a particular process invokes while running. This is useful for application developers who need to troubleshoot programs, but it can also be useful to system administrators who want to dig into the internals of a troublesome application.

Solution

Using a graphical user interface

1. Open the API Monitoring tool (*apimon.exe*) from the Windows 2000 Resource Kit.

2. From the menu, select **File** → **Open** (or click the open folder icon).

3. Browse to the executable you want to monitor and click **OK**.

4. From the menu, select **Tools** → **Start Monitor** (or click the play button). This launches the selected application. Within the API Monitor screen there will be a **DLLs In Use** window and **API Counters** window. The API information will continue to be collected until you stop it.

5. From the menu, select **Tools** → **Stop Monitor** (or click the stop button).

Discussion

If you have any Unix experience, you may be familiar with the *truss* utility. With *truss*, you can view all the system calls and APIs that a particular process is calling. Having this capability can be extremely beneficial when you are trying to debug why a particular application is failing or not behaving correctly. API Monitor provides similar functionality on the Windows platform. It displays the DLLs loaded by the target process, each function it calls, the number of times it calls a function, and the amount of time it took for each function call to complete.

If the API Monitor is the kind of thing that gets you excited, then you'll want to take a look at the Dependency Walker (*depends.exe*) in the Support Tools, which provides even more information.

6.11   Viewing the Handles a Process Has Open

Problem

You want to view all the handles a process has open. This is handy if you want to find out all of the files and registry keys a particular process is using.

Solution

Using a graphical user interface

1. Open the Sysinternals Process Explorer tool (*procexp.exe*).
2. From the menu, select **View** → **View Handles**.
3. Click on the process you want to view. In the bottom window, the list of handles being used by that process will be displayed.

Using a command-line interface

To view all of the handles a process has open, use the following command:

```
> handle -a -p <ProcessName>
```

You can also search for a specific handle using the following command:

```
> handle <HandleName>
```

For example, if you want to find all processes that have the *c:\test* directory open, you would replace *<HandleName>* with *c:\test*.

Using VBScript

There are no scripting interfaces to get this information. To get it programmatically, you must use the Win32 API or .NET Framework, or shell out to the *handle* utility.

Discussion

Have you ever wanted to see all of the resources a particular process is using? Perhaps you have a new application or service and you want to see what files it touches, what registry keys it has open, what Windows stations it uses, etc. The lovely Process Explorer (and *handle.exe* command-line equivalent) can give you this and much more. The cool thing about Process Explorer is that it even lets you close a particular handle if you want to; from the bottom window simply right-click on the handle and select **Close Handle**. This is helpful if you are trying to delete a file or Registry key, but a process has a lock on it.

6.12 Viewing the Network Ports a Process Has Open

Problem

You want to view the network ports on which a process is communicating. This is useful if you want to see the type of traffic a particular process is generating.

Solution

Using a graphical user interface

1. Open the Sysinternals TCPView tool (*tcpview.exe*).

2. The complete list of processes and associated ports are displayed by default. New connections show up in green and terminating connections show up in red.

Using a command-line interface

The following command displays the open ports and the process ID of the process associated with the port. The -o option is new to *netstat.exe* in Windows XP and Windows Server 2003:

```
> netstat -o
```

The Sysinternals *netstatp.exe* command is similar to *netstat.exe*, except it displays the process name associated with each port:

```
> netstatp
```

And for yet another extremely useful port querying tool, check out *portqry.exe* (see MS KB 310099 for more information). With *portqry* you can get even more information than *netstatp*. Run this command to output all of the ports and their associated processes:

```
> portqry -local
```

That command also breaks port usage down by service (e.g., DnsCache). You can watch the port usage for a particular PID and log it to a file. The following command does this for PID 1234:

```
> portqry -wpid 1234 -wt 5 -l portoutput.txt -v
```

The -wt defines the watch time, which is how long *portqry* waits before examining the process again (the default is 60 seconds). The -v option is for verbose output.

Using VBScript

None of the scripting interfaces provide a way to access information about the ports a process has open. However, the *netstatp* tool comes with complete source that shows how to do it via IP Helper functions that can be directly accessed with a non-scripting language.

Discussion

Each connection to and from a client computer is associated with a process. This connection is also associated with a particular port. Most of the open ports you'll see will be numbered above 1024. This is because well-known ports use port numbers lower than 1024 so Windows dynamically allocates ports above that.

A connection has a state, which you'll see when running any of the utilities described in the solution. This state indicates the type of activity going on over the connection. Most of the connections you'll see are in the ESTABLISHED state, which simply means the connection is open and prepared to send or receive traffic. For a list of all the states, see Table 6-4.

Table 6-4. TCP connection states

State	Description
SYN_SEND	Indicates an active open of a connection
SYN_RECEIVED	Server received SYN from the client
ESTABLISHED	Client received server's SYN and session is established
LISTEN	Server is ready to accept a connection
FIN_WAIT_1	Indicates an active close of the connection
TIMED_WAIT	Client enters this state after an active close
CLOSE_WAIT	Indicates a passive close of the connection. Server just received first FIN from a client
FIN_WAIT_2	Client just received acknowledgment of its first FIN from the server
LAST_ACK	Server has sent its own FIN
CLOSED	Server received acknowledgment from client and closed the connection

See Also

MS KB 137984 (TCP Connection States and Netstat Output) and MS KB 310099 (Description of the Portqry.exe Command-Line Utility)

6.13   Script: Process Doctor

Have you ever wanted to know when a particular process terminates on a system? Perhaps an application is failing mysteriously and you find out about it only after a user complains. Or maybe you have an application that fails periodically and you want to start it up immediately after it fails. This is pretty easy to accomplish using both VBScript and the command line.

Using VBScript

With WMI and event handlers, process monitoring is straightforward. The following code monitors the *calc.exe* process, and as soon as it recognizes that it is no longer running, restarts it:

```
' ------ SCRIPT CONFIGURATION ------
strProcess = "calc.exe"  ' Image name of the process you want to monitor
strComputer = "."
' ------ END CONFIGURATION ---------
set objWMI = GetObject("winmgmts:\\" & strComputer & "\root\cimv2")
set colProcesses = objWMI.ExecNotificationQuery(_
                "select * from __instanceDeletionevent " _
            & " within 2 where TargetInstance isa 'Win32_Process' " _
            & " and TargetInstance.Name = '" & strProcess & "'")
do
    set objProcess = colProcesses.NextEvent
    WScript.Echo "Process " & strProcess & _
                " (" & objProcess.TargetInstance.ProcessID & ") terminated"
    intRC = objWMI.Get("Win32_Process").Create(strProcess, , , intProcessID)
    if intRC = 0 Then
        Wscript.Echo strProcess & " started. PID: " & intProcessID
    else
        Wscript.Echo strProcess & " did not start.  Error code: " & intRC
    end if
loop
```

The main method to note in this script is `ExecNotificationQuery`, which executes a WQL query and receives events that result from it. Let's break the query down. The select statement pulls all `__instanceDeletionEvent` objects:

```
"select * from __instanceDeletionEvent "
```

Anytime a process terminates, or a file is deleted, or a service is removed, that event is registered as a deletion event in WMI (`__instanceDeletionEvent`).[*] This is incredibly powerful. The select statement I used matches ALL deletion events, which isn't quite what we want. This is why the next statement is needed:

```
" within 2 where TargetInstance isa 'Win32_Process' "
```

`TargetInstance isa 'Win32_Process'` filters out all deletion events except those of type `Win32_Process`. The `within 2` statement informs WMI how often to check the system (in seconds) to see if anything new matches this query.

At this point, the query would match all terminating processes, so I restrict it to just the one we are interested in:

```
" and TargetInstance.Name = '" & strProcess & "'")
```

---

[*] Likewise, new instances of processes, files, services, etc., are captured as `__instanceCreationEvent` objects and anytime an instance is modified, it is registered as an `__instanceModificationEvent`.

In the case of `Win32_Process` instanceDeletionEvent objects, the `TargetInstance.Name` property equals the name of the process. So here I set that equal to the `strProcess` variable, which contains *calc.exe*.

After I've called `ExecNotificationQuery`, I am ready to enter a loop to start retrieving events. I used a do loop, which makes this script run until you kill it. The first line in the do loop invokes the `NextEvent` method. This is a synchronous call that waits until an event occurs before the script continues. If the *calc.exe* process never dies, the script never moves beyond this step. If it does catch the process terminating, it prints out that process's PID and creates a new instance of the process.

Using a Command-Line Interface

You can do the exact same thing as the VBScript solution using a command line. Here is the complete command:

```
> for /L %v in (1,1,40) do (tasklist /FI "IMAGENAME eq calc.exe" /FO CSV /NH |
findstr "calc.exe" || calc.exe) & sleep 15
```

Let's break this long command line down. The first part is a for loop that starts at 1 and goes to 40 by 1 (i.e., 1, 2, 3, 4 . . . 40). The loop counter is placed in the %v variable.

```
for /L %v in (1,1,40)
```

Next is the command to execute within the loop. The first part of the command simply runs the *tasklist.exe* utility and performs a search for the *calc.exe* process. The last two options tell *tasklist* to print the results (/FO) in a comma-separated list (CSV) and not to print any headers (/NH).

```
do (tasklist /FI "IMAGENAME eq calc.exe" /FO CSV /NH
```

If *calc.exe* is running, this command would produce this output:

```
"calc.exe","4156","Console","0","2,804 K"
```

Whereas if it is not running, it would produce this:

```
INFO: No tasks running with the specified criteria.
```

The second part of the command pipes the output from *tasklist* to the *findstr.exe* utility:

```
| findstr "calc.exe"
```

I do this because we need a way to determine if *calc.exe* is running. All we really want is for *tasklist* to produce some output if it is running and not to generate anything if it isn't. So this *findstr* command helps out by removing the INFO: No tasks . . . . output if *calc.exe* isn't running.

Now, if the *tasklist* and *findstr* commands do not generate any output, the next command executes:

```
|| calc.exe)
```

If they generate output, this command won't execute, which is exactly what we want. It will run *calc.exe* only if *calc.exe* isn't running.

After we've done all this work to determine if *calc.exe* is running and to start it otherwise, we need to take a breather. Remember, this whole thing is in a for loop that will run 40 times. If we didn't put some sort of break in it, it would run 40 consecutive times without a pause. This is where the next command comes into play:

```
& sleep 15
```

This pauses the whole command for 15 seconds. And since we are using a loop with 40 iterations, the whole command will run over a 10-minute period ($15 \times 40/60 = 10$ minutes). If you want this monitor to run for longer, simply change the number of seconds after the *sleep* command or the number of iterations in the for loop.

6.14 Script: Process Terminator

Have you ever wanted to prevent a process from running? Perhaps the process keeps starting and you haven't been able to find what is starting it. Or maybe you know what is causing the process to start, but you can't prevent it from happening. I called the script the Process Doctor because it tries to revive processes that die. In this recipe, I'll describe the opposite. The Process Terminator kills a certain process every time it tries to run.

Using VBScript

The code in this script is very similar to that of the Process Doctor. The primary difference is that instead of looking at instanceDeletionEvent objects, we are looking for instanceCreationEvent objects, that is, new instances of the *calc.exe* process. Here is the script:

```
' ------ SCRIPT CONFIGURATION ------
strProcess = "calc.exe"
strComputer = "."
' ------ END CONFIGURATION ---------

set objWMI = GetObject("winmgmts:\\" & strComputer & "\root\cimv2")
set colProcesses = objWMI.ExecNotificationQuery(_
                "select * from __instanceCreationEvent " _
            & " within 1 where TargetInstance isa 'Win32_Process' " _
            & " and TargetInstance.Name = '" & strProcess & "'")
do
    set objProcess = colProcesses.NextEvent
    WScript.Echo "Terminating process " & strProcess & _
            " (" & objProcess.TargetInstance.ProcessID & ")"
    objProcess.TargetInstance.Terminate
loop
```

Also, instead of creating a new instance of the process when a creation event is found, I terminate the process. For more on terminating process, see Recipe 6.3.

Using a Command-Line Interface

Just as with the Process Doctor, you can perform similar functionality to the Process Terminator using a command line. But fortunately, the command line in this case isn't quite as complicated. Here is the command-line version of the Process Terminator using the *taskkill.exe* command:

```
> for /L %v in (1,1,10) do taskkill /IM calc.exe /F /T & sleep 60
```

The first part is very similar to the Process Doctor command line. This is a for loop that iterates from 1 to 10 by 1's.

```
for /L %v in (1,1,10)
```

The *taskkill* command matches any process with an image name of *calc.exe* and forcefully terminates its process tree (/F and /T):

```
do taskkill /IM calc.exe /F /T
```

Lastly, we sleep for 60 seconds and start the next iteration of the loop:

```
& sleep 60
```

You can also do the same thing using the Sysinternals *pskill.exe* command:

```
> for /L %v in (1,1,10) do pskill calc.exe & sleep 60
```

CHAPTER 7

Services

7.0   Introduction

Windows services are nothing more than continually running processes that are controlled by the Service Control Manager (SCM). Instead of directly creating a service process, you (or the system itself) sends a start or stop message to the SCM, which takes care of starting or stopping the associated process. The DHCP Client provided with the Windows operating system is an example of a service. It is responsible for requesting and renewing DHCP requests (i.e., obtaining an IP address dynamically), and, interestingly, performing dynamic DNS registrations. After the system begins the boot-up process, the SCM starts the DHCP Client service, which kicks off a process that runs in the background to handle DHCP requests. You can stop the DHCP Client service via the Services snap-in, which causes the SCM to terminate the underlying DHCP Client process. If you start the service, the SCM starts the process.

Each service has a corresponding key in the Registry contained under HKEY_LOCAL_ MACHINE\SYSTEM\CurrentControlSet\Services. This stores basic configuration information about the service including service dependencies, the command line to execute to start the service, and startup type (automatic, manual, or disabled). You can find the associated registry key for a service by running the following command:

```
> sc getkeyname "<ServiceDisplayName>"
```

For example, this returns the key for the DHCP Client service:

```
> sc getkeyname "DHCP Client"
[SC] GetServiceKeyName SUCCESS  Name = Dhcp
```

For more information on service registry values, take a look at MS KB 103000 (CurrentControlSet\Services Subkey Entries).

One of the knocks Windows 2000 received was that it had too many services enabled by default. This was both a good and a bad thing. On one hand, it meant that a lot of functionality was turned on out of the box. The downside was that many of the default services, such as IIS, had security issues, so *all* default installations were vulnerable. As a result, Microsoft changed their stance in Windows XP and Windows Server 2003, opting for a more secure approach. Many of the services that were started up by default in Windows 2000 are now disabled at startup in Windows Server 2003. For a list of the changes in the default startup mode, see MS KB 812519 (Services That Are Turned Off by Default in Windows Server 2003). For a list of the default services in Windows Server 2003, see Appendix F.

Using a Graphical User Interface

The primary graphical interface for managing services is the Services snap-in (*services.msc*). Largely unchanged since Windows 2000, the Services snap-in is the one-stop shop for stopping and starting services (Recipe 7.1), setting various service properties such as startup type (Recipe 7.4), service account (Recipe 7.5), recovery options (Recipe 7.6), and viewing service dependences (Recipe 7.10). You can do all of these actions against a remote computer by right-clicking the Services icon in the left pane and selecting "Connect to another computer."

There are a few tasks that you cannot do with the Services snap-in and you have to rely on other tools. For example, if you need to manually install or uninstall a service (Recipes 7.2 and 7.3), you'll need to use the Service Creation Wizard (*srvinstw.exe*), which is available in the Windows 2000 Resource Kit, or the Service Installer (*instsrv.exe*), which is available in the Windows Server 2003 Resource Kit Tools. Likewise, if you want to find services that have certain properties (e.g., find all services run under the Local System account and that have a startup type of Automatic), you'll need to use the *sc.exe* command-line utility (Recipe 7.8).

Using a Command-Line Interface

Table 7-1 lists the command-line utilities used in this chapter. The *sc.exe* utility is installed by default with Windows Server 2003, which makes it the de facto service management command-line tool. You can accomplish virtually any service management task with *sc*. If you are familiar with WMI and the Win32_Service class, which I'll discuss in the next section, you'll also want to take a look at the *wmic.exe* command. With it, you can tap into any Win32_Service properties or methods from the command line.

Table 7-1. Command-line tools used in this chapter

Tool	Windows Server 2003	Windows 2000	Recipes
eventquery.vbs	%SystemRoot%\System32	N/A	7.12
instsrv	Windows Server 2003 Resource Kit	Windows 2000 Resource Kit	7.2, 7.3
net	%SystemRoot%\System32	%SystemRoot%\System32	7.1
ntrights	Windows Server 2003 Resource Kit	Windows 2000 Resource Kit Supplement 1	7.5
psloglist	Sysinternals	Sysinternals	7.12

Table 7-1. Command-line tools used in this chapter (continued)

Tool	Windows Server 2003	Windows 2000	Recipes
psservice	Sysinternals	Sysinternals	7.1, 7.7, 7.8, 7.10
qgrep	Windows Server 2003 Resource Kit	Windows 2000 Resource Kit	7.12
sc	*%SystemRoot%\System32*	Windows 2000 Resource Kit Supplement 1	7.1–7.10
subinacl	MS Download[a]	MS Download*	7.13
wmic	*%SystemRoot%\System32\Wbem*	N/A	7.1, 7.7

[a] *subinacl* is available in the Windows 2000 and Windows Server 2003 Resource Kits, but I advise downloading the latest version from the Microsoft Download site (*http://www.microsoft.com/downloads/details.aspx?FamilyID=e8ba3e56-d8fe-4a91-93cf-ed6985e3927b&displaylang=en* or by going to *http://www.microsoft.com/downloads* and searching for "subinacl"). There have been many updates to the tool and downloading the latest version is the best way to avoid bugs in the earlier versions.

Using VBScript

The primary interface for programmatically managing services is the Win32_Service WMI class. It is used extensively throughout this chapter. Table 7-2 lists the useful properties available with this class, and Table 7-3 contains the methods for this class. All of the properties are read-only. To modify a particular service setting, you have to use a method, such as Change.

Table 7-2. Win32_Service properties

Name	Description
AcceptPause	Boolean that indicates whether the service can be paused (some services cannot).
AcceptStop	Boolean that indicates whether the service can be stopped (some services cannot).
Caption	Short description of the service.
CheckPoint	The service increments this periodically to report its progress during a long start, stop, pause, or continue operation. For example, the service increments this value as it completes each step of its initialization when it is starting up. For services that do not have a start, stop, pause, or continue operation pending, this value should be zero.
Description	Textual description of the service.
DesktopInteract	Boolean that indicates whether the service interacts with the desktop.
DisplayName	Display name of the service.
ErrorControl	Severity of the error if this service fails to start during startup.
ExitCode	Windows error code defining any problems encountered in starting or stopping the service. This property is set to ERROR_SERVICE_SPECIFIC_ERROR (1066) when the error is unique to the service, and information about the error is available in the ServiceSpecificExitCode property.
DatetimeInstallDate	Date and time the service was installed (generally not populated).
Name	Short name for the service. This is the same name that appears as part of the service's Registry key and that you use to manage the service using the *sc.exe* utility.
PathName	Full command-line path the service invokes when starting.
ProcessId	Process ID (PID) of the process the service is being run from.

Table 7-2. Win32_Service properties (continued)

Name	Description
ServiceSpecificExitCode	Service-specific error code for errors that occur while the service is either starting or stopping. The exit codes are defined by the service represented by this class. This value is set only when the ExitCode property value is ERROR_SERVICE_SPECIFIC_ERROR (1066).
ServiceType	The type of service, which can be Kernel Driver, File System Driver, Adapter, Recognizer Driver, Own Process, Share Process, or Interactive Process.
Started	Boolean that indicates whether the service has been started.
StartMode	Startup mode for the service.
StartName	Account under which the service runs.
State	Current state of the service, which can be Stopped, Start Pending, Stop Pending, Running, Continue Pending, Pause Pending, Paused, or Unknown.
SystemName	Name of the system on which the service runs.
TagId	For services that are part of a service group, this ID number determines the relative order within the group where the service starts. A value of 0 or no value indicates the service is not loaded as part of a group.
WaitHint	Estimated time required (in milliseconds) for a start pending, stop, pause, or continue operation. After the specified amount of time has elapsed, the service makes a call to update its status with either an incremented CheckPoint value or a change in state.

Table 7-3. Win32_Service methods

Method Name	Method Description
StartService	Attempts to start the service.
StopService	Attempts to stop the service.
PauseService	Attempts to pause the service.
ResumeService	Attempts to resume the service.
InterrogateService	Requests that the service update its state with the SCM.
UserControlService	Sends user-defined control code to the service.
Create	Creates a new service.
Change	Modifies one or more properties of a service. These include DisplayName, PathName, ServiceType, ErrorControl, StartMode, DesktopInteract, StartName, StartPassword, LoadOrderGroup, LoadOrderGroupDependencies, and ServiceDependencies.
ChangeStartMode	Changes the startup mode of a service.
Delete	Deletes a service.

7.1   Starting and Stopping a Service

Problem

You want to start or stop a service.

Solution

Using a graphical user interface

1. Open the Services snap-in.
2. In the right pane, right-click on the service and select **Start** or **Stop**.

Using a command-line interface:

Run any of the following commands to start a service:

```
> psservice start <ServiceName>
> sc start <ServiceName>
> wmic service <ServiceName> call StartService
> net start <ServiceName>
```

Run any of the following commands to stop a service:

```
> psservice stop <ServiceName>
> sc stop <ServiceName>
> wmic service <ServiceName> call StopService
> net stop <ServiceName>
```

You can use the *wmic*, *psservice*, and *sc* commands against a remote server.

Using VBScript

```
' This code stops and starts (effectively restarts) a service.
' ------ SCRIPT CONFIGURATION ------
strComputer = "<ServerName>"    ' e.g., fs-rtp01 (use . for local server)
strSvcName  = "<ServiceName>"   ' e.g., dnscache
' ------ END CONFIGURATION ---------
set objWMI = GetObject("winmgmts:\\" & strComputer & "\root\cimv2")
set objService = objWMI.Get("Win32_Service.Name='" & strSvcName & "'")

intRC = objService.StopService

WScript.Sleep 5000   ' Give the service 5 seconds to stop

if intRC > 0 then
    WScript.Echo "Error stopping service: " & intRC
else
    WScript.Echo "Successfully stopped service"
end if

intRC = objService.StartService
if intRC > 0 then
    WScript.Echo "Error starting service: " & intRC
else
    WScript.Echo "Successfully started service"
end if
```

Discussion

Starting and stopping a service is a straightforward procedure that every administrator has to do at one point or another. The only potentially tricky thing you need to be aware of when it comes to stopping a service is service dependencies. For example, if ServiceA depends on ServiceB and both services are currently running, you can't stop ServiceB unless you first stop ServiceA (the service that is dependent on it). If you are using the Services snap-in or the command-line tools, they are nice enough to stop all dependent services if there are any (use the /y option with the net stop command). From VBScript, the process is more manual. You first need to look up the dependent services and stop them. You will, in fact, receive an error when you use the StopService method on a service that has active dependencies. For a more robust example that automates stopping dependent services from VBScript, see Recipe 7.14.

See Also

Recipe 7.10, MSDN: StartService Method of the Win32_Service Class, and MSDN: StopService Method of the Win32_Service Class

7.2 Running Any Program or Script as a Service

Problem

You want to run a program or script as a service. This is useful when you want a program to run continuously regardless if someone is logged in.

Solution

The following solutions install the Perl script *monitor.pl* as a service named MyMonitor.

Using a graphical user interface

1. Open the Service Creation Wizard (*srvinstw.exe*).
2. Select **Install a service** and click **Next**.
3. Select the target machine to install the service on and click **Next**.
4. Enter **MyMonitor** for the service name and click **Next**.
5. Enter the path of the *srvany.exe* executable and click **Next**.
6. Select **Service is its own process** and click **Next**.
7. Select the account to run the service under and click **Next**.
8. Select the service startup type and click **Next**.
9. Click **Finish**.
10. Open the Registry Editor (*regedit.exe*).

11. In the left pane, browse to the service's registry key by opening **HKEY_LOCAL_MACHINE** → **SYSTEM** → **CurrentControlSet** → **Services** → **MyMonitor**.

12. Right-click on **MyMonitor** and select **New** → **Key**.

13. Enter **Parameters** and press Enter.

14. Right-click on **Parameters** and select **New** → **String Value**.

15. Enter **Application** and press Enter twice.

16. Enter the path to the Perl executable (e.g., *c:\perl\bin\perl.exe*) and click **OK**.

17. Right-click on **Parameters** and select **New** → **String Value**.

18. Enter **AppParameters** and press Enter twice.

19. Enter the path to the Perl script (e.g., *c:\scripts\monitor.pl*) and click **OK**.

20. Open the Services snap-in.

21. In the left pane, right-click on **MyMonitor** and select **Start**.

Using a command-line interface:

Run the following four commands to install the MyMonitor service:

```
> instsrv MyMonitor "C:\Windows Resource Kits\Tools\srvany.exe"
> reg add HKLM\System\CurrentControlSet\Services\MyMonitor\Parameters
/v Application /d "c:\perl\bin\perl.exe"
> reg add HKLM\System\CurrentControlSet\Services\MyMonitor\Parameters
/v AppParameters /d "C:\scripts\monitor.pl"
> sc start MyMonitor
```

Using VBScript

```
' This code creates and starts the MyMonitor Perl service
' ------ SCRIPT CONFIGURATION ------
strComputer   = "."
strSvcName    = "MyMonitor"
strSrvAnyPath = "c:\Windows Resource Kits\Tools\srvany.exe"
strPerlPath   = "c:\perl\bin\perl.exe"
strPerlScript = "c:\scripts\monitor.pl"
' ------ END CONFIGURATION ---------
const HKLM = &H80000002

' Service Type
Const KERNEL_DRIVER      = 1
Const FS_DRIVER          = 2
Const ADAPTER            = 4
Const RECOGNIZER_DRIVER  = 8
Const OWN_PROCESS        = 16
Const SHARE_PROCESS      = 32
Const INTERACTIVE_PROCESS = 256

INTERACT_WITH_DESKTOP = FALSE
```

```
' Error Control
Const NOT_NOTIFIED     = 0
Const USER_NOTIFIED    = 1
Const SYSTEM_RESTARTED = 2
Const SYSTEM_STARTS    = 3

set objWMI = GetObject("winmgmts:\\" & strComputer & "\root\cimv2")
set objService = objWMI.Get("Win32_Service")
intRC = objService.Create(strSvcName, _
                          strSvcName, _
                          strSrvAnyPath, _
                          OWN_PROCESS, _
                          NOT_NOTIFED, _
                          "Automatic", _
                          INTERACT_WITH_DESKTOP, _
                          "NT AUTHORITY\LocalService",_
                          "")
if intRC > 0 then
    WScript.Echo "Error creating service: " & intRC
    WScript.Quit
else
    WScript.Echo "Successfully created service"
end if

strKeyPath = "SYSTEM\CurrentControlSet\Services\" & _
             strSvcName & "\Parameters"
set objReg = GetObject("winmgmts:\\" & _
                       strComputer & "\root\default:StdRegProv")
objReg.CreateKey HKLM,strKeyPath
objReg.SetStringValue HKLM,strKeyPath,"Application",strPerlPath
objReg.SetStringValue HKLM,strKeyPath,"AppParameters",strPerlScript
WScript.Echo "Created registry values"

set objService = objWMI.Get("Win32_Service.Name='" & strSvcName & "'")
intRC = objService.StartService
if intRC > 0 then
    WScript.Echo "Error starting service: " & intRC
else
    WScript.Echo "Successfully started service"
end if
```

Discussion

Do you have cool script or an executable that you'd like to run continuously? You could use Task Scheduler to periodically run the job, but that doesn't give you much flexibility to stop, start, and monitor the job. Another option is to turn the program into a service as outlined in the solutions. By doing this, the program will run continuously and no one needs to be logged in.

To run a script or executable as a service, you need the help of another program called *srvany.exe* from the Resource Kit. It acts as a wrapper around your script or executable by handling all the service control messages (e.g., stop, start, pause, etc.).

Creating a service consists of setting a few registry keys and values under the `HKLM\`
`SYSTEM\CurrentControlSet\Services\` key. For a SrvAny service, you need to configure several values under the new service's `Parameter` key. The `Application` value
should contain the path to the script or executable you want to run. In this case,
since I'm using Perl, I set this to the Perl executable. And since I need to pass the
name of the Perl script to the executable, I created an `AppParameters` key, which contains any parameters (in this case, the script path) to the executable (specified in
`Application`).

 Not all executables work well when running in the context of a service. Some programs may stop working when a logoff event occurs
and others may not work at all. Your mileage will vary, so test your
custom service thoroughly.

See Also

MS KB 137890 (HOWTO: Create a User-Defined Service), MS KB 821794 (INFO:
Best Practices When You Create Windows Services), and MSDN: Create Method of
the Win32_Service Class

7.3   Removing a Service

Problem

You want to remove a service. When you uninstall an application that previously
installed a service, the service will automatically be removed. However, if you manually installed the service as described in Recipe 7.2, you'll need to manually remove it
to uninstall it.

Solution

Before you can remove a service, you need to make sure the service is not running.
See Recipe 7.1 for more on stopping a service.

Using a graphical user interface

1. Open the Service Creation Wizard (*srvinstw.exe*).
2. Select **Remove a service** and click **Next**.
3. Select the target machine from which to remove the service and click **Next**.
4. Select the service you want to remove and click **Next**.
5. Click **Finish**.
6. Click **OK** to confirm removal of the service.

Using a command-line interface:

The following commands stop a service and remove it:

```
> sc <ServiceName> stop
> instsrv <ServiceName> remove
```

Using VBScript

```
' This code removes a service.
' ------ SCRIPT CONFIGURATION ------
strComputer    = "<ServerName>"   ' e.g., fs-rtp01 (use . for local server)
strSvcName     = "<ServiceName>"  ' e.g., MyMonitor
boolStopService = TRUE            ' e.g., TRUE to attempt to stop the service
' ------ END CONFIGURATION ---------

set objWMI = GetObject("winmgmts:\\" & strComputer & "\root\cimv2")
set objService = objWMI.Get("Win32_Service.Name='" & strSvcName & "'")
if boolStopService = TRUE then
   intRC = objService.StopService

   WScript.Sleep 5000  ' Give the service 5 seconds to stop

   if intRC > 0 then
      WScript.Echo "Error stopping service: " & intRC
      WScript.Quit
   else
      WScript.Echo "Successfully stopped service"
   end if
end if

intRC = objService.Delete
if intRC > 0 then
   WScript.Echo "Error deleting service: " & intRC
else
   WScript.Echo "Successfully deleted service"
end if
```

Discussion

Anytime you uninstall an application, the uninstall program should automatically remove the services that were installed with the application. If you find that it doesn't, you should complain loudly to the company that made that software. If, however, you manually created your own service, the only way to remove it when you no longer want it is to manually delete it. All three solutions use a slightly different method for removing a service, but they are all essentially performing the same task. Removing a service consists of removing the associated entries from the registry (HKLM\SYSTEM\CurrentControlSet\Services\<ServiceName>) and deregistering the service with the SCM.

See Also

Recipe 7.2 and MSDN: Delete Method of the Win32_Service Class

7.4   Setting the Service Startup Type

Problem

You want to configure the startup type (automatic, manual, or disabled) for a service.

Solution

Using a graphical user interface

1. Open the Services snap-in.

2. In the left pane, double-click on the service you want to configure.

3. Choose the startup type under the **General tab**.

4. Click **OK**.

Using a command-line interface:

```
> sc config <ServiceName> start= [boot | system | auto | demand | disabled]
```

The following command disables the Messenger service:

```
> sc config Messenger start= disabled
```

Using VBScript

```
' This code sets the startup type for a service.
' ------ SCRIPT CONFIGURATION ------
strSvcName     = "MyMonitor"
strStartupType = "Automatic"   ' can be "Automatic", "Manual", or "Disabled"
strComputer    = "."
' ------ END CONFIGURATION ---------
set objWMI = GetObject("winmgmts:\\" & strComputer & "\root\cimv2")
set objService = objWMI.Get("Win32_Service.Name='" & strSvcName & "'")
intRC = objService.Change(,,,,strStartupType)
' can alternatively use objService.ChangeStartup(strStartupType) method
if intRC > 0 then
    WScript.Echo "Error setting service startup type: " & intRC
else
    WScript.Echo "Successfully set service startup type"
end if
```

Discussion

The startup type of a service determines whether the service starts when the system boots and whether it can be started at all. The Automatic startup type causes the service to automatically start at system boot up. The Manual startup type means the service will not be started automatically at system boot up unless another automatic service is dependent upon it, but it can be started later by someone with sufficient privileges. The Disabled startup type means that the service is not started at system boot up and cannot be manually started. You have to change the startup type to either Manual or Automatic before you can start a service that is set to Disabled.

You may have noticed that there are two other startup options you can configure with the *sc* utility. These additional startup options are available with the scripting solution as well. They are, however, not applicable to system services. They are used for starting device drivers and can only be configured for drivers. The Boot startup type indicates that the driver is started by the operating system loader. The System startup type means that the driver will be started by the IoInitSystem method (if you are a driver programmer you know what this is, if not, don't worry about it).

See Also

MSDN: Change Method of the Win32_Service Class

7.5   Setting the Service Account and Password

Problem

You want to configure the account and password used by a service.

Solution

Using a graphical user interface

1. Open the Services snap-in.
2. In the left pane, double-click on the service you want to configure.
3. Click the **Log On** tab.
4. Select **This Account**.
5. Enter the domain and username of the account or click **Browse** to find it.
6. Enter and confirm the account's password.
7. Click **OK**.

Using a command-line interface:

```
> sc config <ServiceName> obj= <Domain>\<Username> password= <Password>
```

The following command configures the MyMonitor service to log on using the local administrator account:

```
> sc config MyMonitor obj= FS-RTP01\administrator password= foobar
```

Using VBScript

```
' This code configures the service account
' ------ SCRIPT CONFIGURATION ------
strUser     = "<Domain>\<Username>"   ' e.g., FS-RTP01\administration
strPassword = "<Password>"            ' e.g., foobar
strSvcName  = "<ServiceName>"         ' e.g., MyMonitor
strComputer = "<ServerName>"          ' e.g., fs-rtp01 (use . for local server)
' ------ END CONFIGURATION ---------
set objWMI = GetObject("winmgmts:\\" & strComputer & "\root\cimv2")
set objService = objWMI.Get("Win32_Service.Name='" & strSvcName & "'")
intRC = objService.Change(,,,,,,strUser,strPassword)
if intRC > 0 then
   WScript.Echo "Error setting service account: " & intRC
else
   WScript.Echo "Successfully set service account"
end if
```

Discussion

If you need to configure a user account to run a service under, make sure the account has the *Log on as service* right. Without this system right, the service will not start up correctly. The Services snap-in will automatically grant this right when you configure the log on account for a service. However, neither the command-line or scripting solutions do this. From the command line, you can use the *ntrights.exe* utility:

```
> ntrights +r SeServiceLogonRight -u <User>
```

Here is an example:

```
> ntrights +r SeServiceLogonRight -u RALLENCORP\rallen
```

Unfortunately, WMI doesn't support setting user rights, so if you need to do it programmatically, you'll have to shell out to the *ntrights* command.

There are a couple of issues you need to be aware of if you configure a local or domain account for a service to run under. If you have a password policy enabled in your domain that forces users to change their password after a period of time, make sure you have a process in place to change service account passwords on a regular basis. Another option, albeit much less secure, is to configure service accounts to have nonexpiring passwords. If a service account has an expired password, it will cause the service to fail when starting. The same is true for accounts that are locked out.

To avoid these problems, you can use local system accounts that don't have a password in the traditional sense. Here is an overview of these accounts:

Local System
> This account has full access to the underlying system. It has similar rights to the Administrator account. On a domain controller, it has administrator-level access to all objects in the domain. Be careful when using this account for a service.

Local Service

This account is similar to an authenticated user that is a member of the local Users group on the computer. It has anonymous access to network resources. This account is new in Windows XP and Windows Server 2003.

Network Service

Like the Local Service account, this account has similar access to an authenticated user that is a member of the local Users group. The main difference with this account is that it can access network resources using the credentials of the computer account. This account is new in Windows XP and Windows Server 2003.

See Also

MS KB 279664 (How to Set Logon User Rights with the Ntrights.exe Utility) and MSDN: Change Method of the Win32_Service Class

7.6   Performing an Action Automatically When a Service Fails

Problem

You want to perform an action automatically when a service fails.

Solution

Using a graphical user interface

1. Open the Services snap-in.
2. In the left pane, double-click on the service you want to configure.
3. Click the **Recovery** tab.
4. Configure the failure options you want and click **OK**.

Using a command-line interface:

The following command causes the MyMonitor service to automatically restart after two failures and reboot on the third. Each failure can be up to five seconds apart.

```
> sc failure MyMonitor reset= 3600 reboot="Restarting due to repeated MyMonitor
failure" actions= restart/5000/restart/5000/reboot/5000
```

Using VBScript

The Win32_Service class does not support setting the recovery options of a service.

Discussion

Windows 2000 added a new capability that was sorely missing in previous versions of Windows: the ability to automatically perform a specified action when a service fails. You can configure an action to occur after the first, second, and subsequent failures. The actions you can take include no action (the default), restarting the service, running a program, or restarting the computer. Restarting the service or computer should be used as a last resort because they could mask underlying problems.

You can also reset the failure count after a certain number of days. So let's say that you have a service that regularly fails multiple times a day, but you only want it to restart itself after the first failure every day. You would configure the first failure action to restart the service and set the reset fail count to 1 day.

You can even combine multiple actions by choosing to run a program after service failure. You can create a simple batch file that restarts the service and emails you a report. This gives you a lot of flexibility in how you handle service failures.

7.7   Viewing the List of Services

Problem

You want to view all the services that are installed on a server.

Solution

Using a graphical user interface

1. Open the Services snap-in. The right pane contains all the services installed on the server.
2. Double-click a service to view the description and other service parameters.

Using a command-line interface:

This command lists detailed output for all the running services:

```
> sc \\<ServerName> query
```

And this command lists all services:

```
> psservice \\<ServerName> query
```

If you want only a list of names of all running services, as opposed to detailed output, use this:

```
> sc \\<ServerName> query | findstr SERVICE_NAME
```

Or you can use any of these commands to list the installed services:

```
> srvinfo -nf \\<ServerName>
> psservice \\<ServerName> query | findstr SERVICE_NAME
> wmic /node:"<ServerName>" service list
```

Using VBScript

```
' This code prints the list of services on a machine
' ------ SCRIPT CONFIGURATION ------
strComputer = "<ServerName>"    ' e.g., fs-rtp01 (use . for local server)
boolShowDetails = TRUE          ' set to FALSE to display list w/o details
' ------ END CONFIGURATION ---------
set objWMI = GetObject("winmgmts:\\" & strComputer & "\root\cimv2")
set objServices = objWMI.InstancesOf("Win32_Service")

for each objService in objServices
   WScript.Echo objService.Name
   if boolShowDetails = TRUE then
      for each objProp in objService.Properties_
         ' Print out NULL if the property is blank
         if IsNull(objProp.Value) then
            Wscript.Echo " " & objProp.Name & " : NULL"
         else
         ' If the value is an array, we need to iterate through each element
         ' of the array
            if objProp.IsArray = TRUE then
               For I = LBound(objProp.Value) to UBound(objProp.Value)
                  wscript.echo " " & objProp.Name & " : " & objProp.Value(I)
               next
            else
            ' If the property was  not NULL or an array, we print it
               wscript.echo " " & objProp.Name & " : " & objProp.Value
            end if
         end if
      next
      WScript.Echo ""
   end if
next
```

Discussion

Using a graphical user interface

You can target a remote server by right-clicking the Services icon in the left pane and selecting **Connect to another computer**. Enter the name of the target computer and click **OK**.

Using VBScript

The scripting solution prints each service by using the InstancesOf method on the Win32_Service class. As it loops through each service, it prints all of the properties by looping over the `Properties_` method. It then does a couple of checks to determine the type of value it needs to print.

See Also

Recipe 7.1

7.8   Searching Services

Problem

You want to find one or more services that match certain criteria.

Solution

Using a graphical user interface

The Services snap-in does not allow you to search services.

Using a command-line interface:

With the *sc.exe* command you can query against service type (type= *<TypeName>*), state (state= *<State>*), and group (group= *<GroupName>*).

 For more on service groups, see Recipe 7.11.

Here are two examples:

```
> sc <ServerName> query state= active
> sc <ServerName> query type= driver
```

The *psservice.exe* command is very similar; you can query against service type (type= *<TypeName>*), state (state= *<State>*), and group (group= *<GroupName>*).

For example:

```
> psservice \\<ServerName> query -s active
> psservice \\<ServerName> query -t driver
```

Using VBScript

```
' This code queries services based on the specified
' property name and value
' ------ SCRIPT CONFIGURATION ------
strPropName  = "State"
strPropValue = "'Running'"     ' e.g.,
strComputer  = "<ServerName>"  ' e.g., fs-rtp01 (use . for local server)
' ------ END CONFIGURATION ---------
```

```
set objWMI = GetObject("winmgmts:\\" & strComputer & "\root\cimv2")
set colServices = objWMI.ExecQuery _
                        ("Select * from Win32_Service Where " & _
                         strPropName & " = " & strPropValue)
for each objService in colServices
   Wscript.Echo objService.DisplayName
next

' List of Win32_Service properties:
'  boolean AcceptPause
'  boolean AcceptStop
'  string Caption
'  uint32 CheckPoint;
'  string CreationClassName
'  string Description
'  boolean DesktopInteract
'  string DisplayName
'  string ErrorControl
'  uint32 ExitCode
'  datetime InstallDate
'  string Name
'  string PathName
'  uint32 ProcessId
'  uint32 ServiceSpecificExitCode
'  string ServiceType
'  boolean Started
'  string StartMode
'  string StartName
'  string State
'  string Status
'  string SystemCreationClassName
'  string SystemName
'  uint32 TagId
'  uint32 WaitHint
```

Discussion

See Table 7-2 (in Recipe 7.1) for descriptions of the properties of a service.

See Also

Recipe 7.11

7.9   Finding the Process a Service Is Running From

Problem

You want to find the process from which a service is running from.

Solution

Using a graphical user interface

You can view the executable that is run for a process by opening the Services snap-in and double-clicking a service. You'll see the full path below **Path to executable**.

Using a command-line interface:

The following command displays the process ID (PID) that corresponds to a service:

```
> sc <ServerName> queryex <ServiceName>
```

Using VBScript

```
' This code displays the process ID for a service
' ------ SCRIPT CONFIGURATION ------
strSvcName    = "<ServiceName>"   ' e.g., Messenger
strComputer   = "<ServerName>"    ' e.g., fs-rtp01 (use . for local server)
' ------ END CONFIGURATION ---------
set objWMI = GetObject("winmgmts:\\" & strComputer & "\root\cimv2")
set objService = objWMI.Get("Win32_Service.Name='" & strSvcName & "'")
WScript.Echo "Service: " & strSvcName
WScript.Echo "PID: " & objService.ProcessID
```

Discussion

When it comes down to it, a service is really nothing more than a process that is managed by the SCM, which allows you to send various commands to it (start, stop, pause, etc.). In Recipe 6.6, I described how to find the services that are being run from a single process. In this recipe, I show how to find the process from which a particular service is being run. This can be useful if you attempt to stop a service, but it won't stop. If you can determine the PID or name of the service's process, you can kill the process (Recipe 6.3).

7.10 Viewing the Antecedent and Dependent Services for a Service

Problem

You want to view the services that a particular service depends on (i.e., antecedent services) and services that are dependent on that service. This is helpful to know when you want to stop a service and determine the impact it would have on other services.

Solution

Using a graphical user interface

1. Open the Services snap-in.
2. In the left pane, double-click on the service you want to view.
3. Click the **Dependencies** tab.

Using a command-line interface:

The following command displays the services that depend on the specified service:

```
> sc \\<ServerName> enumdepend <ServiceName>
```

You can also use the following command:

```
> psservice \\<ServerName> <ServiceName> depend
```

The following command displays the services that the specified service depends on:

```
> sc \\<ServerName> qc <ServiceName>
```

Using VBScript

```
' This code lists the antecedent and dependent services for a service
' ------ SCRIPT CONFIGURATION ------
strService = "<ServiceName>"  ' e.g., TapiSrv
strComputer = "<ServerName>"  ' e.g., fs-rtp01 (use . for local server)
' ------ END CONFIGURATION ---------
set objWMI = GetObject("winmgmts:\\" & strComputer & "\root\cimv2")
set colServices = objWMI.ExecQuery("Associators of " _
                    & "{Win32_Service.Name='" & strService & "'} Where " _
                    & "AssocClass=Win32_DependentService Role=Antecedent" )
WScript.Echo "Antecedent services for " & strService & ":"
for each objService in colServices
    Wscript.Echo vbTab & objService.DisplayName
next
WScript.Echo

set colServices = objWMI.ExecQuery("Associators of " _
                    & "{Win32_Service.Name='" & strService & "'} Where " _
                    & "AssocClass=Win32_DependentService Role=Dependent" )
WScript.Echo "Dependent services for " & strService & ":"
for each objService in colServices
    Wscript.Echo vbTab & objService.DisplayName
next
```

Discussion

Service dependencies play a role in how you can stop a service. For example, if ServiceA depends on ServiceB, then ServiceB must be running before ServiceA can start. Similarly, ServiceB cannot be stopped until ServiceA is stopped due to the dependency. A good practical example of this is the Logical Disk Manager Administrative Service. It depends on the Logical Disk Manager service. It wouldn't make a lot of sense for the administrative service to be running, but not the underlying disk manager service (the thing it manages).

Service dependences are configured in each service's registry entry. In the case of the Logical Disk Manager Administrative Service, you can find its registry entry in the following key:

```
HKEY_LOCAL_MACHINE\SYSTEM\CurrentControlSet\Services\dmadmin
```

If you open Registry Editor (*regedit.exe*) and look at that key, you'll see a DependOnService value. The data for this REG_MULTI_SZ value is a list of the services it depends on. One of them is dmserver, which corresponds to the Logical Disk Manager service.

You may also see a DependOnGroup value under a service's registry key. This is similar to DependOnService except that DependOnGroup corresponds to a group of services. For more on service groups, check out Recipe 7.11.

Using VBScript

In the code I needed to use something called an associator. The Associators of clause in a WQL query is similar to a table join in a relational database. It allows you to relate two different types of WMI classes. For services, WMI supports a class called Win32_DependentService, which defines the service dependences for a given service. The first query finds all of the antecedent services (those that depend on the target service):

```
"Associators of {Win32_Service.Name='" & strService & "'} Where " _
    "AssocClass=Win32_DependentService Role=Antecedent"
```

The Associators of clause tells WMI we are going to associate or join another class to the one specified within the curly braces. I set Win32_Service.Name equal to the target service. The Where clause then has two parts, the first sets the associated class, which in this case is Win32_DependentService. The second part (Role=Antecedent) limits the dependent services that are returned to just antecedent services, or ones that depend on the target service. Now look at the second query. The only difference is Role=Dependent returns all of the dependent services of the target service.

7.11   Viewing the Service Load Order

Problem

You want to view the order in which services load during system startup. You typically don't need to worry about the service load order, but it can be helpful if you are experiencing problems with services that are not starting correctly after reboot. Also, device drivers are treated like services. So by viewing the service load order, you can see the device driver load order as well.

Solution

Using a graphical user interface

Open the Sysinternals LoadOrd (*loadord.exe*) utility. See Figure 7-1 for an example of the output.

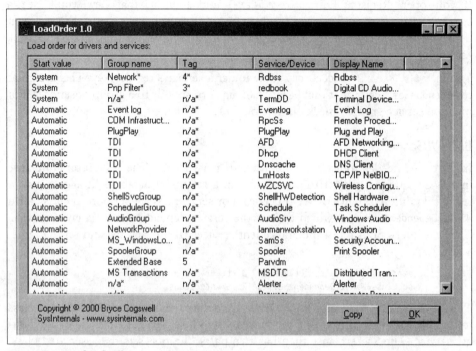

Figure 7-1. LoadOrd utility

Discussion

As I described in Recipe 7.10, Windows supports the concept of service dependencies whereby a service cannot start until the services it depends on have started successfully. Windows also supports the notion of a service load order so that services and groups of services start in a particular order.

A service group is a collection of services that are loaded together at system startup. In Figure 7-1, you can see the group a particular service is in under the Group Name column. The complete list of service groups can be found in the Registry under the following key:

```
HKEY_LOCAL_MACHINE\SYSTEM\CurrentControlSet\Control\GroupOrderList
```

Not all services are part of a group, but the ones that are load before the ones that aren't. The following registry value contains a list of service groups in order of how they are loaded:

```
HKEY_LOCAL_MACHINE\SYSTEM\CurrentControlSet\Control\ServiceGroupOrder\List
```

Each service has registry values under its specific key (HKEY_LOCAL_MACHINE\SYSTEM\CurrentControlSet\System\Services\<*ServiceName*>) that determine which group it is a member of (if any) and its dependencies. Here is a list of these values:

Group
> REG_SZ value that contains the service group name the service belongs to

Tag
> REG_DWORD value that contains a number that dictates the relative order the service starts within a service group

DependOnGroup
> REG_MULTI_SZ value that contains the service groups that must load successfully before this service can start

DependOnService
> REG_MULTI_SZ value that contains the services that must load successfully before this service can start

See Also

MS KB 115486 (HOWTO: Control Device Driver Load Order) and MS KB 193888 (How to Delay Loading of Specific Services)

7.12   Viewing the Startup History of a Service

Problem

You want to view the startup history of a service. Every time a service is started or stopped, a message is logged to the Application event log.

Solution

Using a graphical user interface

1. Open the EventCombMT utility (*eventcombmt.exe*).
2. Right-click on the **Select To Search/Right To Add** box and select **Add Single Server**.
3. Enter the server name, click **Add Server**, and click Close.
4. Highlight the server by clicking on it.
5. Under **Choose Log Files** to search, be sure that **System** is selected.
6. Under **Event Types**, select only **Informational**.

7. Beside **Event IDs**, enter **7035 7036**

8. Beside **Text**, enter the display name of the service (e.g., **The Windows Installer service**).

9. Click the **Search** button.

10. A Windows Explorer window should pop up containing a file with the output of the search. Double-click on the file to view the results.

Using a command-line interface:

The following command displays all the event 7035 and 7036 events that pertain to a particular service. This isn't very efficient because all 7035 and 7036 events are retrieved and piped to a second *qgrep* command to display only the ones we are interested in. Unfortunately, you cannot perform pattern matching of the event message with the *eventquery* command.

```
> eventquery /v /L system /FI "ID eq 7036 or ID eq 7035" | qgrep -e "The
<ServiceDisplayName> service"
```

You can accomplish something similar with the *psloglist* command, but you need to do it in two steps to retrieve the two different event ids:

```
> psloglist -s -i 7035 system | qgrep -e "The <ServiceDisplayName> service"
```

Here is an example:

```
> psloglist -s -i 7036 system | qgrep -e "The DNS Client service"
```

Using VBScript

```
' This code displays the startup history of a servce
' ------ SCRIPT CONFIGURATION ------
strService = "<ServiceDisplayName>" ' e.g., Windows Installer
strLog = "<EventLogName>"            ' e.g., System
strComputer = "<ServerName>"         ' e.g., fs-rtp01 (use . for local server)
' ------ END CONFIGURATION ---------
set objWMI = GetObject("winmgmts:\\" & strComputer & "\root\cimv2")
set colEvents = objWMI.ExecQuery _
            ("Select * from Win32_NTLogEvent " & _
            " Where Logfile = '" & strLog & "' " & _
            "    and ( EventCode = '7036' or EventCode = '7035' ) " & _
            "    and Message like 'The " & strService & " service %'")
set objDate = CreateObject("WbemScripting.SWbemDateTime")
for each objEvent in colEvents
    objDate.Value = objEvent.TimeWritten
    Wscript.Echo objDate.GetVarDate & ":" & objEvent.Message
next
```

Discussion

In the command-line and VBScript solutions, you need to know the service display name in order to find the start and stop events. To determine the display name of a service, you can view it either in the Services snap-in or by running the sc query command.

7.13   Granting the Permission to Manage One or More Services

Problem

You want to grant a user the right to manage (stop and start) a particular service.

Solution

Using a graphical user interface

1. Open the Group Policy Object Editor.
2. Edit the Group Policy object that applies to the computer running the service you want to set security on.
3. In the right pane, expand **Computer Configuration** → **Windows Settings** → **Security Settings** → **System Services**.
4. In the left pane, double-click the service you want to configure.
5. Check the box beside **Define this policy setting**.
6. Select the service startup type.
7. Click the **Edit Security** button.
8. Use the ACL Editor to choose the target security principal and select the permission to apply.
9. Click **OK** to close the ACL Editor.
10. Click **OK** to close the setting properties page.

Using a command-line interface:

The following command grants full control of a service for a user:

```
> subinacl /service \\<ServerName>\<ServiceName> /grant=<User>
```

The following example grants full control of the Messenger service on server fs01 to the AMER\rallen user:

```
> subinacl /service \\fs01\Messenger /grant=AMER\rallen
```

Use this command to view the users who have been granted access to manage a particular service:

```
> subinacl /verbose=1 /service \\<ServerName>\<ServiceName>
```

Here is an example:

```
> subinacl /verbose=1 /service \\fs-rtp01\Messenger
```

To revoke access to a service, use this command:

```
> subinacl /service \\<ServerName>\<ServiceName> /revoke=<UserName>
```

This next command grants the AMER\rallen user control over all services on the server *fs01* and saves the output to *out.txt*:

```
> for /f "tokens=2,*" %s in ( '"psservice.exe | findstr SERVICE_NAME"' ) do subinacl
/verbose=1 /service \\fs01\%s /grant=AMER\rallen >> out.txt
```

Discussion

The access control list (ACL) for a service is stored in the Registry, under the service's Security key—e.g., HKLM\System\CurrentControlSet\Services\<ServiceName>\Security. If you misconfigure the permissions on a service or just want to start over, delete the service's Security key.

 Be sure to download the latest version of *subinacl* from *http://download.microsoft.com/*. Older versions work in unexpected ways. Another alternative you can also use is the *setacl* command, which is very similar in functionality to *subinacl*. *setacl* is available under the GNU Public License from the following web site: *http://setacl.sourceforge.net/*.

See Also

For more on service permissions, visit *http://www.microsoft.com/technet/prodtechnol/windowsserver2003/proddocs/entserver/sys_srv_permissions.asp*.

7.14 Script: Robust Service Restart

A service can be dependent on other services and have other services dependent on it. This is a nice feature because you can configure that in order for ServiceA to run, ServiceB needs to already be running. However, this makes things more complicated when it comes to stopping and starting services. If you want start ServiceA, you also need to make sure ServiceB is running.

When it comes to programmatically restarting services, you could just call the StopService and StartService methods on a service. And since a lot of services don't have any dependencies, this will generally work. But if you happen to try restarting a service that has a dependency, the restart will not be successful. The solution to this is to write a bit of code that can handle restarting services, regardless of dependencies. Here is the code:

```
' This code restarts a service by first stopping all
' dependent services before stopping the target service.
```

```
' Then the target service is started and then all dependent
' services are started.

Option Explicit

' ------ SCRIPT CONFIGURATION ------
Dim strComputer : strComputer = "."           ' e.g., fs-rtp01
Dim strSvcName  : strSvcName  = "<ServiceName>"  ' e.g., dnscache
' ------ END CONFIGURATION ---------
Dim objWMI : set objWMI = GetObject("winmgmts:\\" & strComputer & _
                                    "\root\cimv2")
Dim objService: set objService = objWMI.Get("Win32_Service.Name='" & _
                                    strSvcName & "'")

WScript.Echo "Restarting " & objService.Name & "..."
RecursiveServiceStop  objService
RecursiveServiceStart objService
WScript.Echo "Successfully restarted service"

Function RecursiveServiceStop ( objSvc )

    Dim colServices : set colServices = objWMI.ExecQuery("Associators of " _
                & "{Win32_Service.Name='" & objSvc.Name & "'} Where " _
                & "AssocClass=Win32_DependentService Role=Antecedent" )
    Dim objS
    for each objS in colServices
        RecursiveServiceStop objS
    next

    Dim intRC : intRC = objSvc.StopService
    WScript.Sleep 5000   ' Give the service 5 seconds to stop
    if intRC > 0 then
        WScript.Echo " Error stopping service: " & objSvc.Name
        WScript.Quit
    else
        WScript.Echo " Successfully stopped service: " & objSvc.Name
    end if
End Function

Function RecursiveServiceStart ( objSvc )

    Dim intRC : intRC = objSvc.StartService
    if intRC > 0 then
        WScript.Echo " Error starting service: " & objSvc.Name
        WScript.Quit
    else
        WScript.Echo " Successfully started service: " & objSvc.Name
    end if

    Dim colServices : set colServices = objWMI.ExecQuery("Associators of " _
                & "{Win32_Service.Name='" & objSvc.Name & "'} Where " _
                & "AssocClass=Win32_DependentService Role=Antecedent" )
    Dim objS
    for each objS in colServices
```

```
        RecursiveServiceStart objS
    next

  End Function
```

In order to restart a service, you have to stop all services that are dependent on that service and then stop the service itself. Then to start the service, you have to start the service followed by all dependent services. And that is exactly what this code does. It makes use of a couple of recursive functions that walk through all of the dependent services.

7.15   Script: Service Monitor

Have you ever had a pesky service that would stop for apparently no reason? Well, if you can't afford to buy a service monitoring application, you can write one yourself using WMI and event notifications.

The following code monitors the state of all services and reports any changes:

```
' This code displays the changes in state for the services on a computer.

Option Explicit

' ------ SCRIPT CONFIGURATION ------
Dim strComputer : strComputer = "."
' ------ END CONFIGURATION ---------

Dim objWMI : set objWMI = GetObject("winmgmts:\\" & strComputer _
                                & "\root\cimv2")
Dim colServices : set colServices = objWMI.ExecNotificationQuery( _
                "select * from __instanceModificationEvent " _
            & "within 2 where TargetInstance ISA 'Win32_Service'")
Do
    Dim objSvc : set objSvc = colServices.NextEvent
    If objSvc.TargetInstance.State <> objSvc.PreviousInstance.State Then
        Wscript.Echo objSvc.TargetInstance.Name & _
                " is " & objSvc.TargetInstance.State & _
                " -- it was previously " & _
                objSvc.PreviousInstance.State
    end If
Loop
```

The main method to note in this script is ExecNotificationQuery. This method executes a WQL query and receives events that result from it. Let's break the query down.

The select statement pulls all __instanceModificationEvent objects:

```
"select * from __instanceModificationEvent "
```

So what is a __instanceModificationEvent object? Anytime an instance of a WMI object changes, it registers the change as an instanceModificationEvent. This is incredibly powerful. Whenever a service changes, whether it is a property of a service or service state, that event is registered as a modification event in WMI. That select statement matches all modification events, which isn't quite what we want. This is where the next statement comes into play:

```
" within 2 where TargetInstance ISA 'Win32_Service'"
```

TargetInstance ISA 'Win32_Service' filters all modification events to only those of class Win32_Service. The within 2 statement informs WMI how often to check the system (in seconds) to see if the anything new matches this query.

After we've called ExecNotificationQuery, we are ready to enter a loop to start retrieving events. I used a do loop, which will make this script run until you kill it (i.e., type **Ctrl-C**). The first line in the do loop is the call to NextEvent. This is a synchronous call that waits until an event occurs before the script continues. If no services change, the script won't move beyond this step. If it does catch a service changing in some way, it next checks to see if the state of the service changed (instead of a property being modified). As I mentioned previously, someone could modify another property of a service which would create an instanceModificationEvent. All Win32_Service instanceModificationEvents have a State property.

CHAPTER 8
Event Logs

8.0 Introduction

Event logs provide a standard way for the operating system, services, and applications to record important actions (e.g., application failure), report status messages, keep track of security events, and log boot up messages. In this way, event logs are similar to syslog on the Unix and Linux platforms. They can be an extremely useful resource when you need to troubleshoot specific issues and are often the first places I look when trying to diagnose a problem. As a proactive measure, scan the event logs on your servers frequently to identify any problems that are logged, but may not have resulted in a failure caught by your monitoring software.

Using a Graphical User Interface

There are two graphical tools that you should be familiar with for querying and viewing event log messages. Event Viewer (*eventvwr.msc*) has been around since the days of Windows NT and is provided out of the box under Administrative Tools. It is a simple MMC snap-in that lets you view and filter messages in the available event logs. You can also view the event logs on a remote server with it, but depending on the log size on the remote server and your network connection, this can be a painfully slow process.

As part of the Windows Server 2003 Resource Kit, Microsoft made the Event Comb utility (*eventcombmt.exe*) publicly available. Event Comb is a powerful utility that lets you search the event logs across multiple servers at once. With it, you can restrict your search by event ID, source, type, log, and event description. Event Comb is multithreaded, so it can run against multiple servers simultaneously and you can configure the number of threads that can run at once.

Using a Command-Line Interface

The event log command-line tools available for Windows 2000 have limited functionality. In Windows Server 2003, three new tools were added that provide many more features for searching and creating events and configuring event triggers. Table 8-1 lists command-line tools used in this chapter.

Table 8-1. Command-line tools used in this chapter

Tool	Windows Server 2003	Windows 2000	Recipes
elogdmp	N/A	Windows 2000 Resource Kit	8.9, 8.10
eventcreate	%SystemRoot%\System32	N/A	8.1
eventquery.vbs	%SystemRoot%\System32	N/A	8.2, 8.9, 8.10
eventtriggers	%SystemRoot%\System32	N/A	8.13
logevent	N/A	Windows 2000 Resource Kit	8.1
psloglist	Sysinternals	Sysinternals	8.2
reg	%SystemRoot%\System32	Windows 2000 Support Tools	8.3, 8.5, 8.6
wmic	%SystemRoot%\System32\wbem	N/A	8.7, 8.11

Using VBScript

There are two WMI classes that I use throughout this chapter. The Win32_NTLogEvent class represents individual event log messages and Win32_NTEventlogFile represents the underlying file that contains event log messages. These two classes provide most of the functionality you'll need to retrieve, search, and configure event logs, except for one thing. Neither class supports the ability to create event log messages. In Recipe 8.1, I show how to do this using the Windows Scripting Host LogEvent method.

8.1   Creating an Event

Problem

You want to write an event to an event log. This can be useful if you want to document certain actions you've performed on a server.

Solution

Using a command-line interface

The following command is available on Windows Server 2003:

```
> eventcreate /T <EventType> /ID <EventID> /L <LogName> /SO <EventSource> /D
"<EventDescr>"
```

The following command writes an event to the Application event log with event ID 999 and source SysAdmin:

```
> eventcreate /T INFORMATION /ID 999 /L APPLICATION /SO SysAdmin /D "Restarting
server after service pack install"
```

The *logevent* tool, which is available in the Windows 2000 Resource Kit, can also be used to create events:

```
> logevent -s <EventType> -e <EventID> -r <EventSource> "<EventDescr>"
```

This example is equivalent to the *eventcreate* example where I created an event in the Application log:

```
> logevent -s I -e 999 -r SysAdmin "Restarting server after service pack install"
```

Using VBScript

```
' This code creates an event in the Application event log.
' ------ SCRIPT CONFIGURATION ------
strServer = "\\<ServerName>" ' e.g., fs01
strDescr = "<EventDescr>"     ' e.g., Restarting server after service pack install
' ------ END CONFIGURATION ---------
Const EVENT_SUCCESS = 0
Const EVENT_ERROR   = 1
Const EVENT_WARNING = 3
Const EVENT_INFO    = 4

set objWSHShell = Wscript.CreateObject("Wscript.Shell")
boolRC = objWSHShell.LogEvent(EVENT_INFO, strDescr, strServer)

if boolRC = TRUE then
    WScript.Echo "Successfully created event."
else
    WScript.Echo "Failed to create event."
end if
```

Discussion

Most Windows administrators use the event log as a passive tool, whereby they periodically scan the logs to see if there are any issues that need attention. You can, however, use the event logs in a more active capacity by documenting actions you perform on a server or configuration changes you make. With the command-line solutions I described, it is very easy to create a custom event message. You should consider creating an event every time you perform some significant action on a server, such as installing a new application. This uses the event logs as a poor man's change management system.

Using a graphical user interface

None of the graphical tools (e.g., Event Viewer snap-in) allow you to create custom event log messages.

Using a command-line interface

To create an event on a remote machine, specify the /S option followed by the host name for *eventcreate*, and specify -m followed by \\ and the hostname for *logevent*.

Use /U and /P to specify an alternate user account and password, respectively, with *eventcreate* (there are no similar options for *logevent*).

Using VBScript

With WSH, you can create an event only in the Application log. The WMI Event Log classes do not support creating custom event log messages. However, you can shell out with the *eventcreate* command to create events in other logs.

See Also

MS KB 324145 (HOW TO: Create Custom Events)

8.2 Viewing Events

Problem

You want to view events in an event log.

Solution

Using a graphical user interface

1. Open the Event Viewer (*eventvwr.msc*). To connect to a remote computer, in the left pane right-click the **Event Viewer** icon and select **Connect to another computer**.

2. In the left pane, click on the event log containing the events you want to view.

3. Double-click on an event you want to view in the right pane.

Using a command-line interface

You can use either the *eventquery.vbs* or *psloglist* commands to list the events in an event log. In both of the following examples, the last 10 records from the Application log are displayed. Both commands have numerous other options to view events, so look at the command syntax help for more information.

```
> eventquery.vbs /s <ServerName> /l <LogName> /R <MaxEvents>
```

For example:

```
> eventquery.vbs /s server01 /l Application /R 10
```

Using *psloglist*:

```
> psloglist \\<ServerName> -n <MaxEvents> <LogName>
```

For example:

```
> psloglist \\server01 -n 10 Application
```

Using VBScript

```
' This code displays events in an Event Log.
' ------ SCRIPT CONFIGURATION ------
strLog = "<LogName>"       ' e.g., Application
intNum = <intMax>          ' e.g., 10  (Max number of events to display)
strServer = "<ServerName>" ' e.g., fs01 (use "." for local server)
' ------ END CONFIGURATION ---------

' These constants are taken from WbemFlagEnum
const wbemFlagReturnImmediately = 16
const wbemFlagForwardOnly = 32

' This first part is used to determine how many events are in the log
set objWMI = GetObject("winmgmts:\\" & strServer & "\root\cimv2")
set colLogs = objWMI.ExecQuery("Select * from Win32_NTEventlogFile " & _
            "Where Logfilename = '" & strLog & "'",, _
            wbemFlagReturnImmediately + wbemFlagForwardOnly)
if colLogs.Count > 1 then
   WScript.Echo "Fatal error.  Number of logs found: " & colLogs.Count
   WScript.Quit
end if
for each objLog in colLogs
   intLogMax = objLog.NumberofRecords
next

if intLogMax > intNum then
   intNum = intLogMax - intNum
else
   intNum = intLogMax
end if

' Now I get all of the events up to total of intNum
set colEvents = objWMI.ExecQuery("Select * from Win32_NTLogEvent " & _
            "Where Logfile = '" & strLog & "' and RecordNumber >= " & _
            intNum,,wbemFlagReturnImmediately + wbemFlagForwardOnly)
for each objEvent in colEvents
   Wscript.Echo "Date: " & objEvent.TimeWritten
   Wscript.Echo "Source: " & objEvent.SourceName
   Wscript.Echo "Category: " & objEvent.Category
   Wscript.Echo "Type: " & objEvent.Type
   Wscript.Echo "Event Code: " & objEvent.EventCode
   Wscript.Echo "User: " & objEvent.User
   Wscript.Echo "Computer: " & objEvent.ComputerName
   Wscript.Echo "Message: " & objEvent.Message
   WScript.Echo "------"
next
```

Discussion

An event log message is composed of several fields. Table 8-2 explains each field.

Table 8-2 . Event message fields

Field	Description
Date	Date the event occurred. Example: 3/15/2005.
Time	Local time the event occurred. Example: 12:09:23AM.
Type	Information, Warning, or Error.
User	User account that caused the event to be generated (if applicable). Example: AMER\rallen.
Computer	Computer the event was generated on. Example: RALLEN-WXP.
Source	Application or process that generated the event. Example: Automatic Updates.
Category	Classifies events within a source. Example: Download.
Event ID	Number that identifies the event within the source and category. Example: 2512.
Description	Contents of the event message.

Using VBScript

One thing to note in the VBScript solution is my use of two WMI constants: wbemFlagReturnImmediately and wbemFlagForwardOnly. By default, when you use the ExecQuery method to enumerate a collection, the underlying query has to complete before the code will start iterating over the matching records. When you query large event logs, this can impact the performance of the script significantly while it waits to return thousands of records. If you pass wbemFlagReturnImmediately + wbemFlagForwardOnly (48 is the result) as the third parameter to ExecQuery, performance will be greatly improved. wbemFlagReturnImmediately causes ExecQuery to return immediately and allows you to start enumerating over the matching objects as they are returned. wbemFlagForwardOnly requests an enumerator that you cannot rewind, which means WMI can release the objects after you've viewed them.

See Also

Recipes 8.10, 8.12, and MSDN: Improving Enumeration Performance

8.3   Creating a New Event Log

Problem

You want to create a custom event log. This can be useful if you have a custom application that needs to write a bunch of events to the event log and you do not want to clutter one of the default logs.

Solution

Using a graphical interface

1. Open the Registry Editor (*regedit.exe*).
2. In the left pane, browse to **HKLM → SYSTEM → CurrentControlSet → Services → Eventlog**.
3. Right-click on **Eventlog** and select **New → Key**.
4. Enter the name of the new event log and hit Enter.

Using a command-line interface

Create the following registry key and replace *<LogName>* with the name of the new log:

```
> reg add \\<ServerName>\HKLM\SYSTEM\CurrentControlSet\Services\Eventlog\<LogName>
```

Using VBScript

```
' This code creates a new event log.
' ------ SCRIPT CONFIGURATION ------
strNewLog = "<LogName>"       ' e.g., MyLog
strServer = "<ServerName>"    ' e.g., fs01 (use "." for local server)
' ------ END CONFIGURATION ---------
const HKLM = &H80000002
strKeyPath = "SYSTEM\CurrentControlSet\Services\EventLog\" & strNewLog
set objReg = GetObject("winmgmts:\\" & strServer & "\root\default:StdRegProv")
objReg.CreateKey HKLM, strKeyPath
WScript.Echo "Created Event log " & strNewLog
```

Discussion

When you view events in an event log using a tool such as Event Viewer, you are actually interacting with the Event Log service. It is this service that applications interface with to write and retrieve events. Each event log is defined as a subkey under the HKLM\SYSTEM\CurrentControlSet\Services\Eventlog key. The name of the subkey is the name of the event log. The Event Log service constantly monitors this key for the creation of new subkeys. When it finds a new one, it creates a new event log. After it finds a new subkey, the Event Log service creates a file under the *%SystemRoot%\System32\config* directory to contain the event log messages. If you named the subkey **Test**, the file name would be *Test.evt*. You can then configure the new event log like you would one of the defaults (setting the maximum size, retention period, etc.).

See Also

Recipe 8.1, MS KB 216169 (How to Change the Default Event Viewer Log File Location), and MS KB 315417 (HOW TO: Move Event Viewer Log Files to Another Location in Windows 2000)

8.4   Viewing the Size of an Event Log

Problem

You want to find the size of an event log.

Solution

Using a graphical user interface

1. Open the Event Viewer (*eventvwr.msc*).

2. In the left pane, right-click on the target event log and select **Properties**.

3. The **Size** field contains the size of the event log in kilobytes and bytes.

Using a command-line interface

This command displays the file size for all of the event logs that are stored in the default location on the file system:

```
> dir %systemroot%\system32\config\*evt
```

Using VBScript

```
' This code displays the size of the specified event log in KB
' ------ SCRIPT CONFIGURATION ------
strLog = "LogName>"          ' e.g., Security
strServer = "<ServerName>"   ' e.g., fs01 (use "." for local server)
' ------ END CONFIGURATION ---------
set objWMI = GetObject("winmgmts:\\" & strServer & "\root\cimv2")
set colLogs = objWMI.ExecQuery("Select * from Win32_NTEventlogFile Where : & _
                       Logfilename = '" & strLog & "'")
if colLogs.Count > 1 then
   WScript.Echo "Fatal error.  Number of logs found: " & colLogs.Count
   WScript.Quit
end if
for each objLog in colLogs
   WScript.Echo strLog & " size: " & objLog.FileSize / 1024 & "KB"
next
```

Discussion

Each event log has a corresponding event log file, which contains all of the event log messages (stored in a binary format). The size of an event log is determined by viewing the size of its event log file. By default, the *%systemroot%\system32\config* directory contains these files. Each file name directly corresponds to the name of the event log that uses it with an *.evt* extension (e.g., *Application.evt*).

8.5 Setting the Maximum Size of an Event Log

Problem

You want to set the maximum event log size. You need to make sure you size the event logs properly so they do not consume more disk space than necessary.

Solution

Using a graphical user interface

1. Open the Event Viewer (*eventvwr.msc*).
2. In the left pane, right-click on the target event log and select **Properties**.
3. Beside **Maximum Log Size**, enter the maximum size in kilobytes that the event log can grow to.
4. Click **OK**.

Using a command-line interface

Modify the registry using the following command:

```
> reg add \\<ServerName>\HKLM\SYSTEM\CurrentControlSet\Services\Eventlog\<LogName> /t
REG_DWORD /v MaxSize /d <SizeInBytes>
```

Replace *<LogName>* with the name of the event log you want to configure and *<SizeInBytes>* with the maximum size the log can grow to.

Using VBScript

```
' This code sets the maximum size for an event log.
' ------ SCRIPT CONFIGURATION ------
strLog = "<LogName>"          ' e.g., Application
intSizeBytes = <SizeInBytes>  ' e.g., 1024 * 512  (512KB)
strServer = "<ServerName>"    ' e.g., fs01 (use "." for local server)
' ------ END CONFIGURATION ---------
set objWMI = GetObject("winmgmts:\\" & strServer & "\root\cimv2")
set colLogs = objWMI.ExecQuery("Select * from Win32_NTEventlogFile Where " & _
                        "Logfilename = '" & strLog & "'")
if colLogs.Count <> 1 then
    WScript.Echo "Fatal error.  Number of logs found: " & colLogs.Count
    WScript.Quit
end if
for each objLog in colLogs
    objLog.MaxFileSize = intSizeBytes
    objLog.Put_
```

```
    WScript.Echo strLog & " max size set to " & intSizeBytes
next
```

Discussion

The default maximum size of each event log is 512 KB. Depending on how busy your server is and how many services and applications are running, this size may not be sufficient to store all the events that are generated. With disk space so cheap, consider upping the maximum limit to several megabytes. Ultimately, the maximum size of each of your event logs should be large enough to accommodate the number of events that are generated over the retention period (see Recipe 8.6).

 You can also set the maximum size of the application, system, and security logs via group policy. These settings can be found at the following location within a group policy object: Computer Configuration\Windows Settings\Security Settings\Event Log\.

See Also

MS KB 216169 (How to Change the Default Event Viewer Log File Location) and MS KB 315417 (HOW TO: Move Event Viewer Log Files to Another Location in Windows 2000)

8.6   Setting the Event Log Retention Policy

Problem

You want to set the retention policy for events.

Solution

Using a graphical user interface

1. Open the Event Viewer (*eventvwr.msc*).
2. In the left pane, right-click on the target event log and select **Properties**.
3. You can select one of three options under **When maximum log size is reached**.
4. Click **OK**.

Using a command-line interface

The following command sets the retention policy for events in a particular event log. Two special values you can set for *<TimeInSeconds>* are 0 to overwrite as needed and 4294967295 to never overwrite.

```
> reg add \\<ServerName>\HKLM\SYSTEM\CurrentControlSet\Services\Eventlog\<LogName> /t
REG_DWORD /v Retention /d <TimeInSeconds>
```

Using VBScript

```
' This code sets the number of days events are kept for an event log.
' ------ SCRIPT CONFIGURATION ------
strLog = "<LogName>"          ' e.g., Application
intDays = <NumDays>           ' e.g., 14   (number of days to keep events)
strServer = "<ServerName>"    ' e.g., fs01 (use "." for local server)
' ------ END CONFIGURATION ---------
set objWMI = GetObject("winmgmts:\\" & strServer & "\root\cimv2")
set colLogs = objWMI.ExecQuery("Select * from Win32_NTEventlogFile Where " & _
                               "Logfilename = '" & strLog & "'")
if colLogs.Count <> 1 then
   WScript.Echo "Fatal error.  Number of logs found: " & colLogs.Count
   WScript.Quit
end if
for each objLog in colLogs
   objLog.OverwriteOutdated = intDays
   objLog.Put_
   WScript.Echo strLog & " retention set to " & intDays
next
```

Discussion

There are three basic retention options for event logs:

Overwrite events as needed
Once the maximum event log size is reached, the oldest events get overwritten with new events.

Overwrite events older than a certain number of days
Once the maximum event log size is reached, overwrite only those events that are older than the specified number of days. If there are no events older than the specified day, the event won't be written.

Do not overwrite events
Once the maximum event log size is reached, no events are written.

In the case of the last two options, it is possible for events to not be written to the log because the event log reached its maximum size. With the last option, you need to have a process in place to clear the event log after you've archived the logs. If you do this, be sure to set the maximum size so there is ample space.

You can also set the retention policy of the application, system, and security logs via group policy. These settings can be found at the following location within a group policy object: `Computer Configuration\ Windows Settings\Security Settings\Event Log\`.

If you are trying to decrease the maximum event log size using group policy, be sure to look at MS KB 824245.

See Also

Recipes 8.7, 8.11, and MS KB 824245 (The size of the event log cannot be reduced by using Group Policy)

8.7 Clearing the Events in an Event Log

Problem

You want to clear all of the events in an event log. Typically you do not want to do this unless you've backed up or archived the log. Clearing an event log without saving the events makes it very difficult to track down and troubleshoot problems later.

Solution

Using a graphical user interface

1. Open the Event Viewer (*eventvwr.msc*).

2. In the left pane, right-click on the target event log and select **Clear all Events**.

3. You then have an option to save the log before clearing it. Click **Yes** to save it or **No** to not save it.

Using a command-line interface

The following command clears an event log:

```
> wmic /node:"<ServerName>" nteventlog where "Logfilename = '<LogName>'" Call
ClearEventLog
```

Here is an example that clears the DNS Server log on server *dns01*:

```
> wmic /node:"dns01" nteventlog where "Logfilename = 'DNS Server'" Call ClearEventLog
```

 The *wmic* command cannot be run on Windows 2000. You can target a remote computer that is running Windows 2000, but you must run the command on Windows Server 2003 or Windows XP.

Using VBScript

```
' This code clears all events from the specified event log.
' ------ SCRIPT CONFIGURATION ------
strLog = "<LogName>"          ' e.g., Application
strServer = "<ServerName>"    ' e.g., fs01 (use "." for local server)
' ------ END CONFIGURATION ---------
set objWMI = GetObject("winmgmts:\\" & strServer & "\root\cimv2")
set colLogs = objWMI.ExecQuery("Select * from Win32_NTEventlogFile Where " & _
                               "Logfilename = '" & strLog & "'")
if colLogs.Count <> 1 then
    WScript.Echo "Fatal error.  Number of logs found: " & colLogs.Count
```

```
        WScript.Quit
    end if
    for each objLog in colLogs
        objLog.ClearEventLog
        WScript.Echo strLog & " cleared"
    next
```

Discussion

If you clear the Security event log, event 517 will be automatically generated in the Security log. This event indicates the log was cleared and is important from an auditing perspective. Without event 517, you wouldn't have an idea if the security log had previously been cleared. This doesn't happen for the other logs.

See Also

MS KB 315147 (HOW TO: Clear the Event Logs in Windows 2000)

8.8   Restricting Access to an Event Log

Problem

You want to restrict who can view the event logs on a server.

Solution

The default behavior on Windows 2000 is that anyone can view the event logs (including the Guest account and users connecting with null connections). To restrict this, you need to create the following Registry value: `HKEY_LOCAL_MACHINE\SYSTEM\CurrentControlSet\Services\EventLog\<LogName>\RestrictGuestAccess`, where `<LogName>` is the name of the event log (e.g., Application) you want to restrict. The value should be of type REG_DWORD with the value data set to 1. This limits access to members of the local Administrators group. You can also configure this in group policy. There are three settings that correspond to restricting access to the application, system, and security logs. These settings can be found under `Computer Configuration\Windows Settings\Security Settings\Event Log\`.

With Windows Server 2003, the way event logs are restricted has changed. The `RestrictGuestAccess` registry value is no longer used. It has been replaced with a `CustomSD` value (in the same registry location) that contains a Security Descriptor string (SDDL) that determines what users have access to the event logs. Unfortunately, at the time of this writing, Microsoft has not provided a graphical interface or even a command-line interface for abstracting away the messy details of SDDL. That means if you want to restrict access, you need to learn a little something about SDDL. For a good description of how you can accomplish this, read MS KB 323076 (HOW TO: Set Event Log Security Locally or by Using Group Policy in Windows Server 2003).

Discussion

If you are security conscious, as all good system administrators should be these days, you should be concerned that event logs (except the Security log) on your servers are world-readable by default. The event logs on certain types of servers, such as domain controllers, are a feeding ground of important information for potential attackers. Fortunately, the Security event log is treated differently and not viewable by non-administrators.

Restricting access to the event logs is not as easy as you might hope. In fact, on Windows Server 2003 you have to construct a SDDL string to do it, which can be a little complicated. See the following sites for more information:

- *http://msdn.microsoft.com/library/en-us/debug/base/event_logging_security.asp*
- *http://msdn.microsoft.com/library/en-us/security/security/security_descriptor_string_format.asp*

See Also

MS KB 323076 (HOW TO: Set Event Log Security Locally or by Using Group Policy in Windows Server 2003)

8.9   Searching an Event Log on a Server

Problem

You want to search for events in a specific event log.

Solution

Using a graphical user interface

1. Open the Event Viewer (*eventvwr.msc*).
2. In the left pane, right-click on the event log you want to search and select **Properties**.
3. Click the **Filter** tab.
4. Enter the search criteria and click **OK**.

 Another alternative for searching the event logs on a single host is the Event Comb utility, which I cover in Recipe 8.10.

Using a command-line interface

You can use the *eventquery.vbs* command on Windows Server 2003 to remotely query the event log of a server. The following command displays the last 10 events with event ID 105 on the host fs01:

```
> eventquery.vbs /S fs01 /R 10 /L Application /FI "ID eq 105"
```

On Windows 2000, you can use a combination of the *elogdmp* and *findstr* commands to find specific events. The following command displays events in the Application log that have the string 105 somewhere in the event (it could be in the description, the event ID, etc.):

```
> elogdmp server01 Application | findstr 105
```

Obviously this may not find exactly what you want, but since the output of *elogdmp* is comma-delimited, you can play around with what you pass to *findstr* to improve your odds of returning exactly what you want. For example:

```
> elogdmp server01 Application | findstr ",105,"
```

Using VBScript

```
' This code searches for events matching the specified criteria.
' ------ SCRIPT CONFIGURATION ------
intEventCode = <EventID>              ' Event ID to match; e.g., 105
strLog       = "<EventLogName>"       ' Event log name; e.g., Application
intMaxNum    = <MaxNumberOfEvents>    ' Max events to return (0 for all)
strServer    = "<ServerName>"         ' Use "." for local server
' ------ END CONFIGURATION ---------
set objWMI = GetObject("winmgmts:\\" & strServer & "\root\cimv2")
set colEvents = objWMI.ExecQuery("Select * from Win32_NTLogEvent " & _
                         " Where Logfile = '" & strLog & "'" & _
                         " and EventCode = " & intEventCode)
count = 0
for each objEvent in colEvents
    Wscript.Echo "Date: " & objEvent.TimeWritten
    Wscript.Echo "Source: " & objEvent.SourceName
    Wscript.Echo "Category: " & objEvent.Category
    Wscript.Echo "Type: " & objEvent.Type
    Wscript.Echo "Event Code: " & objEvent.EventCode
    Wscript.Echo "User: " & objEvent.User
    Wscript.Echo "Computer: " & objEvent.ComputerName
    Wscript.Echo "Message: " & objEvent.Message
    WScript.Echo "------"
    WScript.Echo
    count = count + 1
    if intMaxNum > 0 and count >= intMaxNum then
        WScript.Echo "Reached maximum threshold...exiting"
        exit for
    end if
next
```

Discussion

The solutions in this recipe describe how to search events on a single server. If you want to search for events across multiple servers at the same time, look at Recipe 8.10.

8.10 Searching the Event Logs on Multiple Servers

Problem

You want to search for events across multiple computers.

Solution

Using a graphical user interface

1. Open the Event Comb utility (*eventcombmt.exe*). When you first start the tool, it launches a **Simple Instructions** dialog box that contains the following directions:

2. Verify the **Domain** box shows the domain for which you want to search.

3. Right-click the box labeled **Select to Search/Right Click To Add**. Add the servers you want to search—e.g., All the DCs or individual servers.

4. Choose the log files you want to search, e.g., System, Application.

5. Select the event type you would like to search for, e.g., Error, Warning.

6. Enter the event IDs you would like to search for, e.g., 6005, in the **Event IDs** text box.

7. Click **Search** to start your search.

Using a command-line interface

None of the standard command-line tools support searching the event logs across multiple servers. You can, however, use a *for* command to run a query against several servers at once. Here are a couple of examples.

For Windows Server 2003:

```
> for /D %i in ("server01","server02") do eventquery.vbs /S %i /R 10 /L Application /
FI "ID eq 105"
```

For Windows Server 2000:

```
> for /D %i in ("server01","server02") do elogdmp %i Application | findstr ",105,"
```

Using VBScript

```
' This code searches for events that match the specified criteria
' across several servers.
' ------ SCRIPT CONFIGURATION ------
```

```
intEventCode = <EventID>              ' Event ID to match; e.g., 105
strLog       = "<EventLogName>"       ' Event log name; e.g., Application
intMaxNum    = <MaxNumberOfEvents>    ' Max events to return (0 for all)
arrServers   = Array("server01","server02")
' ------ END CONFIGURATION ---------
for each strServer in arrServers
   WScript.Echo vbCrLf & vbCrLf
   WScript.Echo "Searching " & strServer & "...." & vbCrLf
   set objWMI = GetObject("winmgmts:\\" & strServer & "\root\cimv2")
   set colEvents = objWMI.ExecQuery("Select * from Win32_NTLogEvent " & _
                           " Where Logfile = '" & strLog & "'" & _
                           " and EventCode = " & intEventCode)
   count = 0
   for each objEvent in colEvents
      Wscript.Echo "Date: " & objEvent.TimeWritten
      Wscript.Echo "Source: " & objEvent.SourceName
      Wscript.Echo "Category: " & objEvent.Category
      Wscript.Echo "Type: " & objEvent.Type
      Wscript.Echo "Event Code: " & objEvent.EventCode
      Wscript.Echo "User: " & objEvent.User
      Wscript.Echo "Computer: " & objEvent.ComputerName
      Wscript.Echo "Message: " & objEvent.Message
      WScript.Echo "------"
      WScript.Echo
      count = count + 1
      if intMaxNum > 0 and count >= intMaxNum then
         WScript.Echo "Reached maximum threshold...exiting"
         exit for
      end if
   next
next
```

Discussion

The Event Comb utility is an extremely useful and powerful tool to have in your arsenal. Microsoft initially developed it for Windows 2000, but gave it out only to customers experiencing specific issues that required the ability to search the event logs on multiple servers. After the release of Windows Server 2003, Microsoft made it generally available as part of the Account Lockout toolset (*http://www.microsoft.com/downloads/details.aspx?displaylang=en&familyid=7af2e69c-91f3-4e63-8629-b999adde0b9e)* and also in the Windows Server 2003 Resource Kit Tools. Spend some time with it and get familiar with its capabilities.

See Also

MS KB 824209 (How to Use the EventcombMT Utility to Search Event Logs for Account Lockouts)

8.11   Archiving an Event Log

Problem

You want to archive your event logs so you can retrieve them later if necessary.

Solution

Using a graphical user interface

1. Open the Event Viewer (*eventvwr.msc*).
2. In the left pane, right-click on the target event log and select **Save Log File As**.
3. Browse to the location to save the file, enter a name for the file, and click **Save**.

Using a command-line interface

Using the *wmic* utility, you can call the BackupEventLog method that is available with the Win32_NTEventlogfile class:

```
> wmic /node:"<ServerName>" nteventlog where "Logfilename = '<LogName>'" Call
BackupEventLog "<FilePath>"
```

Here is an example of backing up the Application event log:

```
> wmic /node:"fs01" nteventlog where "Logfilename = 'Application'" Call
BackupEventLog "E:\app_back.evt"
```

Using VBScript

```
' This code archives an event log to the specified file.
' ------ SCRIPT CONFIGURATION ------
strLog = "<LogName>"                 ' e.g., Application
strBackupFile = "<FileNameAndPath>"  ' e.g., c:\app_back.evt
strServer = "<ServerName>"           ' e.g., fs01 (use "." for local server)
' ------ END CONFIGURATION ---------
set objWMI = GetObject(_
               "winmgmts:{impersonationLevel=impersonate,(Backup)}!\\" & _
               strServer & "\root\cimv2")
set colLogs = objWMI.ExecQuery("Select * from Win32_NTEventlogFile Where " & _
                         " Logfilename = '" & strLog & "'")
if colLogs.Count <> 1 then
   WScript.Echo "Fatal error.  Number of logs found: " & colLogs.Count
   WScript.Quit
end if
for each objLog in colLogs
   objLog.BackupEventLog strBackupFile
   WScript.Echo strLog & " backed up to " & strBackupFile
next
```

Discussion

You should consider archiving the event logs at least on your most important servers. If nothing else, archive your Security logs so that you can retrieve them if you need to go back and look for suspicious activity. Instead of backing up the log files on the local server, you can also specify a UNC path to a remote file server. If the event logs are using a lot of disk space, you might want to create a simple batch script to archive the event logs and then clear them (see Recipe 8.7). If you are backing up your whole server using a tool like NTBackup, you probably don't need to archive the event logs individually.

8.12   Finding More Information About an Event

Problem

You want to find additional information about the cause or purpose of an event. Often, the information contained in an event is not sufficient to accurately assess or troubleshoot the issue that resulted in it being created.

Solution

You have a few options for finding additional information about a particular event.

When you view the details of an event in the Event Viewer under Windows Server 2003, you will see a link at the bottom of the description for the event. If you click on that link, it will open the Help and Support Center and dynamically query the Microsoft web site to find if anymore information is available for that event. I've tested this with quite a few events and so far and most come back with no additional information. I assume that this will improve over time as Microsoft has a chance to update the site. You can also search for information about events on Microsoft's support web site (*http://support.microsoft.com/*).

A better source of information about events than the Microsoft Help and Support Center is the EventID web site (*http://www.eventid.net/*). There, they have been building a knowledge base about events since 2001. They have over 2800 events in their database that numerous contributors have commented on.

Another option is to search the newsgroup archives. People like to include event log messages in newsgroup posts when they are trying to troubleshoot a problem. It is possible that someone has posted a question about the event you are interested in. The best source for searching newsgroups is the Google Groups web site (*http://groups.google.com*).

8.13   Triggering an Action When an Event Occurs

 You must be running Windows XP or Windows Server 2003 to use event triggers.

Problem

You want to kick off a program or script when a particular event occurs. For example, you may want to send yourself an email when the event occurs or write another event to the event log.

Solution

Using a graphical user interface

Event Viewer doesn't support creating triggers.

Using a command-line interface

Windows Server 2003 comes with a new tool called *eventtriggers* that allows you to configure event log triggers.

```
> eventtriggers /Create /TR "<TriggerName>" /L <LogName> /EID <EventID> /TK <Command>
```

For example:

```
> eventtriggers /Create /TR "Email Trigger" /L Application /EID 177 /TK "cscript
c:\scripts\email.vbs"
```

To view the list of event log triggers configured on a server, run this command:

```
> eventtriggers /query /s <ServerName>
```

To delete a trigger with ID 1, run this command:

```
> eventtriggers /delete /s <ServerName> /TID 1
```

To get a list of configured triggers, run this command:

```
> eventtriggers /query /s <ServerName>
```

Using VBScript

See Recipe 8.14 for an example of how to monitor events as they occur via a script.

Discussion

The *eventtriggers* utility is a powerful new tool that can run on a Windows XP or Windows Server 2003 computer and that runs a command when a specific event occurs. It has three main options for managing event triggers: /Create, /Delete, and /Query. Here is the syntax for the eventtriggers /Create option:

```
Parameter List:
    /S      system          Specifies the remote system to connect to.

    /U      [domain\]user   Specifies the user context under which the
                            command should execute.

    /P      [password]      Specifies the password for the given user
                            context. Prompts for input if omitted.

    /TR     triggername     Specifies a friendly name to associate with
                            the Event Trigger.

    /L      log             Specifies the NT Event Log(s) to monitor
                            events from. Valid types include Application, System,
Security, DNS Server Log, and Directory Log. The wildcard "*" may be used and the
default value is "*".

    /EID    id              Specifies a specific Event ID the Event
                            Trigger should monitor.

    /T      type            Specifies an Event Type that the trigger
                            should monitor. Valid values include "ERROR",
"INFORMATION", "WARNING", "SUCCESSAUDIT", and "FAILUREAUDIT".

    /SO     source          Specifies a specific Event Source the Event
                            Trigger should monitor.

    /D      description     Specifies the description of the Event
                            Trigger.

    /TK     taskname        Specifies the task to execute when the
                            Event Trigger conditions are met.

    /RU     username        Specifies the user account (user context)
                            under which the task runs. For the system
                            account value must be "".

    /RP     password        Specifies the password for the user.
                            To prompt for the password, the value
                            must be either "*" or none.
                            Password will have no effect for the "SYSTEM"
                            account.
```

8.14   Script: Event Watcher

You want to watch events in real time as they occur. The Event Viewer utility works fine to view the events that have occurred on a system at a particular point in time, but it doesn't provide an auto-refresh capability, so if you need to constantly monitor for new events, you have to manually refresh the screen.

Here is a simple piece of code that lets you view events as they happen:

```
' This code displays events for all logs as they occur.

Option Explicit

' ------ SCRIPT CONFIGURATION ------
Dim strComputer : strComputer = "."
' ------ END CONFIGURATION ---------
Dim objWMI : set objWMI = GetObject("winmgmts:\\" & strComputer & "\root\cimv2")
Dim colEvents : set colEvents = objWMI.ExecNotificationQuery( _
                    "Select * from __InstanceCreationEvent WHERE " & _
                    " TargetInstance ISA 'Win32_NTLogEvent'")
Do
    Dim objEvent : set objEvent = colEvents.NextEvent
    WScript.Echo "---------------------------"
    WScript.Echo objEvent.TargetInstance.Logfile & " Event Log"
    WScript.Echo "---------------------------"
    WScript.Echo "Event ID:   " & objEvent.TargetInstance.EventIdentifier
    WScript.Echo "Source:     " & objEvent.TargetInstance.SourceName
    WScript.Echo "Category:   " & objEvent.TargetInstance.CategoryString
    WScript.Echo "Event Type: " & objEvent.TargetInstance.Type
    Dim strText
    for each strText in objEvent.TargetInstance.InsertionStrings
        WScript.Echo "Event Text: " & strText
    next
    WScript.Echo "Computer:   " & objEvent.TargetInstance.ComputerName
    WScript.Echo "User:       " & objEvent.TargetInstance.User
    WScript.Echo "Time:       " & objEvent.TargetInstance.TimeWritten
    WScript.Echo
Loop
```

I've used a temporary WMI event consumer to monitor for new instances of the Win32_NTLogEvent class. The query for this event consumer is set in the colEvents variable. The Win32_NTLogEvent class represents Event Log events. Because I didn't restrict the query further, it will return any event that occurs. You could add additional criteria at the end of the Select statement to restrict the types of events it looks for. This query matches only new events in the Application log:

```
Select * from __InstanceCreationEvent
  Where TargetInstance ISA 'Win32_NTLogEvent'
    And TargetInstance.Logfile = 'Application'
```

This query matches only events in the System log that have an event ID of 1000:

```
Select * from __InstanceCreationEvent
  Where TargetInstance ISA 'Win32_NTLogEvent'
    And TargetInstance.Logfile = 'System'
    And TargetInstance.EventIdentifier = '1000'
```

Following the instantiation of the colEvents variable is a Do loop. This causes the script to run indefinitely (until you type **Ctrl-C** to exit it). The colEvents.NextEvent statement in the Do loop simply causes the script to wait until it finds an event that matches the query previously set. So if no new events occur, you won't see any output from the script, but as soon as one does, you'll see something like the following:

```
C:\>cscript eventmonitor.vbs
Microsoft (R) Windows Script Host Version 5.6
Copyright (C) Microsoft Corporation 1996-2001. All rights reserved.


----------------------------
Application Event Log
----------------------------

Event ID:   101
Source:     EventCreate
Category:
Event Type: Error
Event Text: Just a test
Computer:   rallen-w2k3
User:       rallen-w2k3\admin
Time:       20040319090153.000000-300
```

CHAPTER 9

Registry

9.0 Introduction

The registry is the primary repository for system, application, and user profile configuration information for the Windows operating system. It is a hierarchical database that is structured and used much like a filesystem. The operating system uses the registry to store information as static as environment variables and as dynamic as performance data. The registry is constantly being used by the OS and applications to read, write, and query configuration settings.

Don't Be Scared of the Registry

You have probably seen this warning or one similar to it in an article, book, or Microsoft KB article:

> WARNING: If you use Registry Editor incorrectly, you may cause serious problems that may require you to reinstall your operating system. Microsoft cannot guarantee that you can solve problems that result from using Registry Editor incorrectly. Use Registry Editor at your own risk.

I think this type of warning has made some people overly cautious about modifying or even browsing the registry. I'm here to say that it doesn't have to be that way. Sure, you can muck up the registry, just like you can muck up the operating system or just about any application if you haphazardly delete or modify things. But you are a reasonable person that won't go around making changes on a production system unless you know the impact, so let's put concerns about modifying the registry behind us and move forward. Use the registry as a great source of configuration information and a mechanism to customize the operating system.

Using a Graphical User Interface

Windows 2000 came with two graphical registry editors that had different benefits. The first (*regedit.exe*) was more user-friendly, had better search capabilities, and was easy to work with while the other (*regedt32.exe*) was much more powerful. In Windows Server 2003, most of the features of these two tools were combined into a single tool. Now, Registry Editor has the same look and feel as the user-friendly version in Windows 2000 (*regedit.exe*), but also incorporates some important features such as permission editing from *regedt32.exe*. If you run either *regedit.exe* or *regedt32.exe*, you'll bring up the same tool.

One other graphical tool you should be familiar with is Registry Monitor (*regmon.exe*) from Sysinternals. With it, you can view all of the registry activity on a system in real-time. You can restrict the output to a certain key, and limit the type of activity (read, write, etc.). I cover Registry Monitor in more detail in Recipe 9.12.

Using a Command-Line Interface

The one command-line tool I use extensively throughout this chapter is *reg.exe*. In Windows 2000, *reg.exe* could be found in the Support Tools, but it comes installed by default with Windows Server 2003. With it, you can:

- Search the registry
- Add, modify, and delete registry keys and values
- Import, export, and compare registry files

Using VBScript

WMI has a single class called StdRegProv that provides most of the functions you'll need to programmatically manage the registry. Table 9-1 lists the methods available with this class. This class is a little different from most others in that it doesn't contain properties for object instances (keys, values, etc.). To obtain information about a registry key or value, you have to use one of the methods shown in Table 9-1.

Table 9-1. StdRegProv methods

Method	Description
CheckAccess	Determines if a user has the specified permissions on a registry key
CreateKey	Creates a key
DeleteKey	Deletes a key
DeleteValue	Deletes a value
EnumKey	Enumerates the subkeys of a key
EnumValues	Enumerates the values of a key
GetBinaryValue	Retrieves data from REG_BINARY value
GetDWORDValue	Retrieves data from REG_DWORD value

Table 9-1. StdRegProv methods (continued)

Method	Description
GetExpandedStringValue	Retrieves data from REG_EXPAND_SZ value
GetMultiStringValue	Retrieves data from REG_MULTI_SZ value
GetStringValue	Retrieves data from REG_SZ value
SetBinaryValue	Sets data for REG_BINARY value
SetDWORDValue	Sets data for REG_DWORD value
SetExpandedStringValue	Sets data for REG_EXPAND_SZ value
SetMultiStringValue	Sets data for REG_MULTI_SZ value
SetStringValue	Sets data for REG_SZ value

9.1   Creating and Deleting a Key

Problem

You want to create or delete a registry key.

Solution

Using a graphical user interface

1. Open the Registry Editor (*regedit.exe*).
2. Browse to the location where you want to create or delete a key.
3. To create a key: Right-click the parent key, select **New → Key**, type the name of the key, and hit Enter.
4. To delete a key: Right-click the key you want to delete, select **Delete**, and click **Yes** to confirm.

Using a command-line interface

The following command creates a registry key in the HKLM hive called `Rallencorp`:

```
> reg add \\<ServerName>\HKLM\Software\Rallencorp
```

The following command deletes the same registry key:

```
> reg delete \\<ServerName>\HKLM\Software\Rallencorp
```

You will be prompted to confirm the deletion. Use the /f option to delete the key and bypass the confirmation prompt.

If you have a registry file (i.e., a file with a *.reg* extension), you can also import it using *regedit*:

```
> regedit /s <Filename>
```

The /s option suppresses all windows and dialog boxes. See MS KB 310516 for more on creating registry files.

Using VBScript

```
' This code creates a registry key.
' ------ SCRIPT CONFIGURATION ------
const HKLM = &H80000002
strKeyPath = "<RegKey>"        ' e.g., Software\Rallencorp
strComputer = "<ServerName>" ' e.g., serv01 (use "." for local server)
' ------ END CONFIGURATION ---------
set objReg = GetObject("winmgmts:\\" & strComputer & "\root\default:StdRegProv")
intRC = objReg.CreateKey(HKLM, strKeyPath)
if intRC <> 0 then
    WScript.Echo "Error creating key: " & intRC
else
    WScript.Echo "Successfully created key " & strKeyPath
end if

' This code deletes a registry key.
' ------ SCRIPT CONFIGURATION ------
const HKLM = &H80000002
strKeyPath = "<RegKey>"        ' e.g., Software\Rallencorp
strComputer = "<ServerName>" ' e.g., server01 (use "." for local server)
' ------ END CONFIGURATION ---------
set objReg = GetObject("winmgmts:\\" & strComputer & "\root\default:StdRegProv")
intRC = objReg.DeleteKey(HKLM, strKeyPath)
if intRC <> 0 then
    WScript.Echo "Error deleting key: " & intRC
else
    WScript.Echo "Successfully deleted key " & strKeyPath
end if
```

Discussion

A registry key is nothing more than a container of other keys and registry values. There are six root keys that are used to logically group similar registry data. Table 9-2 lists each of the root keys and describes their purpose.

Table 9-2. The six root keys of the registry

Root key	Description
HKEY_LOCAL_MACHINE	This is the most important root key. It is where most system and application configuration data is stored. It is abbreviated HKLM.
HKEY_CURRENT_USER	This is actually a link to the subkey under HKEY_USERS for the currently logged on user. This is useful because it allows applications to access a single registry path to get any configuration information for the currently logged on user. It is abbreviated HKCU.
HKEY_CURRENT_CONFIG	This is also a link that points under HKLM to hardware information for the current hardware profile. Since you can have different hardware profiles (as you can user profiles), this allows applications to access the one that is currently in use. It is abbreviated HKCC.

Table 9-2. The six root keys of the registry (continued)

Root key	Description
HKEY_CLASSES_ROOT	The subkeys under this key map file extensions to the applications that own them. It is abbreviated HKCR and is a link to HKLM\Software\Classes.
HKEY_PERFORMANCE_DATA	This key is used by applications that want to access performance data. It doesn't actually store the performance data, but serves as an interface to the data. It is abbreviated HKPD.
HKEY_USERS	This key stores profile information for all users of the system. It contains things such as environment variable values and user-specific customization settings. It is abbreviated HKU.

See Also

Recipe 9.2 for setting a value, MS KB 310516 (How to back up, edit, and restore the registry in Windows XP and Windows Server 2003), MS KB 82821 (Registration Info Editor (REGEDIT) Command-Line Switches), and MS KB 310516 (How To Add, Modify, or Delete Registry Subkeys and Values by Using a Registration Entries (.reg) File)

9.2   Setting a Value

Problem

You want to create, modify, or delete a registry value.

Solution

Using a graphical user interface

1. Open the Registry Editor (*regedit.exe*).
2. Browse to the parent key of the value you want to set or delete.
3. To create a value:
4. Right-click on the parent key and select **New** and the type of value you want to create.
5. Type the name of the value and hit enter twice. This should cause the **Edit** dialog box to open.
6. Type the value for the value and click **OK**.
7. To modify a value:
   a. In the right pane, right-click on the value and select **Modify**.
   b. Enter the new data for the value and click **OK**.
8. To delete a value:
   a. In the right pane, right-click on the value and select **Delete**.
   b. Click **Yes** to confirm.

Using a command-line interface

The following command sets a registry value:

```
> reg add \\<ServerName>\<Key> /v <ValueName> /t <ValueType> /d <ValueData>
```

For example:

```
> reg add \\fs01\HKLM\Software\Rallencorp /v Version /t REG_SZ /d "1.2"
> reg add \\.\HKLM\Software\Rallencorp /v Setting1 /t REG_DWORD /d 1024
```

One nice thing about the *reg add* command is that it automatically creates the Rallencorp subkey if it doesn't already exist.

This command deletes a registry value:

```
> reg delete \\<ServerName>\<Key> /v <ValueName>
```

For example:

```
> reg delete \\fs01\HKLM\Software\Rallencorp /v Version
```

Using VBScript

 WMI has different methods for setting each of the registry value datatypes. For example, to set a DWORD, you must use SetDWORDValue, not SetStringValue. See Table 9-1 for the complete list of methods.

```
' This code sets a registry string value
' ------ SCRIPT CONFIGURATION ------
const HKLM = &H80000002
strKeyPath = "<RegKey>"               ' e.g., Software\Rallencorp
strStringValueName = "<ValueName>"    ' e.g., Version
strStringValue = "<ValueData>"        ' e.g., 1.2
strComputer = "<ServerName>"          ' e.g., server01 (use "." for local server)
' ------ END CONFIGURATION ---------
set objReg = GetObject("winmgmts:\\" & strComputer & "\root\default:StdRegProv")
intRC = objReg.SetStringValue(HKLM, strKeyPath, strStringValueName, _
                      strStringValue)
if intRC <> 0 then
   WScript.Echo "Error setting value: " & intRC
else
   WScript.Echo "Successfully set value: " & strStringValueName
end if


' This code deletes a registry value
' ------ SCRIPT CONFIGURATION ------
const HKLM = &H80000002
strKeyPath = "<RegKey>"               ' e.g., Software\Rallencorp
strStringValueName = "<ValueName>"    ' e.g., Version
strComputer = "<ServerName>"          ' e.g., server01 (use "." for local server)
' ------ END CONFIGURATION ---------
set objReg = GetObject("winmgmts:\\" & strComputer & "\root\default:StdRegProv")
intRC = objReg.DeleteValue(HKLM, strKeyPath, strStringValueName)
```

```
if intRC <> 0 then
    WScript.Echo "Error deleting value: " & intRC
else
    WScript.Echo "Successfully deleted value: " & strStringValueName
end if
```

Discussion

Registry keys are used to structure the registry. Registry values are to files what registry keys are to folders. This simple analogy helps describe the purpose of registry values: to store data. Values are made up of three elements: value name, value datatype, and value data. The datatype defines the type of data the value can contain. There are 11 total datatypes; I list the six most common in Table 9-3. If you want to see the more obscure datatypes, see MS KB 256986.

Table 9-3. Most common registry datatypes

Datatype	Description
REG_DWORD	A double word (DWORD). A single word is a 16-bit number, so a double word is a 32-bit number (range from 0–4,294,967,296). Often, this datatype is used when a Boolean value is called for (0 or 1).
REG_SZ	An ASCII or Unicode string. This is another popular datatype, which is frequently used to store names, descriptions, and other text-based data.
REG_MULTI_SZ	Stores multiple independent ASCII or Unicode strings. Each string is null-terminated.
REG_EXPAND_SZ	An ASCII or Unicode string that contains one or more environment variables. This is essentially the same as REG_SZ, except that the embedded environment variables should be evaluated when the data is retrieved by the calling application.
REG_BINARY	Binary data. Avoid storing large binary blobs in the registry with this type so you don't exceed the maximum size of the registry or impact query performance.
REG_LINK	Similar to creating a shortcut on the filesystem, except that a REG_LINK creates a shortcut or link from one section of the registry to another. See Recipe 9.10 for more on creating a REG_LINK.

See Also

Recipe 9.3 and MS KB 256986 (Description of the Microsoft Windows Registry)

9.3   Setting Keys or Values Using Group Policy

Problem

You want to set registry keys or values on client computers using group policy. If you need to configure certain registry settings on a large number of hosts, group policy can help you get the job done.

Solution

Using a graphical user interface

1. Open the Group Policy Management Console (*gpmc.msc*).

2. In the left pane, browse to the group policy object you want to modify.

3. Right-click on the group policy object and select **Edit**. This will launch the Group Policy Object Editor.

4. The predefined registry values you can set are contained under **Administrative Templates** under the **User Configuration** and **Computer Configuration** sections.

If you want to configure registry values that aren't contained in the **User Configuration** and **Computer Configuration** sections, you can create a custom administrative template and apply it to a group policy object. For more on how to do that, see the following whitepaper: *http://www.microsoft.com/WINDOWS2000/techinfo/howitworks/management/rbppaper.asp*

Discussion

Unfortunately, the Group Policy Object Editor doesn't show you the corresponding registry path for each setting under **Administrative Templates**. To get that or to see the complete list of registry settings supported in group policy on Windows Server 2003, Windows 2000, and Windows XP, see the following whitepaper:

> *http://www.microsoft.com/downloads/details.aspx?FamilyId=7821C32F-DA15-438D-8E48-45915CD2BC14.*

 If you need to manage a lot of registry settings via group policy, you might want to evaluate AutoProf Policy Maker Registry Extension, which can greatly simplify the task: *http://www.autoprof.com/policy/registry.html.*

9.4   Exporting Registry Files

Problem

You want to export part of the registry to a registry (*.reg*) file.

Solution

Using a graphical user interface

1. Open the Registry Editor (*regedit.exe*).

2. In the left pane, browse to the key you want to export.

---

3. Right-click on the key and select **Export**.

4. Enter a file name to save the export to and click **Save**.

Using a command-line interface

The following command exports part of the registry to a file:

```
> regedit /e <FilePath> <RegKey>
```

For example:

```
> regedit /e c:\rallencorp.reg HKEY_LOCAL_MACHINE\Software\Rallencorp
```

Using VBScript

```
' This code exports the contents of a key to a registry file.
' Since there are no scripting functions to do this, I simply
' shell out to the regedit tool to do it.

' strCommand = "regedit /e <FilePath> <RegKey>"
strCommand = "regedit /e c:\rallencorp.reg HKEY_LOCAL_MACHINE\Software\Rallencorp"
set objWshShell = WScript.CreateObject("WScript.Shell")
intRC = objWshShell.Run(strCommand, 0, TRUE)
if intRC <> 0 then
   WScript.Echo "Error returned from exporting registry: " & intRC
else
   WScript.Echo "No errors returned from exporting the registry file"
end if
```

Discussion

The Registry Editor allows you to export parts of the registry to a text-based file. You can then modify the file and import it back into the registry (perhaps on another host) using Registry Editor (see Recipe 9.5). These registry files have an extension of *.reg*. Windows recognizes this extension so that if you double-click on a *.reg* file, you will automatically be prompted to import its contents into the registry.

The format for this file is easy to follow. Here is an example registry file containing the contents of the HKLM\Software\Google key:

```
Windows Registry Editor Version 5.00

[HKEY_LOCAL_MACHINE\Software\Google]
"DesktopBarAdminInstall"=dword:00000001

[HKEY_LOCAL_MACHINE\Software\Google\CustomSearch]

[HKEY_LOCAL_MACHINE\Software\Google\Deskbar]
"path"="C:\\PROGRA~1\\Google\\GGTASK~1.DLL"
"Version"=dword:00000051
```

```
[HKEY_LOCAL_MACHINE\Software\Google\Miniviewer]
"path"="C:\\Program Files\\Google\\ggviewer81-47.exe"
"Version"=dword:00000051

[HKEY_LOCAL_MACHINE\Software\Google\NavClient]
"test"="41"
"brand"="GGLD"
"installtime"="1068347808"
"sent"=dword:00000001

[HKEY_LOCAL_MACHINE\Software\Google\NavClient\Obsolete]

[HKEY_LOCAL_MACHINE\Software\Google\Verscheck]
"path"="C:\\Program Files\\Google\\ggverscheck81-47.exe"
"Version"=dword:00000051
```

Exporting the registry is useful if you need to implement a significant change to a system. A registry export can act as both a backup in case things go wrong and a change log to help you determine what was modified after the change.

9.5   Importing Registry Files

Problem

You want to import changes to the registry using a registry (*.reg*) file.

Solution

Using a graphical user interface

1. Open an Explorer (*explorer.exe*) window.
2. Browse to the *.reg* file you want to import.
3. Double-click on the file.
4. Click **Yes** to confirm the import.
5. You can accomplish the same thing within Registry Editor by going to **File** → **Import**.

Using a command-line interface

The following command imports a registry key or subkey:

```
> regedit /s <FilePath>
```

For example:

```
> regedit /s c:\rallencorp.reg
```

Using VBScript

```
' This code imports the contents of a registry file.
' Since there are no scripting functions to do this, I simply
' shell out to the regedit tool to do it.

' strCommand = "regedit /s <FilePath>"
strCommand = "regedit /s c:\rallencorp.reg"
set objWshShell = WScript.CreateObject("WScript.Shell")
intRC = objWshShell.Run(strCommand, 0, TRUE)
if intRC <> 0 then
   WScript.Echo "Error returned from importing registry: " & intRC
else
   WScript.Echo "No errors returned from importing the registry file"
end if
```

Discussion

Importing a registry file is as easy as double-clicking it, but this is where the danger lies. Be careful anytime you import a registry file; make sure it contains exactly what you want to import. If you accidentally import the wrong file, it can unintentionally overwrite values. Since registry files are text based, open a file in a text editor such as Notepad to see what it contains.

9.6   Searching the Registry

Problem

You want to search the registry for the occurrence of a string or number.

Solution

Using a graphical user interface

1. Open the Registry Editor (*regedit.exe*).
2. In the left pane, browse to the key you want to search. If you want to search the entire registry, click on **My Computer** at the top.
3. From the menu, select **Edit → Find**.
4. Enter the string you want to search with and select whether you want to search keys, values, or data.
5. Click the **Find** Next button.
6. If you want to continue searching after a match is found, either select **Edit → Find Next** from the menu or press the **F3** key.

Using a command-line interface

On Windows Server 2003, use the *reg* command to search the registry:

```
> reg query \\<ServerName>\<RegKey> /f <ValueName> /s /k
```

For instance, the following command searches recursively under the specified registry key for all values that contain "Run":

```
> reg query \\server01\HKLM\Software\Microsoft /f Run /s /k
```

Replace the /k switch with /d to perform the same search, but matching only value data (and not key names). Run *reg query /?* for the complete list of search options.

The version of *reg* included with the Windows 2000 Resource Kit does not have all of the search capabilities of the one included with Windows Server 2003. But you can use the *regfind* utility from the Windows 2000 Resource Kit to perform similar searches. Here is the syntax:

```
> regfind -m \\<ServerName> -p <RegKey> -n "<ValueName>"
```

For example:

```
> regfind -m \\server01 -p HKEY_LOCAL_MACHINE\Software\Microsoft -n "Run"
```

View the *regfind* command-line help for all of the search options.

Using VBScript

Unfortunately, the StdRegProv WMI Provider doesn't support searching the registry. Your only options to search the registry via VBScript would be to enumerate over all the keys and values you want to search against (very inefficient), shell out to a command-line utility such as *reg* (see Recipe 9.5 for an example of how to do this), or find a third-party ActiveX control that implements a registry search interface that can be used by scripting languages.

Discussion

The registry contains a significant amount of data. Don't be surprised if your initial search matches a lot of different keys or values that you weren't intending. This is especially true if you search across a whole hive or all of the hives. Try to restrict your search to a specific key when possible.

9.7   Comparing the Registry

Problem

You want to compare the registry on two hosts or compare the registry on the same host after you've installed an application or made other modifications to the registry.

Solution

Using a graphical user interface

1. Use the Registry Editor (*regedit.exe*) to export part of the registry you want to compare for the two target servers (or before and after changes are made on the same server). See Recipe 9.4 for more information on exporting registry files.

2. Open the WinDiff program (*windiff.exe*).

3. From the menu, select **File → Compare Files**.

4. Select the exported registry files you created in step 1.

5. Select **View → Expand** or **View → Outline** from the menu to see the differences.

Discussion

When you export the registry, you are simply exporting the contents of the registry to a text-based file, which you can use to compare against other export files. Windiff is just one example tool that can compare text files and show the differences. Some text editors can do the same (e.g., Textpad is a favorite of mine).

If you only want to see the changes that an application makes during installation, another option is to use the Sysinternals Registry Monitor tool. You can configure Registry Monitor to display only write events for a certain key. For more information on Registry Monitor, see Recipe 9.12.

See Also

MS KB 171780 (How to Use WinDiff to Compare Registry Files)

9.8   Restricting Access to the Registry

Problem

You want to restrict access to a certain registry key or value. This may be necessary if you need to store sensitive data in the registry and want to prevent normal users from seeing it.

Solution

Using a graphical user interface

You must use *regedt32.exe* to set registry permissions on Windows 2000.

1. Open the Registry Editor (*regedit.exe*).

2. In the left pane, browse to the key on which you want to set permissions.

3. Right-click the key and select **Permissions**.

4. To add a new permission, click the Add button. This launches the Object Picker dialog box. Select the user or group you want to add permissions for and click **OK**. The default permission granted to this user or group is read access.

5. To delete a permission, select the user or group you want to remove under **Group or user names** and click the **Remove** button. Click **OK**.

6. To modify a permission, click the **Advanced** button. Select the permission you want to modify under **Permission entries** and click the **Edit** button. Check the boxes corresponding to the permissions you want to grant. Click **OK** until all dialog boxes are closed.

You can also configure registry permissions with group policy. In the left pane of the Group Policy Object Editor, navigate to \Windows Settings\Security Settings\Registry in either the **Computer Config-uration** or the **User Configuration** section. Right-click on **Registry** and select **Add Key**. This allows you to select a target registry key and configure the permissions you wanted on that key.

Using a command-line interface

Use the *subinacl* command to grant access to a registry key. This grants full control for the specified user over a key:

```
> subinacl /verbose=1 /keyreg \\<ServerName>\<KeyPath> /grant=<UserOrGroup>
```

For example:

```
> subinacl /verbose=1 /keyreg \\fs01\HKEY_LOCAL_MACHINE\Software\Rallencorp
/grant=AMER\rallen
```

You can also revoke access to a key using the next command. The following command revokes members of the Users group from being able to access the specified registry key:

```
> subinacl /verbose=1 /keyreg \\<ServerName>\<KeyPath> /revoke=<UserOrGroup>
```

For example:

```
> subinacl /verbose=1 /keyreg \\.\HKEY_LOCAL_MACHINE\Software\Rallencorp
/revoke=Users
```

Lastly, you can view what users and groups have access on a registry key using the /display option with *subinacl* as shown here:

```
> subinacl /verbose=1 /keyreg \\<ServerName>\<KeyPath> /display
```

For example:

```
> subinacl /verbose=1 /keyreg \\fs01\HKEY_LOCAL_MACHINE\Software\Rallencorp /display
```

Discussion

Another useful feature of the permissions function in Registry Editor is Effective Permissions. With it, you can select a user or group and determine what rights it has over a key. And while you can't run this directly on a Windows 2000 system, you can use the remote connection capabilities of Registry Editor to connect to a Windows 2000 system to configure permissions and view effective permissions.

9.9 Backing Up and Restoring the Registry

Problem

You want to back up or restore the registry on a server.

Solution

With the NT Backup utility (*ntbackup.exe*) you can back up the registry by backing up the System State. The System State includes such things as the files necessary to boot the system, the Active Directory database, and the registry. To restore the registry, you have to restore the System State from a previous backup.

Using a graphical user interface

Do the following to back up the System State:

1. Open the NT Backup utility (*ntbackup.exe*) from the Start menu by selecting **Programs → Accessories → System Tools → Backup**.
2. You can click the **Advanced Mode** link to configure backup settings manually or click **Next** to use the wizard interface.
3. Make sure **Back up files and settings** is selected and click Next.
4. To only back up the System State, select **Let me choose what to back up** and click **Next**.
5. Expand **My Computer**, check the box beside **System State**, and click **Next**.
6. Click the **Browse** button to browse to the location where you want to save the back up file and click **Next**.
7. Click **Finish** to start the back up.

Do the following to restore the System State:

1. Browse to the backup file containing the System State you want to restore and double-click the file. This launches the NT Backup utility (*ntbackup.exe*).
2. Click **Next**.
3. Select **Restore files and settings** and click **Next**.

4. Under **Items to restore**, check the box beside **System State** and click **Next**.

5. Click **Finish** to start the restore.

 You may see on the final screen that it states that existing files will not be replaced. This doesn't apply to the System State. Whenever the System State is restored, all System State components are overwritten with the backup version.

Using a command-line interface

The following command backs up the system state to a file:

```
> ntbackup backup systemstate /j "<Description>" /f "<FilePath>"
> ntbackup backup systemstate /j "System State Backup 1" /f "c:\sysstate.bkf"
```

You can't use *ntbackup* from the command line to restore files.

Another option for backing up the registry is to use the *regedit* command to back up specific registry hives to a file. The following command backs up the HKLM hive to a file called *hklm.hiv*:

```
> regedit /e hklm.hiv hkey_local_machine
```

To restore the hive, use the following command:

```
regedit /s hklm.hiv
```

You can use the *reg* command to copy specific subkeys if you don't want to back up an entire hive. For example:

```
> reg save HKLM\Software\Microsoft c:\backup\hklm-sw-ms.hiv
```

To restore the backup to the registry, use the same syntax except replace "save" with "restore":

```
> reg restore <Key> <Filename>
```

Discussion

If you ever run into the case where you have a corrupt registry or perhaps accidentally deleted a section of the registry, the best answer is to restore from your last good system backup. You have to be careful though, restoring the system state restores more than just the registry including system boot files. It also includes the NTDS database for a domain controller.

See Also

MS KB 318149 (How to Maintain Current Registry Backups in Windows NT 4.0 and Windows 2000), MS KB 322755 (HOW TO: Backup, Edit, and Restore the Registry in Windows 2000), and MS KB 322756 (HOW TO: Back Up, Edit, and Restore the Registry in Windows XP and Windows Server 2003)

9.10 Creating a Registry Link

Problem

You want to create a link from one registry key to another. Registry links are used extensively by the operating system, but most people aren't aware that they exist and that they can even be created manually.

Solution

Using a command-line interface

Registry links have never been a highly publicized feature and as a result, there are very few tools that can create them. You can download a tool called *regln* from *http://www.ntinternals.net/regln/* to do the job. This is how you create a registry link with it:

```
> regln <LinkKeyName> <CurrentKeyName>
```

For example:

```
> regln HKLM\SOFTWARE\Rallencorp\Current HKLM\SOFTWARE\Rallencorp\Settings1
```

Use the -d switch to delete a registry link:

```
> regln -d <LinkKeyName>
```

For example:

```
> regln -d HKLM\SOFTWARE\Rallencorp\Current
```

Using VBScript

The StdRegProv WMI Provider does not support creating registry links, so you'll need to shell out to *regln* if you want to create them in a script.

Discussion

You have undoubtedly created a shortcut to a file or folder, perhaps on your desktop, at one point or another. Shortcuts are useful if you have a file that is nested deeply within the filesystem and you don't want to navigate to it each time to access it. Think of registry links in the same way. If there are deeply nested registry keys you need to access on a regular basis, you can use a registry link to make it easier to reach.

Let's say there are a bunch of keys I frequently access that are contained somewhere under the HKEY_LOCAL_MACHINE\Software key. What I could do is create a key called HKEY_LOCAL_MACHINE\Software\Rallencorp and then put all of my registry links under it. Here is an example of creating a link to the Run key:

```
regln HKLM\Software\Rallencorp\Run HKLM\SOFTWARE\Microsoft\Windows\CurrentVersion\Run
```

See Also

More information about the *regln* command can be found at *http://www.tenox.tc/out/regln.txt*.

9.11 Setting the Maximum Registry Size

 This recipe applies only to Windows 2000. On a Windows Server 2003 system, the maximum registry size is constrained only by the amount of physical memory installed.

Problem

You want to set the maximum size to which the registry files can grow.

Solution

For the change to take effect, you must restart the system after changing the size.

Using a graphical user interface

1. Open the **System** applet in the Control Panel.
2. Click the **Advanced** Tab.
3. Click the **Performance Options** button.
4. Click the **Change** button.
5. Modify the maximum registry size setting at the bottom of the dialog box.
6. Click **OK** until all of the windows are closed.

Using a command-line interface

To set the maximum registry size, run the following command:

```
> reg add \\<ServerName>\HKLM\System\CurrentControlSet\Control /v RegistrySizeLimit
/t REG_DWORD /d <SizeInBytes>
```

For example:

```
> reg add \\fs01\HKLM\System\CurrentControlSet\Control /v RegistrySizeLimit /t
REG_DWORD /d 104857600
```

To find the current size of the registry in bytes, run the following command:

```
> dureg -a
```

You can find the *dureg* utility in the Windows 2000 Resource Kit. For some reason it isn't part of the Windows Server 2003 Resource Kit.

Using VBScript

```
' This code sets the maximum registry size on a Windows 2000 server.
' ------ SCRIPT CONFIGURATION ------
intValue     = <SizeInBytes>    ' e.g., 104857600 (size of the registry in bytes)
strComputer = "<ServerName>"   ' e.g., server01 (use "." for local server)
' ------ END CONFIGURATION ---------
const HKLM   = &H80000002
strKeyPath   = "System\CurrentControlSet\Control"
strValueName = "RegistrySizeLimit"
set objReg = GetObject("winmgmts:\\" & strComputer & "\root\default:StdRegProv")
intRC = objReg.SetDwordValue(HKLM, strKeyPath, strValueName, intValue)
if intRC <> 0 then
    WScript.Echo "Error setting value: " & intRC
else
    WScript.Echo "Successfully set value for " & strValueName
end if
```

Discussion

In Windows 2000, the contents of the registry are stored in paged pool, which is an area of physical memory that stores operating system data. By default, paged pool consumes 32 MB of memory, and unused paged pool is written to disk. The default size limit of the registry is 25% of paged pool, or 8 MB. You can configure a higher or lower size limit as I described in the Solution section. This may be needed if you see a message such as this after logging in:

> Your maximum registry size is too small. To ensure that Windows runs properly, increase your registry size.

The registry doesn't automatically consume all of the space that is allocated; it uses only what it needs. The absolute minimum you can configure for the registry is 4 MB and the maximum is 80% of paged pool. The amount of memory allocated for paged pool can be configured by setting the PagedPoolLimit value under HKLM\System\ CurrentControlSet\Control\SessionManager\MemoryManagement.

See Also

MS KB 124594 (Understanding and Configuring Registry Size Limit [RSL])

9.12   Monitoring Registry Activity

Problem

You want to monitor registry accesses. This could involve anything from watching what processes are using the registry to monitoring what a specific user is doing with the registry.

Solution

There are two ways to monitor registry activity. You can view real-time access to the registry with the Sysinternals Registry Monitor (*regmon.exe*) tool. With it you can view the process name, the PID, and the operation performed (e.g., QueryKey, EnumerateValue, SetValue, etc.) for all the processes that have a key or value open. Figure 9-1 shows this tool.

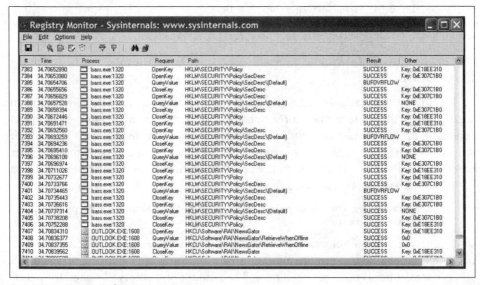

Figure 9-1. Sysinternals Registry Monitor

If you want to monitor registry activity over a long period of time or cannot keep a copy of Registry Monitor open at all times, another option is to enable registry auditing. With registry auditing enabled, you can get detailed information in the Security event log about the successful or failed attempts a particular user or group of users make to the registry. Here is how you set that up:

1. Open the Registry Editor (*regedit.exe*).

2. In the left pane, browse to the key you want to audit. (You can't audit individual registry values.)

3. Right-click on the key and select **Permissions**.

4. Click the **Advanced** button.

5. Click the **Auditing** tab.

6. Click the **Add** button.

7. Use the **Object Picker** to find the user or group for whom you want to audit access.

8. In the **Auditing Entry** box, select the types of things you want to audit. Success is audited separately from **Failure**, so be sure to check all the types you want to audit.

9. Click **OK** until all windows are closed.

10. Open the Local Security Policy snap-in (available from Administrative Tools).

11. In the left pane, expand **Local Policies** and click on **Audit Policy**.

12. In the right pane, double-click on **Audit object access**.

13. Check the box beside **Success** to audit successful actions.

14. Check the box beside **Failure** to audit failed actions.

15. Click **OK**.

Discussion

To enable auditing in the registry, you have to complete two steps. The first consists of configuring what you want to audit in the registry, which you can do with the Registry Editor. (Table 9-4 lists all audit options.) After you've completed this, auditing isn't turned on yet. To do that, you have to go to the Local Policies snap-in (or Group Policy Object Editor in a domain environment) and enable auditing. At this point, any registry access to the keys you configured should be logged to the Security event log.

Table 9-4. Registry audit options

Name	Description
Create Link	Any attempt to create a symbolic link in a particular key
Create Subkey	Any attempt to create subkeys on a selected registry key
Delete	Any attempt to delete a key
Enumerate Subkeys	Any attempt to list the subkeys of a key
Notify	Any notification events from a key in the registry
Query Value	Any attempt to read a value from a key
Read Control	Any attempt to open the discretionary access control list on a key
Set Value	Any attempt to set a value in a key

Table 9-4. Registry audit options (continued)

Name	Description
Write DAC	Any attempt to write a discretionary access control list on a key
Write Owner	Any attempt to change the owner of a key

 It is always a good idea to monitor your event logs closely after you enable auditing. You don't want fill up your Security log unnecessarily because you are auditing too much.

See Also

MS KB 315416 (HOW TO: Use Group Policy to Audit Registry Keys in Windows 2000)

9.13 Viewing Processes That Have a Registry Key Open

Problem

You want to view the processes that have a registry key open. If a process has a key open, you may not be able to modify or delete that key or its values.

Solution

Using a graphical user interface

Open the Sysinternals Registry Monitor (*regmon.exe*) tool. By default, the Registry Monitor shows all processes that have a handle to a registry key or value. You have two options for finding a specific key or value:

- From the menu, select **Edit → Find**. Enter the part of the registry key or value you want to search against. Make sure **Direction** is selected correctly (by default **Down** is selected, but if you want to, search **Up**).

- The second option consists of filtering the output. Select **Options → Filter/ Highlight** from the menu. In the **Include** text box, enter the key or value you want to view. Click **OK** and then **Yes** to confirm.

You can also use the Sysinternals Process Explorer (*procexp.exe*) tool to search for registry handles.

Using a command-line interface

With the Sysinternals *handle* command, you can find a process that has a registry key open. Simply specify the -a switch and some part of the key path or value name you want to search on. Since the search is fuzzy, there is a chance it might match things other than registry access (e.g., an open file), but if your search string is specific enough, you should be able to narrow it down. For example, the following command finds all processes that have a handle to something containing RunOnce in the name (often a registry key):

```
> handle -a RunOnce
```

You can also use *handle* to view all processes that are accessing a key under HKLM\ Software:

```
> handle -a HKLM\Software
```

CHAPTER 10

Network Configuration

10.0 Introduction

System administrators have to wear several different hats. They have to be part server administrator, security professional, storage administrator, and network administrator. In this chapter, I'll cover many of the network-based activities that Windows system administrators have to do, including configuring an IP address and DNS and viewing network activity.

Using a Graphical User Interface

The Network Connections applet hasn't changed significantly since Windows NT, with the exception of adding a few more tabs and buttons. You can do most network configuration tasks with it, but it is not a very efficient or intuitive interface.

For viewing current network activity, I talk about the Sysinternals TCPView (Recipe 10.9) and Microsoft Network Monitor (Recipe 10.11) later in the chapter. Both tools are invaluable for troubleshooting network connectivity issues. Get familiar with them if you haven't already.

Using a Command-Line Interface

Table 10-1 lists all of the command-line tools used in this chapter.

Table 10-1. Command-line tools used in this chapter

Tool	Windows Server 2003	Windows 2000 Server	Recipes
devcon	MS KB 311272	MS KB 311272	10.2
ipconfig	%SystemRoot%\system32	%SystemRoot%\system32	10.1, 10.4, 10.6
linkspeed	Windows Server 2003 Resource Kit	N/A	10.13
netcap	Windows Server 2003 Support Tools	N/A	10.11
netdiag	Windows Server 2003 Support Tools	Windows 2000 Support Tools	10.10
netsh	%SystemRoot%\system32	%SystemRoot%\system32	10.1, 10.3, 10.5, 10.14

Table 10-1. Command-line tools used in this chapter (continued)

Tool	Windows Server 2003	Windows 2000 Server	Recipes
netstat	%SystemRoot%\system32	%SystemRoot%\system32	10.9
netstatp	Sysinternals	Sysinternals	10.9
nltest	Windows Server 2003 Support Tools	Windows 2000 Support Tools	10.7
ping	%SystemRoot%\system32	%SystemRoot%\system32	10.10
reg	%SystemRoot%\system32	Windows 2000 Support Tools	10.7, 10.12
route	%SystemRoot%\system32	%SystemRoot%\system32	10.8
tracert	%SystemRoot%\system32	%SystemRoot%\system32	10.10
wmic	%SystemRoot%\system32\wbem	N/A	10.1, 10.12

Using VBScript

Table 10-2 lists WMI classes used in this chapter, including the recipe numbers where each was used.

Table 10-2. WMI classes used in this chapter

WMI class	Description	Recipes
SNMP_RFC1213_MIB_tcpConnTable	Represents the current TCP connections on a system.	10.9
SNMP_RFC1213_MIB_udpTable	Represents the current UDP connections on a system.	10.9
Win32_IP4RouteTable	Represents the routing table of a network adapter. This class is new to Windows Server 2003.	10.8
Win32_NetworkAdapter	Represents network adapters installed in the computer. This class has several read-only properties that describe the manufacturer hardware and software settings.	10.1, 10.3, 10.4
Win32_NetworkAdapterConfiguration	Represents the network configuration of network adapters. This class has several properties for reading network configuration information and numerous methods for modifying various settings.	10.1, 10.3, 10.4, 10.8, 10.12

10.1   Viewing the Network Configuration

Problem

You want to view the network configuration of a server, including a list of all installed network adapters.

Solution

Using a graphical user interface

1. From the Control Panel, open the **Network Connections** applet.
2. Open the network connection for which you want to view the settings.

3. Click the **Properties** button.

4. Click the **Configure** button to view network adapter properties. Or double-click **Internet Protocol (TCP/IP)** to view network configuration settings.

Using a command-line interface

To view the list of connections and network configuration on the local machine, run the following command:

```
> ipconfig /all
```

To view this information on a remote machine, use the Sysinternals *psexec* command:

```
> psexec \\<ServerName> -u administrator -p MyPass ipconfig /all
```

Another command you can use to view network configuration information is *netsh*, as shown here:

```
> netsh int ip show config
```

Using VBScript

```
' This code displays the network configuration for all connections.
' ------ SCRIPT CONFIGURATION ------
strComputer = "."
' ------ END CONFIGURATION ---------
set objWMI = GetObject("winmgmts:\\" & strComputer & "\root\cimv2")
set colNAs = objWMI.InstancesOf("Win32_NetworkAdapter")
for each objNA in colNAs
    Wscript.Echo objNA.Name
    Wscript.Echo "  Description:  " & objNA.Description
    Wscript.Echo "  Product Name: " & objNA.ProductName
    Wscript.Echo "  Manufacturer: " & objNA.Manufacturer
    Wscript.Echo "  Adapter Type: " & objNA.AdapterType
    Wscript.Echo "  AutoSense:    " & objNA.AutoSense
    Wscript.Echo "  MAC Address:  " & objNA.MACAddress
    Wscript.Echo "  Maximum Speed:" & objNA.MaxSpeed
    Wscript.Echo "  Conn Status:  " & objNA.NetConnectionStatus
    Wscript.Echo "  Service Name: " & objNA.ServiceName
    Wscript.Echo "  Speed:        " & objNA.Speed

    set colNACs = objWMI.ExecQuery(" select * from " & _
                          " Win32_NetworkAdapterConfiguration " & _
                          " where Index = " & objNA.Index)
    ' There should only be one item in colNACs
    for each objNAC in colNACs
        if IsArray(objNAC.IPAddress) then
            for each strAddress in objNAC.IPAddress
                Wscript.Echo "  Network Addr: " & strAddress
            next
        end if
        Wscript.Echo " IP Metric:   " & objNAC.IPConnectionMetric
        Wscript.Echo " IP Enabled:  " & objNAC.IPEnabled
        Wscript.Echo " Filter:      " & objNAC.IPFilterSecurityEnabled
```

```
      Wscript.Echo " Port Security:" & objNAC.IPPortSecurityEnabled
      if IsArray(objNAC.IPSubnet) then
          for each strAddress in objNAC.IPSubnet
              Wscript.Echo " Subnet Mask:  " & strAddress
          next
      end if
      if IsArray(objNAC.DefaultIPGateway) then
          for each strAddress in objNAC.DefaultIPGateway
              Wscript.Echo " Gateway Addr: " & strAddress
          next
      end if
      Wscript.Echo " Database Path:" & objNAC.DatabasePath
      Wscript.Echo " DHCP Enabled: " & objNAC.DHCPEnabled
      Wscript.Echo " Lease Expires:" & objNAC.DHCPLeaseExpires
      Wscript.Echo " Lease Obtained: " & objNAC.DHCPLeaseObtained
      Wscript.Echo " DHCP Server:   " & objNAC.DHCPServer
      Wscript.Echo " DNS Domain:    " & objNAC.DNSDomain
      Wscript.Echo " DNS For WINS: " & objNAC.DNSEnabledForWINSResolution
      Wscript.Echo " DNS Host Name:" & objNAC.DNSHostName
      if IsArray(objNAC.DNSDomainSuffixSearchorder) then
          for each strName in objNAC.DNSDomainSuffixSearchOrder
              Wscript.Echo " DNS Suffix Search Order: " & strName
          next
      end if
      if IsArray(objNAC.DNSServerSearchOrder) then
          for each strName in objNAC.DNSServerSearchOrder
              Wscript.Echo " DNS Server Search Order: " & strName
          next
      end if
      Wscript.Echo " Domain DNS Reg Enabled: " & _
                   objNAC.DomainDNSRegistrationEnabled
      Wscript.Echo " Full DNS Reg Enabled: " & _
                   objNAC.FullDNSRegistrationEnabled
      Wscript.Echo " LMHosts Lookup:      " & objNAC.WINSEnableLMHostsLookup
      Wscript.Echo " WINS Lookup File:    " & objNAC.WINSHostLookupFile
      Wscript.Echo " WINS Scope ID:       " & objNAC.WINSScopeID
      Wscript.Echo " WINS Primary Server: " & objNAC.WINSPrimaryServer
      Wscript.Echo " WINS Secondary:      " & objNAC.WINSSecondaryServer
    next

    WScript.Echo
next
```

Discussion

There are several different ways to get at the host network configuration, as shown
in the Solution section. And since the scripting solution used WMI, there is yet
another way using *wmic*. Here are two commands that display some of the properties of the Win32_NetworkAdapter and Win32_NetworkAdapterConfiguration WMI classes, respectively:

```
> wmic nic list brief
> wmic nicconfig list brief
```

To view all available properties for those classes, replace `brief` with `full` in both commands.

10.2 Disabling a Connection

Problem

You want to disable a network connection for either a virtual interface or a network adapter.

Solution

Using a graphical user interface

1. From the Control Panel open the **Network Connections** applet.
2. Right-click the network connection you want to disable and select **Disable**.

Using a command-line interface

You would think that it would be straightforward to disable a connection from the command line, but unfortunately that is not the case. In fact, the *netsh* command supports disabling connections, but only non-LAN interfaces, which is very disappointing.

But all is not lost! There is an alternative if you really must have a way to disable connections from the command line. The *devcon.exe* tool is the command-line alternative to the Device Manager interface and comes with the Driver Development Kit (DDK). You can download it separately by viewing MS KB 311272 (*http://support.microsoft.com/default.aspx?scid=311272*).

Once you have it downloaded, run this command to get a list of all network devices:

```
> devcon listclass net
```

This displays the list of devices in two columns. The left column contains the hardware ID for each device and the right column contains the description for the device.

After you've found the device you want to disable, run the following command:

```
> devcon disable =net <HardwareID>
```

For example:

```
> devcon disable =net PCI\VEN_14B9^&DEV_A504^&SUBSYS_500014B9^&REV_00
```

There are a couple of important things I need to point out. First, if the hardware ID contains any ampersands (&), you have to escape them using a caret (^). Otherwise, the CMD session will interpret everything after the first & as another command and *devcon* will attempt to match any hardware ID that matches the string up until the first &. This can be dangerous because it can cause you to disable devices you didn't intend to.

Second, if the hardware ID contains two backslashes, remove the second backslash and everything following it. For example, if the `listall` command returned this for a device I wanted to disable:

```
PCI\VEN_14B9&DEV_A504&SUBSYS_500014B9&REV_00\4&39A85202&0&10F0: Cisco Systems PC I
Wireless LAN Adapter
```

I would need to use this as the hardware ID (including the carets):

```
PCI\VEN_14B9^&DEV_A504^&SUBSYS_500014B9^&REV_00
```

Using VBScript

If you thought the command-line way to disable connections was painful, I won't even begin to describe how it can be done via a script. There is a way, but it essentially involves simulating the steps in the graphical solution. Because the script is a major hack and not very reliable, I won't include it here. I am making it available on my web site (*http://www.rallenhome.com/*) in case you are still interested.

A somewhat viable mechanism for using VBScript is to shell out to the *devcon.exe* tool to accomplish your objectives. Don't forget the escaping!

Discussion

Many servers these days come with two network adapters installed to avoid a single point of failure with the network connection. Generally, keep one connection active and use the other as a back up. There are a couple of ways to do this. One is to simply disable one of the connections and manually enable it if the primary fails. Since you probably won't have network connectivity after the primary adapter fails, you'll need another way to access the server, such as an out-of-band console connection of some type.

Another way to do this is to use a feature that many hardware vendors support called *teaming*. With teaming, both adapters are used to form a virtual adapter. If the primary adapter becomes unavailable, the backup takes over automatically. (See your hardware vendor for more details.) The problem with teaming is that, depending on the implementation, it can be unreliable and ultimately cause more configuration headaches than it is worth. I recommend testing teaming configurations thoroughly before implementing them in production.

See Also

MS KB 262265 (Error Message When You Use Netsh.exe to Enable or Disable a Network Adapter)

10.3   Configuring an IP Address

Problem

You want to configure a static IP address or DHCP for a connection.

Solution

Using a graphical user interface

1. From the Control Panel, open the **Network Connections** applet.

2. Double-click the connection you want to configure.

3. Click the **Properties** button.

4. Double-click **Internet Protocol (TCP/IP)**.

5. To enable DHCP, select **Obtain an IP address automatically**. To use a static address, select **Use the following IP address**. Then configure the IP address, subnet mask, and default gateway.

6. Click **OK** until all windows are closed.

Using a command-line interface

The following command configures DHCP for a connection:

```
> netsh int ip set address name="<ConnectionName>" source=dhcp
```

Here is an example for configuring the connection named "Local Area Connection" to use DHCP:

```
> netsh int ip set address name="Local Area Connection" source=dhcp
```

This configures a connection with a static IP and default gateway:

```
> netsh int ip set address name="<ConnectionName>" source=static <IP> <Mask>
<GateWayIP> <Metric>
```

This example configures a static IP address for "Local Area Connection":

```
> netsh int ip set address name="Local Area Connection" source=static 10.3.53.3
255.255.255.0 10.3.53.1 1
```

Using VBScript

```
' This code enables DHCP for the specified connection.
' ------ SCRIPT CONFIGURATION ------
strComputer = "."
strConnection = "Local Area Connection"
' ------ END CONFIGURATION ---------
set objWMI = GetObject("winmgmts:\\" & strComputer & "\root\cimv2")
set colNA = objWMI.ExecQuery("select * " & _
                    " from Win32_NetworkAdapter " & _
                    " where NetConnectionID = '" & strConnection & "'" )
```

```
    for each objNA in colNA
        set colNAConfig = objWMI.ExecQuery _
            ("ASSOCIATORS OF {Win32_NetworkAdapter.DeviceID='" & _
              objNA.DeviceID & "'} " & _
            " WHERE resultClass = win32_NetworkAdapterConfiguration ")
        for each objNAConfig in colNAConfig
            if objNAConfig.DHCPEnabled = True then
                WScript.Echo "DHCP already enabled for " & strConnection
            else
                intRC = objNAConfig.EnableDHCP( )
                if intRC = 0 then
                    WScript.Echo "DHCP Enabled for " & strConnection
                elseif intRC = 1 then
                    WScript.Echo "You must reboot to start using DHCP for " & _
                                 strConnection
                else
                    WScript.Echo "There was an error enabling DHCP for " & _
                                 strconnection & ": " & intRC
                end if
            end if
        next
next

' This code configures an IP address, subnet mask, and default gateway
' for the specified connection.
' ------ SCRIPT CONFIGURATION ------
strComputer = "."
strConnection = "Local Area Connection"
strIP = Array("1.22.2.2")
strMask = Array("255.255.255.0")
strGatewayIP = Array("1.2.3.3")
' ------ END CONFIGURATION ---------
set objWMI = GetObject("winmgmts:\\" & strComputer & "\root\cimv2")
set colNA = objWMI.ExecQuery("select * " & _
                            " from Win32_NetworkAdapter " & _
                            " where NetConnectionID = '" & strConnection & "'" )
for each objNA in colNA
    set colNAConfig = objWMI.ExecQuery _
        ("ASSOCIATORS OF {Win32_NetworkAdapter.DeviceID='" & _
          objNA.DeviceID & "'} " & _
        " WHERE resultClass = win32_NetworkAdapterConfiguration ")
    for each objNAConfig in colNAConfig
        intRC = objNAConfig.EnableStatic(strIP,strMask)
        intRC2 = objNAConfig.SetGateways(strGatewayIP)
        if intRC = 0 and intRC2 = 0 then
            WScript.Echo "IP address configured for " & strConnection
        elseif intRC = 1 or intRC2 = 1 then
            WScript.Echo "You must reboot for the changes to take effect for " & _
                         strConnection
        else
            WScript.Echo "There was an error configuring IP for " & _
                         strconnection & ": " & intRC & " and " & intRC2
        end if
    next
next
```

Discussion

If you use static IP addresses, any time you build a new server, you have to configure an IP address on that server. However, there is no reason why you can't automate the process using either the *netsh* command shown in the command-line solution or WMI. You still have to find an available IP address, which may not be easy to automate depending on your environment, but at least you can provision the IP address in an automated fashion.

This leads to a discussion of using DHCP on servers. You'll find some people dead set against it and others who wouldn't do it any other way. Since network adapters are by default configured to use DHCP, you can remove the step of configuring network settings, such as IP address, DNS servers, etc., on your servers by using DHCP. After the server completes the build process and reboots, it will automatically request an IP address. But as you probably know, DHCP addresses aren't set in stone. The next time the server reboots, it might obtain a different address. And since you more than likely want to add an A record (and possibly a PTR record) in DNS for this server, if it got a new address, those records would no longer be valid.

There are two ways to work around this. First, you can configure a reservation on the DHCP server for a specific IP address. You only need to retrieve the MAC address of the server's network adapter order to configure a reservation (you can get this via the ipconfig /all command). Then see Recipe 14.10 for creating a reservation on the DHCP Server. With this configuration, the server will always receive the same IP address even though it is getting it from DHCP. The benefit of this is that you don't have to manually configure the other settings such as DNS and WINS servers directly on the server. The potential drawback is that if you have to change network adapters for any reason, the reservation would also have to be updated.

The second option is to use dynamic DNS to have the server automatically update DNS based on its current IP address. In fact, you could have the sever itself send the dynamic updates or use DHCP to do that (see Recipe 14.8). That way, even if the server gets a new IP address after every reboot, DNS will be updated automatically. The benefit to this is that it is the most automated solution. There is very little configuration you have to do on a per-server basis (and it is therefore attractive for large environments). The downside is that DNS could have outdated information for a period of time until the server dynamically updates its new information.

See Also

Recipes 14.8 and 14.10

10.4   Renewing or Releasing a DHCP IP Address

Problem

You want to release or renew an IP address obtained via DHCP.

Solution

Using a graphical user interface

1. From the Control Panel, open the **Network Connections** applet.
2. Right-click the DHCP-enabled network connection you want to renew and select **Repair**. This will automatically attempt to renew the connection's IP address.

Using a command-line interface

The following commands renew and release a DHCP IP address, respectively:

```
> ipconfig /renew
> ipconfig /release
```

With either of these commands, you can specify a pattern to match if you want to affect only a subset of adapters. The following command would release the IP address for any adapter that had "Con" (e.g., Local Area Connection 1) in its name:

```
> ipconfig /renew *Con*
```

Using VBScript

```
' This code releases all DHCP IP addresses.
' ------ SCRIPT CONFIGURATION ------
strComputer = "."
' ------ END CONFIGURATION ---------
set objWMI = GetObject("winmgmts:\\" & strComputer & "\root\cimv2")
set objAdapterConfig = objWMI.Get("Win32_NetworkAdapterConfiguration")
intRC = objAdapterConfig.ReleaseDHCPLeaseAll( )
if intRC = 0 then
   WScript.Echo "Released all DHCP IP addresses"
elseif intRC = 1 then
   WScript.Echo "You must reboot to release all DHCP IP addresses"
else
   WScript.Echo "There was an error releasing all DHCP IP addresses: " & intRC
end if


' This code shows performs the same function as the previous example
' but it performs a query for all DHCP enabled IP addresses.  Use this
' if you don't want to release all IP addresses.  Modify the WQL statement
' based on the criteria you need.
' ------ SCRIPT CONFIGURATION ------
strComputer = "."
' ------ END CONFIGURATION ---------
```

```
set objWMI = GetObject("winmgmts:\\" & strComputer & "\root\cimv2")
set colNetworkAdapters = objWMI.ExecQuery _
    ("Select * From Win32_NetworkAdapterConfiguration Where DHCPEnabled = True")
for each objNetworkConfig in colNetworkAdapters
    intRC = objNetworkConfig.ReleaseDHCPLease( )
    if intRC = 0 then
        WScript.Echo "Released IP address for " & objNetworkConfig.Description
    elseif intRC = 1 then
        WScript.Echo "You must reboot to release the IP address for " & _
                     objNetworkConfig.Description
    else
        WScript.Echo "There was an error releasing the IP address for " & _
                     objNetworkConfig.Description & ": " & intRC
    end if
next


' This code renews all DHCP IP addresses.
' ------ SCRIPT CONFIGURATION ------
strComputer = "."
' ------ END CONFIGURATION ---------
set objWMI = GetObject("winmgmts:\\" & strComputer & "\root\cimv2")
set objAdapterConfig = objWMI.Get("Win32_NetworkAdapterConfiguration")
intRC = objAdapterConfig.RenewDHCPLeaseAll( )
if intRC = 0 then
    WScript.Echo "Renewed all DHCP IP addresses"
elseif intRC = 1 then
    WScript.Echo "You must reboot to renew all DHCP IP addresses"
else
    WScript.Echo "There was an error renewing all DHCP IP addresses: " & intRC
end if


' This code renews all adapters made by Intel that are installed on the server.
' ------ SCRIPT CONFIGURATION ------
strComputer = "."
' ------ END CONFIGURATION ---------
set objWMI = GetObject("winmgmts:\\" & strComputer & "\root\cimv2")
set colNAs = objWMI.ExecQuery("select * " & _
                          " from Win32_NetworkAdapter     " & _
                          " where manufacturer = 'Intel' " )
for each objNA in colNAs
    set colSubNAConfig = objWMI.ExecQuery _
        ("ASSOCIATORS OF {Win32_NetworkAdapter.DeviceID='" & _
          objNA.DeviceID & "'} " & _
        " WHERE resultClass = win32_NetworkAdapterConfiguration ")

    for each objNAConfig in colSubNAConfig
        if objNAConfig.DHCPEnabled = True then
            intRC = objNAConfig.RenewDHCPLease( )
            if intRC = 0 then
                WScript.Echo "Renewed IP address for " & objNA.Name
            elseif intRC = 1 then
                WScript.Echo "You must reboot to renew the IP address for " & _
                         objNA.Name
```

```
        else
            WScript.Echo "There was an error renewing the IP address for " & _
                objNA.Name & ": " & intRC
        end if
    end if
next
next
```

Discussion

Fortunately, the whole DHCP release/renew process is automatic and not something you have to do manually. When a client receives a DHCP lease for an IP address, it will automatically attempt to renew that address after 50% of the lease duration. The DHCP Server can grant the renewal, after which the client restarts its lease timer. If the server doesn't respond, the client tries again after 87.5% of the lease duration and then attempts to contact other DHCP Servers.

Even though this process is automatic, there may be times when you need to initiate it yourself—especially if you've made network configuration changes. For example, let's say you configured a reservation on your DHCP Server for a particular host. If that host already has an IP address, you'll need to release the current lease and run the renew command to get the new address.

10.5   Configuring DNS Settings

Problem

You want to configure the DNS settings on a server.

Solution

Using a graphical user interface

To configure the DNS suffix, do the following:

1. From the Control Panel, open the **System** applet.
2. Select the **Computer Name** tab (**Network Identification** tab on Windows 2000).
3. Click the **Change** button (**Settings** button on Windows 2000).
4. Click the **More** button.
5. Enter the suffix under the **Primary DNS suffix of this computer** heading.
6. Check the box beside **Change primary DNS suffix when domain membership changes** if you want the suffix to change to the name of the Active Directory domain the computer joins.
7. Click **OK** until all the windows are closed. You will be prompted to reboot for the changes to take effect.

To modify the list of DNS servers used during name resolution, configure how unqualified names are resolved, and configure DNS dynamic registration, do the following:

1. From the Control Panel, open the **Network Connections** applet.

2. Double-click the connection you want to modify.

3. From this screen you can configure whether to use the DNS servers obtained through DHCP or to manually enter them. In the latter case, you can enter preferred and alternate DNS servers.

4. To configure the other DNS settings, click the **Advanced** button.

5. Select the **DNS** tab.

6. From this screen you can configure additional DNS servers to use during resolution, configure how unqualified names are handled, set a DNS suffix for this connection, and configure DNS registration for this connection.

7. When you are done, click **OK** until all screens are closed.

Using a command-line interface

To view the current DNS configuration for all connections on the local machine, run this command:

```
> netsh int ip show dns
```

To make a connection using DHCP-specified DNS settings, use this command:

```
> netsh int ip set dns "<ConnectionName>" dhcp
```

Here is an example:

```
> netsh int ip set dns "Local Area Connection" dhcp
```

To make a connection using a specified DNS server for name resolution, use this command:

```
> netsh int ip set dns "Local Area Connection" static <IPAddress>
```

Here is an example:

```
> netsh int ip set dns "Local Area Connection" static 10.0.0.1
```

This command allows you to specify only one DNS server for name resolution.

With the same command, you can also configure whether the connection registers the host's name under the primary DNS suffix or the connection-specific suffix. To register just the primary DNS suffix, append "primary" to the end of the command. To register both, append "both." To register nothing, append "none." Here is an example:

```
> netsh int ip set dns "Local Area Connection" static 10.0.0.1 primary
```

Discussion

With Windows Server 2003 Active Directory, you can now configure most DNS client settings via Group Policy. Windows 2000 Group Policy allowed you to only configure the primary DNS suffix (Computer Configuration → Administrative Templates → System → DNS Client → Primary DNS Suffix).

 Be careful with this setting: users who connect to third-party ISPs via their laptops inherit your company's DNS settings, and their third-party connections may fail.

With Windows Server 2003, you can configure the DNS suffix, dynamic updates settings, search list, and DNS servers used for name resolution among many other settings. These settings can be found by navigating the following path of a Group Policy Object: Computer Configuration → Administrative Templates → Network → DNS Client.

See Also

MS KB 178277 (INFO: Setting DNS Domain Suffix Search Order During an Unattended Installation), MS KB 246804 (How to enable or disable dynamic DNS registrations in Windows 2000 and in Windows Server 2003), and MS KB 275553 (How to Configure a Domain Suffix Search List on the Domain Name System Clients)

10.6   Registering DNS Records or Flushing the DNS Cache

Problem

You want to register a server's DNS records dynamically or flush the local DNS cache.

Solution

Using a command-line interface

The following command displays the contents of the local DNS cache:

```
> ipconfig /displaydns
```

And this clears that cache:

```
> ipconfig /flushdns
```

The following command causes the local host to reregister its DNS records via dynamic DNS:

```
> ipconfig /registerdns
```

Using VBScript

```
' This code flushes the local DNS cache.  There are no scripting
' interfaces designed to do this so I have to shell out and run
' the ipconfig /flushdns command.
strCommand = "ipconfig /flushdns"
set objWshShell = WScript.CreateObject("WScript.Shell")
intRC = objWshShell.Run(strCommand, 0, TRUE)
if intRC <> 0 then
   WScript.Echo "Error returned from running the command: " & intRC
else
   WScript.Echo "Command executed successfully"
end if


' This code registers DNS records for the local host.  There are
' no scripting interfaces designed to do this so I have to shell
' out and run the ipconfig /registerhdns command.
strCommand = "ipconfig /registerdns"
set objWshShell = WScript.CreateObject("WScript.Shell")
intRC = objWshShell.Run(strCommand, 0, TRUE)
if intRC <> 0 then
   WScript.Echo "Error returned from running the command: " & intRC
else
   WScript.Echo "Command executed successfully"
end if
```

Discussion

The Windows operating system maintains a name resolution cache of DNS records that the system has queried. This cache is maintained in memory and speeds up future requests for the same record. Each record has an associated time-to-live value. This setting informs clients of the maximum amount of time to cache that particular record. After the time-to-live period expires, Windows removes the record from its cache.

The Windows name resolution cache is maintained by the DNS Cache (DnsCache) service. You can prevent records from being cached by stopping this service (and disabling it if you never want records to be cached again). If you are getting strange results when querying DNS, you may want to view the local DNS cache to see if you are accessing locally cached records instead of what is current on the DNS Server.

The /registerdns option of ipconfig attempts to dynamically reregister DNS records for all IP addresses configured on the system. The DHCP Client (Dhcp) service does the DNS reregistration, so if that service is disabled, the /registerdns option won't work (even if all addresses are statically configured).

See Also

MS KB 245437 (How to Disable Client-Side DNS Caching in Windows), MS KB 264539 (Dynamic DNS Updates Do Not Work if the DHCP Client Service Stops), and MS KB 318803 (How to Disable Client-Side DNS Caching in Windows XP and Windows Server 2003)

10.7   Finding a Computer's Active Directory Site

Problem

You want to find the Active Directory site a computer is part of, which is based on the IP address of the computer.

Solution

Using a command-line interface

In the following command, replace *<HostName>* with the name of the host whose site you want to find.

```
> nltest /server:<HostName> /DsGetSite
```

To force a computer to use a particular site, modify the registry as follows:

```
> reg add HKLM\System\CurrentControlSet\Services\Netlogon\Parameters /v SiteName /t
REG_SZ /d <SiteName>
```

Using VBScript

Although you cannot use it directly from a scripting language such as VBScript, Microsoft provides a DsGetSiteName method that can be used by languages such as Visual Basic and C++ to retrieve site coverage information. In fact, the nltest command shown in the CLI solution is a wrapper around this method.

The IADsTools interface provides a wrapper around this method.

```
set objIadsTools = CreateObject("IADsTools.DCFunctions")
strSite = objIadsTools.DsGetSiteName("<HostName>")
Wscript.Echo "Site: " & strSite


' This code forces the host the script is run on to use a particular site
' ------ SCRIPT CONFIGURATION ------
strSite = "<SiteName>"    ' e.g., Raleigh
' ------ END CONFIGURATION ---------
strNetlogonReg = "SYSTEM\CurrentControlSet\Services\Netlogon\Parameters"
const HKLM = &H80000002
set objReg = GetObject("winmgmts:root\default:StdRegProv")
objReg.SetStringValue HKLM, strNetlogonReg, "SiteName", strSite
WScript.Echo "Set SiteName to " & strSite
```

Discussion

Each domain controller has a server object that is contained within a site. Clients are different—they are associated with a site based on their IP address, and the corresponding subnet that it matches is in the Subnets container. The client site information is important because it determines which domain controller it will authenticate against. If the client's IP address does not match a subnet range of any of the subnets stored in Active Directory, it will randomly pick a site to use, which means it could authenticate against any domain controller in the domain.

Finding the site that contains a client is an important first step when troubleshooting authentication delays or errors. If a client is experiencing significant delays, it could be that the client is authenticating with a random site because it is on a new subnet that has yet to be added to Active Directory. This may also result in a client authenticating over a slow WAN link.

You can bypass the part of the DC Locator process that determines a client's site by hardcoding it in the Registry. This is generally not recommended and should primarily be used as a troubleshooting tool. If a client is experiencing authentication delays due to a misconfigured site or subnet object, you can hardcode its site so they temporarily point to a more optimal location (and domain controller).

See Also

MS KB 247811 (How Domain Controllers Are Located in Windows) and MSDN: DsGetSiteName

10.8   Managing Routes

Problem

You want to view the routing table on a server or possibly configure static routes. Configuring static routes generally isn't needed with today's networks, but it can be necessary especially when working in restricted lab environments that are not fully routed.

Solution

Using a command-line interface

The following command displays all the static and dynamic routes on a system:

```
> route print
```

For a good overview of what each column represents in the route print output, see MS KB 140859.

This command only shows routes that start with 64:

```
> route print 64.*
```

To add a temporary route (one that is erased after the system reboots), use this command:

```
> route ADD <Network> MASK <Mask> <Gateway> METRIC <Metric> IF <Interface#>
```

For example:

```
> route ADD 157.0.0.0 MASK 255.0.0.0  157.55.80.1 METRIC 3 IF 2
```

To add a permanent route, use the same command as before except include the -p switch. To delete a route, use this command:

```
> route DELETE <Network>
```

For example:

```
> route DELETE 157.0.0.0
```

Using VBScript

```
' This code prints similar information to the "route print" command.
' Since the Win32_IP4RouteTable class was first introduced in
' Windows Server 2003, this script does not work against a
' Windows 2000 server.
' ------ SCRIPT CONFIGURATION ------
strComputer = "."
' ------ END CONFIGURATION ---------
set objWMI = GetObject("winmgmts:\\" & strComputer & "\root\cimv2")
set colRoutes = objWMI.InstancesOf("Win32_IP4RouteTable")
for each objRoute in colRoutes

    set colNetworkAdapters = objWMI.ExecQuery(_
                "select * from Win32_NetworkAdapterConfiguration " & _
                " where Interfaceindex = " & objRoute.InterfaceIndex )
    for each objNetworkAdapter in colNetworkAdapters
       for each strIP in objNetworkAdapter.IPAddress
          WScript.Echo "Interface: " & strIP
       next
    next

    WScript.Echo "Network:   " & objRoute.Destination
    WScript.Echo "NetMask:   " & objRoute.Mask
    WScript.Echo "Gateway:   " & objRoute.NextHop
    WScript.Echo "Metric:    " & objRoute.Metric1

    ' Other properties you can display:
    ' WScript.Echo "Age: " & objRoute.Age
```

```
          ' WScript.Echo "Description: " & objRoute.Description
          ' WScript.Echo "Information: " & objRoute.Information
          ' WScript.Echo "Interface Index: " & objRoute.InterfaceIndex
          ' WScript.Echo "Metric 2: " & objRoute.Metric2
          ' WScript.Echo "Metric 3: " & objRoute.Metric3
          ' WScript.Echo "Metric 4: " & objRoute.Metric4
          ' WScript.Echo "Metric 5: " & objRoute.Metric5
          ' WScript.Echo "Name: " & objRoute.Name
          ' WScript.Echo "Protocol: " & objRoute.Protocol
          ' WScript.Echo "Status: " & objRoute.Status
          ' WScript.Echo "Type: " & objRoute.Type

        WScript.Echo
    next


' This code shows how to add a route.
' Since the Win32_IP4RouteTable class was first introduced in
' Windows Server 2003, this script does not work against a
' Windows 2000 server.
' ------ SCRIPT CONFIGURATION ------
strComputer = "."
' ------ END CONFIGURATION ---------
set objLocator = CreateObject("WbemScripting.SWbemLocator")
set objWMI = objLocator.ConnectServer(strComputer, "root/CIMv2")

set objR = objWMI.get("Win32_IP4RouteTable").SpawnInstance_()
objR.Destination = "64.0.0.0"
objR.NextHop = "64.102.57.1"
objR.Mask = "255.0.0.0"
objR.InterfaceIndex = 65539
objR.Metric1 = 22
objR.Protocol = 1
objR.Type = 4
objR.Put_()
Wscript.Echo "Successfully created route"
```

Discussion

If networks are designed properly, system administrators shouldn't have to worry much about how traffic is being routed. Nevertheless, in certain situations where the network is not fully routed or you are experiencing routing issues, you may need to dig into a server's routing tables. You can also add static routes to temporarily get traffic flowing the way you want to or force it to go a certain way. However, I do not recommend configuring permanent static routes if you can avoid it. This type of manual configuration if often overlooked or forgotten and can be a headache to track down later unless the configuration changes are well known by all that are maintaining the server.

See Also

MS KB 140859 (TCP/IP Routing Basics for Windows NT) and MS KB 157025 (Default Gateway Configuration for Multihomed Computers)

10.9 Viewing the Open Ports and Connections

Problem

You want to view the open ports and connections on a server.

Solution

Using a graphical user interface

The Sysinternals TCPView tool is a graphical interface that displays all of the active connections on a host. It displays all of the connection information you might need, including process name and ID, protocol, local address and port, and remote address and port. It is a real-time tool, so it shows connections that are terminating in red and new connections in green. You can close a connection by right-clicking it and selecting **Close Connection**. You can also kill the associated process by selecting **End Process**. See Figure 10-1 for a screenshot of TCPView.

Using a command-line interface

The *netstat* command displays all established connections on a host:

```
> netstat
```

Use the -a option to view all open ports regardless of whether they are active. With the Windows Server 2003 version of *netstat*, you can view the process ID associated with connections by specifying the -o option.

The Sysinternals *netstatp* utility is the command-line version of TCPView. It displays similar information to *netstat*, but it shows the process name and ID associated with the connection by default:

```
> netstatp
```

Using VBScript

```
' This code produces output very similar to the 'netstat -an' command.
' It requires that the target machine have SNMP and the WMI SNMP
' Provider installed.
' ------ SCRIPT CONFIGURATION ------
strComputerIP = "127.0.0.1"
' ------ END CONFIGURATION ---------
set objLocator = CreateObject("WbemScripting.SWbemLocator")
set objWMI = objLocator.ConnectServer("", "root/snmp/localhost")
set objNamedValueSet = CreateObject("WbemScripting.SWbemNamedValueSet")
```

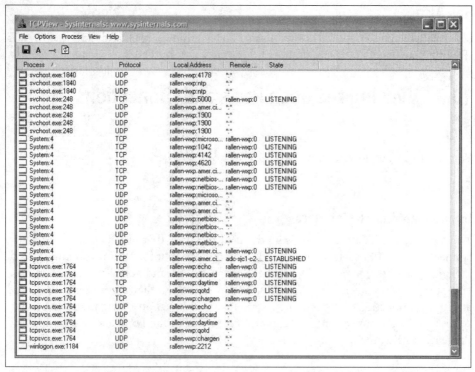

Figure 10-1. Sysinternals TCPView

```
objNamedValueSet.Add "AgentAddress", strComputerIP
objNamedValueSet.Add "AgentReadCommunityName", "public"
objNamedValueSet.Add "AgentWriteCommunityName", "public"

WScript.Echo " Proto  Local Address    Foreign Address       State"
set colTCPConns = objWMI.Instancesof("SNMP_RFC1213_MIB_tcpConnTable",, _
                                  objNamedValueSet )
for each objConn in colTCPConns
     WScript.echo "  TCP   " & objConn.tcpConnLocalAddress & ":" & _
                  objConn.tcpConnLocalPort & _
                  "         " & objConn.tcpConnRemAddress & ":" & _
                  objConn.tcpConnRemPort & "        " & objConn.tcpConnState
next

set colUDPConns = objWMI.Instancesof("SNMP_RFC1213_MIB_udpTable",, _
                                  objNamedValueSet )
for each objConn in colUDPConns
     WScript.echo "  UDP   " & objConn.udpLocalAddress & ":" & _
                  objConn.udpLocalPort & "        *:*"
next
```

Discussion

When you take a look at the list of open connections on a server, you may be surprised to see so many. Unless the server is extremely busy, most should be in the LISTENING state, which simply means the port is open and waiting for a connection. For more on the various states that a connection may be in, see MS KB 137984.

See Also

MS KB 137984 (TCP Connection States and Netstat Output) and MS KB 281336 (How to determine which program uses or blocks specific transmission control protocol ports in Windows)

10.10 Troubleshooting Network Connectivity Problems

Problem

You want to troubleshoot network connectivity problems. This is often necessary if a client is experiencing slow logins or network-based failures when accessing resources.

Solution

First, make sure your network adapter is working. Generally there should be a flashing green light to indicate the adapter is connected and transmitting data.

After you've checked the hardware, you can run several command-line tools to aid in troubleshooting connectivity issues. A good first step is to ping the target host, which can tell you if the remote host is reachable and how long it takes to reach it:

```
> ping <HostNameOrIP>
```

Here are some of the status messages you can receive from *ping*:

Reply
> The host was reachable.

Request timed out
> The target host either did not respond or there is no host configured with the corresponding IP address. You may also see this message if there is a lot of network latency between the two endpoints. You can work around this by using the -w option with ping and specifying the number of milliseconds to wait for each reply.

Unknown host

> If you used a DNS name in the ping command, this indicates that the DNS name was not resolvable by the DNS client.

Destination unreachable

> The ICMP traffic could not reach the network of the target host. This is often due to a routing problem on an intermediate router or a router being down.

If you've pinged a host and the request timed out or the host was unreachable, a good tool to try next is *tracert*, which attempts to trace a route from the source computer to the destination computer.

```
> tracert <HostNameOrIP>
```

This command shows you the path your data takes to get to the destination. If there are connectivity problems with a remote host, this command shows where the problem occurs.

If everything checks out, next run the *netdiag* command on the target system. *netdiag* provides a wealth of information about various network settings configured on the system along with information about DNS, Kerberos, and Active Directory connectivity. Use the /debug option to view detailed output. If you suspect authentication (Kerberos) to be a potential issue, run the *kerbtray* utility to ensure you have functioning Kerberos tickets.

If you are still having network problems, a good last step is to look at the network traffic to see if you can spot any obvious errors being transmitted. See Recipe 10.11 for more information.

See Also

MS KB 169790 (How to Troubleshoot Basic TCP/IP Problems), MS KB 321708 (HOW TO: Use the Network Diagnostics Tool (Netdiag.exe) in Windows 2000), MS KB 219289 (Description of the Netdiag /fix Switch), MS KB 314067 (How to troubleshoot TCP/IP connectivity with Windows XP), and MS KB 325487 (How to troubleshoot network connectivity problems)

10.11 Viewing Network Traffic

Problem

You want to view the network traffic a server sends and receives. This is useful when you need to troubleshoot or debug application problems or system communications failures. Particularly when you are having problems with a particular protocol, such as LDAP or DNS, looking at the associated network traffic can be helpful to see what is being transmitted and received.

Solution

Using a graphical user interface

1. Open the Network Monitor tool (*netmon.exe*). Network Monitor is not installed by default. To install it:

    a. Go to the Control Panel and open the **Add or Remove Programs** applet.

    b. Click on **Add/Remove Windows Components**.

    c. Double-click on **Management and Monitoring Tools**.

    d. Check the box beside **Network Monitor Tools** and click **OK**.

    e. Click **Next**.

    f. Click **Finish**.

2. The first time you start Network Monitor, you will be asked from which network interface you want to capture data. On Windows Server 2003, Microsoft finally made the list of interfaces to choose easy to distinguish because they labeled each one by its connection name (e.g., **Local Area Connection**). With Windows 2000, it doesn't include that information in the label, so choosing an interface is almost a guessing game unless you know the MAC address prefix of your NIC card vendor. A trick you can use to narrow the list of interfaces is to disregard any that have a **Dial-up connection** setting marked as TRUE. After you've selected an interface, click **OK**.

3. From the menu, select **Capture → Start**. If you don't see the **Network Utilization** and **Frames Per Second** indicators fluctuating (a sign traffic is being captured), you likely picked the wrong interface in Step 2. If so, stop the capture by selecting **Capture → Stop** from the menu. Then select **Capture → Networks**. You'll be presented with the same screen as in Step 2 that allows you to select the target interface.

4. When you want to stop the capture, select **Capture → Stop** from the menu. Or if you want to immediately view the traffic, select **Capture → Stop and View**.

5. If the captured data is too much to look at, you can filter it by selecting **Display → Filter** from the menu. From there you can enter Boolean expressions to limit what is displayed.

Using a command-line interface

The Windows Server 2003 Support Tools contains a new tool called *netcap.exe* that can capture packets to a file for viewing later in Network Monitor. Here is an example command line:

```
> netcap /C:d:\netcap.cap /N:1
```

This command captures packets on interface #1 and stores the output in *d:\netcap.cap*. To make sure you are capturing on the correct interface, view the *netcap* help information:

```
> netcap /?
```

At the very end, it displays the list of interfaces on the system and their associated numbers. To view the contents of the capture file, double-click it. This will launch the Network Monitor.

Using VBScript

None of the scripting interfaces allow you to get real-time network traffic information.

Discussion

Network Monitor (NetMon) is not the most user-friendly tool, but it offers powerful features for collecting, filtering, and analyzing a network capture. For more on how to use some of the features of NetMon, see the MS KB articles listed in the See Also section.

 If you are interested in an alternative to NetMon, Ethereal is one of the most popular network traffic analyzers and it is available free from the following site: *http://www.ethereal.com/*.

One thing that is worth noting about NetMon is that it has a default buffer limit of 1 MB. After the data it captures exceeds 1 MB, it begins to overwrite the oldest packets using FIFO (first in, first out). You can increase the size of the buffer to a max of 1 GB. To increase the buffer, select **Buffer Settings** from the **Capture** menu. Enter the maximum number of megabytes and click **OK**.

See Also

MS KB 148942 (How to Capture Network Traffic with Network Monitor), MS KB 310875 (Description of the Network Monitor Capture Utility), and MS KB 812953 (HOW TO: Use Network Monitor to Capture Network Traffic)

10.12 Configuring TCP/IP Filtering

Problem

You want to configure TCP/IP filtering to prevent a server from responding to certain protocols or ports or allow it to respond to certain protocols or ports. This filtering is applied to inbound traffic and does not affect outbound traffic.

Solution

Using a graphical user interface

1. Open the Control Panel.
2. From the **Network Connections** applet, open the connection you want to configure.
3. Click the **Properties** button.
4. Select **Internet Protocol (TCP/IP)**.
5. Click the **Properties** button.
6. Click the **Advanced** button.
7. Click the **Options** tab.
8. Select **TCP/IP filtering**.
9. Click the **Properties** button.
10. Check the box beside **Enable TCP/IP Filtering**.
11. Select **Permit Only** for **TCP Ports, UDP Ports,** and/or **IP Protocols**.
12. Click the **Add** button.
13. Enter the port or protocol number and click **OK**.
14. Repeat the last couple of steps until you've entered all desired ports and protocols.
15. After you are done, close all the dialog screens by clicking either **OK** or **Close**.
16. You will be prompted to reboot for the changes to take effect.

Using a command-line interface

The following command enables TCP/IP filtering:

```
> reg add HKLM\SYSTEM\CurrentControlSet\Services\Tcpip\Parameters /v
EnableSecurityFilters /t REG_DWORD /d 1
```

You must reboot for the changes to take effect. To disable filtering, change /d 1 to /d 0.

Next, configure the protocols and ports you want to filter. This must be done on a per-interface basis. To configure this using the registry, you need to know the GUID assigned to the interface you want to modify. This is a sample interface entry:

```
HKLM\SYSTEM\CurrentControlSet\Services\Tcpip\Parameters\Interfaces\{07383FC4-FF4D-
4E16-9DD6-C27061719D76}
```

To find out what adapter that corresponds with, you can use this command (on Windows Server 2003):

```
> wmic nicconfig get caption,settingid
```

Once you know the GUID of the interface, you can use the reg add command to modify the RawIPAllowedProtocols, TCPAllowedPorts, or UDPAllowedPorts values to filter what you want. Each of those values is of type REG_MULTI_SZ. Here is an example of setting protocols 25 and 80:

```
reg add HKLM\SYSTEM\CurrentControlSet\Services\Tcpip\Parameters\Interfaces\{07383FC4-
FF4D-4E16-9DD6-C27061719D76} /v RawIPAllowedProtocols /t REG_MULTI_SZ /d 25\080
```

You can also use the WMIC utility to configure TCP/IP filtering. These two commands show you how:

```
> wmic /node:"<ServerName>" nicconfig call EnableIPFilterSec(1)
> wmic /node:"<ServerName>" nicconfig where ipenabled=True call EnableIPSec
(<TCPPortList>),(<UDPPortList>),(<ProtoList>)
```

This command allows all TCP and UDP ports, but allows only protocols 80 (http) and 25 (smtp):

```
> wmic nicconfig where ipenabled=True call EnableIPSec (80,25),(0),(0)
```

Using VBScript

```
' This code enables IP Filtering for all adapters and configures
' filtering for all IP-enabled adapters.
' ------ SCRIPT CONFIGURATION ------
strComputer = "."
arrTCPPorts = Array ( 0 )         ' Allow all TCP ports
arrUDPPorts = Array ( 0 )         ' Allow all UDP ports
arrProtos   = Array ( 80, 25 )  ' Allow only HTTP and SMTP
' ------ END CONFIGURATION ---------
set objWMI = GetObject("winmgmts:\\" & strComputer & "\root\cimv2")
set objAdapterConfig = objWMI.Get("Win32_NetworkAdapterConfiguration")
intRC = objAdapterConfig.EnableIPFilterSec( True )
if intRC = 0 then
   WScript.Echo "IP Filtering for all adapters enabled"
elseif intRC = 1 then
   WScript.Echo "IP Filtering enabled for all adapters, " & _
                "but you must reboot for the changes to take effect"
else
   WScript.Echo "There was an error enabling IP Filtering for all " & _
                "adapters: " & intRC
end if

set colNAConfigs = objWMI.ExecQuery( _
                      "select * " & _
                      " from Win32_NetworkAdapterConfiguration " & _
                      " where IPEnabled = True" )
for each objNAConfig in colNAConfigs
   intRC = objNAConfig.EnableIPSec( arrTCPPorts, arrUDPPorts, arrProtos )
   if intRC = 0 then
      WScript.Echo "IP Filtering configured for '" & _
                   objNAConfig.Description & "'"
   elseif intRC = 1 then
      WScript.Echo "IP Filtering configured for '" & objNAConfig.Description & _
                   "', but you must reboot for the changes to take effect"
   else
```

```
        WScript.Echo "There was an error configuring IP Filtering for '" & _
                    objNAConfig.Description & "': " & intRC
    end if
next
```

Discussion

Filtering by port or protocol can be useful in certain situations, but be aware of the
limitations. A good example of when you might want to configure filtering is for
external web servers. If your web server is running on the default HTTP port (80)
and it is running no other networked application, then you only need port 80 open.
But allowing only port 80 traffic also prevents the server from acting as a member in
an Active Directory domain (which requires several ports to be open) and makes
remote administration difficult because you can't connect using the Terminal Services client. Obviously you can add these ports to the list you allow, but remember
that if you do port/protocol filtering, you must have the ports/protocols open that
are needed to support the machine (see Recipe 10.9 for more on how to get the list of
open ports on a system).

See Also

For the list of preassigned port numbers, see the following site: *http://www.iana.org/
assignments/port-numbers*, MS KB 289892 (Internet Protocol Numbers), and MS KB
309798 (HOW TO: Configure TCP/IP Filtering in Windows 2000)

10.13 Measuring Link Speed and Latency
Between Two Hosts

Problem

You want to measure the link speed between two hosts.

Solution

Using a command-line interface

The Windows Server 2003 Resource Kit includes a new tool called *linkspeed*, which
measures the connectivity between two hosts. You run the command from one system and target a remote system:

```
> linkspeed /s \\<ServerName>
> linkspeed /s <ServerDNSName>
```

Alternatively, you can specify the /dc switch to have it test the machine's current
domain controller:

```
> linkspeed /dc
```

I've tested *linkspeed* on Windows 2000. While it runs without fatal errors, it doesn't produce consistent results. It works best when the target system is another Windows Server 2003 machine.

Discussion

Finding the link speed between two hosts is often useful when troubleshooting network connectivity problems. For example, if a client is having problems authenticating to Active Directory, you should learn the link speed between the client and the domain controller with which it is authenticating. A slow speed, perhaps due to congestion, could be the cause. If you want to determine the average link speed between two hosts, you should run the *linkspeed* command several times over multiple days. The results for any particular run of *linkspeed* could vary significantly depending on what is happening in the network at that time.

10.14 Installing the IPv6 Stack

Problem

You want to install and configure the IPv6 stack on a server.

Solution

Windows Server 2003 provides native support for IPv6, but Windows 2000 does not. To install the IPv6 stack for Windows 2000, you need to first download it from *http://www.microsoft.com/downloads/details.aspx?FamilyId=27B1E6A6-BBDD-43C9-AF57-DAE19795A088&displaylang=en*.

Run the executable and extract the files to a folder on your server. Then install the protocol stack by running *setup.exe*. If you are running Service Pack 2 or later (and hopefully you are), you have to perform some additional steps to get the installation to work. By default if you run the setup program it will complain about the system not being at Service Pack 1. Follow the directions on the following site to fix the problem: *http://msdn.microsoft.com/downloads/sdks/platform/tpipv6/faq.asp*.

Once you have the stack installed, you should follow the steps outlined in the graphical user interface instructions to configure it for a particular network connection (which also applies to Windows Server 2003).

Using a graphical user interface

1. Open the Control Panel.
2. From the **Network Connections** applet, double-click the connection you want to install IPv6 for.
3. Click the **Properties** button.

4. Click the **Install** button.

5. Select **Protocol** and click the **Add** button.

6. Select **Microsoft TCP/IP version 6** and click **OK**.

7. Click **Close**.

Using a command-line interface

The following command installs the IPv6 stack. It must be run directly on the target server:

```
> netsh interface ipv6 install
```

If you need to run the command remotely, you can use the *psexec* command:

```
> psexec \\server01 netsh interface ipv6 install
```

Using VBScript

There is no scripting interface to install the stack, but you can shell out and run the *netsh* command as in the following example:

```
' This code installs the IPv6 on the computer the script is run from.
strCommand = "netsh interface ipv6 install"
set objWshShell = WScript.CreateObject("WScript.Shell")
intRC = objWshShell.Run(strCommand, 0, TRUE)
if intRC <> 0 then
   WScript.Echo "Error returned from running the command: " & intRC
else
   WScript.Echo "Command executed successfully"
end if
```

Discussion

IPv6 is the next generation TCP/IP protocol suite intended to replace IPv4. Adoption of IPv6 has been slow, but seems to be steadily gaining momentum. Fortunately, Windows Server 2003 provides better support for IPv6 than it did Windows 2000. For a good overview of IPv6 and how to configure the Windows client, see the following FAQ: *http://msdn.microsoft.com/downloads/sdks/platform/tpipv6/faq.asp*.

See Also

MS KB 325449 (HOW TO: Install and Configure IP Version 6 in Windows Server 2003 Enterprise Server)

CHAPTER 11

Security Best Practices

11.0 Introduction

Security is one of the most important topics today in the world of system administration. In the past, system administrators could get by with not worrying much about security, but with the common occurrence of fast-spreading viruses and worms, everyone has to do their part to make things as secure as possible. The security burden on system administrators is now at an all-time high.

The Windows Server operating systems are famous for their lack of security, but that has largely to do with how Microsoft tried to make Windows easier to use and "on by default" instead of "secure by default." With Windows Server 2003, the operating system is more secure after installation compared to its predecessors. But that is only part of the story. Computers cannot lie in state and remain secure. It is up to system administrators to constantly monitor and be proactive from a security perspective to truly keep systems secure.

And that is what this chapter is about. I cover several security best practices every system administrator should consider when maintaining Windows servers. This chapter is by no means comprehensive, but it does cover many of the basic security precautions that most system administrators should consider.

One thing Microsoft has done a much better job of recently is to publish decent whitepapers about security and securing the Windows OS. Here are a few good ones you might want to look at (all available from *http://download.microsoft.com/*):

- Security Operations Guide for Windows 2000
- Windows Server 2003 Security Guide
- Best Practice Guide for Securing Active Directory Installations
- Securing Windows Server 2003 Active Directory

Basic Tips

Before I dive into the recipes, I'm going to review a few general security precautions. Again, this isn't a comprehensive list, but if you did these and nothing else, you would be doing better than a lot of system administrators out there.

Understand Microsoft's 10 immutable laws of security

Microsoft discusses 10 laws of security on the TechNet web site:

> *http://www.microsoft.com/technet/archive/community/columns/security/essays/*
> *10imlaws.mspx*

Take some time to understand each law (if they aren't self-evident). These laws are some of the most basic tenants of computer security, especially when dealing with Microsoft technologies.

Restrict physical access to computers

You could have the most hardened and locked down servers possible, but if an attacker can gain physical access to them, it is all for naught. Ensure your computers are as physically secure as possible. In remote sites, this can be difficult, and you should keep this in mind when planning to deploy critical services such as a domain controller or Exchange Server.

Don't use administrative accounts during day-to-day use

In the Windows NT days, before Remote Desktop Connection and the *runas* command were available, it wasn't uncommon for administrators to have their own personal account as part of the Domain Admins group. Now, you shouldn't need to do this. Create alternate administrative accounts in Active Directory (e.g., *rallen* for my personal account and *rallen.adm* for my administrative account). Use Remote Desktop Connection or *runas* to run programs that need admin privileges. This will reduce the chance (however unlikely) that you accidentally perform a damaging action on a server. Using your normal user account will also reduce the damage a virus or worm can do if your computer becomes infected.

Keep virus definitions up to date

One of the ways viruses spread so fast is that virus definitions aren't up-to-date on computers. With the blinding speed in which many viruses and worms propagate these days, you have to be on top of the latest definitions and able to push them out as quickly as you get them.

Make sure all critical patches are installed

Even if virus definitions aren't up-to-date, most viruses and worms would be stuck dead in their tracks if everyone installed critical security updates when they come out. Granted, this wasn't as necessary with Windows NT and when Windows 2000 was first introduced, but now, if you don't update your systems within days (and sometimes hours!) of new security updates becoming available, you are just asking to be hit with a new virus or worm. Here is a good site to bookmark and visit periodically to help keep you ahead of the curve with the latest Microsoft security issues: *http://www.microsoft.com/technet/security/current.aspx.*

Avoid casual use of your servers

Have you ever caught yourself browsing the Internet on a production server? It has happened to the best of us, but it is unacceptable. Avoid casual use of your servers as much as possible. In fact, the fewer times you have to use Terminal Service or access the console of your servers, the better—it reduces the chances of something bad happening accidentally. Being on a server unnecessarily can also make it more difficult to troubleshoot and identify the root cause of security incidents. By default, the version of IE that comes with Windows Server 2003 restricts you from viewing most sites; you have to add them to an exception list. Even though it can be annoying, don't disable this feature. It is a good deterrent to casual use.

Audit important activities

Windows provides the capability to log certain actions and activities that are performed on your servers and in Active Directory. By logging important activities, such as the modification of particular administrative groups, you can maintain an audit trail for later reference in case incidents arise. For more information on auditing, see Recipe 11.2.

Check event logs regularly

The event logs can contain a wealth of important security-related information, but they are often overlooked. This is partly due to the amount of noise that is in the event logs in the form of unimportant event messages. Develop a process to centralize and analyze your event logs regularly. Having this process will be even more critical if you are auditing important activities as described previously.

Know what to do when you discover you've been attacked

Most people think it can never happen to them, but the sad truth is it can. In fact, most system administrators don't have near as much security expertise as professional attackers. If a particular attacker (or worse, a group of attackers) takes a fancy to your organization, you'll have to be on top of your game to avoid some type of successful penetration. Some of the best in the business have been attacked. The moral of the story is that you should be prepared for the possibility of being attacked. What would you do? Here are a few good links that might help you develop an incident response plan:

- *http://www.cert.org/tech_tips/root_compromise.html*
- *http://www.cert.org/*
- *http://www.securityfocus.com/*
- *http://microsoft.com/security*

Maintain (and test!) backups

The worst case is that you have a server that gets successfully compromised. Unless you feel extremely confident that you know exactly what was compromised, your best bet would be to reimage the system and restore from a known good backup. That means you need good backups to start with. And if you are performing regular backups, I highly suggest performing a periodic test restore to make sure the backups are good and can be used in an emergency.

11.1   Analyzing Your Security Configuration

Problem

You want to analyze the security configuration of one or more servers to find any vulnerabilities or missing security updates.

Solution

The Microsoft Baseline Security Analyzer (MBSA) is a freely available tool from Microsoft that let's you scan computers for the latest security problems with Windows along with numerous Microsoft products. Some of these include Office, Exchange Server 2003, Microsoft Virtual Machine, and BizTalk. It can also check the configuration of Internet Configuration Firewall, Automatic Updates, and password settings.

MBSA has both a graphical and command-line interface. The MBSA graphical interface allows you to scan a single or multiple computers at one time (up to 10,000). Figure 11-1 shows the MBSA screen for selecting multiple computers. You can choose computers based on domain name and IP address range.

The MBSA command-line interface, *mbsacli.exe*, has the same functionality as the graphical interface. With it, you can easily automate periodic scans of your servers.

For more information on MBSA, including download instructions, see *http://www.microsoft.com/technet/security/tools/mbsahome.mspx*.

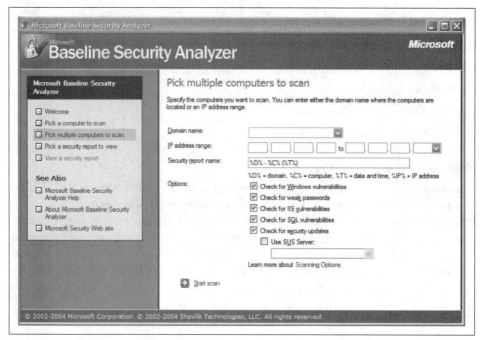

Figure 11-1. MBSA multiple computer selection screen

Discussion

MBSA keeps itself up to date with the latest vulnerabilities and security updates by automatically polling Microsoft when you start the program. As of Version 1.2, you can alternately point MBSA at a SUS server to download the update catalog. This lets you determine what servers in your network are up to date according to your internal SUS server.

See Also

MS KB 320454 (Microsoft Baseline Security Analyzer (MBSA))

11.2   Enabling Auditing

Problem

You want to enable auditing to track certain types of activity that can be useful should you need to backtrack later to determine the cause of security-related issues (e.g., user accidentally deleted, account being compromised).

Solution

Using a graphical user interface

1. Open the Local Security Policy snap-in.

2. In the left pane, expand **Local Policies** → **Audit Policy**.

3. In the right pane, double-click the setting you want to enable, and check the box beside **Success** and/or **Failure** depending on the types of events you want to audit.

You can force new auditing settings to be applied by running the *secedit* command on Windows 2000 or the *gpupdate* command on Windows Server 2003.

Run the following command on Windows 2000:

```
> secedit /refreshpolicy machine_policy
```

And run this command on Windows Server 2003:

```
> gpupdate /target:computer
```

Discussion

Windows supports auditing of various account- and system-related events, which can be invaluable when troubleshooting a security incident. You can enable auditing of nine different types of access on a local server. You can also configure these settings via an Active Directory group policy, which overrides any local settings that you've defined. After auditing has been configured, audit messages are created in the Security event log.

The big question is: which audit settings should you enable? If you turned on everything, your server would start flooding your Security event log and ultimately it wouldn't be very useful. In fact, there are no hard and fast rules for which settings you should enable.

All audit settings have three possible configurations: not configured, Success, and Failure. Not configured means auditing isn't enabled for the setting, Success means log any applicable event that was successful, and Failure means log any applicable event that failed. Often, it is more useful to log Failure events since you want to discover someone who is attempting to perform an activity surreptitiously, which may mean doing it several times until successful.

With some settings, simply enabling Success or Failure won't actually cause any events to be logged. You also have to enable auditing on specific objects, such as a particular file, before events will be audited. This is useful because in some cases, such as files and folders, you may only want to audit certain ones. If auditing were enabled for all files, the amount of events would render auditing unfeasible.

I've listed each of the nine settings in Table 11-1, including information about what type of information is logged and my recommendation for whether you should consider enabling it.

Table 11-1. Audit policy settings

Audit setting	Access type	Recommendation
Account Logon Events	User account log on and log off attempts that are validated by this system.	This setting is most often used on domain controllers, which are generally responsible for authenticating users in a domain environment. Be careful when enabling this because of the large number of events that might be logged.
Account Management	Creation, modification, and deletion of user, group, and computer accounts. Also includes password changes.	Consider enabling both Success and Failure auditing for this setting on member servers, which generally shouldn't have too much account management activity. For domain controllers, you may only want to enable Failure, due to the high number of account management activities.
Directory Service Access	Any type of read or write access to an object in Active Directory.	After enabling this setting, you must also modify the SACL of the object you want to audit. Be careful enabling this on a large container or commonly accessed object in the directory because it can generate a lot of events quickly.
Logon Events	User account log on and log off attempts, and the initiation of network connections.	Unlike the Account Logon Events setting, this setting logs the events on the computer that the request is being made on, not necessarily the computer that is validating the accounts involved. Depending on how busy your servers are, this setting may generate a large number of events.
Object Access	Any type of read or write access to an object on the system (file, folder, printer, registry key, etc.).	After enabling this setting, you must also modify the SACL of the object you want to audit. Be careful enabling this on a frequently accessed object because it can generate a lot of events quickly.
Policy Change	Change to user right policies, audit policies, and trust policies.	Since the number of policy changes is generally low, you might want to consider enabling both Success and Failure auditing for this setting.
Privilege Use	User exercising a user right (e.g., act as part of the operating system, access this computer from the network, log on as a service).	Enabling either Success or Failure for this setting can generate a lot of events, so enable them only if explicitly needed.
Process Tracking	Process creation and termination, and other process-related activities.	Since processes are created and terminated frequently, enabling Success or Failure for this setting can generate a lot of events. Enable it only if explicitly needed.
System Events	System restart or shutdown, and modifications to system security or the security event log.	Since the number of these type of events should be relatively low, consider enabling both Success and Failure.

Be sure to thoroughly test any audit settings before implementing them in production. Even after implementing a change in production, periodically monitor the Security event log to ensure the log isn't being flooded with events.

See Also

MS KB 300549 (HOW TO: Enable and Apply Security Auditing in Windows 2000)

11.3 Renaming the Administrator and Guest Accounts

Problem

You want to rename the administrator and guest accounts on your servers. This is a good practice because these two default accounts are often the target of attackers.

Solution

Using a graphical user interface

To rename a domain administrator or guest account, do the following:

1. From **Administrative Tools**, open the **Active Directory Users and Computers** snap-in.
2. In the left pane, browse to the Users container and click on it.
3. In the right pane, right-click the administrator or guest account and select **Rename**.
4. Type the new name for the account and hit Enter.

To rename a local administrator or guest account, do the following:

1. From **Administrative Tools**, open the **Computer Management** snap-in.
2. In the left pane, expand **System Tools** → **Local Users and Groups** → **Users**.
3. In the right pane, right-click on either the Administrator or Guest account and select **Rename**.
4. Type the new name for the account and press Enter.

Using a graphical user interface

To rename a domain administrator account, use the *dsmove.exe* command (available on Windows Server 2003). The following shows the basic syntax:

```
> dsmove "cn=administrator,cn=users,<DomainDN>" -newname "<NewName>"
```

For example:

```
> dsmove "cn=administrator,cn=users,dc=rallencorp,dc=com" -newname "admn"
```

And this shows how to rename the domain guest account:

```
> dsmove "cn=guest,cn=users,dc=rallencorp,dc=com" -newname "noguest"
```

To rename local accounts, use the *cusrmgr.exe* utility from the Windows 2000 Resource Kit:

```
> cusrmgr -m \\<ServerName> -u admininstrator -r <NewName>
```

For example:

```
> cusrmgr -m \\srv01 -u admininstrator -r admn
```

And to rename the local guest account:

```
> cusrmgr -m \\<ServerName> -u guest -r <NewName>
```

For example:

```
> cusrmgr -m \\srv01 -u guest -r noguest
```

Using VBScript

```
' This code renames a domain account.
' ------ SCRIPT CONFIGURATION ------
strObjectOldName    = "<OldName>"          'e.g., administrator
strObjectNewName    = "<NewName>"          'e.g., RallencorpAdmin
strCurrentParentDN = "<CurrentParentDN>" 'e.g., cn=users,dc=rallencorp,dc=com
' ------ END CONFIGURATION ---------
set objCont = GetObject("LDAP://" & strCurrentParentDN)
objCont.MoveHere "LDAP://cn=" & strObjectOldName & "," & _
                    strCurrentParentDN, "cn=" & strObjectNewName
WScript.Echo strAccount & " successfully renamed"


' This code renames a local account.
' ------ SCRIPT CONFIGURATION ------
strComputer = "<ServerName>"    ' e.g., srv01
strOldName = "<OldName>"        ' e.g., Guest
strNewName = "<NewName>"        ' e.g., RallencorpGuest
' ------ END CONFIGURATION ---------
set objComp = GetObject("WinNT://" & strComputer)
set objUser = GetObject("WinNT://" & strComputer & "/" & strOldName & ",user")
set objNewUser = objComp.MoveHere(objUser.ADsPath, strNewName)
WScript.Echo "Successfully renamed account"
```

Discussion

You can also rename the administrator and guest accounts using group policy or local policy. To do so with group policy, do the following:

1. Edit the target GPO with the Group Policy Object Editor.
2. Navigate to **Computer Configuration** → **Windows Settings** → **Security Settings** → **Local Policies** → **Security Options**.
3. In the right pane, double-click either **Rename administrator account** or **Rename guest account**.
4. Check the box beside **Define this policy setting** and type in the new name for the account.
5. Click **OK**.

If you are worried about using an obscure name for your administrator account like vadar and forgetting what you used later, you can always discover the name by looking up the account by SID. There is also a Joeware tool called *sidtoname* to help do the job. Simply pass the SID of the account to the *sidtoname* command as shown here:

```
D:\>sidtoname S-1-5-21-1801674531-2025429265-839522115-500

SidToName V02.00.00cpp Joe Richards (joe@joeware.net) March 2003

[User]: RALLENCORP\Vadar

The command completed successfully.
```

You can get a complete list of the well-known accounts and their corresponding SIDs in MS KB 243330.

You may be wondering that if you can find out the actual administrator account name by looking up the SID, then what is the point of renaming it. Ultimately, attackers can find out the name of well-known accounts, but there are still many viruses and worms that have attempted to access the administrator account by name. So this is still effective against less sophisticated attackers and viruses.

See Also

MS KB 243330 (Well Known Security Identifiers in Windows Server Operating Systems) and MS KB 320053 (HOW TO: Rename the Administrator and Guest Account in Windows 2000)

11.4 Disabling or Removing Unused Accounts, Services, and Software

Problem

You want to disable or remove anything that you don't explicitly need or use on a frequent basis on your server. The fewer things you have installed or active, the fewer potential vulnerabilities you have.

Solution

There is no one-size-fits-all rule for the accounts and services you should disable. It really depends on how you use your servers and what you use on them. As far as local accounts go, you should really only have a few on your system. The administrator and guest accounts are standard and you may also have built-in accounts for Internet Information Services (IIS) or other applications. In the case of administrator and guest, you can't actually delete those accounts, but you can disable them. If nothing else, you should consider renaming them so that they aren't easy objects of attack (see Recipe 11.3 for more on this).

For services, you should review the services that are actively running and determine which ones you can safely disable. Again, there are no hard and fast rules here, but use Appendix F as your guide. Review the purpose of each service and determine if it needs to be running. For example, if you aren't running any scheduled jobs and don't plan to do so, you don't really need the Task Scheduler service to run. Configure its startup type to Disabled (see Recipe 7.4). For other services that you aren't sure about, don't just disable them on production systems. Test changes on a test system first.

Finally, make sure that all the software installed on your servers is truly needed. Fortunately, Microsoft takes care of providing security updates for the default services that are installed on a system, but it is up to each application vendor to provide you with updates to their software when vulnerabilities are found. Don't forget about those.

See Also

Recipe 11.3

11.5 Enabling Screensaver Locking

Problem

You want to enable screensaver locking to prevent an administrator leaving the console of a server unlocked and exposing it to an intruder.

Solution

Using a graphical user interface

The following instructions enable screensaver locking for the currently logged on user:

1. Right-click the desktop background and select **Properties**.
2. Select the **Screen Saver** tab.
3. Select **Blank** for the screensaver, enter the number of minutes to wait before starting the screensaver and check the box beside **On resume, password protect**.
4. Click **OK**.

The following instructions enable screensaver locking using group policy:

1. Open the Group Policy Management Console (GPMC).
2. In the left pane, navigate to the target group policy, right-click it, and select **edit**. This will launch the Group Policy Object Editor.
3. In the left pane, expand **User Configuration** → **Administrative Templates** → **Control Panel** and click on **Display**.
4. In the right pane, there are five settings you can modify to control screensaver behavior. These include **Hide Screen Saver tab**, **Activate screen saver**, **Screen saver executable name**, **Password protect the screen saver**, and **Screen Saver timeout**.

Using a command-line interface

The following commands enable screensaver locking in the default user profile. Any user who logs in after these commands are run will use these settings. Any user who logged in before these commands are run will retain their original settings.

The following command configures the blank screensaver:

```
> reg add "\\<ServerName>\HKEY_USERS\.DEFAULT\Control Panel\Desktop" /v
SCRNSAVE.EXE /t R
EG_SZ /d scrnsave.scr
> reg add "\\<ServerName>\HKEY_USERS\.DEFAULT\Control Panel\Desktop" /v
ScreenSaveActive/t REG_SZ /d 1
```

The following command sets the screensaver timeout to 10 minutes (600 seconds):

```
> reg add "\\<ServerName>\HKEY_USERS\.DEFAULT\Control Panel\Desktop" /v
ScreenSaveTimeOut /t REG_SZ /d 600
```

The following command enables screensaver locking:

```
> reg add "\\<ServerName>\HKEY_USERS\.DEFAULT\Control Panel\Desktop" /v
ScreenSaverIsSecure /t REG_SZ /d 1
```

Using VBScript

```
' This code enables screensaver locking for all users that log on
' a system even if they've configured other screensaver settings previously.
' ------ SCRIPT CONFIGURATION ------
strComputer = "."
strScreenSaveActive    = "1"
strScreenSaverIsSecure = "1"
strScreenSaveTimeout   = "300"
strScrnSave            = "scrnsave.scr"
' ------ END CONFIGURATION ---------
const HKEY_USERS = &H80000003

set objReg=GetObject("winmgmts:\\" & strComputer & "\root\default:StdRegProv")
objReg.EnumKey HKEY_USERS, "", arrSubKeys

for each strSubkey in arrSubKeys
   WScript.Echo strSubkey
   objReg.EnumValues HKEY_USERS, strSubkey & "\Control Panel\Desktop", _
                     arrValues, arrTypes
   if IsArray(arrValues) then
      WScript.Echo "  setting screen saver values"
      objReg.SetStringValue HKEY_USERS, strSubkey & "\Control Panel\Desktop", _
                     "ScreenSaveActive", strScreenSaveActive
      objReg.SetStringValue HKEY_USERS, strSubkey & "\Control Panel\Desktop", _
                     "ScreenSaverIsSecure", strScreenSaverIsSecure
      objReg.SetStringValue HKEY_USERS, strSubkey & "\Control Panel\Desktop", _
                     "ScreenSaveTimeOut", strScreenSaveTimeOut
      objReg.SetStringValue HKEY_USERS, strSubkey & "\Control Panel\Desktop", _
                     "SCRNSAVE.EXE", strScrnSave
   else
      WScript.Echo "  NOT setting screen saver values"
   end if
   WScript.Echo
next
```

Discussion

If you want to implement a login script or batch file to enable screensaver locking for the currently logged on user of a system, you need to modify the following registry values:

```
HKEY_CURRENT_USER\Control Panel\Desktop
"ScreenSaveActive"="1"
"ScreenSaverIsSecure"="1"
"ScreenSaveTimeOut"="900"
"SCRNSAVE.EXE"="scrnsave.scr"
```

This configures the *scrnsave.scr* screensaver to turn on after 15 minutes (900 seconds) of inactivity.

See Also

MS KB 281250 (Information About Unlocking a Workstation)

11.6   Disabling Storage of the LM Password Hash

Problem

You want to prevent the LM hash for new passwords from being stored in Active Directory. The LM hash is susceptible to brute force attacks and is primarily used for backward compatibility with Windows 95 and 98 clients.

Solution

For Windows 2000, you need to create the following Registry key on all domain controllers: `HKLM\SYSTEM\CurrentControlSet\Control\Lsa\NoLMHash`. Note that this is a key and not a value entry. Also, this is only supported on W2K SP2 and later domain controllers.

For Windows Server 2003, the NoLMHash key has turned into a DWORD value entry under the `HKLM\SYSTEM\CurrentControlSet\Control\Lsa` key. This value should be set to 1. You can accomplish this by modifying the Default Domain Controller Security Policy as described next.

Using a graphical user interface

1. Open the Group Policy Object Editor and target the Default Domain Controller Security Policy.
2. In the left pane, expand **Local Policies** → **Security Options**.
3. In the right pane, double-click on **Network security: Do not store LAN Manager hash value on next password change**.
4. Check the box beside **Define this policy setting**.
5. Click the **Enabled** radio button.
6. Click **OK**.

Discussion

If you do not have Windows 98 or older clients in your domain, you should consider disabling the storage of the LM password hash for users. The LM hash uses an old algorithm (pre-Windows NT 4.0) and is relatively weak compared to the NT hash that is also stored.

 The LM hash is generated only for passwords that are shorter than 15 characters. If you are one of the few people who have a password (or passphrase) longer than that, the LM hash is not stored for you.

See Also

MS KB 299656 (How to Prevent Windows from Storing a LAN Manager Hash of Your Password in Active Directory and Local SAM Databases)

11.7   Requiring Strong Passwords

Problem

You want to enforce the use of strong passwords for user accounts.

Solution

Using a graphical user interface

1. Open the Group Policy Object Editor and target the Default Domain Policy.
2. In the left pane, expand **Computer Configuration** → **Windows Settings** → **Security Settings** → **Account Policies** → **Password Policy**.
3. In the right pane, double-click **Password must meet complexity requirements**.
4. Make sure the box beside **Define this policy setting** is checked and **Enabled** is selected.
5. Click **OK**.

This setting does not have any effect on users' current password. Password complexity is required only after each users' current passwords. For more on how to force users to change their password, see Recipe 6.21 in *Active Directory Cookbook* (O'Reilly).

Discussion

Most users, if given a choice, pick really simple, easy to remember passwords. No matter how tight the security is on your servers, if an attacker can crack a user's password, it is all for naught. To combat this, you can enable password complexity on the Default Domain GPO to require users to choose a password that meets the following criteria:

- Not contain any part of the user's account name
- Contain at least six characters
- Contain characters from three of the following:
  - Uppercase
  - Lowercase
  - Digits
  - Special character (e.g., %(@!)

By enabling this, you can feel a little better that once a user changes his password, that it won't be something trivial (although passwords such as "Mypassword!" still pass the complexity test).

See Also

MS KB 225230 (Enabling Strong Password Functionality in Windows 2000)

11.8 Getting Notified of New Security Vulnerabilities

Problem

You want to be notified when new security vulnerabilities in Microsoft products are found.

Solution

Microsoft provides a notification service that anyone can subscribe to. Simply visit *http://www.microsoft.com/technet/security/bulletin/notify.mspx*.

You'll need to provide an email address to send the notifications to. You may want to use a group mailing list so that multiple people get the notifications.

Discussion

To get a list of the latest security bulletins, visit *http://www.microsoft.com/technet/ security/current.aspx*. From there, you can view monthly security bulletin summaries along with on-demand webcasts that describe the technical details of bulletins.

11.9 Script: Mass Admin Password Changer

What do you do when someone leaves your company that knows the administrator passwords for your systems? Do you go to all of your servers and change the passwords? You should. Do you periodically change all the administrator passwords on your systems by hand? That's where this script comes in handy. All you need is a text file that contains a list of servers, set the new password in the code, and run the script with an account that has administrative privileges on those servers. This way you can quickly change the administration password on a bunch of servers.

Here is the code:

```
Option Explicit
On Error Resume Next
```

```
Dim strServerList : strServerList = "c:\servers.txt"
Dim strServerPass : strServerPass = "c:\pass.txt"
Dim strServerFail : strServerFail = "c:\fail.txt"

Dim strAdminAccount : strAdminAccount = "administrator"
Dim strNewPassword : strNewPassword   = "My!New!Password"

Dim objFSO, objServersFile, objPassFile, objFailFile
Set objFSO  = CreateObject("Scripting.FileSystemObject")
Set objServersFile = objFSO.OpenTextFile(strServerList)
Set objPassFile    = objFSO.CreateTextFile(strServerPass)
Set objFailFile    = objFSO.CreateTextFile(strServerFail)

Do While not objServersFile.AtEndOfStream
    Dim strServer : strServer = objServersFile.ReadLine
    Dim objAdmin
    Set objAdmin = GetObject("WinNT://" & strServer & "/" _
                   & strAdminAccount & ",user")
    if Err then
       objFailFile.WriteLine strServer & " failed: " & Err.Description
       Err.Clear
    else
       objAdmin.SetPassword strNewPassword
       objAdmin.SetInfo
       if Err then
          objFailFile.WriteLine strServer & " failed: " & Err.Description
          Err.Clear
       else
          objPassFile.WriteLine strServer & " successful"
       end if
    end if
Loop

WScript.Echo "Complete."

' Close open files
objServersFile.close
objFailFile.close
objPassFile.close
```

The code is pretty straightforward, but if you'd rather piece together a long command line, I may be able to help there as well. I'm now going to present three different commands that do essentially the same thing as the script, except each pulls the list of servers to change the password on from a different source. They all use the Sysinternals *pspasswd* command to remotely change passwords.

The first does exactly what the script does by iterating over a list of servers in a text file (called *c:\servers.txt*):

```
> for /f %v in (c:\servers.txt) do pspasswd \\%v -u administrator -p <Current> <New>
```

If you want to change the password on just a handful of servers, you may not want to create a text file. With the following command, you can specify the list of hosts:

```
for %v in (localhost,srv01,srv02) do pspasswd \\%v -u administrator -p <Current>
<New>
```

Lastly, you may want to pull your list of servers from Active Directory. The following command iterates over all the computers contained in the *cn=Computers* container in the *dc=rallencorp,dc=com* domain while running on a Windows Server 2003 computer:

```
for /f "usebackq" %v in (`dsquery computer "cn=computers,dc=rallencorp,dc=com"
- limit 0 -o rdn`) do pspasswd \\%~v -u administrator -p <Current> <New>
```

Don't Know Your Administrator Passwords

Upon reading this recipe, one of the technical reviewers for this book, Joe Richards, stated the following:

> Actually, no one should use or know the passwords for the built-in accounts, they should be randomly set to some value greater than 14 characters that are near impossible to memorize and then stuffed into envelopes that are kept in some big pain in the neck manager's office. People should be using their own accounts for everything. Then you simply monitor password ages to make sure they don't change when you don't expect. Every 90 days, sweep through and change the passwords via a script and notify the security manager. If you are confident in the length of the password for brute force cracking then don't even worry about changing it every 90 days. However if you do that, it might be worth watching the last logon time in the script that monitors password age. In one company, the domain administration passwords were 50 random characters, set, tested, and stuffed in an envelope. Each domain had a different password. The procedure was that if someone needed the password it would be changed again that same day. In four or so years, the envelopes were never touched.

CHAPTER 12

Internet Information Services 6.0

12.0 Introduction

Internet Information Services (IIS) is not only a popular platform for hosting web sites, it's also a required component for a number of Windows Server System (WSS) products, including Content Management Server, Exchange Server, Virtual Server, and Systems Management Server. Because these products rely on IIS for many of their core functions, understanding how IIS works is essential if you need to deploy, administer, or troubleshoot such products.

IIS 6.0 has been rewritten almost from scratch for Windows Server 2003, and its improved architecture supports a wide range of new features including application pools, health monitoring, worker process recycling, and web gardens. Security has also been improved in several ways; for example, IIS is no longer installed by default during a Windows Server 2003 installation (except for Windows Server 2003 Web Edition), and when you do install IIS, the default settings allow only static content to be served. In order to configure IIS to deliver dynamic content such as ASP or ASP.NET applications, you must selectively enable these features using the new Web Service Extensions node in IIS Manager. This chapter provides recipes for the most common tasks an IIS administrator faces on a day-to-day basis.

 You cannot upgrade IIS 5.0 on Windows 2000 to IIS 6.0. The only operating system IIS 6.0 runs on is Windows Server 2003. The focus of this chapter is on IIS 6.0.

Application Isolation

IIS 4 first introduced the idea of an out-of-process application, that is, ISAPI or ASP code that runs in a separate memory space from *inetinfo.exe*, the core web server process associated with the IISAdmin and World Wide Web (WWW) services. The advantage of using out-of-process applications was that they could be stopped and started independently from one another, and if one of them crashed it didn't bring down the entire web server.

There were disadvantages, however, out-of-process applications couldn't communicate with each other, ran slowly, and consumed large amounts of memory. As a result, running applications out of process was usually used only during the development phase for troubleshooting unstable applications, and once an application was debugged, it was moved in process with *inetinfo.exe*. And then if any bugs still lingered, the server crashed and had to be manually restarted.

IIS 5 added a new type of application protection called pooled process, which let you run several applications together in a COM+ host process called *dllhost.exe* that was separate from the core *inetinfo.exe* process where the WWW service resides. The advantages of running applications in a pooled process include improved performance and better resource usage over isolated processes. Plus, if one application in the pool dies, it brings down only the other pooled applications and not the entire server.

Additionally, IIS 5 could automatically restart pooled applications if they failed, reducing the number of manual reboots required on your computers. IIS 5 ran all applications as pooled processes by default, but they could also be moved out of process for troubleshooting purposes or in process for top performance. One limitation, however, was that IIS 5 only had one pool for lumping applications together.

The architecture of IIS has been completely revamped in IIS 6 (see Figure 12-1 for a comparison of architectures for different IIS versions). There is now only one kind of application isolation available: application pools. These pools are similar to pooled processes in IIS 5, but now you can create as many pools as you like and group your applications accordingly.

These pools are completely isolated from each other and thus combine the benefits of out of process and pooled process as in IIS 5. And in IIS 6, you can no longer run web-application code in process with *inetinfo.exe*, though this process still encapsulates all FTP, SMTP, or NNTP sites running on the server. Instead, a new service called the Web Administration Service (WAS) replaces IISAdmin as the user-mode component of the WWW service.

This new IIS 6 architecture is named "worker process isolation mode," because any user-developed application code must now run within a worker process (*w3wp.exe*) as its host process instead of the *dllhost.exe* process used by IIS 5. There are several advantages of this new architecture. For example, one worker process can service several applications within a pool, providing isolation between applications running within other pools. One pool can also be serviced by several worker processes in a configuration known as a *web garden*. This increases availability on a single computer the way web farms do using multiple computers.

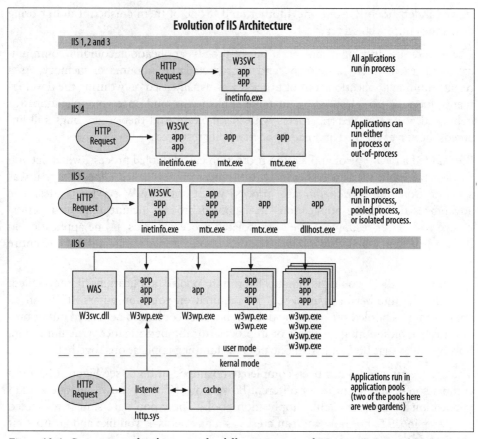

Figure 12-1. Comparison of architectures for different versions of IIS

WAS also monitors the health of worker processes and can terminate blocked processes and create new ones to take their place, further improving performance. And on a multiprocessor computer, a new feature called *processor affinity* lets you assign individual worker processes to specific CPUs to fine-tune performance.

But what happens if you move your existing IIS 5 applications to IIS 6 and they have trouble running on the new architecture? Simply switch your server from worker process isolation mode to IIS 5 isolation mode (see Figure 12-2) and suddenly there are no more application pools, worker processes, WAS, or processor affinity—you've got IIS 5 instead. Or at least something that's similar to it in architecture, which should keep your legacy apps running until you can recode them to take advantage of the new features of worker process isolation mode.

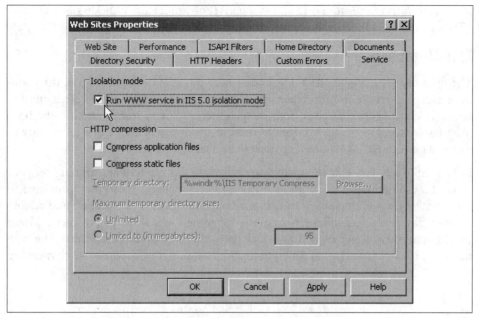

Figure 12-2. Switching from worker process isolation mode to IIS 5 isolation mode

HTTP Request Handling

In previous versions of IIS, the core *inetinfo.exe* process was hooked into the TCP/IP stack to pull out incoming HTTP requests and pass them to the WWW service (*w3svc.dll*) or a *dllhost.exe* helper process as appropriate. In IIS 6, however, the WWW service has been moved out of *inetinfo.exe* into the WAS, and *inetinfo.exe* no longer fields HTTP requests from the stack. Instead, this activity is done by the new kernel mode HTTP listener (*http.sys*). It resides within the TCP/IP stack, listening for incoming HTTP requests and routing them to the appropriate worker process.

This architectural change (within both IIS and the networking subsystem) has several significant results. Responsiveness is improved because *http.sys* can queue HTTP requests if the worker process that services them is blocked or busy. Performance is improved because *http.sys* is a kernel-mode process, in comparison with *inetinfo.exe*, which was a pageable user-mode process. And reliability is improved because *http.sys* cannot encapsulate any user-developed code the way *inetinfo.exe* could in IIS 5. *Http.sys* also caches HTTP responses for both static and dynamic content, generates IIS log entries, and manages establishing and tearing down TCP sessions for HTTP communications.

Note that while *http.sys* means big performance gains for applications running on IIS, it can cause compatibility problems for third-party HTTP applications you have running on your server. Fortunately, there's a workaround using a command-line tool called *httpcfg.exe*, found in the *\Support\Tools* folder on Windows Server 2003 CD. See MS KB 813368 for more information on how to use it.

XML Metabase

The final major change in IIS 6 I'll discuss here pertains to the metabase, the memory-resident database used in place of the registry for storing most IIS configuration settings. The biggest change is from the proprietary binary format used in the IIS 5 metabase to a text-based XML format used in IIS 6. This change makes it easier to edit and customize the metabase to meet your needs.

In fact, IIS 6 lets you edit the metabase even while IIS services are running on your computer, something you couldn't do in earlier versions. (Note that you have to enable this first; see Recipe 12.15.) IIS 6 also makes it easier to back up and restore the metabase, even to a different computer, opening the way for you to create a master IIS computer, clone its settings, and copy them to other computers. The new metabase history feature even generates backups automatically whenever changes are made to the metabase.

 For a more detailed look at IIS 6 and how its architecture and operation differs from previous versions, see Mitch Tulloch's book, *IIS 6 Administration* (Osborne/McGraw-Hill).

Using a graphical user interface

The standard graphical tool for administering IIS is Internet Information Services (IIS) Manager, or IIS Manger for short. This tool is standard on Windows Server 2003 platforms and a version of this tool that runs on Windows XP Professional can be downloaded at *http://www.microsoft.com/downloads/details.aspx?FamilyID=f9c1fb79-c903-4842-9f6c-9db93643fdb7*.

Using a command-line interface

IIS 6 includes a number of command scripts written in VBScript that can be used for common tasks such as creating web sites, backing up the metabase, and so on. In addition, there is the *adsutil.vbs* script that came with IIS 5, which uses ADSI to manipulate the IIS configuration, the *iisreset* command, and the *net* commands, and a couple of useful tools from the IIS 6.0 Resource Kit (you can download the Resource Kit tools from *http://www.microsoft.com/downloads/details.aspx?FamilyID=56fc92ee-a71a-4c73-b628-ade629c89499*). All of the tools used in this chapter are listed in Table 12-1.

Table 12-1. Command-line tools used in Chapter 12

Tool	IIS 6	Recipe(s)
adsutil.vbs	%SystemRoot%\Inetpub\admin-scripts	12.12, 12.13, 12.20, 12.23
iisapp.vbs	%SystemRoot%\system32	12.22
iisback.vbs	%SystemRoot%\system32	12.16
iiscertdeploy.vbs	IIS 6.0 Resource Kit Tools	12.9, 12.11
iiscnfg.vbs	%SystemRoot%\system32	12.3, 12.17
iisext.vbs	%SystemRoot%\system32	12.18
iisftp.vbs	%SystemRoot%\system32	12.2, 12.24, 12.26
iisreset.exe	%SystemRoot%\system32	12.2, 12.15
iisvdir.vbs	%SystemRoot%\system32	12.5
iisweb.vbs	%SystemRoot%\system32	12.2, 12.3, 12.4
net	%SystemRoot%\system32	12.2
selfssl.exe	IIS 6.0 Resource Kit Tools	12.9
sysocmgr.exe	%SystemRoot%\system32	12.1

Using VBScript

IIS is one of Microsoft's most programmable Windows components. And unlike most other components, you have your choice between ADSI and WMI as a programmatic interface. Historically, ADSI was the only interface available to script against IIS, but with Windows Server 2003 and IIS 6, Microsoft added WMI support.

In this chapter, I've used ADSI solely because of its legacy support in older versions of IIS and the fact that a lot of people still use ADSI when scripting IIS. Many of the examples you'll find in other books and on the Web use the ADSI provider. However, depending upon your specific requirements, you may find that WMI provides capabilities that are not present in the ADSI interfaces.

 MSDN has detailed reference information about the ADSI and WMI interfaces. If you have any questions about a specific ADSI class or metabase property, you'll want to search for it in MSDN (*http://msdn.microsoft.com*).

12.1 Installing IIS

Problem

You want to install IIS on a Windows Server 2003 computer.

Solution

Using a graphical user interface

To manually install IIS on a computer that already has Windows Server 2003 installed, do the following:

1. From the Start menu, select Manage Your Server.
2. Click **Add or remove a role**.
3. Click **Next** to detect your network connection.
4. Select the **Application Server (IIS, ASP.NET)** role and click **Next**.
5. If desired, select options to install FrontPage Server Extensions and enable ASP.NET and click **Next**.
6. Click **Next** and insert your Windows Server 2003 product CD when prompted or browse to a network distribution point where the Windows Server 2003 installation files are located.
7. Click **Finish** when the install is completed.

To install additional IIS components (listed under the Discussion section), do the following:

1. From the Control Panel, open the **Add or Remove Programs** applet.
2. Click **Add/Remove Windows Components**.
3. Select **Application Server** and click **Details**.
4. Select the additional components you want to install (more components can be found by selecting **Internet Information Services** and clicking **Details**).
5. Click **OK** as many times as needed, insert your Windows Server 2003 product CD when prompted or browse to a network distribution point where the Windows Server 2003 installation files are located.
6. Click **Finish** when the install is completed.

To perform an unattended install of IIS on a computer with no operating system:

1. Insert the Windows Server 2003 product CD into a Windows XP or Windows Server 2003 computer.
2. When the splash screen appears, click **Perform additional tasks**.
3. Click **Browse this CD**.
4. Double-click the *Support* folder and double-click *Tools*.
5. Double-click *Deploy.cab* to open the compressed folder.
6. Right-click on *setupmgr.exe* and select **Extract**.
7. Specify a location such as **Desktop to extract Setup Manager to** and click **Extract**.

8. Close the *Deploy.cab* window and click **Exit** to close the splash screen.

9. Double-click on *setupmgr.exe* to start Setup Manager and click **Next**.

10. Select **Create new** to create a new answer file and click **Next**.

11. Select **Unattended Setup** to create an unattend.txt file for unattended installation and click **Next**.

12. Select the edition of Windows Server 2003 you plan to install and click **Next**.

13. Select **Fully Automated** and click **Next**.

14. Continue through the wizard to create an answer file named *unattend.txt*.

15. Open your answer file using Notepad.

16. Add the following section to your answer file to install core IIS components and the WWW service:

```
[Components]
iis_common = ON
iis_doc = ON
iis_www = ON
iis_inetmgr = ON
```

17. You can optionally add the following section to your answer file to customize your IIS configuration:

```
[InternetServer]
SvcManualStart = www
PathWWWRoot = C:\webstuff
```

18. Save the changes and use your answer file to perform an unattended installation of Windows Server 2003 using *winnt32.exe* with the /unattend option.

By renaming your answer file to *winnt.sif*, you can perform an automated installation directly from the product CD.

Using a command-line interface

The following command performs an unattended install of IIS on a computer on which Windows Server 2003 is already installed, using an answer file that includes only the [Components] and [InternetServer] sections described in the previous section:

```
> sysocmgr /i:sysoc.inf /u:<PathToAnswerFile>
```

For example, if your answer file is named *iis_install.txt*, is located in the root directory of *C:* drive, and contains the following entries:

```
[Components]
iis_common = ON
iis_doc = ON
iis_www = ON
iis_inetmgr = ON
```

```
[InternetServer]
SvcManualStart = www
PathWWWRoot = C:\webstuff
```

Then you can install IIS using this command:

```
> sysocmgr /i:sysoc.inf /u:C:\iis_install.txt
```

Using VBScript

Unfortunately, there are no scripting interfaces for installing IIS. However, you can run the *sysocmgr* command from the previous section directly within a batch script (*.bat* extension) or using the WScript.Shell Run method within VBScript.

```
' This code simulates the same steps from the command-line solution.
' First, an answer file is created containing the parameters to install
' IIS. Then the sysocmgr command is invoked to perform the installation.
strFile = "c:\iis_install.txt"

constForWriting = 2
set objFSO = CreateObject("Scripting.FileSystemObject")
set objFile = objFSO.OpenTextFile(strFile, constForWriting, True)
objFile.WriteLine("[Components]")
objFile.WriteLine("iis_common = ON")
objFile.WriteLine("iis_doc = ON")
objFile.WriteLine("iis_www = ON")
objFile.WriteLine("iis_inetmgr = ON")
objFile.WriteLine("")
objFile.WriteLine("[InternetServer]")
objFile.WriteLine("SvcManualStart = www")
objFile.WriteLine("PathWWWRoot = C:\webstuff")
objFile.Close

set objWshShell = WScript.CreateObject("WScript.Shell")
intRC = objWshShell.Run("sysocmgr /i:%windir%\inf\sysoc.inf /u:" & _
                        strFile, 0, TRUE)
if intRC <> 0 then
   WScript.Echo "Error returned from sysocmgr command: " & intRC
else
   WScript.Echo "IIS installed"
end if
```

Discussion

Table 12-2 describes some of the IIS components that you can install by adding entries to the [Components] section of your answer file.

Table 12-2. IIS components

Entry	Description
iis_asp	Active Server Pages component
iis_common	Common files needed by other IIS components

Table 12-2. IIS components (continued)

Entry	Description
iis_doc	IIS documentation
iis_ftp	FTP service
iis_inetmgr	Internet Services Manager snap-in for the MMC
iis_www	WWW service
fp_extensions	FrontPage Server Extensions
aspnet	ASP.NET component

For additional IIS components you can install, see the *Ref.chm* help file in the *\Support\ Tools\Deploy.cab* folder on your Windows Server 2003 product CD.

Table 12-3 contains some of the entries you can include in the [InternetServer] section of your answer file.

Table 12-3. IIS unattended configuration options

Entry	Description	Values
PathWWWRoot	Location of home directory for Default Web Site	Specify absolute path to directory (enclose in quotes if path includes spaces)
PathFTPRoot	Location of home directory for Default FTP Site	Specify absolute path to directory (enclose in quotes if path includes spaces)
SvcManualStart	WWW and/or FTP services are stopped and set to Manual after installing IIS	WWW | FTP | WWW,FTP

Note that the entries in the [InternetServer] section require corresponding entries in the [Components] section. For example, if you include an entry for PathWWWRoot in the [InternetServer] section, you must include iis_common, iis_inetmgr, and iis_www in the [Components] section as well. For more information on the entries in these two sections, see the *Ref.chm* help file.

 Don't install IIS on a domain controller unless you have no other option. Installing IIS on a domain controller can significantly increase the attack surface of the domain controller and potentially expose your Active Directory accounts database to malicious attack. For more information, see TechNet Webcast: Successfully Running IIS on a Domain Controller—Level 200 found at *http://msevents.microsoft.com/ CUI/EventDetail.aspx?EventID=1032245355&Culture=en-US.*

See Also

MS KB 323438 (HOW TO: Use Setup Manager to Create an Answer File in Windows Server 2003), MS KB 309506 (How To Perform an Unattended Installation of

IIS 6.0), and MS KB 222444 (How to Add or Remove Windows Components with Sysocmgr.exe)

12.2 Stopping and Starting IIS

Problem

You want to stop and restart IIS as a whole, individual IIS services, or individual sites.

Solution

Using a graphical user interface

1. Open Internet Information Services (IIS) Manager.
2. To restart all IIS services on the server:
   a. In the left pane, right-click on the server node and select **All Tasks → Restart IIS**.
   b. Choose whether to restart IIS, stop IIS, start IIS, or reboot the server and click **OK**.
3. To restart an individual web or FTP site, right-click on the node for the site and select **Stop**, then repeat and select **Start**.

Using a command-line interface

The following command restarts all IIS services on the computer:

```
> iisreset
```

To stop IIS services on a remote computer with IP address 172.16.12.5 do the following:

```
> iisreset 172.16.12.5 /stop
```

To verify that IIS services have been stopped on the remote computer, do the following:

```
> iisreset 172.16.12.5 /status
```

To prevent *iisreset* from being used to stop IIS services, type the following command at the local console of your IIS computer:

```
> iisreset /disable
```

To stop the WWW service only on your IIS computer:

```
> net stop w3svc
```

To start it again:

```
> net start w3svc
```

To stop the IISAdmin service and all dependent IIS services:

```
> net stop /y iisadmin
```

To stop the Default Web Site only while leaving other web sites running, use this command:

```
> iisweb /stop "Default Web Site"
```

To start it again:

```
> iisweb /start "Default Web Site"
```

Using VBScript

```
' This code stops and starts the specific web site.
' ------ SCRIPT CONFIGURATION ------
strComputer = "<ServerName>"  'e.g., web01.rallencorp.com
strPath = "<IISPath>"         'e.g., W3SVC/1
' ------ END CONFIGURATION ---------
set objIIS = GetObject("IIS://" & strComputer & "/" & strPath)

objIIS.Stop
WScript.Echo "Web site " & strComputer & "/" & strPath & " successfully stopped"

objIIS.Start
WScript.Echo "Web site " & strComputer & "/" & strPath & " successfully started"
```

Discussion

In previous versions of IIS, you often had to restart IIS frequently to keep a flaky application running. With IIS 6, you can use application pool recycling (see Recipe 12.23) instead, which restarts only the worker processes associated with that application and leaves other applications running. The only time you should need to restart IIS using the procedures outlined above is when you make a major configuration change to your computer, such as installing a new ISAPI filter or COM component.

Using a graphical user interface

If you can't restart IIS using IIS Manager, it means you may have disabled restarts by running iisreset /disable on your computer previously. Run iireset /enable and try again.

Using a command-line interface

To stop and start the FTP service, use net stop msftpsvc and net start msftpsvc (or the *sc* equivalents), and to stop and start individual FTP sites, use the *iisftp.vbs* command script.

Using a VBScript

If you want to restart a particular web or FTP site, set the strPath variable to the name of the service (e.g., W3SVC) followed by a forward slash and the numeric identifier for the site as seen in IIS Manager. To restart all IIS web services, set strPath to W3SVC.

See Also

Recipes 7.1 and 12.23

12.3   Creating Web Sites

Problem

You want to create a web site.

Solution

Using a graphical user interface

To create a new web site from scratch using a wizard, do the following:

1. Open Internet Information Services (IIS) Manager.
2. In the left pane, expand the server node.
3. Right-click on the **Web Sites** node, select **New → Web Site** to start the **Web Site Creation Wizard**, and click **Next**.
4. Type a descriptive name for your site and click **Next**.
5. Assign an IP address to your site and click **Next**.
6. Specify the path to the home directory for your site, decide whether to allow anonymous access to your site, and click **Next**.
7. Specify web permissions to control access to your site and click **Next**, then **Finish**.

To create a new web site using a previously saved configuration file, do the following:

1. Open Internet Information Services (IIS) Manager.
2. In the left pane, expand the server node.
3. Right-click on the **Web Sites** node and select **New → Web Site (from file)**.
4. Specify the path to the XML file containing your saved IIS configuration, click **Read File**, select the web site you want to import, and click **OK**.
5. If the saved configuration was password protected when it was created, you'll be prompted here for a password; enter it and click **OK**.
6. Right-click on the new web site and select **Start**.

Using a command-line interface

The following command creates a new web site named Human Resources on server with IP 216.44.65.8 and root directory *D:\HR*:

```
> iisweb /create D:\HR "Human Resources" /i 216.44.65.8
```

The following command creates a new site named My Company with root directory *D:\Corp* and IP address "All Unassigned," effectively making My Company the new default web site on the server:

```
> iisweb /create D:\Corp "My Company"
```

The following command creates a site on a standalone server named web04 using local credentials for that computer and leaving the site in a stopped state:

```
> iisweb /create D:\Finance "Accounting Department" /i 216.44.65.8 /dontstart /s
web01 /u web04\Administrator /p <password>
```

The following command creates a site by importing a previously saved password-protected site configuration file named *hr.xml*:

```
> iiscnfg /import /f D:\hr.xml /d <password> /sp /lm/w3svc/1525757177 /dp /lm/w3svc/2
/child
```

The ID number 1525757177 for this site can be found by opening the XML file in Notepad and examining the Location attribute of the IisWebServer tag. For example:

```
<IIsWebServer    Location ="/LM/W3SVC/1525757177"
        AuthFlags="0"
        ServerAutoStart="TRUE"
        ServerBindings="172.16.12.50:80:"
        ServerComment="Human Resources"
    >
</IIsWebServer>
```

You can also retrieve this identifier from IIS Manager by clicking the Web Sites folder in the left pane. The list of web sites and their identifiers will be shown in the right pane.

Using VBScript

```
' This code creates a web site.
' ------ SCRIPT CONFIGURATION ------
strComputer = "<ServerName>" ' computer to connect to
strSiteName = "<SiteName>"    ' web site description
strRootDir = "<DirPath>"      ' root directory for the web site
' The following parameters are optional
' strPort = "<PortNumber>"      ' port for the web site
' strIP = "<IPAddress>"         ' IP address used for the site
' strHostHeader = "<HostName>" ' host header name for the site
' strSiteID = 1234              ' site ID (default is to auto-generate)
' ------ END CONFIGURATION ---------
set objIIS = GetObject("IIS://" & strComputer & "/W3SVC" )
objServerBindings = Array(0)
objServerBindings(0) = strIP & ":" & strPort & ":" & strHostHeader
strNewSiteID = objIIS.CreateNewSite(strSiteName, objServerBindings, _
                                    strRootDir, strSiteID)
WScript.Echo "Successfully created web site " & strSiteName & _
            " with ID " & strNewSiteID
```

Discussion

If you leave the IP address for your new site as All Unassigned, your new site will be the default web site for your computer, which is the web site the server returns when a browser tries to access an IP address not currently assigned to another site. For example, if a computer has three IP addresses 172.16.12.50, 172.16.12.51, and 172.16.12.52 and only the first address has been assigned to a site, then opening the URLs *http://172.16.12.51* or *http://172.16.12.52* will return the default web site. It's a good idea to have a default web site configured with general contact information about your company on a server that will be hosting many sites. Note that if there is already a web site that has All Unassigned for its IP address (such as the Default Web Site created when IIS is installed) then if you assign All Unassigned to another site you won't be able to start that site.

Host headers are a feature of the HTTP/1.1 specification and allow IIS to host multiple web sites that have the same IP address and port number but different DNS identities. You can't use host headers for sites that use SSL, however, and to use host headers you must have DNS name resolution working on your network. Also, don't assign any host header names to the Default Web Site. One good side of host headers is that when you have thousands of web sites hosted on a single IIS computer, using host headers to identify them incurs a smaller performance hit than using individual IP addresses.

Using VBScript

The one tricky thing about this code is setting up the ServerBindings array. For whatever reason, instead of making the web site IP address, port, and host header part of the parameters to the CreateNewSite method, they must be concatenated together in an array element and separated by a colon.

See Also

Recipes 12.4, 12.17, MS KB 304187 (IIS: Home Directory Cannot Point to Mapped Drives), and MS KB 816568 (HOW TO: Manage Web Sites and Web Virtual Directories by Using Command-Line Scripts in IIS 6.0)

12.4 Hosting Multiple Web Sites

Problem

You want to host multiple web sites on the same computer.

Solution

Using a graphical user interface

To uniquely identify each web site by IP address:

1. Start the Web Site Creation Wizard described in the previous recipe.
2. When the IP Address and Port Settings screen appears, select any unused IP address from the list and continue with the wizard.
3. Users can now access each site using URLs such as *http://172.16.12.50, http:// 172.15.12.51*, and so on. You can also use a DNS server to define friendly DNS names for each site if desired.

To uniquely identify each web site by port number:

1. Start the **Web Site Creation Wizard** described in the previous recipe.
2. When the **IP Address and Port Settings** screen appears, specify any port number above 1023 and continue with the wizard.
3. Users can now access each site using an URL such as *http://172.16.12.50:8081, http://172.16.12.50:8082*, and so on. You can also use a DNS server to define a friendly DNS name for your server, but users will still need to know the port number for each site they want to access, for example *http://www.mtit.com:8081, http://www.mtit.com:8082*, and so on.

To uniquely identify each web site by host header name:

1. Start the **Web Site Creation Wizard** described in the previous recipe.
2. When the **IP Address and Port Settings** screen appears, type a unique host header name for the site and continue with the wizard.
3. Users can now access the web site with host header name *www1.mtit.com* using the URL *http://www1.mtit.com*, the web site with host header name *www2.mtit.com* using the URL *http://www2.mtit.com*, and so on.

You can also modify the IP address or port number of an existing web site, or assign it a host header name, by doing the following:

1. Open Internet Information Services (IIS) Manager.
2. In the left pane, expand the **Web Sites** node under the server node.
3. Right-click on the node for the web site you want to configure and select **Properties**.
4. Select the **Web Site** tab.
5. Change the IP address assigned to the site if desired.
6. Change the default port number (80) to something different if desired.
7. Click **Advanced**, click **Add**, and specify a host header if desired (you can repeat to assign multiple host headers for your site).

Using a command-line interface

The following commands create two web sites on the local server that are uniquely identified by IP addresses:

```
> iisweb /create D:\HR "Human Resources" /i 172.16.12.51
> iisweb /create D:\Finance "Accounting Department" /i 172.16.12.52
```

The following commands create two web sites on the local server that are uniquely identified by port numbers (the first site uses the default port 80):

```
> iisweb /create D:\HR "Human Resources" /i 172.16.12.50
> iisweb /create D:\Finance "Accounting Department" /b 8080 /i 172.16.12.50
```

The following commands create two web sites that are uniquely identified by their host header names:

```
> iisweb /create D:\HR "Human Resources" /i 172.16.12.50 /d hr.mtit.com
> iisweb /create D:\Finance "Accounting Department" /i 172.16.12.50 /d acct.mtit.com
```

To list all web sites on the local server, use the following command:

```
> iisweb /query
```

Using VBScript

```
' This code displays all the web sites on a server.
' ------ SCRIPT CONFIGURATION ------
strComputer = "<ServerName>" ' e.g., web01.rallencorp.com
' ------ END CONFIGURATION ---------
set objIIS = GetObject("IIS://" & strComputer & "/W3SVC")
for each objSite in objIIS
   if (objSite.Class = "IIsWebServer") then
      WScript.Echo objSite.ServerComment & " (" & objSite.Name & ")"
   end if
next
```

Discussion

The maximum number of web sites you can create on an IIS 6 computer depends on the available RAM. For example, a computer with 256 MB of RAM can host only 64 sites, and if you try to create a 65th site you'll get error 1131 in the System event log. In lieu of adding more RAM, you can work around this limitation by creating a new DWORD value named MaxEndPoints in the following registry key:

```
HKLM\SYSTEM\CurrentControlSet\Services\HTTP\Parameters
```

Set MaxEndPoints to one more than the number of web sites you need to host, but don't exceed 1024.

The web site limitation based on RAM is in place for a good reason. Microsoft does this so they can count on a certain amount of RAM per web site. Unless you have a good reason and you really know what you're doing, it probably doesn't make sense to mess around with the MaxEndPoints key.

Using VBScript

This code works by obtaining a reference to the top-level IIS service (W3SVC), enumerating all of the child objects, and printing the child objects of the class IIsWebServer, which represent web sites. The W3SVC object can also have IIsWebInfo and IIsFilter child objects, so if you don't check for the IIsWebServer class, you may end up printing more than just web sites.

See Also

Recipe 12.3 and MS KB 324287 (HOW TO: Use Host Header Names to Configure Multiple Web Sites in Internet Information Services 6.0)

12.5 Creating Virtual Directories

Problem

You want to create a virtual directory for a web site.

Solution

Using a graphical user interface

To create a new virtual directory using a wizard, do the following:

1. Open Internet Information Services (IIS) Manager.

2. In the left pane, expand the **Web Sites** node under the server node.

3. Right-click on the node for the web site you want to configure, select **New** → **Virtual Directory** to start the **Virtual Directory Creation Wizard**, and click **Next**.

4. Specify an alias for your virtual directory and click **Next**.

5. Specify the absolute path (for a local virtual directory) or UNC path (for a remote virtual directory) to the folder or share where the content is located and click **Next**.

6. Specify web permissions to control access to your virtual directory and click **Next**, then **Finish**.

To create a virtual directory using a previously saved configuration file, do the following:

1. Open Internet Information Services (IIS) Manager.
2. In the left pane, expand the **Web Sites** node under the server node.
3. Right-click on the node for the web site you want to configure and select **New → Virtual Directory (from file)**.
4. Specify the path to the XML file containing the saved IIS configuration, click **Read File**, select the virtual directory you want to import, and click **OK**.
5. If the saved configuration was password protected when it was created, you'll be prompted here for a password; enter it, and click **OK**.

To create a virtual directory using Windows Explorer, do the following:

1. Open Windows Explorer, right-click the physical directory you want to create an alias for, and click **Sharing and Security**.
2. Select the **Web Sharing** tab.
3. Specify the web site in which your virtual directory will be located.
4. Click **Share this folder**.
5. Type an alias for your virtual directory, modify its web permissions if desired, and click **OK** twice.

Using a command-line interface

The following command creates a virtual directory within the Human Resources web site and maps alias employees to physical directory *D:\resumes*:

```
> iisvdir /create "Human Resources" employees D:\resumes
```

To list virtual directories within the Human Resources site:

```
> iisvdir /query "Human Resources"
```

To delete the previously created virtual directory:

```
> iisvdir /delete "Human Resources\employees"
```

Using VBScript

```
' This code creates a virtual directory in the default Web Site
' ------ SCRIPT CONFIGURATION ------
strComputer = "rallen-w2k3"
strVdirName = "<VdirName>"   'e.g., employees
strVdirPath = "<Path>"       'e.g., D:\resumes
' ------ END CONFIGURATION ---------
set objIIS = GetObject("IIS://" & strComputer & "/W3SVC/1")
set objweb site = objIIS.GetObject("IISWebVirtualDir","Root")
set objVdir = objweb site.Create("IISWebVirtualDir",strVdirName)
objVdir.AccessRead = True
objVdir.Path = strVdirPath
```

```
objVdir.SetInfo
WScript.Echo "Successfully created virtual directory: " & objVdir.Name
```

Discussion

A virtual directory is a directory that behaves from the client perspective as if it is a subdirectory of a web site, whereas the actual directory may reside in a different location on the web server's hard drive or even on a different server on the network. A local virtual directory is one that maps to a folder on the local computer's file structure, while a remote virtual directory is one that maps to a shared folder on the network. The main purpose of virtual directories is to provide administrators with flexibility in how they host content for web sites.

Using a command-line interface

The *iisvdir.vbs* command can be used only to create local virtual directories, not remote ones. In other words, if the directory containing the web content is a shared folder on a different server (such as a file server) and you want to create a virtual directory on your IIS computer that maps to this shared folder, you can't use the *iisvdir.vbs* script to do this.

See Also

MS KB 816568 (HOW TO: Manage Web Sites and Web Virtual Directories by Using Command-Line Scripts in IIS 6.0), MS KB 247376 (WWW and FTP Virtual Directories Are Not Displayed in Directory Listings), and MS KB 311626 (How to: Rename a Virtual Directory in IIS 6.0)

12.6 Configuring Web Permissions

Problem

You want to control access to content on your web server using web permissions.

Solution

Using a graphical user interface

To control access to content for all web sites on your server, do the following:

1. Open Internet Information Services (IIS) Manager.
2. In the left pane, right-click on the **Web Sites** node and select **Properties**.
3. Select the **Home Directory** tab.
4. Select the web permissions you want to allow and click **OK**.
5. If the **Inheritance Overrides** dialog box appears, click **Select All** and click **OK** (repeat if this box appears again).

To control access to content in a particular web site, do the following:

1. Open Internet Information Services (IIS) Manager.
2. In the left pane, expand the **Web Sites** node, right-click on your web site, and select Properties.
3. Select the **Home Directory** tab.
4. Select the web permissions you want to allow and click **OK**.
5. If the **Inheritance Overrides** dialog box appears, click **Select All**, and click **OK** (repeat if this box appears again).

To control access to content in a particular virtual directory, do the following:

1. Open Internet Information Services (IIS) Manager.
2. In the left pane, right-click on your web site, right-click on the virtual directory within it you want to control, and select **Properties**.
3. Select the **Virtual Directory** tab.
4. Select the web permissions you want to allow and click **OK**.

To control access to a particular file in a web site or virtual directory, do the following:

1. Open Internet Information Services (IIS) Manager.
2. In the left pane, right-click on your web site or virtual directory.
3. Right-click on the file you want to restrict and select **Properties**.
4. Select the **File** tab.
5. Select the web permissions you want to allow and click **OK**.

Using VBScript

```
' This code configures web permissions on a web site.
' ------ SCRIPT CONFIGURATION ------
strComputer = "<ServerName>"  'e.g., web01
strSiteID = "<SiteID>"        'e.g., 1
' ------ END CONFIGURATION ---------
set objweb site = GetObject("IIS://" & strComputer & "/W3SVC/" & strSiteID)
objweb site.AccessRead = True
objweb site.AccessWrite = True
objweb site.AccessSource = True
objweb site.AccessScript = False
objweb site.AccessExecute = False
objweb site.SetInfo
WScript.Echo "Successfully modified permissions for web site: " & _
             objweb site.ServerComment


' This code configures web permissions on a virtual directory.
' ------ SCRIPT CONFIGURATION ------
strComputer = "<ServerName>"  'e.g., web01
strSiteID = "<SiteID>"        'e.g., 1
```

```
strVdir = "<VdirPath>"          'e.g., Root/employees
' ------ END CONFIGURATION ---------
set objweb site = GetObject("IIS://" & strComputer & "/W3SVC/" & strSiteID)
set objVdir = objweb site.GetObject("IISWebVirtualDir",strVdir)
objVdir.AccessRead = True
objVdir.AccessWrite = True
objVdir.AccessSource = True
objVdir.AccessScript = False
objVdir.AccessExecute = False
objVdir.SetInfo
WScript.Echo "Successfully modified permissions for virtual directory: " & _
          objVdir.Name
```

Discussion

Web permissions are a set of simple permissions that are applied equally to all users who try to access content on IIS. You specify web permissions for a site or virtual directory when you run the wizard to create that site or directory. Table 12-4 lists web permissions available in IIS.

Table 12-4. IIS web permissions

Web permission	Description
Read	Users can read or download files from the directory using a web browser.
Write	Users can modify or upload files to the directory using WebDAV clients.
Directory Browsing	Users can enumerate the files in the directory if no default document is defined or present.
Script Source Access	Users can read the code of ASP pages (if Read is enabled) or modify the code (if Write is enabled).
Execute Permissions	Controls whether scripts and other executable programs can run.

Web permissions are different from NTFS permissions in several ways. First, web permissions apply equally to all users who try to access content on IIS, while different users or groups can have different NTFS permissions applied to them depending on the need. Second, web permissions are defined at the virtual directory level while NTFS permissions are applied to physical directories. And third, NTFS permissions are far more granular than web permissions. Because of these differences, web permissions are mainly useful for controlling access to public Internet sites where visitors are anonymous. NTFS permissions on the other hand are important for controlling access to private intranet sites where users must be authenticated before they can access content.

While web permissions are useful, NTFS permissions should still be considered your first line of defense in controlling access to content on your web server. If NTFS and web permissions conflict, the most restrictive applies. So if you have open web permissions, but the underlying NTFS permissions are restricted, it will result in users not getting access to the content. Consider web permissions as a proxy to NTFS for web users.

See Also

MS KB 321506 (Web Permissions Behave Unexpectedly with Script Engines)

12.7 Configuring IP Address and Domain Name Restrictions

Problem

You want to restrict access to content on your web server by IP address or domain name.

Solution

Using a graphical user interface

To restrict access to all sites on your server, do the following:

1. Open Internet Information Services (IIS) Manager.
2. In the left pane, right-click on the **Web Sites** node and select **Properties**.
3. Select the **Directory Security** tab and click **Edit** under **IP address and domain name restrictions**.
4. Select either **Granted access** or **Denied access** depending on whether you want to define a rule to allow or deny access to your server.
5. Click **Add** and specify either a single IP address, an entire subnet of addresses, or a DNS domain name depending on how you want to restrict access to your server. Click **OK**.
6. If the **Inheritance Overrides** dialog box appears, click **Select All** and click **OK** (repeat if this box appears again).

To restrict access to a particular web site, do the following:

1. Open Internet Information Services (IIS) Manager.
2. In the left pane, expand the **Web Sites** node, right-click on your web site, and select **Properties**.
3. Select the **Directory Security** tab and click **Edit** under **IP address and domain name restrictions**. Follow the same directions as described previously.

To restrict access to a particular virtual directory, do the following:

1. Open Internet Information Services (IIS) Manager.
2. In the left pane, expand the **Web Sites** node, right-click on a particular virtual directory within your web site and select **Properties**.

3. Select the **Directory Security** tab and click **Edit** under **IP address and domain name restrictions**. Follow the same directions as described previously.

To restrict access to a particular file:

1. Open Internet Information Services (IIS) Manager.

2. In the left pane, expand the **Web Sites** node, right-click on a particular file within a virtual directory or site, and select **Properties**.

3. Select the **File Security** tab and click **Edit** under **IP address and domain name restrictions**. Follow the same directions as described previously.

Using VBScript

```
' This code configures IP and domain restrictions for a web site.
' ------ SCRIPT CONFIGURATION ------
strComputer = "<ServerName>"   'e.g., web01.rallencorp.com
strSiteID = "<SiteID>"         'e.g., 1
' ------ END CONFIGURATION ---------
set objweb site = GetObject("IIS://" & strComputer & "/W3SVC/" & strSiteID)
set objIPRestrict = objweb site.Get("IPSecurity")
objIPRestrict.IPDeny = Array("10.1.2.0,255.255.255.0","192.168.179.34")
objIPRestrict.DomainDeny = Array("unrulydomain.biz")
objweb site.IPSecurity = objIPRestrict
objweb site.SetInfo
WScript.Echo "Successfully set IP and domain restrictions for web site: " & _
             objweb site.ServerComment

WScript.Echo ""
WScript.Echo "IP Deny:"
arrDeny = objweb site.Get("IPSecurity").IPDeny
for i = 0 to Ubound(arrDeny)
  WScript.Echo arrDeny(i)
next
arrDeny = objweb site.Get("IPSecurity").DomainDeny
WScript.Echo ""
WScript.Echo "Domain Deny:"
for i = 0 to Ubound(arrDeny)
  WScript.Echo arrDeny(i)
next
```

Discussion

When a user tries to access web content, IIS first checks to see whether there is any IP address or domain name restriction that denies access to the user. If not, IIS then tries to authenticate the user with any of the methods described in the next recipe. If authentication is successful, IIS checks to see what the requested content's web permissions are to determine what access level to grant the user. If the web permissions grant the user some level of access to the requested content, IIS compares the user's account (if provided) with the content's NTFS permissions to determine the user's final level of access.

One good use of IP and domain restrictions is when you're running IIS on a corporate intranet. By allowing only IP addresses for subnets on your network, you can prevent external users on the Internet from accessing content on your IIS computer (unless they spoof their address, of course). If you have a public-facing web server, you can also use this feature to block attacks from specific IP addresses or domain names when an attack has been detected. In most cases though, your perimeter firewall is the main place you should consider configuring these kinds of settings, not IIS. Avoid using domain name blocking as it requires costly reverse DNS lookups for each user request, which will negatively effect IIS performance.

Using VBScript

Setting IP and domain restrictions via ADSI is convoluted and deserves explanation. First, you have to call GetObject with a reference to a web site or virtual directory in the usual way. If you specify a web site, the IP and domain restrictions will apply across the entire web site, whereas referencing a virtual directory will enforce the restrictions only on that directory. Next is a call to get a reference to the IPSecurity object. Instead of setting properties directly on the web site or virtual directory, you have to modify this IPSecurity object. Two property methods of note include IPDeny and DomainDeny. Set them by passing in an array of values. For IPDeny you need an array of IP addresses, and for DomainDeny you need an array of domain names. With IPDeny, you can restrict a whole subnet by specifying a value in the format of "<Network>,<Mask>", which I included in the code.

After that, you have to set the IPSecurity property method to the value of the IPSecurity object we've been working with. Now, you just need to call SetInfo to commit the change.

After the call to SetInfo, I illustrate how to view the current values of IPDeny and DomainDeny. This serves as a check to make sure what I set previously was committed as expected.

See Also

Recipe 12.6

12.8 Configuring Web Site Authentication

Problem

You want to authenticate users before they can access content on your web server.

Solution

Using a graphical user interface

1. Open Internet Information Services (IIS) Manager.

2. In the left pane, browse to the web site, directory, or file you want configure, right-click it, and select **Properties**.

3. Select the **Directory Security** tab and click **Edit** under **Authentication and access control**.

4. Select the authentication methods you want to enable on your web server and click **OK**.

5. If the **Inheritance Overrides** dialog box appears, click **Select All** and click **OK** (repeat if this box appears again).

Using VBScript

```
' This code configurations authentication for a web site.
' ------ SCRIPT CONFIGURATION ------
strComputer = "<ServerName>"
strSiteID = "<SiteID>"

intFlag = 1 + 4
' Here are the available authentication values:
'       1 = Anonymous
'       2 = Basic
'       6 = MD5
'       4 = NTLM
'      64 = Passport
' For the intFlag variable, simply add together the
' numbers that represent the auth settings you want
' to configure.
' ------ END CONFIGURATION ---------

set objweb site = GetObject("IIS://" & strComputer & "/W3SVC/" & strSiteID)
objweb site.AuthFlags = intFlag
objweb site.SetInfo
WScript.Echo "Successfully modified auth settings for: " & _
             objweb site.ServerComment
```

Discussion

Authentication complements permissions as another tool for controlling access to content on IIS. When a user tries to access a web site, the user must first be authenticated. For a publicly hosted site designed for Internet users, anonymous access is the usual authentication method. For private intranets, some form of credential-based authentication must be used to guard against unauthorized access to company files. As Table 12-5 shows, IIS supports a number of different authentication methods to control access to your web server's content.

Table 12-5. IIS authentication methods

Authentication method	Description	Level of security	Usage
Anonymous Access	Uses the IUSR_servername account to grant guest access to users without the need to have them supply credentials	None	Content on public-facing Internet servers
Basic Authentication	Transmits users' credentials in clear text over the network	Low	Use only in conjunction with SSL
Digest Authentication	Uses an encrypted challenge/response scheme to authenticate the user's credentials	Medium	Public content on private intranet servers
Integrated Windows Authentication	Uses Kerberos or NTLM to authenticate Windows accounts of users	High	Content on private intranet servers
.NET Passport Authentication	Requires that users sign up for .NET Passport	Highest	Servers that require Passport authentication

If you enable multiple authentication methods including Anonymous Access, only Anonymous Access will be used. If you enable multiple authentication methods and Anonymous Access is *not* enabled, the most secure authentication method is attempted first and continues until reaching the least secure method unless the user successfully authenticates.

If authentication must take place through a proxy server, use Digest Authentication instead of Integrated Windows Authentication. Note that Digest Authentication requires Internet Explorer 5 or higher on the client end.

Unlike web sites, which support all five of the authentication methods described in Table 12-5, FTP sites on IIS support only Anonymous Access and Basic Authentication.

Using VBScript

Configuring authentication settings via ADSI is straightforward. You just need to set the AuthFlags property on a web site or virtual directory object. AuthFlags is a bit flag, which means you have to add the values associated with the desired settings and use that total as the value for AuthFlags. I included in the code the list of possible authentication settings and their corresponding values.

See Also

MS KB 324274 (How To Configure IIS Web Site Authentication in Windows Server 2003) and MS KB 324276 (HOW TO: Configure Internet Information Services Web Authentication in Windows Server 2003)

12.9 Obtaining and Installing SSL Certificates

Problem

You want to obtain a server certificate from a Certificate Authority (CA) and install it on your IIS computer to enable SSL on a web site.

Solution

Using a graphical user interface

To obtain a certificate from a third-party CA and install it on a web site named MTIT Corp, first generate a certificate request as follows:

1. Open Internet Information Services (IIS) Manager.

2. In the left pane, expand the MTIT Corp web site, right-click on the site, and select **Properties**.

3. Select the **Directory Security** tab.

4. Click the **Server Certificate** button to start the **Web Server Certificate Wizard** and click **Next**.

5. Select **Prepare the request now but send it later** and click **Next**.

6. Type the name of the web site (in this example, MTIT Corp) and click **Next**.

7. Leave the bit length at 1024 or choose a higher value if desired for greater security and click **Next**.

8. Type the name of your organization and organizational unit (e.g., department or division) and click **Next**.

9. Type the DNS name of your web site and click **Next**.

10. Type the specified geographical information and click **Next**.

11. Save your certificate request file as *C:\certreq.txt*.

To submit your certificate request to a third-party CA such as Verisign, do the following:

Go to the CA's web site (e.g., *www.verisign.com*) and follow instructions for submitting your certificate request to obtain a server certificate. Typically, you will have to paste the contents of your *certreq.txt* file into a form as part of the process. You will receive an email from the site with the certificate at the end of the message, bracketed between lines that say BEGIN CERTIFICATE and END CERTIFICATE.

To install your server certificate on your web site, do the following:

1. Copy the entire section from `BEGIN CERTIFICATE` to `END CERTIFICATE` (including these two lines) from the CA's email message to the clipboard by selecting the text and pressing **Ctrl-C**.

2. Use Notepad to create a new text file, press **Ctrl-V** to paste the certificate information into the file, and save it as a *.cer* file; for example, *C:\newcert.cer*.

3. Open Internet Information Services (IIS) Manager.

4. In the left pane, expand the console tree to display the MTIT Corp web site, right-click on the site, and select **Properties**.

5. Select the **Directory Security** tab.

6. Click the **Server Certificate** button to start the **Web Server Certificate Wizard** and click **Next**.

7. Select **Process the pending request and install the certificate** and click **Next**.

8. Specify the path to the *.cer* file containing the certificate (e.g., *C:\newcert.cer*) and click **Next**.

9. Accept 443 as the standard SSL port number, click **Next**, and then **Finish**.

To verify the certificate has been installed, do the following:

1. Open Internet Information Services (IIS) Manager.

2. In the left pane, expand the console tree to display the MTIT Corp web site, right-click on the site, and select **Properties**.

3. Select the **Directory Security** tab.

4. Click the **View Certificate** button.

Using a command-line interface

For simple testing purposes, the following command uses the *selfssl* utility from the IIS 6 Resource Kit Tools to install a self-signed SSL certificate on your Default Web Site:

```
> selfssl
```

Type **y** and press Enter when prompted.

The following command installs a server certificate using a *.cer* file and a password-protected *.pfx* file obtained from a third-party CA using the *IISCertDeploy.vbs* command script included in the IIS 6 Resource Kit Tools:

```
> iiscertdeploy -new C:\newcert.cer -c C:\newcert.pfx -p <password> -i w3svc/
1005026399
```

Note that this command installs the certificate on the web site that has site ID number 1005026399.

To determine the ID number of a web site without delving into the metabase, right-click on the web site in IIS Manager and select **Properties**, select the **Web Site** tab, click the **Properties** button, and note the numeric portion of the string beginning W3SVC beside **Log file name**.

Using VBScript

For a good example script on how to import a certificate, see *iiscertdeploy.vbs* in the IIS 6 Resource Kit.

Discussion

If you want to use IIS for hosting public SSL (https) sites for e-commerce or other reasons, you'll need to obtain a server certificate (i.e., a certificate that verifies the identify of a web server to clients that try to access it) from a commercial CA such as Verisign and install the certificate on your web server. Such certificates can cost hundreds of dollars or more per year, but most CA's also provide time-limited certificates for free that you can use to test your SSL site before purchasing a commercial server certificate.

If you have used Windows Certificate Services to install your own CA, the process of requesting and installing a server certificate is different. See the Knowledge Base articles in the See Also section for more information. Using your own CA is useful on a corporate intranet or extranet scenario, but not on a general Internet site, because any clients that need to access your site using SSL must first have your CA's root certificate installed on them. In other words, if you want your secure site to be accessible to anonymous users on the Internet, you'll have to obtain an install a server certificate from a third-party CA such as Verisign instead of using Certificate Services.

See Also

Recipe 12.10, MS KB 324284 (HOW TO: Secure XML Web Services with Secure Socket Layer in Windows Server 2003), and MS KB 816794 (HOW TO: Install Imported Certificates on a Web Server in Windows Server 2003)

12.10 Enabling SSL on a Web Site

Problem

You want to enable SSL on a web site on which you have previously installed a server certificate.

Solution

Using a graphical user interface

To enable SSL on the MTIT Corp web site where we installed a server certificate in Recipe 12.9, do the following:

1. Open Internet Information Services (IIS) Manager.
2. In the left pane, expand the console tree to display the MTIT Corp web site, right-click on the site, and select **Properties**.
3. Select the **Directory Security** tab.
4. Under **Secure Communications**, click **Edit**.
5. Select the checkbox labeled **Require Secure Channel (SSL)** and click **OK** twice.

To verify that SSL works, do the following:

1. Open Internet Explorer on the IIS server and try to open an URL with the IP address of the MTIT Corp web site; for example, *http://172.16.11.210*. You should get an HTTP 403.4 error message: "Forbidden: SSL is required to view this resource."
2. Try to open a secure URL with the IP address of the MTIT Corp web site, for example *https://172.16.11.210*. You should be able to view the default document (home page) of the site.

Using VBScript

```
' This code enables 128-bit SSL on a web site.
' ------ SCRIPT CONFIGURATION ------
strComputer = "<ServerName>"
strSiteID = "<SiteID>"

' Taken from AccessSSLFlags
'   8 = AccessSSL
'   256 = AccessSSL128
intFlag = 8 + 256
' ------ END CONFIGURATION ---------
set objweb site = GetObject("IIS://" & strComputer & "/W3SVC/" & strSiteID)
objweb site.AccessSSLFlags = intFlag
objweb site.SetInfo
WScript.Echo "Successfully modified SSL settings for: " & _
            objweb site.ServerComment
```

Discussion

If a Security Alert dialog box appears (see Figure 12-3 for an example) when you try step 7 in the graphical solution, your browser's certificate root store (the list of CAs your browser trusts) may not contain a root certificate that can validate your server certificate. This can happen, for example, if you obtain and install a limited-time test certificate from a third-party CA so you can test an SSL web site you are developing before you go ahead and purchase a server certificate and roll your server into production. In this case, the solution is to download the test root certificate (a *.cer file) from the CA and install it into Internet Explorer's root store as follows:

1. Open Internet Explorer and select **Tools → Internet Options**.
2. Select the **Content** tab and click the **Certificates** button.
3. Select the **Trusted Root Certification Authorities** tab.
4. Click **Import** to start the Certificate Import Wizard and click **Next**.
5. Browse to the test root certificate (*.cer) file that you downloaded from the CA and open it.
6. Click **Next** twice and then **Finish**.

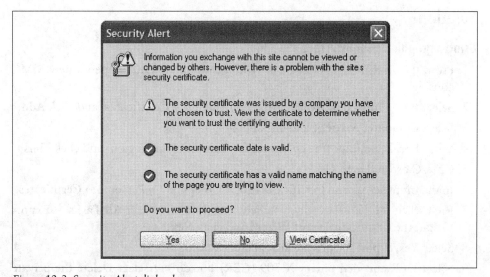

Figure 12-3. Security Alert dialog box

The Security Alert box in Figure 12-3 should now not appear when you try to open the https:// URL for your SSL-enabled web site.

The other settings on the Secure Communication dialog box deserve some mention. While server certificates identify web servers to clients, web clients can also have their own certificates, called client certificates, that they can use to prove their identify to the server. By default, SSL-enabled sites on IIS are configured to ignore client certificates—i.e., to authenticate clients regardless of whether they can prove their identity using a certificate. If desired, you can configure SSL sites to require that clients have certificates. This is often used in high-security environments where both sides (client and server) must be trusted. Client certificates can also be mapped to user accounts so that the client's certificate is used for authentication purposes instead of the user's credentials. For more information on client certificate mapping, see MS KB 315588.

See Also

Recipe 12.9 and MS KB 315588 (HOW TO: Secure an ASP.NET Application Using Client-Side Certificates)

12.11 Backing Up SSL Certificates

Problem

You want to back up your server certificate and its associated private key.

Solution

Using a graphical user interface

1. From the Start menu, select **Run**, type `mmc` and click **OK** to open a new MMC console.

2. Select **File → Add/Remove snap-in**, click **Add**, click **Certificates**, and click **Add**.

3. Select **Computer Account** and click **Next**.

4. Select **Local computer** (the computer this console is running on) and click **Finish**.

5. Click **Close** and then **OK**.

6. In the left pane, expand **Certificates (Local Computer) → Personal → Certificates**.

7. Right-click on the previously installed certificate and select **All Tasks → Export** to start the Certificate Export Wizard and click **Next**.

8. Select **Yes, export the private key**, and click **Next**.

9. Select **DER encoded binary X.509 (CER)** but do *not* select **Delete the private key if export is successful** and click **Next**.

10. Specify a name and path for the export file such as *C:\Certback\back.cer*, click **Next**, and then **Finish**.

Note that you can also choose to export the certificate to a shared folder on a remote server, which may be a better option if you want to centralize certificate backups for multiple web servers.

Using a command-line interface

Using the *IISCertDeploy.vbs* command script included in the IIS 6 Resource Kit Tools, the following command backs up a server certificate previously installed on a web site that has ID number 1005026399:

```
> iiscertdeploy -e C:\Certback\back.pfx -p <password> -i w3svc/1005026399
```

Note that the certificate is backed up as a password-protected *.pfx* file. Do not lose your password or you won't be able to restore your backed-up certificate if necessary.

Using VBScript

For a good example script on how to export or back up a certificate, see *iiscertdeploy.vbs* in the IIS 6 Resource Kit.

Discussion

Backing up your server certificate is important in case you need to replace your SSL-enabled web server with a different computer. Be sure you back up certificates and any private keys to a secure location.

To restore a backed-up server certificate to a different IIS computer, follow the previous procedure, but at step 7, select **All Tasks → Import** and complete the Certificate Import Wizard.

 Do *not* select the option **Delete the private key if export is successful** when you run the Certificate Export Wizard; otherwise, SSL will no longer work on your site and will have to be reconfigured.

See Also

Recipe 12.9

12.12 Configuring Web Site QoS Settings

Problem

You want to tune IIS performance by configuring quality of service (QoS) settings.

Solution

Using a graphical user interface

To limit the number of simultaneous incoming HTTP connections for a web site, do the following:

1. Open Internet Information Services (IIS) Manager.
2. In the left pane, expand the console tree to display your web site, right-click on the site, and select **Properties**.
3. Select the **Performance** tab.
4. Change the **Web site connections** setting from its default value of **Unlimited** to a value you specify.
5. Click **OK**.

To configure the connection timeout value for a web site, do the following:

1. Open Internet Information Services (IIS) Manager.
2. In the left pane, expand the console tree to display your web site, right-click on the site, and select **Properties**.
3. Select the **Web Site** tab.
4. Make sure that **Enable HTTP Keep-Alives** is selected (which is the default).
5. Change the value of **Connection timeout** as desired.
6. Click **OK**.

To control the amount of network bandwidth used by a web site, do the following:

1. Open Internet Information Services (IIS) Manager.
2. In the left pane, expand the console tree to display your web site, right-click on the site, and select **Properties**.
3. Select the **Performance** tab.
4. Select the checkbox labeled **Limit the total network bandwidth available to this web site**.
5. Specify the maximum desired bandwidth allowed in kilobytes per second.
6. Click **OK**.

Using a command-line interface

The following command helps prevent attackers from consuming resources by unnecessarily keeping connections open on your IIS computer:

```
> cscript %systemroot%\inetpub\adminscripts\adsutil.vbs SET W3SVC/MinFileBytesPerSec
500
```

Using VBScript

```
' This code sets various QoS settings
' ------ SCRIPT CONFIGURATION ------
strComputer = "<ServerName>"
' ------ END CONFIGURATION ---------
set objWS = GetObject("IIS://" & strComputer & "/W3SVC")
objWS.Put "ConnectionTimeout", 120
objWS.Put "HeaderWaitTimeout", 2
objWS.Put "MinFileBytesPerSec", 240
objWS.Put "AllowKeepAlive", True
objWS.Put "MaxBandwidth", &HFFFFFFFF
objWS.Put "MaxEndpointConnections", &HFFFFFFFF
objWS.SetInfo
WScript.Echo "QoS settings configured for web site: " & objWS.ServerComment
```

Discussion

The main use for *limiting connections* is to deal with denial of service (DoS) attacks designed to overload your computer with bogus connection attempts. If the web site connections setting is left as Unlimited, it means IIS tries to handle all incoming requests even if it overloads the server until connections are refused. However, if a connection limit is specified and this limit is reached, an "HTTP 403.9 Forbidden: Too many users" error message is returned. You can also configure a connection limit globally for all web sites using the properties of the Web Sites node.

The main purpose of *connection timeouts* is to enable IIS to reclaim TCP resources from idle clients so other users can connect. Setting this value too high may result in fewer clients being able to connect, while a setting that is too low may result in disconnected client sessions. You can also configure this setting globally for all web sites using the properties of the Web Sites node.

The main use for *bandwidth throttling* is to ensure a web site has sufficient bandwidth for users to access it. This is particularly useful on a computer hosting multiple web sites. You can also configure this setting using the properties of the Web Sites node, but in this case (unlike the other QoS settings), only web sites that do not have bandwidth throttling enabled are affected by this global setting. In other words, global bandwidth throttling does not override bandwidth throttling configured at the site level.

By default, IIS drops any connection if its throughput rate falls below 240 bytes per second. But attackers exploit this by opening TCP connections with your computer and sending data at rates slightly higher than 240 bytes per sec, so setting the MinFileBytesPerSec metabase property to 500 or higher may help foil such attacks. But first test how this affects how your web applications work from a user's point of view before changing this setting in a production environment.

See Also

MS KB 332087 (QoS Is Not Installed When Bandwidth Throttling Is Enabled Directly in the IIS Metabase), MS KB 314402 (PRB: Slow Clients Disconnected When Server Uses Large Synchronous Write Methods), MS KB 238210 (HTTP Keep-Alive header sent whenever ASP Buffering is enabled), and MS KB 817439 (IIS 6.0 changes to the metabase property ConnectionTimeout affect other settings in IIS)

12.13 Configuring Web Site Logging

Problem

You want to log visits to your web sites.

Solution

Using a graphical user interface

To enable logging for all web sites on the server, do the following:

1. Open Internet Information Services (IIS) Manager.
2. In the left pane, expand the console tree to display the **Web Sites** node, right-click on this node, and select **Properties**.
3. Select the **Web Site** tab.
4. Select the **Enable logging** checkbox.
5. Select a log file format as desired (**W3C Extended Log File Format** is recommended).

To enable logging for an individual web site, do the following:

1. Open Internet Information Services (IIS) Manager.
2. In the left pane, expand the console tree to display your web site, right-click on the site, and select **Properties**.
3. Select the **Web Site** tab.
4. Select the **Enable logging** checkbox.
5. Select a log file format as desired (**W3C Extended Log File Format** is recommended).

To enable or disable logging for content stored in your web site's home directory, do the following:

1. Open Internet Information Services (IIS) Manager.
2. In the left pane, expand the console tree to display your web site, right-click on the site, and select **Properties**.
3. Select the **Home Directory** tab.
4. Select or clear the **Log visits** checkbox as desired.

To enable or disable logging for content stored in a virtual directory:

1. Open Internet Information Services (IIS) Manager.
2. In the left pane, expand the console tree to display your web site, select a virtual directory within your site, right-click on the virtual directory, and select **Properties**.
3. Select the **Virtual Directory** tab.
4. Select or clear the **Log visits** checkbox as desired.

To enable or disable logging for an individual file, do the following:

1. Open Internet Information Services (IIS) Manager.

2. In the left pane, expand the console tree to display your web site, right-click on a particular file within the home directory or some other virtual directory, and select **Properties**.

3. Select the **File** tab.

4. Select or clear the **Log visits** checkbox as desired.

Using a command-line interface

The following command enables Centralized Binary Logging, which is new to IIS 6:

```
> cscript %systemroot%\inetpub\adminscripts\adsutil.vbs SET W3SVC/
CentralBinaryLoggingEnabled
```

After running this command you need to restart IIS (see Recipe 12.2) at which point IIS log files will have the format *rayymmdd.ibl* (*ra* stands for "raw") and will be found in *%SystemRoot%\system32\logfiles\w3svc*. Once you've enabled Centralized Binary Logging, any further changes you make to IIS logging settings in the GUI are ignored. These **.ibl* log files can be read using the Log Parser (*LogParser.exe*) utility included in the IIS 6 Resource Kit Tools.

This command causes W3C Extended log files to roll over (create new log files) for all web sites at midnight local time:

```
> cscript %systemroot%\inetpub\adminscripts\adsutil.vbs SET W3WVC\
LogFileLocaltimeRollover
```

Note that even if you do this, IIS still records times in W3C Extended log files using UTC, not local time.

Using VBScript

```
' This code enables logging
' ------ SCRIPT CONFIGURATION ------
strComputer = "<ServerName>"
strSite = "<Site>" ' e.g., W3SVC/222
intEnableLog = 1  ' 1 to enable; 0 to disable
' ------ END CONFIGURATION ---------
set objWS = GetObject("IIS://" & strComputer & "/" & strSite)
objWS.Put "LogType", intEnableLog
' objWS.Put "LogDirectory", "d:\logs" ' uncomment this to set the log dir
objWS.SetInfo
WScript.Echo "Logging enabled for web site: " & objWS.ServerComment
```

Discussion

Table 12-6 summarizes the different log file formats available for IIS.

Table 12-6. IIS log formats

Log file format	Description
W3C Extended Log File Format	A customizable format developed by the World Wide Web Consortium
IIS Log File Format	A fixed format developed by Microsoft for earlier versions of IIS
NCSA Log File Format	A fixed format developed by the National Center for Supercomputing Applications for the original ncsa-httpd web server
ODBC Logging	Enables logging to an ODBC-compliant database, such as Microsoft SQL Server
Centralized Binary Logging	Enables multiple web sites to write to a single log file using a proprietary binary format

 Don't use ODBC Logging on IIS 6 because it disables kernel mode caching, which can significantly degrade web server performance.

See Also

MS KB 324279 (HOW TO: Configure Web Site Logging in Windows Server 2003), MS KB 814870 (INFO: IIS 6.0 Log Management Documentation), MS KB 242898 (IIS Log File Naming Syntax), MS KB 291279 (IIS Log File Is Not Created When There Is No Activity on a Web Site), MS KB 194699 (Extended Log File Format Always in GMT), MS KB 271196 (IIS Log File Entries Have the Incorrect Date and Time Stamp), and MS KB 832975 (Additional properties are now available for logging in the Httperr#.log file in IIS 6.0)

12.14 Configuring Web Site Redirection

Problem

You want to redirect requests for files in your web site to a different site, directory, or file.

Solution

Using a graphical user interface

To redirect requests to files in your web site's home directory, do the following:

1. Open Internet Information Services (IIS) Manager.
2. In the left pane, expand the console tree to display your web site, right-click on the site, and select **Properties**.
3. Select the **Home Directory** tab.
4. Select the option named **A redirection to a URL**.
5. Select the option **The exact URL entered above**, if you want to redirect requests to a specific file. For example, type **/temp/default.htm** in the **Redirect to** box if

you want to redirect requests for files in your home directory to the *default.htm* file in the */temp* virtual directory.

6. Select the option **A directory below URL entered**, if you want to redirect requests to files in a subdirectory. For example, type **/newsite** in the **Redirect to** box if you want to redirect requests for files in your home directory to a new version of your site in the */newsite* subdirectory.

7. Select the option A **permanent redirection for this resource**, if you want to send an "HTTP 301 Permanent Redirect" status message to clients requesting files from your home directory.

To redirect requests to files in a virtual directory, do the following:

1. Open Internet Information Services (IIS) Manager.

2. In the left pane, expand the console tree to display your web site, right-click on a virtual directory, and select **Properties**.

3. Select the **Virtual Directory** tab.

4. Follow steps 5 through 7 above.

To redirect requests to a particular file, do the following:

1. Open Internet Information Services (IIS) Manager.

2. In the left pane, expand the console tree to display your web site, right-click on a particular file, and select **Properties**.

3. Select the **File** tab.

4. Select the option **The exact URL entered above** and specify the full URL of the file you want to redirect to.

Using VBScript

```
' This code creates a redirect for a virtual directory
' and maintains the path info during redirection
' ------ SCRIPT CONFIGURATION ------
strComputer = "<ServerName>"
' ------ END CONFIGURATION ---------
set objVirtualDir = GetObject("IIS://" & strComputer & "/W3SVC/1/Root/CGIs")
objVirtualDir.Put "HttpRedirect", _
                "http://www.rallencorp.com/NewSite/CGIs$S$Q, EXACT_DESTINATION"
objVirtualDir.SetInfo
WScript.Echo "Redirect set for virtual directory"


' This code creates permanent redirect for an entire web site
' and does NOT maintain path info during redirection
' ------ SCRIPT CONFIGURATION ------
strComputer = "<ServerName>"
' ------ END CONFIGURATION ---------
set objWS = GetObject("IIS://" & strComputer & "/W3SVC/222/Root")
```

```
objWS.Put "HttpRedirect", _
          "http://www.rallencorp.com/newsite, PERMANENT & EXACT_DESTINATION"
objWS.SetInfo
WScript.Echo "Redirect set for web site"
```

Discussion

Redirection is useful when you are reorganizing your web site by moving content around or creating a new version of your site. If you fail to configure redirection in such situations, users will experience frustrating "HTTP 404 File Not Found" error messages when visiting bookmarked pages.

Using VBScript

The HttpRedirect metabase property is very flexible. It can be configured to redirect based on a variety of criteria. For the complete list of options available for this property, see the HttpRedirect page in MSDN (*http://msdn.microsoft.com/library/default.asp?url=/library/en-us/iissdk/iis/ref_mb_httpredirect.asp*).

See Also

MS KB 298498 (IIS generates courtesy redirect when folder without trailing slash is requested)

12.15 Enabling Direct Metabase Editing

Problem

You want to edit the metabase while IIS is still running. You may need to do this to configure metabase properties that are not accessible from the GUI.

Solution

Using a graphical user interface

1. Open Internet Information Services (IIS) Manager.
2. In the left pane, right-click on the node representing your IIS server and select **Properties**.
3. Select the **Enable Direct Metabase Edit** checkbox and click **OK**.

You can now use Notepad or some other text editor to edit the *%SystemRoot%\system32\inetsrv\MetaBase.xml* file as desired while IIS is running.

Using a command-line interface

To enable edit-while-running from the local server's command line, you have to first stop all IIS services:

```
> iisreset /stop
```

Use a text editor to open the metabase configuration file *%SystemRoot%\system32\inetsrv\MetaBase.xml* and change the line:

```
EnableEditWhileRunning = "0"
```

to:

```
EnableEditWhileRunning = "1"
```

Save your changes and then type the following command to restart IIS services:

```
> iisreset /start
```

Using VBScript

```
' This code enables the direct metabase editing setting
' ------ SCRIPT CONFIGURATION ------
strComputer = "<ServerName>"
' ------ END CONFIGURATION ---------
set objServer = GetObject("IIS://" & strComputer)
objServer.EnableEditWhileRunning = 1
objServer.EnableHistory = 1
objServer.SetInfo
WScript.Echo "Successfully enabled direct metabase editing on server " & _
             objServer.Name
```

Discussion

When IIS is running, it uses an in-memory copy of the metabase. If you make a change to the metabase, the change takes effect immediately in the in-memory metabase, and 60 seconds later IIS writes the changes to the *MetaBase.xml* file on disk. If, however, another metabase change is made before the 60 seconds are up, the timer resets to 60 seconds again (this can happen five times). Saving your IIS configuration or stopping the IISAdmin service also flushes the in-memory metabase to disk.

Be careful when modifying the metabase directly—if you make a mistake and the metabase becomes corrupted, IIS may not start and you'll have to restore the metabase from backup (see Recipe 12.16). When possible, try to avoid editing the metabase directly and use the GUI or a programmatic method instead.

The IIS 6 Resource Kit Tools includes Version 1.6 of Metabase Explorer (*MBExplorer.exe*), a graphical tool that you can use to view and edit the metabase on local or remote IIS computers. MBExplorer replaced MetaEdit tool on older versions of IIS. Figure 12-4 shows MBExplorer focused on the default web site.

> For a bird's eye view of the hierarchical structure of the IIS 6 metabase, see the article "Inside the XML Metabase of IIS6" by Mitch Tulloch (*http://www.windowsdevcenter.com/pub/a/windows/2004/07/13/iis_metabase.html*). For a more detailed look at the metabase, see Mitch's book, *IIS 6 Administration*, from Osborne/McGraw-Hill.

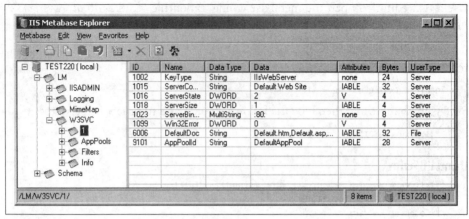

Figure 12-4. MBExplorer view of the default web site

Using VBScript

To enable direct metabase editing using ADSI, you have to set the EnableEditWhileRunning and EnableHistory properties to 1. The EnableHistory property causes IIS to create a backup copy of the metabase every time the in-memory version of the metabase is written to disk. This is a precautionary measure to ensure that you don't get yourself into too much trouble by corrupting the metabase. With the history feature, you can restore previous versions of the metabase.

See Also

Recipe 12.16, MS KB 814871 (INFO: IIS 6.0 Metabase Documentation), and MS KB 267904 (SAMPLE: Metaacl.exe Modifying Metabase Permissions for the IIS Admin Objects)

12.16 Backing Up and Restoring the Metabase

Problem

You want to back up or restore the metabase. You may need to restore it if the metabase becomes corrupt or your server bites the dust.

Solution

Using a graphical user interface

To back up the metabase, do the following:

1. Open Internet Information Services (IIS) Manager.
2. In the left pane, right-click on the node representing your IIS server and select **All Tasks → Backup/Restore Configuration**.

3. Click the **Create Backup** button and type a name for your backup.

4. If you want to password protect your backup, select the **Encrypt backup using password** checkbox, and type and confirm a password.

5. Click **OK** and then **Close**.

To restore a previously backed up metabase configuration, do the following:

1. Open Internet Information Services (IIS) Manager.

2. In the left pane, right-click on the node representing your IIS server and select **All Tasks → Backup/Restore Configuration**.

3. Select the metabase backup you want to restore and click the **Restore** button.

4. Click Yes to restart IIS services and enter the password if your metabase backup is password protected.

5. Click **OK** and then **Close** when the restore is finished.

To restore the metabase from a metabase history (automatic backup) file, do the following:

1. Open Internet Information Services (IIS) Manager.

2. In the left pane, right-click on the node representing your IIS server and select **All Tasks → Backup/Restore Configuration**.

3. Select the metabase history file (named Automatic Backup) you want to restore and click the **Restore** button.

4. Click **Yes** to restart IIS services.

5. Click **OK** and then **Close** when the restore is finished.

To restore the metabase to its initial configuration when IIS was installed, do the following:

1. Open Internet Information Services (IIS) Manager.

2. In the left pane, right-click on the node representing your IIS server and select **All Tasks → Backup/Restore Configuration**.

3. Select the backup named **Initial Backup** and click the **Restore** button.

4. Click **Yes** to restart IIS services.

5. Click **OK** and then **Close** when the restore is finished.

Using a command-line interface

The following command backs up the metabase using the *iisback.vbs* script and names the two backup files *28july04.MD0* (for *MetaBase.xml*) and *28july04.SD0* (for *MBSchema.xml*):

```
> iisback /backup /b 28july04
```

To view a list of the current metabase backups, use the following command:

```
> iisback /list
```

If you create another backup with the same name as the previous one, the version number will be incremented by one. To overwrite version 0 of the backup instead and create a new backup, do the following:

```
> iisback /backup /b 28july04 /v 0 /overwrite
```

The following command restores the password-protected backup named My Metabase Backup:

```
> iisback /restore /b "My Metabase Backup" /e <password>
```

Using VBScript

For a good example script on how to backup and restore the metabase, see the code for *iisback.vbs* in the IIS 6 Resource Kit.

Discussion

Table 12-7 lists the three kinds of metabase backups. The Subfolder column contains the subfolders under *%SystemRoot%\system32\inetsrv* in which the backup is stored.

Table 12-7. Types of metabase backups

Name of backup	Subfolder	Description
Initial Backup	\MetaBack	Automatically created when IIS is installed
Automatic Backup	\History	Automatically created whenever configuration changes have been made since the in-memory metabase was last flushed to disk
<any_name>	\MetaBack	Manually created by an administrator as described in this recipe

Whenever the metabase is backed up, both the metabase configuration file (*MetaBase.xml*) and metabase schema (*MBSchema.xml*) are backed up. The automatically generated initial backups are named as follows:

- The initial backup of *MetaBase.xml* file is named *Initial Backup - created automatically by IIS setup.MD1*.
- The initial backup of *MBSchema.xml* file is named *Initial Backup - created automatically by IIS setup.SC1*.

History files are named using major and minor version numbers as follows:

- *MetaBase_<majorversion>_<minorversion>.xml*
- *MBSchema_<majorversion>_<minorversion>.xml*

For example:

- *MetaBase_0000000043_0000000000.xml*
- *MBSchema_0000000043_0000000000.xml*

The major version number is incremented when you:

- Manually restart IIS using IIS Manager
- Manually stop IIS using IIS Manager or net stop
- Right-click on the IIS computer node in IIS Manager and select **All Tasks** → **Save Configuration to Disk**
- Wait for IIS to automatically flush the in-memory metabase to disk when configuration changes have been made

The minor version number increments after you've enabled edit-while-running (see Recipe 12.15), manually edited the metabase configuration file (*%SystemRoot%\ system32\inetsrv\MetaBase.xml*), and saved the changes. If the major version number is incremented, the minor version number is reset to zero.

Manually created backup files are named according to the name you assign, for example:

- *28July04.MD0*
- *28July04.SC0*

If you create a second backup the same day, the new files would be named:

- *28July04.MD1*
- *28July04.SC1*

Regularly creating password-protected metabase backups is a good idea for two reasons:

- The security properties of the metabase are encrypted. These include, for example, AdminACL, which contains the discretionary access control list (DACL) that controls access to metabase keys.
- You can restore the backup to a different IIS 6 computer if your original computer crashes.

If you had an SSL-enabled web site on your crashed computer, however, you'll need to install your server certificate on your new computer and restart IIS on the new computer.

See Also

Recipe 12.15 and MS KB 324277 (How To Create a Metabase Backup by Using IIS 6.0 in Windows Server 2003)

12.17 Exporting and Importing the Metabase

Problem

You want to export or import a portion of the metabase. This can be useful when you want to clone the configuration of a web site or virtual directory by copying it to another IIS computer.

Solution

Using a graphical user interface

You can export the metabase configuration for an individual web site, all web sites, an individual FTP site, all FTP sites, an individual virtual directory, a file, an individual application pool, or all application pools as follows:

1. Open Internet Information Services (IIS) Manager.
2. In the left pane, right-click on the node whose metabase configuration you want to export and select **All Tasks → Save Configuration to a File**.
3. Type a name for the exported file and, if desired, browse to a different directory where you want to save the file.
4. Optionally password protect the export file by typing a password and confirming it.
5. Click **OK**.

For example, to export the portion of the metabase that contains configuration settings for a web site named My Web Site, do the following:

1. Open Internet Information Services (IIS) Manager.
2. In the left pane, right-click on **My Web Site** and select **All Tasks → Save Configuration to a File** and continue as above.

To import the previously saved configuration for **My Web Site** back into the Metabase, do the following:

1. Open Internet Information Services (IIS) Manager.
2. In the left pane, right-click on **Web Sites** and select **New → Web Site (from file)**.
3. Type the path to the saved configuration file or click **Browse** to select it.
4. Click the **Read File** button to display a list of web sites contained in the saved configuration file.
5. Select the web site named **My Web Site** and click **OK**.
6. Specify a password if prompted and click **OK**.
7. Right-click on the web site and select **Start** to start it.

You can similarly import the configuration for an FTP site, virtual directory, or application pool.

Using a command-line interface

The following command exports the configuration of the Default Web Site to a configuration file named *default.xml*:

```
> iiscnfg /export /f default.xml /sp /lm/w3svc/1 /children
```

Here /sp specifies the source path, i.e., the metabase key, you want to export. In this case, I used /lm/w3svc/1, which represents the Default Web Site (site ID = 1 under the W3SVC service). The /children option recursively exports subkeys (child keys) as well.

This command exports the configuration of a site with ID number 66485902 and password protects the export file so you can import it onto a different IIS computer:

```
> iiscnfg /export /f anothersite.xml /sp /lm/w3svc/66485902 /children /p <password>
```

If you leave out the /children option, only the configuration of the virtual root will be exported, and not the configuration of any virtual directories below the root.

Let's now import the configuration of the Default Web Site, which we exported above as *default.xml*, but first let's delete the Default Web Site:

```
> iisweb /delete "Default Web Site"
```

To recreate the Default Web Site, import its previously saved configuration:

```
> iiscnfg /import /f default.xml /sp /lm/w3svc/1 /dp /lm/w3svc/1 /children
```

Here /dp stands for the destination path, i.e., the metabase key, into which you want to import the configuration data. Again, /children ensures that subkeys are imported as well.

We can even import a second copy of the Default Web Site and assign it the site ID number 2 as follows:

```
> iiscnfg /import /f default.xml /sp /lm/w3svc/1 /dp /lm/w3svc/2 /children
```

Note that in IIS Manager, the copy of the site won't start unless you assign it a unique IP address.

Discussion

Metabase export files don't include encrypted properties (such as AdminACL) the way metabase backup files do. If you want to export a configuration that can be imported into a different IIS computer, be sure to password protect the export file and remove any computer-specific information it contains such as metabase properties referencing the IUSR or IWAM accounts used by IIS, the AdminACL, and any properties that use passwords before exporting it. Also, be sure to recreate the content folders on the target computer exactly as on the source computer.

12.18 Enabling Dynamic Content

Problem

You want to allow dynamic web applications to run on IIS.

Solution

Using a graphical user interface

To enable Active Server Pages (ASP), ASP.NET, Internet Data Connector, Server Side Includes, or WebDAV on your server, do the following:

1. Open Internet Information Services (IIS) Manager.
2. In the left pane, expand the server node in the console tree and select **Web Service Extensions**.
3. Right-click on the web service extension you want to enable and select **Allow**.

If the ASP.NET extension is not displayed, you have to install ASP.NET first as follows:

1. From the Start menu, select **Control Panel → Add or Remove Programs**.
2. Click **Add/Remove Windows Components**.
3. Select **Application Server** and click **Details**.
4. Select **ASP.NET** and click **OK** followed by **Next**.

To enable a specify CGI application or ISAPI DLL to run on your server, do the following:

1. Open Internet Information Services (IIS) Manager.
2. In the left pane, expand the server node in the console tree and select **Web Service Extensions**.
3. Click the link **Add a new web service extension**.
4. Type a descriptive name for the new extension.
5. Type the full path to the CGI application or ISAPI DLL.
6. Select the checkbox labeled **Set extension status** to **Allowed** and click **OK**.

To enable all CGI applications or ISAPI DLLs to run on your server, do the following:

1. Open Internet Information Services (IIS) Manager.
2. In the left pane, expand the server node in the console tree and select **Web Service Extensions**.
3. Right-click either **All Unknown ISAPI Extensions** or **All Unknown CGI Extensions** and select **Allow**.

Using a command-line interface

The following command lists all web service extensions installed (but not necessarily enabled) on the computer:

```
> iisext /listext
```

This command enables ASP:

```
> iisext /enfile C:\Windows\system32\inetsrv\asp.dll
```

To verify the ASP extension has been enabled, do the following:

```
> iisext /listfile
```

The output from this command will display a 1 beside extensions that are enabled and a 0 beside ones that are disabled.

To add and enable a new web service extension for a CGI form handler application called *form.exe* located in the *C:\Inetpub\wwwroot\cgi-bin* directory, do the following:

```
> iisext /addfile C:\Inetpub\wwwroot\cgi-bin\form.exe 1 MyForm 1 "CGI Form Handler"
```

The first 1 enables the extension and the second 1 allows it to be removed later if desired. The string MyForm is the extension's internal service name, while "CGI Form Handler" is the name displayed in the IIS Manager. Be sure to also give the *\cgi-bin* folder Scripts and Executables permission in IIS Manager (see Recipe 12.6).

Using VBScript

```
' This code shows how to enable several extensions.
' ------ SCRIPT CONFIGURATION ------
strComputer = "<ServerName>"
' ------ END CONFIGURATION ---------
set objWS = GetObject("IIS://" & strComputer & "/W3SVC")
objWS.EnableApplication("WebDAV")
objWS.EnableApplication("Active Server Pages")
objWS.EnableApplication("Server Side Includes")
objWS.EnableApplication("Internet Data Connector")
objWS.EnableApplication("ASP.NET")
objWS.SetInfo
WScript.Echo "Web Services Extensions enabled"
```

Discussion

Table 12-8 lists the internal service names and executables for several different web service extensions. For the scripting solution, use the name in the Extension column with the EnableApplication method to enable a certain extension.

Table 12-8. IIS web service extensions

Extension	Internal name	Executable
Active Server Pages	ASP	*%windir%\system32\inetsrv\asp.dll*
ASP.NET	ASP.NET v1.1.4322	*%windir%\Microsoft.NET\Framework\v1.1.4322\aspnet_isapi.dll*

Table 12-8. IIS web service extensions (continued)

Extension	Internal name	Executable
Internet Data Connector	HTTPODBC	*%windir%\system32\inetsrv\httpodbc.dll*
Server Side Includes	SSINC	*%windir%\system32\inetsrv\ssinc.dll*
WebDAV	WEBDAV	*%windir%\system32\inetsrv\httpext.dll*

See Also

Recipe 12.16, MS KB 332060 (IIS 6.0: Definition of Term Web Service Extension), MS KB 315122 ("HTTP Error 404 - File or Directory not found" error message when you request dynamic content with IIS 6.0), MS KB 328360 (How to enable and disable ISAPI extensions and CGI applications in IIS 6.0), MS KB 327403 (How To: Rename Web Service Extensions in IIS 6.0), MS KB 812405 (PRB: ASP.NET 1.0 Does Not Appear in the Web Service Extension List in IIS 6.0), MS KB 328505 (HOW TO: List Web Server Extensions and Extension Files in IIS 6.0), and MS KB 160422 (How IIS launches a CGI application)

12.19 Creating Application Pools

Problem

You want to create a new application pool.

Solution

Using a graphical user interface

1. Open Internet Information Services (IIS) Manager.
2. In the left pane, expand the server node in the console tree and select **Application Pools**.
3. Right-click on **Application Pools** and select **New → Application Pool**.
4. Type a descriptive name for the new pool.
5. Choose whether to use an existing pool as a template (select the existing pool whose configuration settings you want to copy) or leave the configuration settings for the new pool at their default values.
6. Click **OK** to create the new pool.

Using VBScript

```
' This code creates an app pool.
' ------ SCRIPT CONFIGURATION ------
strComputer = "<ServerName>"
strAppPoolName = "<AppPoolName>"
' ------ END CONFIGURATION ---------
```

```
set objAppPools = GetObject("IIS://" & strComputer & "/w3svc/AppPools")
set objNewAppPool = objAppPools.Create("IIsApplicationPool", strAppPoolName)

' Recycle this app pool every 2,000 requests
objNewAppPool.AppPoolRecycleRequests = True
objNewAppPool.PeriodicRestartRequests = 2000

' Run this app pool as NETWORK SERVICE (just like the default app pool)
objNewAppPool.AppPoolIdentityType = 2

' Save new app pool
objNewAppPool.SetInfo( )

WScript.Echo "App Pool created successfully: " & objNewAppPool.Name
```

Discussion

Application pools are used to assign worker processes for dynamic applications running on IIS. An application pool can have one or more worker processes servicing one or more applications assigned to that pool, and if multiple worker processes service the pool, the pool is called a *web garden*. When IIS is installed, a Default Application Pool is created, and if you create a new application (see Recipe 12.21) it is automatically added to the default pool. By right-clicking on the pool, you can stop and start it, recycle worker processes associated with the pool, configure the settings for the pool, or save its configuration.

Application pools are generally created to isolate applications along process boundaries. That way, if an application in one pool fails, applications running in different pools are unaffected. Note that IIS must be running in worker process isolation mode in order to create and use application pools (IIS 5.0 isolation mode does not support application pools).

See Also

Recipe 12.22

12.20 Configuring Application Pool Identities

Problem

You want to configure the identity of an application pool.

Solution

Using a graphical user interface

1. Open Internet Information Services (IIS) Manager.
2. In the left pane, expand the server node in the console tree and select **Application Pools**.

3. Right-click on the target application pool and select **Properties**.

4. Select to the **Identity** tab.

5. Select either one of the three predefined identities or a custom user account and click **OK**.

Using a command-line interface

The following two commands assign a custom user account for an application pool identity and set the password for the account:

```
> cscript %systemroot%\inetpub\adminscripts\adsutil.vbs SET W3SVC/AppPools/
<AppPoolName>/WAMUserName <Username>
> cscript %systemroot%\inetpub\adminscripts\adsutil.vbs SET W3SVC/AppPools/
<AppPoolName>/WAMUserPass <Password>
```

Replace *<AppPoolName>* with the name of the target application pool, *<Username>* with the name, and *<Password>* with the user's password.

Using VBScript

```
' This code configures an app pool identity.
' ------ SCRIPT CONFIGURATION ------
strComputer = "<ServerName>"
strAppPoolName = "<AppPoolName>"
strUser   = "<Username>"  ' e.g., RALLENCORP\myiisuser
strPasswd = "<Password>"
' ------ END CONFIGURATION ---------

set objAppPool = GetObject("IIS://" & strComputer & "/w3svc/AppPools/" & _
                           strAppPoolName)
objAppPool.AppPoolIdentityType = 3
objAppPool.WAMUserName = strUser
objAppPool.WAMUserPass = strPasswd
objAppPool.SetInfo( )

WScript.Echo "App Pool identity modified successfully: " & objAppPool.Name
```

Discussion

When an application in the pool executes, the worker process impersonates the identity of the process token associated with the client requesting the application pool. An application pool's identity is the security context in which the worker processes assigned to the pool run when no application is running within the pool. The three predefined identities that can be assigned to a pool are shown in Table 12-9.

Table 12-9. Predefined application pool identities

Identity	Description
Network Service	Built-in identity with few privileges
Local Service	Same as Network Service but can only access resources on local computer
Local System	Powerful built-in identity with numerous privileges

By default, new application pools (and the Default Application Pool) use Network Service as their identity. If you want to create a custom user account for a pool, be sure to give it a complex password and make it a member of the IIS_WPG built-in group, which gives the account the privileges needed to be able to instantiate new worker processes on the computer.

12.21 Creating Applications

Problem

You want to create a new application for a web site or virtual directory.

Solution

Using a graphical user interface

To create a new application for a web site, do the following:

1. Open Internet Information Services (IIS) Manager.
2. In the left pane, expand the console tree and select your web site.
3. Right-click on the web site and select **Properties**.
4. Select the **Home Directory** tab.
5. If the Default Application is already defined for the site, click **Remove**.
6. Click **Create** and type a name for your new application.
7. Assign appropriate execute permissions for your application.
8. Assign your application to the appropriate application pool.
9. Click **Apply**.

To create a new application for a virtual directory, do the following:

1. Open Internet Information Services (IIS) Manager.
2. In the left pane, expand the console tree and select a virtual directory under your web site.
3. Right-click on the virtual directory and select **Properties**.

4. Select the **Virtual Directory** tab.

5. If a default application name is already defined for the site, click **Remove**.

6. Click **Create** and type a name for your new application.

7. Assign appropriate execute permissions for your application.

8. Assign your application to the appropriate application pool.

9. Click **Apply**.

Discussion

IIS terminology can be confusing, specifically:

Application

A group of files (usually ASP scripts) contained in a web site's home directory or a virtual directory (and possibly subdirectories) that clients (web browsers) can access to perform some programmatic function. For example, an ASP application could consist of a set of web pages with scripts in them to act as a front-end for a SQL database. Simply putting the web pages and scripts in a directory doesn't create an application; you still need to create an application by defining an application starting point (see below) so you can set boundaries for ASP sessions and so on.

Application starting point

Any subdirectory beneath the home directory (or any other virtual directory) for which you remove the parent application and define a new application. All subdirectories beneath this directory then become part of the new application. For example, by default the application name for the Default Web Site is Default Application. If you create a virtual directory named */Stuff* within the Default Web Site, */Stuff* is automatically assigned a new application starting point called Stuff and therefore is a separate application from the Default Application. To make */Stuff* part of the Default Application instead, simply remove its application starting point. An easy way of telling whether a virtual directory is an application starting point is to look at the icon for the virtual directory in IIS Manager: a gear icon indicates a new application starting point, while a folder with the world on it indicates that the directory belongs to a parent application.

Application pool

A logical way of grouping applications together to assign them processing resources so they can execute efficiently and be isolated from one another (so that if one fails the others won't fail also). In the example just described, when you create the new /Stuff virtual directory, you can verify that Stuff defines a separate application when you select the Default Application Pool and see two applications (Default Application and Stuff) beneath it.

See Also

Recipe 12.22

12.22 Isolating Applications into Pools

Problem

You want to isolate an application from other applications so that when the application fails, it won't bring down other applications on the server.

Solution

Using a graphical user interface

1. Create a new application pool for your application (see Recipe 12.19)

2. Open Internet Information Services (IIS) Manager.

3. In the left pane, expand the console tree and select the web site (or virtual directory) where your application starting point is defined.

4. Right-click on the web site (or virtual directory) and select **Properties**.

5. Select the **Home Directory** (or **Virtual Directory**) tab.

6. Assign your application to the appropriate application pool and click **Apply**.

Using a command-line interface

The following command displays the process ID (PID) of all worker processes running on the computer, plus the application pool each worker process is assigned to:

```
> iisapp
```

The following command displays the application pool to which the worker process having PID 2765 is assigned:

```
> iisapp /p 2765
```

Using VBScript

```
' This code assigns an application to an app pool.
' ------ SCRIPT CONFIGURATION ------
strComputer = "<ServerName>"
strAppPoolName = "<AppPoolName>"
strApp = "<AppPath>" ' e.g., /W3SVC/1/Root/CGI
' ------ END CONFIGURATION ---------

set objVirtualDir = GetObject("IIS://" & strComputer & strApp)
objVirtualDir.AppPoolId = strAppPoolName
objVirtualDir.SetInfo( )
```

```
WScript.Echo "Application " & objApp.Name & _" isolated to App Pool " _
          & strAppPoolName
```

Discussion

In previous versions of IIS, a poorly written application could cause the entire web server to fail. IIS 6 gets around this by allowing you to isolate applications into pools so that a badly-behaving application will affect only other applications running in the same pool, but have no impact on applications running in different pools. Note that application pools are available only in worker process isolation mode (to change isolation modes use the checkbox on the Services tab of the Web Sites Properties sheet).

To isolate an application when IIS is running in IIS 5 isolation mode, do this instead:

1. Open Internet Information Services (IIS) Manager.
2. In the left pane, expand the console tree and select the web site (or virtual directory) where your application starting point is defined.
3. Right-click on the web site (or virtual directory) and select **Properties**.
4. Select the **Home Directory** (or **Virtual Directory**) tab.
5. Assign appropriate execute permissions to your application to isolate it as desired.

The choices for application isolation in this mode are:

Low (IIS Process)
    The application runs in-process together with *inetinfo.exe* (not recommended because if the application fails, IIS itself will crash).

Medium (Pooled Process)
    The application runs in a separate memory pool together with other designated applications (if any).

High (Isolated)
    The application runs out of process in its own *dllhost.exe* host process.

See Also

Recipe 12.19

12.23 Configuring Application Pool Recycling

Problem

You want to configure an application pool to recycle (restart its associated worker processes) under certain conditions.

Solution

Using a graphical user interface

To configure an application pool to recycle automatically, do the following:

1. Open Internet Information Services (IIS) Manager.

2. In the left pane, expand the server node in the console tree and select **Application Pools**.

3. Right-click on an application pool and select **Properties**.

4. Select the **Recycling** tab.

5. Choose one of the different options for recycling (see the Discussion section) and click **Apply**.

To recycle an application pool manually, do the following:

1. Open Internet Information Services (IIS) Manager.

2. In the left pane, expand the server node in the console tree and select **Application Pools**.

3. Right-click on an application pool and select **Recycle**.

Using a command-line interface

You can't configure application pool recycling from the command line, but once recycling has been configured, you can make IIS log recycling events in the System event log using the following command:

```
> cscript %systemroot%\inetpub\adminscripts\adsutil.vbs set w3svc/AppPools/
<AppPoolName>/<EventName> true
```

Replace *<AppPoolName>* with the name of your application pool and *<EventName>* with one of the recycling events listed in Table 12-10.

Table 12-10. System events related to application pool recycling

Event name	Description	Event code
AppPoolRecycleTime	Worker process ID recycled after reaching its elapsed time interval	1074
AppPoolRecycleRequests	Worker process ID recycled after reaching its processing request limit	1075
AppPoolRecycleSchedule	Worker process ID recycled after reaching its scheduled recycle time	1076
AppPoolRecycleMemory	Worker process ID recycled after reaching its virtual memory limit	1077
AppPoolRecycleIsapiUnhealthy	Worker process ID recycled due to an unhealthy ISAPI extension being loaded	1078
AppPoolRecycleOnDemand	All worker processes in the specified pool have been recycled at the request of an administrator	1079

Table 12-10. System events related to application pool recycling (continued)

Event name	Description	Event code
AppPoolRecycleConfigChange	All worker processes in the specified pool have been recycled because the pool's configuration has been changed	1080
AppPoolRecyclePrivateMemory	Worker process ID recycled after reaching its private bytes memory limit	1177

Using VBScript

```
' This code enables app pool recycling
' ------ SCRIPT CONFIGURATION ------
strComputer = "<ServerName>"
strAppPoolName = "<AppPoolName>"
' ------ END CONFIGURATION ---------

set objAppPool = GetObject("IIS://" & strComputer & "/w3svc/AppPools/" _
                           & strAppPoolName)
objAppPool.AppPoolRecycleRequests = True
objAppPool.PeriodicRestartRequests = 2000
objAppPool.SetInfo( )

WScript.Echo "App Pool recycling set successfully: " & objAppPool.Name
```

Discussion

Recycling an application pool restarts any worker processes assigned to the pool. Application pools may be configured to recycle based on different conditions:

- After an elapsed time interval (the default is 1740 minutes or 29 hours).
- After an elapsed number of processing requests.
- At scheduled times each day.

Application pools can also be configured to recycle if they consume too much memory, which is typically used for buggy applications that leak memory.

Using a command-line interface

Table 12-10 lists the different System events that can be logged for application pool recycling.

See Also

MS KB 332088 (How to modify Application Pool Recycling events in IIS 6.0)

12.24 Creating FTP Sites

Problem

You want to create an FTP site.

Solution

Using a graphical user interface

First, you need to install the FTP service:

1. From the Start menu, select **Control Panel → Add or Remove Programs**.
2. Click **Add/Remove Windows Components**.
3. Select the checkbox for **Application Server** and click **Details**.
4. Select the checkbox for **Internet Information Services (IIS)** and click **Details**.
5. Select the checkbox for **File Transfer Protocol (FTP) Service**, click **OK** twice, and then **Next**.
6. Click **Finish** after the wizard completes.

To create a new FTP site from scratch using a wizard, do the following:

1. Open Internet Information Services (IIS) Manager.
2. In the left pane, expand the server node in the console tree.
3. Right-click on the **FTP Sites** node, select **New → FTP Site** to start the FTP Site Creation Wizard, and click **Next**.
4. Type a descriptive name for your site and click **Next**.
5. Assign an IP address to your site and click **Next**.
6. Select the option **Do not isolate users** and click **Next**.
7. Specify the path to the FTP home directory for your site and click **Next**.
8. Specify access permissions to control access to your site and click **Next** then **Finish**.

To create a new FTP site using a previously saved configuration file, do the following:

1. Open Internet Information Services (IIS) Manager.
2. In the left pane, expand the server node in the console tree.
3. Right-click on the **FTP Sites** node and select **New → FTP Site (from file)**.
4. Specify the path to the XML file containing your saved IIS configuration, click **Read File**, select the FTP site you want to import, and click **OK**.
5. If prompted for a password, enter it and click **OK**.
6. In the left pane, right-click on the new FTP site and select **Start**.

Using a command-line interface

The following command creates a new FTP site named My FTP Site with root directory *C:\ftpstuff* and IP address 172.16.12.50, and leaves the site in a stopped state:

```
> iisftp /create C:\ftpstuff "My FTP Site" /i 172.16.12.50 /dontstart
```

To start the new site, do the following:

```
> iisftp /start "My FTP Site"
```

You can also stop and start all FTP sites on your server using the following commands:

```
> net stop msftpsvc
> net start msftpsvc
```

To display a list of all FTP sites on your server, use the following command:

```
> iisftp /query
```

Using VBScript

```
' This code creates a ftp site.
' ------ SCRIPT CONFIGURATION ------
strComputer = "<ServerName>"    ' computer to connect to
strSiteName = "<SiteName>"      ' web site description
strRootDir = "<RootDirectory>"  ' root directory for the ftp site
strPort = "21"                  ' port for the web site
' The following parameters are optional
' strIP = "<IPAddress>"         ' IP address used for the site
' strHostHeader = "<HostName>"  ' host header name for the site
strSiteID = "<SiteID>"          ' site ID (default is to auto-generate)
' ------ END CONFIGURATION ---------
set objIIS = GetObject("IIS://" & strComputer & "/msftpsvc" )
set objNewFtpServer = objIIS.Create("IIsFtpServer",strSiteID)
objNewFtpServer.ServerComment = strSiteName
objServerBindings = Array(0)
objServerBindings(0) = strIP & ":" & strPort & ":" & strHostHeader
objNewFtpServer.ServerBindings = objServerBindings
objNewFtpServer.SetInfo

set objNewDir = objNewFTPServer.Create("IIsFtpVirtualDir", "ROOT")
objNewDir.Path = strRootDir
objNewDir.AccessRead = True
objNewDir.SetInfo

WScript.Echo "Successfully created ftp site " & objNewFtpServer.ServerComment
```

Discussion

When you install the FTP Service component of IIS, a Default FTP Site is automatically created. Like the Default Web Site, this FTP site listens on all unassigned IP addresses, if you only need one FTP site, you can customize this one (for example, by specifying content location, configuring authentication methods, specifying a directory listing style, and so on) instead of creating additional new FTP sites. You can also use the *iisftp.vbs* command script to create virtual directories for FTP sites. The syntax of this command is similar to the *iisvdir.vbs* script used to create virtual directories for web sites (discussed in Recipe 12.5). Be sure to see MS KB 142853 mentioned below for a difference in how virtual directories work with FTP vs. web sites.

Using VBScript

This code is similar, though not identical, to the code for creating a web site shown in Recipe 12.5. There are a couple of notable differences. First, instead of calling a CreateNewSite method, it calls Create and passes IIsFtpServer and the site ID to it. That method returns an object that represents the new FTP site. It then modifies several properties including ServerBindings (see Recipe 12.5). After that, the script calls SetInfo to commit the changes, but we still aren't quite done.

By default, there are no virtual directories configured for new FTP sites, so we have to create our own. I call the Create method against the new FTP server object and set up the directory (note that this doesn't actually create the directory on the filesystem).

See Also

Recipe 12.5, MS KB 323384 (How To Set Up an FTP Server in Windows Server 2003), MS KB 311669 (IIS: MMC for FTP Site Does Not Display Files or Folders in the Right Pane), MS KB 142853 (Virtual Directories Not Visible on FTP Clients), and MS KB 814865 (INFO: FTP Site Administration Documentation in IIS 6.0)

12.25 Configuring FTP Authentication

Problem

You want to authenticate users before they can access content on your FTP server.

Solution

Using a graphical user interface

1. Open Internet Information Services (IIS) Manager.
2. In the left pane, expand the console tree and select the **FTP Sites** node.
3. Right-click on your FTP site and select **Properties**.
4. Select the **Security Accounts** tab.
5. To allow anonymous users access to your FTP site, select **Allow anonymous connections**.
6. To force users to supply credentials to access your FTP site, deselect **Allow anonymous connections**.

Using VBScript

```
' This enables anonymous-only access to a web site
' and configures the default user account and password.
' ------ SCRIPT CONFIGURATION ------
strComputer = "<ServerName>"
strSiteID = "<SiteID>"
```

```
'  ------ END CONFIGURATION ---------
set objFtpSite = GetObject("IIS://" & strComputer & "/MSFTPSVC/" & strSiteID)

objFtpSite.AllowAnonymous     = True
objFtpSite.AnonymousOnly      = True
objFtpSite.AnonymousUserName  = "DOMAIN\iisuser"
objFtpSite.AnonymousUserPass  = "!!sUser"
objFtpSite.SetInfo

WScript.Echo "Successfully modified Anonymous settings for: " & _
            objFtpSite.ServerComment
```

Discussion

If anonymous connections are disabled, users are authenticated to your site using Basic Authentication. In this situation, the user is prompted for the credentials of his Windows user account. When the user enters his credentials and clicks OK, the user's password will be appended to the URL and transmitted in clear text across the network, which is not secure.

If you want to configure anonymous FTP, select both **Allow anonymous connections** and **Allow only anonymous connections**, which means that users are never prompted for their credentials when trying to access your site. In this case, if you are accessing the FTP site using Internet Explorer, no credentials are prompted for. If you are using a command-line FTP client, however, you have to type **anonymous** as your username and a password.

See Also

MS KB 314932 (HOW TO: Create an FTP Folder with Read Access but Not List Access)

12.26 Configuring FTP User Isolation

Problem

You want to create an FTP site that gives each user her own virtual root directory.

Solution

Using a graphical user interface

First, you need to create the appropriate folder structure using Windows Explorer:

1. Create or choose a folder as the home directory for your new FTP site (e.g., *C:\ FtpHome*).

2. Create a subfolder beneath this home folder and give the subfolder a name identical to the NetBIOS name of your domain (e.g., MTIT for mtit.com).

3. Now create sub-subfolders for each domain user and give each sub-subfolder a name identical to the Pre-Windows 2000 logon name of each user (e.g., *bsmith* for *bsmith@mtit.com*).

4. Your folder tree should look something like this:

   \FtpHome
   \FtpHome\MTIT
   \FtpHome\MTIT\bsmith
   \FtpHome\MTIT\mjones

Now create a new FTP site that uses FTP User Isolation to map each user's account to their own FTP virtual root:

1. Open Internet Information Services (IIS) Manager.

2. In the left pane, expand the server node in the console tree.

3. Right-click on the **FTP Sites** node and select **New** → **FTP Site** to start the FTP Site Creation Wizard and click **Next**.

4. Type a descriptive name for your site and click **Next**.

5. Assign an IP address to your site and click **Next**.

6. Select the option **Isolate users** and click **Next**.

7. Specify the path to the home directory for your site and click **Next**.

8. Give users both **Read** and **Write** access permissions, click **Next**, then **Finish**.

Using a command-line interface

First, create a folder structure as described above. Then use the following command to create a new FTP site named My FTP Site with root directory *C:\FtpHome* and IP address 172.16.12.50, and implement FTP user isolation:

```
> iisftp /create C:\FtpHome "My FTP Site" /i 172.16.12.50 /isolation Local
```

Using VBScript

```
' This code creates a ftp site.
' ------ SCRIPT CONFIGURATION ------
strComputer = "<ServerName>"     ' computer to connect to
strSiteName = "<SiteName>"       ' web site description
strRootDir = "<RootDirectory>"   ' root directory for the ftp site
strPort = "21"                   ' port for the web site
' The following parameters are optional
' strIP = "<IPAddress>"          ' IP address used for the site
' strHostHeader = "<HostName>"   ' host header name for the site
strSiteID = "<SiteID>"           ' site ID (default is to auto-generate)
' ------ END CONFIGURATION ---------
set objIIS = GetObject("IIS://" & strComputer & "/msftpsvc" )
set objNewFtpServer = objIIS.Create("IIsFtpServer",strSiteID)
objNewFtpServer.ServerComment = strSiteName
objServerBindings = Array(0)
```

```
objServerBindings(0) = strIP & ":" & strPort & ":" & strHostHeader
objNewFtpServer.ServerBindings = objServerBindings

objNewFtpServer.UserIsolationMode = 1  ' 0 = No isolation
                                       ' 1 = Isolation
                                       ' 2 = AD isolation
objNewFtpServer.SetInfo

set objNewDir = objNewFTPServer.Create("IIsFtpVirtualDir", "ROOT")
objNewDir.Path = strRootDir
objNewDir.AccessRead = True
objNewDir.SetInfo

WScript.Echo "Successfully created ftp site " & objNewFtpServer.ServerComment
```

Discussion

IIS 6 supports three different isolation methods:

Do not isolate users
    All users share the same FTP home directory (this is the default with earlier versions of IIS).

Isolate users
    Each user has his own private FTP directory that appears to him to be the root directory of the FTP site. Users are authenticated either against Active Directory (in a Windows 2000 or Windows Server 2003 domain environment) or against a local SAM database (in a workgroup).

Isolate users using Active Directory
    Each user has her own private FTP directory that appears to her to be the root directory of the FTP site. Users are authenticated against a specified container within Active Directory (requires either a Windows Server 2003 domain or extending of the Windows 2000 AD schema).

The solution described in this recipe is for the *Isolate users* approach. For information on how to programmatically use the *Isolate users using Active Directory* approach, see MS KB 555205 (FTP User Isolation Using Active Directory Using Visual C#).

 The isolation level of an FTP site must be chosen when you create the site. You can't convert an ordinary FTP site into an isolated one or vice versa, at least according to Microsoft. However, if you create the necessary folder structure described in the first three steps above, you can then convert an ordinary FTP site into an isolated one by changing the UserIsolationMode metabase property for the site from 0 to 1.

See Also

MS KB 555018 (How To Set Up Isolated Ftp Site)

CHAPTER 13

Domain Name System (DNS)

13.0 Introduction

The Domain Name System (DNS) is one of the most critical services on your network. When DNS isn't working, users are unable to browse the web, send or receive email, and, in the case of Active Directory, log on to a domain. Both clients and domain controllers use DNS to locate domain controllers in a particular site or that serve a particular function. Fortunately, the Microsoft DNS Server has steadily improved over the years to the point where it is robust and reliable.

DNS has been around since the early 1980s, so it is a mature protocol. Rarely does DNS change in a significant way. However, Active Directory introduced an innovative change to how DNS data is stored. Instead of using the antiquated primary and secondary zone transfer method to replicate zone data between servers, Active Directory–integrated zones store zone data in Active Directory and take advantage of the same replication process domain controllers use to replicate data. This adds multimaster capabilities to DNS that current standards do not allow for. The one catch with Active Directory–integrated zones is that the DNS Server must run on a domain controller. Overloading DNS Server responsibilities on your domain controllers may not be something you want to do if you plan on supporting a large volume of DNS requests, but it is definitely something to consider for medium to small sites.

For more on the Microsoft DNS Server beyond what this chapter covers, I recommend *DNS on Windows Server 2003* (O'Reilly). There are also numerous web sources for learning about DNS. Here are some of the ones I recommend:

- DNS Resources Directory (*http://www.dns.net/dnsrd/*)
- RFC 1032—Domain Administrators Guide
- RFC 1033—Domain Administrators Operations Guide
- RFC 1034—Domain Names—Concepts and Facilities
- RFC 1035—Domain Names—Implementation and Specification

- Kirkpatrick, Gil (CTO of Netpro). "Authentication Topology: Configure DNS SRV Records to Speed Authentication," Windows & .Net Magazine, March 2003. Available for free download from *http://www.netpro.com/forum/files/ Authentication_Topology.pdf*.

Using a Graphical User Interface

The primary graphical user interface for managing the DNS Server is the DNS snap-in (*dnsmgmt.msc*). This MMC snap-in is installed under Administrative Tools when you install the DNS Server.

The DNS snap-in communicates to the DNS Server over RPC to the DNS Server service. That means if the DNS Server service is stopped, you won't be able to configure DNS using the snap-in.

The DNS snap-in works fine when you are dealing with small zones, but performance is pretty bad when you want to modify or add a resource record in a zone that has several thousand resource records. Consider using *dnscmd.exe* instead if you find yourself in that situation.

Using a Command-Line Interface

The command-line counterpart to the DNS snap-in is *dnscmd.exe*, which is available in the Support Tools on the Windows Server 2003 or Windows 2000 Server CD. *dnscmd.exe* includes the proverbial kitchen sink of options for managing a Microsoft DNS Server. Most of the command-line examples in this chapter use *dnscmd.exe*, but I'll also cover other useful utilities such as *sysocmgr.exe*, for installing the DNS server; and *sc.exe*, which can be used to query, start, and stop the DNS server. See Table 13-1 for the complete list of command-line tools covered in this chapter.

Table 13-1. Command-line tools used in this chapter

Command	Windows Server 2003	Windows 2000 Server	Recipes
dnscmd.exe	Windows Server 2003 Support Tools	Windows 2000 Support Tools	13.2–11, 13.13–16
ipconfig.exe	%SystemRoot%\system32	%SystemRoot%\system32	13.14
nslookup.exe	%SystemRoot%\system32	%SystemRoot%\system32	13.10, 13.12, 13.14
sc.exe	%SystemRoot%\system32	Windows 2000 Resource Kit	13.2
sysocmgr.exe	%SystemRoot%\system32	%SystemRoot%\system32	13.1

The DNS server is one of the few Microsoft services that can be configured completely from a command line. The *dnscmd.exe* utility has been around since Windows NT. Microsoft has added new options with every major operating system release. With it, you can modify server settings and create, query, and manipulate zones and resource records. In the Windows Server 2003 version, there are even *dnscmd.exe* commands for managing Active Directory application partitions.

Using VBScript

The WMI DNS Provider was first released as part of Windows 2000 Resource Kit Supplement 1, but unfortunately it wasn't ready for prime time. That version was buggy, didn't include all the documented features, and in several cases, behaved differently from what the documentation described. Also, since the DNS Provider was included as part of a Resource Kit, it was not fully supported by Microsoft, which meant that if you encountered problems you were largely on your own. That said, much of the functionality you probably need is present in the Windows 2000 version, so it may be suitable for your use.

With Windows Server 2003, the DNS Provider is fully functional and supported, although some discrepancies still exist between the Microsoft documentation and the implementation, at least in the version that was available at the time this book went to press. It is installed automatically whenever you install the DNS Server service.

The three main areas of interest when it comes to managing DNS include server configuration, zone management, and the creation and deletion of resource records. The DNS Provider has several classes available to manipulate each of these components, all stored under the root\MicrosoftDNS namespace. With the MicrosoftDNS_Server class, you can manipulate server configuration settings, start and stop the DNS Server service, and initiate scavenging. The MicrosoftDNS_Zone class allows you to create, delete, and modify zone configuration. The MicrosoftDNS_ResourceRecord class and child classes provide methods for manipulating the various resource record types.

Several additional classes supported by the DNS Provider manage other aspects of DNS including the root hints (MicrosoftDNS_RootHints), DNS server cache (MicrosoftDNS_Cache), and server statistics (MicrosoftDNS_Statistics) classes. For more information on these classes, including sample scripts in VBScript and Perl, check out the following section in the Microsoft Developer Network Library (*http://msdn.microsoft.com/library/*): **Win32 and COM Development** → **Networking** → **Network Protocols** → **Domain Name System (DNS)** → **SDK Documentation** → **Domain Name System (DNS)**.

13.1   Installing the DNS Server

Problem

You want to install the DNS Server.

Solution

Using a graphical user interface

1. From the Control Panel, open the Add or Remove Programs applet.
2. Click on **Add/Remove Windows Components**.
3. Double-click on **Network Services**.
4. Check the box beside **Domain Name System (DNS)**.
5. Click **OK**.
6. Click **Next**.
7. Click **Finish**.

Using a command-line interface

Create a file using a text editor, such as *notepad.exe*, with the following contents:

```
[netoptionalcomponents]
dns=1
```

Next, run the *sysocmgr* utility with following parameters (assuming the file you just created is named *c:\dns_install.txt*):

```
> sysocmgr /i:%windir%\inf\sysoc.inf /u:c:\dns_install.txt
```

Using VBScript

Unfortunately, there are no native scripting interfaces for installing DNS Server. However, you can run the *sysocmgr* command from the previous section directly within a batch script (*.bat* extension) or using the WScript.Shell Run method within VBScript.

```
' This code simulates the same steps from the command-line solution.
' First an answer file is created containing the parameters to install
' the DNS Server. Then the sysocmgr command is invoked to perform the
' installation.
strFile = "c:\dns_install.txt"

constForWriting = 2
set objFSO = CreateObject("Scripting.FileSystemObject")
set objFile = objFSO.OpenTextFile(strFile, constForWriting, True)
objFile.WriteLine("[netoptionalcomponents]")
objFile.WriteLine("dns=1")
objFile.Close

set objWshShell = WScript.CreateObject("WScript.Shell")
intRC = objWshShell.Run("sysocmgr /i:%windir%\inf\sysoc.inf /u:" & _
                        strFile, 0, TRUE)
if intRC <> 0 then
   WScript.Echo "Error returned from sysocmgr command: " & intRC
else
```

```
    WScript.Echo "DNS Server installed"
end if
```

Discussion

The Microsoft DNS Server is an optional operating system component that you can install on any Windows 2000 Server or Windows Server 2003 machine. The *sysocmgr* utility has additional options for suppressing dialog boxes (/x and /q). For the complete list of sysocmgr options, run `sysocmgr /?` from a command line.

 You can also install the DNS Server using the **Manage Your Server or Configure Your Server** wizards.

See Also

Recipes 2.4 and 13.2

13.2   Starting and Stopping the DNS Server

Problem

You want to start or stop the DNS Server.

Solution

Using a graphical user interface

1. From the Administrative Tools, open the DNS snap-in (*dnsmgmt.msc*).

2. In the left pane, right-click on the server and select **All Tasks**. From here you can select either **Stop** to stop the DNS Server or **Start** to start it.

Using a command-line interface

You can use the *net.exe* command to stop or start the DNS Server service on the local machine:

```
> net stop dns
> net start dns
```

If you want to stop or start DNS Server remotely, use the *sc.exe* command:

```
> sc \\<ServerName> stop dns
> sc \\<ServerName> start dns
```

Using VBScript

```
' This code restarts the DNS Server on the specified host.
' ------ SCRIPT CONFIGURATION ------
```

```
strServer  = "<ServerName>"   ' e.g., dns1.rallencorp.com
' ------ END CONFIGURATION ---------
on error resume next

set objDNS = GetObject("winMgmts:\\" & strServer & "\root\MicrosoftDNS")
set objDNSServer = objDNS.Get("MicrosoftDNS_Server.Name=""."""")

objDNSServer.StopService
if Err Then
  WScript.Echo "StopService failed: " & Err.Description
  Wscript.Quit
end if

objDNSServer.StartService
if Err Then
  WScript.Echo "StartService failed: " & Err.Description
  Wscript.Quit
end if

WScript.Echo "Restart successful"
```

Discussion

DNS Server runs as a service, which means you can also use the Services snap-in (*services.msc*) to start and stop it. When you stop DNS Server, it will no longer respond to DNS queries. You will also not be able to configure DNS Server while it is in a stopped state. This is because the DNS management tools, such as the DNS snap-in and *dnscmd*, communicate with DNS Server using RPC calls directly to that service. If the service is stopped, those tools won't work.

If you do not want DNS Server to respond to queries, but you still want to be able to configure it, there is another option; DNS Server can be paused. For clients, this is effectively the same as stopping the service because it will not respond to DNS queries, but because the service remains up, you can use the management tools to configure it. To pause the DNS Server, follow the same steps outlined in the graphical user interface section, but select **Pause** from the list of **All Tasks**. To unpause (or resume) the server, select **Resume**.

From a command line, use these commands to pause and resume the server, respectively:

```
> sc \\<ServerName> pause dns
> sc \\<ServerName> continue dns
```

 From VBScript, the MicrosoftDNS_Server class doesn't support pausing and resuming the DNS Server, but the Win32_Service class does.

If you want to take only a single zone offline, you can pause just that zone. *dnscmd* supports pausing and resuming zones, as shown here:

```
> dnscmd <ServerName> /zonepause <ZoneName>
> dnscmd <ServerName> /zoneresume <ZoneName>
```

This works as you might expect. When a zone is in the paused state, DNS Server will not respond to client queries for records in that zone, but you can still make configuration changes to it.

See Also

Recipe 7.1, MSDN: MicrosoftDNS_Server, and MSDN: MicrosoftDNS_Zone

13.3   Modifying DNS Server Configuration

Problem

You want to modify DNS Server settings. This will be one of the first things you need to do after installing DNS Server.

Solution

Using a graphical user interface

1. From the Administrative Tools, open the DNS snap-in (*dnsmgmt.msc*).
2. Connect to the DNS Server you want to modify. In the left pane, right-click on **DNS** and select **Connect to DNS Server**. Select **The following computer** and enter the target server name. Click **OK**.
3. Right-click on the server and select **Properties**.
4. Choose from the various tabs to edit settings.
5. Click **OK** after you've completed the modifications to commit the changes.

Using a command-line interface

With the following command, replace *<Setting>* with the name of the setting to modify and *<Value>* with the value to set:

```
> dnscmd <ServerName> /config /<Setting> <Value>
```

The following command enables the EnableDnsSec setting on *dns01*:

```
> dnscmd dns01 /config /EnableDnsSec 1
```

The following command disables the NoTcp setting on the local host:

```
> dnscmd /config /NoTcp 0
```

The following command sets the DsPollingInterval setting to 60 on *dns02*:

```
> dnscmd dns02 /config /DsPollingInterval 60
```

For the complete list of settings, run dnscmd /config from the command line.

Using VBScript

```
' This code shows how to set a DNS Server property.
strServer = "<ServerName>"
set objDNS = GetObject("winMgmts:\\" & strServer & "\root\MicrosoftDNS")
set objDNSServer = objDNS.Get("MicrosoftDNS_Server.Name=""."""")
objDNSServer.<Setting> = <Value>    ' e.g., objDNSServer.AllowUpdate = TRUE
objDNSServer.Put_

' This code displays all the settings on a DNS Server.
' ------ SCRIPT CONFIGURATION ------
strServer  = "<ServerName>"  ' e.g., dns1.rallencorp.com
' ------ END CONFIGURATION ---------

' Instantiate a WMI object for the target server
set objDNS = GetObject("winmgmts:\\" & strServer & "\root\MicrosoftDNS")
' Get an instance of the MicrosoftDNS_Server  class
set objDNSServer = objDNS.Get("MicrosoftDNS_Server.Name=""."""")

' Iterate over each property using Properties_
Wscript.Echo objDNSServer.Properties_.Item("Name") & ":"
for each objProp in objDNSServer.Properties_
    if IsNull(objProp.Value) then
       Wscript.Echo " " & objProp.Name & " : NULL"
    else
       if objProp.IsArray = TRUE then
          for I = LBound(objProp.Value) to UBound(objProp.Value)
               wscript.echo " " & objProp.Name & " : " & objProp.Value(I)
          next
       else
          Wscript.echo " " & objProp.Name & " : " & objProp.Value
       end if
    end if
next
```

Discussion

Using a graphical user interface

DNS Server supports a variety of settings to configure everything from scavenging and forwarders to logging. With the DNS snap-in, the settings are spread over several tabs in the Properties property page.

Using a command-line interface

You can get a list of available settings, many of which can't be configured from the DNS snap-in, by running dnscmd /config from a command line. For the CLI and VBScript solutions, the setting names are nearly identical. Be careful when using the dnscmd /config command because very little error checking is done on the values you specify.

Each setting is stored in the registry on the DNS Server under the `HKEY_LOCAL_MACHINE\`
`SYSTEM\CurrentControlSet\Services\DNS\Parameters` key. The `dnscmd /config` command simply writes the value you specify to a registry value and does not verify if the input is valid. See the following web site for more information on what values are expected for each setting: *http://msdn.microsoft.com/library/en-us/dns/dns/microsoftdns_server.asp*.

Using VBScript

Be sure to call the `Put_` method after you finish configuring settings in order for the changes to be committed to the server.

See Also

MSDN: MicrosoftDNS_Server

13.4 Creating a Zone

Problem

You want to create a forward or reverse lookup zone. A forward lookup zone maps names to IP addresses or other names, and a reverse lookup zone maps IP addresses to names.

Solution

Using a graphical user interface

Use the following instructions to create a forward zone:

1. From the Administrative Tools, open the DNS snap-in (*dnsmgmt.msc*).

2. Connect to the DNS Server you want to modify. In the left pane, right-click on **DNS** and select **Connect to DNS Server**. Select **The following computer** and enter the target server name. Click **OK**.

3. Expand the server in the left pane and click **Forward Lookup Zones**.

4. Right-click on **Forward Lookup Zones** and select **New Zone**.

5. Click **Next**.

6. Select the zone type and click **Next**.

7. If you selected Active Directory to store the zone data, you will be asked for the servers to which you want to replicate the DNS data. Click Next after you make your selection. (This applies to only Windows Server 2003.)

8. Enter the zone name and click **Next**.

9. Fill out the information for the remaining screens. They will vary depending on whether you are creating a primary, secondary, or stub zone.

Use these instructions to create a reverse zone:

1. From the Administrative Tools, open the DNS snap-in (*dnsmgmt.msc*).
2. Connect to the DNS Server you want to modify. In the left pane, right-click on **DNS** and select **Connect to DNS Server**. Select **The following computer** and enter the target server name. Click **OK**.
3. Expand the server in the left pane and click on **Reverse Lookup Zones**.
4. Right-click on **Reverse Lookup Zones** and select **New Zone**.
5. Click **Next**.
6. Select the zone type and click **Next**.
7. If you selected Active Directory to store the zone data, you will be asked which servers you want to replicate the DNS data to. Click **Next** after you make your selection. (This applies to only Windows Server 2003.)
8. Type the **Network ID** or enter a **Reverse lookup zone name** and click **Next**.
9. Fill out the information for the remaining screens. They will vary depending on if you are creating a primary, secondary, or stub zone.

Using a command-line interface

The following command creates an Active Directory–integrated forward or reverse zone:

```
> dnscmd <ServerName> /zoneadd <ZoneName> /DsPrimary
```

This example adds an Active Directory–integrated forward zone called *rallencorp.com* on *dns01*:

```
> dnscmd dns01 /zoneadd rallencorp.com /DsPrimary
```

This example adds an Active Directory–integrated reverse zone for *8.10.192.in-addr.arpa* on *dns01*:

```
> dnscmd dns01 /zoneadd 8.10.192.in-addr.arpa /DsPrimary
```

This command creates a file-based zone:

```
> dnscmd <ServerName> /zoneadd <ZoneName> /Primary /file <FileName>
```

This example creates a file-based zone on the local host for the zone *foobar.com*:

```
> dnscmd . /zoneadd foobar.com /Primary /file foobar.com.dns
```

This command creates a file-based secondary zone:

```
> dnscmd <ServerName> /zoneadd <ZoneName> /Secondary <MasterIPAddress> [ /file
<FileName> ]
```

This example creates a file-based secondary zone for *10.10.192.in-addr.arpa*:

```
> dnscmd dns01 /zoneadd 10.10.192.in-addr.arpa /Secondary 192.168.2.5
```

When you create a file-based primary or secondary zone, the file that stores the contents of the zone is created under *%SystemRoot%\ system32\dns*.

Using VBScript

```
' This code creates an AD-integrated forward or reverse zone.
' ------ SCRIPT CONFIGURATION ------
strServer  = "<ServerName>"   ' e.g., dns01.rallencorp.com
strNewZone = "<ZoneName>"     ' e.g., othercorp.com or 8.10.192.in-addr.arpa.
' ------ END CONFIGURATION ---------
set objDNS = GetObject("winMgmts:\\" & strServer & "\root\MicrosoftDNS")
set objDNSZone = objDNS.Get("MicrosoftDNS_Zone")
strNull = objDNSZone.CreateZone(strNewZone, 0 , True)
WScript.Echo "Created zone " & strNewZone
```

Discussion

Using a command-line interface

When you create an Active Directory–integrated zone with the /DsPrimary switch, you can also include a /dp switch and specify an application partition to add the zone to. Here is an example:

```
> dnscmd /zoneadd <ZoneName> /DsPrimary /dp domaindnszones.rallencorp.com
```

See Also

Recipe 13.7, MS KB 323445 (HOW TO: Create a New Zone on a DNS Server in Windows Server 2003), MSDN: DNS WMI Provider, and MSDN: CreateZone Method of the MicrosoftDNS_Zone Class

13.5   Viewing a DNS Server's Zones

Problem

You want to view the supported zones on a DNS Server.

Solution

Using a graphical user interface

1. From the Administrative Tools, open the DNS snap-in (*dnsmgmt.msc*).

2. Connect to the DNS Server you want to view. In the left pane, right-click on **DNS** and select **Connect to DNS Server**. Select **The following computer** and enter the target server name. Click **OK**.

3. In the left pane, expand the target server and click **Forward Lookup Zones** or **Reverse Lookup Zones** to view the supported zones in the right pane.

Using a command-line interface

Run the following command to view the zones on a local DNS Server:

```
> dnscmd <ServerName> /enumzones
```

The following command enumerates the zones on server *dns01*:

```
> dnscmd dns01 /enumzones
```

Using VBScript

```
' This code lists the zones that are supported by the specified server.
' ------ SCRIPT CONFIGURATION ------
strServer = "<ServerName>"  ' e.g., dns01.rallencorp.com
' ------ END CONFIGURATION ---------
set objDNS = GetObject("winMgmts:\\" & strServer & "\root\MicrosoftDNS")
set objDNSServer = objDNS.Get("MicrosoftDNS_Server.Name="".""")
set objZones = objDNS.ExecQuery("Select * from MicrosoftDNS_Zone " & _
                                "Where DnsServerName = '" & _
                                objDNSServer.Name & "'")
WScript.Echo "Zones on " & objDNSServer.Name
for each objZone in objZones
    WScript.Echo " " & objZOne.Name
next
```

Discussion

Using a graphical user interface

When you click on either **Forward Lookup Zones** or **Reverse Lookup Zones** in the left pane, the right pane contains a **Type** column that displays each zone's type.

Using a command-line interface

Using the /enumzones switch without any additional parameters displays all zones on the server. However, you can specify additional filters that limit the types of zones returned. With the Windows 2000 version of *dnscmd*, you can specify up to two filters:

```
Filter1:
    /Primary
    /Secondary
    /Cache
    /Auto-Created
Filter2:
    /Forward
    /Reverse
```

With the Windows Server 2003 version of *dnscmd*, the filter behavior has changed. Instead of having two levels of criteria, you can specify one or more of the following:

```
/Primary
/Secondary
/Forwarder
/Stub
```

```
/Cache
/Auto-Created
/Forward
/Reverse
/Ds
/File
/DomainDirectoryPartition
/ForestDirectoryPartition
/CustomDirectoryPartition
/LegacyDirectoryPartition
/DirectoryPartition <PartitionName>
```

For more information on what each of these filters mean, run `dnscmd /enumzones /?`.

Using VBScript

To get the list of zones, I used a WQL query to find all `MicrosoftDNS_Zone` objects. You can add additional criteria to the WQL Select statement to return a subset of zones supported by the server if you need to. Look up the properties of the `MicrosoftDNS_Zone` class in MSDN to see the additional properties you can add to the query.

See Also

MSDN: MicrosoftDNS_Zone

13.6 Converting a Zone to an Active Directory– Integrated Zone

Problem

You want to convert a primary zone to an Active Directory–integrated zone. This causes the contents of the zone to be stored and replicated in Active Directory instead of in a text file, as is the case with a standard primary zone.

Solution

Using a graphical user interface

1. From the Administrative Tools, open the DNS snap-in (*dnsmgmt.msc*).
2. Connect to the DNS Server you want to modify. In the left pane, right-click on **DNS** and select **Connect to DNS Server**. Select **The following computer** and enter the target server name. Click **OK**.
3. If you want to convert a forward zone, expand the **Forward Lookup Zone** folder. If you want to convert a reverse zone, expand the **Reverse Lookup Zone folder**.
4. Click on the zone you want to convert, then right-click it, and select **Properties**.

5. Beside **Type**, click the **Change** button.

6. Check the box beside **Store the zone in Active Directory**.

7. Click **OK** and click **OK** again.

Using a command-line interface

Use the following command to convert a standard primary zone to Active Directory–integrated:

```
> dnscmd <ServerName> /zoneresettype <ZoneName> /DsPrimary
```

For example:

```
> dnscmd dns02 /zoneresettype myzone.com /DsPrimary
```

Using VBScript

```
' This code converts a zone to AD-integrated.
' ------ SCRIPT CONFIGURATION ------
strZone   = "<ZoneName>"     ' e.g., rallencorp.com
strServer = "<ServerName>"   ' e.g., dc1.rallencorp.com
' ------ END CONFIGURATION ---------
set objDNS = GetObject("winMgmts:\\" & strServer & "\root\MicrosoftDNS")
set objDNSServer = objDNS.Get("MicrosoftDNS_Server.Name="".""")
set objDNSZone = objDNS.Get("MicrosoftDNS_Zone.ContainerName=""" & _
                    strZone & """,DnsServerName=""" & _
                    objDNSServer.Name & """,Name=""" & strZone & """")
strNull = objDNSZone.ChangeZoneType(0, True)
objDNSZone.Put_
WScript.Echo "Converted " & strZone & " to AD-integrated"
```

Discussion

The only time DNS data is stored in Active Directory is if you have a zone that is Active Directory–integrated. Standard primary and secondary zones that are not Active Directory–integrated store DNS data locally on the file system of each DNS Server. If you have an Active Directory–integrated zone under Windows 2000, a container is created in Active Directory at *cn=<ZoneName>,cn=MicrosoftDNS,cn=System,<DomainDN>*, where *<ZoneName>* is the name of the zone.

For Windows Server 2003, you can use application partitions to store DNS data in an alternate location. By default, there are three options for storing DNS data in Windows Server 2003–based forests:

1. Store DNS data on all domain controllers in a domain (only option for Windows 2000).

2. Store DNS data on all domain controllers that are DNS Servers in the domain.

3. Store DNS data on all domain controllers that are DNS Servers in the forest.

The default location for the second option is *dc=DomainDNSZones,<DomainDN>* and for the third option, it is *dc=ForestDNSZones,<ForestDN>*. These two locations are actually application partitions that are replicated only to the domain controllers that are DNS Servers in the domain or forest, respectively.

Inside the *cn=MicrosoftDNS* container is a dnsZone object for each Active Directory–integrated zone. Inside of the dnsZone container are dnsNode objects, each of which store all resource records associated with a particular node. In the following textual representation of an A record, the *dc1.rallencorp.com* name is considered a node (generally the left side of the resource record).

```
dc1.rallencorp.com. 600 IN A 6.10.57.21
```

There could be multiple resource records associated with the *dc1.rallencorp.com* name, so each dnsNode object has a multivalued dnsRecord attribute. The dnsNode object represents the name and the values of the dnsRecord attribute for all of its resource records. Unfortunately, the contents of that attribute are stored in a binary format and are not directly readable.

See Also

MS KB 198437 (How to Convert DNS Primary Server to Active Directory Integrated), MS KB 227844 (Primary and Active Directory Integrated Zones Differences), and MSDN: ChangeZoneType Method of the MicrosoftDNS_Zone Class

13.7 Moving Active Directory–Integrated Zones into an Application Partition

 This recipe requires the Windows Server 2003 domain functional level.

Problem

You want to move an Active Directory–integrated zone into an application partition to reduce unnecessary replication traffic to domain controllers that are not DNS Servers.

Solution

Using a graphical user interface

1. From the Administrative Tools, open the DNS snap-in (*dnsmgmt.msc*).

2. Connect to the DNS Server you want to modify. In the left pane, right-click on **DNS** and select **Connect to DNS Server**. Select **The following computer** and enter the target server name. Click **OK**.

3. Expand the server in the left pane and expand either **Forward Lookup Zones** or **Reverse Lookup Zones** depending on the type of zone.

4. Click on the name of the zone.

5. Right-click on the zone and select **Properties**.

6. Click on the **Change** button beside **Replication**.

7. Select the application partition where you want to move the zone.

8. Click **OK** and click **OK** again.

Using a command-line interface

The following command moves a zone to the default application partition that replicates to all domain controllers that are DNS Servers in the domain:

```
> dnscmd <ServerName> /zonechangedirectorypartition <ZoneName> /domain
```

The following command moves a zone into the application partition that replicates to all domain controllers in a forest that are DNS Servers:

```
> dnscmd <ServerName> /zonechangedirectorypartition <ZoneName> /forest
```

Using VBScript

At the time of publication of this book, the DNS WMI Provider did not support programmatically moving a zone into an application partition.

Discussion

With Windows 2000 Active Directory, Active Directory–integrated zones replicate to every domain controller in the domain they are stored. So if you have domain controllers that aren't acting as DNS Servers, which is often the case, those domain controllers replicate the Active Directory–integrated zone data even though they don't really use it. This can be confusing and result in increased and unnecessary replication traffic to replicate changes with the zones.

A domain controller serves as a DNS Server only if you explicitly install the DNS Server service. Just because a zone is Active Directory–integrated doesn't mean every domain controller acts as a DNS Server.

Windows Server 2003 provides an elegant solution to this issue by using application partitions. Application partitions are user-defined partitions that can be configured to replicate with any domain controller in a forest. This provides much more flexibility for how you store and replicate your Active Directory–integrated zones. You could, in fact, have a couple domain controllers from each domain act as DNS Servers for all of your Active Directory domains and replicate DNS data only to them.

See Also

Recipe 13.6 and Chapter 17 of *Active Directory Cookbook* (O'Reilly)

13.8   Creating a Stub Zone

 Stub zones are a new feature in Windows Server 2003, so this recipe will not work on Windows 2000.

Problem

You want to create a stub zone to improve the efficiency of name resolution, avoid creating secondaries in some situations, or keep delegated zone information current without manual intervention.

Solution

Using a graphical user interface

1. Open the DNS snap-in (*dnsmgmt.msc*).
2. Connect to the DNS Server you want to modify. In the left pane, right-click on **DNS** and select **Connect to DNS Server**. Select **The following computer** and enter the target server name. Click **OK**.
3. Expand the server in the left pane and click on **Forward Lookup Zones**.
4. Right-click on **Forward Lookup Zones** and select **New Zone**.
5. Click **Next**.
6. Select the option beside **Stub Zone** and click **Next**.
7. Enter the zone name and click **Next**.
8. Fill out the information for the remaining screens, which vary depending on whether you are creating a file-based or Active Directory–integrated zone.

Using a command-line interface

To create a file-based stub zone, use the following command:

```
> dnscmd <ServerName> /zoneadd <ZoneName> /stub <ServerList> /file <FileName>
```

<ZoneName> should be the name of the zone you want to create the stub for; <ServerList> should be a space-separated list of IP addresses of servers that are authoritative for the stub; and the /file <FileName> parameter is optional for file-based stub zones only and should specify the filename where the zone information is stored.

Here is an example:

```
> dnscmd /zoneadd rallencorp.com /stub 6.10.6.24 17.7.16.18
```

To create an Active Directory–integrated stub zone, replace the /stub option with /dsstub and do not include a /file option; For example:

```
> dnscmd /zoneadd rallencorp.com /dsstub 6.10.6.24 17.7.16.18
```

Using VBScript

```
' This code creates a file-based stub zone
' ------ SCRIPT CONFIGURATION ------
strServer = "<ServerName>"    ' e.g., dns01
strNewZone = "<ZoneName>"     ' e.g., rallencorp.com
strFileName = "<FileName>"    ' e.g., rallencorpstubzone.dns (THIS IS OPTIONAL)
arrMasterIPs = Array("<IP1>","<IP2>") ' replace <IP1,2> with IPs of master server
' ------ END CONFIGURATION ---------
on error resume next
set objDNS = GetObject("winMgmts:\\" & strServer & "\root\MicrosoftDNS")
set objDNSZone = objDNS.Get("MicrosoftDNS_Zone")
strNull = objDNSZone.CreateZone(strNewZone,2,false,strFileName, _
                                strFileName, arrMasterIPs)

if Err then
    WScript.Echo "Error occurred creating zone: " & Err.Description
else
    WScript.Echo "Zone created."
end if


' This code creates an Active Directory-integrated stub zone
' ------ SCRIPT CONFIGURATION ------
strServer = "<ServerName>"    ' e.g., dns01
strNewZone = "<ZoneName>"     ' e.g., rallencorp.com
arrMasterIPs = Array("<IP1>","<IP2>") ' replace <IP1,2> with IPs of master server
' ------ END CONFIGURATION ---------
on error resume next
set objDNS = GetObject("winMgmts:\\" & strServer & "\root\MicrosoftDNS")
set objDNSZone = objDNS.Get("MicrosoftDNS_Zone")
strNull = objDNSZone.CreateZone(strNewZone,2,true,,strFileName, arrMasterIPs)
if Err then
    WScript.Echo "Error occurred creating zone: " & Err.Description
else
    WScript.Echo "Zone created."
end if
```

Discussion

Stub zones are a new kind of zone supported in Windows Server 2003 that let you create a more efficient and automated name resolution topology. Consider the following scenario. You are preparing to deploy Active Directory and you plan on creating a subdomain called *ad.rallencorp.com* to be the root of your AD forest. You create the delegation on your root DNS servers (by creating NS records) for *ad.rallencorp.com* that points at one of the domain controllers the AD team is using to host the AD DNS namespace. Your root DNS servers will be authoritative for *rallencorp.com* and the domain controllers using Active Directory–integrated DNS will be authoritative for *ad.rallencorp.com*. There is nothing unusual here, but there is some support overhead in maintaining the delegation relationship between the root DNS servers and the AD DNS servers (i.e., maintaining the list of NS records). Normally, you wouldn't want to delegate to just one server because that is a single point of failure. And the AD team may enable DNS on several domain controllers. With Microsoft DNS on Windows 2000, your only option would be to manually create NS records for each domain controller on your root servers. With Windows Server 2003, you can actually automate the process by creating a stub zone.

In this example, you'd create a stub zone on your root DNS server for *ad.rallencorp.com*. You then specify a couple of "master" server IPs (i.e., pick a couple of the domain controllers running DNS) and you are done. Periodically the root servers will go out to the master IPs and refresh their list of NS records for the stub zone automatically. In fact, you can't modify the contents of a stub zone because it is maintained through this automatic process. Changes must be made in the source zone before they'll show up in the stub zone.

There are three resource record types you'll see in a stub zone:

Start of Authority (SOA)
> This record contains various zone properties such as the primary nameserver(s), administrative contact, default time to live, etc.

Name Server (NS)
> There will be one NS record for each authoritative name server for the source zone of the stub zone.

Glue Address (A)
> There will be at least one A record for every name server that has an NS record. These glue records are necessary so that clients can determine the IP address of a host defined in an NS record (which only contains host names).

 Stub zones aren't for everyone and they generally won't have a place in organizations that don't have subdomains or a discontiguous namespace.

See Also

Recipe 13.9 and MS KB 811118 (Support WebCast: Microsoft Windows Server 2003 DNS: Stub Zones and Conditional Forwarding)

13.9 Configuring Conditional Forwarding

 Conditional forwarding is a new feature in Windows Server 2003, so this recipe will not work on Windows 2000.

Problem

You want to configure conditional forwarding to streamline name resolution in your environment.

Solution

Using a graphical user interface

1. Open the DNS snap-in (*dnsmgmt.msc*).
2. Connect to the DNS Server you want to modify. In the left pane, right-click on **DNS** and select **Connect to DNS Server**. Select **The following computer** and enter the target server name. Click **OK**.
3. Right-click on the server and select **Properties**.
4. Click the **Forwarders** tab.
5. To configure a global forwarder, make sure **All other DNS domains** is selected under **DNS domain**, type an IP under **Selected domain's forwarder IP address list**, click **Add**, and **Apply**.
6. To configure a forwarder for a specific domain, click the **New** button.
7. Enter the domain name and click **OK**.
8. Add IPs as described for global forwarders.
9. From the **Forwarders** tab, you can also set the number of seconds the server waits before forward queries times out, and you can disable the use of recursion for certain domains. Both of these can be set on a per-domain basis.

Using a command-line interface

The following command sets the default forwarders. Replace `<IPsOfForwarders>` with a space-separated list of IP addresses for the name servers to forward requests to:

```
> dnscmd <ServerName> /resetforwarders <IPsOfForwaders>
```

For example:

```
> dnscmd dns01 /resetforwarders 10.22.3.4 10.22.3.5
```

The following command creates a domain-based forwarder:

```
> dnscmd <ServerName> /zoneadd <DomainName> /forwarder <IPsOfForwarders>
```

The following command configures the default forwarder timeout:

```
> dnscmd <ServerName> /config /forwardingtimeout <NumSeconds>
```

The following command configures the forwarder timeout for a specific domain:

```
> dnscmd <ServerName> /config <DomainName> /forwardertimeout <NumSeconds>
```

Using VBScript

```
' This code enumerates the default forwarders.
' ------ SCRIPT CONFIGURATION ------
strServer  = "<ServerName> "  ' e.g., dns1.rallencorp.com
' ------ END CONFIGURATION ---------

set objDNS = GetObject("winMgmts:\\" & strServer & "\root\MicrosoftDNS")
set objDNSServer = objDNS.Get("MicrosoftDNS_Server.Name="".""")
for each strForwarder in objDNSServer.Forwarders
   Wscript.Echo strForwarder
next


' This code sets the default forwarders.
' ------ SCRIPT CONFIGURATION ------
strServer  = "<ServerName>"  ' e.g., dns1.rallencorp.com
arrForwarders = Array("<IP1>","<IP2>")
' ------ END CONFIGURATION ---------

set objDNS = GetObject("winMgmts:\\" & strServer & "\root\MicrosoftDNS")
set objDNSServer = objDNS.Get("MicrosoftDNS_Server.Name="".""")
objDNSServer.Forwarders = arrForwarders
objDNSServer.Put_
Wscript.Echo "Successfully set default forwarders"


' This code sets the forwarders for a specific domain.
' ------ SCRIPT CONFIGURATION ------
strServer = "<ServerName>"   ' e.g., dns01
strNewZone = "<ZoneName>"     ' e.g., othercorp.com
arrMasterIPs = Array("<IP1>","<IP2>") ' replace <IPx> with IPs of master server
' ------ END CONFIGURATION ---------
on error resume next
set objDNS = GetObject("winMgmts:\\" & strServer & "\root\MicrosoftDNS")
set objDNSZone = objDNS.Get("MicrosoftDNS_Zone")
strNull = objDNSZone.CreateZone(strNewZone,3,false,"",arrMasterIPs)
if Err then
   WScript.Echo "Error occurred creating zone: " & Err.Description
else
   WScript.Echo "Domain forwarder created."
end if
```

Discussion

Name servers have long supported the notion of forwarders. The idea is that instead of forwarding all unresolved queries to the root Internet name servers, you'd forward those queries to a specific server or set of servers. This allows you to control the flow of name resolution.

Microsoft extended this capability in Windows Server 2003 to support conditional forwarding. With conditional forwarding, you can forward unresolved queries for specific domains to different name servers. The most common use of conditional forwarding is when you have two or more discontiguous namespaces. Consider the example in Figure 13-1. Here, both *rallencorp.com* and *othercorp.com* are owned by the same company. Normally, for name servers of *rallencorp.com* to resolve queries for *othercorp.com*, the queries would first have to be forwarded to the root Internet name servers. With conditional forwarding, you can specify that all requests for *othercorp.com* are to be sent to *othercorp.com* name servers and all other unresolved queries are to be sent to the Internet.

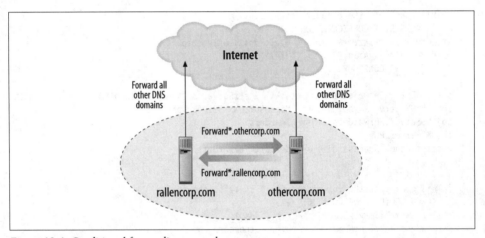

Figure 13-1. Conditional forwarding example

See Also

Recipe 13.8, MS KB 304491 (Conditional Forwarding in Windows Server 2003), and MS KB 811118 (Support WebCast: Microsoft Windows Server 2003 DNS: Stub Zones and Conditional Forwarding)

13.10 Configuring Zone Transfer

Problem

You want to enable zone transfers to specific secondary name servers.

Solution

Using a graphical user interface

1. Open the DNS snap-in (*dnsmgmt.msc*).

2. In the left pane, expand the server node and expand either **Forward Lookup Zone** or **Reverse Lookup Zone** depending on the type of zone you want to manage.

3. Right-click on the zone and select **Properties**.

4. Select the **Zone Transfers** tab.

5. Select either the option to restrict zone transfers to those servers listed on the **Name Servers** tab, or the option to restrict zone transfers to specific IP addresses, as desired. See the Discussion section for more on these two options.

Using a command-line interface

The following command enables zone transfers for the *test.local* zone and specifies they can only occur with servers that have NS records in the zone (i.e., servers listed within the Name Servers tab of the DNS snap-in):

```
> dnscmd <ServerName> /ZoneResetSecondaries test.local /SecureNs
```

The next command enables zone transfers for same zone, but specifies they can only occur with hosts whose IP addresses are 172.16.11.33 and 172.16.11.34:

```
> dnscmd <ServerName> /ZoneResetSecondaries test.local /SecureList 172.16.11.33
172.16.11.34
```

Using VBScript

```
' This code creates a name server (NS) record on a DNS server.

strDNSServer = "<servername>"
strContainer = "<containername>"
strOwner = "<ownername>"
intRecordClass = 1
intTTL = 600
strNSHost = "<nameservername>"
strComputer = "."

set objWMIService = GetObject _
    ("winmgmts:\\" & strComputer & "\root\MicrosoftDNS")
set objItem = objWMIService.Get("MicrosoftDNS_NSType")
errResult = objItem.CreateInstanceFromPropertyData _
    (strDNSServer, strContainer, strOwner, intRecordClass, intTTL, strNSHost)


' This code configures the allowed secondaries for zone transfer and notify

' XFR constants
const ZONE_SECSECURE_NO_SECURITY = 0
```

```
const ZONE_SECSECURE_NS_ONLY      = 1
const ZONE_SECSECURE_LIST_ONLY    = 2
const ZONE_SECSECURE_NO_XFR       = 3

' NOTIFY constants
const ZONE_NOTIFY_OFF             = 0
const ZONE_NOTIFY_ALL_SECONDARIES = 1
const ZONE_NOTIFY_LIST_ONLY       = 2

' ------ SCRIPT CONFIGURATION ------
strZone   = "<ZoneName>"    ' e.g., rallencorp.com
strServer = "<ServerName>"  ' e.g., dc1.rallencorp.com

' use one of the above XFR constants
intSecureSecondaries = ZONE_SECSECURE_LIST_ONLY
arrSecondaries = Array("1.1.1.2","1.1.1.3")

' use one of the above NOTIFY constants
intNotify = ZONE_NOTIFY_LIST_ONLY
arrNotify = Array("<IP1>","<IP2>")
' ------ END CONFIGURATION ---------

set objDNS = GetObject("winMgmts:\\" & strServer & "\root\MicrosoftDNS")
set objDNSServer = objDNS.Get("MicrosoftDNS_Server.Name="".""")
set objDNSZone = objDNS.Get("MicrosoftDNS_Zone.ContainerName=""" & _
                    strZone & """,DnsServerName=""" & _
                    objDNSServer.Name & """,Name=""" & strZone & """")
strNull = objDNSZone.ResetSecondaries(arrSecondaries,intSecureSecondaries, _
                                arrNotify,intNotify)
objDNSZone.Put_
WScript.Echo "Updated secondaries for zone transfer and notify"
```

Discussion

Your DNS implementation may require that you allow some zone transfers to occur,
but you want to restrict which hosts can initiate zone transfers with your name servers. Since allowing anyone to initiate a zone transfer with your server could provide
them with information for mapping out your network, it is critical that you limit
which hosts can pull zone transfers from your servers.

If you are using only Active Directory–integrated zones, the **Name Servers** tab will be
automatically populated with a list of all name servers authoritative for the selected
zone, and this is the recommended choice when you have a large network with many
name servers deployed. If any of your name servers are using standard zone files,
however, you will need to populate this tab manually for any secondary name servers you deploy.

Specifying a list of IP addresses for hosts that can initiate zone transfers may be more
secure since it is more specific, but this approach has the trade-off of adding the
additional management overhead of keeping track of the name servers' IP addresses
on your network, so you should only follow this approach if your network is small

and you have relatively few name servers deployed. Another disadvantage of this approach is that if you forget to add some name servers' IP addresses to your list, zone information stored on these servers could become stale, causing name resolution to fail for some of your clients. This could result in some of your users experiencing difficulties in accessing network resources.

Note that on Windows 2000 name servers, the default setting allows zone transfers with any host that requests them. This setting is inherently insecure as it allows attackers to use *nslookup* to display all resource records on your servers, so be sure to use the steps outlined in this recipe to change the setting on your servers to one of the two settings described here. Windows Server 2003 DNS is more secure by default because in the case of file-based zones, it is configured to allow zone transfers only with servers listed on the Name Servers tab of a zone. In the case of Active Directory–integrated zones, it is configured to disallow zone transfers entirely since they generally aren't needed in an Active Directory environment.

See Also

Recipe 13.4

13.11 Creating and Deleting Resource Records

Problem

You want to create or delete resource records.

Solution

Using a graphical user interface

1. Open the DNS snap-in (*dnsmgmt.msc*).
2. Connect to the DNS Server you want to modify. In the left pane, right-click on **DNS** and select **Connect to DNS Server**. Select **The following computer** and enter the target server name. Click **OK**.
3. If you want to add or delete a record in a forward zone, expand the **Forward Lookup Zone** folder. If you want to add or delete a record for a reverse zone, expand the **Reverse Lookup Zone** folder.

To create a resource record, do the following:

1. In the left pane, right-click the zone and select the option that corresponds to the record type you want to create—e.g., **New Host (A)**.
2. Fill in all required fields.
3. Click **OK**.

To delete a resource record, do the following:

1. In the left pane, click on the zone where the record is.
2. In the right pane, right-click on the record you want to delete and select **Delete**.
3. Click **Yes** to confirm.

Using a command-line interface

To add a resource record, use the following command:

```
> dnscmd <ServerName> /recordadd <ZoneName> <NodeName> <RecordType> <RRData>
```

The following example adds an A record in the *rallencorp.com* zone:

```
> dnscmd dc1 /recordadd rallencorp.com myhost01 A 19.25.52.25
```

To delete a resource record, use the following command:

```
> dnscmd <ServerName> /recorddelete <ZoneName> <NodeName> <RecordType> <RRData>
```

The following example deletes an A record in the *rallencorp.com* zone:

```
> dnscmd dns01 /recorddelete rallencorp.com myhost01 A 19.25.52.25
```

Using VBScript

```
' This code shows how to add an A record and PTR record using
' the DNS WMI Provider.

' This code must be executed directly on a DNS Server.

' ------ SCRIPT CONFIGURATION ------
strForwardRRAdd = "myhost01.rallencorp.com. IN A 19.25.52.25"
strReverseRRAdd = "25.52.25.19.in-addr.arpa IN PTR myhost01.rallencorp.com"
strForwardDomain = "rallencorp.com"
strReverseDomain = "25.19.in-addr.arpa."
' ------ END CONFIGURATION ---------

set objDNS = GetObject("winMgmts:root\MicrosoftDNS")
set objRR = objDNS.Get("MicrosoftDNS_ResourceRecord")
set objDNSServer = objDNS.Get("MicrosoftDNS_Server.Name=""."""")

' Create the A record
strNull = objRR.CreateInstanceFromTextRepresentation( _
                objDNSServer.Name, _
                strForwardDomain, _
                strForwardRRAdd, _
                objOutParam)
set objRR2 = objDNS.Get(objOutParam)
WScript.Echo "Created Record: " & objRR2.TextRepresentation

' Create the PTR record
strNull = objRR.CreateInstanceFromTextRepresentation( _
                objDNSServer.Name, _
                strReverseDomain, _
```

```
                            strReverseRRAdd, _
                            objOutParam)
    set objRR2 = objDNS.Get(objOutParam)
    WScript.Echo "Created Record: " & objRR2.TextRepresentation


    ' This code shows how to delete an A and PTR record for the record
    ' I created in the previous example.

    strHostName  = "myhost01.rallencorp.com."

    set objDNS = GetObject("winMgmts:root\MicrosoftDNS")
    set objDNSServer = objDNS.Get("MicrosoftDNS_Server.Name="".""")

    set objRRs = objDNS.ExecQuery(" select * " & _
                        " from MicrosoftDNS_ResourceRecord " & _
                        " where OwnerName = """ & strHostName & """" & _
                        " Or RecordData = """ & strHostName & """")
    if objRRs.Count < 1 then
       WScript.Echo "No matches found for " & strHostName
    else
       for each objRR in objRRs
          objRR.Delete_
          WScript.Echo "Deleted " & objRR.TextRepresentation
       next
    end if
```

Discussion

Using a graphical user interface

The DNS snap-in is good for creating a small number of records, but if you need to add or delete more than a couple of dozen, I recommend writing a batch file around *dnscmd* or preferably the DNS WMI Provider.

Using a command-line interface

Adding A, CNAME, and PTR resource records is pretty straightforward as far as the data you must enter, but other record types, such as SRV, require quite a bit more data. Run dnscmd /recordadd /? and dnscmd /recorddelete /? for the required parameters for each record type.

Using VBScript

In the first example, I created A and PTR records using the CreateInstanceFromTextRepresentation method, which is a MicrosoftDNS_ResourceRecord method that allows you to create resource records by passing in the textual version of the record. This is the textual representation of the A record used in the example:

```
myhost01.rallencorp.com IN A 19.25.52.25
```

The first parameter to this method is the DNS Server name, the second is the name of the domain to add the record to, the third is the resource record, and the last is an out parameter that returns a reference to the new resource record.

In the second example, I find all resource records that match a certain hostname and delete them. This is done by first using a WQL query to find all resource records where the OwnerName equals the target host name (this will match any A records) and where RecordData equals the target host name (this will match any PTR records). The Delete_ method is called on each matching record, removing them on the DNS Server.

See Also

MSDN: MicrosoftDNS_ResourceRecord

13.12 Querying Resource Records

Problem

You want to query resource records. You might want to do this if you need to find the IP address that is mapped to a particular host name or vice versa.

Solution

Using a graphical user interface

The DNS snap-in does not provide an interface for searching resource records.

Using a command-line interface

In the following command, replace <RecordType> with the type of resource record you want to find (e.g., A, CNAME, SRV) and <RecordName> with the name or IP address of the record to match.

```
> nslookup -type=<RecordType> <RecordName>
```

Using VBScript

```
' This code prints the resource records that match
' the specified name
' ------ SCRIPT CONFIGURATION ------
strQuery = "<RecordName>"
' ------ END CONFIGURATION ---------

set objDNS = GetObject("winMgmts:root\MicrosoftDNS")
set objDNSServer = objDNS.Get("MicrosoftDNS_Server.Name="".""")
set objRRs = objDNS.ExecQuery(" select * " & _
                    " from MicrosoftDNS_ResourceRecord" & _
                    " where  OwnerName = """ & strQuery & """" & _
```

```
                          " Or  DomainName = """ & strQuery & """" & _
                          " Or RecordData = """ & strQuery & """")
        if objRRs.Count < 1 then
           WScript.Echo "No matches found for " & strHostName & " of " _
                     & strRecordType & " type"
        else
           for each objRR in objRRs
              WScript.Echo objRR.TextRepresentation
           next
        end if
```

Discussion

Using a command-line interface

You can leave off the -type switch and the command will find any A, PTR, and CNAME records that match <RecordName>. You can also run *nslookup* from interactive mode, which you can enter by typing *nslookup* at a command prompt with no additional parameters.

Using VBScript

In the VBScript code, I used a WQL query to find all matching resource records. This is a good example of how powerful the DNS WMI Provider can be. The query finds any object of the MicrosoftDNS_ResourceRecord class that has an OwnerName, DomainName, or RecordData field equal to the <RecordName>. This is not the most efficient query if the server supports multiple large zones, so you may want restrict it to search for specific types of records by adding criteria to match RecordType = <Type>.

See Also

MSDN: MicrosoftDNS_ResourceRecord

13.13 Scavenging Old Resource Records

Problem

You want to scavenge old resource records. DNS scavenging is the process whereby resource records are automatically removed if they are not updated after a period of time. Typically, this applies only to resource records that were added via DDNS, but you can also scavenge manually added records (or static records). DNS scavenging is a recommended practice (although disabled by default) so that your DNS zones are automatically kept clean of stale resource records.

Solution

The following solutions show how to enable automatic scavenging on all Active Directory–integrated zones.

Using a graphical user interface

1. From the Administrative Tools, open the DNS snap-in (*dnsmgmt.msc*).

2. Connect to the DNS Server you want to modify. In the left pane, right-click on **DNS** and select **Connect to DNS Server**. Select **The following computer** and enter the target server name. Click **OK**.

3. Click on the server, right-click on it, and select **Set Aging/Scavenging for all zones**.

4. Check the box beside **Scavenge stale resource records**.

5. Configure the **No-Refresh** and **Refresh** intervals as necessary and click **OK**.

6. Check the box beside **Apply these settings to the existing Active Directory-integrated zones** and click **OK**.

7. Right-click on the server again and select **Properties**.

8. Select the **Advanced** tab.

9. Check the box beside **Enable automatic scavenging of stale resource records**.

10. Configure the scavenging period as required.

11. Click **OK**.

Using a command-line interface

The following commands configure the various scavenging parameters I describe later in the Discussion section:

```
> dnscmd <ServerName> /config /ScavengingInterval <ScavengingMinutes>
> dnscmd <ServerName> /config /DefaultAgingState 1
> dnscmd <ServerName> /config /DefaultNoRefreshInterval <NoRefreshMinutes>
> dnscmd <ServerName> /config /DefaultRefreshInterval <RefreshMinutes>
```

The following command enables aging of records for a specific zone (so old records will eventually be scavenged):

```
> dnscmd <ServerName> /config <ZoneName> /aging 1
```

The following command enables aging for all primary zones on a server:

```
> dnscmd <ServerName> /config ..AllZones /aging 1
```

Using VBScript

```
' This code enables scavenging for all Active Directory-integrated zones
' ------ SCRIPT CONFIGURATION ------
strServer = "<ServerName>"
intScavengingInterval = <ScavengingMinutes>
intNoRefreshInterval  = <NoRefreshMinutes>
intRefreshInterval    = <RefreshMinutes>
' ------ END CONFIGURATION ---------
set objDNS = GetObject("winMgmts:\\" & strServer & "\root\MicrosoftDNS")
set objDNSServer = objDNS.Get("MicrosoftDNS_Server.Name="".""")
```

```
objDNSServer.ScavengingInterval        = intScavengingInterval
objDNSServer.DefaultNoRefreshInterval   = intNoRefreshInterval
objDNSServer.DefaultRefreshInterval     = intRefreshInterval
objDNSServer.DefaultAgingState          = TRUE
objDNSServer.Put_
WScript.Echo "Configured server scavenging settings"

set objZones = objDNS.ExecQuery("Select * from MicrosoftDNS_Zone " & _
                        "Where DnsServerName = '" & _
                            objDNSServer.Name & "'" & _
                        " And DsIntegrated = TRUE")
WScript.Echo "Configuring Active Directory-integrated zones: "
for each objZone in objZones
    WScript.Echo " " & objZone.Name & " HERE: " & objZone.Aging
    objZone.Aging = 1
    objZone.Put_
next
```

Discussion

There are four settings you must be aware of before enabling scavenging. Use caution when enabling scavenging because an incorrect configuration could lead to resource records getting deleted by mistake.

The first setting you need to configure is the *scavenging interval*. This is the interval in which the DNS Server kicks off the scavenging process. It is disabled by default so that scavenging does not take place unless you enable this setting. When enabled, the default value is 168 hours (7 days).

The second setting is the *default aging state* for new zones; if you want all new zones to be configured for scavenging, set this to 1.

The next two settings control how records get scavenged. The *no refresh interval* determines how long before a dynamically updated record can be updated again. This setting is necessary to reduce how often a DNS Server has to update its timestamp of the resource record. The default value is 168 hours (7 days). That means that after a resource record has been dynamically updated, the server will not accept another dynamic update for the same record for 7 days. If the IP address or some other data for the record changes sooner than 7 days, the server will process the update.

The *refresh interval* setting is the amount of time after the no refresh interval that a client has to update its record before it is considered old or stale. The default value for this setting is also 168 hours (7 days).

If you use the default values, the combination of the no refresh interval and refresh interval would mean that a dynamically updated record would not be considered stale for up to 14 days after its last update. In actuality, it could be up to 21 days before the record gets deleted if the record became stale right after the last scavenge process completed: 7 days (no refresh) + 7 days (refresh) + up to 7 days (scavenge process).

13.14 Clearing the DNS Cache

Problem

You want to clear the DNS cache. The DNS cache contains resource records that are cached for a period of time in memory so that repeated requests for the same record can be returned quickly. There are two types of DNS cache. One pertains to the resolver on any Windows client (servers and workstations), and the other to the cache used by DNS Server. Clearing the cache is useful after you've made a change to DNS and you want the client resolver or DNS Server not to use the previously cached entry.

Solution

To flush the client resolver cache, use the following command:

```
> ipconfig /flushdns
```

To flush the DNS Server cache, use any of the following solutions:

Using a graphical user interface

1. From the Administrative Tools, open the DNS snap-in (*dnsmgmt.msc*).
2. Connect to the DNS Server you want to modify. In the left pane, right-click on **DNS** and select **Connect to DNS Server**. Select **The following computer** and enter the target server name. Click **OK**.
3. Right-click on the server and select **Clear Cache**.

Using a command-line interface

The following command clears the server cache:

```
> dnscmd <ServerName> /clearcache
```

Using VBScript

```
' This code clears the DNS Server cache.
' ------ SCRIPT CONFIGURATION ------
strServer = "<ServerName>"    ' e.g., dc1.rallencorp.com
' ------ END CONFIGURATION ---------

set objDNS = GetObject("winmgmts:\\" & strServer & "\root\MicrosoftDNS")
set objDNSServer = objDNS.Get("MicrosoftDNS_Server.Name="".""")
set objDNSCache  = objDNS.Get("MicrosoftDNS_Cache.ContainerName=""..Cache""" & _
                     ",DnsServerName=""" & objDNSServer.Name & _
                     """,Name=""..Cache""")
```

```
objDNSCache.ClearCache
WScript.Echo "Cleared server cache"
```

Discussion

The client resolver cache is populated whenever you perform a lookup on a workstation or server: for example, with the *nslookup* command. You can view this cache by running `ipconfig /displaydns` from a command line. This cache is maintained by the DNS Client service (*dnscache*), so another way of flushing the cache is to restart that service.

The second type of cache is only for DNS Servers. It contains a copy of records the DNS Server has sent to clients when resolving queries. You can view this cache by browsing the **Cached Lookups** folder for a server in the DNS snap-in. This folder is not shown by default, so you'll need to select **Advanced** from the **View** menu.

With both the client and server cache, the records are removed from the cache after the record's Time To Live (TTL) value expires. The TTL is used to age records so that clients and servers have to rerequest them at a later point and receive any changes that may have been made.

13.15 Enabling DNS Server Debug Logging

Problem

You want to enable DNS debug logging to troubleshoot issues related to DNS queries or updates.

Solution

Using a graphical user interface

1. From the Administrative Tools, open the DNS snap-in (*dnsmgmt.msc*).
2. Connect to the DNS Server you want to modify. In the left pane, right-click on **DNS** and select **Connect to DNS Server**. Select **The following computer** and enter the target server name. Click **OK**.
3. Right-click on the server and select **Properties**.
4. Click on the **Debug Logging** tab (or the **Logging** tab for Windows 2000).
5. Select what you want to log and the location of the log file (the log file location is hardcoded to *%systemroot%\system32\dns\dns.log* on Windows 2000).
6. Click **OK**.

Using a command-line interface

Use the following four commands to enable debug logging. For the log level add together the event codes you want logged and specify the result in hex. The available event codes are listed in Table 13-2.

```
> dnscmd <ServerName> /Config /LogLevel <EventFlagSumInHex>
```

Table 13-2. DNS debug logging event codes

Hexadecimal value	Decimal value	Descriptions
0x0	0	No logging. (This is the default)
0x1	1	Queries transactions
0x10	16	Notifications transactions
0x20	32	Updates transactions
0xFE	254	Non-queries transactions
0x100	256	Question packets
0x200	512	Answer packets
0x1000	4096	Send packets
0x2000	8192	Receive packets
0x4000	16384	UDP packets
0x8000	32768	TCP packets
0xFFFF	65535	All packets
0x10000	65536	AD write transactions
0x20000	131072	AD update transactions
0x1000000	16777216	Full packets
0x80000000	2147483648	Write-through transactions

Use the following command to specify the location of the log file:

```
> dnscmd <ServerName> /Config /LogFilePath <DirectoryAndFilePath>
```

Use the following command to log only entries that pertain to certain IP addresses:

```
> dnscmd <ServerName> /Config /LogIPFilterList <IPAddress1>[,<IPAddress2>...]
```

Use the following command to specify the maximum log file size:

```
> dnscmd <ServerName> /Config /LogFileMaxSize <NumberOfBytesInHex>
```

Use the following command to disable debug logging:

```
> dnscmd <ServerName> /Config /LogLevel 0
```

Using VBScript

```
' This code enables DNS debug logging.
' ------ SCRIPT CONFIGURATION ------
strServer    = "<ServerName>"              ' e.g., dc1
' The log level must be in decimal, not hex like dnscmd
```

```
intLogLevel   = <EventFlagSumInDecimal>      ' e.g., 65535
arrFilterList = Array("<IPAddress1>")        ' e.g., 192.168.1.12
strFilePath   = <DirectoryAndFilePath>       ' e.g., c:\dnslog.txt
intFileSize   = <NumberOfBytesInDecimal>     ' e.g., 50000000
' ------ END CONFIGURATION ---------

set objDNS = GetObject("winMgmts:\\" & strServer & "\root\MicrosoftDNS")
set objDNSServer = objDNS.Get("MicrosoftDNS_Server.Name="".""")
objDNSServer.LogLevel = intLogLevel
objDNSServer.LogIPFilterList = arrFilterList
objDNSServer.LogFilePath = strFilePath
objDNSServer.LogFileMaxSize = intFileSize
objDNSServer.Put_
WScript.Echo "Enabled DNS Debug Logging on " & strServer

' To disable debug logging, set the intLogLevel variable to 0
```

Discussion

With the DNS Server debug log, you can record all DNS operations received and initiated by the server, including queries, updates, zone transfers, etc. If you need to troubleshoot a particular host, you can use the LogIPFilterList setting in *dnscmd* or the WMI DNS Provider to restrict the log to operations performed only for or by that host.

The most important debug log setting is the log level. With the DNS snap-in, you can select from a list of available options. With Windows Server 2003, the DNS snap-in provides an intuitive interface for selecting the required options. On Windows 2000, you are presented with a list of check boxes and you have to figure out which ones need to be used in conjunction with one another. You have a similar issue with CLI and VBScript solutions, where you need to determine what log level you want to set.

Table 13-2 contains all of the event codes with their hexadecimal and decimal values.

DNS debug logging can come in handy if you want to look at the dynamic update requests a particular DNS Server is processing. For example, if a client or DHCP server is attempting to dynamically register records, you can enable the Update Transactions log category on the DNS Server you think should be processing the updates. If you don't see any update transactions, that can indicate another server is processing the dynamic update requests.

 Transactions are not immediately written to the debug log file as they occur. They are buffered and written to the file after a certain number of requests are processed.

See Also

MSDN: MicrosoftDNS_Server

13.16 Viewing DNS Server Utilization Statistics

Problem

You want to view DNS Server utilization statistics.

Solution

Using a graphical user interface

1. From the Administrative Tools, open the Performance Monitor.
2. Click on **System Monitor** in the left pane.
3. In the right pane, click the + button. This will bring up the page to add counters.
4. Under **Select counters from computer**, enter the name of the DNS Server you want to target.
5. Select the **DNS** performance object.
6. Select the counters you want to add and click the **Add** button.
7. Click **Close**.

Using a command-line interface

Use the following command to display utilization statistics:

```
> dnscmd <ServerName> /statistics
```

Using VBScript

```
' This code displays all statistics for the specified DNS Server
' ------ SCRIPT CONFIGURATION ------
strServer = "<ServerName>"    ' e.g., dc1.rallencorp.com
' ------ END CONFIGURATION ---------
set objDNS = GetObject("winmgmts:\\" & strServer & "\root\MicrosoftDNS")
set objDNSServer = objDNS.Get("MicrosoftDNS_Server.Name="".""")
set objStats = objDNS.ExecQuery("Select * from MicrosoftDNS_Statistic ")
for each objStat in objStats
    WScript.Echo " " & objStat.Name & " : " & objStat.Value
next
```

Discussion

DNS Server keeps track of dozens of performance metrics. These metrics include the number of queries, updates, transfers, directory reads, and directory writes processed by the server. If you can pump these metrics into an enterprise management system, you can track DNS usage and growth over time.

These statistics can also be useful to troubleshoot load-related issues. If you suspect a DNS Server is being overwhelmed with DNS update requests, you can look at the

Dynamic Update Received/sec counter and see if it is processing an unusually high number of updates.

Using a command-line interface

Each statistics category has an associated number (i.e., statid). You can obtain a subset of the statistics by providing a statid after the /statistics option. For a complete list of categories and their statid, run the following command:

```
> dnscmd /statistics /?
```

Here is an example of viewing the Query (statid = 2) and Query2 (statid = 4) statistics:

```
> dnscmd /statistics 6
DNS Server . statistics:

Queries and Responses:
----------------------
Total:
     Queries Received =       14902
     Responses Sent   =       12900
UDP:
     Queries Recvd    =       14718
     Responses Sent   =       12716
     Queries Sent     =       23762
     Responses Recvd  =           0
TCP:
     Client Connects  =         184
     Queries Recvd    =         184
     Responses Sent   =         184
     Queries Sent     =           0
     Responses Recvd  =           0


Queries:
--------
Total        =     14902
    Notify   =         0
    Update   =      2207
    TKeyNego =       184
    Standard =     12511
       A     =      1286
       NS    =        29
       SOA   =      2263
       MX    =         0
       PTR   =         1
       SRV   =      8909
       ALL   =         0
       IXFR  =         0
       AXFR  =         0
       OTHER =        23

Command completed successfully.
```

Using VBScript

You can obtain a subset of statistics by adding a where clause to the WQL query. The following query would match only counters that start with **Records**:

```
select * from MicrosoftDNS_Statistic where Name like 'Records%'
```

See Also

MSDN: MicrosoftDNS_Statistic

13.17 Preventing Cache Pollution on DNS Servers

Problem

You want to prevent the DNS cache on a name server from becoming polluted with false information.

Solution

Using a graphical user interface

1. Open the DNS snap-in and connect to the name server you want to manage.
2. Right-click on the name server node and select **Properties**.
3. Select the **Advanced** tab.
4. Select the checkbox labeled **Secure against cache pollution**.
5. Click **OK**.

Using a command-line interface

The following command adds the value SecureResponses to the HKLM\SYSTEM\ CurrentControlSet\Services\DNS\Parameters registry key and assigns it a value of 1:

```
> reg /add HKLM\SYSTEM\CurrentControlSet\Services\DNS\Parameters /v SecureResponses
/t REG_DWORD /d 1
```

Using VBScript

You can provide the same function with the following code:

```
set objWSHShell = CreateObject("WScript.Shell")
strRegKey = "HKLM\SYSTEM\CurrentControlSet\Services\DNS\Parameters"
objWSHShell.RegWrite regkey & "SecureResponses", 1
```

One additional method of doing something similar with VBScript is to clear the DNS cache of resource records. The following code utilizes WMI to clear the DNS cache on the current computer:

```
strComputer = "."
set objWMI = GetObject("winmgmts:\\" & strComputer & "\root\MicrosoftDNS")
```

```
set colItems = objWMI.ExecQuery("Select * From MicrosoftDNS_Cache")
for each objItem in colItems
    objItem.ClearCache( )
next
```

Discussion

The DNS Server cache is used to temporarily store the result of DNS queries from clients so that if the same query is received within a short time interval, the server can respond with the cached information instead of performing a lookup. This results in increased performance and reduced processor load. If attackers can inject false information into the DNS cache or modify existing information within the cache, they can redirect DNS queries from legitimate clients to a rogue name server impersonating as a legitimate server.

Enabling the cache pollution prevention setting affects how a name server processes the results of a recursive query issued against another name server. For example, if the local server queries the remote server for a host in one namespace (e.g., testone.com) and the response from the second server includes a referral to a host in a different namespace (e.g., testtwo.com), the local server discards the response and does not cache it in its name server cache. Note that this setting is enabled by default in Windows 2000 and Windows Server 2003, so you only need to perform this task if you have previously disabled the setting.

The tradeoff with enabling this setting is that sometimes valid responses end up being dropped; for example, if the company owning the second namespace provides DNS services to the company owning the first namespace (for example, if an ISP owned testtwo.com and hosts services for testone.com). This is not a huge issue, however, since it just means that such responses aren't cached; it doesn't mean your name server can't perform a recursive lookup against the other server each time a query is received. The only impact of not being able to cache such responses is the small delay incurred by not being able to retrieve successful lookups from the local server's cache.

See Also

MS KB 241352 (How to Prevent DNS Cache Pollution)

13.18 Preventing Windows Clients from Attempting Dynamic Updates

Problem

You've disabled dynamic updates entirely on your name servers for security reasons and want to ensure that clients don't waste processing cycles by sending dynamic updates to your servers.

Solution

Using a graphical user interface

To disable dynamic updates for a specific interface such as Local Area Connection, do the following:

1. For Windows 2000, click **Start** → **Settings** → **Network and Dialup Connections**. For Windows XP click **Start** → **Control Panel** → **Network Connections**.
2. Double-click on **Local Area Connection** and click **Properties**.
3. Double-click on **Internet Protocol (TCP/IP)** and click **Advanced**.
4. Select the **DNS** tab and clear the checkbox labeled **Register this connection's address in DNS**.

To disable dynamic updates globally for all interfaces on a client, do the following:

1. Open Registry Editor (*regedit.exe*).
2. In the left pane, navigate to the following key: `HKLM\CurrentControlSet\Services\Tcpip\Parameters`.
3. From the menu, select **Edit** → **New** → **DWORD Value**, type `DisableDynamicUpdate`, and click **OK**.
4. Double-click on **DisableDynamicUpdate** and assign it a value of 1.
5. Close Registry Editor and reboot the client computer.

On Windows Server 2003, you can also use Group Policy to disable dynamic updates on Windows XP and 2003 clients:

1. Open the Active Directory Users and Computers (ADUC) snap-in.
2. In the left pane, right-click on the domain or OU that contains the computer objects for your client computers and select **Properties**.
3. Select the **Group Policy** tab, select the appropriate Group Policy Object (GPO), and click **Edit**.
4. In the left pane of the Group Policy Editor, select **Computer Configuration** → **Administrative Templates** → **Network** → **DNS Client**.
5. Double-click on the policy named **Dynamic Update**.
6. Change the policy setting to **Disabled**.

Using a command-line interface

The following command disables dynamic updates on a client configured with a static IP address and sets the name server address to 10.0.0.1:

```
> netsh interface ip set dns "Local Area Connection" static 10.0.0.1 register=none
```

To disable dynamic updates on a client machine that uses DHCP to acquire an IP address, use the following command:

```
> netsh interface ip set dns "Local Area Connection" dhcp register=none
```

And the following command globally disables dynamic updates for all interfaces on the client:

```
> reg /add HKLM\SYSTEM\CurrentControlSet\Services\Tcpip\Parameters /v
DisableDynamicUpdates /t REG_DWORD /d 1
```

Reboot the system to make this change take effect.

Using VBScript

The following VBScript automates the same registry change as outlined in the previous *reg* command:

```
set objWSHShell = CreateObject("WScript.Shell")
strRegKey = "HKLM\SYSTEM\CurrentControlSet\Services\Tcpip\Parameters\"
objWSHShell.RegWrite strRegKey & "DisableDynamicUpdates", 1
```

Discussion

Disabling dynamic updates on clients will prevent them from attempting to register their A and PTR records with the name server. Note that when you set the DisableDynamicUpdates registry value to 1 on the client, the checkbox labeled "Register this connection's addresses in DNS," located on the DNS tab of the TCP/IP Advanced Properties page for each connection, is unaffected. If you later change your mind and want your client to attempt dynamic updates, change the registry value to 0 and reboot your machine.

See Also

MS KB 246804 (How to enable or disable dynamic DNS registrations in Windows 2000 and in Windows Server 2003) and MS KB 294785 (New Group Policies for DNS in Windows Server 2003)

13.19 Script: DNS Server Configuration Checker

Configuring a large number of DNS Servers can be a chore. And unless you have a script that routinely checks the configuration on all of your DNS Servers, it's very likely that over time those servers will not have identical configurations. One administrator may make a change on one server and not another. If the servers don't have identical configurations, when problems pop up you may end up spending a lot of time troubleshooting false negatives because of the discrepancies.

Using the WMI DNS Provider, we can write a script that checks the configuration of a number of servers and updates them as necessary. To perform the configuration checking, we'll store each setting in a VBScript Dictionary object. Another option would be to store the settings in a text file and read them into a Dictionary object when the script starts up. The script iterates over a list of servers, checks the settings on each server, and modifies settings as necessary.

Here is the script's code:

```
option explicit
on error resume next

Dim arrServers
Dim strUsername, strPassword
Dim dicDNSConfig

' Array of DNS Servers to check
arrServers = Array("dns01.rallencorp.com","dns02.rallencorp.com")

' User and password that can modify the config on the DNS Servers
strUsername = "dnsadmin"
strPassword = "dnspwd"

' This dictionary object will contain the key value pairs for all
' the settings that you want to check and configure on the DNS Servers.
Set dicDNSConfig = CreateObject("Scripting.Dictionary")
dicDNSConfig.Add "AllowUpdate",             1
dicDNSConfig.Add "LooseWildCarding",        TRUE
dicDNSConfig.Add "MaxCacheTTL",             900
dicDNSConfig.Add "MaxNegativeCacheTTL",     60
dicDNSConfig.Add "EventLogLevel",           0
dicDNSConfig.Add "StrictFileParsing",       TRUE
dicDNSConfig.Add "DisableAutoReverseZones", TRUE

Dim arrDNSConfigKeys
arrDNSConfigKeys = dicDNSConfig.keys

Dim objLocator
Set objLocator = CreateObject("WbemScripting.SWbemLocator")

Dim x, y, boolRestart
For x = LBound(arrServers) to UBound(arrServers)
   boolRestart = False

   WScript.echo arrServers(x)

   Dim objDNS, objDNSServer
   Set objDNS = objLocator.ConnectServer(arrServers(x), _
                                  "root\MicrosoftDNS", _
                                  strUserName, strPassword)
   set objDNSServer = objDNS.Get("MicrosoftDNS_Server.Name="".""")

   for y = 0 To dicDNSConfig.Count - 1
      Dim strKey
      strKey = arrDNSConfigKeys(y)
```

```
        WScript.Echo "  Checking " & strKey
        if dicDNSConfig.Item(strKey) <> objDNSServer.Properties_.Item(strKey) then
            objDNSServer.Properties_.Item(strKey).value = dicDNSConfig(strKey)
            objDNSServer.Put_
            boolRestart = TRUE
            if Err Then
                WScript.Echo "    Error setting " & strKey & " : " & _
                             Err.Description
                Wscript.Quit
            else
                WScript.Echo "    " & strKey & " updated"
            end if
        end if
    Next

    if boolRestart then
        objDNSServer.StopService
        if Err Then
            WScript.Echo "StopService failed: " & Err.Description
            Wscript.Quit
        end if

        objDNSServer.StartService
        if Err Then
            WScript.Echo "StartService failed: " & Err.Description
            Wscript.Quit
        end if
        WScript.Echo "Restarted"
    end if

    WScript.Echo ""
next
```

Besides the use of the Dictionary object, most of the script is a combination of several recipes in this chapter. I added a server array so that you can check multiple servers at once. For each server, the script simply checks each key in the Dictionary object to see if its value matches the key on the name server. If not, it modifies the server and commits the change via Put_. After it's done looping through all the settings, it restarts the DNS Server service if a change has been made to its configuration. It then proceeds to the next server.

One enhancement to automate the process even more would be to dynamically query the list of name servers instead of hardcoding them in an array. You would need to look up the NS records for one or more zones for which your name servers are authoritative. As long as an NS record is added for each new name server, the script would automatically discover new name servers on subsequent runs (kind of like a stub zone).

CHAPTER 14

DHCP Server

14.0 Introduction

The Dynamic Host Configuration Protocol (DHCP) is prevalent within most organizations. If you have more than three or four client computers, statically configuring IP addresses and network settings can be a support burden. DHCP makes the job of assigning IP addresses much easier because instead of manually configuring each computer on your network, DHCP does it for you. Dynamically assigning IP addresses and reclaiming them when they are no longer being used also makes more efficient use of your address space.

DHCP is a simple yet effective protocol that allows a computer booting up with no prior TCP/IP network configuration to obtain an IP address, called a *lease*, and various network settings, called *options*, such as the default router, DNS servers, and default domain name. For details on how DHCP works, see RFC 2131: *http://www.ietf.org/rfc/rfc2131.txt*.

The Microsoft DHCP Server is one of the most popular DHCP servers available. It's included with the Windows Server operating system and is simple to configure and maintain. In this chapter, I'll cover several recipes that walk you through the setup and configuration of DHCP Server.

Using a Graphical User Interface

DHCP Server comes with the DHCP MMC snap-in (*dhcpmgmt.msc*) that can be used to configure and manage scopes, superscopes, leases, reservations, and options. This is the graphical tool I use for most recipes in this chapter.

Using a Command-Line Interface

The *netsh* tool allows you to configure from the command line just about everything you can control with the DHCP snap-in, plus some additional advanced settings that you can't even access with the snap-in. The *netsh* tool can be run in a variety of different ways. There is an interactive mode that you get to by simply typing **netsh** at a command line. If it is a DHCP Server, type **dhcp server** and press the Enter key to configure the local computer. *Netsh* will return an error if the local computer doesn't have DHCP Server running. Alternatively, you can type **dhcp server \\<ServerName>** to configure a remote DHCP Server. Type **list** and press the Enter key to get a list of all available commands you can run from within a given mode.

Netsh supports a command-line mode that lets you run a single command and return to the command prompt. Instead of typing **netsh** and pressing Enter, type the full path of the command. For example:

```
> netsh dhcp server dump
```

Finally, *netsh* supports a batch mode that lets you run multiple *netsh* commands at a time. Simply write each command to a text file. Then run the following command:

```
> netsh exec <Filename>
```

where `<Filename>` is the path to the file containing the commands.

The only other command-line tools I cover in this chapter are *dhcploc* and *sysocmgr*. *dhcploc* is useful for finding all the DHCP Servers on a given subnet. You can find it in the Windows 2000 Resource Kit Supplement 1 or in the Windows Server 2003 Support Tools. See Recipe 14.18 for more information. I use *sysocmgr* in Recipe 14.1 to install DHCP Server and it can be found in *%systemroot%/system32*.

Using VBScript

Both the graphical and command-line tools for managing DHCP Server are robust and flexible. Unfortunately, Microsoft has no corresponding programmatic interfaces for managing DHCP Server from scripts. There are no WSH or WMI APIs for DHCP Server. Microsoft did throw its customers a bone by providing a DLL called *dhcpobjs.dll* in the Windows 2000 Resource Kit. It provides an interface that scripts can use to manage various aspects of DHCP Server, but it has a few problems. It isn't truly supported by Microsoft since it is part of a Resource Kit. This wouldn't be a huge issue, but it turns out that *dhcpobjs* is pretty buggy; especially when dealing with a large number of scopes and leases. There are numerous threads in the Microsoft newsgroups about people running into problems when using *dhcpobjs*. So if you use it, understand that it isn't the most stable interface. It is also poorly documented.

The only other option is to call out to the *netsh* command from within scripts. Programming purists will hate the thought of doing this, but if you want to automate the configuration and maintenance of your DHCP Servers, this is really your only option. You can use the Run method I've used numerous times in this book to run *netsh*. The following code snippet shows how to use Run to set the audit log location:

```
strServer = "\\dhcp01"  ' set this to "" to target the local computer
strCommand = "netsh dhcp server " & strServer & " set auditlog d:\dhcp\audit"

set objWshShell = WScript.CreateObject("WScript.Shell")
intRC = objWshShell.Run(strCommand, 0, TRUE)
if intRC <> 0 then
   WScript.Echo "Error returned from running the command: " & intRC
else
   WScript.Echo "Command executed successfully"
end if
```

The main issue with the Run method is you don't have access to standard error or standard out to capture any output generated by the command. If you are going to use *netsh* extensively in scripts, you may want to use the Exec method instead, which has options for accessing standard out and standard error. The following code performs the same function as the previous code, except it prints everything sent to standard out and, if an error occurs, everything sent to standard error:

```
strServer = ""
strCommand = "netsh dhcp server " & strServer & " set auditlog d:\dhcp\audit"

WScript.Echo "Running command: " & strCommand
WScript.Echo
set objShell = CreateObject("Wscript.Shell")
set objProc  = objShell.Exec(strCommand)

Do
   WScript.Sleep 100
Loop Until objProc.Status <> 0

if objProc.ExitCode <> 0 then
   WScript.Echo "EXIT CODE: " & objProc.ExitCode
   WScript.Echo "ERROR: " & objProc.StdErr.ReadAll
end if

WScript.Echo "OUTPUT: " & objProc.StdOut.ReadAll
```

With Exec, it is a good idea to check the Status property to ensure the command completed. The script uses this feature to test for command completion and if it hasn't completed, the script sleeps for 100 milliseconds and check again. It then looks at the ExitCode. A nonzero exit code indicates an error and if that occurs, I print the code and the text sent to standard error. Lastly, I print the output from standard out.

 I don't include scripting examples using *netsh* in this chapter, but they are available on my web site: *http://www.rallenhome.com/books/*.

14.1 Installing DHCP Server

Problem

You want to install the DHCP Server service.

Solution

Using a graphical user interface

1. From the Control Panel, open the Add or Remove Programs applet.
2. Click **Add/Remove Windows Components**.
3. Double-click **Network Services**.
4. Check the box beside **Dynamic Host Configuration Protocol (DHCP)**.
5. Click **OK**.
6. Click **Next**.
7. Click **Finish**.

 You can also install DHCP Server from the Manage Your Server wizard.

Using a command-line interface

First, create a file using a text editor such as Notepad with the following contents:

```
[netoptionalcomponents]
dhcpserver=1
```

Next, use the *sysocmgr.exe* utility with the following parameters (assuming the file you just created is named *c:\dhcp_install.txt*):

```
> sysocmgr /i:%windir%\inf\sysoc.inf /u:c:\dhcp_install.txt
```

Using VBScript

Unfortunately, there aren't any scripting APIs for installing the DHCP Server. One option would be to run the *sysocmgr* command from within a script.

Discussion

The DHCP Server service is an optional Windows Component, so you can install it using the Add or Remove Programs applet in the Control Panel. There are no configuration options when you install the DHCP Server, so installation is a breeze. After you've installed the service, you'll need to authorize the server, if you have an Active Directory environment, as described in Recipe 14.2.

If the server you installed DHCP on is multihomed (i.e., has multiple active network adapters), you'll want to make sure the correct network adapters are enabled for use by the DHCP Server. You can enable or disable adapters for use by DHCP Server by doing the following:

1. Open the DHCP snap-in.
2. In the left pane, click on the server node.
3. From the menu, select **Action → Properties**.
4. Select the **Advanced** tab.
5. Click the **Bindings** button.
6. Make sure the interfaces where the DHCP Server should respond are checked.
7. Click **OK** until all dialog boxes are closed.

 DHCP-enabled interfaces (from a client perspective) will not show up in the list of available interfaces; the DHCP Server will use only interfaces that have statically assigned IP addresses.

See Also

Recipes 2.4 and 14.2

14.2   Authorizing a DHCP Server

Problem

You want to permit (i.e., authorize) a DHCP Server to process DHCP requests from clients. This is necessary only if the DHCP Server is a member of an Active Directory domain.

Solution

Using a graphical user interface

 Windows 2000 DHCP Servers cannot be authorized with the Windows Server 2003 version of the DHCP snap-in unless the DHCP Server has Service Pack 2 or higher installed.

1. Open the DHCP snap-in.
2. In the left pane, right-click on **DHCP** and select **Add Server**.
3. Type in the name of the DHCP Server you want to target and click **OK**.
4. Click on the server entry in the left pane.
5. Right-click on the server and select **Authorize**.

If the DHCP Server is not a member of an Active Directory domain, you will not see the **Authorize** option.

Using a command-line interface

The following command authorizes a DHCP Server in Active Directory:

```
> netsh dhcp add server <DHCPServerName> <DHCPServerIP>
```

This example shows how to authorize the DHCP Server named dhcp01.rallen-corp.com with IP 192.168.191.15:

```
> netsh dhcp add server dhcp01.rallencorp.com 192.168.191.15
```

Using VBScript

See Recipe 14.0 for more information on how to run the *netsh* command from within a script. The following script prints out the list of authorized DHCP Servers in Active Directory:

```
' ------ SCRIPT CONFIGURATION ------
strForestRootDN = "<ForestRootDN>"  ' e.g., dc=rallencorp,dc=com
' ------ END CONFIGURATION ---------
set objCont = GetObject("LDAP://CN=DhcpRoot,CN=NetServices,CN=Services," & _
                        "CN=Configuration," & strForestRootDN)
colDHCPServers = objCont.GetEx("dhcpServers")
for each strDHCPServer in colDHCPServers
   Wscript.Echo strDHCPServer
next
```

Discussion

Windows 2000 and Windows Server 2003–based DHCP servers that belong to an Active Directory domain must be authorized before they can give out leases to clients. This feature helps reduce the danger of a rogue Windows 2000 or Windows Server 2003 DHCP Server that an end-user sets up, perhaps unintentionally. A rogue DHCP Server can provide incorrect lease information or deny lease requests altogether, ultimately causing a denial of service for clients on your network.

If the DHCP Server service is enabled on a domain controller, it is automatically authorized. A DHCP Server that is a member server of an Active Directory domain performs a query in Active Directory to determine whether it is authorized. If it is, it will respond to DHCP requests; if not, it will not respond to requests.

A standalone DHCP server that is not a member of an Active Directory domain sends out a DHCPINFORM message when it first initializes. If an authorized DHCP Server responds to the message, the standalone server will not respond to any further DHCP requests. If it does not receive a response from a DHCP Server, it will respond to client requests and give out leases.

DHCP servers are represented in Active Directory as objects of the dhcpClass class, which can be found in the *cn=NetServices,cn=Services,cn=Configuratation,<ForestRootDN>* container. The relative distinguished name of these objects is the DHCP Server's IP address. There is also an object in the same container named cn=dhcpRoot, which is created after the first DHCP Server is authorized. It has an attribute named dhcpServers that contains all authorized servers. I enumerated this attribute in the VBScript solution to display all authorized servers.

By default, only members of the Enterprise Admins group can authorize DHCP Servers. You, however, can delegate the rights to authorize a DHCP Server. Do the following to delegate the necessary permissions to a group called DHCP Admins:

1. Open ADSI Edit from the Support Tools while logged on as a member of the Enterprise Admins group.

2. In the left pane, expand the **Configuration Container** → **CN=Configuration** → **CN=Services** → **CN=NetServices**.

3. Right-click on **CN=NetServices** and select **Properties**.

4. Select the **Security** tab.

5. Click the **Advanced** button.

6. Click the **Add** button.

7. Use the object picker to select the DHCP Admins group.

8. Check the boxes under **Allow** for **Create dHCPClass objects** and **Delete dHCP-Class objects**.

9. Click **OK** until all dialog boxes are closed.

10. Back in the left pane of ADSI Edit, right-click on **CN=dhcpRoot** (if you've previously authorized DHCP Servers) and select **Properties**.

11. Select the **Security** tab.

12. Click the **Advanced** button.

13. Click the **Add** button.

14. Use the object picker to select the DHCP Admins group.

15. Check the boxes under **Allow** for **Write**.

16. Click **OK** until all dialog boxes are closed.

Using a graphical user interface

You can quickly determine whether a DHCP Server has been authorized by looking at its server node in the left pane of the DHCP snap-in. If the icon has a little red flag, that means it isn't authorized, if it is green, then it is authorized.

Using a command-line interface

To see the list of authorized servers using the command line, run the following command:

```
> netsh dhcp show server
```

See Also

MS KB 279908 (Unexpected Results in the DHCP Service Snap-In After Using NETSH to Authorize DHCP), MS KB 300429 (HOW TO: Install and Configure a DHCP Server in an Active Directory Domain in Windows 2000), and MS KB 303351 (How to Use Netsh.exe to Authorize, Unauthorize, and List DHCP Servers in Active Directory), MS KB 306925 (Cannot Authorize New DHCP Server in Active Directory), and MS KB 323360 (HOW TO: Install and Configure a DHCP Server in an Active Directory Domain in Windows Server 2003)

14.3   Configuring Server Options

Problem

You want to configure DHCP options at the server level. These server options will be applied to all of the scopes on the server unless overridden within a scope.

Solution

Using a graphical user interface

1. Open the DHCP snap-in.
2. In the left pane, right-click on **DHCP** and select **Add Server**.
3. Type in the name of the DHCP Server you want to target and click **OK**.
4. Expand the server entry in the left pane.
5. Click on **Server Options**, then right-click it and select **Configure Options**.
6. Check the box beside the option you want to configure.
7. This will make the **Data entry** section of the dialog box active.
8. Enter the value(s) for the option and click **OK**.

Using a command-line interface

The following command configures a server option:

```
> netsh dhcp server \\<ServerName> set optionvalue <OptCode> <DataType> <OptValue>
```

In the following example, the "domain name" option (code 015) is configured with a value of "rallencorp.com" on the DHCP server named dhcp01:

```
> netsh dhcp server \\dhcp01 set optionvalue 015 STRING rallencorp.com
```

You can view all of the server options that have been configured with this command:

```
> netsh dhcp server \\<ServerName> show optionvalue
```

Using VBScript

See Recipe 14.0 for more information on how to run the *netsh* command from within a script.

Discussion

When a DHCP Server responds to a client request for a lease, the server also responds with any configured *options* for the scope. Options are nothing more than bits of configuration information, such as the servers to use for name resolution, the default domain name, default router, etc. Some options may be specific to a particular scope, for example, the default router for a subnet; these options are called scope options. Other options may be more global, such as the default domain name; these options are called server options. If you have more than a handful of scopes to configure global settings on, it can be tedious to change them later if you've configured them individually as scope options. This is where server options come in. Instead of configuring the default domain name option on each individual scope, you can configure it at the server level. All scopes will then use this server option. You can override any server options by configuring the same option on a scope.

See Also

Recipe 14.8

14.4 Enabling Address Conflict Detection

Problem

You want to enable address conflict detection on a DHCP Server. With conflict detection enabled, the DHCP Server will ping the IP address it wants to grant a lease for to make sure no other computers are using that IP address. If the ping request receives a reply, the server will mark the IP as BAD_ADDRESS.

Solution

Using a graphical user interface

1. Open the DHCP snap-in.
2. In the left pane, right-click on **DHCP** and select **Add Server**.
3. Type in the name of the DHCP Server you want to target and click **OK**.

4. Right-click the server in the left pane and select **Properties**.

5. Click the **Advanced** tab.

6. Enter the number of ping attempts beside **Conflict detection attempts**. I highly recommend you use either 1 or 2.

7. Click **OK**.

Using a command-line interface

The following command configures conflict detection:

```
> netsh dhcp server \\<ServerName> set detectconflictretry <PingAttempts>
```

This command displays the current conflict detection setting:

```
> netsh dhcp server \\<ServerName> show detectconflictretry
```

Using VBScript

See Recipe 14.0 for more information on how to run the *netsh* command from within a script.

Discussion

Enabling address conflict detection is generally a good idea so clients don't obtain an IP address in use by another computer. The DHCP Server will ping the IP address it is about to grant to ensure nothing responds. You can configure the number of ping attempts, but one or two should be sufficient in most cases.

You might wonder why conflict detection is even necessary. There are three situations where a DHCP Server can give a lease for an IP address that is already in use:

1. A user hardcodes an IP address that is within a scope's IP address range.

2. The DHCP Server's database becomes corrupted or lost and the server does not know which clients it previously gave leases to. Since its lease database is empty, the server may start handing out previously allocated leases.

3. A buggy DHCP client does not use its lease correctly.

Enabling conflict detection adds some overhead to the lease request process. Each ping attempt must timeout, which takes about a second per attempt, before the server can grant the lease. For this reason, you don't want to configure more than one or two ping attempts.

See Also

MS KB 161430 (DHCP: Detecting and Flagging Duplicate IP Addresses)

14.5   Creating a Scope

Problem

You want to create a scope. A scope is group of settings that define how the DHCP Server is supposed to handle requests for a given network.

Solution

Using a graphical user interface

1. Open the DHCP snap-in.
2. In the left pane, right-click on **DHCP** and select **Add Server**.
3. Type in the name of the DHCP Server you want to target and click **OK**.
4. Right-click the server in the left pane and select **New Scope**.
5. Click **Next** to begin the **New Scope Wizard**.
6. Enter a name and description for the scope and click **Next**.
7. Enter the beginning and end of the IP address range, the subnet mask, and bit length, and click **Next**.
8. In the next screen, you can enter any IP addresses you want to exclude. Click **Next** after you are done or if you don't need to add any exclusions.
9. Enter the lease duration and click **Next**.
10. You will now be presented with a choice to configure scope options. If you want to configure them, select **Yes** or **No** and click **Next**.
11. If you selected to configure scope options, you will be presented with a screen to set the default gateway IP address for the scope. Click **Next** after you are done.
12. On the next screen, you configure the default domain name and DNS servers to be used by clients of the scope. Click **Next** after you are done.
13. Next, you can enter one or more WINS Servers. Click **Next** after you are done.
14. The last screen allows you to activate the scope or leave it inactive. Click **Next**.
15. Click **Finish**.

Using a command-line interface

It takes several commands to create and configure a scope. The following command creates a scope:

```
> netsh dhcp server add scope <SubnetID> <SubnetMask> "<ScopeName>"
"<ScopeDescription>"
```

For instance, the following command creates a scope for the subnet 192.168.1.0:

```
> netsh dhcp server add scope 192.168.1.0 255.255.255.0 "Floor1" "Scope used for
desktop users on floor 1"
```

These next three commands configure an IP range, an excluded IP range, and activate the scope, respectively:

```
netsh dhcp server scope 192.168.1.0 add iprange 192.168.1.1 192.168.1.254
netsh dhcp server scope 192.168.1.0 add excluderange 192.168.1.1 192.168.1.10
netsh dhcp server scope 192.168.1.0 set state 1
```

Using VBScript

See Recipe 14.0 for more information on how to run the *netsh* command from within a script.

Discussion

Before creating scopes, decide how you are going to manage them. Develop a naming convention for the scopes that make them easy to identify their networks. Use good descriptions. You may want to add contact information to the description of a specific scope if there are certain people you need to contact when problems arise on that network (e.g., running out of leases). Use contiguous IP address space as much as possible and avoid using excluded IP ranges to keep a straightforward scope layout.

Once you create a scope, you may need to do one or more of the following:

Activate the scope
> When you create a scope, it is deactivated (or disabled) by default. You'll need to activate it before the DHCP Server will start offering leases from it.

Create a superscope
> If you've created this scope on a secondary subnet and plan to use it in addition to an existing scope on a single network, you'll need to create a superscope and add both the secondary and primary scopes to the superscope.

Create reservations
> If you plan on allocating IP addresses to your servers via DHCP, you may want to ensure they always receive the same IP address by creating reservations.

Configure scope options
> With each scope, you can configure scope options to give out settings (e.g., default router) that are specific to a given network.

See Also

Recipes 14.6, 14.7, 14.8, and 14.11

14.6 Creating a Superscope

Problem

You want to create a superscope, which allows you to manage multiple scopes on the same physical network.

Solution

Using a graphical user interface

1. Open the DHCP snap-in.
2. In the left pane, right-click on **DHCP** and select **Add Server**.
3. Type the name of the DHCP Server you want to target and click **OK**.
4. Right-click the server in the left pane and select **New Superscope**. This option will display only if there are scopes configured that have not been added to a superscope yet.
5. Click **Next** to begin the **New Superscope Wizard**.
6. Enter a name for the superscope and click **Next**.
7. Select the scopes to add to the superscope and click **Next**.
8. Click **Finish**.

Using a command-line interface

The following command creates a superscope named "Building 5" and adds the scope identified by subnet 192.168.1.0 to it:

```
> netsh dhcp server scope 192.168.1.0 set superscope "Building 5" 1
```

The following command displays all the superscopes on a server:

```
> netsh dhcp server show superscope
```

The following command deletes the superscope named "Building 5":

```
> netsh dhcp server delete superscope "Building 5"
```

Using VBScript

See Recipe 14.0 for more information on how to run the *netsh* command from within a script.

Discussion

Superscopes allow you to manage a collection of scopes as one entity. You can activate or deactivate all the scopes in a superscope at one time and view the combined lease statistics for all scopes in the superscope.

Superscopes are most often used when you need to create a secondary subnet to increase the number of available leases for a particular network. For example, let's say you created a scope for network 10.1.2.0/24 with 250 leases (leaving four IP addresses available for static use). Once the scope runs out of available leases, you can create a secondary subnet that is used on the same physical network. To make that work with the DHCP Server, you have to create a superscope and add the original and secondary scopes to the superscope.

One of the features of a superscope is the ability to activate and deactivate it. When you activate a superscope, it activates all scopes contained within it. And when you deactivate a superscope, it deactivates all scopes.

When you delete a superscope, none of the scopes contained within it are deleted. The scopes will become standalone and not be part of a superscope (unless you add them to another superscope later).

See Also

Recipe 14.5

14.7 Activating or Deactivating a Scope

Problem

You want to activate or deactivate a scope. A DHCP Server will not respond to lease requests for a given scope unless that scope is activated. When you deactivate a scope, you prevent clients from obtaining leases from it.

Solution

Using a graphical user interface

1. Open the DHCP snap-in.
2. In the left pane, right-click on DHCP and select **Add Server**.
3. Type in the name of the DHCP Server you want to target and click **OK**.
4. Expand the server in the left pane.
5. Click on the scope you want to activate or deactivate.
6. Right-click on the scope and select either **Activate** or **Deactivate**.
7. Click **Yes** to confirm.

Using a command-line interface

The following command activates a scope:

```
> netsh dhcp server \\<ServerName> scope <SubnetID> set state 1
```

And this command deactivates a scope:

```
> netsh dhcp server \\<ServerName> scope <SubnetID> set state 0
```

Using VBScript

See Recipe 14.0 for more information on how to run the *netsh* command from within a script.

Discussion

Once you create a scope, you have to activate it before clients can obtain leases from it. But before you activate a scope, be sure to configure any necessary scope options. If you activate a scope before configuring options, clients may obtain leases, but still not be able to communicate on the network if settings such as the default router are not set.

 Deactivating a scope is an easy way to disable a scope temporarily. Clients will still be able to use their existing lease, but will not be able to renew it.

See Also

Recipes 14.5 and 14.8

14.8 Configuring Scope Options

Problem

You want to configure scope options. While you want to configure as many options as possible at the server level, some options that are specific to a scope need to be configured within the scope. An example of this is the default router option (code 3) when you have multiple subnets and only one DHCP Server.

Solution

Using a graphical user interface

1. Open the DHCP snap-in.
2. In the left pane, right-click on **DHCP** and select **Add Server**.
3. Type in the name of the DHCP Server you want to target and click **OK**.
4. Expand the server entry in the left pane.
5. Expand the scope you want to set options for.

6. Click on the **Scope Options** icon. In the right pane, you will see the list of options currently configured for the scope. This will include any server options that have been configured.

7. To modify an option, double-click it in the right pane. To configure a new scope option, right-click on the **Scope Options** icon and select **Configure Options**.

8. Check the box beside the option you want to configure. This will make the **Data entry** section of the dialog box active.

9. Enter the value(s) for the option and click **OK**.

Using a command-line interface

The following command configures a scope option:

```
> netsh dhcp server \\<ServerName> scope <SubnetID> set optionvalue <OptCode>
<DataType> <OptValue>
```

In this example, the "default router" option (code 3) is configured with a value of 192.168.10.1:

```
> netsh dhcp server \\dhcp01 scope 192.168.10.0 set optionvalue 3 IPADDRESS
192.168.10.1
```

You can view all of the scope options for a scope with this command:

```
> netsh dhcp server \\<ServerName> scope <SubnetID> show optionvalue
```

Using VBScript

See Recipe 14.0 for more information on how to run the *netsh* command from within a script.

Discussion

When a DHCP Server responds to a client request for a lease, the server also responds with any configured *options* for the scope. Options are nothing more than bits of configuration information, such as the servers to use for name resolution, the default domain name, default router, etc. Some options may be specific to a particular scope (for example, the default router for a subnet) or may be more global (such as the default domain name). The former are called scope options and the latter are called server options. I covered server options in Recipe 14.3.

See Also

Recipe 14.3

14.9   Enabling Dynamic DNS Updates from the DHCP Server

Problem

You want to configure the DHCP Server to perform dynamic DNS updates on behalf of clients.

Solution

Using a graphical user interface

To set the global dynamic DNS update configuration, do the following:

1. Open the DHCP snap-in.
2. In the left pane, right-click on **DHCP** and select **Add Server**.
3. Type in the name of the DHCP Server you want to target and click **OK**.
4. Right-click the server node and select **Properties**.
5. Click the **DNS** tab.
6. Check the box beside **Enable DNS dynamic updates according to the settings below**.
7. Select the radio button beside the desired option. You can have A and PTR records updated only when requested by DHCP clients, or have them always updated, even if the DHCP client doesn't request it.
8. Unless you have a good reason otherwise, you should check the box beside **Discard A and PTR records when lease is deleted**.
9. Check the box beside **Dynamically update DNS A and PTR records for DHCP clients that do not request updates** if you have legacy clients such as Windows NT or Windows 9x that you want to register dynamically in DNS.
10. Click **OK**.

To set the dynamic DNS update configuration for a specific scope, do the following:

1. Open the DHCP snap-in.
2. In the left pane, right-click on **DHCP** and select **Add Server**.
3. Type in the name of the DHCP Server you want to target and click **OK**.
4. Right-click on the target scope and select **Properties**.
5. Click the **DNS** tab.
6. Configure the settings as described above.
7. Click **OK**.

Using a command-line interface

You can configure all of the dynamic DNS update settings with *netsh*. This is the format for the command:

```
> netsh dhcp server set dnsconfig <Enable> <Update> <DeleteOld> <Legacy>
```

There are four bits (0 for off or 1 for on) corresponding to each flag. The first setting is for enabling dynamic updates. If the second flag is 0, A and PTR records are always updated, and if it is 1, they are updated only if requested. The third flag, when set to 1, deletes A and PTR records when leases expire. The fourth flag, when set to 1, will cause the DHCP Server to send updates even if the client doesn't support it.

The following command enables dynamic updates (1), always performs dynamic updates (1), deletes records for expired leases (1), and does not perform updates for legacy clients (0):

```
> netsh dhcp server set dnsconfig 1 1 1 0
```

 netsh doesn't support setting dynamic update settings on a per-scope basis as you can do with the GUI.

Using VBScript

See Recipe 14.0 for more information on how to run the *netsh* command from within a script.

Discussion

Dynamically assigning IP addresses to clients makes IP address management easier, but your clients may not always want to refer to other computers by IP address. If you are running the Windows Internet Naming Service (WINS) in your environment, client computers automatically register their names with that service, which allows users to use the NetBIOS protocol to resolve computer names. If you prefer to rely on the Domain Name System (DNS), clients will need to dynamically register their hostname via dynamic DNS updates. You could allow each client to register their own A and PTR records, but then each client would send its own set of DNS updates to your DNS servers. If you have hundreds of clients, that would be hundreds of computers that send dynamic updates. There are also some security issues with allowing clients to do this. Another option is to use the DHCP Server to send dynamic updates on behalf of clients.

 For a detailed explanation on how DHCP works with DNS, visit *http://www.microsoft.com/resources/documentation/WindowsServ/2003/standard/proddocs/en-us/Default.asp?url=/resources/documentation/WindowsServ/2003/standard/proddocs/en-us/sag_DHCP_imp_InteroperabilityDNS.asp*.

See Also

Recipe 14.19

14.10 Managing the Leases for a Scope

Problem

You want to view or delete the active leases for a scope.

Solution

Using a graphical user interface

1. Open the DHCP snap-in.
2. In the left pane, right-click on **DHCP** and select **Add Server**.
3. Type in the name of the DHCP Server you want to target and click **OK**.
4. Expand the target scope.
5. Click on **Address Leases**. The list of allocated leases will be displayed in the right pane.
6. To delete a lease, right-click the target lease in the right pane and select **Delete**.
7. Confirm the deletion by selecting **Yes**.

 If you are interested in scope utilization, you can view the statistics on a per-scope basis by right-clicking the scope and selecting **Display Statistics**.

Using a command-line interface

The following command displays the allocated leases for scope 10.1.2.0:

```
> netsh dhcp server scope 10.1.2.0 show clients
```

The following command deletes the lease for IP address 10.1.2.5:

```
> netsh dhcp server scope 10.1.2.0 delete lease 10.1.2.5
```

Using VBScript

See Recipe 14.0 for more information on how to run the *netsh* command from within a script.

Discussion

If you delete a lease, you'll also need to make sure the client isn't actively using that IP address anymore. Simply deleting the lease on the DHCP Server makes that lease available again for other clients to use. It doesn't actually do anything to the client itself. You can release a lease on the client by running `ipconfig /release`. Then run `ipconfig /renew` to request a new lease.

The *netsh* command supports a few other options for deleting leases. Instead of specifying the lease IP address, you can instead specify a hostname. The following command deletes the lease associated with the host rallen-wxp in the scope 10.1.2.0:

```
> netsh dhcp server scope 10.1.2.0 delete lease \\rallen-wxp
```

If there are multiple leases that have been allocated to rallen-wxp, only the first one will be deleted. You can also delete all leases marked as BAD_ADDRESS (which indicates the server attempted to assign the lease IP, but some other device is using that address). The following command deletes all BAD_ADDRESS leases:

```
> netsh dhcp server scope 10.1.2.0 delete lease allbadaddresses
```

Finally, you can delete all leases obtained by a RAS server using the following command:

```
> netsh dhcp server scope 10.1.2.0 delete lease allrasserveraddresses
```

14.11 Creating a Reservation

Problem

You want to create a lease reservation for a computer so that it always receives the same IP address.

Solution

Using a graphical user interface

1. Open the DHCP snap-in.
2. In the left pane, right-click on **DHCP** and select **Add Server**.
3. Type in the name of the DHCP Server you want to target and click **OK**.
4. Expand the target scope.
5. Right-click on **Reservations** and select **New Reservation**.
6. Enter the name, IP address, MAC address, and description for the reservation.
7. Click **Add**.
8. The reservation will now show up under **Address Leases** and will be marked as inactive until the target client requests a lease.

Using a command-line interface

The following is the general syntax for adding a reservation:

```
> netsh dhcp server scope <ScopeID> add reservedip <ReservedIP> <MAC_Address>
<ClientName> <ClientComment>
```

The following command creates a reservation for IP address 10.1.2.5:

```
> netsh dhcp server scope 10.1.2.0 add reservedip 10.1.2.5 000102C8B474 rallen-wxp
"Robbie's laptop"
```

Using VBScript

See Recipe 14.0 for more information on how to run the *netsh* command from within a script.

Discussion

In some situations, it is not ideal to let hosts obtain an IP address dynamically. For example, web servers need to be referable by a friendly hostname (e.g., *www.rallencorp.com*), which is associated with an IP address. If that IP address changes, the DNS record for the hostname also needs to change. The propagation delay while the record is updated could result in some clients getting errors when trying to access the web site. The solution for this, and any other server with DNS dependency, is to create a reservation.

When you create a reservation, you associate a MAC address with an IP address. You can get the MAC address for a specific network adapter by running ipconfig /all and looking beside Physical Address. After you create the reservation, the next time that network adapter requests a lease, the DHCP Server will recognize the MAC address and assign it the IP address of the reservation.

You may be wondering that since you have to go to the trouble of creating a reservation for servers with static IP addresses, why use DHCP at all for these hosts. The primary benefit of still using DHCP is for the auto-configuration options and the ability to change settings such as DNS Server or WINS Servers across a large number of hosts. Using DHCP means you have to configure fewer things manually on the server. However, if you are provisioning network settings another way, perhaps via group policy, this might not be enough justification.

14.12 Enabling DHCP Audit Logging

Problem

You want to enable DHCP Server audit logging to monitor activity the server is receiving or to use the logs as an audit trail in case a problem arises in the future.

 Enabling logging on a busy DHCP Server can negatively impact performance. Monitor the server closely after initially turning on logging.

Solution

Using a graphical user interface

1. Open the DHCP snap-in.
2. In the left pane, right-click on **DHCP** and select **Add Server**.
3. Type in the name of the DHCP Server you want to target and click **OK**.
4. Right-click the server node and select **Properties**.
5. On the General tab, check the box beside **Enable DHCP audit logging**.
6. Click **OK**.

Using a command-line interface

Surprisingly, *netsh* doesn't allow you to enable DHCP audit logging. You can only modify the audit log file path (see Recipe 14.13). However, this setting is controlled via the registry. The following command enables auditing by setting the ActivityLogFlag value:

```
> reg add HKLM\System\CurrentControlSet\Services\DhcpServer\Parameters /v
ActivityLogFlag /t REG_DWORD /d 1
```

To disable auditing, use the same command except use /d 0 in place of /d 1.

Discussion

After you enable auditing on a DHCP Server, all DHCP requests, database mainte-nance events, and various errors will be logged to a file. By default, a separate file is generated for each day of the week and stored in *%SystemRoot%\system32\dhcp*. See Recipe 14.13 for more on how to store audit logs in a different directory. The files are named *DhcpSrvLog-xxx.log* where *xxx* is the day of the week (e.g., *DhcpSrvLog-Mon.log*). After the first week, the previous week's file is overwritten.

The events logged to the audit log (a plain text file) have the following format:

```
ID,Date,Time,Description,IP Address,Host Name,MAC Address
```

Table 14-1 contains each of these fields and their corresponding description. The ID is a number that represents a certain event. When a new log is started (or overwrit-ten), the list of event codes and their descriptions is written at the top for easy refer-ence. For client-specific audit entries (e.g., a DHCP request), all fields will be populated. For database or DHCP authorization events, some of the fields will be blank.

Table 14-1. DHCP audit log fields

Field	Description
ID	The event ID code. Some of the common codes and corresponding descriptions are written at top of the log file.
Date	Date the event was logged.
Time	Time the event was logged.
Description	Description of the event.
IP Address	IP address of DHCP client.
Host Name	Host name of DHCP client.
MAC Address	MAC address of DHCP client.

The DHCP Server monitors how the log files grow and the available disk space to determine if it should stop logging prematurely to prevent it from consuming too much space. There are two conditions that cause auditing to stop:

- When disk space runs below 20 MB on the filesystem the log files are on.
- When a single log file reaches the preset maximum size (the default is 1 MB).

Fortunately, you can modify these default values by editing the registry. There are three registry values that control DHCP Server disk monitoring located under HKLM\SYSTEM\CurrentControlSet\Services\DHCPServer\Parameters:

DhcpLogDiskSpaceCheckInterval
> This specifies the number of audit entries recorded between disk verification checks. The default is 50, which means 50 events have to be recorded before the disk verification check occurs.

DhcpLogFilesMaxSize
> The maximum size in megabytes for all seven log files. By default, this is 7, which means each log file can only grow to be 1 MB before the DHCP Server stops logging for that day.

DhcpLogMinSpaceOnDisk
> The minimum size in megabytes that must exist on the filesystem for logging to continue. The default is 20, which means the DHCP Server will stop logging altogether if disk space goes below 20 MB on the filesystem.

 You may need to create these values (as REG_DWORD) if they don't already exist.

See Also

Recipe 14.13, MS KB 328891 (Changes in Windows Server 2003 DHCP Logging), and MS KB 843215 (The daily DHCP audit log file is deleted after you restart the DHCP service in Windows Server 2003)

14.13 Modifying the DHCP Database and Audit Log Paths

Problem

You want to move the DHCP database or audit logs from the default location (*%SystemRoot%\system32\dhcp*) to another directory or filesystem.

Solution

Using a graphical user interface

1. Open the DHCP snap-in.
2. In the left pane, right-click on **DHCP** and select **Add Server**.
3. Type in the name of the DHCP Server you want to target and click **OK**.
4. Right-click the server node and select **Properties**.
5. Click the **Advanced** tab.
6. Modify the audit file or database path as needed and click **OK**.

Using a command-line interface

The following command sets the database path to *d:\dhcp*:

```
> netsh dhcp server set databasepath d:\dhcp
```

The following command sets the audit log file path to *d:\dhcp\logs*:

```
> netsh dhcp server set auditlog d:\dhcp\logs
```

Using VBScript

See Recipe 14.0 for more information on how to run the *netsh* command from within a script.

Discussion

Based on your disk configuration, the default location for the DHCP Server database and audit logs may not be sufficient. In any case, you are better off moving these paths off of the system drive, especially if you have multiple disks on the server. In a high-load scenario, disk access to the DHCP database can have an impact on DHCP response times. If you can move the database and logs to a separate disk, the DHCP Server won't compete with the operating system to access the filesystem.

By default, the DHCP database is named *dhcp.mdb*. You can change this too if necessary, although not by using the DHCP snap-in. Use the following command to change the name of the database to *rallencorp-dhcp.mdb*:

```
> netsh dhcp server set databasename rallencorp-dhcp.mdb
```

 After modifying the database or audit log paths or the database name, you have to restart the DHCP Server service for the changes to take effect.

See Also

Recipe 14.12

14.14 Backing Up the DHCP Database

Problem

You want to back up the DHCP database.

Solution

Using a graphical user interface

1. Open the DHCP snap-in on the target DHCP Server.
2. In the left pane, click the server node.
3. From the menu, select **Action → Backup**.
4. Select the folder to store the backup files in and click **OK**.

Using a command-line interface

You can't initiate a backup from *netsh*, but you can configure how frequently the automatic backups occur and where backup files are stored. The following command changes the default backup time to 24 hours (1,440 minutes):

```
> netsh dhcp server set databasebackupinterval 1440
```

The following command changes the backup location to *d:\dhcp\backups*:

```
> netsh dhcp server set databasebackuppath d:\dhcp\backups
```

You can also dump the DHCP Server configuration to a text file and import it later using *netsh*. Here is how you export it:

```
> netsh dhcp server dump > dhcpconfig.dmp
```

The *dump* option does not export any lease information.

Using VBScript

See Recipe 14.0 for more information on how to run the *netsh* command from within a script.

Discussion

The DHCP Server service automatically performs a backup of the DHCP database and DHCP Server registry configuration key every 60 minutes (and overwrites the previous back up). You can also perform a manual backup as outlined in the GUI solution. Backup files are stored in *%SystemRoot%\system32\dhcp\backup* by default, but you can change that location as described in the CLI solution. You should change this path to another drive so that a disk failure doesn't impact both the active database and the backup files.

The DHCP Server takes care of performing regular database backups, but you'll still need to use a backup tool such as NTBackup to archive those backups on a regular basis. As long as you are backing up the *%SystemRoot%\system32\dhcp* directory and the system state (which includes the registry), you can restore the database and server configuration on the same server or on another server if necessary.

See Also

Recipes 14.15, 14.16, MS KB 173396 (How to Restore a Corrupted DHCP Database File), and MS KB 325473 (How to move a DHCP database to a computer that is running Windows Server 2003)

14.15 Restoring the DHCP Database

Problem

You want to restore the DHCP database.

Solution

Using a graphical user interface

1. Open the DHCP snap-in on the target DHCP Server.

2. In the left pane, click the server node.

3. From the menu, select **Action → Restore**.

4. Select the folder that contains the backup files (the default location will automatically be opened) and click **OK**.

5. If the DHCP Server service is running, you'll be prompted to restart it for the changes to take effect. Click **Yes**.

Using a command-line interface

You can't initiate a restore from *netsh*, but if you've exported the DHCP Server configuration with the dump option (see Recipe 14.14), you can import it elsewhere. The following command imports the configuration saved to the file *dhcpconfig.dmp*:

```
> netsh exec dhcpconfig.dmp
```

Discussion

In Recipe 14.14, I outline how the DHCP Server automatically makes a copy of the DHCP database every 60 minutes. The DHCP database contains all the scope information, reservations, leases, and options. The server also backs up a portion of the DHCP Server registry key, which contain settings related to database path and audit logs among other global settings. Most of these registry values can be set with *netsh*. Run `netsh dhcp server set /?` to get a list.

If you restore via the DHCP snap-in, both the database and registry key are restored. In order for the change to take effect, you have to restart the DHCP Server if it is already running.

One thing that is not restored, because it is not backed up, is the DNS credentials (user name, password, and domain) used for making dynamic DNS updates. If your DHCP Server is not performing dynamic DNS updates on behalf of your clients, you do not need to worry about this; but if you are, then you'll need to manually restore these settings. See Recipe 14.19 for more information on these settings.

See Also

Recipes 14.14, 14.19, MS KB 173396 (How to Restore a Corrupted DHCP Database File), MS KB 145881 (How to Use Jetpack.exe to Compact a WINS or DHCP Database), and MS KB 283251 (How to Use the Jetpack Utility on a Clustered WINS/ DHCP Database)

14.16 Importing and Exporting DHCP Server Configuration

Problem

You want to export the DHCP Server configuration and use it on another server.

Solution

Using a graphical user interface

The Windows 2000 Resource Kit contains a tool called *dhcpexim*, which is a simple GUI for exporting and importing DHCP Server configuration. However, I've tested it on Windows Server 2003 and have not been able to make it work properly. Based on other newsgroup postings on the subject, it doesn't appear the Windows 2000 version of *dhcpexim* works with Windows Server 2003. So until a new version is released (which may never happen), your only option on Windows Server 2003 is the CLI solution described next.

Using a command-line interface

The following command exports DHCP Server configuration to *c:\dhcp.txt*:

```
> netsh dhcp server export C:\dhcp.txt all
```

To import this configuration on another server, copy *c:\dhcp.txt* to the target server and run the following command on that server (I'm assuming the DHCP Server has already been installed):

```
> netsh dhcp server import C:\dhcp.txt all
```

Using VBScript

See Recipe 14.0 for more information on how to run the *netsh* command from within a script.

Discussion

The *netsh* tool makes it easy to import and export DHCP Server configuration information. In the CLI solution, I showed how to export all scope information, but you can specify a subset if you want only certain ones. The following command exports only the scopes pertaining to 10.1.2.0 and 10.1.3.0:

```
> netsh dhcp server export C:\dhcp.txt 10.1.2.0 10.1.3.0
```

 According to the usage information for export and import commands, the DHCP Server service will not respond to clients while these commands are being run. Keep this in mind if you have many scopes to export; it can take several minutes and clients may not be able to acquire a lease during this time.

See Also

MS KB 130642 (How to Move a DHCP Database to Another Windows Server)

14.17 Viewing DHCP Utilization Statistics

Problem

You want to view statistics on the number of DHCP requests a particular server has processed.

Solution

You can view a snapshot of the number of DHCP requests a server has processed by doing the following:

1. Open the DHCP snap-in.
2. In the left pane, right-click on **DHCP** and select **Add Server**.
3. Type in the name of the DHCP Server you want to target and click **OK**.
4. Right-click the server and select **Action → Display Statistics**.

You can get similar information by running the following command:

```
> netsh dhcp server \\<ServerName> show mibinfo
```

You can also trend DHCP statistics over a period of time using Performance Monitor:

1. Open the Performance Monitor snap-in.
2. Click the plus (add) button in the right pane.
3. Under **Performance object**, select **DHCP Server**.
4. Under **Select counters from list**, click on a counter you want to view and click the **Add** button. You can also click on the **Explain** button to view more information about a specific counter.
5. Click **Close** when you are done.

Discussion

Any time you look at the performance statistics, you need an understanding of the baseline performance. For example, if you look at the number of DHCP acknowledgments per second and find that your server is currently at 7, how do you know if that is more or less than normal? You really need to become familiar with how much traffic your server is getting so that if you suspect your server is becoming overloaded, you have a frame of reference.

Also, with DHCP the time of day is important. When users arrive in the morning and fire up their computers, there will be a lot of DHCP Discover requests by client computers. Depending on your lease duration, you may see additional spikes throughout the day. For example, if your lease duration is set to four hours, clients will begin to extend the lease after two hours. Then at the end of the day, when your users shut down their computers, you may see a lot of DHCP Release request activity.

Table 14-2 lists counters you can track in Performance Monitor. Most of these counters are rates (i.e., the number of transactions per second). If you want the overall number per transaction, open the Display Statistics dialog in the DHCP snap-in.

Table 14-2. DHCP server performance monitor counters

Counter name	Counter description
Acks/sec	Rate of DHCP Acks sent by the DHCP server
Active Queue Length	Number of packets in the processing queue of the DHCP server
Conflict Check Queue Length	Number of packets in the DHCP server queue waiting on conflict detection (ping)
Declines/sec	Rate of DHCP Declines received by the DHCP server
Discovers/sec	Rate of DHCP Discovers received by the DHCP server
Duplicates Dropped/sec	Rate at which the DHCP server received duplicate packets
Informs/sec	Rate of DHCP Informs received by the DHCP server
Milliseconds per packet (Avg)	Average time per packet taken by the DHCP server to send a response
Nacks/sec	Rate of DHCP Nacks sent by the DHCP server
Offers/sec	Rate of DHCP Offers sent out by the DHCP server
Packets Expired/sec	Rate at which packets are expired in the DHCP server message queue
Packets Received/sec	Rate at which packets are received by the DHCP server
Releases/sec	Rate of DHCP Releases received by the DHCP server
Requests/sec	Rate of DHCP Requests received by the DHCP server

For good rules of thumb concerning what to watch for when observing the DHCP performance counters, go to *http://msdn.microsoft.com* and search on "DHCP Server Object." In the Performance Monitor Reference, Microsoft describes all of the counters and provides guidance on how to determine bottlenecks based on what you are seeing.

If you determine that you are seeing an unusually high rate of DHCP requests, you'll want to learn what clients are generating the bulk of the traffic. For more on enabling DHCP auditing, see Recipe 14.12.

See Also

Recipe 14.12

14.18 Finding the DHCP Servers on a Subnet

Problem

You want to find the DHCP Servers that are active on a particular subnet. This is useful if you believe there is a rogue DHCP Server causing problems for your clients.

Solution

The *dhcploc* command lets you see a computer's DHCP traffic for a broadcast domain. Simply pass in the IP address of the machine from which you are running the command:

```
> dhcploc 192.168.32.24
```

You will not see any output from the command until it captures some DHCP traffic. You can try running `ipconfig /renew` to force some traffic to be generated. You can also press the "**d**" key when you have *dhcploc* running to have it generate a DIS-COVER message.

Here is some sample output from the command:

```
9:34:58 (IP)0.0.0.0        NACK    (S)192.168.31.84    ***
9:36:38 (IP)192.168.190.130 OFFER  (S)192.168.12.226   ***
9:36:38 (IP)192.168.196.231 ACK    (S)192.168.13.53
9:36:53 (IP)192.168.196.231 ACK    (S)192.168.13.53
9:37:05 (IP)192.168.196.234 OFFER  (S)192.168.13.53
9:37:05 (IP)192.168.193.232 OFFER  (S)192.168.12.198
9:37:06 (IP)192.168.190.132 OFFER  (S)192.168.12.221   ***
```

The first column contains a timestamp, the second column is the IP address of the target computer, the third is the DHCP request type, the fourth is the IP address of the DHCP Server, and the fifth is a flag that indicates whether the DHCP Server is authorized. If it is not authorized, you'll see three stars (***). In the previous output, you can see that 192.168.31.84, 192.168.12.226, and 192.168.12.221 are all unauthorized DHCP Servers.

dhcploc can also send alerts if it detects an unauthorized server. This allows you to start *dhcploc*, leave it running, and let it proactively notify you when it discovers an unauthorized server. To do so, specify the /a: option followed by the list of users to alert as shown here:

```
> dhcploc /a:"rallen" 192.168.32.24
```

Discussion

dhcploc works by capturing all of the DHCP traffic it sees on the network. Since most DHCP traffic is sent via broadcast, every computer in the broadcast domain (e.g., all computers connected to a hub on a local segment), can look at DHCP traffic. Most computers simply discard the traffic unless it is destined for them, but *dhcploc* captures all DHCP traffic.

Do not run *dhcploc* from a DHCP Server. DHCP traffic will be delivered to *dhcploc* instead of the DHCP Server. By running the command directly on a DHCP Server, it is likely the server won't be able to respond to any client requests.

See Also

Recipe 14.2 and MS KB 186462 (DHCPLOC Should Not Be Run from DHCP Servers)

14.19 Running DHCP Server on a Domain Controller

Problem

You want to run the DHCP Server service on a domain controller. It is not recommended that you run DHCP on a domain controller unless you modify the DHCP Server configuration to use alternate credentials when making dynamic DNS updates. This recipe explains how.

Solution

Using a graphical user interface

1. Open the DHCP snap-in.
2. In the left pane, right-click on **DHCP** and select **Add Server**.
3. Type in the name of the DHCP Server you want to target and click **OK**.
4. Right-click the server and select **Properties**.
5. Click the **Advanced** tab.
6. Click the **Credentials** button.
7. Enter the username, domain, and password for the account you want to use.
8. Click **OK** until all dialog windows are closed.

Using a command-line interface

Use the following command to display the current DNS credentials used by the DHCP Server:

```
> netsh dhcp server show dnscredentials
```

Use the following command to configure new DNS credentials on the DHCP Server:

```
> netsh dhcp server set dnscredentials <Username> <Domain> <Password>
```

Use the following command to remove the DNS credentials used by the DHCP Server:

```
> netsh dhcp server delete dnscredentials dhcpfullforce
```

Using VBScript

See Recipe 14.0 for more information on how to run the *netsh* command from within a script.

Discussion

By default, the DHCP Server runs under the credentials of the computer account that is hosting it. If it happens to be running on a domain controller, it runs under the domain controller's computer account. A domain controller has full permissions over any Active Directory–integrated zones it replicates. The result of the DHCP Server running on a domain controller means that if the DHCP Server has been configured to dynamically register DNS records on behalf of clients, it can potentially update any record stored in an Active Directory–integrated zone. Ultimately, that leaves the zones vulnerable to name hijacking, whereby a client can cause records to be overwritten that shouldn't be. This can cause all sorts of havoc if an attacker starts replacing important records in your zones.

Microsoft recommends that you avoid this completely by not running the DHCP Server on a domain controller. But as of Windows 2000 Service Pack 1, you can work around this issue by configuring the DHCP Server to use alternate credentials when making dynamic updates. The account doesn't need any special permissions in order to dynamically update records. After you've configured alternate credentials, check the event log for any errors pertaining to logon issues (perhaps the username or password are incorrect) or dynamic update errors.

 If you back up a DHCP Server's configuration using NTBackup, DNS credentials are not backed up. This is done intentionally to prevent someone from hijacking names by restoring a DHCP Server from backup. You must manually restore the DNS credentials if you have to restore a DHCP Server.

See Also

Recipe 14.14 and MS KB 255134 (Installing Dynamic Host Configuration Protocol (DHCP) and Domain Name System (DNS) on a Domain Controller)

CHAPTER 15

Active Directory

15.0   Introduction

Active Directory is an LDAP-based directory that supports the LDAP v3 specification defined in RFC 2251. In this chapter, I'm going to cover some of the most common tasks that you'll need to do to support an Active Directory infrastructure. However, Active Directory is a complex intermixed set of technologies that cannot be covered comprehensively in a single chapter. If you want more information after finishing this chapter, read *Active Directory* (O'Reilly) to get a thorough understanding of Active Directory's capabilities or *Active Directory Cookbook* (O'Reilly) for more examples, scripts, and tips.

A Really Brief Introduction

A forest is a logical structure that is a collection of domains, plus the configuration and schema naming contexts, and application partitions. Forests are considered the primary security boundary in Active Directory. By that I mean, if you need to definitively restrict access to a domain to block access by administrators from other domains, you need to implement a separate forest (and subsequently a domain in that forest), instead of using a domain within a given forest. This is due to the transitive trust relationship between all domains in a forest and the extensive permissions that members of the Domain Admins group have. Unlike domains and trusts, a forest is not represented by a container or any other type of object in Active Directory. At a minimum, a forest consists of three naming contexts: the forest root domain, the Configuration Naming Context (NC), and the Schema NC. The Partitions container in the Configuration NC lists partitions that are associated with a forest. Here are the types of partitions that can be part of a forest:

Configuration NC

Contains data that is applicable across all of the domains and thus is replicated to all domain controllers in the forest. Some of this data includes the site topology, list of partitions, published services, display specifiers, and extended rights.

Schema NC

Contains the objects that describe how data can be structured and stored in Active Directory. The `classSchema` objects in the Schema NC represent class definitions for objects. The `attributeSchema` objects describe what data can be stored with classes. The Schema NC is replicated to all domain controllers in a forest.

Domain NC

A domain is a naming context that holds domain-specific data including user, group, and computer objects.

Application partitions

Configurable partitions that can be rooted anywhere in the forest and can be replicated to any domain controller in the forest. These are not available with Windows 2000.

Each Active Directory domain is served by one or more domain controllers. A Domain controller is authoritative for a single domain, but can store partial read-only copies of objects in other domains in the forest if it is enabled as a global catalog server. All domain controllers in a forest also replicate the Configuration and Schema Naming Contexts.

Active Directory is a multimaster directory, meaning that updates can be made on any domain controller in a domain, but some tasks cannot be distributed to all servers due to concurrency issues. For example, if two different domain controllers made conflicting updates to the schema, the impact could be severe and could result in data loss. For this reason, Active Directory supports Flexible Single Master Operations (FSMO) roles. For each role there is only one domain controller that acts as the role owner and performs the tasks associated with the role. See Recipe 15.18 for more information on FSMO roles.

15.1 Creating a New Active Directory Forest

Problem

You want to promote a domain controller into an existing forest or create a new forest.

Solution

Using a graphical user interface

Run *dcpromo* from a command line or **Start** → **Run**.

On a Windows 2000:

1. Select **Domain controller for a new domain** and click **Next**.

2. Select **Create a new domain tree** and click **Next**.

3. Select **Create a new forest of domain trees** and click **Next**.

4. Follow the rest of the configuration steps to complete the wizard.

On a Windows Server 2003:

1. Select **Domain controller for a new domain** and click **Next**.

2. Select **Domain in a new forest** and click **Next**.

3. Follow the rest of the configuration steps to complete the wizard.

Discussion

To create a new forest you need to create a forest root domain. To do this, you need to use the *dcpromo* executable to promote a Windows 2000 or Windows Server 2003 server to be a domain controller for the new forest root domain. The *dcpromo* program has a wizard interface that requires you to answer several questions about the forest and domain you want to promote the server into. After *dcpromo* finishes, you will be asked to reboot the computer to complete the promotion process.

The two options *dcpromo* offers to create a new domain are adding the domain to an existing domain tree or starting a new domain tree. If you want to create a new domain that is a subdomain (contained within the same namespace) of a parent domain, you are creating a domain in an existing domain tree. If you are creating the first domain in a forest or a domain outside the namespace of the forest root, you are creating a domain in a new domain tree.

Each domain increases the support costs of Active Directory due to the need for maintaining additional domain controllers and time spent configuring and maintaining the domain. When designing an Active Directory forest, your goal should be to keep the number of domains to a minimum.

A good test to use before running *dcpromo* is the *dcdiag* command with the /test: dcpromo option. This command will examine the existing DNS infrastructure to see if any changes are required to accommodate the new domain controller (DC). With the /test option you must also specify /DnsDomain:*<ADDomainName>* where *<ADDomainName>* is the domain name that the DC will be promoted into. Then you need to include an option that specifics the type of operation you plan to perform, which can be one of

/NewForest, /NewTree, /ChildDomain, or /ReplicaDC. See the *dcdiag* help information (run dcdiag /?) for more information.

 The /test:dcpromo option is available only with the Windows Server 2003 version of *dcdiag*.

See Also

MS KB 238369 (HOW TO: Promote and Demote Domain Controllers in Windows 2000) and MS KB 255248 (HOW TO: Create a Child Domain in Active Directory and Delegate the DNS Namespace to the Child Domain)

15.2   Promoting a Domain Controller from Media

 This recipe requires that the server being promoted run Windows Server 2003.

Problem

You want to promote a new domain controller using a backup from another domain controller as the initial source of the directory contents (DIT) instead of replicating the entire DIT over the network.

Solution

Using a graphical user interface

1. You first need to back up the system state of an existing domain controller in the domain where the new server will go, by running the MS Backup utility found at **Start → Programs → Accessories → System Tools → Backup**.

2. Once you have a good backup, you need to restore it to the new server, which can also be done using MS Backup. You should restore the files to an alternate location, not to their original location.

3. Next, run *dcpromo* with the /adv option from a command line or **Start → Run**:

   ```
   > dcpromo /adv
   ```

4. After the *dcpromo* wizard starts, select **Additional Domain Controller for an existing domain** and click **Next**.

5. Under **Copy Domain Information**, select **From these restored backup files**, browse to the backup files you created in step 2, and click **Next**.

6. Enter credentials of a user who is part of the Domain Admins group in the domain you are promoting the domain controller into and click **Next**.

7. Choose the folders to store the Active Directory database and log files and click **Next**.

8. Choose the folder to store SYSVOL and click **Next**.

9. Enter a Restore Mode password and click **Next**.

10. Click **Next** to start the promotion.

Discussion

Being able to promote a domain controller using the system state backup of another domain controller is a new feature in Windows Server 2003. With Windows 2000, a new domain controller had to replicate the entire DIT over the network from an existing domain controller. For organizations that had either a really large Active Directory DIT file or very poor network connectivity to a remote site, replicating the full contents over the network presented challenges. Under these conditions, the promotion process could take a prohibitively long time to complete. Now with the *dcpromo install from media* option, the initial promotion process can be substantially quicker. After you've done the initial install from media (i.e., backup tape or CD/DVD), the domain controller replicates the changes since the backup was taken.

> Be sure that the backup files you are using are much less than 60 days old. If you install a domain controller using backup files that are older than 60 days, you could get in trouble with zombie objects getting re-injected after being purged (due to the default 60-day tombstone lifetime).

See Also

Recipe 15.6

15.3   Uninstalling Active Directory

Problem

You want to demote a domain controller or completely tear down a domain or forest because you no longer need it.

Solution

Do the following to demote a domain controller to be a member server:

1. Run the *dcpromo* command from a command line or **Start → Run**.

2. Click **Next**.

3. If the server is the last domain controller in the domain, check the box beside **This server is the last domain controller in the domain**.

4. Click **Next**.

5. Type and confirm the password for the local Administrator account.

6. Click **Next** twice to begin the demotion.

If you want to completely remove a domain, you have to demote each domain controller in the domain, which is accomplished by running *dcpromo* on the domain controllers and following the steps outlined above. For the last domain controller in the domain, be sure to select **This server is the last domain controller in the domain** in the *dcpromo* wizard so that the objects associated with the domain get removed.

 If the domain you want to remove has subdomains, you must remove the subdomains before proceeding.

After all domain controllers have been demoted and depending on how your environment is configured, you may need to remove WINS and DNS entries that were associated with the domain controllers and domain unless they were automatically removed via WINS deregistration and DDNS during the demotion process. The following commands can help determine if all entries have been removed:

```
> netsh wins server \\<WINSServerName> show name <NetbiosName> 1c
> nslookup <DomainControllerName>
> nslookup -type=SRV _ldap._tcp.dc._msdcs.<DomainDNSName>
> nslookup <DomainDNSName>
```

You will also want to remove any trusts that have been established for the domain (see Recipe 15.20 for more details).

To remove a forest, you need to follow this process for all domains in that forest.

Discussion

Before you demote a domain controller, ensure that all of the FSMO roles have been transferred to other servers (see Recipe 15.19); otherwise, they will be transferred to random domain controllers as part of the demotion process, which may not be optimal for your installation. Also, if the server is a global catalog, ensure that other global catalog servers exist in the forest and can handle the load. If the DC was also a DNS server, make sure clients are pointed to an alternate server.

It is important to demote a server before decommissioning or rebuilding it so that its associated objects in Active Directory are removed, its DNS locator resource records are dynamically removed, and replication with the other domain controllers is not interrupted. If a domain controller does not successfully demote, or if you do not get the chance to demote it because of failed hardware, see MS KB 216498 for manually removing a domain controller from Active Directory. With Windows Server 2003, there is a new *dcpromo* command-line option called /forceremoval that provides a cleaner way to forcefully remove a broken domain controller from Active Directory. See MS KB 332199 for more information.

You can use a brute force method to remove a forest by simply reinstalling the operating system on all domain controllers in the forest. This method is not recommended except in lab or test environments. The brute force method is not a clean way to do it because the domain controllers are unaware the forest is being removed and may generate errors until they are rebuilt. You'll also need to make sure any DNS resource records for the domain controllers are removed from your DNS servers, since the domain controllers will not dynamically remove them as they do during the demotion process.

The "brute force" method for removing a forest is also messy because it leaves all the domain controller and server objects, along with the domain object and associated domain naming context in the forest. If you use that approach you will eventually see a bunch of replication and NTFRS errors in the event log from failed replication events. If this happens to you, see MS KB 230306 for how to remove an orphaned domain.

See Also

Recipe 15.20, MS KB 216498 (HOW TO: Remove Data in Active Directory After an Unsuccessful Domain Controller Demotion), MS KB 230306 (HOW TO: Remove Orphaned Domains from Active Directory), MS KB 238369 (HOW TO: Promote and Demote Domain Controllers in Windows 2000), MS KB 255229 (Dcpromo Demotion of Last Domain Controller in Child Domain Does Not Succeed), MS KB 307304 (HOW TO: Remove Active Directory with the Dcpromo Tool in Windows 2000), and MS KB 332199 (Using the DCPROMO /FORCEREMOVAL Command to Force the Demotion of Active Directory Domain Controllers)

15.4   Upgrading from Windows 2000 to Windows Server 2003

Problem

You want to upgrade your existing Windows 2000 Active Directory domain controllers to Windows Server 2003. Before doing this, you must run the ADPrep tool, which extends the schema and adds several objects in Active Directory that are necessary for new features and enhancements.

Solution

First, run the following command on the Schema FSMO domain controller with the credentials of an account that is in both the `Enterprise Admins` and `Schema Admins` groups:

```
> adprep /forestprep
```

After the updates from `/forestprep` have replicated throughout the forest, run the following command on the Infrastructure FSMO domain controller in each domain with the credentials of an account in the `Domain Admins` group:

```
> adprep /domainprep
```

If the updates from `/forestprep` have not replicated to at least the Infrastructure FSMO servers in each domain, an error will be returned when running `/domainprep`. To debug any problems you encounter, see the ADPrep log files located at *%SystemRoot%\System32\Debug\Adprep\Logs*.

 adprep can be found in the *\i386* directory on the Windows Server 2003 CD. The tool relies on several files in that directory, so you cannot simply copy that file out to a server and run it. You must run it either from a CD or from a location where the entire directory has been copied.

To determine if `adprep /domainprep` completed, check for the existence of the following object, where *<DomainDN>* is the distinguished name of the domain:

```
cn=Windows2003Update,cn=DomainUpdates,cn=System,<DomainDN>
```

To determine if `adprep /forestprep` completed, check for the existence of the following object, where *<ForestRootDN>* is the distinguished name of the forest root domain:

```
cn=Windows2003Update,cn=ForestUpdates,cn=Configuration,<ForestRootDN>
```

Discussion

The *adprep* command prepares a Windows 2000 forest and domains for Windows Server 2003. Both `/forestprep` and `/domainprep` must be run before you can upgrade any domain controllers to Windows Server 2003 or install new Windows Server 2003 domain controllers.

The *adprep* command serves a similar function to the Exchange 2000 setup `/forestprep` and `/domainprep` commands, which prepare an Active Directory forest and domains for Exchange 2000. The `adprep /forestprep` command extends the schema and modifies some default security descriptors, which is why it must run on the Schema FSMO domain controller and under the credentials of someone in both the `Schema Admins` and `Enterprise Admins` groups. In addition, the `adprep /forestprep` and

/domainprep commands add new objects throughout the forest, many of which are necessary for new features supported in Windows Server 2003 Active Directory.

If you've installed Exchange 2000 or Services For Unix 2.0 in your forest prior to running *adprep*, there are schema conflicts with the *adprep* schema extensions that you'll need to fix first. MS KB 325379 and 314649 have a detailed list of compatibility issues and resolutions.

One of the nice features of adprep is it stores its progress in Active Directory. For /domainprep, a container with a distinguished name of cn=DomainUpdates,cn=System,*<DomainDN>* is created that has child object containers cn=Operations and cn=Windows2003Update. After adprep completes a task, such as extending the schema, it creates an object under the cn=Operations container to signify its completion. Each object has a GUID for its name, which represents some internal operation for adprep. For /domainprep, 52 of these objects are created. After all of the operations have completed successfully, the cn=Windows2003Update object is created to indicate /domainprep has completed. Figure 15-1 shows an example of the container structure created by /domainprep.

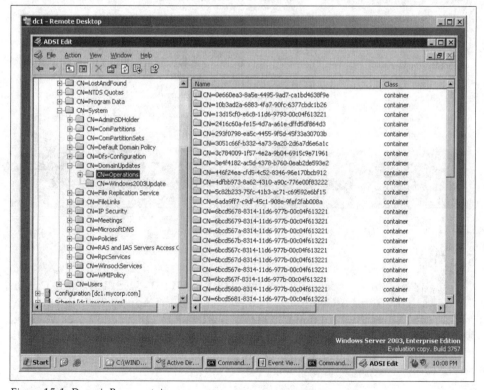

Figure 15-1. DomainPrep containers

For /forestprep, a container with the distinguished name of cn=ForestUp-dates,cn=Configuration,<ForestRootDN> is created with child object containers cn=Operations and cn=Windows2003Update. The same principles apply as for /domainprep except that there are 36 operation objects stored within the cn=Operations container. After /forestprep completes, the cn=Windows2003Update object will be created that marks the successful completion of /forestprep. Figure 15-2 shows an example of the container structure created by /forestprep.

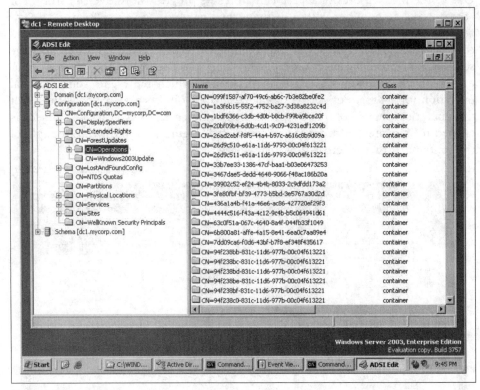

Figure 15-2. ForestPrep containers

See Also

Chapter 14 of *Active Directory* (O'Reilly), MS KB 331161 (List of Fixes to Use on Windows 2000 Domain Controllers Before You Run the Adprep/Forestprep Command), MS KB 314649 (Windows Server 2003 ADPREP Command Causes Mangled Attributes in Windows 2000 Forests That Contain Exchange 2000 Servers), and MS KB 325379 (How to Upgrade Windows 2000 Domain Controllers to Windows Server 2003)

15.5 Raising the Functional Level

Problem

You want to raise the functional level of a Windows Server 2003 domain or forest. You should raise the functional level of a domain as soon as possible after installing a new Windows Server 2003 domain or upgrading from Windows 2000 to take advantage of the new features and enhancements. Once all the domains in a forest are at the Windows Server 2003 functional level, you can raise the forest functional level.

Solution

Do the following to raise the functional level of a domain:

Using a graphical user interface

1. Open the Active Directory Domains and Trusts snap-in.
2. In the left pane, browse to the domain you want to raise, right-click it, and select **Raise Domain Functional Level**.
3. Select the new functional level you want to set and click **OK**.
4. After a few seconds you should see a message stating whether the operation was successful.

Using a command-line interface

To retrieve the current functional level of a domain, use the following command:

```
> dsquery * <DomainDN> -scope base -attr msDS-Behavior-Version
```

Or use the enumprop command found in the Windows 2000 Resource Kit:

```
> enumprop /ATTR:msDS-Behavior-Version "LDAP://<DomainDN>"
```

To change the functional level to Windows Server 2003, create an LDIF file called *raise_domain_func_level.ldf* with the following contents:

```
dn: <DomainDN>
changetype: modify
replace: msDS-Behavior-Version
msDS-Behavior-Version: 2
-
```

Next, run the *ldifde* command to import the change:

```
> ldifde -i -f raise_domain_func_level.ldf
```

Using VBScript

```
' This code changes the functional level of the specified domain to
' the Windows Server 2003 domain functional level
' ------ SCRIPT CONFIGURATION ------
```

```
strDomain = "<DomainDNSName>"    ' e.g., amer.rallencorp.com
' ------ END CONFIGURATION ---------

set objDomain = GetObject("LDAP://" & strDomain)
objDomain.GetInfo
if objDomain.Get("msDS-Behavior-Version") <> 2 then
   Wscript.Echo "Changing domain to Windows Server 2003 functional level..."
   objDomain.Put "msDS-Behavior-Version", 2
   objDomain.SetInfo
else
   Wscript.Echo "Domain already at Windows Server 2003 functional level "
end if
```

Do the following to raise the functional level of a forest:

Using a graphical user interface

1. Open the Active Directory Domains and Trusts snap-in.
2. In the left pane, right-click on **Active Directory Domains and Trusts** and select **Raise Forest Functional Level**.
3. Select **Windows Server 2003 Functional Level** and click OK.
4. After a few seconds you should see a message stating whether the operation was successful.

Using a command-line interface

To retrieve the current forest functional level, use the following command:

```
> dsquery * <ForestRootDN> -scope base -attr msDS-Behavior-Version
```

Or use the *enumprop* command found in the Windows 2000 Resource Kit:

```
> enumprop /ATTR:msDS-Behavior-Version "LDAP://<ForestRootDN>"
```

To change the functional level to Windows Server 2003, create an LDIF file called *raise_forest_func_level.ldf* with the following contents:

```
dn: cn=partitions,cn=configuration,<ForestRootDN>
changetype: modify
replace: msDS-Behavior-Version
msDS-Behavior-Version: 2
-
```

Next, run the *ldifde* command to import the change:

```
> ldifde -i -f raise_forest_func_level.ldf
```

Using VBScript

```
' This code changes the functional level of the forest the
' user running the script is logged into to Windows Server 2003.

set objRootDSE = GetObject("LDAP://RootDSE")
set objDomain = GetObject("LDAP://cn=partitions," & _
                          objRootDSE.Get("configurationNamingContext") )
```

```
if objDomain.Get("msDS-Behavior-Version") <> 2 then
   Wscript.Echo "Attempting to change forest to " & _
                "Windows Server 2003 functional level..."
   objDomain.Put "msDS-Behavior-Version", 2
   objDomain.SetInfo
else
   Wscript.Echo "Forest already at Windows Server 2003 functional level"
end if
```

Discussion

In Windows Server 2003 Active Directory, functional levels have replaced the domain mode that was used in Windows 2000 to signify what operating systems are allowed to run on the domain controllers in the domain. With Windows Server 2003, there are functional levels for both domains and forests, whereas with Windows 2000 the domain mode applied only to domains. But just as with domain modes, changing a functional level is a one-way operation. After you make the change, there is no reverting back (i.e., unless you restore the entire domain or forest).

The msDS-Behavior-Version attribute of the domainDNS object (e.g., dc=amer,dc=rallencorp,dc=com) holds the current domain functional level. Table 15-1 shows the three functional levels, their associated msDS-Behavior-Version values, and the operating systems that can be used on each's domain controllers.

Table 15-1. Windows Server 2003 functional levels

Functional level	msDS-Behavior-Version	Valid operating systems
Windows 2000	0	Windows 2000 Windows NT (when in mixed mode) Windows Server 2003
Windows Server 2003 Interim	1	Windows NT 4.0 Windows Server 2003
Windows Server 2003	2	Windows Server 2003

When a domain is at the Windows 2000 functional level, the domain can be in mixed mode or native mode. Various new features of Windows Server 2003 Active Directory are enabled with each domain functional level. See Chapter 1 of *Active Directory* (O'Reilly) for more details.

The value contained in msDS-Behavior-Version is mirrored in the domainFunctionality attribute of the RootDSE. That means you can perform anonymous queries against the RootDSE of a domain to quickly determine its current functional level.

> One of the benefits of the GUI solution is that if a problem is encountered, you can save and view the output log generated from the snap-in, which will contain information on any errors that were encountered.

Windows Server 2003 forest functional levels are very similar to domain functional levels. In fact, Table 15-1 also applies to forest functional levels, except that the list of available operating systems applies to all domain controllers in the forest, not just a single domain. So even if just one of the domains in the forest is at the Windows 2000 domain functional level, you cannot raise the forest above the Windows 2000 forest functional level. If you attempt to do so, you will receive an error that the operation cannot be completed. After you raise the last Windows 2000 domain functional level to Windows Server 2003, you can then raise the forest functional level.

You may wonder why there is a need to differentiate between forest and domain functional levels. The primary reason is new features. Some new Windows Server 2003 Active Directory features require all domain controllers in the forest to run Windows Server 2003. To ensure all domain controllers are running a certain operating system throughout a forest, Microsoft had to apply the functional level concept to forests as well as domains. For more information on the new features that are available with each functional level, see Chapter 1 of *Active Directory* (O'Reilly).

The forest functional level is stored in the msDS-Behavior-Version attribute of the Partitions container in the Configuration NC. For example, in the *rallencorp.com* forest it would be stored in cn=partitions,cn=configuration,dc=rallencorp,dc=com. The value contained in msDS-Behavior-Version is mirrored to the forestFunctionality attribute of the RootDSE, which means you can find the functional level of the forest by querying the RootDSE.

See Also

Chapter 1 of *Active Directory* (O'Reilly), Recipe 15.14, and MS KB 322692 (HOW TO: Raise the Domain Functional Level in Windows Server 2003)

15.6   Backing Up Active Directory

Problem

You want to back up Active Directory to tape or disk.

Solution

Back up the System State, which includes the Active Directory–related files on the domain controller. Here are the directions for backing up the System State using the MS Backup utility that comes installed on Windows 2000 and Windows Server 2003 computers.

Using a graphical user interface

1. Go to **Start** → **All Programs** (or **Programs** for Windows 2000) → **Accessories** → **System Tools** → **Backup**.
2. Click the **Advanced Mode** link.
3. Click the **Backup** tab.
4. Check the box beside **System State**.
5. Check the box beside any other files, directories, or drives you would also like to back up.
6. For **Backup destination**, select either **File** or **Tape** depending on where you want to back up the data.
7. For **Backup media or file name**, type either the name of a file or select the tape where to save the backup.
8. Click the **Start Backup** button twice.

Using a command-line interface

The NTBackup utility supports several command-line parameters that you can use to initiate backups without ever bringing up the GUI.

For the complete list of supported commands on Windows 2000, see MS KB 300439 (How to Use Command Line Parameters with the "Ntbackup" Command).

For the complete list of supported commands on Windows Server 2003, see MS KB 814583 (HOW TO: Use Command Line Parameters With the Ntbackup Command in Windows Server 2003).

Discussion

Fortunately, domain controllers can be backed up while online, which makes the process relatively easy. And since Active Directory is included as part of the System State on domain controllers, you are required to back up only the System State, although you can back up other folders and drives as necessary. On a domain controller, the System State includes the following:

- Boot files
- Registry
- COM+ class registration database
- Active Directory files
- System Volume (SYSVOL)
- Certificates database (if running Certificate Server)

See Also

MS KB 216993 (Backup of the Active Directory Has 60-Day Useful Life), MS KB 240363 (HOW TO: Use the Backup Program to Back Up and Restore the System State in Windows 2000), MS KB 300439 (How to Use Command Line Parameters With the "Ntbackup" Command), MS KB 326216 (HOW TO: Use the Backup Feature to Back Up and Restore Data in Windows Server 2003), and MS KB 814583 (HOW TO: Use Command Line Parameters with the Ntbackup Command in Windows Server 2003)

15.7   Restoring Active Directory

Problem

You want to perform a nonauthoritative or authoritative restore of a domain controller. A nonauthoritative restore can be useful if you want to quickly restore a domain controller that failed due to a hardware problem. An authoritative restore is needed if data was deleted from Active Directory that you want to bring back.

Solution

To restore a domain controller without restoring any objects (i.e., nonauthoritative restore), do the following:

1. First, boot the domain controller into Directory Services Restore Mode.
2. Open the NT Backup utility; go to **Start → All Programs** (or **Programs** for Windows 2000) → **Accessories → System Tools → Backup**.
3. Click the **Advanced Mode** link.
4. Under the **Welcome** tab, click the **Restore Wizard** button and click **Next**.
5. Check the box beside **System State** and any other drives you want to restore and click **Next**.
6. Click the **Advanced** button.
7. Select **Original location** for **Restore files to**.
8. For the **How to Restore** option, select **Replace existing files** and click **Next**.
9. For the **Advanced Restore Options**, be sure that the following are checked: **Restore Security Settings**, **Restore junction points**, and **Preserve existing mount volume points**. Then click **Next**.
10. Click **Finish**.
11. Restart the computer.

When the system starts up, any changes that have occurred in the domain since the backup was taken will be replicated to it.

If you want to restore a single object (i.e., authoritative restore), *before* you restart (step 11), run the following command:

```
> ntdsutil "auth restore" "restore object <ObjectDN>" q
```

Here is an example:

```
> ntdsutil "auth restore" "restore object cn=jsmith,ou=Sales,dc=rallencorp,dc=com" q
```

To restore an entire subtree (again, an authoritative restore) run the following:

```
> ntdsutil "auth restore" "restore subtree ou=Sales,dc=rallencorp,dc=com" q
```

Note the only difference is that I specified subtree instead of object and I included the distinquished name (DN) of an organizational unit (OU) instead of a user account. Restart the computer after you are done. This will cause that single object or subtree to replicate out to all domain controllers. Any other changes that have taken place in the domain will replicate to this server.

> There are some issues related to restoring user, group, computer, and trust objects that you should be aware of. See MS KB 216243 and MS KB 280079 for more information.

If you want to restore all of the objects in an Active Directory domain (i.e., a complete authoritative restore), do the following *before* step 11:

Run the following command to restore the entire database:

```
> ntdsutil "auth restore" "restore database" q
```

Then restart the computer.

Discussion

If you encounter a failed domain controller that you cannot bring back up (e.g., multiple hard disks fail), you have two options for restoring it. One option is to remove the domain controller completely from Active Directory (as outlined in Recipe 15.3) and then repromote it back in. This is known as the *restore from replication* method, because you are essentially bringing up a brand new domain controller and will let replication restore all the data on the server. On Windows Server 2003 domain controllers, you can also use the *install from media* option described in Recipe 15.2 to expedite this process.

The other option, nonauthoritative restore, is described in the first part of the Solution section; you can restore the domain controller from a good backup. This method involves booting into Directory Services Restore Mode, restoring the system state and any necessary system drives, and then rebooting. As long as the domain controller comes up clean, it should start participating in Active Directory replication once again and sync any changes that have occurred since the last backup.

In some cases, you may not want to restore an entire domain controller, but only certain objects in Active Directory. If an administrator or user accidentally deletes an important object or entire subtree from Active Directory, you can restore that particular object or set of objects. Fortunately, the process isn't very painful. The key is having a good backup that contains the objects you want to restore. If you don't have a backup that has the objects in it, you are out of luck.

 Well, that is not completely true with Windows Server 2003 since you can restore deleted objects, but that is beyond the scope of this recipe.

To restore one or more objects, you need to follow the same steps as performing a nonauthoritative restore. The only difference is that after you do the restore, you need to use the *ntdsutil* command to mark the objects in question as authoritative on the restored domain controller. After you reboot the domain controller, it will replicate any objects that have been added or modified since the last backup, except for the objects or subtrees that were marked as authoritative. For those objects, Active Directory increments the USN in such a way that they will become authoritative and replicate out to the other domain controllers.

You can also use *ntdsutil* without first doing a restore in situations where an object has been deleted accidentally, but the change has not yet replicated to all domain controllers. The trick here is that you need to find a domain controller that has not had the deletion replicated yet and either stop it from replicating or make the object authoritative before it receives the replication update.

The last restore method I describe is a complete authoritative restore. In a production environment, you should never have to perform this type of restore. It is a drastic measure and you will inevitably lose data as a result. Before you even attempt such a restore, you may want to contact Microsoft Support to make sure all options have been exhausted. That said, you should test the authoritative restore process in a lab environment, and make sure you have the steps properly documented in case you ever need to use it. Microsoft created a really good whitepaper on performing forest recoveries called *Best Practices: Active Directory Forest Recovery*, which you can download from *http://download.microsoft.com*.

For a detailed discussion of the advantages and disadvantages of each option, see Chapter 13 in *Active Directory* (O'Reilly).

See Also

MB KB 216243 (Authoritative Restore of Active Directory and Impact on Trusts and Computer Accounts), MS KB 240363 (HOW TO: Use the Backup Program to Back Up and Restore the System State in Windows 2000), MS KB 241594 (HOW TO: Perform an Authoritative Restore to a Domain Controller in Windows 2000), and MS

KB 280079 (Authoritative Restore of Groups Can Result in Inconsistent Membership Information Across Domain Controllers)

15.8 Searching for Objects in a Domain

Problem

You want to find objects that match certain criteria in a domain.

Solution

Using a graphical user interface

1. Open LDP from the Support Tools (*ldp.exe*).
2. From the menu, select **Connection** → **Connect**.
3. For **Server**, enter the name of a domain controller (or leave blank to do a server-less bind).
4. For **Port**, enter 389. To perform a forest-wide search using the Global Catalog, enter 3268.
5. Click **OK**.
6. From the menu, select **Connection** → **Bind**.
7. Enter credentials of a user.
8. Click **OK**.
9. From the menu, select **Browse** → **Search**.
10. For **BaseDN**, type the base distinguished name where to start the search.
11. For **Scope**, select the appropriate scope.
12. For **Filter**, enter an LDAP filter.
13. Click **Run**.

If you expect your search to return a large number of objects (e.g., more than 1000), you'll need to enable the Paged LDAP control to see them all in LDP.

1. Click the **Options** button.
2. For **Timeout** (s), enter a value such as 10.
3. For **Page size**, enter the number of objects to be returned with each page, (e.g., 1000).
4. Under **Search Call Type**, select **Paged**.
5. Click **OK**.
6. A page of results (i.e., 1000 entries) will be displayed each time you click on **Run** until all results have been returned.

Using a command-line interface

Use the following command to perform a search against a domain controller:

```
> dsquery * <BaseDN> -scope <Scope> -filter "<Filter>" -attr "<AttrList>"
```

The following example searches for all siteLink objects in the Configuration container:

```
> dsquery * "cn=configuration,dc=rallencorp,dc=com" -scope subtree -filter "(object
category=sitelink)" -attr "name"
```

Use the following command to perform a search against the global catalog:

```
> dsquery * <BaseDN> -gc -scope <Scope> -filter "<Filter>" -attr "<AttrList>"
```

Use the following command to perform a search in which you expect there to be a large number of matching entries:

```
> dsquery * <BaseDN> -limit 0 -scope <Scope> -filter "<Filter>" -attr "<AttrList>"
```

Using VBScript

```
' This code searches for objects based on the specified criteria.
' ------ SCRIPT CONFIGURATION ------
strBase   = "<LDAP://<BaseDN>>;" ' BaseDN should be the search base
strFilter = "<Filter>;"          ' Valid LDAP search filter
strAttrs  = "<AttrList>;"         ' Comma-seperated list
strScope  = "<Scope>"            ' Should be on of Subtree, Onelevel, or Base
' ------ END CONFIGURATION ---------

set objConn = CreateObject("ADODB.Connection")
objConn.Provider = "ADsDSOObject"
objConn.Open "Active Directory Provider"
set objRS = objConn.Execute(strBase & strFilter & strAttrs & strScope)
objRS.MoveFirst
while Not objRS.EOF
    Wscript.Echo objRS.Fields(0).Value
    objRS.MoveNext
wend


' This code enables paged searching
' ------ SCRIPT CONFIGURATION ------
strBase   = "<LDAP://<BaseDN>>;"
strFilter = "<Filter>;"
strAttrs  = "<AttrList>;"
strScope  = "<Scope>"
' ------ END CONFIGURATION ---------

set objConn = CreateObject("ADODB.Connection")
objConn.Provider = "ADsDSOObject"
objConn.Open "Active Directory Provider"
set objComm = CreateObject("ADODB.Command")
objComm.ActiveConnection = objConn
objComm.Properties("Page Size") = 1000
objComm.CommandText = strBase & strFilter & strAttrs & strScope
```

```
set objRS = objComm.Execute
objRS.MoveFirst
while Not objRS.EOF
    Wscript.Echo objRS.Fields(0).Value
    objRS.MoveNext
wend
```

Discussion

Most tools that can be used to search Active Directory require a basic understanding of how to perform LDAP searches using a base DN, search scope, and search filter as described in RFC 2251 and 2254. The base DN is where the search begins in the directory tree. The search scope defines how far down in the tree to search from the base DN. The search filter is a prefix notation string that contains equality comparisons of attribute and value pairs.

The scope can be base, onelevel (or one), or subtree (or sub). A base scope will match only the base DN, onelevel will match only objects that are contained directly under the base DN, and subtree will match everything below the base DN (not including the base DN).

The search filter syntax is a powerful way to represent simple and complex queries. An example filter that matches all user objects would be (&(objectclass=user)(objectcategory=Person)). For more information on filters, see RFC 2254.

When you perform a normal LDAP search over port 389, you are searching against a particular partition in Active Directory: the Domain naming context, Configuration naming context, Schema naming context, or application partition. If you have multiple domains in your forest, this type of search applies only to the specified domain.

The global catalog facilitates forest-wide searches. The global catalog contains a subset of the attributes for all objects in the forest (excluding objects in application partitions). Think of it as a subset of all the naming contexts combined. All objects will be contained in the global catalog, except for objects in application partitions, but only some of the attributes will be available. For that reason, if you perform a global catalog search and do not get values for attributes you expected, make sure those attributes are included in the global catalog, also known as the partial attribute set (PAS).

You might notice that searches with large numbers of matches stop displaying after 1000. Domain controllers return only a maximum of 1,000 entries from a search unless paging is enabled. This is done to prevent queries from consuming a lot of resources on domain controllers by retrieving the results all at once.

Paged support is implemented via an LDAP control. LDAP controls were defined in RFC 2251 and the Paged control in RFC 2696. Controls are extensions to LDAP that were not built into the protocol, so not all directory vendors support the same ones.

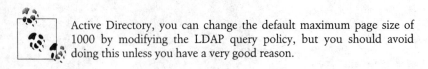 Active Directory, you can change the default maximum page size of 1000 by modifying the LDAP query policy, but you should avoid doing this unless you have a very good reason.

Active Directory returns a maximum of only 262,144 entries even when paged searching is enabled. This value is defined in the LDAP query policy and can be modified like the maximum page size.

Using a graphical user interface

A word of caution when using LDP to display a large number of entries: by default only 2048 lines will be displayed in the right pane. To change that value, go to Options → General and change the Line value under Buffer Size to a larger number.

Using a command-line interface

<AttrList> should be a comma-separated list of attributes to return. If left blank, all attributes that have a value will be returned. With -limit set to 0, paging will be enabled and all matching objects will be returned. If -limit is not specified, only 100 matches will be returned.

Using VBScript

The VBScript solution used ADO to perform the search. When using ADO, you must first create a connection object with the following three lines:

```
set objConn = CreateObject("ADODB.Connection")
objConn.Provider = "ADsDSOObject"
objConn.Open "Active Directory Provider"
```

At this point, you can pass parameters to the Execute method, which will return a ResultSet object. You can iterate over the ResultSet by using the MoveFirst and MoveNext methods.

To enable paged searching in ADO, you must instantiate an ADO Command object. A Command object allows you set various properties of a query, including size limit, time limit, and page size. See MSDN for the complete list.

See Also

RFC 2251 (Lightweight Directory Access Protocol (v3)), RFC 2254 (Lightweight Directory Access Protocol (v3)), MSDN: Searching with ActiveX Data Objects (ADO), and for a good whitepaper on performing queries with LDAP, see: *http:// www.microsoft.com/windows2000/techinfo/howitworks/activedirectory/ldap.asp*

15.9   Creating an Object

Problem

You want to create an object in Active Directory.

Solution

In each solution below, an example of adding a user object named jsmith is shown. Modify the examples as needed to include whatever class and attributes you need to create.

Using a graphical user interface

1. Open ADSI Edit.
2. If an entry for the naming context you want to browse is not already displayed, do the following:
   a. Right-click on **ADSI Edit** in the right pane and click **Connect to....**
   b. Fill in the information for the naming context, container, or OU you want to add an object to. Click on the **Advanced** button if you need to enter alternate credentials.
3. In the left pane, browse to the container or OU you want to add the object to. Once you've found the parent container, right-click on it and select **New → Object**.
4. Under **Select a Class**, select **user**.
5. For the cn, enter jsmith and click **Next**.
6. For sAMAccountName, enter jsmith and click **Next**.
7. Click the **More Attributes** button to enter additional attributes and values.
8. Click **Finish**.

Using a command-line interface

Create an LDIF file called *create_object.ldf* with the following contents:

```
dn: cn=jsmith,cn=users,dc=rallencorp,dc=com
changetype: add
objectClass: user
samaccountname: jsmith
```

Then run the following command:

```
> ldifde -v -i -f create_object.ldf
```

It is also worth noting that you can add a limited number of object types with the *dsadd* command. Run dsadd /? from a command line for more details.

Using VBScript

```
set objUsersCont = GetObject(LDAP://cn=users,dc=rallencorp,dc=com")
set objUser = objUsersCont.Create("user", "CN=jsmith")
objUser.Put "sAMAccountName", "jsmith" ' mandatory attribute in W2K
objUser.SetInfo
```

Discussion

To create an object in Active Directory, you have to specify the objectClass, relative distinguished name (RDN) value, and any other mandatory attributes that are not automatically set by Active Directory. Some of the automatically generated attributes include objectGUID, instanceType, and objectCategory.

In the jsmith example, the objectclass was user, the RDN value was jsmith, and the only other mandatory attribute that had to be set was sAMAccountName. Admittedly, this user object is unusable in its current state because it will be disabled by default and no password is set, but it should give you an idea of how to create an object.

Using a graphical user interface

Other tools such as AD Users and Computers could be used to do the same thing, but ADSI Edit is useful as a generic object editor.

One attribute that you will not be able to set via ADSI Edit is the password (unicodePwd attribute). It is stored in binary form and cannot be edited directly. If you want to set the password for a user through a GUI, you can do it with the AD Users and Computers snap-in.

Using a command-line interface

For more on *ldifde*, see Recipe 15.15.

With *dsadd* you can set numerous attributes when creating an object. The downside is that as of the publication of this book, you can create only the following object types: computer, contact, group, ou, quota, and user.

Using VBScript

The first step to create an object is to call GetObject on the parent container. Then call the Create method on that object and specify the objectClass and RDN for the new object. The sAMAccountName attribute is then set by using the Put method. Lastly, SetInfo commits the change. If SetInfo is not called, the creation will not be committed to the domain controller.

See Also

Recipe 15.15, MSDN: IADsContainer::GetObject, MSDN: IADsContainer::Create, MSDN: IADs::Put, and MSDN: IADs::SetInfo

---

15.10 Modifying an Object

Problem

You want to modify one or more attributes of an object.

Solution

The following examples set the last name (sn) attribute for the jsmith user object.

Using a graphical user interface

1. Open ADSI Edit.
2. If an entry for the naming context you want to browse is not already displayed, do the following:
3. Right-click on **ADSI Edit** in the right pane and click **Connect to…**.
4. Fill in the information for the naming context, container, or OU you want to add an object to. Click on the **Advanced** button if you need to enter alternate credentials.
5. In the left pane, browse to the container or OU that contains the object you want to modify. Once you've found the object, right-click on it and select **Properties**.
6. Edit the sn attribute.
7. Enter Smith and click **OK**.
8. Click **Apply**.

Using a command-line interface

Create an LDIF file called *modify_object.ldf* with the following contents:

```
dn: cn=jsmith,cn=users,dc=rallencorp,dc=com
changetype: modify
add: sn
sn: Smith
-
```

Then run the following command:

```
> ldifde -v -i -f modify_object.ldf
```

You can modify a limited number of object types with the *dsmod* command. Run dsmod /? from a command line for more details.

Using VBScript

```
strObjectDN = "cn=jsmith,cn=users,dc=rallencorp,dc=com"
set objUser = GetObject("LDAP://" & strObjectDN)
objUser.Put "sn", "Smith"
objUser.SetInfo
```

Discussion

Using a graphical user interface

If the parent container of the object you want to modify has a lot of objects in it, you may want to add a new connection for the DN of the target object. This will be easier than trying to hunt through a container full of objects. You can do this by right-clicking **ADSI Edit** and selecting **Connect to…**. Under **Connection Point**, select **Distinguished Name** and enter the DN of the object.

Using a command-line interface

For more on *ldifde*, see Recipe 15.15.

As of the publication of this book, the only types of objects you can modify with *dsmod* are computer, contact, group, ou, server, quota, and user.

Using VBScript

If you need to do anything more than assign or replace a value for an attribute, you'll need to use the PutEx method instead of Put. PutEx allows for greater control in assigning multiple values, deleting specific values, and appending values.

PutEx requires three parameters: an update flag, an attribute name, and an array of values to set or unset. The update flags are defined by the ADS_PROPERTY_OPERATION_ENUM collection and listed in Table 15-2.

Table 15-2. ADS_PROPERTY_OPERATION_ENUM

Name	Value	Description
ADS_PROPERTY_CLEAR	1	Remove all value(s) of the attribute.
ADS_PROPERTY_UPDATE	2	Replace the current values of the attribute with the ones passed in. This will clear any previously set values.
ADS_PROPERTY_APPEND	3	Add the values passed in to the set of existing values of the attribute.
ADS_PROPERTY_DELETE	4	Delete the values passed in.

Finally, SetInfo commits the change. If SetInfo is not called, the creation will not get committed to the domain controller.

In the following example, each update flag is used while setting the otherTelephoneNumber attribute:

```
strObjectDN = "cn=jsmith,cn=users,dc=rallencorp,dc=com"

const ADS_PROPERTY_CLEAR  = 1
const ADS_PROPERTY_UPDATE = 2
const ADS_PROPERTY_APPEND = 3
const ADS_PROPERTY_DELETE = 4
```

```
set objUser = GetObject("LDAP://" & strObjectDN)

' Add/Append two values
objUser.PutEx ADS_PROPERTY_APPEND, "otherTelephoneNumber", _
              Array("555-1212", "555-1213")
objUser.SetInfo
' Now otherTelephoneNumber = 555-1212, 555-1213

' Delete one of the values
objUser.PutEx ADS_PROPERTY_DELETE, "otherTelephoneNumber", Array("555-1213")
objUser.SetInfo
' Now otherTelephoneNumber = 555-1212

' Change values
objUser.PutEx ADS_PROPERTY_UPDATE, "otherTelephoneNumber", Array("555-1214")
objUser.SetInfo
' Now otherTelephoneNumber = 555-1214

' Clear all values
objUser.PutEx ADS_PROPERTY_CLEAR, "otherTelephoneNumber",  vbNullString
objUser.SetInfo
' Now otherTelephoneNumber = <empty>
```

See Also

MSDN: IADs::Put, MSDN: IADs::PutEx, MSDN: IADs::SetInfo, and MSDN: ADS_PROPERTY_OPERATION_ENUM

15.11 Moving an Object

Problem

You want to move an object to a different container or OU in the same domain.

Solution

Using a graphical user interface

1. Open ADSI Edit.
2. If an entry for the naming context you want to browse is not already displayed, do the following:
3. Right-click on **ADSI Edit** in the right pane and click **Connect to...**.
4. Fill in the information for the naming context, container, or OU where the object is currently. Click on the **Advanced** button if you need to enter alternate credentials.
5. In the left pane, browse to the container or OU that contains the object you want to modify. Once you've found the object, right-click on it and select **Move**.
6. Browse to the new parent of the object, select it and click **OK**.

Using a command-line interface

```
> dsmove "<ObjectDN>" -newparent "<NewParentDN>"
```

Using VBScript

```
' This code moves an object from one location to another in the same domain.
' ------ SCRIPT CONFIGURATION ------
strNewParentDN = "LDAP://<NewParentDN>"
strObjectDN    = "LDAP://cn=jsmith,<OldParentDN>"
strObjectRDN   = "cn=jsmith"
' ------ END CONFIGURATION ---------

set objCont = GetObject(strNewParentDN)
objCont.MoveHere strObjectDN, strObjectRDN
```

Discussion

Using a graphical user interface

If the parent container of the object you want to move has a lot of objects in it, you may want to add a new connection entry for the DN of the object you want to move. This may save you time searching through the list of objects in the container. You can do this by right-clicking **ADSI Edit** and selecting **Connect to...**. Under **Connection Point**, select **Distinguished Name** and enter the DN of the object you want to move.

Using a command-line interface

The *dsmove* utility can work against any type of object (there are no limitations as with *dsadd* and *dsmod*). The first parameter is the DN of the object to be moved. The second parameter is the new parent container of the object. The -s parameter can additionally be used to name a specific server to work against.

Using VBScript

The MoveHere method can be tricky, so an explanation of how to use it to move objects is in order. First, you need to call GetObject on the new parent container. Then call MoveHere on the parent container object with the ADsPath of the object to move as the first parameter and the RDN of the object to move as the second.

The reason for the apparent duplication of cn=jsmith in the MoveHere method is that the same method can also be used for renaming objects within the same container.

See Also

MS KB 313066 (HOW TO: Move Users, Groups, and Organizational Units Within a Domain in Windows 2000) and MSDN: IADsContainer::MoveHere

---

15.12 Moving an Object to a Different Domain

Problem

You want to move an object to a different domain within the same forest.

Solution

Using a command-line interface

```
> movetree /start /s SourceDC /d TargetDC /sdn SourceDN /ddn TargetDN
```

In the following example, the cn=jsmith object in the *amer.rallencorp.com* domain will be moved to the *emea.rallencorp.com* domain:

```
> movetree /start /s dc-amer1 /d dc-emea1
  /ddn cn=jsmith,cn=users,dc=amer,dc=rallencorp,dc=com
  /sdn cn=jsmith,cn=users,dc=emea,dc=rallencorp,dc=com
```

Using VBScript

```
set objObject = GetObject("LDAP://TargetDC/TargetParentDN")
objObject.MoveHere "LDAP://SourceDC/SourceDN", vbNullString
```

In the following example, the cn=jsmith object in the *amer.rallencorp.com* domain will be moved to the *emea.rallencorp.com* domain:

```
set objObject = GetObject( _
   "LDAP://dc-amer1/cn=users,dc=amer,dc=rallencorp,dc=com")
objObject.MoveHere _
   "LDAP://dc-emea1/cn=jsmith,cn=users,dc=emea,dc=rallencorp,dc=com", _
   vbNullString
```

Discussion

You can move objects between domains assuming you follow a few guidelines:

- The user requesting the move must have permissions to modify objects in the parent container of both domains.
- You need to explicitly specify the target DC (serverless binds usually do not work). This is necessary because the "Cross Domain Move" LDAP control is being used behind the scenes.
- The move operation must be performed against the RID master for both domains. This is so that the move is a single master operation, which prevents conflicts (i.e., moving to two different domains from different DCs).
- Both domains must be in native mode.

- When you move a user object to a different domain, its `objectSID` is replaced with a new SID (based on the new domain), and the old SID is added to the `sIDHistory` attribute.
- For group objects, you can move only universal groups. To move global or domain local groups, you must first convert them to universal.

There is currently no direct method to move user accounts between domains in different forests. This requires a restructuring tool such as ADMT 2.0, which actually creates new objects rather than actually moving the original objects. You can download ADMT from *http://download.microsoft.com*.

See Also

Chapter 4 of *Active Directory Cookbook* (O'Reilly) for more on LDAP controls, MS KB 238394 (How to Use the MoveTree Utility to Move Objects Between Domains in a Single Forest), and MSDN: IADsContainer::MoveHere

15.13 Renaming an Object

Problem

You want to rename an object and keep it in its current container or OU.

Solution

Using a graphical user interface

1. Open ADSI Edit.
2. If an entry for the naming context you want to browse is not already displayed, do the following:
   a. Right-click on **ADSI Edit** in the right pane and click **Connect to...**.
   b. Fill in the information for the naming context, container, or OU that contains the object you want to rename. Click on the **Advanced** button if you need to enter alternate credentials.
3. In the left pane, browse to container or OU where the object you want to modify is. Once you've found the object, right-click on it and select **Rename**.
4. Enter the new name and click **OK**.

Using a command-line interface

```
> dsmove "<ObjectDN>" -newname "<NewName>"
```

Using VBScript

```
' This code renames an object and leaves it in the same location.
' ------ SCRIPT CONFIGURATION ------
strCurrentParentDN = "<CurrentParentDN>"
strObjectOldName   = "cn=<OldName>"
strObjectNewName   = "cn=<NewName>"
' ------ END CONFIGURATION ---------

set objCont = GetObject("LDAP://" & strCurrentParentDN)
objCont.MoveHere "LDAP://" & strObjectOldName & "," & _
                 strCurrentParentDN, strObjectNewName
```

Discussion

Before you rename an object, ensure no applications reference it by name. You can make objects rename-safe by requiring all applications storing a reference to objects use the GUID of the object, not the name. The GUID (stored in the objectGUID attribute) is guaranteed to be unique and does not change when an object is renamed.

It is worth pointing out that by rename, I strictly mean renaming the object itself in the directory. If a user had a name change and thus need to be renamed, you may need to modify multiple attributes, such as sn (surname), sAMAccountName, userPrincipalName, etc.

Using a graphical user interface

If the parent container of the object you want to rename has a lot of objects in it, you may want to add a new connection for the DN of the object you want to rename. This may save you time searching through the list of objects in the container. You can do this by right-clicking **ADSI Edit** and selecting **Connect to…**. Under **Connection Point**, select **Distinguished Name** and enter the DN of the object you want to rename.

Using a command-line interface

The two parameters that are needed to rename an object are the original DN of the object and the new RDN (-newname). The -s option can also be used to specify a server name to work against.

Using VBScript

The MoveHere method can be tricky to use, so an explanation of how to use it to rename objects is in order. First, you need to call GetObject on the parent container of the object you want to rename. Then call MoveHere on the parent container object and specify the ADsPath of the object to rename as the first parameter. The new RDN including prefix (e.g., cn=) of the object should be the second parameter.

See Also

MSDN: IADsContainer::MoveHere

15.14 Deleting an Object

Problem

You want to delete an object or container from Active Directory.

Solution

Using a graphical user interface

1. Open ADSI Edit.
2. If an entry for the naming context you want to browse is not already displayed, do the following:

    a. Right-click on **ADSI Edit** in the right pane and click **Connect to....**

    b. Fill in the information for the naming context, container, or OU where the object you want to delete is contained. Click on the **Advanced** button if you need to enter alternate credentials.

3. In the left pane, browse to the object you want to delete.
4. Right-click on the object and select **Delete**.
5. Click **Yes** to confirm.

Using a command-line interface

Use the following command to delete a single object:

```
> dsrm "<ObjectDN>"
```

Use the following command to delete a container and its child objects:

```
> dsrm "<ObjectDN>" -subtree
```

Using VBScript

```
strObjectDN = "<ObjectDN>"
set objUser = GetObject("LDAP://" & strObjectDN)
objUser.DeleteObject(0)
```

Discussion

There is not much difference between deleting a leaf node and deleting a container that has child objects. However, there is a distinction in what is happening in the background.

Deleting an object that has no children can be done with a simple LDAP delete operation. On the other hand, to delete a container and its children, the tree delete LDAP control has to be used. If you were to do the deletion from an LDAP-based tool like LDP, you would first need to enable the **Subtree Delete** control, which has an OID of 1.2.840.113556.1.4.805. LDP provides another option to do a **Recursive Delete** from the client side. That will essentially iterate through all the objects in the container, deleting them one by one. The **Subtree Delete** is more efficient, especially when dealing with large containers.

Using a graphical user interface

If the parent container of the object you want to delete has a lot of objects in it, you may want to add a new connection entry for the DN of the object you want to delete. This may save you time searching through the list of objects in the container and could help avoid accidental deletions. You can do this by right-clicking **ADSI Edit** and selecting **Connect to…**. Under **Connection Point**, select **Distinguished Name** and enter the DN of the object you want to delete.

Using a command-line interface

The *dsrm* utility can be used to delete any type of object (no limitations based on object type as with *dsadd* and *dsmod*). The only required parameter is the DN of the object to delete. You can also specify -noprompt to keep it from asking for confirmation before deleting. The -s parameter can be used as well to specify a specific server to target.

Using VBScript

Using the DeleteObject method is straightforward. Passing 0 as a parameter is required but does not have any significance at present.

An alternate and perhaps safer way to delete objects is to use the IADsContainer::Delete method. To use this method, you must first bind to the parent container of the object. You can then call Delete by passing the object class and RDN of the object you want to delete. Here is an example for deleting a user object:

```
set objCont = GetObject("LDAP://ou=Sales,dc=rallencorp,dc=com")
objCont.Delete "user", "cn=rallen"
```

Delete is safer than DeleteObject because you have to be more explicit about what you are deleting. With DeleteObject you only need to specify a distinguished name and it will delete it. If you happen to mistype the DN or the user input to a web page that uses this method is mistyped, the result could be disastrous.

See Also

MS KB 258310 (Viewing Deleted Objects in Active Directory), MSDN: IADsContainer::Delete, and MSDN: IADsDeleteOps::DeleteObject

15.15 Exporting and Importing Objects Using LDIF or CSV

Problem

You want to import or export objects in mass. There are two ways to do this: via an LDIF file or comma-separated value file.

Solution

Using a graphical user interface

None of the standard Microsoft GUI tools support importing or exporting Active Directory data with LDIF or CSV.

Using a command-line interface

The following command exports objects using LDIF:

```
> ldifde -f output.ldf -l <AttrList> -p <Scope> -r "<Filter>" -d "<BaseDN>"
```

To import objects using the *ldifde* utility, you must first create an LDIF file with the objects to add, modify, or delete. Here is an example LDIF file that adds a user, modifies the user twice, and then deletes the user:

```
dn: cn=jsmith,cn=users,dc=rallencorp,dc=com
changetype: add
objectClass: user
samaccountname: jsmith
sn: JSmith
useraccountcontrol: 512

dn: cn=jsmith,cn=users,dc=rallencorp,dc=com
changetype: modify
add: givenName
givenName: Jim
-
replace: sn
sn: Smith
-

dn: cn=jsmith,cn=users,dc=rallencorp,dc=com
changetype: delete
```

Once you've created the LDIF file, you just need to run the *ldifde* command to import the new objects.

```
> ldifde -i -f input.ldf
```

The following command exports objects from a CSV file:

```
> csvde -f output.csv -l <AttrList> -p <Scope> -r "<Filter>" -d "<BaseDN>"
```

To import objects using the *csvde* utility, you must first create a CSV file containing the objects to add. The first line of the file should contain a comma-separated list of attributes you want to set, with DN being the first attribute. Here is an example:

```
DN,objectClass,cn,sn,userAccountControl,sAMAccountName,userPrincipalName
```

The rest of the lines should contain entries to add. If you want to leave one of the attributes unset, leave the value blank (followed by a comma). Here is a sample CSV file that would add two user objects.

```
DN,objectClass,sn,userAccountControl,sAMAccountName,userPrincipalName
"cn=jim,cn=users,dc=rallencorp,dc=com",user,Smith,512,jim,jim@rallencorp.com
"cn=john,cn=users,dc=rallencorp,dc=com",user,,512,john,john@rallencorp.com
```

Once you've created the CSV file, you need to run the *csvde* command to import the new objects:

```
> csvde -i -f input.csv
```

Using VBScript

None of the COM or VBScript-based interfaces support importing or exporting Active Directory data natively with LDIF or CSV. However, if you use Perl, you can use the Net::LDAP::LDIF module, which supports reading and writing LDIF files.

Discussion

The LDAP Data Interchange Format (LDIF) specification defined in RFC 2849 describes a well-defined file-based format for representing directory entries. The format is intended to be both human and machine parseable, which adds to its usefulness. LDIF is the de facto standard for importing and exporting a large number of objects.

While LDIF is useful for exchanging data between different LDAP servers, CSV is useful for exchanging data between Microsoft utilities, notably Excel. Once you have a CSV file containing entries, you can use Excel to view, sort, and manipulate the data.

The first line of a CSV file, as you can see from the example in the solution, lists the fields set by subsequent lines. Each subsequent line specifies values for one entry to be added. If you have a spreadsheet containing objects you want to import, first save it as a CSV file and use *csvde* to import it. You cannot modify attributes of an object or delete objects using *csvde*.

Using a command-line interface

In *ldifde*, the -f option specifies the name of the file to use to save the entries to, -s is the DC to query, -l is the comma-separated list of attributes to include, -p is the search scope, -r is the search filter, and -d is the base DN. If you encounter any problems using *ldifde*, the -v option enables verbose mode and can help identify problems.

To import with *ldifde*, simply specify the -i option to turn on import mode and -f *<filename>* for the file. It can also be beneficial to use the -v option to turn on verbose mode to get more information in case of errors.

The parameters used by *csvde* are nearly identical to those used by *ldifde*. The -f option specifies the name of the file to use to save the entries to, -s is the DC to query, -l is the comma-separated list of attributes to include, -p is the search scope (base, onelevel, or subtree), -r is the search filter, and -d is the base DN. If you encounter any issues, the -v option enables verbose mode and can help identify problems.

To import with *csvde*, simply specify the -i option to turn on import mode and -f *<filename>* for the file. It can also be beneficial to use the -v option to turn on verbose mode to get more information in case of errors.

See Also

RFC 2849 (The LDAP Data Interchange Format (LDIF) - Technical Specification), MS KB 237677 (Using LDIFDE to Import and Export Directory Objects to Active Directory), and MS KB 327620 (HOW TO: Use Csvde to Import Contacts and User Objects into Active Directory)

15.16 Finding the Closest Domain Controller

Problem

You want to find the closest domain controller for a particular domain.

Solution

Using a command-line interface

The following command finds the closest domain controller in the specified domain (*<DomainDNSName>*). By default, it will return the DC closest to the computer nltest is being run from, but you can optionally use the /server option to target a remote computer. You can also optionally specify the /site option to find a domain controller that belongs to a particular site.

```
> nltest /dsgetdc:<DomainDNSName> [/site:<SiteName>] [/server:<ClientName>]
```

Using VBScript

```
' This code finds the closest domain controller in the domain
' that the computer running the script is in.
' ------ SCRIPT CONFIGURATION ------
```

```
strDomain = "<DomainDNSName>"   ' e.g., emea.rallencorp.com
' ------ END CONFIGURATION ---------

set objIadsTools = CreateObject("IADsTools.DCFunctions")
objIadsTools.DsGetDcName( Cstr(strDomain) )
Wscript.Echo "DC: " & objIadsTools.DCName
Wscript.Echo "DC Site: " & objIadsTools.DCSiteName
Wscript.Echo "Client Site: " & objIadsTools.ClientSiteName
```

Discussion

The DC locator process as described in MS KB 314861 and MS KB 247811 defines how clients find the closest domain controller. The process uses the site topology stored in Active Directory to calculate the site where a particular client is. After the client site has been identified, it is a matter of finding a domain controller that is either a member of that same site or that is covering that site.

The Microsoft DsGetDcName Directory Services API method implements the DC Locator process, but unfortunately cannot be used directly from a scripting language, such as VBScript. The IADsTools interface provides a wrapper around DsGetDcName, which is what I used. The nltest /dsgetdc command is also a wrapper around the DsGetDcName method, and is a handy tool when troubleshooting client issues related to finding an optimal domain controller.

Using a command-line interface

You can use *nltest* to return the closest domain controller that is serving a particular function. Some of the available functions include a global catalog server (/GC option), time server (/TIMESERV option), KDC (/KDC option), and PDC (/PDC option). Run nltest /? from a command line for the complete list.

Using VBScript

As with *nltest*, you can specify additional criteria for finding a domain controller by calling the SetDsGetDcNameFlags method before calling DsGetDcName. SetDsGetDcNameFlags accepts a comma-delimited string of the following flags:

- DS_FORCE_REDISCOVERY
- DS_DIRECTORY_SERVICE_REQUIRED
- DS_DIRECTORY_SERVICE_PREFERRED
- DS_GC_SERVER_REQUIRED
- DS_PDC_REQUIRED
- DS_IP_REQUIRED
- DS_KDC_REQUIRED
- DS_TIMESERV_REQUIRED
- DS_WRITABLE_REQUIRED

- DS_GOOD_TIMESERV_PREFERRED
- DS_AVOID_SELF
- DS_IS_FLAT_NAME
- DS_IS_DNS_NAME
- DS_RETURN_DNS_NAME
- DS_RETURN_FLAT_NAME

See Also

For more information on the IADsTools interface, see *IadsTools.doc* in the Support Tools; MS KB 247811 (How Domain Controllers Are Located in Windows); MS KB 314861 (How Domain Controllers Are Located in Windows XP); and MSDN: DsGetDcName, and MSDN: MicrosoftDNS

15.17 Enabling and Disabling the Global Catalog

Problem

You want to enable or disable the global catalog on a particular domain controller.

Solution

Using a graphical user interface

1. Open the Active Directory Sites and Services snap-in.
2. Browse to the nTDSDSA object (NTDS Settings) underneath the server object for the domain controller whose global catalog you want to enable or disable.
3. Right-click on **NTDS Settings** and select **Properties**.
4. Under the **General** tab, check (to enable) or uncheck (to disable) the box beside **Global Catalog**.
5. Click **OK**.

Using a command-line interface

In the following command, *<ServerObjectDN>* should be the server object DN, not the DN of the nTDSDSA object:

```
> dsmod server "<ServerObjectDN>" -isgc yes|no
```

For example, the following command enables the global catalog on *dc1* in the Raleigh site:

```
> dsmod server
"cn=DC1,cn=servers,cn=Raleigh,cn=sites,cn=configuration,dc=rallencorp,dc=com" -isgc
yes
```

Using VBScript

```
' This code enables or disables the GC for the specified DC
' ------ SCRIPT CONFIGURATION ------
strDC = "<DomainControllerName>"   ' e.g., dc01.rallencorp.com
strGCEnable = 1                    ' 1 = enable, 0 = disable
' ------ END CONFIGURATION ---------

set objRootDSE = GetObject("LDAP://" & strDC & "/RootDSE")
objNTDS = GetObject("LDAP://" & strDC & "/" & _
                    objRootDSE.Get("dSServiceName"))
objNTDS.Put "options", strGCEnable
objNTDS.SetInfo
```

Discussion

The first domain controller promoted into a forest is by default also made a global catalog server. If you want additional servers to contain the global catalog, you have to enable it. The global catalog on a domain controller becomes enabled when the low-order bit on the options attribute on the nTDSDSA object under the server object for the domain controller is set to 1. The DN of this object for *dc1* in the Default-First-Site-Name site looks like this: *cn=NTDS Settings,cn=DC1,cn=Default-First-Site-Name,cn=Sites,cn=Configuration, dc=rallencorp,dc=com*.

After enabling the global catalog, it can take some time before the domain controller can start serving as a global catalog server. The length of time is based on the amount of data that needs to replicate and the type of connectivity between the domain controller's replication partners. Once a server has completed initial replication of the global catalog, the isGlobalCatalogReady attribute in the RootDSE will be marked TRUE. Another way to determine if a domain controller has been at least flagged to become a global catalog is by checking if the options attribute on the nTDSDSA object for the server has been set to 1. Note that this does not necessarily mean the server is accepting requests as a global catalog. After replication is complete, you should see Event 1119 in the Directory Services log stating the server is advertising itself as a global catalog. At that point, you should also be able to perform LDAP queries against port 3268 on that server.

 If you have Exchange installed in the forest, you'll also need to reboot the server before it will be used as a global catalog by Exchange servers and clients.

See Also

MS KB 313994 (HOW TO: Create or Move a Global Catalog in Windows 2000)

15.18 Finding the FSMO Role Holders

Problem

You want to find the domain controllers that are acting as one of the FSMO role holders.

Solution

Using a graphical user interface

For the Schema Master:

1. Open the Active Directory Schema snap-in.
2. Right-click on **Active Directory Schema** in the left pane and select **Operations Master**.

For the Domain Naming Master:

1. Open the Active Directory Domains and Trusts snap-in.
2. Right-click on **Active Directory Domains and Trusts** in the left pane and select **Operations Master**.

For the PDC Emulator, RID Master, and Infrastructure Master:

1. Open the Active Directory Users and Computers snap-in.
2. Make sure you've targeted the correct domain.
3. Right-click on **Active Directory Users and Computers** in the left pane and select **Operations Master**.
4. There are individual tabs for the PDC, RID, and Infrastructure roles.

Using a command-line interface

In the following command, you can leave out the /Domain *<DomainDNSName>* option to query the domain in which you are currently logged on:

```
> netdom query fsmo /Domain:<DomainDNSName>
```

You can also use the dsquery server command to list the FSMO role owners as shown here where *<Role>* can be schema, name, infr, pdc, or rid:

```
> dsquery server -hasfsmo <Role>
```

Using VBScript

```
' This code prints the FSMO role owners for the specified domain.
' ------ SCRIPT CONFIGURATION ------
strDomain = "<DomainDNSName>"  ' e.g., emea.rallencorp.com
' ------ END CONFIGURATION ---------
```

```
set objRootDSE = GetObject("LDAP://" & strDomain & "/RootDSE")
strDomainDN  = objRootDSE.Get("defaultNamingContext")
strSchemaDN = objRootDSE.Get("schemaNamingContext")
strConfigDN = objRootDSE.Get("configurationNamingContext")

' PDC Emulator
set objPDCFsmo = GetObject("LDAP://" & strDomainDN)
Wscript.Echo "PDC Emulator: " & objPDCFsmo.fsmoroleowner

' RID Master
set objRIDFsmo = GetObject("LDAP://cn=RID Manager$,cn=system," & strDomainDN)
Wscript.Echo "RID Master: " & objRIDFsmo.fsmoroleowner

' Schema Master
set objSchemaFsmo = GetObject("LDAP://" & strSchemaDN)
Wscript.Echo "Schema Master: " & objSchemaFsmo.fsmoroleowner

' Infrastructure Master
set objInfraFsmo = GetObject("LDAP://cn=Infrastructure," & strDomainDN)
Wscript.Echo "Infrastructure Master: " & objInfraFsmo.fsmoroleowner

' Domain Naming Master
set objDNFsmo = GetObject("LDAP://cn=Partitions," & strConfigDN)
Wscript.Echo "Domain Naming Master: " & objDNFsmo.fsmoroleowner
```

Discussion

Several Active Directory operations are sensitive, such as updating the schema, and therefore need to be done on a single domain controller. Active Directory cannot guarantee the proper execution of these functions in a situation where they may be invoked from more than one DC. The FSMO mechanism is used to limit these functions to a single DC.

There are five designated FSMO roles that correspond to these sensitive functions. A FSMO role can apply either to an entire forest or to a specific domain. Each role is stored in the fSMORoleOwner attribute on various objects in Active Directory depending on the role. Table 15-3 lists FSMO roles:

Table 15-3. FSMO roles

Role	Description	fSMORoleOwner location	Domain- or forest-wide?
Schema	Processes schema updates	*CN=Schema,CN=Configuration, <ForestDN>*	Forest
Domain Naming	Processes the addition, removal, and renaming of domains	*CN=Partitions,CN=Configuration, <ForestDN>*	Forest
Infrastructure	Maintains references to objects in other domains	*CN=Infrastructure,<DomainDN>*	Domain

Table 15-3. FSMO roles (continued)

Role	Description	fSMORoleOwner location	Domain- or forest-wide?
RID	Handles RID pool allocation for the domain controllers in a domain	*CN=Rid Manager$, CN=System,<DomainDN>*	Domain
PDC Emulator	Acts as the domain master browser and as the PDC for downlevel clients and Backup Domain Controllers (BDCs)	*<DomainDN>*	Domain

Using VBScript

If you want to get the DNS name for each FSMO, you'll need to get the parent object of the nTDSDSA object and use the dNSHostName attribute. The code for getting the Schema Master could be changed to the following to retrieve the DNS name of the DC:

```
set objSchemaFsmo = GetObject("LDAP://cn=Schema,cn=Configuration," & strForestDN)
set objSchemaFsmoNTDS = GetObject("LDAP://" & objSchemaFsmo.fsmoroleowner)
set objSchemaFsmoServer = GetObject(objSchemaFsmoNTDS.Parent)
Wscript.Echo "Schema Master: " & objSchemaFsmoServer.Get("dNSHostName")
```

See Also

MS KB 197132 (Windows 2000 Active Directory FSMO Roles), MS KB 223346 (FSMO Placement and Optimization on Windows 2000 Domain Controllers), MS KB 234790 (HOW TO: Find Servers That Hold Flexible Single Master Operations Roles), and MS KB 324801 (HOW TO: View and Transfer FSMO Roles in Windows Server 2003)

15.19 Transferring or Seizing a FSMO Role

Problem

You want to transfer a FSMO role to a different domain controller. This is necessary if you need to take a current FSMO role holder down for maintenance. If a current FSMO role holder is unavailable, you'll need to seize the role on another domain controller.

Solution

Using a graphical user interface

1. Use the same directions as described in Recipe 15.18 for viewing a specific FSMO, except target (i.e., right-click and select **Connect to Domain Controller**) the domain controller you want to transfer the FSMO to before selecting **Operations Master**.

2. Click the **Change** button.

3. Click **OK** twice.

4. You should then see a message stating whether the transfer was successful.

Using a command-line interface

The following transfers the PDC Emulator role to `<NewRoleOwner>`. See the discussion for more about transferring the other roles:

```
> ntdsutil roles conn "co t s <NewRoleOwner>" q "transfer PDC" q q
```

The following seizes the PDC Emulator role to run on `<NewRoleOwner>`:

```
> ntdsutil roles conn "co t s <NewRoleOwner>" q "seize PDC" q q
```

Using VBScript

```
' This code transfers the PDC Emulator role to the specified owner.
' See the discussion to see about transferring the other roles.
' ------ SCRIPT CONFIGURATION ------
strNewOwner = "<NewRoleOwner>"  ' e.g., dc2.rallencorp.com
' ------ END CONFIGURATION ---------
Set objRootDSE = GetObject("LDAP://" & strNewOwner & "/RootDSE")
objRootDSE.Put "becomePDC", 1
objRootDSE.SetInfo
```

Seizing a FSMO role is typically not something you need to do programmatically, but you can do it. All you need to do is set the `fSMORoleOwner` attribute for the object that represents the FSMO role as described in Recipe 15.18 with the distinguished name of nTDSDSA object of the new role owner.

Discussion

The first domain controller in a new forest is assigned the two forest-wide FSMO roles (schema and domain naming). The first domain controller in a new domain gets the other three domain-wide roles. It is very likely you'll need to move the roles around to different domain controllers at some point. Also, when you need to take down a domain controller that is currently a FSMO role owner, you'll want to transfer the role beforehand. If you plan to install a hotfix or do some other type of maintenance that necessitates only a quick reboot, you may not want to go to the trouble of transferring the FSMO role.

Some FSMO roles are more time critical than others. For example, the PDC Emulator role is used extensively, but the Schema Master is needed only when extending the schema. If a FSMO role owner becomes unavailable before you can transfer it, you'll need to seize the role.

Seizing a FSMO role should not be done lightly. The general recommendation is to seize a FSMO role only when you cannot possibly bring the previous role holder back online. One reason that seizing a role is problematic is that you could possibly lose data. For example, let's say that you extended the schema and immediately after it was extended, the Schema FSMO went down. If you could not bring that server back online, those extensions may have not replicated before the server went down. You would need to determine if the schema extensions replicated and, if not, re-extend the schema. A similar problem can result from losing the RID FSMO, where duplicate RID pools may be allocated.

Using a command-line interface

Any role can be transferred using ntdsutil by replacing "transfer PDC" in the solution with one of the following:

- "transfer domain naming master"
- "transfer infrastructure master"
- "transfer RID master"
- "transfer schema master"

Using VBScript

FSMO roles can be transferred programmatically by setting the become<FSMORole> operational attribute on the RootDSE of the domain controller to transfer the role to. The following are the available attributes that can be set that correspond to each FSMO role:

- becomeDomainMaster
- becomeInfrastructureMaster
- becomePDC
- becomeRidMaster
- becomeSchemaMaster

See Also

Recipe 15.18, MS KB 223787 (Flexible Single Master Operation Transfer and Seizure Process), MS KB 255504 (Using Ntdsutil.exe to Seize or Transfer FSMO Roles to a Domain Controller), and MS KB 324801 (HOW TO: View and Transfer FSMO Roles in Windows Server 2003)

15.20 Creating and Removing a Trust

Problem

You want to create or delete a trust from an AD domain to a Windows NT domain, Kerberos realm, or another AD domain.

Solution

Using a graphical user interface

1. Open the Active Directory Domains and Trusts snap-in.

2. In the left pane, right-click the domain you want to add a trust for and select **Properties**.

3. Click on the **Trusts** tab.

4. Click the **New Trust** button.

5. After the **New Trust Wizard** opens, click **Next**.

6. Complete the rest of the wizard steps. They will vary depending on the type of trust you create.

Using a command-line interface

```
> netdom trust <TargetDomainName> /Domain:<ADDomainName> /ADD
        [/UserD:<ADDomainName>\ADUser> /PasswordD:*]
        [/UserO:<TargetDomainName>\TargetUser> /PasswordO:*]
        [/TwoWay]
```

For example, to create a trust from the NT4 domain RALLENCORP_NT4 to the AD domain RALLENCORP, use the following command:

```
> netdom trust RALLENCORP_NT4 /Domain:RALLENCORP /ADD
        /UserD:RALLENCORP\administrator /PasswordD:*
        /UserO:RALLENCORP_NT4\administrator /PasswordO:*
```

You can make the trust bidirectional, i.e., two-way, by adding a /TwoWay option to the example.

The following command deletes a trust:

```
> netdom trust <TrustingDomain> /Domain:<TrustedDomain> /Remove /verbose
  [/UserO:<TrustingDomainUser> /PasswordO:*]
  [/UserD:<TrustedDomainUser> /PasswordD:*]
```

Using VBScript

None of the scripting interfaces support the capability to create a trust, but you can delete them as shown here:

```
' This code deletes a trust in the specified domain.
' ------ SCRIPT CONFIGURATION ------
' Set to the DNS or NetBIOS name for the Windows 2000,
' Windows NT domain or Kerberos realm trust you want to delete.
strTrustName = "<TrustName>"
' Set to the DNS name of the source or trusting domain
strDomain    = "<DomainDNSName>"
' ------ END CONFIGURATION ---------
```

```
set objRootDSE = GetObject("LDAP://" & strDomain & "/RootDSE")
set objTrust = GetObject("LDAP://cn=System," & _
                         objRootDSE.Get("defaultNamingContext") )
objTrust.Delete "trustedDomain", "cn=" & strTrustName
set objTrustUser = GetObject("LDAP://cn=Users," & _
                         objRootDSE.Get("defaultNamingContext") )
objTrustUser.Delete "trustedDomain", "cn=" & strTrustName & "$"
WScript.Echo "Successfully deleted trust for " & strTrustName
```

Discussion

It is common when migrating from a Windows NT environment to Active Directory to set up trusts to down-level master account domains or resource domains. This allows AD users to access resources in the NT domains without providing alternate credentials. Windows NT does not support transitive trusts and therefore your only option is to create a nontransitive trust. That means you'll need to set up individual trusts between the NT domain and every Active Directory domain that contains users that need to access the NT resources.

In Windows Server 2003, Active Directory introduced a new trust type called a forest trust. A forest trust allows you to create a single transitive trust between two forest root domains and have it apply to all subdomains. In Windows 2000 forests, you have to set up individual trusts between all the domains in one forest with all the domains in another.

Trusts are stored in Active Directory as two objects; a trustedDomain object in the System container and a user object in the Users container. Both of these objects need to be removed when deleting a trust. The GUI and CLI solutions take care of that in one step, but in the VBScript example both objects needed to be explicitly deleted. It is also worth noting that each solution deleted only one side of the trust. If the trust was to a remote AD forest or NT 4.0 domain, you also need to delete the trust in that domain.

See Also

MS KB 306733 (HOW TO: Create a Trust Between a Windows 2000 Domain and a Windows NT 4.0 Domain), MS KB 308195 (HOW TO: Establish Trusts with a Windows NT-Based Domain in Windows 2000), MS KB 309682 (HOW TO: Set up a One-Way Non-Transitive Trust in Windows 2000), MS KB 325874 (HOW TO: Establish Trusts with a Windows NT-Based Domain in Windows Server 2003), and MS KB 816301 (HOW TO: Create an External Trust in Windows Server 2003)

15.21 Viewing the Trusts for a Domain

Problem

You want to view the trusts that are configured in a domain.

Solution

Using a graphical user interface

1. Open the Active Directory Domains and Trusts snap-in.
2. In the left pane, right-click the domain you want to view and select **Properties**.
3. Click on the **Trusts** tab.

Using a command-line interface

```
> netdom query trust /Domain:<DomainDNSName>
```

Using VBScript

```vbscript
' This code prints the trusts for the specified domain.
' ------ SCRIPT CONFIGURATION ------
strDomain = "<DomainDNSName>"    ' e.g., rallencorp.com
' ------ END CONFIGURATION ---------

' Trust Direction Constants taken from NTSecAPI.h
set objTrustDirectionHash = CreateObject("Scripting.Dictionary")
objTrustDirectionHash.Add "DIRECTION_DISABLED", 0
objTrustDirectionHash.Add "DIRECTION_INBOUND",  1
objTrustDirectionHash.Add "DIRECTION_OUTBOUND", 2
objTrustDirectionHash.Add "DIRECTION_BIDIRECTIONAL", 3

' Trust Type Constants - taken from NTSecAPI.h
set objTrustTypeHash = CreateObject("Scripting.Dictionary")
objTrustTypeHash.Add "TYPE_DOWNLEVEL", 1
objTrustTypeHash.Add "TYPE_UPLEVEL", 2
objTrustTypeHash.Add "TYPE_MIT", 3
objTrustTypeHash.Add "TYPE_DCE", 4

' Trust Attribute Constants - taken from NTSecAPI.h
set objTrustAttrHash = CreateObject("Scripting.Dictionary")
objTrustAttrHash.Add "ATTRIBUTES_NON_TRANSITIVE", 1
objTrustAttrHash.Add "ATTRIBUTES_UPLEVEL_ONLY", 2
objTrustAttrHash.Add "ATTRIBUTES_QUARANTINED_DOMAIN", 4
objTrustAttrHash.Add "ATTRIBUTES_FOREST_TRANSITIVE", 8
objTrustAttrHash.Add "ATTRIBUTES_CROSS_ORGANIZATION", 16
objTrustAttrHash.Add "ATTRIBUTES_WITHIN_FOREST", 32
objTrustAttrHash.Add "ATTRIBUTES_TREAT_AS_EXTERNAL", 64

set objRootDSE = GetObject("LDAP://" & strDomain & "/RootDSE")
set objTrusts  = GetObject("LDAP://cn=System," & _
                           objRootDSE.Get("defaultNamingContext") )
objTrusts.Filter = Array("trustedDomain")
Wscript.Echo "Trusts for " & strDomain & ":"

for each objTrust in objTrusts
   for each strFlag In objTrustDirectionHash.Keys
      if objTrustDirectionHash(strFlag) = objTrust.Get("trustDirection") then
```

```
            strTrustInfo = strTrustInfo & strFlag & " "
         end If
      next

      for each strFlag In objTrustTypeHash.Keys
         if objTrustTypeHash(strFlag) = objTrust.Get("trustType") then
            strTrustInfo = strTrustInfo & strFlag & " "
         end If
      next

      for each strFlag In objTrustAttrHash.Keys
         if objTrustAttrHash(strFlag) = objTrust.Get("trustAttributes") then
            strTrustInfo = strTrustInfo & strFlag & " "
         end If
      next

      WScript.Echo " " & objTrust.Get("trustPartner") & " : " & strTrustInfo
      strTrustInfo = ""
   next
```

Discussion

Using a graphical user interface

You can view the properties of a particular trust by clicking on a trust and clicking the **Properties** button.

Using a command-line interface

You can include the /Direct option if you want to view only direct trust relationships. If you don't use /Direct, implicit trusts that occur due to transitive trust relationships will also be listed.

Using VBScript

This script uses dictionary objects to ease the mapping of the various integer values for attributes such as trustType and trustDirection to descriptive names. A dictionary object in VBScript is analogous to a hash or associative array in other programming languages. The Add method accepts a key and value pair to add to the dictionary. The Keys method returns the keys of the dictionary as a collection. To access a value of the dictionary, you simply pass the key name as a parameter to the dictionary object, such as objDictionary(strKey).

Another option to query trusts programmatically is with the Trustmon WMI Provider. The Trustmon Provider is new to Windows Server 2003. See Recipe 15.22 for an example.

See Also

Recipes 15.22, MS KB 228477 (HOW TO: Determine Trust Relationship Configurations), and MSDN: TRUSTED_DOMAIN_INFORMATION_EX

15.22 Verifying and Resetting Trusts

Problem

You want to verify that a trust is working correctly. This is the first diagnostic step to take if users notify you that authentication to a remote domain appears to be failing. If you've determined a trust is broken, you need to reset it, which will allow users to authenticate across it again.

Solution

Using a graphical user interface

For the Windows 2000 version of the Active Directory Domains and Trusts snap-in:

1. In the left pane, right-click on the trusting domain and select **Properties**.
2. Click the **Trusts** tab.
3. Click the domain that is associated with the trust you want to verify.
4. Click the **Edit** button.
5. Click the **Verify** button.
6. If the validation function fails, you'll be given an option to reset the trust.

For the Windows Server 2003 version of the Active Directory Domains and Trusts snap-in:

1. In the left pane, right-click on the trusting domain and select Properties.
2. Click the **Trusts** tab.
3. Click the domain that is associated with the trust you want to verify.
4. Click the **Properties** button.
5. Click the **Validate** button.
6. If the validation function fails, you'll be given an option to reset the trust.

Using a command-line interface

The following command verifies a trust:

```
> netdom trust <TrustingDomain> /Domain:<TrustedDomain> /Verify /verbose
   [/User0:<TrustingDomainUser> /Password0:*]
   [/UserD:<TrustedDomainUser> /PasswordD:*]
```

The following command resets a trust:

```
> netdom trust <TrustingDomain> /Domain:<TrustedDomain> /Reset /verbose
  [/UserO:<TrustingDomainUser> /PasswordO:*]
  [/UserD:<TrustedDomainUser> /PasswordD:*]
```

Using VBScript

```
' The following code lists all of the trusts for the
' specified domain using the Trustmon WMI Provider.
' The Trustmon WMI Provider is supported only on Windows Server 2003.
' ------ SCRIPT CONFIGURATION ------
strDomain = "<DomainDNSName>"  ' e.g., amer.rallencorp.com
' ------ END CONFIGURATION ---------
set objWMI = GetObject("winmgmts:\\" & strDomain & _
                       "\root\MicrosoftActiveDirectory")
set objTrusts = objWMI.ExecQuery("Select * from Microsoft_DomainTrustStatus")
for each objTrust in objTrusts
    Wscript.Echo objTrust.TrustedDomain
    Wscript.Echo " TrustedAttributes: " & objTrust.TrustAttributes
    Wscript.Echo " TrustedDCName: "     & objTrust.TrustedDCName
    Wscript.Echo " TrustedDirection: "  & objTrust.TrustDirection
    Wscript.Echo " TrustIsOk: "         & objTrust.TrustIsOK
    Wscript.Echo " TrustStatus: "       & objTrust.TrustStatus
    Wscript.Echo " TrustStatusString: " & objTrust.TrustStatusString
    Wscript.Echo " TrustType: "         & objTrust.TrustType
    Wscript.Echo ""
next


' This code shows how to search specifically for trusts
' that have failed, which can be accomplished using a WQL query that
' contains the query: TrustIsOk = False
' ------ SCRIPT CONFIGURATION ------
strDomain = "<DomainDNSName>"  ' e.g., amer.rallencorp.com
' ------ END CONFIGURATION ---------

set objWMI = GetObject("winmgmts:\\" & strDomain & _
                       "\root\MicrosoftActiveDirectory")
set objTrusts = objWMI.ExecQuery("select * " _
                     & " from Microsoft_DomainTrustStatus " _
                     & " where TrustIsOk = False ")
if objTrusts.Count = 0 then
   Wscript.Echo "There are no trust failures"
else
   WScript.Echo "Trust Failures:"
   for each objTrust in objTrusts
      Wscript.Echo " " & objTrust.TrustedDomain & " : " & _
                      objTrust.TrustStatusString
      Wscript.Echo ""
   next
end if


' This code resets the specified trust.
' ------ SCRIPT CONFIGURATION ------
```

```
' Set to the DNS or NetBIOS name for the Windows 2000,
' Windows NT domain or Kerberos realm you want to reset the trust for.
strTrustName = "<TrustToCheck>"

' Set to the DNS name of the source or trusting domain.
strDomain    = "<TrustingDomain>"
' ------ END CONFIGURATION ---------

' Enable SC_RESET during trust enumerations
set objTrustProv = GetObject("winmgmts:\\" & strDomain & _
             "\root\MicrosoftActiveDirectory:Microsoft_TrustProvider=@")
objTrustProv.TrustCheckLevel = 3  ' Enumerate with SC_RESET
objTrustProv.Put_

' Query the trust and print status information
set objWMI = GetObject("winmgmts:\\" & strDomain & _
                     "\root\MicrosoftActiveDirectory")
set objTrusts = objWMI.ExecQuery("Select * " _
                   & " from Microsoft_DomainTrustStatus " _
                   & " where TrustedDomain = '" & strTrustName & "'" )
for each objTrust in objTrusts
    Wscript.Echo objTrust.TrustedDomain
    Wscript.Echo " TrustedAttributes: " & objTrust.TrustAttributes
    Wscript.Echo " TrustedDCName: "     & objTrust.TrustedDCName
    Wscript.Echo " TrustedDirection: "  & objTrust.TrustDirection
    Wscript.Echo " TrustIsOk: "         & objTrust.TrustIsOK
    Wscript.Echo " TrustStatus: "       & objTrust.TrustStatus
    Wscript.Echo " TrustStatusString: " & objTrust.TrustStatusString
    Wscript.Echo " TrustType: "         & objTrust.TrustType
    Wscript.Echo ""
next
```

Discussion

Verifying a trust consists of checking connectivity between the domains, and determining if the shared secrets of a trust are synchronized between the two domains. Resetting a trust synchronizes the shared secrets (i.e., passwords) for the trust. The PDC role holder in both domains is used to synchronize the password so they must be reachable.

Using a graphical user interface

The Active Directory Domains and Trusts screens have changed somewhat between Windows 2000 and Windows Server 2003. The Verify button has been renamed Validate.

Using a command-line interface

If you want to verify a Kerberos trust, use the /Kerberos option with the *netdom* command. If you are resetting a Kerberos realm trust, you'll need to specify the /PasswordT option.

Using VBScript

The WMI Trustmon Provider is new to Windows Server 2003. It provides a nice interface for querying and checking the health of trusts. One of the benefits of using WMI to access this kind of data is that you can use WQL, the WMI Query Language, to perform complex queries to find trusts with certain properties. WQL is a subset of the Structured Query Language (SQL) commonly used to query databases. In the second VBScript example, I used WQL to find all trusts that have a problem. You could expand the query to include additional criteria, such as trust direction, trust type, and so on.

See Also

MSDN: Trustmon Provider

15.23 Enabling Diagnostics Logging

Problem

You want to enable diagnostics event logging because the current level of logging is not providing enough information to help pinpoint the problem you are troubleshooting.

Solution

Using a graphical user interface

1. Run *regedit.exe* from the command line or **Start → Run**.
2. In the left pane, expand **HKEY_LOCAL_MACHINE → System → CurrentControlSet → Services → NTDS → Diagnostics**.
3. In the right pane, double-click on the diagnostics logging entry you want to increase, and enter a number (0–5) based on how much you want logged.
4. Click **OK**.

Using a command-line interface

```
> reg add HKLM\SYSTEM\CurrentControlSet\Services\NTDS\Diagnostics /v
"<LoggingSetting>" /t REG_DWORD /d <0-5>
```

Using VBScript

```
' This code sets the specified diagnostics logging level
' ------ SCRIPT CONFIGURATION ------
strDC   = "<DomainControllerName>"  ' e.g., dc01
strLogSetting = "<LoggingSetting>"   ' e.g., 1 Knowledge Consistency Checker
```

```
intFlag = <FlagValue>               ' Flag value in decimal, e.g., 5
' ------ END CONFIGURATION ---------
const HKLM = &H80000002
strRegKey = "SYSTEM\CurrentControlSet\Services\NTDS\Diagnostics"
set objReg = GetObject("winmgmts:\\" & strDC & "\root\default:StdRegProv")
objReg.SetDwordValue HKLM, strRegKey, strLogSetting, intFlag
WScript.Echo "Diagnostics logging for " & strLogSetting _
             & " set to " & intFlag
```

Discussion

A useful way to troubleshoot specific problems you are encountering with Active
Directory is to increase the diagnostics logging level. Diagnostics logging can be
enabled by component. For example, if you determine the KCC is not completing
every 15 minutes, you can enable diagnostics logging for the one Knowledge Consistency Checker setting.

These settings are stored under HKLM\SYSTEM\CurrentControlSet\Services\NTDS\
Diagnostics. By default, all settings are set to 0, which disables diagnostic logging,
but you can increase any one of them by setting it to a number from 1 through 5. As
a general rule, a value of 1 is used for minimum logging, 3 for medium logging, and 5
for maximum logging. It is a good practice to ease your way up to 5 because some
diagnostics logging settings can generate a huge number of events in the event log,
which may make it difficult to read, along with increasing resource utilization on the
domain controller.

Here is the complete list of diagnostics logging settings for Windows Server 2003. Note
that settings 20–24 are not available on Windows 2000–based domain controllers.

```
 1 Knowledge Consistency Checker
 2 Security Events
 3 ExDS Interface Events
 4 MAPI Interface Events
 5 Replication Events
 6 Garbage Collection
 7 Internal Configuration
 8 Directory Access
 9 Internal Processing
10 Performance Counters
11 Initialization/Termination
12 Service Control
13 Name Resolution
14 Backup
15 Field Engineering
16 LDAP Interface Events
17 Setup
18 Global Catalog
19 Inter-site Messaging
20 Group Caching
```

```
21 Linked-Value Replication
22 DS RPC Client
23 DS RPC Server
24 DS Schema
```

See Also

MS KB 220940 (How to Enable Diagnostic Event Logging for Active Directory Services)

15.24 Script: Displaying the Structure of a Forest

Do you know the structure of your Active Directory forest? You could use a tool such as ADSI Edit and expand all of the OUs and containers in each domain, but if you have a lot of OUs, this would be very time consuming.

With a pretty simple script, you can enumerate all the domains, OUs, and containers in a forest. And you don't need any type of privileged rights to do it. Here is the script:

```
' This code prints out the forest tree hierarchy

' BEGIN SECTION 1
set objRootDSE = GetObject("LDAP://RootDSE")
strBase    = "<LDAP://cn=Partitions," & _
                objRootDSE.Get("ConfigurationNamingContext") & ">;"
strFilter  = "(&(objectcategory=crossRef)(systemFlags=3));"
strAttrs   = "name,trustParent,nCName,dnsRoot,distinguishedName;"
strScope   = "onelevel"
set objConn = CreateObject("ADODB.Connection")
objConn.Provider = "ADsDSOObject"
objConn.Open "Active Directory Provider"
set objRS = objConn.Execute(strBase & strFilter & strAttrs & strScope)
objRS.MoveFirst
' END SECTION 1


' BEGIN SECTION 2
set dicSubDomainTrue = CreateObject("Scripting.Dictionary")
set dicDomainHierarchy = CreateObject("Scripting.Dictionary")
set dicDomainRoot = CreateObject("Scripting.Dictionary")
' END SECTION 2


' BEGIN SECTION 3
while not objRS.EOF
    dicDomainRoot.Add objRS.Fields("name").Value, objRS.Fields("nCName").Value
    if objRS.Fields("trustParent").Value <> "" then
        dicSubDomainTrue.Add objRS.Fields("name").Value, 0
        set objDomainParent = GetObject("LDAP://" & _
                            objRS.Fields("trustParent").Value)
```

```
                    dicDomainHierarchy.Add objRS.Fields("name").Value, _
                                    objDomainParent.Get("name")
        else
            dicSubDomainTrue.Add objRS.Fields("name").Value, 1
        end if
        objRS.MoveNext
    wend
    ' END SECTION 3

    ' BEGIN SECTION 4
    for each strDomain in dicSubDomainTrue
        if dicSubDomainTrue(strDomain) = 1 then
            DisplayDomains strDomain, "", dicDomainHierarchy, dicDomainRoot
        end if
    next

    Function DisplayDomains ( strDomain, strSpaces, dicDomainHierarchy, dicDomainRoot)
        WScript.Echo strSpaces & strDomain
        DisplayObjects "LDAP://" & dicDomainRoot(strDomain), "  " & strSpaces
        for each strD in dicDomainHierarchy
            if dicDomainHierarchy(strD) = strDomain then
                DisplayDomains strD, "  " & strSpaces, dicDomainHierarchy, _
                            dicDomainRoot
            end if
        next
    End Function

    ' DisplayObjects takes the ADsPath of the object to display
    ' child objects for and the number of spaces (indention) to
    ' use when printing the first parameter
    Function DisplayObjects( strADsPath, strSpace)
        set objObject = GetObject(strADsPath)
        Wscript.Echo strSpace & objObject.Name
        objObject.Filter = Array("container","organizationalUnit")
        for each objChildObject in objObject
            DisplayObjects objChildObject.ADsPath, strSpace & "  "
        next
    End Function

    ' END SECTION 4
```

This script is a little more complicated than most of the scripts in this book, but you should be able to handle it. Let's walk through it.

In SECTION 1, I set up an ADO query to find all domains in a forest. This is a little trickier than you might imagine. Domains are represented in the Configuration naming context as crossRef objects; but since LDAP referrals can also be created as crossRef objects, I have to look for a specific type of crossRef object, ones that have a systemFlags attribute equal to **3**. This signifies Active Directory domains.

In SECTION 2, I set up three dictionary objects that I'll use throughout the script. Here is a brief overview of each dictionary object:

dicSubDomainTrue

> This is used to identify whether domains contain subdomains. The keys will be domain names and values will be 0 if the domain has no subdomains or 1 if it does. This dictionary will be used later to enumerate the domain hierarchy.

dicDomainHierarchy

> This is used to store the parent domain of a subdomain. The keys will be the domain names and the values will be each domain's parent domain name.

dicDomainRoot

> This is used to store the default naming context for each domain. The keys will be the domain names and the values will be the DN of each domain's root.

In SECTION 3, I enumerate over each of the values returned by the ADO query started in SECTION 1. I first set the domain root in the dicDomainRoot dictionary. Next, I evaluate if the trustParent attribute contains a value. If it does, then I know the domain I'm currently on has a parent domain. If trustParent does not contain a value, I know that it is the root domain of the forest or domain tree. If it does have a parent, I set an entry for the domain in dicSubDomainTrue to 0 to signify that I haven't found a subdomain for this domain yet. I then set an entry in dicDomainHierarchy to contain the domain and parent domain as key value pairs.

At this point, I've set up all the data structures I need to start printing out the structure of a forest. In SECTION 4, I start iterating over each domain in the forest. I'll enter only the domains that are roots of their forests. Then I call the DisplayDomains function. DisplayDomains prints the name of the current domain and calls DisplayObjects to print each container and organizationalUnit object in the domain. This effectively prints the structure of that domain. After it is done with that, it starts to loop over the keys in dicDomainHierarchy to find all child domains that have the current domain set as their parent. If it finds a subdomain of the current domain, it calls DisplayDomains (recursively) on that domain and the process repeats.

CHAPTER 16

Domain User, Group, and Computer Accounts

16.0 Introduction

The three most common types of objects you'll need to manage in an Active Directory forest include users, groups, and computers. You'll need to create user objects to represent the employees, customers, or students in your environment. It is important to understand how to properly configure and automate the management of user objects so you can cut down on much of the day-to-day tasks required to support these objects.

A group is a simple concept that has been used in many different types of systems over the years. In generic terms, a group is just a collection of things. Groups are used most frequently in a security context whereby you set up a group of users and apply certain permissions or rights to that group. Using a group is much easier when applying security than using individual users because you have to apply the security only once instead of once per user.

In Active Directory, groups are flexible objects that can contain virtually any other type of object as a member. Active Directory groups can be used for many different purposes including controlling access to resources, defining a filter for the application of group policies, and as an email distribution list.

The scope and type of a group defines how the group can be used in a forest. The type of a group can be either security or distribution. Security groups can be used to restrict access to resources whereas distribution groups can be used only as a simple grouping mechanism. Both group types can be used as email lists. The scope of a group determines where members of the group can be located in the forest and where in the forest you can use the group in ACLs. The supported group scopes include universal, global, and domain local. Universal groups and domain local groups can have members that are part of any domain in the forest. Global groups can only have members that are part of the same domain the group is in.

As far as Active Directory is concerned, computers are very similar to users. In fact, computer objects inherit directly from the user object class, which is used to represent user accounts. That means computer objects have all of the attributes of user objects and then some. Computers need to be represented in Active Directory for many of the same reasons users do, including the need to access resources securely, utilize GPOs, and have permissions granted or restricted on them.

To participate in a domain, computers need a secure channel to a domain controller. A secure channel is an authenticated connection that can transmit encrypted data. To set up the secure channel, a computer has to present a password to a domain controller. The domain controller then verifies that password against the password stored in Active Directory with the computer's account. Without the computer object, and subsequently the password stored within it, there would be no way for the domain controller to verify a computer is what it claims to be.

16.1   Creating a User Account

Problem

You want to create a user account in Active Directory.

Solution

Using a graphical user interface

1. Open the Active Directory Users and Computers (ADUC) snap-in.
2. If you need to change domains, right-click on **Active Directory Users and Computers** in the left pane, select **Connect to Domain**, enter the domain name and click **OK**.
3. In the left pane, browse to the parent container of the new user, right-click on it, and select **New → User**.
4. Enter the values for the first name, last name, full name, and user logon name fields as appropriate and click **Next**.
5. Enter and confirm the password, set any of the password flags, and click **Next**.
6. Click **Finish**.

Using a command-line interface

```
> dsadd user "<UserDN>" -upn <UserUPN> -fn "<UserFirstName>" -ln "<UserLastName>" -
display "<UserDisplayName>" -pwd <UserPasswd>
```

Using VBScript

```
' The following code creates a user object and sets several attributes.
set objParent = GetObject("LDAP://<ParentDN>")
set objUser   = objParent.Create("user", "cn=<UserName>") ' e.g., joes
objUser.Put "sAMAccountName", "<UserName>"    ' e.g., joes
objUser.Put "userPrincipalName", "<UserUPN>" ' e.g., joes@rallencorp.com
objUser.Put "givenName", "<UserFirstName>"    ' e.g., Joe
objUser.Put "sn", "<UserLastName>"           ' e.g., Smith
objUser.Put "displayName", "<UserFirstName> <UserLastName>" ' e.g., Joe Smith
objUser.SetInfo
objUser.SetPassword("<Password>")
objUser.AccountDisabled = FALSE
objUser.SetInfo
```

Discussion

In Windows 2000 Active Directory, the only mandatory attribute that must be set when creating a user is sAMAccountName, which is the account name that is used to interoperate with down-level domains. For Windows Server 2003, if you don't specify a value for sAMAccountName, it will be auto-populated for you. If you allow UPN logons, you'll want to make sure the userPrincipalName attribute is set.

> With Windows Server 2003, you can also create user accounts using the inetOrgPerson class, which is commonly used in other LDAP directories to represent users. For more on inetOrgPerson, see RFC 2798.

Using a graphical user interface

To set additional attributes, double-click on the user account after it has been created. There are several tabs to choose from that contain attributes that are grouped together based on function (e.g., Profile).

Using a command-line interface

Several additional attributes can be set with the dsadd user command. Run dsadd user /? for the complete list.

Using VBScript

Take a look at Recipe 16.9 for more information on the userAccountControl attribute and the various flags that can be set for it.

See Also

Recipes 16.2 and 16.9 and MSDN: ADS_USER_FLAG_ENUM

16.2 Creating a Large Number of Users

Problem

You want to create a large number of user objects, either for testing purposes or to initially populate Active Directory with your employee, customer, or student user accounts.

Solution

The following examples will create 1000 users in the *rallencorp.com* domain under the Bulk operational unit (OU). The password is set, but no other attributes are configured. You can modify the examples to populate whatever attributes you need. Also remember that if you've enabled password complexity in your domain, you'll need to set a more complex password or the examples will fail.

Using a command-line interface

```
> for /L %i in (1,1,1000) do dsadd user cn=User%i,ou=bulk,dc=rallencorp,dc=com -pwd
User%i
```

Using VBScript

```
' This code creates a large number of users with incremented user names
' e.g., User1, User2, User3, ....
' ------ SCRIPT CONFIGURATION ------
intNumUsers = 1000          ' Number of users to create
strParentDN = "<ParentDN>" ' e.g., ou=bulk,dc=emea,dc=rallencorp,dc=com
' ------ END CONFIGURATION ---------

' Taken from ADS_USER_FLAG_ENUM
Const ADS_UF_NORMAL_ACCOUNT = 512

set objParent = GetObject("LDAP://" & strParentDN)
for i = 1 to intNumUsers
    strUser = "User" & i
    Set objUser = objParent.Create("user", "cn=" & strUser)
    objUser.Put "sAMAccountName", strUser
    objUser.Put "userAccountControl", ADS_UF_NORMAL_ACCOUNT
    objUser.SetInfo
    objUser.SetPassword(strUser)
    objUser.AccountDisabled=FALSE
    objUser.SetInfo
    WScript.Echo "Created " & strUser
next
WScript.Echo ""
WScript.Echo "Created " & intNumUsers & " users"
```

Discussion

Using ADSI and on Windows Server 2003, the new DS command-line utilities, you can create hundreds and even thousands of users easily and quickly. I ran both the CLI and VBScript solutions in a test domain to create 1,000 user objects on a single processor machine. The VBScript solution took less than 1.5 minutes and the CLI solution took less than five minutes. Admittedly, they are not populating very many attributes, but it shows that you can quickly populate Active Directory with user accounts very easily. You can also modify the examples to pull from a data source, such as an employee database, and use real data. If you have a spreadsheet that contains all of your user information, see Chapter 1 for more on how to interact with Excel programmatically.

See Also

Recipes 16.1

16.3   Modifying an Attribute for Several Users at Once

Problem

You want to modify an attribute for several users at once.

Solution

Using a graphical user interface

This requires the Windows Server 2003 version of the Active Directory Users and Computers snap-in.

1. Open the ADUC snap-in.
2. If you need to change domains, right-click on **Active Directory Users and Computers** in the left pane, select **Connect to Domain**, enter the domain name, and click **OK**.
3. In the left pane, browse to the parent container of the objects you want to modify.
4. In the right pane, highlight each object you want to modify, right-click, and select **Properties**.

5. Check the box beside the attribute(s) you want to modify and edit the attribute fields.

6. Click **OK**.

Using a command-line interface

The following command sets the home directory of all users under a parent container (*<ParentDN>*) to be on a particular file server (*<FileServer>*). The user (i.e., $username$) is automatically replaced with the sAMAccountName for the user.

```
> for /F "usebackq delims=""" %i in (`dsquery user "<ParentDN>" -limit 0 -scope
onelevel`) do dsmod user -hmdir "\\<FileServerName>\$username$" %i
```

Using VBScript

```
' This code sets the home drive of all users under a container
' to be on a file server where the share name is the same as the user's
' sAMAccountName.
set objParent = GetObject("LDAP://<ParentDN>")
objParent.Filter = Array("user")
for each objUser in objParent
    Wscript.Echo "Modifying " & objUser.Get("sAMAccountName")
    objUser.HomeDirectory = "\\<FileServerName>\" & _
                            objUser.Get("sAMAccountName")
    objUser.SetInfo
next
```

Discussion

It is often necessary to update several users at once due to an organizational, location, or file server change. In each solution, I showed how to modify all users within a parent container, but you may need to use different criteria for locating the users.

With ADUC, you are limited to modifying multiple users that belong to the same container. You can, however, create a Saved Query with the Windows Server 2003 version of ADUC that returns users based on any criteria you specify. You can then highlight those users and modify them as described in the GUI solution.

With the CLI solution, you can modify the dsquery user command to search on whatever criteria you are interested. The same applies in the VBScript solution, but you'll need to use an ADO query instead of the Filter method if you want to do anything more complex.

 Microsoft PSS provides a tool called ADModify, which can also be used for performing bulk operations. You can download the tool from *ftp://ftp.microsoft.com/PSS/Tools/Exchange%20Support%20Tools/ADModify/*.

16.4   Unlocking a User

Problem

You want to unlock a locked-out user.

Solution

Using a graphical user interface

1. Open the ADUC snap-in.
2. In the left pane, right-click on the domain and select **Find**.
3. Select the appropriate domain beside **In**.
4. Type the name of the user beside Name and click **Find Now**.
5. In the **Search Results**, right-click on the user and select **Unlock**.
6. Click **OK**.

Using a command-line interface

Joe Richards has written a tool called *unlock* that lets you find locked out users and unlock them in one shot. The following command displays all locked out accounts on the default domain controller:

```
> unlock . * -view
```

The following command unlocks the user rallen on dc01:

```
> unlock dc01 rallen
```

This command unlocks all locked users on the default domain controller:

```
> unlock . *
```

You can download *unlock* from *http://www.joeware.net/win/free/tools/unlock.htm*.

Using VBScript

```
' This code unlocks a locked user.
' ------ SCRIPT CONFIGURATION ------
strUsername = "<UserName>"          ' e.g., jsmith
strDomain = "<NetBiosDomainName>" ' e.g., RALLENCORP
' ------ END CONFIGURATION ---------

set objUser = GetObject("WinNT://" & strDomain & "/" & strUsername)
if objUser.IsAccountLocked = TRUE then
   objUser.IsAccountLocked = FALSE
   objUser.SetInfo
   WScript.Echo "Account unlocked"
else
   WScript.Echo "Account not locked"
end if
```

Discussion

If you've enabled account lockouts in a domain (see Recipe 16.7), users will inevitably get locked out. A user can get locked out for a number of reasons, but generally it is either because a user mistypes his password a number of times (because he forgot it) or a user changes his password and does not log off and log on again.

You can use ADSI's IADsUser::IsAccountLocked method to determine if a user is locked out. You can set IsAccountLocked to FALSE to unlock a user. Unfortunately, there is a bug with the LDAP provider version of this method, so you have to use the WinNT provider instead. See MS KB 250873 for more information on this bug.

See Also

Recipe 16.7, MS KB 250873 (Programmatically Changing the Lockout Flag in Windows 2000), and MSDN: Account Lockout

16.5 Troubleshooting Account Lockout Problems

Problem

A user is having account lockout problems and you need to determine where it is getting locked from and how he or she is getting locked out.

Solution

Using a graphical user interface

LockoutStatus is a new tool available for Windows 2000 or Windows Server 2003 that can help identify which domain controllers are locking out users. It works by querying the lockout status of a user against all domain controllers in the user's domain.

To determine the lockout status of a user, open *LockoutStatus* and select **File →** **Select Target** from the menu. Enter the target user name and the domain of the user. Click **OK**. At this point, each domain controller in the domain will be queried and the results will be displayed.

Discussion

The *Lockoutstatus.exe* tool is just one of many that are available in the new "Account Lockout and Management" tool set provided by Microsoft. These new lockout tools are intended to help administrators with account lockout problems that are very difficult to troubleshoot given the tools available under Windows 2000. Along with the tool mentioned in the Solution, here are a few others that are included in the set:

ALockout.dll
> A script that uses this DLL is included that can enable logging of application authentication, which can point out if an application is using bad credentials that cause account lockouts.

ALoInfo.exe
> Displays services and shares that are using a particular account name. It can also print all the users and their password age.

NLParse.exe
> Filter tool for the *netlogon.log* files. You can use it to extract just the lines that relate to account lockout information.

All of the new Account Lockout tools can be downloaded from:

> *http://microsoft.com/downloads/details.aspx?familyid=7AF2E69C-91F3-4E63-8629-B999ADDE0B9E&displaylang=en.*

See Also

MS KB 813500 (Support WebCast: Microsoft Windows 2000 Server and Windows Server 2003: Password and Account Lockout Features)

16.6 Viewing and Modifying the Account Lockout and Password Policies

Problem

You want to view the account lockout and password policies for a domain.

Solution

Using a graphical user interface

1. Open the Default Domain Policy console (under Administrative Tools on a domain controller).

2. In the left menu, expand **Default Domain Policy** → **Computer Configuration** → **Windows Settings** → **Security Settings** → **Account Policies**.

3. Click on **Password Policy** or **Account Lockout Policy** and double-click the property you want to set or view in the right frame.

Using a command-line interface

```
> enumprop /ATTR:
lockoutduration,lockoutthreshold,lockoutobservationwindow,maxpwdage,minpwdage,minpwdl
ength,pwdhistorylength,pwdproperties "LDAP://<DomainDN>"
```

Using VBScript

```
' This code displays the current settings for the password
' and account lockout policies.
' ------ SCRIPT CONFIGURATION ------
strDomain = "<DomainDN>"   ' e.g., rallencorp.com
' ------ END CONFIGURATION ---------
set objRootDSE = GetObject("LDAP://" & strDomain & "/RootDSE")
set objDomain  = GetObject("LDAP://" & _
                           objRootDSE.Get("defaultNamingContext") )

' Hash containing the domain password and lockout policy attributes
' as keys and the units (e.g., minutes) as the values
set objDomAttrHash = CreateObject("Scripting.Dictionary")
objDomAttrHash.Add "lockoutDuration", "minutes"
objDomAttrHash.Add "lockoutThreshold", "attempts"
objDomAttrHash.Add "lockoutObservationWindow", "minutes"
objDomAttrHash.Add "maxPwdAge", "minutes"
objDomAttrHash.Add "minPwdAge", "minutes"
objDomAttrHash.Add "minPwdLength", "characters"
objDomAttrHash.Add "pwdHistoryLength", "remembered"
objDomAttrHash.Add "pwdProperties", " "

' Iterate over each attribute and print it
for each strAttr in objDomAttrHash.Keys
   if IsObject( objDomain.Get(strAttr) ) then
      set objLargeInt = objDomain.Get(strAttr)
      if objLargeInt.LowPart = 0 then
         value = 0
      else
         value = Abs(objLargeInt.HighPart * 2^32 + objLargeInt.LowPart)
         value = int ( value / 10000000 )
         value = int ( value / 60 )
      end if
   else
      value = objDomain.Get(strAttr)
   end if
   WScript.Echo strAttr & " = " & value & " " & objDomAttrHash(strAttr)
next

'Constants from DOMAIN_PASSWORD_INFORMATION
Set objDomPassHash = CreateObject("Scripting.Dictionary")
objDomPassHash.Add "DOMAIN_PASSWORD_COMPLEX", &h1
objDomPassHash.Add "DOMAIN_PASSWORD_NO_ANON_CHANGE", &h2
objDomPassHash.Add "DOMAIN_PASSWORD_NO_CLEAR_CHANGE", &h4
objDomPassHash.Add "DOMAIN_LOCKOUT_ADMINS", &h8
objDomPassHash.Add "DOMAIN_PASSWORD_STORE_CLEARTEXT", &h16
objDomPassHash.Add "DOMAIN_REFUSE_PASSWORD_CHANGE", &h32
```

```
' The PwdProperties attribute requires special processing because
' it is a flag that holds multiple settings.
for each strFlag In objDomPassHash.Keys
  if objDomPassHash(strFlag) and objDomain.Get("PwdProperties") then
    WScript.Echo "  " & strFlag & " is enabled"
  else
    WScript.Echo "  " & strFlag & " is disabled"
  end If
next
```

Discussion

You can set several parameters to control account lockout and password complexity on the Default Domain GPO. These settings are applied domain-wide and cannot be set on a per-OU basis.

The properties that can be set for the **Account Lockout Policy** include:

Account lockout duration
> Number of minutes an account will be locked before being automatically unlocked. A value of 0 indicates accounts will be locked out indefinitely; i.e., until an administrator manually unlocks them.

Account lockout threshold
> Number of failed logon attempts after which an account will be locked.

Reset account lockout counter after
> Number of minutes after a failed logon attempt that the failed logon counter for an account will be reset to 0.

The properties that can be set for the **Password Policy** include:

Enforce password history
> Number of passwords to remember before a user can reuse a previous password.

Maximum password age
> Maximum number of days a password can be used before a user must change it.

Minimum password age
> Minimum number of days a password must be used before it can be changed.

Minimum password length
> Minimum number of characters a password must be.

Password must meet complexity requirements
> If enabled, passwords must meet all of the following criteria:
> - Not contain all or part of the user's account name
> - Be at least six characters in length
> - Contain characters from three of the following four categories:
>   — English uppercase characters (A–Z)
>   — English lowercase characters (a–z)

— Base-10 digits (0–9)

— Nonalphanumeric characters (e.g., !, $, #, %)

Store passwords using reversible encryption

If enabled, passwords are stored in such a way that they can be retrieved and decrypted. This is essentially the same as storing passwords in plain text.

Using a graphical user interface

On a domain controller or machine that has *adminpak.msi* installed, the Default Domain Policy snap-in is present from the Start menu under Administrative Tools. On a member server, you need to open the GPO snap-in and locate the Default Domain policy.

Using a command-line interface

There is no standard CLI that can modify a GPO, but you can use *enumprop* to view each of the attributes on the domain object that make up the account lockout and password policy settings.

Using VBScript

The VBScript solution required quite a bit of code to perform a simple task: printing out the account lockout and password policy settings. First, I created a Dictionary object with each of the six attributes as the keys and the unit's designation for each key (e.g., minutes) as the value. I then iterated over each key, printing it along with the value retrieved from the domain object.

Some additional code was necessary to distinguish between the values returned from some of the attributes. In the case of the time-based attributes, such as lockoutDuration, an IADsLargeInteger object was returned from the Get method instead of a pure integer or string value. IADsLargeInteger objects represent 64-bit, also known as Integer8, numbers. 32-bit systems, which make up the majority of systems today, have to break 64-bit numbers into two parts (a high and low part) in order to store them. Unfortunately, VBScript cannot natively handle a 64-bit number and stores it as a double precision. To convert a 64-bit number into something VBScript can handle, we have to first multiply the high part by 4,294,967,296 (2^{32}) and then add the low part to the result:

```
value = Abs(objLargeInt.HighPart * 2^32 + objLargeInt.LowPart)
```

Then I divided by 10,000,000 or 10^7, which represents the number of 100 nanosecond intervals per second:

```
value = int ( value / 10000000 )
```

Next, I used the int function to discard any remainder and finally I divided the result by 60 (number of seconds):

```
value = int ( value / 60 )
```

Note that the result is only an approximation in minutes and can be off by several minutes, hours, or even days, depending on the original value.

The last part of the code iterates over another Dictionary object that contains constants representing various flags that can be set as part of the `pwdProperties` attribute.

See Also

MS KB 221930 (Domain Security Policy in Windows 2000), MS KB 255550 (Configuring Account Policies in Active Directory), MSDN: IADsLargeInteger, and MSDN: DOMAIN_PASSWORD_INFORMATION

16.7   Enabling and Disabling a User Account

Problem

You want to enable or disable a user.

Solution

Using a graphical user interface

1. Open the ADUC snap-in.
2. In the left pane, right-click on the domain and select **Find**.
3. Select the appropriate domain beside **In**.
4. Type the name of the user beside **Name** and click **Find Now**.
5. In the **Search Results**, right-click on the user and select **Enable Account** or **Disable Account**.
6. Click **OK**.

Using a command-line interface

To enable a user, use the following command:

```
> dsmod user <UserDN> -disabled no
```

To disable a user, use the following command:

```
> dsmod user <UserDN> -disabled yes
```

Using VBScript

```
' This code will enable or disable a user.
' ------ SCRIPT CONFIGURATION ------
' Set to FALSE to disable account or TRUE to enable account
strDisableAccount = FALSE
strUserDN = "<UserDN>" ' e.g., cn=jsmith,cn=Users,dc=rallencorp,dc=com
' ------ END CONFIGURATION ---------
set objUser = GetObject("LDAP://" & strUserDN)
```

```
if objUser.AccountDisabled = TRUE then
    WScript.Echo "Account for " & objUser.Get("cn") & " currently disabled"
    if strDisableAccount = FALSE then
        objUser.AccountDisabled = strDisableAccount
        objUser.SetInfo
        WScript.Echo "Account enabled"
    end if
else
    WScript.Echo "Account currently enabled"
    if strDisableAccount = TRUE then
        objUser.AccountDisabled = strDisableAccount
        objUser.SetInfo
        WScript.Echo "Account disabled"
    end if
end if
```

Discussion

Account status is used to control whether a user is allowed to log on. When an account is disabled, the user is not allowed to log on to her workstation with the account or access Active Directory–controlled resources. Much like the lockout status, the account status is stored as a flag in the userAccountControl attribute (see Recipe 16.9).

There is an IADsUser::AccountDisabled property that allows you to determine and change the status. Set the method FALSE to enable the account or TRUE to disable.

See Also

Recipe 16.9

16.8 Setting a User's Password

Problem

You want to set the password for a user.

Solution

Using a graphical user interface

1. Open the ADUC snap-in.
2. In the left pane, right-click on the domain and select **Find**.
3. Select the appropriate domain beside **In**.
4. Type the name of the user beside **Name** and click **Find Now**.
5. In the **Search Results**, right-click on the user and select **Reset Password**.
6. Enter and confirm the new password.
7. Click **OK**.

Using a command-line interface

This command changes the password for the user specified by *<UserDN>*. Using * after the -pwd option causes you to be prompted you for the new password. You can replace * with the password you want to set, but it is not a good security practice since other users that are logged into the machine may be able to see it.

```
> dsmod user <UserDN> -pwd *
```

Using VBScript

```
' This code sets the password for a user.
' ------ SCRIPT CONFIGURATION ------
strUserDN = "<UserDN>"      ' e.g., cn=jsmith,cn=Users,dc=rallencorp,dc=com
strNewPasswd = "NewPasword"
' ------ END CONFIGURATION ---------
set objUser = GetObject("LDAP://" & strUserDN)
objUser.SetPassword(strNewPasswd)
Wscript.Echo "Password set for " & objUser.Get("cn")
```

Discussion

The password for a user is stored in the unicodePwd attribute. You cannot directly modify that attribute, but have to use one of the supported APIs. With the VBScript solution you can use the IADsUser::SetPassword method as shown or IADsUser::ChangePassword. The latter requires the existing password to be known before setting it. This is the method you'd want to use if you've created a web page that accepts the previous password before allowing a user to change it.

See Also

MS KB 225511 (New Password Change and Conflict Resolution Functionality in Windows), MS KB 264480 (Description of Password-Change Protocols in Windows 2000), MSDN: IADsUser::SetPassword, and MSDN: IADsUser::ChangePassword

16.9   Setting a User's Account Options

Problem

You want to view or update the userAccountControl attribute for a user. This attribute controls various account options; for example, the user must change his password at next logon and whether the account is disabled.

Solution

Using a graphical user interface

1. Open the ADUC snap-in.
2. In the left pane, right-click on the domain and select **Find**.

3. Select the appropriate domain beside **In**.

4. Beside **Name**, type the name of the user and click **Find Now**.

5. In the **Search Results**, double-click on the user.

6. Select the **Account** tab.

7. Many of the userAccountControl flags can be set under **Account options**.

8. Click **OK** after you're done.

Using a command-line interface

The dsmod user command has several options for setting various userAccountControl flags, which are listed in the Discussion section. Each switch accepts yes or no as a parameter to either enable or disable the setting.

Using VBScript

```
' This code enables or disables a bit value in the userAccountControl attr.
' ------ SCRIPT CONFIGURATION ------
strUserDN = "<UserDN>"      ' e.g., cn=rallen,ou=Sales,dc=rallencorp,dc=com
intBit = <BitValue>         ' e.g., 65536
boolEnable = <TrueOrFalse> ' e.g., TRUE
' ------ END CONFIGURATION ---------
strAttr = "userAccountControl"
set objUser = GetObject("LDAP://" & strUserDN)
intBitsOrig = objUser.Get(strAttr)
intBitsCalc = CalcBit(intBitsOrig, intBit, boolEnable)
if intBitsOrig <> intBitsCalc then
    objUser.Put strAttr, intBitsCalc
    objUser.SetInfo
    WScript.Echo "Changed " & strAttr & " from " & _
                 intBitsOrig & " to " & intBitsCalc
else
    WScript.Echo "Did not need to change " & strAttr & " (" & _
                 intBitsOrig & ")"
end if

Function CalcBit(intValue, intBit, boolEnable)
    CalcBit = intValue
    if boolEnable = TRUE then
       CalcBit = intValue Or intBit
    else
       if intValue And intBit then
          CalcBit = intValue Xor intBit
       end if
    end if
End Function
```

Discussion

The userAccountControl attribute on user (and computer) objects could be considered the kitchen sink of miscellaneous and sometimes completely unrelated user account properties. If you have to do much creating and managing user objects, you'll need to become intimately familiar with this attribute.

The userAccountControl attribute is a bit flag, which means you have to take a couple extra steps to search against or modify it. For more on searching and modifying a bit flag attribute, see Recipes 4.10 and 4.13 in *Active Directory Cookbook* (O'Reilly).

The dsmod user command can be used to modify a subset of userAccountControl properties, as shown in Table 16-1. Table 16-2 lists userAccountControl properties as defined in the ADS_USER_FLAG_ENUM enumeration.

Table 16-1. dsmod user options for setting userAccountControl

dsmod user switch	Description
-mustchpwd	Sets whether the user must change password at next logon
-canchpwd	Sets whether the user can change his password
-disabled	Set account status to enabled or disabled
-reversiblepwd	Sets whether the user's password is stored using reversible encryption
-pwdneverexpires	Sets whether the user's password never expires

Table 16-2. ADS_USER_FLAG_ENUM values

Name	Value	Description
ADS_UF_SCRIPT	1	Logon script is executed
ADS_UF_ACCOUNTDISABLE	2	Account is disabled
ADS_UF_HOMEDIR_REQUIRED	8	Home Directory is required
ADS_UF_LOCKOUT	16	Account is locked out
ADS_UF_PASSWD_NOTREQD	32	A password is not required
ADS_UF_PASSWD_CANT_CHANGE	64	Read-only flag that indicates if the user cannot change his password
ADS_UF_ENCRYPTED_TEXT_PASSWORD_ALLOWED	128	Store password using reversible encryption
ADS_UF_TEMP_DUPLICATE_ACCOUNT	256	Account provides access to the domain, but not to any other domain that trusts the domain
ADS_UF_NORMAL_ACCOUNT	512	Enabled user account
ADS_UF_INTERDOMAIN_TRUST_ACCOUNT	2048	A permit to trust account for a system domain that trusts other domains
ADS_UF_WORKSTATION_TRUST_ACCOUNT	4096	Enabled computer account
ADS_UF_SERVER_TRUST_ACCOUNT	8192	Computer account for backup domain controller
ADS_UF_DONT_EXPIRE_PASSWD	65536	Password will not expire
ADS_UF_MNS_LOGON_ACCOUNT	131072	MNS logon account
ADS_UF_SMARTCARD_REQUIRED	262144	Smart card is required for logon
ADS_UF_TRUSTED_FOR_DELEGATION	524288	Allow Kerberos delegation

Table 16-2. ADS_USER_FLAG_ENUM values (continued)

Name	Value	Description
ADS_UF_NOT_DELEGATED	1048576	Do not allow Kerberos delegation even if ADS_UF_TRUSTED_FOR_DELETATION is enabled
ADS_UF_USE_DES_KEY_ONLY	2097152	Requires DES encryption for keys
ADS_UF_DONT_REQUIRE_PREAUTH	4194304	Account does not require Kerberos preauthentication for logon
ADS_UF_PASSWORD_EXPIRED	8388608	Read-only flag indicating account's password has expired. Used only with the WinNT provider.
ADS_UF_TRUSTED_TO_AUTHENTICATE_FOR_DELEGATION	16777216	Account is enabled for delegation

See Also

MSDN: ADS_USER_FLAG_ENUM

16.10 Setting a User's Profile Attributes

Problem

You want to set one or more of the user profile attributes.

Solution

Using a graphical user interface

1. Open the ADUC snap-in.
2. In the left pane, right-click on the domain and select **Find**.
3. Select the appropriate domain beside **In**.
4. Beside **Name**, type the name of the user and click **Find Now**.
5. In the **Search Results**, double-click on the user.
6. Click the **Profile** tab.
7. Modify the various profile settings as necessary.
8. Click **OK**.

Using a command-line interface

```
> dsmod user "<UserDN>" -loscr ScriptPath -profile ProfilePath -hmdir HomeDir -hmdrv
DriveLetter
```

Using VBScript

```
' This code sets the various profile related attributes for a user.
strUserDN = "<UserDN>"    ' e.g., cn=jsmith,cn=Users,dc=rallencorp,dc=com
```

```
set objUser = GetObject("LDAP://" & strUserDN)
objUser.Put "homeDirectory", "\\fileserver\" & objUser.Get("sAMAccountName")
objUser.Put "homeDrive", "z:"
objUser.Put "profilePath", "\\fileserver\" & _
            objUser.Get("sAMAccountName") & "\profile"
objUser.Put "scriptPath", "login.vbs"
objUser.SetInfo
Wscript.Echo "Profile info for " & objUser.Get("sAMAccountName") & " updated"
```

Discussion

The four attributes that make up a user's profile settings include the following:

homeDirectory
> UNC path to home directory

homeDrive
> Drive letter (e.g., z:) to map home directory

profilePath
> UNC path to profile directory

scriptPath
> Path to logon script

When you set the homeDirectory attribute, the referenced folder needs to already exist. For an example on creating shares for users, see MS KB 234746.

See Also

MS KB 234746 (How to Create User Shares for All Users in a Domain with ADSI), MS KB 271657 (Scripted Home Directory Paths Require That Folders Exist), and MS KB 320043 (HOW TO: Assign a Home Directory to a User)

16.11 Finding a User's Last Logon Time

 This recipe requires the Windows Server 2003 forest functional level.

Problem

You want to determine the last time a user logged in to a domain.

Solution

Using a graphical user interface

If you install the *AcctInfo.dll* extension to ADUC, you can view the last logon timestamp.

1. Open the ADUC snap-in.

2. In the left pane, right-click on the domain and select **Find**.

3. Select the appropriate domain beside **In**.

4. Beside **Name**, type the name of the user you want to modify and click **Find Now**.

5. In the **Search Results**, double-click on the user.

6. Click the **Additional Account Info** tab.

7. View the value for **Last-Logon-Timestamp**.

 AcctInfo.dll can be downloaded from the Microsoft download site:
http://microsoft.com/downloads/details.aspx?FamilyId=7AF2E69C-91F3-4E63-8629-B999ADDE0B9E&displaylang=en.

Using VBScript

```
' This code prints the last logon timestamp for a user.
' ------ SCRIPT CONFIGURATION ------
strUserDN = "<UserDN>"  ' e.g., cn=rallen,ou=Sales,dc=rallencorp,dc=com
' ------ END CONFIGURATION ---------

set objUser = GetObject("LDAP://" & strUserDN)
set objLogon = objUser.Get("lastLogonTimestamp")
intLogonTime = objLogon.HighPart * (2^32) + objLogon.LowPart
intLogonTime = intLogonTime / (60 * 10000000)
intLogonTime = intLogonTime / 1440
WScript.Echo "Approx last logon timestamp: " & intLogonTime + #1/1/1601#
```

Discussion

Trying to determine when a user last logged on has always been a challenge in the Microsoft NOS environment. In Windows NT, you could retrieve a user's last logon timestamp from a PDC or BDC, but this timestamp was the last time the user logged on to the PDC or BDC. That means in order to determine the actual last logon, you'd have to query every domain controller in the domain. In large environments this wasn't practical. With Windows 2000 Active Directory, things did not improve much. A lastLogon attribute is used to store the last logon timestamp, but unfortunately, this attribute isn't replicated. So again, to get an accurate picture, you'd have to query every domain controller in the domain for the user's last logon attribute and keep track of the most recent one.

With Windows Server 2003, we finally have a viable solution. A new attribute called lastLogonTimestamp was added to the user objects schema. This attribute is similar to the lastLogon attribute that was available previously, with two distinct differences. First, and most importantly, this attribute is replicated. That means when a user logs in, the `lastLogonTimestamp` attribute gets populated and then replicates to all domain controllers in the domain.

The second difference is that since `lastLogonTimestamp` is replicated, Microsoft needed to add safeguards to ensure that a user can repeatedly login over a short period of time, without any impact on replication. For this reason, the `lastLogonTimestamp` is updated only if the last update occurred a week or more earlier. This means that the `lastLogonTimestamp` attribute could be up to a week off in terms of accuracy with a user's actual last logon. Ultimately, this shouldn't be a problem for most situations because `lastLogonTimestamp` is intended to address the common problem where administrators want to run a query and determine which users have not logged in over the past month, or longer.

16.12 Creating a Group Account

Problem

You want to create a group account.

Solution

Using a graphical user interface

1. From the Administrative Tools, open the **Active Directory Users and Computers** snap-in.

2. If you need to change domains, right-click on **Active Directory Users and Computers** in the left pane, select **Connect to Domain**, enter the domain name, and click **OK**.

3. In the left pane, browse to the parent container of the new group, right-click on it, and select **New → Group**.

4. Enter the name of the group and select the group scope (global, domain local, or universal) and group type (security or distribution).

5. Click **OK**.

Using a command-line interface

In the following command, `<GroupDN>` should be replaced with the distinguished name of the group account to create; `<GroupScope>` should be l, g, or u for domain local group, global group, or universal group, respectively; and -secgrp should be set to yes if the group is a security group or no otherwise. Another recommended option to set is -desc to specify a description of the group.

```
> dsadd group "<GroupDN>" -scope <GroupScope> -secgrp yes|no -desc "<GroupDesc>"
```

Here is an example:

```
> dsadd group "cn=mygroup,cn=users,dc=rallencorp,dc=com" -scope g -secgrp yes -desc
"A test group"
```

Using VBScript

```
' The following code creates a global security group.
' ------ SCRIPT CONFIGURATION ------
strGroupParentDN = "<GroupParentDN>"   ' e.g., ou=Groups,dc=rallencorp,dc=com
strGroupName     = "<GroupName>"       ' e.g., ExecAdminsSales
strGroupDescr    = "<GroupDesc>"       ' e.g., Executive Admins for Sales group
' ------ END CONFIGURATION ---------
' Constants taken from ADS_GROUP_TYPE_ENUM
Const ADS_GROUP_TYPE_DOMAIN_LOCAL_GROUP = 1
Const ADS_GROUP_TYPE_GLOBAL_GROUP       = 2
Const ADS_GROUP_TYPE_LOCAL_GROUP        = 4
Const ADS_GROUP_TYPE_SECURITY_ENABLED   = -2147483648
Const ADS_GROUP_TYPE_UNIVERSAL_GROUP    = 8

set objOU = GetObject("LDAP://" & strGroupParentDN)
set objGroup = objDomain.Create("group","cn=" & strGroupName)
objGroup.Put "groupType", ADS_GROUP_TYPE_GLOBAL_GROUP _
                         Or ADS_GROUP_TYPE_SECURITY_ENABLED
objGroup.Put "description", strGroupDescr
objGroup.SetInfo
```

Discussion

In each solution, a group was created in an Active Directory domain with no members. (For more information on how to add and remove members, see Recipe 16.15.) The groupType attribute contains a flag indicating both group scope and type. The available flag values are defined in the ADS_GROUP_TYPE_ENUM enumeration. Recipe 16.16 contains more information on setting the group scope and type.

See Also

MS KB 231273 (Group Type and Scope Usage in Windows), MS KB 232241 (Group Management with ADSI in Windows 2000), MS KB 320054 (HOW TO: Manage Groups in Active Directory in Windows 2000), and MSDN: ADS_GROUP_TYPE_ENUM

16.13 Viewing the Members of a Group

Problem

You want to view the members of a group.

Solution

Using a graphical user interface

1. Open the ADUC snap-in.
2. If you need to change domains, right-click on **Active Directory Users and Computers** in the left pane, select **Connect to Domain**, enter the domain name, and click **OK**.
3. In the left pane, right-click on the domain and select **Find**.
4. Enter the name of the group and click **Find Now**.
5. Double-click on the group in the bottom results pane.
6. Click the **Members** tab.

Using a command-line interface

The following command displays the direct members of a group:

```
> dsget group "<GroupDN>" -members
```

Add the -expand option to enumerate all nested group members:

```
> dsget group "<GroupDN>" -members -expand
```

Using VBScript

```
' This code prints the direct members of the specified group.
' ------ SCRIPT CONFIGURATION ------
strGroupDN = "<GroupDN>" ' e.g., cn=SalesGroup,ou=Groups,dc=rallencorp,dc=com
' ------ END CONFIGURATION ---------

set objGroup = GetObject("LDAP://" & strGroupDN)
Wscript.Echo "Members of " & objGroup.Name & ":"
for each objMember in objGroup.Members
    Wscript.Echo objMember.Name
next


' This code prints the nested membership of a group.
' ------ SCRIPT CONFIGURATION ------
strGroupDN = "<GroupDN>"  ' e.g., cn=SalesGroup,ou=Grps,dc=rallencorp,dc=com
' ------ END CONFIGURATION ---------
strSpaces  = " "
set dicSeenGroupMember = CreateObject("Scripting.Dictionary")
Wscript.Echo "Members of " & strGroupDN & ":"
DisplayMembers "LDAP://" & strGroupDN, strSpaces, dicSeenGroupMember

Function DisplayMembers ( strGroupADsPath, strSpaces, dicSeenGroupMember)

    set objGroup = GetObject(strGroupADsPath)
    for each objMember In objGroup.Members
        Wscript.Echo strSpaces & objMember.Name
```

```
        if objMember.Class = "group" then
            if dicSeenGroupMember.Exists(objMember.ADsPath) then
                Wscript.Echo strSpaces & "    ^ already seen group member " & _
                                    "(stopping to avoid loop)"
            else
                dicSeenGroupMember.Add objMember.ADsPath, 1
                DisplayMembers objMember.ADsPath, strSpaces & "  ", _
                            dicSeenGroupMember
            end if
        end if
    next

    End Function
```

Discussion

The member attribute of a group object contains the distinguished names of the directly added group members. This is in contrast to indirect group members, which are group members due to nested group membership. To view the complete group membership, recurse through each group's members.

In the second VBScript example, I used a dictionary object to prevent an infinite loop. The dictionary object stores each group member; before the DisplayMembers function is called, a check is performed to determine if the group has already been evaluated. If so, a message is displayed indicating the group will not be processed again. If this type of checking was not employed and you had a situation where group A was a member of group B, group B was a member of group C, and group C was a member of group A, the loop would repeat without terminating.

See Also

MSDN: IADsMember

16.14 Viewing a User's Group Membership

Problem

You want to view a user's group membership.

Solution

Using a graphical user interface

1. Open the ADUC snap-in.
2. In the left pane, right-click on the domain and select **Find**.
3. Select the appropriate domain beside **In**.
4. Type the name of the user beside **Name** and click **Find Now**.

5. In the **Search Results**, double-click on the user.

6. Click the **Member Of** tab.

7. To view all indirect group membership (from nested groups), you'll need to double-click on each group.

Using a command-line interface

The following command displays the groups *<UserDN>* is a member of. Use the -expand switch to list nested group membership as well:

```
> dsget user <UserDN> -memberof [-expand]
```

Using VBScript

```
' This code displays the group membership of a user.
' It avoids infinite loops due to circular group nesting by
' keeping track of the groups that have already been seen.
' ------ SCRIPT CONFIGURATION ------
strUserDN = "<UserDN>"   ' e.g., cn=jsmith,cn=Users,dc=rallencorp,dc=com
' ------ END CONFIGURATION ---------

set objUser = GetObject("LDAP://" & strUserDN)
Wscript.Echo "Group membership for " & objUser.Get("cn") & ":"
strSpaces = ""
set dicSeenGroup = CreateObject("Scripting.Dictionary")
DisplayGroups "LDAP://" & strUserDN, strSpaces, dicSeenGroup

Function DisplayGroups ( strObjectADsPath, strSpaces, dicSeenGroup)

   set objObject = GetObject(strObjectADsPath)
   WScript.Echo strSpaces & objObject.Name
   on error resume next ' Doing this to avoid an error when memberOf is empty
   if IsArray( objObject.Get("memberOf") ) then
      colGroups = objObject.Get("memberOf")
   else
      colGroups = Array( objObject.Get("memberOf") )
   end if

   for each strGroupDN In colGroups
      if Not dicSeenGroup.Exists(strGroupDN) then
         dicSeenGroup.Add strGroupDN, 1
         DisplayGroups "LDAP://" & strGroupDN, strSpaces & " ", dicSeenGroup
      end if
   next

End Function
```

Discussion

The memberOf attribute on user objects is multivalued and lists the distinguished names for the groups of which the user is a member. memberOf is actually linked with the member attribute on group objects, which holds the distinguished names of its members. For this reason, you cannot directly modify the memberOf attribute; you must modify the member attribute on the group instead.

The primary group of a user, which the user is technically a member of, will not be shown in either the CLI or VBScript solutions. This is because the primary group is not stored in the memberOf attribute like the rest of the groups.

See Also

Recipe 16.13

16.15 Adding and Removing Members of a Group

Problem

You want to add or remove group members.

Solution

Using a graphical user interface

1. Follow the same steps as in Recipe 16.13 to view the members of the group.
2. To remove a member, click on the member name, click the **Remove** button, click **Yes**, and click **OK**.
3. To add a member, click on the **Add** button, enter the name of the member, and click **OK** twice.

Using a command-line interface

The -addmbr option adds a member to a group:

```
> dsmod group "<GroupDN>" -addmbr "<MemberDN>"
```

The -rmmbr option removes a member from a group:

```
> dsmod group "<GroupDN>" -rmmbr "<MemberDN>"
```

The -chmbr option replaces the complete membership list:

```
> dsmod group "<GroupDN>" -chmbr "<Member1DN Member2DN ...>"
```

Using VBScript

```
' This code adds a member to a group.
' ------ SCRIPT CONFIGURATION ------
strGroupDN = "<GroupDN>"  ' e.g., cn=SalesGroup,ou=Groups,dc=rallencorp,dc=com
strMemberDN = "<MemberDN>" ' e.g., cn=jsmith,cn=users,dc=rallencorp,dc=com
' ------ END CONFIGURATION ---------
```

```
set objGroup = GetObject("LDAP://" & strGroupDN)
' Add a member
objGroup.Add("LDAP://" & strMemberDN)

' This code removes a member from a group.
' ------ SCRIPT CONFIGURATION ------
strGroupDN = "<GroupDN>"   ' e.g., cn=SalesGroup,ou=Groups,dc=rallencorp,dc=com
strMemberDN = "<MemberDN>" ' e.g., cn=jsmith,cn=users,dc=rallencorp,dc=com
' ------ END CONFIGURATION ---------

set objGroup = GetObject("LDAP://" & strGroupDN)
' Remove a member
objGroup.Remove("LDAP://" & strMemberDN)
```

Discussion

Since there are no restrictions on what distinguished names you put in the member attribute, you can essentially have any type of object as a member of a group, which makes groups very useful. While OUs are typically used to structure objects that share certain criteria, group objects can be used to create loose collections of objects.

The benefit of using group objects as a collection mechanism is that the same object can be a member of multiple groups, whereas an object can only be a part of a single OU. Another key difference is that you can assign permissions on resources to groups because they are considered security principals in Active Directory, whereas OUs are not. This is different from some other directories, such as Novell Netware, where OUs act more like security principals.

See Also

Recipe 16.13, MSDN: IADsGroup::Add, and MSDN: IADsGroup::Remove

16.16 Changing the Scope or Type of a Group

Problem

You want to change the scope or type of a group.

Solution

Using a graphical user interface

1. Open the ADUC snap-in.
2. If you need to change domains, right-click on **Active Directory Users and Computers** in the left pane, select **Connect to Domain**, enter the domain name, and click **OK**.
3. In the left pane, right-click on the domain and select **Find**.
4. Enter the name of the group you want to modify and click **Find Now**.

5. Double-click on the group in the results pane.

6. In the group properties dialog box, select the new scope or type and click **OK**.

Using a command-line interface

The following example changes the group scope for *<GroupDN>* to *<NewScope>*, which should be l for domain local group, g for global group, or u for universal group.

```
> dsmod group "<GroupDN>" -scope <NewScope>
```

The following example changes the group type for *<GroupDN>*. For the -secgrp switch, specify yes to change to a security group or no to make the group a distribution list.

```
> dsmod group "<GroupDN>" -secgrp yes|no
```

Using VBScript

```
' This code sets the scope and type of the specified group
' to a universal security group.
' ------ SCRIPT CONFIGURATION ------
strGroupDN = "<GroupDN>"  ' e.g., cn=SalesGroup,ou=Groups,dc=rallencorp,dc=com
' ------ END CONFIGURATION ---------

' Constants taken from ADS_GROUP_TYPE_ENUM
ADS_GROUP_TYPE_DOMAIN_LOCAL_GROUP = 1
ADS_GROUP_TYPE_GLOBAL_GROUP       = 2
ADS_GROUP_TYPE_LOCAL_GROUP        = 4
ADS_GROUP_TYPE_SECURITY_ENABLED   = -2147483648
ADS_GROUP_TYPE_UNIVERSAL_GROUP    = 8

set objGroup = GetObject("LDAP://" & strGroupDN )
objGroup.Put "groupType", ADS_GROUP_TYPE_UNIVERSAL_GROUP _
                     Or ADS_GROUP_TYPE_SECURITY_ENABLED
objGroup.SetInfo
```

Discussion

Group scope and type are stored as a flag in the groupType attribute on group objects. To directly update groupType, you must logically OR the values associated with each type and scope as shown in the API solution. Note that there is no specific value for the distribution list type. If you want to create a distribution list, do not include the ADS_GROUP_TYPE_SECURITY_ENABLED flag when setting groupType.

 For a good description of the usage scenarios for each group type, see Chapter 11 in *Active Directory* (O'Reilly).

See Also

MS KB 231273 (Group Type and Scope Usage in Windows), MSDN: ADS_GROUP_
TYPE_ENUM, and MSDN: What Type of Group to Use.

16.17 Creating a Computer Account

Problem

You want to create a computer account.

Solution

Using a graphical user interface

1. From the Administrative Tools, open the **Active Directory Users and Computers** snap-in.

2. If you need to change domains, right-click on **Active Directory Users and Computers** in the left pane, select **Connect to Domain**, enter the domain name and
   click **OK**.

3. In the left pane, browse to the parent container for the computer, right-click on
   it, and select **New → Computer**.

4. Enter the name of the computer and click **OK**.

Using a command-line interface

Use the following command to create a computer account in Active Directory:

```
> dsadd computer "<ComputerDN>" -desc "<Description>"
```

Using VBScript

```
' This code creates a computer account in Active Directory.
' ------ SCRIPT CONFIGURATION ------
strBase  = "<ParentComputerDN>"  ' e.g., cn=Computers,dc=rallencorp,dc=com
strComp  = "<ComputerName>"      ' e.g., joe-xp
strDescr = "<Description>"       ' e.g., Joe's Windows XP workstation
' ------ END CONFIGURATION ---------

' ADS_USER_FLAG_ENUM
Const ADS_UF_WORKSTATION_TRUST_ACCOUNT = &h1000

set objCont = GetObject("LDAP://" & strBase)
set objComp = objCont.Create("computer", "cn=" & strComp)
objComp.Put "sAMAccountName", strComp & "$"
objComp.Put "description", strDesc
objComp.Put "userAccountControl", ADS_UF_WORKSTATION_TRUST_ACCOUNT
objComp.SetInfo
Wscript.Echo "Computer account for " & strComp & " created"
```

Discussion

Creating a computer account in Active Directory is not much different from creating a user account. In the CLI and API solutions, I set the description attribute, but it is not mandatory. The only mandatory attribute for computer accounts is sAMAccountName, which should be set to the name of the computer with $ appended (e.g., joe-wxp$).

These solutions simply create a computer account. You'll still need to join a computer with the same name as the computer account to a domain as I describe in Recipe 16.18.

See Also

MS KB 222525 (Automating the Creation of Computer Accounts), MS KB 283771 (HOW TO: Pre-stage Windows 2000 Computers in Active Directory), MS KB 315273 (Automating the Creation of Computer Accounts), MS KB 320187 (HOW TO: Manage Computer Accounts in Active Directory in Windows 2000), and MSDN: ADS_USER_FLAG_ENUM

16.18 Joining a Computer to a Domain

Problem

You want to join a computer to a domain after the computer account has already been created in Active Directory.

Solution

Using a graphical user interface

1. Log on to the computer you want to join and open the Control Panel.
2. Open the **System** applet.
3. Click the **Computer Name** tab.
4. Click the **Change** button.
5. Under **Member of**, select **Domain**.
6. Enter the domain you want to join and click **OK**.
7. You may be prompted to enter credentials of a user that has permission to join the computer.
8. Reboot the computer.
9. Note that the tab names in the **System** applet vary between Windows 2000, Windows XP, and Windows Server 2003.

Using a command-line interface

Run the following command to join a computer to a domain:

```
> netdom join <ComputerName> /Domain <DomainName> /UserD <DomainUserUPN> /PasswordD *
/UserO <ComputerAdminUser> /PasswordO * /Reboot
```

Using VBScript

```
' This code joins a computer to a domain.
' The JoinDomainOrWorkGroup( ) method was introduced in Windows XP
' so this code works only against Windows XP and Windows Server 2003.
' ------ SCRIPT CONFIGURATION ------
strComputer      = "<ComputerName>"        ' e.g., joe-xp
strDomain        = "<DomainName>"          ' e.g., rallencorp.com
strDomainUser    = "<DomainUserUPN>"       ' e.g., administrator@rallencorp.com
strDomainPasswd  = "<DomainUserPasswd>"
strLocalUser     = "<ComputerAdminUser>"   ' e.g., administrator
strLocalPasswd   = "<ComputerUserPasswd>"
' ------ END CONFIGURATION ---------

'#######################
' Constants
'#######################
Const JOIN_DOMAIN           = 1
Const ACCT_CREATE           = 2
Const ACCT_DELETE           = 4
Const WIN9X_UPGRADE         = 16
Const DOMAIN_JOIN_IF_JOINED = 32
Const JOIN_UNSECURE         = 64
Const MACHINE_PASSWORD_PASSED = 128
Const DEFERRED_SPN_SET      = 256
Const INSTALL_INVOCATION    = 262144

'##########################
' Connect to Computer
'##########################
set objWMILocator = CreateObject("WbemScripting.SWbemLocator")
objWMILocator.Security_.AuthenticationLevel = 6
set objWMIComputer = objWMILocator.ConnectServer(strComputer, _
                                    "root\cimv2", _
                                         strLocalUser, _
                                         strLocalPasswd)
set objWMIComputerSystem = objWMIComputer.Get( _
                              "Win32_ComputerSystem.Name='" & _
                              strComputer & "'")

'##########################
' Join Computer
'##########################
rc = objWMIComputerSystem.JoinDomainOrWorkGroup(strDomain, _
                                    strDomainPasswd, _
                                    strDomainUser, _
                                    vbNullString, _
                                    JOIN_DOMAIN)
```

```
        if rc <> 0 then
            WScript.Echo "Join failed with error: " & rc
        else
            WScript.Echo "Successfully joined " & strComputer & " to " & strDomain
        end if
```

Discussion

Before you can join a computer to Active Directory, you must first create a computer account for it as described in Recipe 16.17. At that point you can join the computer to the domain.

Using a graphical user interface

If you have the correct permissions in Active Directory, you can actually create a computer account at the same time as you join it to a domain via the instructions described in the GUI solution. Since the System applet doesn't let you specify an OU for the computer account, if it needs to create a computer account, it will do so in the default Computers container (cn=computers).

Using a command-line interface

The *netdom* command attempts to create a computer account for the computer during the join operation if one does not already exist. An optional /OU switch can be included to specify the OU in which to create the computer account. To do so, you'll need to have permission to create and manage computer accounts in the OU.

There are some restrictions on running the netdom join command against a remote computer. If a Windows XP machine has the ForceGuest security policy setting enabled, you cannot join it remotely. Running the *netdom* command directly on the machine works regardless of the ForceGuest setting.

Using VBScript

In order for the Win32_ComputerSystem::JoinDomainOrWorkGroup method to work remotely, you have to use an AuthenticationLevel equal to 6 so that the traffic between the two machines (namely the passwords) is encrypted. You can also create computer accounts using JoinDomainOrWorkGroup by including the ACCT_CREATE flag in combination with JOIN_DOMAIN.

Just like with the *netdom* utility, you cannot run this script against a remote computer if that computer has the ForceGuest setting enabled.

See Also

http://www.microsoft.com/technet/prodtechnol/winxppro/reskit/prde_ffs_ypuh.asp (for more information on the ForceGuest setting), MS KB 238793 (Enhanced Security Joining or Resetting Machine Account in Windows 2000 Domain), MS KB 251335

(Domain Users Cannot Join Workstation or Server to a Domain), MS KB 290403 (How to Set Security in Windows XP Professional That Is Installed in a Workgroup), MSDN: Win32_ComputerSystem::JoinDomainOrWorkgroup, and MSDN: NetJoinDomain

16.19 Renaming a Computer

Problem

You want to rename a computer.

Solution

Using a graphical user interface

1. Log on to the computer either directly or with a remote console application, such as Terminal Services.

2. Open the Control Panel and double-click on the **System** Applet.

3. Select the **Computer Name** tab and click the **Change** button.

4. Under **Computer Name**, type the new name of the computer and click **OK** until you've closed all of the **System** applet screens.

5. Reboot the machine.

Using a command-line interface

The following command renames a computer and the corresponding Active Directory computer account:

```
> netdom renamecomputer <ComputerName> /NewName <NewComputerName> /UserD
<DomainUserUPN> /PasswordD * /UserO <ComputerAdminUser> /PasswordO * /Reboot
```

The renamecomputer option is only available in Windows XP and Windows Server 2003 (not Windows 2000).

Using VBScript

```
' This code renames a computer in AD and on the host itself.
' The Rename( ) method was introduced in Windows XP so this code works
' only against Windows XP and Windows Server 2003.
' ------ SCRIPT CONFIGURATION ------
strComputer     = "<ComputerName>"        e.g., joe-xp
strNewComputer  = "<NewComputerName>"      e.g., joe-pc
strDomainUser   = "<DomainUserUPN>"        e.g., administrator@rallencorp.com
strDomainPasswd = "<DomainUserPasswd>"
strLocalUser    = "<ComputerAdminUser>"   e.g., joe-xp\administrator
strLocalPasswd  = "<ComputerAdminPasswd>"
' ------ END CONFIGURATION ---------
```

```
'##########################
' Connect to Computer
'##########################
set objWMILocator = CreateObject("WbemScripting.SWbemLocator")
objWMILocator.Security_.AuthenticationLevel = 6
set objWMIComputer = objWMILocator.ConnectServer(strComputer, _
                                        "root\cimv2", _
                                              strLocalUser, _
                                              strLocalPasswd)
set objWMIComputerSystem = objWMIComputer.Get( _
                              "Win32_ComputerSystem.Name='" & _
                              strComputer & "'")
'##########################
' Rename Computer
'##########################
rc = objWMIComputerSystem.Rename(strNewComputer, _
                              strDomainPasswd, _
                              strDomainUser)
if rc <> 0 then
    WScript.Echo "Rename failed with error: " & rc
else
    WScript.Echo "Successfully renamed " & strComputer & " to " & _
                strNewComputer
end if

WScript.Echo "Rebooting..."
set objWSHShell = WScript.CreateObject("WScript.Shell")
objWSHShell.Run "rundll32 shell32.dll,SHExitWindowsEx 2"
```

Discussion

Renaming a computer consists of two operations: renaming the computer object in
Active Directory and renaming the hostname on the machine itself. To do it in one
step, which each of the three solutions do, you must have permission in Active Directory to rename the account and administrator permissions on the target machine.
For the rename operation to be complete, you must reboot the computer.

 In some cases, renaming a computer can adversely affect services running on the computer. For example, you cannot rename a machine
that is a Windows 2000 domain controller or a Windows Certificate
Authority without first removing those services (which may have negative consequences). It also requires significant additional effort to
rename a server running either SQL Server or Exchange Server.

Using a graphical user interface

After you rename the computer, you will be prompted to reboot the machine. You
can cancel out if necessary, but you'll need to reboot at some point to complete the
rename operation.

Using a command-line interface

You can also have *netdom* reboot the machine by including a /Reboot switch, which automatically reboots the computer after the rename is complete.

Using VBScript

The Win32_ComputerSystem::Rename method must be run on the local machine unless the computer is a member of a domain. Unlike the GUI and CLI solutions, you cannot specify alternate credentials for the connection to the computer other than domain credentials. For this reason, the user and password you use with the Rename method must have administrative privileges on the target machine (i.e., part of the Administrators group) and on the computer object in Active Directory.

See Also

MS KB 228544 (Changing Computer Name in Windows 2000 Requires Restart), MS KB 238793 (Enhanced Security Joining or Resetting Machine Account in Windows 2000 Domain), MS KB 260575 (HOW TO: Use Netdom.exe to Reset Machine Account Passwords of a Windows 2000 Domain Controller), MS KB 325354 (HOW TO: Use the Netdom.exe Utility to Rename a Computer in Windows Server 2003), and MSDN: Win32_ComputerSystem::Rename

16.20 Resetting a Computer Account

Problem

You want to test the secure channel of a computer and reset the computer account if it is failing.

Solution

Use the following command to test a secure channel for a computer:

```
> nltest /server:<ComputerName> /sc_query:<DomainName>
```

If this command returns errors, such as ERROR_NO_LOGON_SERVERS, try resetting the secure channel using the following command:

```
> nltest /server:<ComputerName> /sc_reset
```

If that doesn't help, you'll need to reset the computer account as described next.

Using a graphical user interface

1. From the Administrative Tools, open the **Active Directory Users and Computers** snap-in.

2. If you need to change domains, right-click on **Active Directory Users and Computers** in the left pane, select **Connect to Domain**, enter the domain name, and click **OK**.

3. In the left pane, right-click on the domain and select **Find**.

4. Beside **Find**, select **Computers**.

5. Type the name of the computer and click **Find Now**.

6. In the **Search Results** pane, right-click on the computer and select **Reset Account**.

7. Click **Yes** to verify.

8. Click **OK**.

9. Rejoin the computer to the domain (Recipe 16.18).

Using a command-line interface

You can use the *dsmod* utility to reset a computer's password. You will need to rejoin the computer to the domain after doing this:

```
> dsmod computer  "<ComputerDN>" -reset
> dsmod computer "cn=rallen-wxp,cn=computers,dc=rallencorp,dc=com"
```

Another option is to use the *netdom* command, which can reset the computer so that you do not need to rejoin it to the domain:

```
> netdom reset <ComputerName> /Domain <DomainName> /UserO <UserUPN> /PasswordO *
> netdom reset rallen-wxp /Domain rallencorp.com /UserO rallen@rallencorp.com /
PasswordO *
```

Using VBScript

```
' This resets an existing computer object's password to the initial default.
' You'll need to rejoin the computer to the domain after doing this.
set objComputer = GetObject("LDAP://<ComputerDN>")
objComputer.SetPassword "<ComputerName>"
```

Discussion

Every member computer in an Active Directory domain establishes a secure channel with a domain controller. The computer's password is stored locally in the form of an LSA secret and in Active Directory. This password is used by the NetLogon service to establish the secure channel with a domain controller. If for some reason the LSA secret and computer password become out of sync, the computer will no longer be able to authenticate in the domain. The nltest /sc_query command can query a computer to verify its secure channel is working. Here is sample output from the command when things are working:

```
Flags: 30 HAS_IP  HAS_TIMESERV
Trusted DC Name \\dc1.rallencorp.com
Trusted DC Connection Status Status = 0 0x0 NERR_Success
The command completed successfully
```

Here is sample output when things are not working:

```
Flags: 0
Trusted DC Name
Trusted DC Connection Status Status = 1311 0x51f ERROR_NO_LOGON_SERVERS
The command completed successfully
```

When you've identified that a computer's secure channel has failed, you'll need to reset the computer, which consists of setting the computer object password to the name of the computer. This is the default initial password for new computers. Every 30 days Windows 2000 and newer systems automatically change their passwords in the domain. After you've set the password, rejoin the computer to the domain since it will no longer be able to communicate with a domain controller due to unsynchronized passwords (the domain controller doesn't know the password has been reset). However, if you use the netdom reset command, it tries to reset the password on both the computer and in Active Directory, which if successful, means you do not need to rejoin it to the domain.

See Also

Recipe 16.18, MS KB 216393 (Resetting Computer Accounts in Windows 2000 and Windows XP), and MS KB 325850 (HOW TO: Use Netdom.exe to Reset Machine Account Passwords of a Windows Server 2003 Domain Controller)

CHAPTER 17

Exchange Server 2003

17.0   Introduction

Exchange Server 2003 is Microsoft's messaging and collaboration server application. It enables you to send and receive email and other interactive messages through computer networks. Exchange is designed to integrate directly with Microsoft Outlook and has a rich application programming interface (API) that can be utilized to integrate custom applications, making it a very flexible framework for business collaboration.

Although Windows Server 2003 has built-in SMTP and POP3 support, it isn't enough for serious corporate needs. If you like analogies, SMTP/POP3 services are to Exchange what the Model-T is to the modern automobile. You can certainly recognize the basic pieces, but there have been notable extensions to those pieces to make the product more flexible and powerful for today's needs. Some additional features in the product are IMAP, Web Email Support via Outlook Web Access (OWA), a robust calendaring system, advanced message routing, distribution lists, public folders, configurable spam filtering, and considerable functionality for controlling message flow and client experience.

Exchange was one of the first Active Directory–enabled applications. This is an unsurprising fact as Active Directory is based in great part on the directory technology "borrowed" from Exchange. It is probably also unsurprising that Exchange is a heavy consumer of Active Directory, for the same reason, and extremely dependent upon Active Directory functioning well. Because of this tight integration, you should try to incorporate Exchange requirements into your overall Active Directory design as early as possible. Failure to do so can have significant impact on the quality of service of both the Active Directory and Exchange. The integration of Exchange could require your Active Directory design to change considerably.

Exchange has a large feature-set, and several books have been written that cover designing, implementing, and running Exchange. What I present here is a small set of appetizer recipes covering some of the more basic functions, including installing a new instance of Exchange Server 2003 and some basic administration tasks. If you would like to get the full seven-course meal, you should consider getting the *Exchange Server Cookbook* from O'Reilly.

Using a Graphical User Interface

Exchange has traditionally been administrated from the GUI. There are two primary Microsoft GUI tools for administrating Exchange, both based on the Microsoft Management Console (MMC).

The first is a tool you probably already know: the Active Directory Users and Computers (ADUC) tool. Microsoft has extended the functionality of this Active Directory tool to manage many aspects of the users and groups used by Exchange. This makes sense since most Active Directory administrators are already familiar with this tool and the information being updated is primarily in Active Directory. If you are working only with managing users' Exchange information, you will most likely spend your time with this tool.

The second tool is the Exchange System Manager (ESM), which is used for configuring and monitoring the overall Exchange environment, including servers, policies, queues, routing connectors, and other configuration specific settings.

You can find these tools on any server running Exchange, and they can also be installed onto non-Exchange servers and clients for remote administration of Exchange. See Recipe 17.6 for more on this topic. All graphical solutions in this chapter require the Exchange management tools to be present on the workstation or server being used.

Using a Command-Line Interface

As previously mentioned, Exchange was traditionally managed from the GUI, so the availability of command-line tools for basic Exchange management functions isn't what you would call staggering. The primary reason for this is the complexity of the Exchange system. Simply put, Exchange can do a lot of different things and needs specific customizations for each deployment. Using custom scripts tends to be the most efficient way for most organizations to handle Exchange functions from the command line.

If you really prefer non-scripted CLI though, most of the configuration information for Exchange is kept in Active Directory. This means you can use your usual Active Directory command-line tools to query and set Exchange information. You simply have to understand what specific attributes are used to control that specific functionality in Exchange. This may be less intuitive than one would hope, but with sufficient testing and research you can do a considerable amount with Exchange via Active Directory command-line tools, such as *ldifde*. The general process most administrators follow when trying to work this out is to use the GUI to do something and then look at the resulting Active Directory object created or modified and then trying to duplicate it via script or CLI. Of course, you will want to do this in a test lab before utilizing your results in a production environment.

Unless otherwise noted, all command-line solutions require the Exchange management tools to be present on the workstation or server being used. See Recipe 17.6 for more on installing these tools.

Table 17-1 lists the command-line tools used in this chapter and the recipes they are used in.

Table 17-1. Command-line tools used in this chapter

Tool	Windows Server 2003	Windows 2000	Recipes
Idifde	%SystemRoot%\system32	%SystemRoot%\system32	17.9, 17.10, 17.12, 17.18–17.22, 17.24
ExchMbx	http://www.joeware.net	http://www.joeware.net	17.9–17.12, 17.16, 17.18–17.20
Dsadd	%SystemRoot%\system32	N/A	17.20

Using VBScript

Through the WMI, ADSI, and CDOEXM scripting interfaces you have the capability to automate many Exchange tasks. Table 17-2 lists all WMI classes used in this chapter. Unfortunately, the CDOEXM interface isn't available by default on Windows computers, so you will need to load the Exchange management tools on computers that run any scripts using that interface.

Table 17-2. WMI classes used in this chapter

WMI class	Description	Recipes
Exchange_Mailbox	WMI class that represents Exchange mailboxes	17.13–17.15, 17.17
Exchange_DSAccessDC	WMI Class that represents DSAccess	17.26

WMI and ADSI are covered in Appendixes B and C, respectively. Since CDOEXM is specific to Exchange programming, I'll cover it in more depth here. CDOEXM stands for Collaboration Data Objects for Exchange Management and is a COM library supplied by Microsoft for developing messaging and administration applications for Exchange. You can find the documentation for CDOEXM in the Microsoft Online MSDN Library and the Exchange Server 2003 Software Development Kit (SDK). There are additional WMI classes available for Exchange that are not used for recipes in this chapter (see the Exchange SDK for more information).

Notes on Managing Exchange

Managing Exchange is a little different from managing most other Microsoft applications. The computer where you run the tools or scripts must be a member of a domain in the forest where the Exchange organization resides. This is true whether you are using a script or the GUI. Exchange doesn't allow you to select other organizations to manage. This can be troublesome for someone managing multiple Exchange organizations or a mobile worker who moves between sites or companies and likes to run her workstation in workgroup mode instead of being a member of any specific domain.

Permissions are very important and often misunderstood in Exchange. Permissions can be set up very simply or in a very complicated way; it is tough to find a middle ground. The simplest method is to give your Exchange administrators Domain Admin access. This is pretty standard in small companies where the Exchange administrators are doing all aspects of administration. But this practice is usually unacceptable in larger companies where separation of duties and more security is required. See Recipe 17.7 for more discussion and details on permissions.

Finally, it is preferable to run Exchange in Active Directory native mode (for Windows 2000) or at the Windows Server 2003 forest functional level. Running Exchange in an Active Directory mixed-mode environment can be troublesome. If you must run in this mode, try to keep the timeframe as short as possible and anticipate that things will not work exactly as expected during that time.

17.1   Preparing Active Directory for Exchange

Problem

You want to prepare your Active Directory forest and domains for installation of your first Exchange Server.

Solution

Using a graphical user interface

The first phase of the installation is called ForestPrep and needs to be run once on the Schema flexible single master operations (FSMO) domain controller:

1. Log on to the Schema FSMO forest root domain controller with an account that has both Enterprise and Schema Admin rights.

2. Prepare the domain controller for a schema update. See Recipe 10.2 in *Active Directory Cookbook* (O'Reilly).

3. Per your corporate standards, create either a global or universal group for the initial Exchange administration delegation. Name the group in a descriptive way like ExchangeRootAdmins. See Chapter 7 in *Active Directory Cookbook* (O'Reilly) for assistance on creating groups.

4. Insert the Exchange Server CD into the CD-ROM.

5. On the **Start** menu, click **Run** and type:

   ```
   <driveletter>:\setup\i386\setup.exe /forestprep
   ```

where **<*driveletter*>** is your CD-ROM's drive letter. This path may vary for certain versions of Exchange Server, such as MSDN or Select versions.

6. On the **Welcome** screen, click Next.

7. On the **License Agreement** screen, read through the agreement and if you agree, click **I agree** and click **Next**.

8. If the **Product Identification** screen is presented, enter your Exchange Server product key and click **Next**.

This screen may not appear for certain versions of Exchange Server, such as the MSDN or Select versions.

9. On the **Component Selection** screen, verify that the action specified is **ForestPrep** and click **Next**.

10. On the **Server Administrator Account** screen, enter the group created in step 3 and click **Next**.

11. On the **Completing the Microsoft Exchange Wizard** screen, click **Finish**.

The second phase is called DomainPrep and needs to be run once for the forest root domain and once for every domain in the forest that will contain mail-enabled objects. Preferably you will run this process on every domain in the forest. Prior to starting DomainPrep, wait for the schema updates from the ForestPrep to replicate.

1. Log on to a machine that is part of the domain with an account that is a member of the Domain Admins group.

2. Insert the Exchange Server CD into CD-ROM.

3. On the **Start** menu, click **Run** and type:

        <driveletter>:\setup\i386\setup.exe /domainprep

   where **<*driveletter*>** is your CD-ROM's drive letter. This path may vary for certain versions of Exchange Server, such as MSDN or Select versions.

4. On the **Welcome** screen, click **Next**.

5. On the **License Agreement** screen, read through the agreement and if you agree, click **I agree** and click **Next**.

6. If the **Product Identification** screen is presented, enter your Exchange Server product key and click **Next**.

This screen may not appear for certain versions of Exchange Server, such as the MSDN or Select versions.

7. On the **Component Selection** screen, verify that the action specified is **Domain-Prep** and click **Next**.

8. Depending on how your domain is configured for Pre-Windows 2000 Compatible Access, you may get a pop-up with a message saying "The domain '<domainname>' has been identified as an insecure domain for mail-enabled groups with hidden distribution list (DL) membership..." If you get this pop-up, click **OK**.

9. On the **Completing the Microsoft Exchange Wizard** screen, click **Finish**.

Using a command-line interface

You cannot run ForestPrep from the command line. You can, however, run an unattended DomainPrep. You will need to create an unattended installation configuration file, which is described in Recipe 17.5. For further details on this process, see the Exchange Server 2003 Deployment Guide.

You can load the Exchange schema additions to your forest before running Forest-Prep. With this method, you can import the Exchange-specific schema modifications months in advance. For details on this process, see MS KB 327757.

Discussion

Microsoft Exchange will not run in an Active Directory forest unless the forest and the domains have been properly prepared. Microsoft did not make the assumption that everyone would use Exchange and therefore did not include all of the Exchange attributes and classes in the base Active Directory schema. The ability to dynamically extend the schema for Active Directory makes it possible for only those people running Exchange to install the Exchange infrastructure.

In addition to schema changes, you have to make security changes to Active Directory and the domain policy, as well as create some basic Exchange infrastructure objects. All of this is completed in the Exchange ForestPrep and DomainPrep processes. Do not confuse these with the Windows 2003 ForestPrep and DomainPrep processes (using the *adprep* command); the concept is the same, but the specific changes are different.

You need to run the ForestPrep process once per forest to make the schema changes, create the Exchange organization structure in the Configuration container, and set up Exchange-specific permissions. The ForestPrep process is also responsible for the initial delegation of Exchange rights to a specific user or group for administrative control. I recommend that you create a security group in your root domain for this delegation. In a single domain forest, which will never get another domain, you could use a domain local group. In a multidomain forest, you must use a global or universal group. The group assigns rights to objects in the Configuration container. Whether you use a global or universal group is up to you; either will do the job. The

ForestPrep process requires the user to be part of both the Enterprise and Schema Admins groups.

You need to run the DomainPrep process in the root domain of the forest and for every domain that will contain mail-enabled objects. Normally, you run Domain-Prep on every domain in an Active Directory forest. The process creates Exchange-security principals, modifies the domain security policy, creates some Exchange specific infrastructure objects, and assigns permissions to the domain's Active Directory partition. The DomainPrep process requires the user to be a member of the Domain Admins group of the domain being prepared.

Depending on whether your domain has Pre-Windows 2000 Compatible Access enabled or not, you may get a scary looking message during the DomainPrep process that tells you your domain is insecure for mail-enabled groups with hidden distribution list membership. Instead of making quick changes to your domain that could break other applications, investigate if you need that compatibility access. If you do not need the access, by all means, lock down the Pre-Windows 2000 Compatible Access group as specified.

Just like any application, there are requirements for the installation of Exchange Server 2003. The requirements are broken into forest and machine requirements. For ForestPrep and DomainPrep, there are no machine requirements. However, the forest requirements are:

- Domain controllers must run Windows 2000 Server Service Pack 3 or Windows Server 2003.
- Global catalog servers must run Windows 2000 Server Service Pack 3 or Windows Server 2003. You should have at least one global catalog server per domain where you intend to install Exchange.
- DNS and WINS must be properly configured.

Due to the depth of changes made to the overall structure of Active Directory, the ForestPrep process requires Schema and Enterprise Admin rights and the Domain-Prep requires Domain Admin rights. This prevents anyone but the centralized administration group responsible for the overall Active Directory forest from initially installing Exchange into the forest.

For a more in-depth discussion of the Exchange Server 2003 deployment requirements, considerations, and the specifics of what the "prep" processes do, please see the Exchange Server 2003 Deployment Guide. This is a free download from Microsoft available at *http://www.microsoft.com/downloads*. Type **Exchange Server 2003 Deployment Guide** in the keywords and click **Go**.

See Also

MS KB 314649 (Windows Server 2003 adprep /forestprep Command Causes Mangled Attributes in Windows 2000 Forests That Contain Exchange 2000 Servers), MS

KB 327757 (How To Extend the Active Directory Schema for Exchange Without Installing Exchange), Chapters 7 and 10 in *Active Directory Cookbook* (O'Reilly), and Exchange Server 2003 Deployment Guide

17.2 Installing the First Exchange Server

Problem

You want to install the first Exchange Server of an Exchange organization.

Solution

Using a graphical user interface

1. Install and configure prerequisite services. See the Discussion section for more on these services.

2. Log on to a server that is member of an Exchange-enabled domain with an account that is a member of the delegated group in Recipe 17.1. This account should also be a local administrator of the server.

3. Go to the Windows Update site and install any critical security patches. Click on **Start** → **All Programs** → **Windows Update**.

4. Insert the Exchange Server CD into the CD-ROM drive.

5. On the **Start** menu, click **Run**, type **<driveletter>:\setup\i386\setup.exe**, and click **OK**. **<driveletter>** is the drive letter of your CD-ROM drive. The path to *setup.exe* may vary for certain versions of Exchange Server, such as MSDN or Select versions.

6. On the **Welcome** screen, click **Next**.

7. On the **License Agreement** screen, read through the agreement and if you agree, click **I agree** and click **Next**.

8. If the **Product Identification** screen is presented, enter your Exchange Server product key and click **Next**.

> This screen may not appear for certain versions of Exchange Server, such as the MSDN or Select versions.

9. On the **Component Selection** screen in the **Action** column, verify that the action selected is **Typical**. Verify that the install path is correct for your installation and click **Next**. It is a common practice is to load Exchange onto a drive other than the system drive.

10. On **Installation Type** screen, verify that **Create a new Exchange Organization** is selected and click **Next**.

11. On the **Organization Name** screen, enter the name you want for your Exchange organization and click Next. You can leave the default name of First Organization or name it something specific to your installation (e.g., RALLEN-CORPMAIL).

12. On the **License Agreement** screen, select **I agree** and then click **Next**.

13. Review the **Installation Summary** screen and click **Next**.

14. On the **Completing the Microsoft Exchange Wizard** screen, click **Finish**.

15. Download and install the latest Exchange 2003 Service Pack. As of the time of this writing, that is Service Pack 1. See Recipe 17.4 for more on installing Exchange service packs.

Using a command-line interface

You cannot install the first Exchange Server of the Organization via the command line.

Discussion

The first Exchange server you install is special. This is because in addition to installing the Exchange Server software on the server, the process is also creating Active Directory objects in the Configuration container for the Exchange organization. As such, the installation is slightly different from any other Exchange Server installation you will do in the forest (see Recipe 17.3). The difference is in steps 10 and 11, which will not be present for any other Exchange Server Installations within the Exchange organization. In these steps, you will choose whether to create a new Exchange organization or join an existing Exchange 5.5 organization. The additional considerable amount of work involved in joining an existing Exchange 5.5 organization is outside the scope of this chapter. See the *Exchange Server Cookbook* (O'Reilly) for more information.

Exchange Server has several software prerequisites. You must have these prerequisites in place prior to installing Exchange, or Exchange will refuse to install. The prerequisites vary by operating system.

The Windows 2000 SP3+ prerequisites are:

- Windows Server 2003 Administration Tools Pack (*adminpak.msi*)
- Internet Information Services (IIS)
- World Wide Web Publishing (WWW) Service
- Simple Mail Transport Protocol (SMTP) Service
- Network News Transfer Protocol (NNTP) Service

Window Server 2003 requires the Windows 2000 prerequisites plus these additional items:

- .NET Framework
- ASP.NET

See Chapter 12 for more details on the installation of IIS.

See Also

Recipe 17.4, MS KB 822593 (Description of the /ChooseDC Switch in Exchange Server 2003), and MS KB 822893 (Setup Options for Exchange Server 2003)

17.3   Installing Additional Exchange Servers

Problem

You want to install an additional Exchange Server.

Solution

Using a graphical user interface

1. Install and configure prerequisite services. See the Discussion section for more on these services.

2. Log on to a server that is member of an Exchange-enabled domain with an account that is a member of the group delegated in Recipe 17.1. This account should also be an administrator of the server.

3. Go to the Windows Update site and install any critical security patches. Click on **Start** → **All Programs** → **Windows Update**.

4. Insert the Exchange Server CD into the CD-ROM drive.

5. On the **Start** menu, click **Run**, type *<driveletter>*:**\setup\i386\setup.exe**, and click **OK**. *<driveletter>* is your CD-ROM's drive letter. This path may vary for certain versions of Exchange Server, such as MSDN or Select versions.

6. On the **Welcome** screen, click **Next**.

7. On the **License Agreement** screen, read through the agreement and if you agree, click **I agree** and click **Next**.

8. If the **Product Identification** screen is presented, enter your Exchange Server **product key** and click **Next**.

> This screen may not appear for certain versions of Exchange Server, such as the MSDN or Select versions.

9. On the **Component Selection** screen in the **Action** column, verify that the action specified is **Typical**. Verify that the install path is correct for your installation and click **Next**. A common practice is to load Exchange onto a drive other than the system drive.

10. On the **License Agreement** screen, select **I agree** and click **Next**.

11. Review the **Installation Summary** screen and click **Next**.

12. On the **Completing the Microsoft Exchange Wizard** screen, click **Finish**.

13. Download and Install latest Exchange 2003 Service Pack. As of the time of this writing, that is Service Pack 1. See Recipe 17.4 for more on installing Exchange service packs.

Using a command-line interface

Any Exchange server installations after the initial Exchange server can be handled through the command line with the unattended installation process. You will need to generate and use an unattended installation INI file. See Recipe 17.5 for more on the INI file creation process.

Once you have an unattended file, use the following command to install Exchange:

```
> <driveletter>:\setup\i386\setup.exe /unattendfile <unattendfile>
```

If there is an error during the install process, it will be recorded in the Exchange Server setup log, which by default will be located in the root of the system drive, generally *c:*.

Discussion

Exchange Server has several software prerequisites for its installation. You must have these prerequisites met prior to installing Exchange or else Exchange will refuse to install. See Recipe 17.2 for more details on the prerequisites.

Using a command-line interface

If you have only one or two Exchange servers, automating the Exchange Server service pack installation will probably not appeal to you. However, if you have several Exchange Servers, using the unattended installation features of Exchange can certainly lead to time savings, efficiency, and consistency.

See Also

Recipes 17.4 and 17.5, MS KB 822593 (Description of the /ChooseDC Switch in Exchange Server 2003), and MS KB 822893 (Setup Options for Exchange Server 2003)

17.4   Installing an Exchange Service Pack

Problem

You want to update your Exchange Server with the latest Exchange service pack.

Solution

Using a graphical user interface

1. Download the latest service pack from Microsoft. This can be found at *http://www.microsoft.com/exchange/*. The current Exchange service pack at the time of this writing for Exchange 2003 is Service Pack 1.

2. On the **Start** menu, click **Run**, type the path to the service pack executable (e.g., *E3SP1ENG.exe*), and click **OK**.

3. When asked for a folder to extract the files to, type *C:\Temp\Exchange2003* and click **OK**.

4. On the **Extraction Complete** screen, click **OK**.

5. On the **Start** menu, click **Run**, type the full path to *update.exe*, and click **OK**. This will vary by service pack and language version, but here is an example path: *C:\Temp\Exchange2003\E3SP1ENG\setup\i386\update.exe*.

6. On the **Welcome** screen, click **Next**.

7. On the **License Agreement** screen, read through the agreement and if you agree, click **I agree** and click **Next**.

8. On the **Component Selection** screen in the **Action** column, verify that the action specified is **Update** and click **Next**. If an operating system update is required first, you will get a pop-up explaining what needs to be done. See the Discussion section for more information.

9. On the **Installation Summary** screen, verify actions and click **Next**.

10. On the **Completing the Microsoft Exchange Wizard** screen, click **Finish**.

Using a command-line interface

Service Pack installations can be handled through unattended installations just like regular Exchange server installations. You will need to generate and use the appropriate unattended installation INI file. See Recipe 17.5 for more on INI file creation.

Once you have an unattended file, use the following command to update.

```
> <driveletter>:\<path_to_sp_files>\update.exe /unattendfile <unattendfile>
```

Note that if there is an error during the installation process, it will be recorded in the Exchange Server setup log, which by default will be located in the root of the system drive, generally *c:*.

Discussion

Installing service packs is very important for keeping a secure, well-run system. This procedure needs to be followed both for servers running Exchange and any machines loaded with the Exchange administration tools. When applying any service pack, you may be prompted to install some other hot fix or service pack first for the operating system. For example, when installing Exchange SP1 on Windows Server 2003, you must also have the hot fix from MS KB 831464.

Using a command-line interface

If you have only one or two Exchange servers, automating the Exchange Server service pack installation will probably not appeal to you. However, if you have several Exchange Servers, using the unattended installation feature of Exchange can certainly lead to time savings, efficiency, and consistency.

See Also

Recipes 2.11 and 17.5, MS KB 831464 (FIX: IIS 6.0 compression corruption causes access violations), and MS KB 822893 (Setup Options for Exchange Server 2003)

17.5 Creating Unattended Installation Files for Exchange and Exchange Service Pack

Problem

You want to create an unattended installation file for command-line installations and upgrades of Exchange Server.

Solution

Using a graphical user interface

1. Follow the procedures for Exchange Server installation (see Recipe 17.3), Exchange Server Management Tools installation (see Recipe 17.6), or Exchange Server Service Pack installation (see Recipe 17.4) to the point where you enter the setup or update command.

2. Append to the run command the option /createunattend *<driveletter>*:*<path>*\ *<filename>*.ini. Note that *<filename>* should describe the installation or update. Examples include *e2k3-unattended-sp1-install.ini* and *e23k-tools-install.ini*.

3. Follow all of the screen prompts of the normal installation or upgrade.

4. On the **Completing the Microsoft Exchange Wizard** screen, click **Finish**.

5. Your unattended installation file should be in the location specified in the /createunattend option.

Discussion

Using unattended installation is a great way to install Exchange on many servers, deploy the Exchange tools to many administrator workstations, update service packs for Exchange on many servers, or maintain consistency in installation configurations.

The basic process is simply to add the /createunattend switch to the command line for either the *setup* or *update* command. You can also, if you choose, create an encrypted unattended installation file by using the /encryptedmode option. To see a complete list of options, run the *setup* or *update* executable with the /? option. After you create the file, you can use it to install Exchange as shown in the command-line solution in Recipe 17.3.

See Also

Recipes 17.3, 17.4, and 17.6 and MS KB 822893 (Setup Options for Exchange Server 2003)

17.6   Installing Exchange Management Tools

Problem

You want to install Exchange Management tools onto a workstation or server that isn't running Exchange.

Solution

Using a graphical user interface

1. Install and configure prerequisite services. See the Discussion section for the list of these services.

2. Go to the Windows Update site and install any critical security patches.

3. Load the Exchange Server CD into your CD-ROM drive.

4. On the **Start** menu, click **Run**, type *<driveletter>*:\setup\i386\setup.exe, and click **OK**. *<driveletter>* is your CD-ROM's drive letter. This path may vary for certain versions of Exchange Server, such as MSDN or Select versions.

5. On the **Welcome** screen, click **Next**.

6. On the **License Agreement** screen read through the agreement and if you agree, click **I agree** and click **Next**.

7. If the **Product Identification** screen is presented, enter your Exchange Server product key and click **Next**.

This screen may not appear for certain versions of Exchange Server such as the MSDN or Select versions.

8. On the **Component Selection** screen, select **Custom** in the top row of the **Action** column. Select the **Install** next to **Microsoft Exchange System Management Tools**. Verify that the installation path is correct for your installation and click **Next**.

9. Review the **Installation Summary** screen and click **Next**.

10. On the **Completing the Microsoft Exchange Wizard** screen, click **Finish**.

11. Download and install the latest Exchange 2003 Service Pack. As of the time of this writing, that is Service Pack 1. See Recipe 17.4 for more information.

Using a command-line interface

Any Exchange Management Tool installations can be handled through the command line with the unattended installation process. You will need to generate and use the appropriate unattended installation INI file. See Recipe 17.5 for more on creating an INI file.

Once you have an unattended file, use the following command to install it.

```
> <driveletter>:\setup\i386\setup.exe /unattendfile <unattendfile>
```

Note that if there is an error during the installation process, it will be recorded in the Exchange Server setup log, which by default will be located in the root of the system drive, generally *c:*.

Discussion

Exchange Server has several software prerequisites for the Exchange Management Tools software, without which they will refuse to install. You must have the Windows Server 2003 Administration Tools Pack (*adminpak.msi*) installed on Windows XP SP1+, Windows 2000 SP3+, or Windows Server 2003 along with the following services:

- Internet Information Services (IIS)
- World Wide Web Publishing (WWW) Service
- Simple Mail Transport Protocol (SMTP) Service

See Chapter 12 for more details on installation of these prerequisites.

Finally, Microsoft recommends against installing Exchange tools on a machine that runs Outlook. I've not had an issue with loading the Exchange tools on a workstation that had Outlook, but it is a point that I must mention. See MS KB 266418 for more details.

Using a command-line interface

If you have only one or two machines you want to install the tools on, automating the Exchange Server Management Tools installation will probably not be any value to you. However, if you have several machines you need to load the tools on, using the unattended installation feature can lead to time savings, efficiency, and consistency.

See Also

Recipe 17.5, MS KB 822593 (Description of the /ChooseDC Switch in Exchange Server 2003), MS KB 822893 (Setup Options for Exchange Server 2003), and MS KB 266418 (Microsoft does not recommend installing Exchange Server and Outlook on the same computer)

17.7   Delegating Exchange for the First Time

Problem

You want to delegate permissions to manage Exchange. This recipe allows you to configure the basic delegation of the three Exchange roles to users or groups.

Solution

Using a graphical user interface

1. Log on to a machine with an account that is in the initially delegated Exchange Group from Recipe 17.2.

2. Per your corporate standards, create three groups called ExchangeViewAdmins, ExchangeAdmins, and ExchangeFullAdmins. The groups can be any scope. See Chapter 7 in *Active Directory Cookbook* (O'Reilly) for assistance on creating groups and the ramifications of the different group scopes.

3. Open the Exchange System Manager (ESM) snap-in.

4. In the left pane, right-click on the Organization name (e.g., RALLENCORP-MAIL) and select **Delegate Control**.

5. On the Welcome screen, click **Next**.

6. On the **Users and Groups** screen, click **Add**.

7. On the **Delegate Control** screen, click **Browse**.

8. On the **Select Users**, **Computers**, **Or Groups** screen, type into the text box the name of the group to which you want to delegate **Exchange View Admin** rights (e.g., RALLENCORP\ExchangeViewAdmins).

9. Back on the **Delegate Control** screen, verify that **Exchange View Only Administrator** is listed in the role drop-down menu and click **OK**.

10. Repeat steps 6–9 for ExchangeAdmins and ExchangeFullAdmins, selecting the appropriate permissions in the role drop-down menu.

11. If you used a group in the root delegation in Recipe 17.2, you may still see one or more accounts listed in the **Users and Groups** box. Remove these from the list by selecting them and clicking **Remove**.

12. Review the list of **Users and Groups** and click **Next**. You should have the following groups and roles listed:

    * ExchangeAdmins with role Exchange Administrator
    * ExchangeFullAdmins with role Exchange Full Administrator
    * ExchangeViewAdmins with role Exchange View Only Administrator

13. On the **Completed Wizard** screen, click **Finish**.

14. Add the accounts of the administrators to the various groups with your favorite group management tool.

Discussion

Exchange delegation is a delicate and complicated topic. Most of the Exchange permissions are granted through access control lists (ACLs) on objects in Active Directory. These permissions in Active Directory can be delegated in a very granular way. Exchange consolidates the permissions into three main layers of delegation called roles:

* Exchange View Only Administrator allows you to look at the Exchange System.
* Exchange Administrator allows you to fully administer Exchange Server computer information.
* Exchange Full Administrator allows you to fully administer Exchange.

Be aware that none of these Exchange Roles give you access rights on user objects themselves. You can be an Exchange Full Administrator and not be able to mailbox-enable a single user. For that, you need to determine what rights you want the Exchange Admins to have on user objects and grant them separately.

Unfortunately, it is beyond the scope of this chapter to dig into all of the various ways to delegate rights to Active Directory objects. I'll assume for the remainder of this chapter that any administrator who needs to make changes to a user or group, such as mail-enabling or mailbox-enabling a user, mail-enabling a distribution group, creating a contact, etc., is a member of the Account Operators group with the additional permissions outlined in the next paragraph delegated in Active Directory.

By default, Account Operators have permissions to manage user objects, inetOrgPerson objects, and group objects. They do not have permissions to manage contacts or query-based distribution lists. In order for an Account Operator to be able to fully manage mail-specific contents of Active Directory, permissions to create, delete, and manage contacts (i.e., objects with an objectclass of contact) and query-based distribution groups (i.e., objects with an objectclass of `msExchDynamicDistributionList`) have to be added separately. For details on Active Directory security and delegation, see Chapter 14 of *Active Directory Cookbook* (O'Reilly).

In this security-aware world we now live in, I would be lax if I didn't talk about delegation best practices. Security best practices dictate for a separation of duties for different types of administrators. This is also known as the principle of least privileges. Exchange is definitely large enough to follow this type of model and has a couple of levels where these separations can most logically be made.

The first level involves the Help Desk or Call Center Exchange troubleshooters. These are people who you don't want making changes. You only want them to look at what is in place so they can properly escalate to the next level of support if the issue is truly an Exchange issue. These admins will need only view only access to Exchange and Active Directory. This would map to the Exchange View Only Admin Role.

The second level are the Exchange Data Administrators, administrators who are responsible for manipulating which users do and don't get Mailboxes and managing contacts and distribution lists. They will need to be able to manipulate users and other mail-enabled objects, but not manipulate the overall Exchange system configuration. This level is often automated and the functionality wrapped into some sort of provisioning system as the requests and responses should be standard. This level of permission will need Exchange view access and various create/delete/change permissions on the user, contact, and group objects in the forest. This would map to the Exchange View Only Admin Role coupled with the specially delegated Account Operator as specified earlier. The primary tool these admins use will be the ADUC snap-in.

> This functionality, placed in a custom web-based application with a proper authentication and authorization system, could be pushed to the Help Desk or even out to the business users so that business management can directly manage who can and can't have email. Microsoft also helps in the automation of this level by distributing a tool in the Exchange Resource Kit for automatically handling distribution lists called AutoDL. This tool has the concept of Distribution List subscriptions and managed Distribution Lists and has a web front-end for ease of use by nontechnical users.

Finally, you have Exchange Service Administrators; these are the main Exchange administrators who actually manage the overall service. They need to be able to manipulate the servers and the system configuration but don't generally need to manipulate the mail objects, such as users, groups, and contacts. This level would map to Exchange or Exchange Full Admin Roles. This level also requires local Administrator rights on the Exchange Servers. There could be times that these Admins will need additional permissions in Active Directory on User objects, most notably if they are moving mailboxes, as discussed in Recipe 17.16, or reconnecting mailboxes, as discussed in Recipe 17.14. The primary tool these administrators will use will be the ESM snap-in.

Depending on the size of your company and the security concerns you have, you may have none of these divisions, a subset of these divisions, or possibly even more divisions.

See Also

MS KB 823018 (Overview of Exchange Administrative Role Permissions in Exchange 2003), MS KB 316792 (Minimum permissions necessary to perform Exchange-related tasks), Chapters 7 and 14 of *Active Directory Cookbook* (O'Reilly), Active Directory Delegation Whitepaper and Appendix (*www.microsoft.com/downloads*), and *http://www.microsoft.com/technet/prodtechnol/exchange/2003/library/ex2k3ad.mspx*

17.8   Stopping and Starting Exchange Server

Problem

You want to stop or start Exchange Server.

Solution

Stopping and starting Exchange consists of stopping and starting the Exchange-related services. The basics of stopping and starting services are covered in Recipe 7.1. See the Discussion of this recipe for the list of Exchange services.

Discussion

There are several services involved with Exchange Server. Stopping different services will accomplish different things. The services are interdependent, so when you stop or start various services you may see a message about having to stop dependent services. If you do stop dependent services, don't forget to restart them again when you restart the service you began with.

To shut down Exchange completely on a given machine, you need to stop all of the following services:

Microsoft Exchange Event (MSExchangeES)
> This service was used for launching event-based scripts in Exchange 5.5 when folders changes were detected. Exchange 2000 offered the ability to create Event Sinks directly, so this use of this service has decreased. This service is not started by default.

Microsoft Exchange IMAP4 (IMAP4Svc)
> This service supplies IMAP4 protocol message server functionality. This service is disabled by default. To use IMAP4 you must enable this service, configure it to auto-start, and start the service.

Microsoft Exchange Information Store (MSExchangeIS)
This service is used to access the Exchange mail and public folder stores. If this service is not running, users will not be able to use Exchange. This service is started by default.

Microsoft Exchange Management (MSExchangeMGMT)
This service is responsible for various management functions available through WMI, such as message tracking, etc. This service is started by default.

Microsoft Exchange MTA Stacks (MSExchangeMTA)
This service is used to transfer X.400 messages sent to and from foreign systems, including Exchange 5.5 Servers. This service was extremely important in Exchange 5.5, which used X.400 as the default message transfer protocol. Before stopping or disabling this service, review MS KB 810489. This service is started by default.

Microsoft Exchange POP3 (POP3Svc)
This service supplies POP3 protocol message server functionality. This service is disabled by default. To use POP3 you must enable this service, configure it to auto-start, and start the service.

Microsoft Exchange Routing Engine (RESvc)
This service is used for routing and topology information for routing SMTP-based messages. This service is started by default.

Microsoft Exchange System Attendant (MSExchangeSA)
This service handles various cleanup and monitoring functions. One of the most important functions of the System Attendant is the Recipient Update Service (RUS), which is responsible for mapping attributes in Active Directory to the Exchange subsystem and enforcing recipient policies. When you "create" a mailbox for a user, you simply set some attributes on a user object. The RUS takes that information and does all of the work in the background with Exchange to really make the mailbox. If you mailbox- or mail-enable objects and they don't seem to work, the RUS is one of the first places you will look for an issue. If you need to enable diagnostics for the RUS, the parameters are maintained in a separate service registry entry, this service entry is called MSExchangeAL. This isn't a real service; it is simply the supplied location to modify RUS functionality. This service is started by default.

Microsoft Exchange Site Replication Service (MSExchangeSRS)
This service is used in Organizations that have Exchange 5.5 combined with Exchange 2000/2003. This service is not started by default.

Network News Transfer Protocol (NNTP) (NntpSvc)
This service is responsible for supplying NNTP Protocol Server functionality. This service is started by default.

Simple Mail Transfer Protocol (SMTP) (SMTPSVC)
This service is responsible for supplying SMTP Protocol Server functionality. This service is started by default.

Different servers could be running a combination of different services based on the complexity of the environment and the specific function of the server. Not all Exchange Servers will run all Exchange Services.

See Also

MS KB 263094 (XADM: Internal Names of Exchange 2000 Server Services) and Chapter 7

17.9 Mail-Enabling a User

Problem

You want to mail-enable a user.

Solution

Using a graphical user interface

1. Open the ADUC snap-in.

This needs to be run on a workstation or server that has the Exchange Management Tools loaded (see Recipe 17.6).

2. If you need to change domains, right-click on **Active Directory Users and Computers** in the left pane, select **Connect to Domain**, enter the domain name, and click **OK**.

3. In the left pane, browse to the parent container of the user, right-click on the user, and select **Exchange Tasks**.

4. On the **Welcome** screen, click **Next**.

5. Select **Establish E-mail Address** and click **Next**.

6. Verify the mail alias is what you want.

7. Click **Modify**, select the external email address type (generally **SMTP Address**), click **OK**, enter an external email address, and click **OK**.

There is an **Advanced** tab on the **Internet Address Properties** screen. On this tab, you have the option to override the default handling of email sent to this recipient. (e.g., you can force all email to be delivered as HTML or plain text, etc.)

8. On the **Completion** screen, click **Finish**.

Using a command-line interface

```
> exchmbx -b "<User DN>" -me <smtp email address>
```

Replace *<User DN>* with the user's distinguished name and *<smtp email address>* with the user's external email address.

To mail-enable user joe with the email address *joe@unixmail.rallencorp.com*, execute the following command. The command should be contained on one line.

```
> exchmbx -b "cn=joe,cn=users,dc=rallencorp,dc=com" -me joe@unixmail.rallencorp.com
```

For an alternative Microsoft native tool method, create an LDIF file called *mailenable_user.ldf* with the following contents:

```
dn: <User DN>
changetype: modify
replace: targetAddress
targetaddress: SMTP:<smtp email address>
-
replace: mailNickName
mailNickname: <mail nickname>
-
replace: mAPIRecipient
mAPIRecipient: FALSE
-
replace: legacyExchangeDN
legacyExchangeDN: <legacy exchange DN>
-
replace: internetEncoding
internetEncoding: 1310720
-
```

Replace *<User DN>* with the user's distinguished name, *<smtp email address>* with the user's external email address, and *<legacy exchange DN>* with the proper legacy exchange distinguished name value. Then run the following command:

```
>ldifde -i -f mailenable_user.ldf
```

Using VBScript

```
' This code mail enables a user.
' ------ SCRIPT CONFIGURATION ------
strUserDN = "<UserDN>"    ' e.g., cn=jsmith,cn=Users,dc=rallencorp,dc=com
strEmailAddr = "<EmailAddress>" 'e.g., jsmith234@freemail.net
' ------ END CONFIGURATION ---------
set objUser = GetObject("LDAP://" & strUserDN)
objUser.MailEnable strEmailAddr
objUser.Put "internetEncoding",1310720
objUser.SetInfo( )
Wscript.Echo "Successfully mail-enabled user."
```

Discussion

A mail-enabled user is a user who has at least one email address defined within Exchange, but does not have a mailbox. This does not give any access rights to the user within the Exchange system; it simply allows Exchange users to select the mail-enabled users from the global address list (GAL) and easily send email to them. You would use a mail-enabled user when you have a user who needs to log into the domain, but has an email address external to the forest's Exchange organization. The email address could be external to the company or it could just be external to the Exchange organization of that forest. Examples would be users with mailboxes on external email systems or users with mailboxes on internal non-Exchange servers.

 Mail-enabling a user requires Exchange Data Administrator permissions. See the Discussion for Recipe 17.7.

When you create a mail-enabled user with the ADUC or with VBScript, you call out to the CDOEXM interface, which is the Microsoft-supported method of managing Exchange attributes on users, groups, and contacts. The specific method in this case is `MailEnable`. In the background, the specific changes made by the `MailEnable` method are on the user object in Active Directory and include changes to the following attributes:

- `targetAddress`
- `mailNickname`
- `mAPIRecipient`
- `legacyExchangeDN`

In addition to those attributes, the `internetEncoding` attribute should also be set for proper message handling. This is the attribute that is updated if you go into the Advanced tab of the Internet Address Properties screen. The default value for this attribute is 1310720, which tells Exchange to use the default settings of the Internet Mail Service. You can specify other values to force email to be converted to various formats. Table 17-3 lists alternate values for the `internetEncoding` attribute.

Table 17-3. internetEncoding attribute values

Value	Meaning
1310720	Use Internet Mail Service settings.
917504	Allow plain text.
1441792	Allow plain text or HTML.
2228224	Allow plain text/uuencoding.
131072	Allow plain text/uuencoding with BinHex.

Once all of those attributes are in place, the RUS sets additional attributes on the user object to make it usable for Exchange.

Using a graphical user interface

Mail-enabling a user is a little more confusing if you are creating new users because you don't get prompted to mail-enable them. To create a mail-enabled user from scratch, create the user and, when prompted to create a mailbox, clear the **Create an Exchange Mailbox** checkbox. Once the user is created, follow the directions described in the solution.

Using a command-line interface

Command-line administration tools for Exchange are rather rare. Luckily, the ExchMbx tool is available as a free download from Joe Richards' web site *http://www.joeware.net*. This tool can turn a difficult process into something simple. If you need to modify the `internetEncoding` attribute as mentioned above, add the `-internetencoding` option to the parameter list specifying the proper value from Table 17-3. For example:

```
> exchmbx -b <UserDN> -me <SmtpEmailAddress> -internetencoding 917504
```

If you prefer Microsoft native solutions, the LDIF solution I described will work, but it can be dangerous because there is the possibility of duplicating critical values within the Exchange organization. If you put duplicate `mailNickname` or `legacyExchangeDN` values into the system, you will have bad results in your Exchange organization, and almost certainly, start producing nondelivery reports (NDR) for the mail objects involved.

The `mailNickname` attribute generally can be set to be the same as the `sAMAccountName`, which has to be unique in the domain. But what should you do you with `legacyExchangeDN`? If you aren't tied to a legacy 5.5 organization, you can follow the simple format the system currently uses. If you have a legacy 5.5 organization, you need to follow the structure for that organization. For assistance with this, contact Microsoft PSS or Microsoft Consulting Services.

The general format of `legacyExchangeDN` is:

```
/o=<Org>/ou=<AdministrativeGroup>/cn=<RecipientContainer>/cn=<mailnickname>
```

Assuming your `mailNickName` is unique (it had better be) and you know the values for the other variables, you can quickly construct a `legacyExchangeDN` like:

```
/o=CORPMAIL/ou=NORTHAMER/cn=Recipients/cn=NICOLEHANSKNECHT
```

You should always verify that the `legacyExchangeDN` you chose is not already used by searching Active Directory, because someone may have changed an existing user's `mailNickname` but, correctly, did not touch the `legacyExchangeDN` value. You could, of course, "fix" the `legacyExchangeDN` of that previously existing user so that it properly fits the pattern, but you would impact the user's email functionality.

The attribute legacyExchangeDN is used in Exchange internally for addressing email. If you try to respond to an email sent to you by a user within the same Exchange organization who has had her legacyExchangeDN changed, you will get an NDR and the mail will not be delivered. So if a user has a name change from Chris Smith to Chris Jones and her sAMAccountName and mailNickname both change from *csmith* to *cjones*, her legacyExchangeDN must remain the same so that anyone within the Exchange organization will be able to easily respond to emails she sent as *csmith*. The point is that you should always check that the legacyExchangeDN value you are setting is unique. The simple solution to follow if the value is already present is to append a –1, –2, or whatever dash value is required to get to a unique value.

You have the option of *not* specifying the legacyExchangeDN in the LDIF file. If the attribute is empty, Exchange will populate it for you. If there is already a value, Exchange will not change the attribute.

Unfortunately, if you are mail enabling an object that was previously mail- or mailbox-enabled it could have an existing value for legacyExchangeDN; this value may or may not be unique. One very specific case is that some tools will set the legacyExchangeDN value to ADCDisabled when an object is mail or mailbox disabled to alert the ADC to the object's status.

You can modify the internetEncoding attribute value in the LDIF file to any value in Table 17-3.

If you want to mail-enable multiple users at once, remove the -b option from the parameter list and pipe the distinguished names into ExchMbx from another tool or from a file. Run exchmbx /? for usage details.

Using VBScript

Creating a mail-enabled user from VBScript is quite simple; one call to the MailEnable method and the work is done. As I indicated in the CLI solution, you can modify the internetEncoding value to some other value in Table 17-3, depending on your needs.

See Also

Recipe 17.10, MS KB 275636 (Creating Exchange Mailbox-Enabled and Mail-Enabled Objects in Active Directory.), and MS KB 281740 (XCON: Internet Mail Service Settings Are Not Overridden for Custom Recipients in Distribution List) for the values of internetEncoding.

17.10 Mail-Disabling a User

Problem

You want to mail-disable a user.

Solution

Using a graphical user interface

1. Open the ADUC snap-in.

 This needs to be run on a workstation or server that has the Exchange Management Tools loaded (see Recipe 17.6).

2. If you need to change domains, right-click on **Active Directory Users and Computers** in the left pane, select **Connect to Domain**, enter the domain name, and click **OK**.

3. In the left pane, browse to the parent container of the user, right-click on the user, and select **Exchange Tasks**.

4. On the **Welcome** screen, click **Next**.

5. Select **Remove Exchange Attributes** and click **Next**.

6. Read the warning and click **Next**.

7. On the **Completion** screen, click **Finish**.

Using a command-line interface

```
> exchmbx -b "<User DN>" -clear
```

Replace <User DN> with the user's distinguished name.

For an alternative Microsoft native tool method, create an LDIF file called *clearmailattribs.ldf* with the following contents:

```
dn: <UserDN>
changetype: modify
replace: altRecipient
altRecipient:
-
replace: authOrig
authOrig:
-
...
<SEE DISCUSSION, NOT A COMPLETE LDIF FILE>
...
```

Replace *<UserDN>* with the user's distinguished name. Note that this is not a complete LDIF file as there are many attributes that must be cleared (see the Discussion section). Once you've created the LDIF file, run the following command:

```
> ldifde -i -f clearmailattribs.ldf
```

Using VBScript

```
' This code mail disables a user.
' ------ SCRIPT CONFIGURATION ------
strUserDN = "<UserDN>"    ' e.g., cn=jsmith,cn=Users,dc=rallencorp,dc=com
' ------ END CONFIGURATION ---------
set objUser = GetObject("LDAP://" & strUserDN)
objUser.MailDisable
objUser.SetInfo( )
Wscript.Echo "Successfully mail-disabled user."
```

Discussion

This recipe removes the Active Directory Exchange attributes for a previously mail-enabled user. This is a simple process from ADUC and from VBScript, but behind the scenes several attributes are being updated. For a complete list of the attributes that are modified, see MS KB 307350.

> Mail-disabling a user requires Exchange Data Administrator permissions. See the Discussion for Recipe 17.7.

Using a graphical user interface

This process is identical to the process for deleting a user's mailbox.

Using a command-line interface

The ExchMbx solution is simple and, unlike the VBScript solution, can be used on either mail- or mailbox-enabled users.

> If you want to clear the Exchange mail attributes on several objects at once remove the -b option from the parameter list and pipe the distinguished names into ExchMbx from another tool or from a file. Run exchmbx /? for usage details.

The LDIF solution requires some additional explanation. The LDIF file shown in the solution is not complete. You must clear many more attributes than listed. Check out MS KB 307350 for the current listing of attributes that should be cleared when removing Exchange attributes (there were about 90 at the time of this writing).

Using VBScript

The VBScript solution leverages the CDOEXM `MailDisable` method to mail-disable the user. Unfortunately, you can not use this method to mailbox-disable a user. So when you call this method, you should be sure that the user is mail-enabled versus mailbox-enabled. If you use this method on a mailbox-enabled user, you will get an error such as "E-mail addresses cannot be removed from this user because it has a mailbox." The quick way to ascertain whether a user has a mailbox or is simply mail-enabled is to check for the existence of the `homeMDB` attribute. If a user object has `homeMDB` populated, there is an associated mailbox for that account.

See Also

Recipe 17.9 and MS KB 307350 (XGEN: Using the "Remove Exchange Attributes" Option)

17.11 Mailbox-Enabling a User

Problem

You want to create a mailbox for a user. This is also known as mailbox-enabling a user.

Solution

Using a graphical user interface

1. Open the ADUC snap-in.

> This needs to be run on a workstation or server that has the Exchange Management Tools loaded (see Recipe 17.6).

2. If you need to change domains, right-click on **Active Directory Users and Computers** in the left pane, select **Connect to Domain**, enter the domain name, and click **OK**.

3. In the left pane, browse to the parent container of the user, right-click on the user, and select **Exchange Tasks**.

4. On the **Welcome** screen, click **Next**.

5. Select **Create Mailbox** and click **Next**.

6. Verify the mail alias is what you want, select the server you want the mailbox on, select which store where you want the mailbox, and click **Next**.

7. On the **Completion** screen, click **Finish**.

Using a command-line interface

```
> exchmbx -b "<UserDN>" -cr "<server>:<storage group>:<mail store>"
```

Or alternatively, run the following command:

```
> exchmbx -b <UserDN> -cr "<Home MDB URL>"
```

To mailbox-enable user joe with a mailbox on Exchange Server SRV1, Storage group SG1, and mailbox store DB1, execute the following command:

```
> exchmbx -b "cn=joe,cn=users,dc=rallencorp,dc=com" -cr "srv1:sg1:db1"
```

 I highly recommend that you keep your storage group and mailbox store names short, simple, and "space" free. Spaces are troublesome to deal with at the command prompt and have caused many administrators unneeded grief. If you do not use spaces and other special characters, you can dispense with the quotes in all of the command-line examples.

Replace *<UserDN>* with the user's distinguished name, *<server>* with the Exchange server name, *<storage group>* with the storage group, *<mail store>* with the mail store, and *<Home MDB URL>* with the full homeMDB URL for the desired mailbox store.

Using VBScript

```
' This code creates a mailbox for a user.
' ------ SCRIPT CONFIGURATION ------
strUserDN = "<UserDN>"    ' e.g., cn=jsmith,cn=Users,dc=rallencorp,dc=com
strHomeMDB = "<Home MDB DN>"
' e.g. CN=Mailbox Store (SERVER),CN=First Storage Group,CN=InformationStore,
' CN=SERVER,CN=Servers,CN=First Administrative Group,CN=Administrative Groups,
'       CN=RALLENCORPMAIL,CN=Microsoft Exchange,CN=Services,
'       CN=Configuration,DC=rallencorp,DC=com"
' ------ END CONFIGURATION ---------
set objUser = GetObject("LDAP://" & strUserDN)
objUser.CreateMailBox strHomeMDB
objUser.SetInfo( )
Wscript.Echo "Successfully mailbox-enabled user."
```

Discussion

A mailbox-enabled user is a user who has a mailbox defined in the Exchange organization where the user object exists. This is the most common object in an Exchange organization.

 Mailbox-enabling a user requires Exchange Data Administrator permissions. See the Discussion for Recipe 17.7.

When you create a mailbox for a user with the GUI or VBScript, you call out to the `CreateMailbox` CDOEXM interface. In the background, the specific changes made by the `CreateMailbox` method are on the user object in Active Directory and include changes to the following attributes:

- `mDBUseDefaults`
- `msExchUserAccountControl`
- `homeMTA`
- `msExchHomeServerName`
- `homeMDB`
- `mailNickname`
- `msExchMailboxGuid`
- `msExchMailboxSecurityDescriptor`
- `legacyExchangeDN`

Once all of those attributes are in place, the RUS sets additional attributes on the user object. The mailbox cannot be used nor receive email until the RUS has gone through this stamping process.

Using a graphical user interface

Creating a mailbox when you create a new user is a trivial task with ADUC because you simply need to specify the email alias and where in the Exchange organization the mailbox should reside. All of the guesswork on where the mailbox can go is removed because you have to select the location from the drop-down menu.

Using a command-line interface

Prior to the ExchMbx tool, there was no simple way to mailbox-enable a user from the command line. The LDIFDE method is not feasible because the `msExchMailboxSecurityDescriptor` attribute is a binary value and difficult to manipulate with LDIF files and text editors. For flexibility, ExchMbx allows you to specify the entire `homeMDB` URL, or you can specify the server, storage group, and mailbox store.

 If you want to mailbox-enable multiple users at once, remove the `-b` option from the parameter list and pipe the distinguished names into ExchMbx from another tool or from a file. Run `exchmbx /?` for usage details.

Using VBScript

The trickiest part of creating a mailbox for a user with VBScript is to know what to use for the `homeMDB` attribute. If you use the wrong value you will get the error: "The server is not operational," which isn't helpful feedback. This is where the GUI method is nice, because it looks up all of the possible values for you and lets you select from the list.

I present an alternative scripting method in Recipe 17.16, which lets you specify three well-known pieces of information to locate the proper homeMDB value. Finally, another alternative would be to search Active Directory for all valid homeMDB values, display them, and have the person running the script select from the list just like ADUC does. This third method involves searching against the Configuration container of Active Directory with the following filter: (objectcategory=msExchPrivateMDB).

See Also

MS KB 275636 (Creating Exchange Mailbox-Enabled and Mail-Enabled Objects in Active Directory) and MS KB 253770 (XADM: Tasks Performed by the Recipient Update Service)

17.12 Deleting a User's Mailbox

Problem

You want to delete a user's mailbox. This is also known as mailbox-disabling a user.

Solution

Using a graphical user interface

1. Open the ADUC snap-in.

 This needs to be run on a workstation or server that has the Exchange Management Tools loaded (see Recipe 17.6).

2. If you need to change domains, right-click on **Active Directory Users and Computers** in the left pane, select **Connect to Domain**, enter the domain name, and click **OK**.

3. In the left pane, browse to the parent container of the user, right-click on the user, and select **Exchange Tasks**.

4. On the **Welcome** screen, click **Next**.

5. Select **Remove Exchange Attributes** and click **Next**.

6. Read the warning and click **Next**.

7. On the **Completion** screen, click **Finish**.

Using a command-line interface

See the command-line example for Recipe 17.10.

Using VBScript

```
' This code mail disables a user.
' ------ SCRIPT CONFIGURATION ------
strUserDN = "<UserDN>"   ' e.g., cn=jsmith,cn=Users,dc=rallencorp,dc=com
' ------ END CONFIGURATION ---------
set objUser = GetObject("LDAP://" & strUserDN)
objUser.DeleteMailbox
objUser.SetInfo( )
Wscript.Echo "Successfully deleted user's mailbox."
```

Discussion

Although the recipe title is "Deleting a User's Mailbox," these solutions don't really delete the mailbox. They actually just clear the Exchange attributes from the user object and that disassociates the mailbox from the user. The mailbox will still exist in the Exchange store. The length of time it will exist depends on the mailbox retention period, which is, by default, 30 days. While the mailbox exists in that state, it can be reconnected to the same or a different user object.

 Deleting user mailboxes requires Exchange Data Administrator permissions. See the Discussion for Recipe 17.7.

Using a graphical user interface

This process in ADUC is identical to that of mail-disabling a user (see Recipe 17.10).

Using VBScript

The VBScript solution leverages the CDOEXM DeleteMailbox method to delete the mailbox for the user. Unfortunately, you cannot use this method to mail-disable a user. So when you call this method, you should be sure that the user is mailbox-enabled versus mail-enabled. If you use this method on a mail-enabled user, you will get an error, such as "This user does not have a mailbox." The quick way to ascertain whether or not a user has a mailbox or is simply mail-enabled is to check for the existence of the homeMDB attribute. If a user object has homeMDB populated, there is an associated mailbox for that account.

See Also

Recipes 17.13, and 17.14, MS KB 307350 (XGEN: Using the "Remove Exchange Attributes" Option), and MS KB 274343 (How to Recover a Deleted Mailbox in Exchange)

17.13 Purging a Deleted Mailbox

Problem

You want to purge a deleted mailbox from the Exchange Store.

Solution

Using a graphical user interface

1. Open the Exchange System Manager (ESM) snap-in.

2. In the left pane, browse to the mailboxes container of the server, storage group, and database where you want to purge a mailbox.

3. In the left pane, scroll down until you find the mailbox that you wish to purge. The mailbox should have a small red circle with a white X in it, indicating it is disconnected.

4. Right-click the mailbox and select **Purge**.

5. When prompted if you are sure you want to continue, click **Yes**.

Using VBScript

```
' This code purges a deleted mailbox.
' ------ SCRIPT CONFIGURATION ------
strComputer = "<Exchange Server>" 'e.g., ExchServer2
strMailbox = "<Mailbox Alias>"     'e.g., jsmith
' ------ END CONFIGURATION ---------

set objWMI = GetObject("winmgmts:\\" & strComputer & _
                        "\root\MicrosoftExchangeV2")
set objDiscMbx = objWMI.ExecQuery("Select * from Exchange_Mailbox WHERE " _
                         & "MailboxDisplayName='" & strMailbox & "'",,48)
for each objMbx in objDiscMbx
  objMbx.Purge
next
Wscript.Echo "Successfully purged mailbox."
```

Discussion

A mailbox that has been deleted still has physical presence in the Exchange store. This recipe wipes that mailbox completely from the store. Once a mailbox has been purged, the only way to retrieve it is through restoring from a backup, which could be a lengthy process given the need to recover the entire store. In other words, don't do this unless you are sure of the consequences.

Purging a mailbox requires Exchange Service Administrator permissions. See the Discussion for Recipe 17.7.

Using a graphical user interface

You may run into a case where ESM doesn't show you a mailbox is disconnected when in fact you know it is. This can happen if you delete the mailbox and immediately look at it in ESM. In order to clear that condition, you will need to right-click on the mailboxes container and select Run Cleanup Agent, causing some house cleaning to be done. The mailbox should then show up as disconnected.

Using VBScript

The Purge method is part of the Exchange_Mailbox class, which is new for Exchange 2003. In Exchange 2000, there was no method available to purge a mailbox via a script.

Be extremely careful with this script because it could easily remove all disconnected mailboxes on a given Exchange server. In the SELECT statement of the WMI query, if the WHERE clause is removed, the purge loop below that would then clear every mailbox that was disconnected, so be careful.

Because this script uses Exchange WMI extensions, it can be run from any machine that has WMI; the machine does not need the Exchange Management Tools loaded.

See Also

Exchange Server 2003 SDK: WMI Reference

17.14 Reconnecting a Deleted Mailbox

Problem

You want to reconnect a mailbox in the Exchange Store to a user object.

Solution

Using a graphical user interface

1. Open the Exchange System Manager (ESM) snap-in.
2. In the left pane, browse to the mailboxes container of the server, storage group, and database where you want to reconnect a mailbox.

3. In the right pane, scroll down until you find the mailbox you wish to reconnect. The mailbox should have a small red circle with a white X on it indicating it is disconnected.

4. Right-click the mailbox and select **Reconnect**.

5. Choose a user object in the directory you wish to reconnect this mailbox to.

6. A dialog box indicating the **Reconnect Operation has completed successfully** should pop up. Click **OK**.

Using VBScript

```
' This code reconnects a mailbox to a user.
' ------ SCRIPT CONFIGURATION ------
strComputer = "<Exchange Server>" ' e.g., ExchServer2
strUser = "<Userid>"              ' e.g., jsmith
strMailbox = "<Mailbox Alias>"    ' e.g., jsmith
' ------ END CONFIGURATION ---------

set objWMI = GetObject("winmgmts:\\" & strComputer & _
                        "\root\MicrosoftExchangeV2")
set objDiscMbx = objWMI.ExecQuery("Select * from Exchange_Mailbox WHERE " _
                        & "MailboxDisplayName='" & strMailbox & "'",,48)
for each objMbx in objDiscMbx
   objMbx.Reconnect strUser
next
Wscript.Echo "Successfully reconnected mailbox."
```

Discussion

When you tell the system to delete an Exchange mailbox, it isn't really deleted. It is simply disassociated or disconnected from the user object. These mailboxes are referred to as orphaned or disconnected. Deleted mailboxes stay in this disconnected state for a configurable period, by default 30 days, and can be recovered any time in that period. To truly remove a mailbox before that time, you must purge the mailbox after the deletion. This recipe shows how to reconnect that disconnected mailbox back to the original user object, or, if you prefer, an alternate user object.

 Reconnecting a mailbox requires Exchange Service Administrator permissions plus additional permissions on user objects. See the Discussion for Recipe 17.7 and MS KB 316792.

Using a graphical user interface

You may run into a case where the ESM doesn't show you a mailbox is disconnected when, in fact, you know it is. This can happen if you delete the mailbox and immediately look at it in ESM. In order to clear that condition, you will need to right-click on the mailboxes container and select **Run Cleanup Agent**, causing some house cleaning to be done. The mailbox should then show up as disconnected.

On the Exchange 2000 Server CD in the *Support\Utils* folder, is a tool called *mbconn.exe*, which can also be used to reconnect mailboxes. This tool is not included on the Exchange 2003 Server CD. However, it still functions fine against Exchange 2003.

Using VBScript

The Reconnect method is part of the Exchange_Mailbox class, which is new for Exchange 2003. In Exchange 2000, there was no method available to reconnect a mailbox via a script. Unfortunately, there are some serious flaws with this implementation of the Reconnect method, which severely limits its usability in some environments.

The first flaw is that the WMI method must run directly on the Exchange Server with the disconnected mailbox, so the script must run on the Exchange server. You can't, for instance, have a script that runs from a workstation that will reconnect mailboxes on any of your Exchange servers.

The second flaw is that you cannot specify the domain of the user you want to reconnect to the mailbox. In a single domain Exchange environment, this will be fine. Trying to reconnect a mailbox in a forest with the same user name in multiple domains could give unexpected results.

See Also

Recipe 17.15, Exchange Server 2003 SDK, MS KB 274343 (How to Recover a Deleted Mailbox in Exchange), MS KB 316792 (Minimum permissions necessary to perform Exchange-related tasks), and Exchange Server 2003 SDK: WMI Reference

17.15 Enumerating Disconnected Mailboxes

Problem

You want to enumerate all disconnected mailboxes on a server.

Solution

Using a graphical user interface

1. Open the Exchange System Manager (ESM) snap-in.

2. In the left pane, browse to the mailboxes container of the server, storage group, and database where you want to view disconnected mailboxes.

3. In the right pane, scroll down through the list, taking note of all mailboxes with a small red circle with a white X in it.

Using VBScript

```
' This code enumerates disconnected mailboxes.
' ------ SCRIPT CONFIGURATION ------
strComputer = "<Exchange Server>" 'e.g., ExchServer2
' ------ END CONFIGURATION ---------

set objWMI = GetObject("winmgmts:\\" & strComputer & _
                        "\root\MicrosoftExchangeV2")

set objDiscMbx = objWMI.ExecQuery("Select * from Exchange_Mailbox",,48)
for each objMbx in objDiscMbx
  if (objMbx.DateDiscoveredAbsentInDS <> "") then
    Wscript.Echo objMbx.MailBoxDisplayName & " " & _
                 objMbx.DateDiscoveredAbsentInDS
  end if
next
Wscript.Echo "Successfully enumerated disconnected mailboxes."
```

Discussion

When you tell the system to delete an Exchange mailbox, it isn't really deleted. It is simply disassociated or disconnected from the user object. These mailboxes are referred to as orphaned or disconnected. This recipe shows you how to enumerate the disconnected mailboxes you have on a specified server.

 Viewing mailbox details in the ESM requires Exchange View Admin role access. However in order to do this with a script, the WMI provider also requires local administrator permissions on the Exchange server. See the Discussion for Recipe 17.7.

Using a graphical user interface

You may run into a case where ESM doesn't show you a mailbox is disconnected when, in fact, you know it is. This can happen if you delete the mailbox and immediately look at it in ESM. In order to clear that condition, you will need to right-click on the **Mailboxes** container and select **Run Cleanup Agent**, causing some house cleaning to be done. The mailbox should then show up as disconnected.

Using VBScript

This is one of the occasions where a script is faster and easier than the corresponding GUI. There is no method to just enumerate disconnected mailboxes in ESM. You actually have to go down the list and look at every mailbox. If you have thousands of mailboxes, this could be tedious. If you have thousands of mailboxes across many servers, it can quickly become unmanageable.

The DateDiscoveredAbsentInDS property is part of the Exchange_Mailbox class, which is new for Exchange 2003.

Since this script uses Exchange WMI extensions, it can be run from any machine that has WMI. The machine does not have to have the Exchange Management Tools loaded.

See Also

Exchange Server 2003 SDK: WMI Reference

17.16 Moving a Mailbox

Problem

You want to move a mailbox to a new database, storage group, or server.

Solution

Using a graphical user interface

1. Open the ADUC snap-in.

This needs to be run on a workstation or server that has the Exchange Management Tools loaded (see Recipe 17.6).

2. If you need to change domains, right-click on **Active Directory Users and Computers** in the left pane, select **Connect to Domain**, enter the domain name, and click **OK**.

3. In the left pane, browse to the parent container of the user, right-click on the user, and select **Exchange Tasks**.

4. On the **Welcome** screen, click **Next**.

5. Select **Move Mailbox** and click **Next**.

6. Select new values for **Server** and **Mailbox Store** and click **Next**.

7. Select how you want to handle corrupted messages and click **Next**.

8. Specify when to start processing the move task and click **Next**.

9. When the **Completed** screen is shown, click **Finish**. If there are errors, select the **View Detailed Report** checkbox to get a failure report.

Using a command-line interface

```
> exchmbx -b <UserDN> -move "<server>:<storage group>:<mail store>"
```

Or alternatively, run the following command:

```
> exchmbx -b <UserDN> -move "<Home MDB URL>"
```

Replace *<UserDN>* with the user's distinguished name, *<server>* with the Exchange server name, *<storage group>* with the storage group, *<mail store>* with the mail store, and *<Home MDB URL>* with the full homeMDB URL for the desired mailbox store.

To move an existing mailbox for user joe to Exchange Server Srv1, Storage group SG1, and mailbox store DB1, execute the following command:

```
> exchmbx -b "cn=joe,cn=users,dc=rallencorp,dc=com" -move "srv1:sg1:db1"
```

Using VBScript

```
' This code moves a mailbox.
' ------ SCRIPT CONFIGURATION ------
strUserDN = "<UserDN>" ' e.g., cn=jsmith,cn=Users,dc=rallencorp,dc=com
strServer = "<Exchange Server>"        ' e.g., ExchServer2
strSGName = "<Storage Group Name>"        ' e.g., SG1
strMailStoreName = "<MailBox Store Name>" ' e.g., DB1
' ------ END CONFIGURATION ---------
' Find Storage Group URL and Generate Mailbox Store URL
strSearch = "cn=" & strSGName  & ","
set objSrv = CreateObject("CDOEXM.ExchangeServer")
objSrv.DataSource.Open strServer
for each strSg in objSrv.StorageGroups
    if (instr(1,strSg,strSearch,1)>0) then
        strSGUrl = strSg
        exit for
    end if
next
strMBUrl = "LDAP://cn=" & strMailStoreName & "," & strSGUrl

' Attach to user and move mailbox
set objUser = GetObject("LDAP://" & strUserDN)
objUser.MoveMailbox(strMBUrl)
Wscript.Echo "Successfully moved mailbox."
```

Discussion

Mailbox moves are commonly done in many Exchange organizations due to servers getting upgraded, server hardware issues, users migrating from Exchange 5.5 to Exchange 2003, or the administrators wanting to readjust mailbox location for load balancing.

 Moving a mailbox requires Exchange Service Administrator permissions plus additional permissions on user objects. See the Discussion for Recipe 17.7 and MS KB 842033.

A mailbox move is an odd operation in terms of permissions. Logically, moving a mailbox is basically a combination of create and delete operations, which is something an Exchange Data Administrator can do just fine. However, to actually move a mailbox, you must have Exchange Administrator Role permissions with a subset of the permissions Exchange Data Administrator have on users. See MS KB 842033 for details of the permissions needed.

If you don't handle user mailbox administration through an automated web site, I recommend that you delegate permissions to the attributes listed in the knowledge base articles to some Active Directory group. Once delegated, add the Exchange Administrator Role users to that group and have them handle all mailbox moves.

Using a graphical user interface

The move mailbox wizard is the only Exchange wizard that allows you to schedule when the changes will be made. This is obviously a handy feature for mailbox moves because it isn't something you generally want to do midday. This allows Exchange administrators who like to sleep at night to schedule the work to be done, and go home with everyone else.

Using a command-line interface

Prior to the ExchMbx tool, there was no simple way to move a mailbox from the command line. The command structure to move a mailbox is similar to the command structure to create a mailbox (see the command-line solution in Recipe 17.11).

If you want to move multiple mailboxes at once, remove the -b option from the parameter list and pipe the distinguished names into Exch-Mbx from another tool or from a file. Run exchmbx /? for usage details.

Using VBScript

The trickiest part of moving a mailbox for a user is to know what the Home MDB URL is for the database where you want to move the user. The method used here allows you to specify three well-known components and arrive at the answer. In Recipe 17.11, I use another method to do this by entering the exact value for the mailbox store URL. A third alternative would be to search Active Directory for all valid homeMDB values, display them, and have the person running the script select from the list like ADUC does. To get the list of mailbox store URLs, search against the Configuration container in Active Directory (e.g., *cn=Configuration,dc=rallencorp,dc=com*) with the following filter (objectCategory=msExchPrivateMDB).

See Also

MS KB 842033 ("Access Denied" error message when you move mailboxes by using the Exchange Task Wizard in Exchange Server 2003), MS KB 316792 (Minimum permissions necessary to perform Exchange-related tasks), and MS KB 821829 (Moving Mailboxes in Exchange Server 2003)

17.17 Viewing Mailbox Sizes and Message Counts

Problem

You want to view the sizes and message counts of all mailboxes on a server.

Solution

Using a graphical user interface

1. Open the Exchange System Manager (ESM) snap-in.

2. In the left pane, browse to the mailboxes container of the server, storage group, and database where you want to view mailboxes.

3. In the right pane, scroll down through the list of mailboxes, noting the **Size** and **Total Items** columns.

Using VBScript

```
' This code displays all mailboxes and their sizes
' ------ SCRIPT CONFIGURATION ------
strComputer = "<Exchange Server>" 'e.g., ExchServer2
' ------ END CONFIGURATION ---------

set objWMI = GetObject("winmgmts:\\" & strComputer & _
                       "\root\MicrosoftExchangeV2")
set objMbxs = objWMI.ExecQuery("Select * from Exchange_Mailbox",,48)
for each objMbx in objMbxs
  Wscript.Echo objMbx.MailBoxDisplayName & " " & objMbx.size & "KB  " _
               & objMbx.TotalItems & " items"
Next
Wscript.Echo "Script completed successfully."
```

Discussion

Mailbox sizes and message counts are items on Exchange systems that administrators routinely want to know about for the purposes of reporting and metrics. Administrators want to know if their mail system is balanced and if users are spread across the mailbox stores evenly. Knowing the number of users and the size of their mailboxes in each mailbox store, the administrator can make better decisions about where new user mailboxes should be placed or if some leveling of mailboxes is required.

 Viewing mailbox details in the ESM requires Exchange View Admin role access. However, in order to do this with a script, the WMI provider requires local administrator permissions on the Exchange server. See the Discussion for Recipe 17.7.

Using a graphical user interface

Click on the header of each of the columns displayed in the right pane of the ESM to sort by that value.

Using VBScript

This script can be modified to show several things for mailboxes. Some of the more notable items besides Size and Items are LastLogonTime, LastLoggedOnUserAccount, and DateDiscoveredAbsentInDS. Please reference the Exchange 2003 SDK for a complete list of items available in the Exchange_Mailbox class.

> Since this script uses Exchange WMI extensions, it can be run from any machine that has WMI; the machine does not have to have the Exchange Management Tools loaded.

See Also

Exchange Server 2003 SDK: WMI Reference

17.18 Mail-Enabling a Contact

Problem

You want to mail-enable a contact.

Solution

Using a graphical user interface

1. Open the ADUC snap-in.

> This needs to be run on a workstation or server that has the Exchange Management Tools loaded (see Recipe 17.6).

2. If you need to change domains, right-click on **Active Directory Users and Computers** in the left pane, select **Connect to Domain**, enter the domain name, and click **OK**.

3. In the left pane, browse to the parent container of the contact, right-click on the contact, and select **Exchange Tasks**.

4. On the **Welcome** screen, click **Next**.

5. Select **Establish E-mail Address** and click **Next**.

6. Verify the mail alias.

7. Click **Modify**, select external email address type (generally **SMTP Address**), and click **OK**. Enter an external email address and click **OK**.

8. Select the associated administrative group and click **Next**.

9. On the **Completion** screen, click **Finish**.

Using a command-line interface

```
> exchmbx -b "<ContactDN>" -me <smtp email address>
```

Replace *<ContactDN>* with the contact's distinguished name and the *<smtp email address>* with the contact's external email address.

For an alternative method, create an LDIF file called *mailenable_contact.ldf* with the following contents:

```
dn: CN=<ContactDN>
changetype: modify
replace: targetAddress
targetaddress: SMTP:<smtp email address>
-
replace: mailNickName
mailNickname: <mail nickname>
-
replace: mAPIRecipient
mAPIRecipient: FALSE
-
replace: legacyExchangeDN
legacyExchangeDN: <legacy exchange DN>
-
replace: internetEncoding
legacyExchangeDN: 1310720
-
```

Replace *<ContactDN>* with the contact's distinguished name, *<smtp email address>* with the contact's external email addresss, and *<legacy exchange DN>* with the proper legacy exchange distinguished name value. Then run the following command:

```
>ldifde -i -f mailenable_user.ldf
```

Using VBScript

```
' This code mail enables a contact.
' ------ SCRIPT CONFIGURATION ------
strContactDN = "<ContactDN>" ' e.g., cn=jsmith,ou=Contacts,dc=rallencorp,dc=com
strEmailAddr = "<EmailAddress>" 'e.g., jsmith234@freemail.net
' ------ END CONFIGURATION ---------
set objContact = GetObject("LDAP://" & strContactDN)
objContact.MailEnable strEmailAddr
objContact.Put "internetEncoding",1310720
objContact.SetInfo( )
Wscript.Echo "Successfully mail-enabled contact."
```

Discussion

A mail-enabled contact is a contact that has at least one email address defined within Exchange. A contact cannot have a mailbox because it is not a security principal, so there is no way to safely authenticate the object. You use a mail-enabled contact when you have an email address external to the forest's Exchange organization that you want to be listed in your GAL. The email address could be external to the company or it could just be external to that forest's Exchange organization. Examples would be people from other companies or users who do not use the Active Directory of the Exchange organization.

 Mail-enabling a contact requires Exchange Data Administrator permissions. See the Discussion for Recipe 17.7.

When you create a mail-enabled contact with the GUI or VBScript, you are using the CDOEXM interface library. The specific method called in this case is `MailEnable`. In the background, the specific changes made by the `MailEnable` method are on the contact object in Active Directory. They include changes to the following attributes:

- `targetAddress`
- `mailNickname`
- `mAPIRecipient`
- `legacyExchangeDN`

In addition to those attributes, the `internetEncoding` attribute also needs to be set for proper message handling. See the Discussion in Recipe 17.9 for details.

Once all of those attributes are in place, the RUS sets additional attributes on the contact object to make it usable for Exchange.

Using a graphical user interface

Creating a mail-enabled contact from scratch is very similar to mail-enabling an existing contact.

Using a command-line interface

See the command-line discussion in Recipe 17.9 for details.

Using VBScript

See the VBScript discussion in Recipe 17.9 for details.

See Also

Recipes 17.10, and 17.19, and MS KB 275636 (Creating Exchange Mailbox-Enabled and Mail-Enabled Objects in Active Directory.)

17.19 Mail-Disabling a Contact

Problem

You want to mail-disable a contact.

Solution

Using a graphical user interface

1. Open the ADUC snap-in.

 This needs to be run on a workstation or server that has the Exchange Management Tools loaded (see Recipe 17.6).

2. If you need to change domains, right-click on **Active Directory Users and Computers** in the left pane, select **Connect to Domain**, enter the domain name, and click **OK**.

3. In the left pane, browse to the parent container of the user, right-click on the user, and select **Exchange Tasks**.

4. On the **Welcome** screen, click **Next**.

5. Select **Remove Exchange Attributes** and click **Next**.

6. Read the warning and click **Next**.

7. On the **Completion** screen, click **Finish**.

Using a command-line interface

See the command-line example for Recipe 17.10.

Using VBScript

```
' This code mail disables a contact.
' ------ SCRIPT CONFIGURATION ------
strContactDN = "<ContactDN>"
'              e.g., cn=jsmith,ou=Contacts,dc=rallencorp,dc=com
' ------ END CONFIGURATION ---------
set objContact = GetObject("LDAP://" & strContactDN)
objContact.MailDisable
objContact.SetInfo( )
Wscript.Echo "Successfully mail-disabled contact."
```

Discussion

This recipe shows how to remove the Active Directory Exchange attributes for a previously mail-enabled contact. The solutions are identical to the solutions for mail-disabling users, shown in the Discussion for Recipe 17.10.

 Mail-enabling a contact requires Exchange Data Administrator permissions. See the Discussion for Recipe 17.7.

See Also

Recipe 17.10 and MS KB 307350 (XGEN: Using the "Remove Exchange Attributes" Option)

17.20 Creating a Mail-Enabled Distribution List

Problem

You want to create a mail-enabled distribution list.

Solution

Using a graphical user interface

1. Open the ADUC snap-in.

 This needs to be run on a workstation or server that has the Exchange Management Tools loaded (see Recipe 17.6)

2. If you need to change domains, right click on **Active Directory Users and Computers** in the left pane, select **Connect to Domain**, enter the domain name, and click **OK**.

3. In the left pane, browse to the parent container of the new DL, right-click on it, and select **New → Group**.

4. Enter group name, select group scope, select group type, and click **Next**.

5. Verify that **Create an Exchange e-mail address** is selected and click **Next**.

6. Click **Finish**.

Using a command-line interface

The following command creates a group:

```
> dsadd group "<GroupDN>" -scope <Group Scope> -secgrp yes|no
```

The following command mail-enables a group:

```
> exchmbx -b "<GroupDN>" -me
```

Replace *<GroupDN>* with the group's distinguished name, *<Group Scope>* with l, g, or u for local group, global group, or universal group, respectively. -secgrp should be set to yes if this is to be a security group, no otherwise.

To create and mail-enable a distribution universal group named UniDL, execute the following commands:

```
> dsadd group "cn=UniDL,ou=grps,dc=rallencorp,dc=com" -scope u -secgrp no
> exchmbx -b "cn=UniDL,ou=grps,dc=rallencorp,dc=com" -me
```

For an alternative method, create an LDIF file called *create_dl.ldf* with the following contents:

```
dn: CN=<group name>,<Parent DN>
changetype: add
objectClass: group
cn: <group name>
sAMAccountName: <group name>
groupType: <group type>
mailNickname: <mail nickname>
legacyExchangeDN: <legacy exchange DN>
reportToOriginator: TRUE
```

Replace *<ParentDN>* with the distinguished name of the container where you want the group created, *<group name>* with the name you want the group to be called, *<group type>* with the group's scope and type value, *<mail nickname>* with the group's mail nickname, and *<legacy exchange DN>* with the proper legacy exchange distinguished name value. As mentioned in Recipe 17.9, you can skip specifying the legacyExchangeDN if you want Exchange to populate the value for you.

To create a Universal Distribution List group with an Exchange generated legacyExchangeDN, create the file with the following contents:

```
dn: CN=UniMailGroup,CN=groups,DC=rallencorp,DC=com
changetype: add
objectClass: group
cn: UniMailGroup
sAMAccountName: UniMailGroup
groupType: 8
mailNickname: UniMailGroup
reportToOriginator: TRUE
```

Then run the following command:

```
> ldifde -i -f create_dl.ldf
```

Using VBScript

```
' This code creates and mail enables a Distribution List
' ------ SCRIPT CONFIGURATION ------
strParentDN = "<ParentDN>"    ' e.g., ou=groups,dc=rallencorp,dc=com
```

```
strGroupName = "<GroupName>"   ' e.g., JoewareUsers
' ------ END CONFIGURATION ---------
' Constants taken from ADS_GROUP_TYPE_ENUM
Const ADS_GROUP_TYPE_DOMAIN_LOCAL_GROUP = 1
Const ADS_GROUP_TYPE_GLOBAL_GROUP       = 2
Const ADS_GROUP_TYPE_LOCAL_GROUP        = 4
Const ADS_GROUP_TYPE_SECURITY_ENABLED   = -2147483648
Const ADS_GROUP_TYPE_UNIVERSAL_GROUP    = 8

set objOU = GetObject("LDAP://" & strParentDN)
set objGroup = objOU.Create("group","cn=" & strGroupName)
objGroup.Put "groupType", ADS_GROUP_TYPE_UNIVERSAL_GROUP
objGroup.Put "sAMAccountName", strGroupName
objGroup.MailEnable
objGroup.SetInfo
Wscript.Echo "Successfully created mail-enabled DL."
```

Discussion

Anyone who has used a distribution list knows how useful they can be. It is much easier to send email to a single email address than to tens or hundreds or even thousands of addresses. Exchange allows you to mail-enable any group object in Active Directory. Then, when someone sends email to that group, every mail-enabled or mailbox-enabled user in the group will receive a copy of the email.

 Creating a mail-enabled group requires Exchange Data Administrator permissions. See the Discussion for Recipe 17.7.

Active Directory groups can have a group type of security or distribution. While distribution lists are usually of type distribution, you can mail-enable security groups as well. In fact, if anyone in the Exchange Organization uses a distribution group to grant permissions to anything in Exchange, whether it is a calendar or a folder or any other object, Exchange converts the distribution group to a mail-enabled security group. This is something to be aware of because more than one administrator has found himself in a position trying to explain why distribution groups had mysteriously changed into security groups.

A popular question I've often heard is: What scope should my distribution groups have? The official response is: whatever scope you need. If you have a multidomain environment, you should probably use a universal group. Mail-enabled groups have to be fully expandable on any global catalog that gets the request to expand the membership. The only group scope that qualifies in a normal multidomain environment is a universal group. If you have a single-domain environment, any group scope will work fine.

When you create a mail-enabled group with the GUI or VBScript, you are using the CDOEXM interface. This interface is the Microsoft-supported method of managing

Exchange attributes on users, groups, and contacts. `MailEnable` is the specific method called. In the background, the specific changes made by the `MailEnable` method are on the group object in Active Directory and include changes to the following attributes:

- `reportToOriginator`
- `mailNickname`
- `legacyExchangeDN`

Once those attributes have been set, the RUS sets additional attributes on the group object to make the group usable by Exchange.

Using a graphical user interface

Using the GUI to create distribution groups is straightforward. Mail-enabling an existing group is similar to mail-enabling a user or contact, except you don't have to specify an email address.

Using a command-line interface

The main things to be concerned with the command-line version of this recipe are the group scope, group type value, and, for the LDIF solution, the specifics concerning the mail attributes `mailNickname` and `legacyExchangeDN` mentioned in Recipe 17.9. The group type determines the scope of the group and whether it is also security enabled. See the constants defined in the VBScript example for the values to use. The email address can not be specified for mail-enabled groups, that attribute will be handled by the RUS.

Using VBScript

This script creates a universal distribution group. All of the constants are included for group scope and type, so you can modify the code to suit your needs. If you need to make a group a security group, simply or in the `TYPE_SECURITY_ENABLED` flag like so:

```
ADS_GROUP_TYPE_UNIVERSAL_GROUP or TYPE_SECURITY_ENABLED
```

See Also

Recipe 17.7, MS KB 839949 (Troubleshooting mail transport and distribution groups in Exchange 2000 Server and in Exchange Server 2003), MS KB 275636 (Creating Exchange Mailbox-Enabled and Mail-Enabled Objects in Active Directory.), MS KB 251631 (XADM: How to Create Distribution Lists in Exchange 2000 Server), and *http://www.microsoft.com/technet/prodtechnol/exchange/2000/deploy/access.mspx*

17.21 Creating a Query-Based Distribution List

Problem

You want to create a query-based distribution list.

> Creating a mail-enabled query-based distribution list requires the Exchange organization be in Exchange Native Mode. See MS KB 829577.

Solution

Using a graphical user interface

1. Open the ADUC snap-in.

> This needs to be run on a workstation or server that has the Exchange Management Tools loaded (see Recipe 17.6).

2. If you need to change domains, right-click on **Active Directory Users and Computers** in the left pane, select **Connect to Domain**, enter the domain name, and click **OK**.

3. In the left pane, browse to the parent container of the new object, right-click on it and select **New → Query-based Distribution Group**.

4. Enter the group name and mail alias and click **Next**.

5. Select the search base, enter the specifics of the filter, and then click **Next**.

> The filter should be a standard LDAP filter—e.g., (&(objectcategory=user)(homeMDB=*)(employeeType=FT)).

6. Verify the summary and click Finish.

Using a command-line interface

First, you need to create an LDIF file called *add_qbdl.ldf* with the following contents:

```
dn: CN=<QB DL Name>,<ParentDN>
changetype: add
cn: <QB DL Name>
displayName: <QB DL Name>
objectClass: msExchDynamicDistributionList
```

```
mailNickname: <mail nickname>
legacyExchangeDN: <legacy Exchange DN>
msExchDynamicDLFilter: <LDAP Filter>
msExchDynamicDLBaseDN: <BaseDN>
reportToOriginator: TRUE
systemFlags: 1610612736
```

Replace *<QB DL Name>* with the name of the address list, *<mail nickname>* with the mail nickname, *<legacy Exchange DN>* with the appropriate legacy Exchange DN value, *<LDAP Filter>* with the specific LDAP filter you want to be used to determine group membership, *<BaseDN>* with the base distinguished name you want used in combination with the filter, and *<ParentDN>* with the distinguished name of the container you want the group created in. Then run the following command:

```
> ldifde -i -f add-qbdl.ldf
```

Using VBScript

```
' This code creates and mail enables a Query-Based Distribution List.
' ------ SCRIPT CONFIGURATION ------
strParentDN  = "<Parent DN>"    ' e.g., ou=groups,dc=rallencorp,dc=com
strGroupName ="<DL Name>"       ' e.g., Sales Dept
strBaseDN = "<Base DN>"         ' e.g., ou=mail,dc=rallencorp,dc=com
strFilter = "<Filter>"          ' e.g., (&( department=sales)(homemdb=*))
strLegacyDN = "<Legacy DN of Recipients>" & "/cn=" & strGroupName
' e.g. /o=RALLENCORPMAIL/ou=First Administrative Group/cn=Recipients

' ------ END CONFIGURATION ---------
' Set Dynamic values
set objOU = GetObject("LDAP://" & strParentDN)
set objGroup = objOU.Create("msExchDynamicDistributionList","cn=" & _
                            strGroupName)
objGroup.Put "msExchDynamicDLBaseDN", strBaseDN
objGroup.Put "msExchDynamicDLFilter", strFilter
objGroup.Put "displayName", strGroupName
objGroup.Put "mailNickname", strGroupName
objGroup.Put "legacyExchangeDN",strLegacyDN

' Set static values
objGroup.Put "systemFlags",1610612736
objGroup.Put "reportToOriginator",TRUE

objGroup.SetInfo
Wscript.Echo "Successfully created query-based DL."
```

Discussion

Exchange Server 2003 has introduced a new type of distribution list: the query-based DL. These are, as implied by name, distribution lists that are built on the fly based on a query; specifically an LDAP query against Active Directory.

Creating a mail-enabled query based distribution list requires Exchange Data Administrator permissions. See the Discussion for Recipe 17.7.

This is an extremely powerful addition for Exchange, but you have to be careful because you can get into trouble with it. Unlike address lists, the query-based DL is resolved each time it is used with an actual LDAP query against Active Directory. This means that the query needs to be efficient. Used enough, a poorly designed query for the DL could severely impact Exchange and Active Directory performance. You will want to use indexed attributes and avoid bitwise operators, the NOT operator, and medial search strings as per normal Active Directory efficient programming guidelines. A medial search string is a search string that has a wildcard somewhere other than at the end of the string (e.g., *llen or j*e). See MSDN for more details (search for "Creating Efficient Active Directory Queries").

For Windows Server 2003 Active Directory, Microsoft made an undocumented change concerning how the Query Processor (QP) worked with linked attributes. Linked attributes, due to how they are stored, are implicitly indexed but the Windows 2000 QP did not take advantage of these indices. In Windows Server 2003 Active Directory, the QP will use the implicit indexes for all linked attributes and greatly speed up searches using those attributes. This has tremendous implications around attributes such as homeMDB and member and the speed at which you can search on those attributes.

Unlike every other object you can mail-enable, when you create a query-based DL you are *not* using the CDOEXM interface. However, when you create this object with ADUC, the Exchange Management tools must be loaded or the distribution list object will not be properly populated and will not function properly. When creating the object from script or command line, you directly set all of the Active Directory attributes of the msExchDynamicDistributionList object. The specific changes that need to be made are to the following attributes:

- displayName
- mailNickname
- reportToOriginator
- legacyExchangeDN
- systemFlags
- msExchDynamicDLBaseDN
- msExchDynamicDLBaseFilter

Using a graphical user interface

Using the GUI is probably the safest way to generate a query for these DLs unless you are very familiar with how to make efficient Active Directory queries. The GUI is configured to help direct you to create queries that are more efficient. If they are created in the ADUC, you will not have to deal with the legacyExchange and mailNickname issues discussed below.

Using a command-line interface

This example follows the standard LDIF method of importing or modifying an object used in other examples. See the command-line interface discussion from Recipe 17.9.

> In Recipe 17.9, there is discussion indicating that you can avoid specifying the legacyExchangeDN attribute and Exchange will auto-generate a value for you. Unfortunately, this functionality is *not* extended to the Query-Based DL at this time.

Using VBScript

This is the only script in this chapter for mail-enabling objects that doesn't have a nice simple interface. It seems when Microsoft came up with the query-based distribution list object, they totally forgot about people who script and use the command line. You would expect that you could use the CDOEXM MailEnable method, but unfortunately it doesn't work. This is the only script in this chapter that has no choice but to deal with the legacyExchangeDN and mailNickname attributes. See the notes on these two attributes in the command-line interface discussion from Recipe 17.9.

See Also

MS KB 251631 (XADM: How to Create Distribution Lists in Exchange 2000 Server), MS KB 822897 (How to Troubleshoot Query-Based Distribution Groups), MS KB 829577 (Mixed mode vs. native mode in Exchange Server 2003), and MSDN: Creating More Efficient Microsoft Active Directory-Enabled Applications

17.22 Creating an Address List

Problem

You want to create an address list.

Solution

Using a graphical user interface

1. Open the Exchange System Manager (ESM) snap-in.
2. In the left pane, browse to the **Recipients** → **All Address Lists** container.
3. Right-click on the **All Address Lists** container and select **New** → **Address List**.
4. Enter the address list name.
5. Click on **Filter Rules**, configure the filter settings, and click **OK**.

 The filter should be a standard LDAP filter—e.g., (&(objectcategory=user)(homeMDB=*)(employeeType=FT)).

6. Click Finish.

Using a command-line interface

First, create an LDIF file called *add_al.ldf* with the following contents:

```
dn: CN=<Address List Name>,<ParentDN>
changetype: add
cn: <Address List Name>
displayName: <Address List Name>
objectClass: addressBookContainer
purportedSearch: <LDAP Filter>
systemFlags: 1610612736
```

Replace *<Address list Name>* with the name of the address list and *<ParentDN>* with the distinguished name of the Address Lists container in Active Directory (e.g., *cn=All Address Lists, cn=Address Lists Container, cn=RALLENCORPMAIL, cn=Microsoft Exchange, cn=Services, cn=Configuration, dc=rallencorp, dc=com*). Then, run the following command:

```
>ldifde -i -f add-al.ldf
```

Using VBScript

```
' This code creates an Address List.
' ------ SCRIPT CONFIGURATION ------
strParentDN  = "<DN to All Address Lists Container>"
' e.g., CN=All Address Lists,CN=Address Lists Container,
' CN=RALLENCORPMAIL,CN=Microsoft Exchange,
' CN=Services,CN=Configuration,DC=rallencorp,DC=com

strObjClass = "addressBookContainer"
strALName = "<Address List Name>"    ' e.g., Sales Dept
strFilterAttrib = "purportedSearch"
strFilter = "<LDAP Filter>"    ' e.g., (&(department=sales)(homemdb=*))
```

```
' ------ END CONFIGURATION ---------
' Set Dynamic values
set objOU = GetObject("LDAP://" & strParentDN)
set objNewObj = objOU.Create(strObjClass,"cn=" & strALName)
objNewObj.Put "displayName",strALName
objNewObj.Put strFilterAttrib,strFilter

' Set static values
objNewObj.Put "systemFlags",1610612736

' Save object
objNewObj.SetInfo
Wscript.Echo "Successfully created address list."
```

Discussion

Address lists are special groupings of email accounts that allow users to quickly find specific email users that are part of some logical grouping in the GAL. The RUS is responsible for creating and maintaining the address list links to the mail-enabled objects. The RUS links an address list to mail-enabled objects by adding the address list's distinguished name to the object's showInAddressBook multivalue attribute. Once an address list has been created, it can take hours or days for the RUS to fully populate the list by stamping all related objects' showInAddressBook attributes, depending on the size of your organization.

 Managing address lists requires Exchange Service Administrator permissions. See the Discussion for Recipe 17.7.

A curious point about address lists is that even though an LDAP filter is used to specify who should and shouldn't be in the list, Exchange doesn't actually use the filter to do an LDAP lookup against Active Directory. Instead, the RUS does its own compare on objects one by one. This is why you can't specify a search base where the address list should start; it encompasses the entire forest including the configuration container. This means you need to be very careful with the filter so that it is limited to the objects you truly want displayed. A positive aspect of this implementation is that it doesn't matter if you select indexed attributes for the filter. Since the RUS isn't using LDAP to resolve the objects from the filter, performance is not affected by any indexes on the attributes. One final note: be careful if you use the preview button in the Exchange System Manager to verify the list's validity. That method will use an LDAP query against Active Directory to display the values, and has no bearing on whether the list is built yet or even what will end up on it. It is possible in certain cases that the preview will not match with what you actually get in the address list.

Address lists are represented in Active Directory by the addressBookContainer class. This is a simple class. The main value, the address list filter, is stored in the purportedSearch attribute.

Using a graphical user interface

Using the GUI for this process is straight forward and is the most likely way you'll want to create address lists unless you need to create a lot of them on the fly or you are importing them from a test lab.

Using a command-line interface

As mentioned previously, you need to be very careful with the filter you specify for the purportedSearch attribute. The slightest mistake can cause the filter to not produce any results or produce an incorrect or incomplete result set. A filter such as (!attrib=value) instead of (!(attrib=value)), while acceptable to Active Directory's LDAP parser, will cause undefined results when interpreted by the RUS. The only way to verify that the list has been properly built is to manually compare what the query should generate with what has been generated.

To do this comparison, first generate a list of distinguished names that are members of the address list. This is done by using LDAP to query for all mail-enabled objects that have the address list distinguished name listed in the showInAddressBook attribute (e.g., *(&(mailNickname=*)(showinaddressbook=cn=All Users,cn=All Address Lists,cn=Address Lists Container,cn=RALLENCORP,cn=Microsoft Exchange,cn=Services, cn=Configuration,dc=rallencorp,dc=com))*). Next, generate a list of distinguished names that are matched by the query you used for the address list. Finally, compare these lists.

Using VBScript

Using VBScript is very similar to using the command-line method. You simply set the same attributes on a newly created object. As in the command-line method, the most important attribute is the purportedSearch attribute; see the command-line Discussion for more details.

See Also

MS KB 319213 (HOW TO: Use Address Lists to Organize Recipients in Exchange 2003) and MS KB 253828 (How the Recipient Update Service Populates Address Lists)

17.23 Creating a Recipient Policy

Problem

You want to create a recipient policy to configure an alternate email address or mailbox manager policy.

Solution

Using a graphical user interface

1. Open the Exchange System Manager (ESM) snap-in.
2. In the left pane, browse to the **Recipients** → **Recipient Policies** container.
3. Right-click on **Recipient Policies** and select **New** → **Recipient Policy**.
4. Select the property pages you want on the recipient policy form and click **OK**.
5. Enter the recipient policy name.
6. Click on **Filter Rules**, click **Modify**, select the search criteria, click **OK**.
7. Read the warning message that is displayed and click **OK**.
8. Set the desired policies on the **E-Mail Addresses (Policy)** and Mailbox **Manager Settings (Policy)** tabs.
9. When you are done, click **OK**.

Discussion

Recipient policies are used for controlling how the RUS stamps mail-enabled objects. It is in charge of stamping objects with the correct email addresses as well as Mailbox Manager settings, such as automatically deleting and reporting on messages that exceed certain ages and sizes. Companies that have multiple divisions and want different email addresses for users in the different divisions use multiple recipient policies for configuring the email addresses. Each recipient policy has a filter that specifies the mailboxes it should configure with its rules.

Recipient policy is too involved to do simply from the command line or through VBScript. Several of the values in the Active Directory `msExchRecipientPolicy` class are binary types, which are not trivial to manipulate with LDIF or VBScript. If you wish to programmatically create recipient policies, you can do it, but you will need to use something a bit more involved, such as Visual Basic or C++.

 Managing recipient policies requires Exchange Service Administrator permissions. See the Discussion for Recipe 17.7.

One note of warning: do not test the manipulation of recipient policies in your production environment. Changes to recipient policies get stamped on many or possibly all mail-enabled objects in the directory, and you could unintentionally bring down entire sections of your mail delivery system. Due to its widespread effect, you could have great difficulty getting it all back up and running quickly. One company that shall remain unnamed had gone through a merger process and was trying to standardize some of their mail systems. Unfortunately, they unintentionally changed the primary email address of more than 100,000 employees with one small incorrect recipient policy change. Due to the type of mistake, this wasn't noticed internally. It took a couple of days for people outside of the company to notice and report the issue to the company before it was corrected. In the meanwhile, most email going into the company from the outside was not properly delivered.

See Also

MS KB 249299 (HOW TO: Configure Recipient Policies in Exchange), MS KB 319201 (How To Use Recipient Policies to Control E-mail Addresses in Exchange 2000), MS KB 259381 (XADM: How to Create a Custom Recipient Policy Based on Routing Groups), MS KB 319188 (How to use recipient policies to control mailboxes in Exchange 2000 and Exchange 2003), MS KB 325921 (How to Configure E-mail Addresses Based on Domain Membership), and MS KB 328738 (XADM: How the Recipient Update Service Applies Recipient Policies)

17.24 Creating a Storage Group

Problem

You want to create a new storage group to allow for more mailbox stores, faster backups, or a logical organization of mailboxes.

Solution

Using a graphical user interface

1. Open the Exchange System Manager (ESM) snap-in.
2. In the left pane, browse to the server that you want to create a new storage group for.
3. Right-click on the server and select **New → Storage Group**.
4. Enter a name, transaction log location, system path location for storage of temporary and recovered files, and click **OK**.

Using a command-line interface

First, create an LDIF file called *add_sg.ldf* with the following contents:

```
dn: CN=<Storage Group Name>,<ParentDN>
changetype: add
objectClass: msExchStorageGroup
cn: <Storage Group Name>
showInAdvancedViewOnly: TRUE
systemFlags: 1610612736
msExchESEParamEnableIndexChecking: TRUE
msExchESEParamEnableOnlineDefrag: TRUE
msExchESEParamSystemPath: <Path to store system files>
msExchESEParamPageFragment: 8
```

```
msExchESEParamPageTempDBMin: 0
msExchRecovery: TRUE
msExchESEParamZeroDatabaseDuringBackup: 0
msExchESEParamBaseName: E01
msExchESEParamCircularLog: 0
msExchESEParamEventSource: MsExchangeIS
msExchESEParamCheckpointDepthMax: 20971520
msExchESEParamCommitDefault: 0
msExchESEParamLogFilePath: <Path to log files>
msExchESEParamDbExtensionSize: 256
msExchESEParamLogFileSize: 5120
```

Replace *<Storage Group Name>* with the name of the storage group, *<ParentDN>* with the distinguished names of the storage groups container for the appropriate server, *<Path to store system files>* with the filesystem path where you want system files (temporary and recovered files), and *<Path to log files>* with the filesystem path where you want exchange log files. Then run the following command:

```
>ldifde -i -f add-sg.ldf
```

Using VBScript

```
' This code creates a Storage Group.
' ------ SCRIPT CONFIGURATION ------
strServer = "<Exchange Server>"        ' e.g., ExchServer2
strName   = "<Storage Group Name>"     ' e.g., SG1
strPath   = "<File Path>" & strName    ' e.g., D:\Program Files\ExchSrvr
' ------ END CONFIGURATION ---------

' Create URL to Storage Group
Set objSrv = CreateObject("CDOEXM.ExchangeServer")
objSrv.DataSource.Open strServer

' This for loop is a bit of a hack to retrieve the first Storage Group
' in the collection. VBScript doesn't let you access specific elements
' of a collection the way Jscript can.
for each strSg in objSrv.StorageGroups
   strTemp = strSg
   exit for
next
strTemp = mid(strTemp,instr(2,strTemp,"cn",1))
strSGUrl = "LDAP://cn=" & strName & "," & strTemp

' Create/configure Storage Group and save it
set objSG = CreateObject("CDOEXM.StorageGroup")
objSG.MoveSystemFiles(strPath)
objSG.MoveLogFiles(strPath)
objSG.DataSource.SaveTo strSGUrl
Wscript.Echo "Successfully created storage group."
```

Discussion

Storage groups are used for physically breaking your databases up into smaller management groups. This is done for several reasons. Chief among them are so you have more numerous but smaller databases, a logical organization of mailboxes, or faster Exchange backups and restores. The Exchange Server can run one simultaneous backup for each storage group. So if you have 10 databases spread across two storage groups, you can have two backups running in parallel; if you have 10 databases spread across five storage groups, you can have five backups running in parallel.

 Managing storage groups requires Exchange Service Administrator permissions. See the Discussion for Recipe 17.7.

Depending on the version (Standard versus Enterprise) of Exchange, you can have up to four storage groups per server and up to five mailbox stores per storage group. ESM enforces these limits, but it is possible to directly modify Active Directory to exceed them. If you create more databases or storage groups than allowed by your version, the additional databases will not mount.

Storage groups are represented in Active Directory by the msExchStorageGroup class. This class has several attributes that have fairly intuitive string values and names and can be matched up to the options in ESM. Unfortunately, the raw Active Directory objects and attributes and their valid values for Exchange are not well documented. You can experiment with their settings, but do so only in a lab environment.

Using a command-line interface

A bad aspect of creating storage groups by direct Active Directory object manipulation is that you will not get warnings concerning the maximum number of storage groups allowed.

Using VBScript

The process of calling the CDOEXM interfaces to create storage groups is rather straightforward once you have the URL for the object's location in Active Directory. In this solution, to get the storage group container's distinguished name for the server, the script loops through all storage groups on the sever and sets strTemp to the URL value of the last storage group. This value is then parsed to get the parent container for the storage groups to build the new storage group URL.

See Also

MS KB 821748 (HOW TO: Add New Mailbox Stores in Exchange Server 2003)

17.25 Creating a Mailbox Store

Problem

You want to create a mailbox store. The primary reason for creating additional mailbox stores is to decrease the size of the individual stores while supporting many users on one server.

Solution

Using a graphical user interface

1. Open the Exchange System Manager (ESM) snap-in.
2. In the left pane, browse to the server and storage group where you want to create a new mailbox store.
3. Right-click on the storage group and select **New** → **Mailbox Store**.
4. Enter a name for the store, configure the settings on each tab, and click **OK**.
5. When prompted to mount the store, click **Yes**.

Using VBScript

```
' This code creates a Mailbox Store.
' ------ SCRIPT CONFIGURATION ------
strServer = "<Exchange Server>"          ' e.g., ExchServer2
strSGName = "<Storage Group Name>"       ' e.g., SG1
strMailStoreName = "<MailBox Store Name>"  ' e.g., DB1
' ------ END CONFIGURATION ---------

' Find Storage Group URL
strSearch = "CN=" & strSGName  & ","
set objSrv = CreateObject("CDOEXM.ExchangeServer")
objSrv.DataSource.Open strServer
for each strSg in objSrv.StorageGroups
    if (instr(1,strSg,strSearch,1)>0) then strSGUrl = strSg
next

' Generate Mailbox Store URL
strMBUrl = "LDAP://CN=" & strMailStoreName & "," & strSGUrl

' Create/configure Mailbox Store and save it
set objMb = CreateObject("CDOEXM.MailBoxStoreDB")
objMb.DataSource.SaveTo strMBUrl

' Mount DataBase
objMB.Mount
Wscript.Echo "Successfully created mailbox store."
```

Discussion

Mailbox stores, which are also called mailbox databases, are where mailboxes are located. There are quite a few configuration settings for mailbox stores which are beyond the scope of this chapter, but going through the ESM GUI when manually creating a mailbox store should give you an idea of what can be configured.

> Managing mailbox stores requires Exchange Service Administrator permissions. See the Discussion for Recipe 17.7.

Depending on the version (Standard or Enterprise) of Exchange, you can have up to four storage groups per server and up to five mailbox stores per storage group. ESM enforces these limits, but it is possible to directly modify Active Directory to exceed these limits. If you create more databases or storage groups than allowed, the additional databases will not mount.

Mailbox stores are represented in Active Directory by the msExchPrivateMDB class. This class is not as simple as some of the other classes used by Exchange. In addition, several of the attributes hold binary data, so working directly with these Active Directory objects can be difficult via VBScript or command-line methods. One of the more notable attributes of the mailbox store objects is a back-link attribute called homeMDBBL. This multivalued attribute links back to all of the user objects that have mailboxes in this mailbox store.

> If you are using Windows 2000 Active Directory, you will find it is much faster to enumerate the mailboxes on an Exchange Server by looking at the homeMDBBL attribute versus the homeMDB attributes on the users. In Windows Server 2003 Active Directory, there was a change in how the Query Processor handles linked attributes resulting in minimal difference between using homeMDB and homeMDBBL attributes.

Using a command-line interface

Due to the binary attributes the mailbox store objects contain, they are not good candidates for the LDIFDE command-line tool.

Using VBScript

The process of calling the CDOEXM interface is rather straightforward once you have the URL for the object's location in Active Directory. As with the GUI, there are many properties that can be configured through VBScript. To get a complete list of the various methods and properties available for the MailBoxStoreDB interface, see the Exchange Server 2003 SDK.

See Also

MS KB 821748 (HOW TO: Add New Mailbox Stores in Exchange Server 2003)

17.26 Listing Domain Controllers and Global Catalog Servers Used by an Exchange Server

Problem

You want to list the domain controllers and global catalog servers currently being used by an Exchange Server.

Solution

Using a graphical user interface

1. Open the Exchange System Manager (ESM) snap-in.
2. In the left pane, browse to the **Servers** container.
3. Right-click on the target server and select **Properties**.
4. Click on the **Directory Access** tab and view the domain controllers being used.

Using VBScript

```
' This code enumerates domain controllers being used.
' ------ SCRIPT CONFIGURATION ------
strComputer = "<Exchange Server>" 'e.g., ExchServer2
' ------ END CONFIGURATION ---------

set objWMI = GetObject("winmgmts:\\" & strComputer & _
                       "\root\MicrosoftExchangeV2")

set objDCList = objWMI.ExecQuery("Select * from Exchange_DSAccessDC",,48)
for each objDc in objDCList
  Wscript.Echo "DCName: objDc.name"
  strTemp = "Automatic"
  if (dc.ConfigurationType=0) then strTemp="Manual"
  Wscript.Echo "  Selection: " & strTemp
  Wscript.Echo "  Is Fast  : " & objDc.IsFast
  Wscript.Echo "  In Sync  : " & objDc.IsInSync
  Wscript.Echo "  Is Up    : " & objDc.IsUp
  Wscript.Echo "  Ldap Port: " & objDc.LDAPPort
  strTemp = "Global Catalog"
  if (objDc.type=0) then strTemp = "Config"
  if (objDc.type=1) then strTemp = "Local Domain"
  Wscript.Echo "  Role     : " & strTemp
  Wscript.Echo "-----------"
Next
Wscript.Echo "Script completed successfully."
```

Discussion

Exchange is very dependent upon Active Directory domain controllers. The list of domain controllers currently being used by a server is usually one of the first pieces of information you should gather when you encounter an Exchange issue. While this can be done through the GUI, it is much easier to get the data through a script.

 Unfortunately, you must have at least local administrator rights on the Exchange Server being queried to get this information.

While the GUI provides only a listing of the domain controllers and global catalog servers in use, the WMI provider offers considerably more information. This additional information can be extremely important during troubleshooting, so you should have this script or something similar available to your Exchange Admins for troubleshooting purposes.

Using VBScript

 Because this script uses Exchange WMI extensions, it can be run from any machine that has WMI. The machine does not have to have the Exchange Management Tools loaded.

See Also

Exchange Server 2003 SDK: WMI Reference

17.27 Mounting and Dismounting Mailbox Stores

Problem

You want to mount or dismount a mailbox store.

Solution

Using a graphical user interface

1. Open the Exchange System Manager (ESM) snap-in.
2. In the left pane, browse to the server and storage group that contains the mailbox store you want to manipulate.
3. Right-click on the mailbox store and select **Dismount Store**.
4. Click **Yes** when prompted to continue.

Using VBScript

```
' This code mounts/dismounts a Mailbox Store.
' ------ SCRIPT CONFIGURATION ------
strServer       = "<Exchange Server>"      ' e.g., ExchServer2
strSGName       = "<Storage Group Name>"   ' e.g., SG1
strMailStoreName = "<Database Name>"       ' e.g., DB1
' ------ END CONFIGURATION ---------

' Find Storage Group URL
strSearch = "CN=" & strSGName  & ","
set objSrv = CreateObject("CDOEXM.ExchangeServer")
objSrv.DataSource.Open strServer
for each sg in oSrv.StorageGroups
    if (instr(1,sg,strSearch,1)>0) then strSGUrl = sg
next

' Generate Mailbox Store URL
strMBUrl = "LDAP://CN=" & strMailStoreName & "," & strSGUrl

' Open Mailbox Store
set objMb = CreateObject("CDOEXM.MailBoxStoreDB")
objMb.DataSource.Open strMBUrl

if (objMb.Status = 0) then
    Wscript.Echo "Mailbox store is mounted, dismounting..."
    objMb.Dismount
else
    Wscript.Echo "Mailbox store is dismounted, mounting..."
    objMb.Mount
end if
Wscript.Echo "Script completed successfully."
```

Discussion

There will be times that you need to dismount a mailbox store on the fly. This could be for integrity checking, mailbox restorations, or to make email unavailable to some users for some reason. When you dismount a mailbox store, users with mailboxes in that store will be unable to retrieve their mail; users with mailboxes in other mailbox stores will be unaffected.

> Managing mailbox stores requires Exchange Service Administrator permissions. See the Discussion for Recipe 17.7.

Using a graphical user interface

When a store is stopped, it has a white circle with a red downward pointing arrow over the normal mailbox store icon.

Using VBScript

The mailbox store mount/dismount script shows off three basic functions: how to check status of a mailbox store, how to mount, and how to dismount. Once again, the method to get the mailbox store URL can vary between the three methods mentioned in Recipes 17.11 and 17.16.

See Also

MS KB 314211 (HOW TO: Make a Data Store Temporarily Inaccessible to Users in Exchange 2000 Server) and Exchange Server 2003 SDK: WMI Reference

Introduction to WSH

Since the release of Windows 2000, each operating system Microsoft has produced comes with a technology called the Windows Script Host, more commonly known as WSH, which allows scripts to execute directly on the client computer. WSH-based scripts can open and read files, attach to network resources, automate Word and Excel to create reports and graphs, automate Outlook to manipulate email and news, change values in the registry, and so on. The reason these scripts can be so versatile is that WSH supports scripting access to all Component Object Model (COM) objects installed on the client computer.

COM is a Microsoft technology that defines each host component as a set of objects, thus allowing you to automate and manipulate virtually anything you require on a client computer. When someone needs to create or manage a new component on a Windows-based host, he creates a COM interface, which can be thought of as the definition of the object, and the entire set of operations that can be performed on that object. Interfaces normally are stored in Dynamic Link Library (DLL) files.

So, for example, if you want to manipulate a file, you actually need to manipulate a file COM object. The file COM object definition will be stored in an interface held in a DLL. The interface will define all of the operations, such as creating the file, deleting the file, writing to the file, and so on. The interface will also define a series of object properties, such as the filename and owner, which can be accessed and modified. Operatings that affect an object are known as methods.

In addition to methods and properties provided by interfaces, each scripting language that you use will offer a series of defined functions, such as writing to the screen or adding two numbers together.

You can write scripts that execute using WSH and access any COM objects available to you using the methods and properties defined in the interface for that object as well as any functions in your chosen scripting language. By default, you can use Microsoft VBScript or Microsoft JScript (Microsoft's version of JavaScript). WSH is fully extensible, so other language vendors can provide installation routines that update WSH on a client to allow support for other languages. A good example is PerlScript, the WSH scripting language that provides support for the Perl language and is available from ActiveState (*http://www.activestate.com/*).

How to Write Scripts

WSH scripts are easy to write. The following example is a very simple one in VBScript called *SIMPLE.VBS*.

```
MsgBox "Hi World!"
```

All you have to do is open your favorite text editor and add the command. You then save the file with a specific filename extension, VBS for VBScript and JS for Jscript. Then you can double-click the script and it will run using WSH. If you open Task Manager (press Ctrl+Shift+Esc) you will notice a *wscript.exe* process running, this is the WSH process that is executing the script. Figure A-1 shows the output of the script, which is a simple dialog box with a text string in it. The script uses the VBScript MsgBox function.

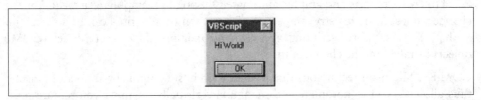

Figure A-1. Output from a very simple script

Now let's take a look at a slightly more complex script called *SIMPLE ADSI.VBS*. This script makes use of ADSI to display the description of a user.

```
Dim objUser 'A variable representing my user

set objUser = GetObject("LDAP://cn=Betty Parsons," & _
              "ou=Pre-Sales,ou=Sales,dc=rallencorp,dc=com")
MsgBox objUser.Description

set objUser = Nothing
```

The first line is a variable declaration. We are declaring that objUser is the name for an object from which we are going to retrieve information contained within Active Directory. The Dim keyword is used to declare a variable and the apostrophe (') indicates that everything following it is a comment that will not be executed.

The second line is too long to print on the page, so we have broken it into two with an underscore (_) continuation character at the end of the line. It tells the interpreter that it should read the next line as if it were joined to the end of the first. The ampersand character (&) is used to concatenate the separated strings together. The entire line, ignoring the underscore, uses the objUser variable to hold a reference to a user object via a call to VBScript's GetObject function, passing the distinguished name of the user.

The third line simply uses the VBScript MsgBox function again to print out the description of the Betty Parsons user object. The dot signifies that Description is a property method available for the specific type of object we are accessing, which in this case is a user.

The last line simply discards the reference to Betty Parsons, and objUser becomes empty again. Strictly speaking, at the end of a script, the system discards all references anyway, but we are including it for completeness.

So, printing out properties of objects in Active Directory isn't hard at all.

WSH 2.0 Versus 5.6

WSH 2.0 comes bundled with Windows 2000 and Windows 98, while WSH 5.6 comes bundled with Windows Server 2003 and Windows XP. WSH is also available for download for Windows 95 and Windows NT. Do not be alarmed by the dramatic increase in version numbers; 5.6 was the next major version after 2.0. In fact, for most people writing scripts, the differences between 2.0 and 5.6 are not significant enough to worry about. Version 5.6 offers a new security model and perhaps most importantly, the ability to execute scripts remotely.

As of WSH 2.0, two types of file formats are supported. The first is the traditional script files, which contain pure VBScript or JScript and have a language-specific file extension (e.g., *.vbs*), and the second is Windows Script File (WSF), which has a *.wsf* extension.

WSF is actually an Extensible Markup Language (XML) file, with the scripting code embedded inside <script>...</script> tags, which is embedded in <job>...</job> tags. The following example shows how the *SIMPLE.VBS* example would look using the WSF format:

```
<job>
<script language="VBScript">

MsgBox "Hello World"

</script>
</job>
```

The XML specifies that the file contains a single script (a job) and that the script to be run is written in VBScript. At its simplest, to write WSF scripts with VBScript instead of the traditional script files, all you have to do is prefix your code with the first two lines and end your code with the last two lines as shown in *SIMPLE.VBS*.

I encourage you to find out more about WSH to fully utilize its capabilities. For more information on WSH, including advanced functionality and running scripts using WSF, see the Microsoft Scripting web site: *http://msdn.microsoft.com/scripting/*.

—with Alistair Lowe-Norris

Introduction to WMI

The Windows Management Instrumentation (WMI) API was developed by Microsoft in 1998 in response to developers' and system administrators' ever growing need for a common, scriptable API to manage the components of the Windows operating system. Before WMI, if you wanted to manage some component of the operating system, you had to resort to using one of the component-specific Win32 APIs, such as the Registry API or the Event Log API. Each API typically had its own implementation quirks and required way too much work to do simple tasks. The other big problem with the Win32 APIs was that scripting languages, such as VBScript, could not access them. This limited how much an inexperienced programmer or system administrator could programmatically manage systems. WMI changes all this by providing a single API that can be used to query and manage the Event Log, the Registry, system processes, the file system, and almost any other operating system component.

The WMI architecture relies heavily upon the concept of providers. These providers gather and supply information to the underlying objects being queried. Depending on the WMI information you are trying to retrieve, WMI will contact the specific provider that can retrieve the information (e.g., SNMP or the Registry).

WMI is installed as part of the following operating systems: Windows 2000 Professional, Windows 2000 Server, Windows XP, and Windows 2003 server. WMI is available as an installable option on Windows 98 and is included as part of service pack 4 for Windows NT 4.0 systems. If you are going to use WMI on these older operating systems, I suggest you download the latest version of the WMI client from MSDN (*http://msdn.microsoft.com/*).

The learning curve to develop WMI scripts is relatively short if you have any experience with a scripting language. In fact, once you understand how to reference, enumerate, and query objects of a particular class with WMI, it is straightforward to adapt the code to work with any managed component, including DNS. And fortunately, by understanding just a few guidelines, you can convert VBScript code to Perl and vice versa.

Referencing an Object

To reference objects in WMI, you use a UNC-style path name. Here is an example of how to reference the C: drive on the host *srv01*:

```
\\srv01\root\CIMv2:Win32_LogicalDisk.DeviceID="C:"
```

The first part of the path (\\srv01\) is a reference to the computer on which the object resides. To reference the computer on which the script is running, you can use a dot (.) for the computer name. The second part (root\CIMv2) is the namespace within which the object resides. Each WMI provider uses a unique namespace to store its associated objects. The third part (Win32_LogicalDisk) is the class of the object being referenced. The fourth part is the key/value pairs representing an object of that class. Generically, the path can be described as follows:

```
\\ComputerName\NameSpace:ClassName.KeyName="KeyValue"[,KeyName2="KeyValue2"...]
```

Now that we know how to reference WMI objects, let's access an object using VBScript's GetObject function. In order for GetObject to understand we are referencing WMI objects, we have to include one additional piece of information: the moniker. If you've done any Active Directory scripting before, you're probably familiar with the LDAP: and WinNT: monikers used in ADSI. For WMI, we need to use the winmgmts: moniker:

```
set objDisk = GetObject("winmgmts:\\srv01" & _
                        "\root\CIMv2:" & _
                        "Win32_LogicalDisk.DeviceID='C:'")
```

To accomplish the same thing in Perl, we need to use the Win32::OLE module. Here is the same code written in Perl:

```
use Win32::OLE;
$objDisk = Win32::OLE->GetObject("winmgmts:\\\\srv01" .
                        "\\root\\CIMv2:" .
                        "Win32_LogicalDisk.DeviceID='C:'");
```

Enumerating Objects of a Particular Class

Now let's enumerate all logical disks on a machine. To do so, we need to use the InstancesOf method. An example should make this clear:

```
strComputer = "."
set objWMI = GetObject("winmgmts:\\" & strComputer & "\root\cimv2")
set objDisks = objWMI.InstancesOf("Win32_LogicalDisk")
for each objDisk in objDisks
    Wscript.Echo "DeviceID: " &  objDisk.DeviceID
    Wscript.Echo "FileSystem: " &  objDisk.FileSystem
    Wscript.Echo "FreeSpace: " & objDisk.FreeSpace
    Wscript.Echo "Name: " & objDisk.Name
    Wscript.Echo "Size: " & objDisk.Size
    WScript.Echo ""
next
```

Here we get a WMI object which points to the root\CIMv2 namespace, after which we call the InstancesOf method and pass the Win32_LogicalDisk class. That method returns a collection of Win32_LogicalDisk objects, which we then iterate over with a for loop.

Since we used a for loop in the last example, we'll show the equivalent code in Perl:

```perl
use Win32::OLE 'in';
my $strComputer = ".";
my $objWMI = Win32::OLE->GetObject("winmgmts:\\\\$strComputer\\root\\cimv2");
my $objDisks = $objWMI->InstancesOf("Win32_LogicalDisk");
for my $objDisk (in $objDisks) {
    print "DeviceID: ", $objDisk->DeviceID,"\n";
    print "FileSystem: ", $objDisk->FileSystem    ,"\n";
    print "FreeSpace: ", $objDisk->FreeSpace,"\n";
    print "Name: ", $objDisk->Name,"\n";
    print "Size: ", $objDisk->Size,"\n";
    print "\n";
}
```

As you can see, the Perl code is very similar to the VBScript code. One thing to note is that we had to import the in function on the first line because we use it later in the for loop to iterate over the $objDisks collection. VBScript provides this function natively within the language, whereas Perl does not.

Having the capability to easily obtain all instances of a certain type of class is very powerful. As you can imagine, you could adapt the code to retrieve a list of all CPUs, services, processes, etc., on a specific computer. The only issue with the last example is that prior to writing the script, we needed to know which property methods of the Win32_LogicalDisk class we wanted to print. We can instead retrieve all properties of the Win32_LogicalDisk class using the Properties_ method on each object as shown here:

```vbscript
strComputer = "."
strWMIClass = "Win32_LogicalDisk"
set objWMI = GetObject("winmgmts:\\" & strComputer & "\root\cimv2")
set objDisks = objWMI.InstancesOf(strWMIClass)
for each objDisk in objDisks
    for each objProp in objDisk.Properties_
        ' Print out NULL if the property is blank
        if IsNull(objProp.Value) then
            Wscript.Echo " " & objProp.Name & " : NULL"
        else
        ' If the value is an array, we need to iterate through each element
        ' of the array
            if objProp.IsArray = TRUE then
                For I = LBound(objProp.Value) to UBound(objProp.Value)
                    wscript.echo " " & objProp.Name & " : " & objProp.Value(I)
                next
            else
        ' If the property was not NULL or an array, we print it
                wscript.echo " " & objProp.Name & " : " & objProp.Value
```

```
        end if
      end if
    next
    WScript.Echo ""
  next
```

Searching with WQL

So far I've shown how to instantiate specific objects, such as a logical drive, and how to enumerate all the instances of a particular class using the InstancesOf method. Knowing how to do both of these functions will take us a long way with WMI, but we are missing one other important capability: the ability to find objects that meet certain criteria.

The creators of WMI found an elegant way to handle this problem. They implemented a subset of the Structured Query Language (SQL) known as the WMI Query Language (WQL). WQL greatly increases the power of WMI by giving the programmer a wide range of flexibility in locating objects. Unfortunately, WQL only supports read-only operations. You can not modify, update, or delete values in the WMI repository with WQL.

With WQL, we can even perform the same function as the InstancesOf method we used earlier. The following query retrieves all the Win32_LogicalDisk objects on a system:

```
select * from Win32_LogicalDisk
```

We can use any property available on Win32_LogicalDisk objects as criteria in our search. As an example, let's say we wanted to find all NTFS logical disks that have less than 100 MB of available space. The query would look like the following:

```
select * from Win32_LogicalDisk
where FreeSpace < 104857600
and   filesystem = 'NTFS'
```

Pretty easy, huh? Now let's put WQL to use. First we need to get a WMI object to the namespace we want to query. After we've done that, we can call the ExecQuery method on that object and pass the WQL query to use. The next example uses the "less than 100 MB" query we just described to print out all logical disks on the local computer that match that criterion:

```
strComputer = "."
set objWMI = GetObject("winmgmts:\\" & strComputer & "\root\cimv2")
set objDisks = objWMI.ExecQuery _
            ("select * from Win32_LogicalDisk " & _
             "where FreeSpace < 104857600 " & _
             "and filesystem = 'NTFS' ")
for each objDisk in objDisks
    Wscript.Echo "DeviceID: " & objDisk.DeviceID
    Wscript.Echo "Description: " & objDisk.Description
    Wscript.Echo "FileSystem: " & objDisk.FileSystem
    Wscript.Echo "FreeSpace: " & objDisk.FreeSpace
next
```

Authentication with WMI

So far, the examples we've shown assume that the caller of the script has the necessary rights to access the WMI information on the target computer. In most cases in which you are trying to automate a task, that may not be the case. Luckily, using alternate credentials in WMI is very straightforward.

Previously, to connect to a WMI namespace, we would have used the following:

```
strComputer = "srv01.rallencorp.com"
set objWMI = GetObject("winmgmts:\\" & strComputer & "\root\cimv2")
```

But let's say that the person calling the script does not have any privileges on *srv01*. We must now use the following:

```
strComputer = "srv01.movie.edu"
strUserName = "administrator"
strPassword = "password"

set objLocator = CreateObject("WbemScripting.SWbemLocator")
set objWMI = objLocator.ConnectServer(strComputer, "root\cimv2", _
                              strUserName, strPassword)
```

We've replaced the single call to GetObject with a call to CreateObject to instantiate a WbemScripting.SWbemLocator object. The SWbemLocator object has a method called ConnectServer, which allows us to specify the target machine, username, and password.[*] We can then use the object returned from ConnectServer to get the instances of a class, perform a WQL search, or carry out any other function.

---

[*] Obviously, it is less than ideal to include passwords in plain text scripts. An alternative would be to require the user to use the *runas* command to authenticate as the privileged user, or if you plan on running the script via Scheduled Tasks, to provide credentials when you configure the task.

Introduction to ADSI

In February 1997, Microsoft released a set of generic interfaces, called the Active Directory Service Interfaces (ADSI), to access and manipulate different directory services. ADSI is a collection of classes and methods that allows developers using any language that supports the component object model (COM) to access and manipulate objects on workstations and servers or in a directory service, such as Active Directory. Contrary to its name, it was written to be generic and extensible rather than specific to Active Directory. This means that developers can write code to access objects on various directory servers without the need to know vendor-specific library routines or APIs. ADSI is also extensible so developers of other directory services can write the underlying Dynamic Link Library (DLL) code that will allow ADSI to interact with their systems. This is possible because Microsoft publishes the specifications that a Directory Service Provider (code that implements the ADSI specification for a particular directory service) must meet to work correctly with ADSI. This means that whenever you call an ADSI procedure or reference any object via ADSI against a valid provider, you can feel confident that the procedure will perform according to ADSI's formal documentation no matter what the provider is. While there are several directory service provider-specific extensions, ADSI also supports Lightweight Directory Access Protocol (LDAP), which provides the majority of functionality that most directory vendors need.

LDAP is a network protocol that is the primary mechanism for accessing directory services over TCP/IP and has become the de facto standard for directory service access on the Internet. A directory server simply has to support LDAP 2.0 or later, and ADSI can instantly access the directory service without a provider-specific DLL.

ADSI's native support for LDAP means that it can access a very large list of directory services. For older directories such as NT4, vendors have written providers to support ADSI. The list of supported directory services includes the following:

- Active Directory
- Microsoft Exchange Server

- Windows NT 4.0
- NetWare 3.x's bindery-based system
- Novell Directory Service (NDS) and eDirectory
- Netscape iPlanet / Sun ONE
- OpenLDAP
- IBM Lotus Notes
- Microsoft's Internet Information Server (IIS) objects

Before you can start writing scripts that use ADSI, you first need to understand the basic COM concept of interfaces, as well as ADSI's concepts of namespaces, programmatic identifiers (ProgIDs), and ADsPaths.

Objects and Interfaces

A method is a procedure or function that is defined on an object that interacts with the object. For instance, an interface to access Active Directory group objects would have Add and Remove methods, so that members could be added or removed from a group. Methods are normally represented as `Interface::MethodName` when referenced, and this is the form we adopt in this book. Objects also have properties that are retrieved using the `IADs::Get` (get a single-value attribute) or `IADs::GetEx` (get a multivalue attribute) methods and set or replaced using the `IADs::Put` (modify a single-value attribute) or `IADs::PutEx` (modify a multivalue attribute) methods.

Each ADSI object supports an IADs interface that provides six basic pieces of information about that object:

Name
    Relative name for the object (relative distinguished name [RDN] in the case of Active Directory)

ADsPath
    Unique identifier for object

GUID
    128-bit Globally Unique Identifier of object

Class
    Objectclass of the object

Schema
    ADsPath to the objectclass of the object

Parent
    ADsPath to the parent object

If you wanted to retrieve the GUID property of an object named objX in VBScript, you would use the following:

```
strGUID = objX.Get("GUID")
```

You can see that we are calling the IADs::Get method on the object called objX; the dot (.) indicates the invocation of a property or method. The IADs::Get method takes one parameter, the property to retrieve, which in this case is the GUID, and passes it out to a variable that we have called strGUID. To relieve you from having to use the IADs::Get method for the most common properties, certain interfaces allow you to access common properties with property methods. In these specific cases, you may use the dotted method notation to retrieve the property by using the property method of the same name. So in the previous GUID example, the GUID property has a property method of the same name (i.e., IADs::GUID). We could, therefore, retrieve the GUID with:

```
strGUID = objX.GUID
```

We won't go into the interfaces in any more depth here, we just want to give you a feel for how methods and properties can be accessed on an object via ADSI interfaces. Although an object can support more than one interface without a problem, each object supports only the interfaces that are relevant to it. For example, the user object does not support the methods that work for groups. There are approximately 40 interfaces that all begin with the prefix IADs. Interfaces can relate to many different types of objects, including objects that reside in directory services (e.g., IADsUser, IADsGroup), transient objects that don't exist in a directory service (e.g., IADsPrintJob), and security-related objects (e.g., IADsOpenDSObject, IADsAccessControlList). Note that not every object has a specific IADs interface (e.g., IADsUser) that applies to its objectclass, so in those cases, you have to use the more generic IADs or IADsContainer interfaces.

Because each directory service is slightly different, not every ADSI interface method and property works in every directory service. If you make a method call to a directory service provider that doesn't support a particular method, you'll receive an error specifying that the provider doesn't support that method. According to the ADSI specification, each service provider must reject inappropriate calls with the correct ADSI error message.

Namespaces, ProgIDs, and ADsPaths

To reference different types of servers (e.g., Windows NT 4.0, NetWare, etc.) with ADSI, you must use the namespaces that correspond to the ADSI providers used by that directory service. ADSI uses a unique prefix called a ProgID to distinguish between these namespaces. Each ProgID is synonymous with a particular namespace and directory provider.

In a script, you specify the ProgID at the beginning of the object reference. The ProgID is used behind the scenes to correctly connect and bind to the corresponding directory service. For example, you specify *WinNT://* to access individual Windows NT 3.51, 4.0, Windows 2000, and Windows Server 2003 systems while you use

LDAP:// to access Active Directory and other LDAP directories. When ADSI encounters the ProgID, ADSI loads an appropriate ADSI-provider DLL to correctly process the bind request and method invocations.

 ProgIDs are case-sensitive. *WinNT://* will work, whereas *WINNT://* will not.

Telling ADSI you want to bind via a particular namespace isn't enough. You also need to reference the object that you want to access in that namespace. A unique identifier known as an ADsPath can be used to reference each object in a namespace. Take, for example, the following WinNT namespace ADsPaths.

These two reference JoeB, a user in DOMAIN:

```
WinNT://DOMAIN/JoeB
WinNT://DOMAIN/JoeB, User
```

These two reference COMP12345, a computer in DOMAIN:

```
WinNT://DOMAIN/COMP12345
WinNT://DOMAIN/COMP12345, Computer
```

These two reference Users, a group in DOMAIN:

```
WinNT://DOMAIN/Users
WinNT://DOMAIN/Users, Group
```

This references JoeB, a user on computer MOOSE in DOMAIN:

```
WinNT://DOMAIN/MOOSE/JoeB
```

This references JoeB, a user on computer MOOSE in WORKGROUP:

```
WinNT://WORKGROUP/MOOSE/JoeB
```

This references JoeB, a user on computer MOOSE:

```
WinNT://MOOSE/JoeB
```

As these examples show, you can reference each object by using only its name or, more properly, by using its name and type, if multiple identically named objects with different types exist.

Each namespace has a unique format for the ADsPath string, so you need to make sure that you're using the correct ADsPath notation. For example, each of these ADs-Paths references a unique object.

This one references JoeB, a user in DOMAIN:

```
WinNT://DOMAIN/JoeB, User
```

This next one references JoeB, a user in the Finance Organizational Unit (OU) within the rallencorp organization of the IntraNetWare tree called MyNetWareTree:

```
NDS://MyNetWareTree/O=RALLENCORP/OU=FINANCE/CN=JoeB
```

This one references JoeB, a NetWare 3.x or 4.x (bindery services) user that exists on server *MYSERVER:*

```
NWCOMPAT://MYSERVER/JoeB
```

Finally, this one references the default WWW service component of IIS running on the local host:

```
IIS://localhost/w3svc/1
```

In the preceding examples, NDS: refers to IntraNetWare 5.x and 4.x. (Because IntraNetWare 5.x is LDAP-compliant, you also can use LDAP paths with it.) NWCOMPAT: refers to NetWare 4.x, 3.2, 3.12, and 3.11 servers in bindery-emulation mode. IIS: refers to metabase paths on a host running IIS 3.0 or later.

One of the most commonly used namespaces is the LDAP namespace. You can use LDAP with ADSI to access a variety of directory services, including Active Directory. Although you can use the WinNT namespace to access Active Directory, you need to use the LDAP namespace to fully utilize all of ADSI's methods and properties. For this reason, our primary focus will be on the LDAP namespace.

You can use several formats to refer to LDAP directories. For example, all the following ADsPaths reference the Administrator object within the Users container of the *moose* directory server in the *rallencorp.com* zone:

```
LDAP://cn=administrator,cn=users,dc=rallencorp,dc=com
LDAP://moose.rallencorp.com/cn=administrator,cn=users,dc=rallencorp,dc=com
LDAP://moose/cn=administrator,cn=users,dc=rallencorp,dc=com
LDAP://DC=com/DC=rallencorp/CN=Users/CN=Administrator
LDAP://moose.rallencorp.com/DC=com/DC=rallencorp/CN=Users/CN=Administrator
```

In these examples, CN stands for common name and DC stands for domain component. These examples show that you can specify the LDAP namespace ADsPath going down or up the hierarchical Directory Information Tree (DIT). Most people have adopted the naming style used in the first three examples, where the most specific element of an object is used first. Also note that you can specify a fully qualified domain controller name after *LDAP://*, using a forward slash character (/) to separate the server name from the rest of the path.

If a name includes some unusual characters, such as a forward slash or a comma, you can use double quotation marks ("") or a single backslash (\) to specify that the character should be interpreted as part of the ADsPath itself. For example, if you have a user called AC/DC on the server, then this is wrong:

```
LDAP://cn=ac/dc,cn=users,dc=amer,dc=rallencorp,dc=com
```

This will interpret the path using cn=ac followed by dc followed by cn=users and so on. As dc on its own is not a valid part of the path, the ADsPath is invalid. Here are the two ways to specify the path correctly:

```
LDAP://cn=ac\/dc,cn=users,dc=amer,dc=rallencorp,dc=com
LDAP://"cn=ac/dc",cn=users,dc=amer,dc=rallencorp,dc=com
```

Obviously, as the backslash is a special character, to use it in a name, you would need to do one of the following for an object called cn=hot\cold:

```
LDAP://cn=hot\\cold,cn=users,dc=amer,dc=rallencorp,dc=com
LDAP://"cn=hot\cold",cn=users,dc=amer,dc=rallencorp,dc=com
```

The first specifies that the following character is to be interpreted as part of the name, and the latter specifies that the whole first name is a valid string.[*]

When to Use the LDAP and WinNT Namespaces

Contrary to popular belief, just because the WinNT namespace is used to access Windows NT servers, does not mean it is of little use to Windows 2000 and Windows Server 2003. While the LDAP namespace is used to access Active Directory, the WinNT namespace is used to access users, groups, and other objects on individual computers. Active Directory exists only on DCs in your forest. If you have a server or a client that is a member of a workgroup or a domain, that machine also will have objects on it. These could be local users, such as Administrator or Guest, printers, shares, and so on. Obviously, these objects are not part of Active Directory if they are unique to the machine. As individual machines do not support direct access via LDAP, you have to use the WinNT namespace.

Retrieving Objects

Now that you know how to use ADsPaths to distinguish between different namespaces, we'll demonstrate how to establish a connection and authenticate to the server containing the directory service you want to access. Authenticating a connection isn't always necessary; some directories, such as Active Directory, allow anonymous read-only access to certain parts of the directory tree if you configure it that way. In general though, allowing anonymous access is not a good practice. It can make things much more difficult to troubleshoot if you discover that one of your domain controllers is being impacted by an overzealous client. When using ADSI, if authentication is not done explicitly, the credentials of the account the script is running under will be used. If the account running the script is not part of the Active Directory you want to query or in a trusted domain, you will not be able to do very much. That's why performing explicit authentication in ADSI scripts is generally the best way to go.

---

[*] Unfortunately, the latter, while valid, will not work with VBScript's GetObject function due to the extra quotation marks ("").

If you just want to bind using the current account's credentials to a directory server to get a reference to an object, use the GetObject function:

```
Dim strPath       'path to the directory server
Dim objMyDomain   'root object of the directory

strPath = "LDAP://dc=amer,dc=rallencorp,dc=com"
Set objMyDomain = GetObject(strPath)
```

The code begins by declaring two variables with VBScript Dim statements. The first variable, strPath, is an ADsPath. The prefix str specifies that this ADsPath is a text string. The second variable, objMyDomain, is a reference to the object in the directory that the ADsPath represents. The prefix obj specifies that the variable is an object.

Next, we assign the strPath variable to the path of the directory server you want to bind to, in this case, LDAP://dc=amer,dc=rallencorp,dc=com. You need to enclose this path in quotation marks, because it's a text string.

Finally, we use VBScript's Set statement with the GetObject method to create a reference between the variable you declared and the existing object with which we want to interact. In this case, we're creating a reference between objMyDomain and the existing object that the ADsPath LDAP://dc=amer,dc=rallencorp,dc=com represents (i.e., the domain object of the *amer.rallencorp.com* domain). After we've established this reference, we can use other IADs-based interfaces to interact with that object.

—with Alistair Lowe-Norris

List of Default Environment Variables

Environment variables are useful when working with the CMD shell or when automating tasks. To use an environment variable, enclose the variable name with percent signs (%). For example, this command prints the SystemRoot environment variable:

```
> echo %systemroot%
```

You can generally use environment variables with most commands. This makes them very useful in batch scripts. This command changes the working directory to the *system32* directory:

```
> cd %systemroot%\system32
```

For more on environment variables, see Recipe 2.11.

The following are the default environment variables available with Windows 2000 and Windows Server 2003:

ALLUSERSPROFILE
> The path to the *All Users* Profile.
>
> Example: *C:\Documents and Settings\All Users\Desktop*

APPDATA
> User-specific path where applications store data by default.
>
> Example: *C:\Documents and Settings\Administrator\Application Data*

CD
> Current working directory.
>
> Example: *C:*

CMDCMDLINE
> The path to the CMD executable.
>
> Example: *C:\WINDOWS\system32\cmd.exe*

CMDEXTVERSION
> The version number of the Command Processor Extensions.
>
> Example: 2

COMPUTERNAME

The name of the computer.

Example: SRV01

COMSPEC

The path to the CMD executable.

Example: *C:\WINDOWS\system32\cmd.exe*

DATE

The current date.

Example: Fri 01/16/2004

ERRORLEVEL

The error code returned from the most recently used command. A value other than 0 indicates an error condition.

Example: 0

HOMEDRIVE

The drive where the currently logged on user's home directory is located.

Example: *C:*

HOMEPATH

The path to the currently logged on user's home directory.

Example: *\Documents and Settings\Administrator*

HOMESHARE

The network path to the currently logged on user's home directory (if on a network share).

Example: *\\fs01\rallen*

LOGONSEVER

In workgroup mode, this will be local server. When the computer is part of a domain, this will be the local server for cached logons or a domain controller for authenticated logons.

Example: *AD01*

NUMBER_OF_PROCESSORS

The number of processors installed on the system.

Example: 1

OS

The operating system name.

Example: Windows_NT

PATH

The search path for programs.

Example: *C:\Perl\bin\;C:\Program Files\Res Kits\Tools\;C:\Program Files*

PATHEXT
> The list of extensions the operating system uses to find unqualified file names.
>
> Example: .COM;.EXE;.BAT;.CMD;.VBS;.VBE;.JS;.JSE;.WSF;.WSH

PROCESSOR_ARCHITECTURE
> The processors chip architecture (e.g., x86 or IA64)
>
> Example: x86

PROCESSOR_IDENTFIER
> A description of the processor.
>
> Example: x86 Family 15 Model 0 Stepping 7, GenuineIntel

PROCESSOR_LEVEL
> The processor level.
>
> Example: 15

PROCESSOR_REVISION
> The revision number of the processor.
>
> Example: 0007

PROMPT
> The variables used to generate the command prompt.
>
> Example: PG

RANDOM
> A random number between 0 and 32767 generated by the operating system.
>
> Example: 19803

SYSTEMDRIVE
> The drive on which the operating system was installed.
>
> Example: C:

SYSTEMROOT
> The path to the root directory containing the operating system files.
>
> Example: C:\WINDOWS

TEMP and TMP
> The user-specific path to the directory used to house temporary files.
>
> Example: C:\DOCUME~1\ADMINI~3\LOCALS~1\Temp\1

TIME
> The current time.
>
> Example: 0:07:22.67

USERDOMAIN
> The domain of the currently logged on user.
>
> Example: RALLENCORP

USERNAME

The username of the currently logged on user.

Example: administrator

USERPROFILE

The user-specific path to user profile data.

Example: *C:\Documents and Settings\Administrator*

WINDIR

The path to the root directory containing the operating system files.

Example: *C:\WINDOWS*

List of Default Processes

If you fire up Taskmgr or Process Viewer on any Windows 2000 or Windows Server 2003 system, you will see a core set of processes. These processes run by default on any system and handle things such as logons, managing certain services, and controlling the Windows shell. The complete list of these processes is in Table E-1.

Table E-1. Default Windows processes

Process name	Purpose
Csrss.exe	An essential subsystem that is responsible for managing console windows, user-mode threads, and some parts of the 16-bit virtual MS-DOS environment. Csrss stands for client/server run-time subsystem.
Explorer.exe	Responsible for the user shell. If you've ever experienced the Start menu, taskbar, or Windows Explorer freezing up, terminating and restarting this process can help.
Lsass.exe	Responsible for authenticating users and issuing the access token associated with each user session.
Mstask.exe	Corresponds to the Task Scheduler service and is responsible for running scheduled tasks.
Services.exe	Service Control Manager (SCM), which is responsible for handling service management requests such as start, stop, and pause.
Smss.exe	Session Manager, which is the first user-mode process to run after a system starts up. The kernel starts this process, which in turn, starts other user-mode processes, such as *csrss.exe* and *winlogon.exe*.
Spoolsv.exe	Responsible for spooling print and fax jobs.
Svchost.exe	Started by any service that is run from a dynamic link library. See MS KB 250320 for more information on how to locate services that use this process.
System	Handles all kernel mode threads.
System Idle Process	Single-threaded process that accounts for unused processor time. In Taskmgr, this process will show up using all unused processor time. On a lightly loaded server, it can use as much as 99% of the CPU.
Winlogon.exe	Handles logon and logoff requests by users.

Table E-1. Default Windows processes (continued)

Process name	Purpose
Winmgmt.exe	A Windows 2000-only process that is responsible for loading all WMI providers. It is responsible for managing all WMI requests and responses from client computers. If any WMI provider fails, it causes all WMI providers to become unavailable.
Wmiprvse.exe	In Windows Server 2003, the winmgmt.exe process was replaced with this. Instead of all WMI providers being loaded by a single process, a separate instances of *wmiprvse.exe* is spawned for each active provider. Thus, if a single provider fails, only that provider is affected.

List of Default Services

Table F-1 contains a list of the default services you'll find installed on a Windows Server 2003 system and their default startup type and status.

Table F-1. List of default services in Windows Server 2003

Display name	Service name	Startup type/status	Description
Alerter	alerter	Disabled/Stopped	Notifies selected users and computers of administrative alerts. If the service is stopped, programs that use administrative alerts will not receive them.
Application Layer Gateway Service	alg	Manual/Stopped	Provides support for application-level protocol plug-ins and enables network connectivity.
Application Management	appmgmt	Manual/Stopped	Processes installation, removal, and enumeration requests for Active Directory IntelliMirror group policy programs. If the service is disabled, users will be unable to install, remove, or enumerate any IntelliMirror programs.
Automatic Updates	wuauserv	Automatic/Started	Enables the download and installation of critical Windows updates. If the service is disabled, the operating system can be manually updated at the Windows Update Web site.
Background Intelligent Transfer Service	bits	Manual/Started	Transfers data between clients and servers in the background. If BITS is disabled, features such as Windows Update will not work correctly.
ClipBook	clipsrv	Disabled/Stopped	Enables ClipBook Viewer to store information and share it with remote computers.
COM+ Event System	eventsystem	Manual/Started	Supports System Event Notification Service (SENS), which distributes events to subscribing Component Object Model (COM) components.
COM+ System Application	comsysapp	Manual/Stopped	Manages the configuration and tracking of COM+-based components. If the service is stopped, most COM+-based components will not function properly.

Display name	Service name	Startup type/status	Description
Computer Browser	browser	Automatic/Started	Maintains an updated list of computers on the local network and supplies this list to computers designated as browsers.
Cryptographic Services	cryptsvc	Automatic/Started	Provides three management services: Catalog Database Service, which confirms the signatures of Windows files; Protected Root Service, which adds and removes Trusted Root Certification Authority certificates from this computer; and Key Service, which helps enroll this computer for certificates.
DHCP Client	dhcp	Automatic/Started	Registers and updates IP addresses and Domain Name System (DNS) records for this computer. If this service is stopped, this computer will not receive dynamic IP addresses and DNS updates.
Distributed File System	dfs	Automatic/Started	Integrates disparate file shares into a single, logical namespace and manages these logical volumes distributed across a local or wide area network.
Distributed Link Tracking Client	trkwks	Automatic/Started	Enables client programs to track linked files that are moved within an NTFS volume, to another NTFS volume on the same computer, or to an NTFS volume on another computer.
Distributed Link Tracking Server	trksvr	Disabled/Stopped	Enables the Distributed Link Tracking Client service within the same domain to provide more reliable and efficient maintenance of links within the domain.
Distributed Transaction Coordinator	msdtc	Automatic/Started	Coordinates transactions that span multiple resource managers, such as databases, message queues, and file systems.
DNS Client	dnscache	Automatic/Started	Resolves and caches DNS names for this computer.
Error Reporting Service	ersvc	Automatic/Started	Collects, stores, and reports unexpected application crashes to Microsoft. If this service is stopped, Error Reporting will occur only for kernel faults and some types of user mode faults.
Event Log	eventlog	Automatic/Started	Enables event log messages issued by Windows-based programs and components to be viewed in Event Viewer. This service cannot be stopped.
File Replication	ntfrs	Manual/Stopped	Allows files to be automatically copied and maintained simultaneously on multiple servers.

Display name	Service name	Startup type/status	Description
Help and Support	helpsvc	Automatic/Started	Enables Help and Support Center to run on this computer. If this service is stopped, Help and Support Center will be unavailable.
HTTP SSL	httpfilter	Manual/Stopped	Implements the secure hypertext transfer protocol (HTTPS) for the HTTP service, using the Secure Socket Layer (SSL).
Human Interface Device Access	hidserv	Disabled/Stopped	Enables generic input access to Human Interface Devices (HID), which activates and maintains the use of predefined hot buttons on keyboards, remote controls, and other multimedia devices. If this service is stopped, hot buttons controlled by this service will no longer function.
IMAPI CD-Burning COM Service	imapiservice	Disabled/Stopped	Manages CD recording using Image Mastering Applications Programming Interface (IMAPI). If this service is stopped, this computer will be unable to record CDs.
Indexing Service	cisvc	Disabled/Stopped	Indexes contents and properties of files on local and remote computers; provides rapid access to files through flexible querying language.
Internet Connection Firewall (ICF)/Internet Connection Sharing (ICS)	sharedaccess	Disabled/Stopped	Provides network address translation, addressing, name resolution, and/or intrusion prevention services for a home or small office network.
Intersite Messaging	ismserv	Disabled/Stopped	Controls the exchange of messages (i.e., replication) between domain controllers using either remote procedure call (RPC) or SMTP.
IPSEC Services	policyagent	Automatic/Started	Provides end-to-end security between clients and servers on TCP/IP networks.
Kerberos Key Distribution Center	kdc	Disabled/Stopped	On domain controllers, this service enables users to log on to the network using the Kerberos authentication protocol. If this service is stopped on a domain controller, users will be unable to log on to the network using that DC.
License Logging	licenseservice	Disabled/Stopped	Monitors and records client access licensing for portions of the operating system (such as IIS, Terminal Server, and File/Print) as well as products that aren't a part of the OS, such as SQL and Exchange Server. If this service is stopped, licensing will be enforced, but will not be monitored.

Display name	Service name	Startup type/status	Description
Logical Disk Manager	dmserver	Automatic/Started	Detects and monitors new hard disk drives and sends disk volume information to Logical Disk Manager Administrative Service for configuration. If this service is stopped, dynamic disk status and configuration information may become out of date.
Logical Disk Manager Administrative Service	dmadmin	Manual/Stopped	Configures hard disk drives and volumes.
Messenger	messenger	Disabled/Stopped	Transmits net send and Alerter service messages between clients and servers. This service is not related to Windows Messenger.
Microsoft Software Shadow Copy Provider	swprv	Manual/Stopped	Manages software-based volume shadow copies taken by the Volume Shadow Copy service. If this service is stopped, software-based volume shadow copies cannot be managed.
Net Logon	netlogon	Manual/Stopped	Maintains a secure channel between this computer and the domain controller for authenticating users and services. If this service is stopped, the computer may not authenticate users and services and the domain controller cannot register DNS records.
NetMeeting Remote Desktop Sharing	mnmsrvc	Disabled/Stopped	Enables an authorized user to access this computer remotely by using NetMeeting over a corporate intranet. If this service is stopped, remote desktop sharing will be unavailable.
Network Connections	netman	Manual/Started	Manages objects in the Network and Dial-Up Connections folder, in which you can view both local area network and remote connections. If this service is disabled, you will not be able to view local area network and remote connections.
Network DDE	netdde	Disabled/Stopped	Provides network transport and security for DDE for programs running on the same computer or on different computers. If this service is stopped, DDE transport and security will be unavailable.
Network DDE DSDM	netddedsdm	Disabled/Stopped	Manages Dynamic Data Exchange (DDE) network shares. If this service is stopped, DDE network shares will be unavailable.
Network Location Awareness (NLA)	nla	Manual/Started	Collects and stores network configuration and location information, and notifies applications when this information changes.
NT LM Security Support Provider	ntlmssp	Manual/Stopped	Provides security to RPC programs that use transports other than named pipes.

Display name	Service name	Startup type/status	Description
Performance Logs and Alerts	sysmonlog	Manual/Stopped	Collects performance data from local or remote computers based on preconfigured schedule parameters, then writes the data to a log or triggers an alert. If this service is stopped, performance information will not be collected.
Plug and Play	plugplay	Automatic/Started	Enables a computer to recognize and adapt to hardware changes with little or no user input. Stopping or disabling this service will result in system instability.
Portable Media Serial Number	wmdmpmsn	Manual/Stopped	Retrieves the serial number of any portable media player connected to this computer. If this service is stopped, protected content might not be downloaded to the device.
Print Spooler	spooler	Automatic/Started	Manages all local and network print queues and controls all printing jobs. If this service is stopped, printing on the local machine will be unavailable.
Protected Storage	protectedstorage	Automatic/Started	Protects storage of sensitive information, such as private keys, and prevents access by unauthorized services, processes, or users. If this service is stopped, protected storage will be unavailable.
Remote Access Auto Connection Manager	rasauto	Manual/Stopped	Detects unsuccessful attempts to connect to a remote network or computer and provides alternative methods for connection. If this service is stopped, users will need to manually connect.
Remote Access Connection Manager	rasman	Manual/Stopped	Manages dial-up and virtual private network (VPN) connections from this computer to the Internet or other remote networks. If this service is stopped, the operating system might not function properly.
Remote Desktop Help Session Manager	rdsessmgr	Manual/Stopped	Manages and controls Remote Assistance. If this service is stopped, Remote Assistance will be unavailable.
Remote Procedure Call (RPC)	rpcss	Automatic/Started	Serves as the endpoint mapper and COM Service Control Manager. If this service is stopped or disabled, programs using COM or RPC services will not function properly.
Remote Procedure Call (RPC) Locator	rpclocator	Manual/Stopped	Enables RPC clients using the RpcNs* family of APIs to locate RPC servers. If this service is stopped or disabled, RPC clients using RpcNs* APIs may be unable to locate servers or fail to start.

Display name	Service name	Startup type/status	Description
Remote Registry	remoteregistry	Automatic/Started	Enables remote users to modify registry settings on this computer. If this service is stopped, the registry can be modified only by users on the local computer.
Removable Storage	nlmssvc	Manual/Stopped	Manages and catalogs removable media and operates automated removable media devices. If this service is stopped, programs that are dependent on Removable Storage, such as Backup and Remote Storage, will operate more slowly.
Resultant Set of Policy Provider	rsopprov	Manual/Stopped	Enables a user to connect to a remote computer, access the Windows Management Instrumentation database for that computer, and either verify the current Group Policy settings made for the computer or check settings before they are applied. If this service is stopped, remote verification will be unavailable. If this service is disabled, any services that explicitly depend on it will fail to start.
Routing and Remote Access	remoteaccess	Disabled/Stopped	Enables multiprotocol LAN-to-LAN, LAN-to-WAN, VPN, and network address translation (NAT) routing services for clients and servers on this network.
Secondary Logon	seclogon	Automatic/Started	Lets processes start under alternate credentials. If this service is stopped, this type of logon access will be unavailable.
Security Accounts Manager	samss	Automatic/Started	The startup of this service signals other services that the Security Accounts Manager (SAM) is ready to accept requests. Disabling this service will prevent other services in the system from being notified when the SAM is ready, which may in turn prevent those services from starting correctly.
Server	lanmanserver	Automatic/Started	Supports file, print, and named-pipe sharing over the network for this computer. If this service is stopped, these functions will be unavailable.
Shell Hardware Detection	shellhwdetection	Automatic/Started	Provides notifications for AutoPlay hardware events.
Smart Card	scardsvr	Manual/Stopped	Manages access to smart cards read by this computer. If this service is stopped, the computer will be unable to read smart cards.
Special Administration Console Helper	sacsvr	Manual/Stopped	Allows administrators to remotely access a command prompt using Emergency Management Services.

Display name	Service name	Startup type/status	Description
System Event Notification	sens	Automatic/Started	Monitors system events and notifies subscribers to COM+ Event System of these events. If this service is stopped, COM+ Event System subscribers will not receive system event notifications.
Task Scheduler	schedule	Automatic/Started	Enables a user to configure and schedule automated tasks on this computer. If this service is stopped, these tasks will not be run at their scheduled times.
TCP/IP NetBIOS Helper	lmhosts	Automatic/Started	Provides support for the NetBIOS over TCP/IP (NetBT) service and NetBIOS name resolution for clients on the network, therefore enabling users to share files, print, and log on to the network.
Telephony	tapisrv	Manual/Stopped	Provides Telephony API (TAPI) support for clients using programs that control telephony devices and IP-based voice connections.
Telnet	tlntsvr	Disabled/Stopped	Enables a remote user to log on to this computer and run programs, and supports various TCP/IP Telnet clients, including UNIX-based and Windows-based computers.
Terminal Services	termservice	Manual/Started	Allows users to connect interactively to a remote computer. Remote Desktop, Fast User Switching, Remote Assistance, and Terminal Server depend on this service. Stopping or disabling this service may make your computer unreliable. To prevent remote use of this computer, clear the checkboxes on the Remote tab of the System properties control panel item.
Terminal Services Session Directory	tssdis	Disabled/Stopped	Enables a user connection request to be routed to the appropriate terminal server in a cluster. If this service is stopped, connection requests will be routed to the first available server.
Themes	themes	Disabled/Stopped	Provides user experience theme management.
Uninterruptible Power Supply	ups	Manual/Stopped	Manages an uninterruptible power supply (UPS) connected to the computer.
Upload Manager	uploadmgr	Manual/Stopped	Manages synchronous and asynchronous file transfers between clients and servers on the network. If this service is stopped, synchronous and asynchronous file transfers between clients and servers on the network will not occur.
Virtual Disk Service	vds	Manual/Stopped	Provides software volume and hardware volume management service.

Table F-1. List of default services in Windows Server 2003 (continued)

Display name	Service name	Startup type/status	Description
Volume Shadow Copy	vss	Manual/Stopped	Manages and implements Volume Shadow Copies used for backup and other purposes. If this service is stopped, shadow copies will be unavailable for backup and the backup may fail.
WebClient	webclient	Disabled/Stopped	Provides WebDAV integration into the Explorer shell.
Windows Audio	audiosrv	Automatic/Started	Manages audio devices for Windows-based programs. If this service is stopped, audio devices and effects will not function properly.
Windows Image Acquisition (WIA)	stisvc	Disabled/Stopped	Provides image acquisition services for scanners and cameras.
Windows Installer	msiserver	Manual/Stopped	Adds, modifies, and removes applications provided as a Windows Installer (*.msi) package.
Windows Management Instrumentation	winmgmt	Automatic/Started	Provides a common interface and object model to access management information about operating system, devices, applications, and services. If this service is stopped, most Windows-based software will not function properly.
Windows Management Instrumentation Driver Extensions	wmi	Manual/Stopped	Monitors all drivers and event trace providers that are configured to publish Windows Management Instrumentation (WMI) or event trace information.
Windows Time	w32time	Automatic/Started	Maintains date and time synchronization on all clients and servers in the network. If this service is stopped, date and time synchronization will be unavailable.
WinHTTP Web Proxy Auto-Discovery Service	winhttpauto-proxysvc	Manual/Stopped	Implements the Web Proxy Auto-Discovery (WPAD) protocol for Windows HTTP Services (WinHTTP). WPAD is a protocol to enable an HTTP client to automatically discover a proxy configuration. If this service is stopped or disabled, the WPAD protocol will be executed within the HTTP client's process instead of an external service process; there would be no loss of functionality as a result.
Wireless Configuration	wzcsvc	Automatic/Started	Enables automatic configuration for IEEE 802. 11 adapters. If this service is stopped, automatic configuration will be unavailable.

Table F-1. List of default services in Windows Server 2003 (continued)

Display name	Service name	Startup type/status	Description
WMI Performance Adapter	wmiapsrv	Manual/Stopped	Provides performance library information from WMI providers to clients on the network. This service runs only when Performance Data Helper is activated.
Workstation	lanmanwork- station	Automatic/Started	Creates and maintains client network connections to remote servers. If this service is stopped, these connections will be unavailable.

Index

We'd like to hear your suggestions for improving our indexes. Send email to *index@oreilly.com*.

SYSTEMDRIVE default environment
    variable, 627
systeminfo.exe command, 49
SYSTEMROOT default environment
    variable, 627

T

tasklist.exe command, 169
tasks
    deleting, 156
    listing automatic, 152
    listing scheduled, 158
    running
        via Group Policy, 151
        via login scripts, 149–151
        when users log on, 147–149
        with alternate credentials, 142–145
        with remote servers, 145
    scheduling, 153–156
TCP/IP (Transmission Control
        Protocol/Internet Protocol)
    filtering, 284–287
    LDAP network protocol for accessing
        directories, 618
TCPView tool, 179, 279
TechNet web site, Microsoft's 10 laws of
        security, 291
TEMP default environment variable, 627
terminating processes, 167, 183
testing
    backups, 293
    computer accounts, 539
    secure channels, 43–45
    servers, 43–45
text editors, 376
TIME default environment variable, 627
time, setting, 34–37
Time To Live (TTL), 405
time zones, setting, 34–37
TMP default environment variable, 627
tools
    accessing, 3–5
    API monitoring, 177
    command-line, 15
    Process Explorer, 166
        searching, 170
    running (with alternate credentials), 5
    TCPView, 179
    (see also utilities)

traffic, viewing, 282–284
transferring
    DNS zones, configuring, 394–397
    FSMO roles, 490–492
Transmission Control Protocol/Internet
        Protocol (see TCP/IP)
triggering actions (event logs), 233
troubleshooting
    connections, 281
    critical failures, 55–58
    Help and Support Center, 15
    processes, 180–183
    services, performing actions
        automatically, 198
    user objects (in Active Directory), 512
trusts
    verifying, 497–500
    viewing, 494
TTL (Time To Live), 405
types of group accounts, modifying, 531

U

unattended IIS configuration options, 317
undeleting files, 104
uninstalling
    Active Directory, 453–455
    Windows Component, 27–30
Unknown host status message (ping), 282
unlock tool, 511
unlocking user objects (in Active
        Directory), 511
updates
    Automatic Updates
        configuring, 23–26
        disabling, 26
    DNS, preventing, 411
    dynamic DNS, enabling from DHCP
        Server, 432
    SUS, 24
    virus definitions, 291
    Windows Update, disabling, 26
upgrades, Active Directory (Windows 2000
        to Windows Server 2003), 455–458
uptime, viewing, 59
user accounts
    Active Directory
        configuring options, 519–522
        configuring passwords, 518
        configuring profiles, 522

About the Author

Robbie Allen is a Technical Leader at Cisco Systems, where he is involved in the deployment of Active Directory, DNS, DHCP, and several Network Management solutions. He enjoys working on Unix and Windows, and his favorite programming language is Perl. Robbie was named a Windows Server MVP in 2004 and 2005 for his contributions to the Windows community and the publication of several popular O'Reilly books. Robbie is currently studying at MIT in the System Design and Management program. For more information, see Robbie's web site at *http://www.rallenhome.com*.

Colophon

Our look is the result of reader comments, our own experimentation, and feedback from distribution channels. Distinctive covers complement our distinctive approach to technical topics, breathing personality and life into potentially dry subjects.

The animal on the cover of *Windows Server Cookbook* is a Chacma baboon (*Papio ursinus*). The Chacma is commonly referred to as the Savannah Baboon, or even dog-faced monkey due to its close-set eyes, heavy brow, dog-like muzzle, and sharp upper canine teeth. Its two-inch-long canines are larger than those of both lions and leopards, and at a sprint this large baboon can reach speeds of 35–40 miles per hour. The Chacma is also easily distinguishable by its fur, which ranges in color from yellowish-gray to almost black. This species can be found everywhere in Southern Africa except in the dry areas of Namibia, while its close relative the yellow baboon occupies much of the North.

Chacma baboons feed on just about every part of a tree and have a rich diet that includes grasses, seeds, rhizomes, berries, mushrooms, fruit, eggs, small insects, earthworms, birds, lizards, and occasionally scrub hares and baby impalas. Sometimes male Chacmas even kill and eat infants of their own species that are unrelated to them. Baboons are diurnal and are always on the move so they don't strip an environment of its vegetation. When they travel, they move in a specific formation, with the dominant male in the lead, the dominant female behind him, and the rest of the males encircling the females and babies. Baboons are unique in that all the members of a troop are related in one way or another. Most baboon troops are comprised of 30 to 40 members, but troops can range in size from 10 to 200.

Baboons have a complex social system based on dominance. The troop leaders' dominance is drilled into the rest of the troop from an early age, and if they become disobedient, they are likely to receive violent discipline. Older males can become quite bad-tempered, and when two males get into a fight, the male who chooses to end the fight will grab an infant from a mother to prevent his rival from attacking. But baboons are also capable of forming strong friendships. Some male and female baboons bond very closely, spending a lot of time together feeding, grooming, resting, and copulating.

Matt Hutchinson was the production editor for *Windows Server Cookbook*. Octal Publishing, Inc. provided production services. Darren Kelly, Mary Anne Mayo, and Colleen Gorman provided quality control.

Ellie Volckhausen designed the cover of this book, based on a series design by Edie Freedman. The cover image is a 19th-century engraving from *The Royal Natural History*. Karen Montgomery produced the cover layout with Adobe InDesign CS using Adobe's ITC Garamond font.

David Futato designed the interior layout. This book was converted by Andrew Savakis to FrameMaker 5.5.6 with a format conversion tool created by Erik Ray, Jason McIntosh, Neil Walls, and Mike Sierra that uses Perl and XML technologies. The text font is Linotype Birka; the heading font is Adobe Myriad Condensed; and the code font is LucasFont's TheSans Mono Condensed. The illustrations that appear in the book were produced by Robert Romano, Jessamyn Read, and Lesley Borash using Macromedia FreeHand MX and Adobe Photoshop CS. The tip and warning icons were drawn by Christopher Bing. This colophon was written by Lydia Onofrei.

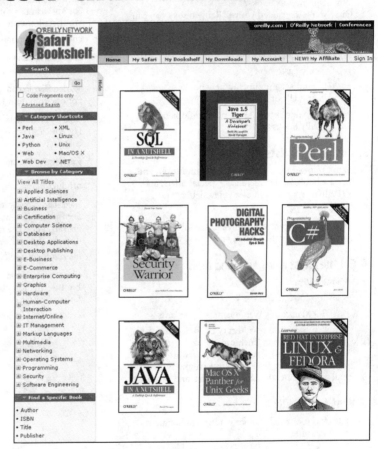

Keep in touch with O'Reilly

1. Download examples from our books

To find example files for a book, go to:

www.oreilly.com/catalog

select the book, and follow the "Examples" link.

2. Register your O'Reilly books

Register your book at *register.oreilly.com*

Why register your books?
Once you've registered your O'Reilly books you can:

- Win O'Reilly books, T-shirts or discount coupons in our monthly drawing.

- Get special offers available only to registered O'Reilly customers.

- Get catalogs announcing new books (US and UK only).

- Get email notification of new editions of the O'Reilly books you own.

3. Join our email lists

Sign up to get topic-specific email announcements of new books and conferences, special offers, and O'Reilly Network technology newsletters at:

elists.oreilly.com

It's easy to customize your free elists subscription so you'll get exactly the O'Reilly news you want.

4. Get the latest news, tips, and tools

www.oreilly.com

- "Top 100 Sites on the Web"—PC Magazine
- CIO Magazine's Web Business 50 Awards

Our web site contains a library of comprehensive product information (including book excerpts and tables of contents), downloadable software, background articles, interviews with technology leaders, links to relevant sites, book cover art, and more.

5. Work for O'Reilly

Check out our web site for current employment opportunities:

jobs.oreilly.com

6. Contact us

O'Reilly Media
1005 Gravenstein Hwy North
Sebastopol, CA 95472 USA

TEL: 707-827-7000 or 800-998-9938
       (6am to 5pm PST)

FAX: 707-829-0104

order@oreilly.com
For answers to problems regarding your order or our products. To place a book order online, visit:

www.oreilly.com/order_new

catalog@oreilly.com
To request a copy of our latest catalog.

booktech@oreilly.com
For book content technical questions or corrections.

corporate@oreilly.com
For educational, library, government, and corporate sales.

proposals@oreilly.com
To submit new book proposals to our editors and product managers.

international@oreilly.com
For information about our international distributors or translation queries. For a list of our distributors outside of North America check out:

international.oreilly.com/distributors.html

adoption@oreilly.com
For information about academic use of O'Reilly books, visit:

academic.oreilly.com

Related Titles Available from O'Reilly

Windows Administration

Active Directory Cookbook

Active Directory, *2nd Edition*

DHCP on Windows 2000

DNS on Windows 2000, *2nd Edition*

DNS on Windows Server 2003

Managing Microsoft Exchange Server

Managing the Windows 2000 Registry

MCSE in a Nutshell

PC Hardware in a Nutshell, *3rd Edition*

Securing Windows NT/2000 Servers for the Internet

Windows 2000 Administration in a Nutshell

Windows 2000 Commands Pocket Reference

Windows 2000 Performance Guide

Windows NT TCP/IP Network Administration

Windows Server 2003 in a Nutshell

Windows Server Hacks

Windows XP Unwired

Wireless Hacks